I0253949

ANCIENT SYRIAC DOCUMENTS

RELATIVE TO

THE EARLIEST ESTABLISHMENT OF CHRISTIANITY

IN EDESSA AND THE NEIGHBOURING COUNTRIES,

FROM THE YEAR AFTER OUR LORD'S ASCENSION

TO THE BEGINNING OF THE FOURTH CENTURY;

DISCOVERED, EDITED, TRANSLATED, AND ANNOTATED

BY THE LATE

W. CURETON, D.D., F.R.S.,

CANON OF WESTMINSTER,

MEMBER OF THE IMPERIAL INSTITUTE OF FRANCE,

ETC. ETC.

WITH A PREFACE BY

W. WRIGHT, PH.D., LL.D.,

ASSISTANT IN THE DEPARTMENT OF MSS., BRITISH MUSEUM.

WILLIAMS AND NORGATE,

14 HENRIETTA STREET, COVENT GARDEN, LONDON;

AND 20 SOUTH FREDERICK STREET, EDINBURGH.

1864.

W. M. WATTS, CROWN COURT, TEMPLE BAR.

PREFACE.

The Syriac texts contained in this volume were discovered and transcribed by its lamented author so long ago as 1848; for in the preface to the *Festal Letters of Athanasius*, p. xxiii, note, he says: "I have found amongst the Syriac manuscripts in the British Museum a considerable portion of the original Aramaic document, which Eusebius cites as preserved in the archives of Edessa, and various passages from it, quoted by several authors, with other testimonies which seem to be sufficient to establish the fact of the early conversion of many of the inhabitants of that city, and among them, of the king himself, although his successors afterwards relapsed into Paganism. These, together with accounts of the martyrdom of some of the first bishops of that city, forming a most interesting accession to our knowledge of the early propagation of Christianity in the East down to about A.D. 300, I have already transcribed, and hope to publish, with a translation, and such illustrations as may appear necessary. I regret that the little leisure which I have for such labours will not allow me even to speculate upon the probable time when I may be able to fulfil this intention."

The printing of these documents was actually commenced about three years ago, but progressed at first very slowly, owing to the demands made upon Dr. Cureton's time by his parochial and other duties. Indeed, up to May 1863, when he met with the accident that ultimately caused his death, only, I believe, about forty pages had been printed. As soon, however, as he was again able to attend to business, he pushed forward the printing both of text and translation as rapidly as possible, availing himself to some extent of my assistance in correcting the proofs of the former; and happily his strength held out long enough to enable him to all but finish his task. When his health finally gave way, there remained only the preface to be written; but of that, although it was all arranged in his mind, he did not, it would seem, commit a single line to paper.

The main scope and object of this work—of which I can safely say that it is, with one exception, the most generally interesting of all Dr. Cureton's publications—is clearly enough stated in the passage from one of his own writings quoted above. He was himself firmly persuaded of the genuineness of the epistles attributed to Abgar, king of Edessa, and our Lord; an opinion which he shared with such illustrious scholars as Baronius,* Tillemont,† Cave,‡ R. Mountague, bishop of Norwich,§ and Grabe.|| Whether right in this particular point or not, his book indubitably proves the conversion of King Abgar Ukkâmâ and a considerable number of the Edessenes at the hands of Addai or Thaddæus, one of the seventy Disciples; and presents us with authentic documents relative to the persecutions of the early Christians in that city, from the time of the first martyr Sharbîl, down to that of the last, Ḥabib.

To those who, like myself, study the ancient Syriac literature principally from a linguistic interest, this volume offers several documents of high importance; in particular the two discourses on the martyrs of Edessa by Mâr Jacob, bishop of Sĕrûg, one of the earliest and finest of Syrian writers, but of whose metrical homilies only one

* *Annales*, Lucca, 1738, tom. i. pp. 83, 84. † *Mémoires*, Paris, 1701, tome i. p. 362.
‡ *Hist. Literar.*, Oxford, 1740, vol. i. p. 2.
§ *Origines Ecclesiast.*, London, 1640, tom. i. pars poster., p. 61 foll.
|| *Spicilegium SS. Patrum*, Oxford, 1714, tom. i. p. 1 foll. and p. 314 foll.

other specimen has hitherto been published, I mean that on Simeon Stylites in the *Acta Martyrum* of S. E. Assemani (t. ii. p. 230.)

With regard to the share which I have taken in the production of this volume, only a very few words of explanation are necessary.

As mentioned above, I aided my departed friend in correcting the proof sheets of the Syriac text from p. ܠܐ to the end; and he made it his last request to me that I would undertake to usher the work into the world. To this I consented somewhat reluctantly, simply from a consciousness of my total incompetence to do it and him justice. As a mere linguist I am not his equal, nor is my historical knowledge to be compared with his. He had studied the questions connected with this volume for years and from every point of view; whereas I was new to them, having scarcely ventured at all into that particular field of history, nor having, for the present at least, the necessary leisure to do so. I have therefore confined myself entirely to a careful revision of the Syriac texts, which I have collated line for line with the original manuscripts. In this way I have been able, I hope, to note every error or misprint of any consequence; but I have not thought it necessary to swell the list of errata, and thereby uselessly augment the size of the volume, by pointing out every instance in which a mark of punctuation has been omitted or misplaced. Nor have I deemed it worth while to spend time in the revision of the translation and notes, being aware that the attentive reader can easily correct for himself the comparatively few and trifling misprints that occur in them.

I cannot conclude this preface without briefly tracing the literary career of my lamented friend; and in doing so, I shall avail myself of an article in the *Times* newspaper for Thursday, June 30, of the present year, the materials for which were contributed by myself and other friends.

William Cureton was born at Westbury in Shropshire, in the year 1808; received his earlier education at the Free Grammar School of Newport in the same county; and proceeded to Oxford with a Careswell exhibition at the age of eighteen. For private reasons, which reflected the highest credit on him, he entered Christ Church as a servitor, and graduated in 1830. In the following year he took holy orders, and was appointed Under-Librarian of the Bodleian Library in 1834. He continued in that post till 1837, when he was called to the British Museum as Assistant-Keeper of the MSS., having been selected for this office principally on account of his oriental scholarship.

The first duty assigned to him here was the preparation of a classified catalogue of the Arabic portion of the collection; and of this the first part, comprising the Christian writings and the divisions of Mohammedan theology, law and history, was published in 1846.

As early, however, as 1841 his Arabic studies had been interrupted by the acquisition by the Trustees of the famous Nitrian collection of Syriac manuscripts. This event furnished him with materials for researches, at once varied and profound, in a new field. On the arrival of the manuscripts—the first portion in 1841, the second in 1843—he threw himself heart and soul into the study of the Syriac language and literature. On him in the first instance devolved the task of classifying the volumes, of gathering together, collating, and arranging the numberless fragments and loose leaves of which the Nitrian collection consisted, and of drawing up a brief summary of their contents for the catalogue of additional manuscripts in the Museum.

One of the first results of these labours was an article in the *Quarterly Review*, No. cliii, Dec. 1845, giving an account of the way in which the manuscripts were procured, and a rough sketch of their contents; and in the same year appeared the first edition of the ancient Syriac version of the Epistles of St. Ignatius to St. Polycarp, the Ephesians, and the Romans. The views propounded by Dr. Cureton—that we have here the genuine epistles of St. Ignatius in their original form; that the previously known recensions of these three epistles are much altered and interpolated; and that all others ascribed to that Father are supposititious—views such as these were certain to excite much controversy in the theological world. Commenced by Wordsworth in the *English Review*, No. viii, July 1845, the strife was continued by S. Lee (*British Magazine*, vol. xxx), Bunsen, Baur, Hilgenfeld, Denzinger, Hefele, Jacobson, and others, of whom the first two supported Cureton, while the rest combated his views. Cureton himself took the field against Wordsworth in his *Vindiciæ Ignatianæ* (1846), a calm but crushing refutation of his opponent's allegation that the Syriac version was "a miserable epitome by an Eutychian heretic." The year 1849 saw the publication of the *Corpus Ignatianum*, an enlarged edition of the work of 1845, almost contemporaneously with which appeared Petermann's edition of the Ignatian epistles. Since then the discussion has been continued by Lipsius (1859) on the side of Cureton, and Merx (1861) on that of his opponents, and is not even yet brought to a final settlement. Cureton, however, remained stedfast to the views stated with such clearness and learning in the *Corpus Ignatianum*; and would, if his life had been spared, have once again stepped forward to sum up and conclude the controversy.

While the Ignatian controversy was at its height, Dr. Cureton edited the text of a portion of the Syriac version of the long-lost *Festal Letters of Athanasius*, of which he had been the fortunate discoverer. The preface to these letters contains an interesting account of the Nitrian collection, more especially of a third portion, which reached the Museum in 1847. These letters have been translated into English by Burgess (1854), and form one of the volumes of Pusey's Library of the Fathers. A German translation from the pen of the well-known Syriac scholar Larsow had already appeared in 1852.

In 1851 Cureton edited for the Trustees of the British Museum the palimpsest fragments of the *Iliad*, which are contained in the Nitrian manuscript now numbered Add. 17,210.

In 1853 there issued from the University Press of Oxford an important contribution to our historical knowledge—the third part of the *Ecclesiastical History of John, bishop of Ephesus*, edited by Cureton, from the Add. ms. 14,640. Of this he intended to publish a translation; but other labours prevented him, and his wishes were carried out by the Rev. R. Payne Smith, under-librarian of the Bodleian Library, whose version appeared in 1860. There is also a German translation by Schönfelder (1862).

Two years later this indefatigable scholar published his *Spicilegium Syriacum*, containing remains ascribed to Bardesanes, Melito of Sardes, and Ambrose, with an English translation and notes; and in 1858 he edited perhaps the most valuable of all his works, and one which has given rise to scarcely less controversy than the Ignatian Epistles. He discovered in the Add. ms. 14,451, which belongs to the latter half of the fifth century, the remains of an ancient recension of the Syriac Gospels, differing notably from the ordinary Pĕshiṭtā version. In his preface he dwelt on these divergences, more especially in the text of the Gospel of St. Matthew; summed up the evidence in favour of the Hebrew original of that Gospel; and endeavoured to prove that this particular manuscript represented the Hebrew far more faithfully than the Pĕshiṭtā does—at least in the shape in which it is generally known to European scholars. His views have been warmly espoused by that able critic Dr. Tregelles, and as warmly combated by other scholars, such as Hermansen (Copenhagen, 1859). It was Dr. Cureton's intention to have returned in after years to this subject, and to have made known additional evidence which he had collected upon these points.

Three years later Cureton brought out the last work that he was destined to finish—*the History of the Martyrs in Palestine* by Eusebius of Cæsarea, taken from the same venerable manuscript from which Dr. S. Lee edited the *Theophania* of that Father.

Dr. Cureton was an active promoter, if not the founder, of the Society for the publication of Oriental Texts, of which he was the honorary secretary until about the year 1850. For it he edited Esh-Shahrastâni's *Book of Religious and Philosophical Sects*, published in two parts in 1842 and 1846, and En-Nesefi's *Pillar of the Creed of the Sunnites*, published in 1843; having previously brought out in the same year Rabbī Tanchūm's *Commentary on the Book of Lamentations*. He was also an active member of the Committee of the Oriental Translation Fund, of which he became deputy-chairman in 1848, and chairman in 1863, on the death of Mr. Botfield. In 1859 he was appointed by the Queen Crown Trustee of the British Museum, a post of which he discharged the duties most zealously and efficiently. Of the estimation in which he was held on the Continent it is proof sufficient to mention that he was D.D. of the University of Halle, corresponding member of the German Oriental Society, and foreign associate of the Institute of France, besides being connected with many other learned bodies throughout Europe.

The eminence attained by Dr. Cureton was mainly founded on his Syriac publications, distinguished as they are by the intrinsic value of the works selected, by the accuracy of his texts, and the scholarship and honesty displayed in his translations and notes. In these qualities of judicious selection, accuracy, scholarship and freedom from prejudice, Cureton stands pre-eminent among all the Englishmen and foreigners who have followed him in the work of editing Syriac writings. I may add, too, that he was most liberal in communicating his knowledge of the contents of the Nitrian collection to all students who sought his assistance; and that not a few, nor the least important, of the publications from these manuscripts by other editors were undertaken at his suggestion and with his aid. Those who choose to refer to the *Nova Patrum Bibliotheca* of Cardinal Mai (tom. vi., p. x.), or to the *Spicilegium Solesmense* of Dom Pitra (tom. ii., p. xxxviii.), will find there well merited eulogies of his learning and liberality. I myself have received since his death several letters from foreign scholars, expressing the greatest grief for his loss, and I cannot deny myself the melancholy pleasure of quoting one of these, from the pen of that distinguished classic and orientalist the Rev. Antonio Ceriani, one of the Doctors of the Ambrosian Library. "La notizia della morte del Dr. Cureton mi tornò assai dolorosa; era ben lontano dall' aspettarmela. La letteratura Siriaca ha perduto in lui, io credo, *il migliore editore di testi*, che sapeva anche tradurre bene in modo che potessero approfittarne anche i profani, e accompagnare di buone note. E per i suoi lavori, e per la parte grande che ebbe all' acquisto di tanta parte dei MSS. Siriaci di Sceti, che altrimenti sarebbero forse andati smarriti, egli lascia sicuramente dietro di sè un bel nome. Pur troppo però deve essere dolorosa la sua perdita ai suoi amici, che ben difficilmente potevano averne uno più dotto e più amorevole. Quando io era a Londra, venni trattato da lui come un fratello; mi offerse anche copie di MSS. Siriaci da pubblicare, che io non accettai solo, perchè avendo già determinati i miei lavori, difficilmente avrei potuto soddisfare al suo voto; e volli perciò che potessero servire a qualche giovine di buona volontà."

Verily Cureton's life was one of unremitting and well directed labour, and the bread which he has cast upon the waters will doubtless be found after many days.

ܕܐܠܗܐ ܗܘ ܕܢܬܠ ܚܝܘܗܝ ܐܬܬܢܝܚ ܘܗܘܐ ܘܡܥܗܕܢܘܬܐ ܥܠܡ
ܙܘܥܝܬܐ. ܗܘ ܕܝܗܒ ܠܗ ܡܘܗܒܬܐ ܙܕܩܐ ܒܗܘܢ ܕܡܬܬܥܗܕܘܢ.
ܘܥܡܘܗܝ ܕܢܬܚܪ ܡܠܝܐ ܕܒܪܬ ܡܠܬܐ ܗܘ ܕܐܬܪܚܪܐ: ܕܬܒ
ܒܨܒܘܬܗ ܕܐܬܪ ܐܬܪܬܘ ܡܠܐܟܘܬܐ ܕܚܟܡܬܐ ܗܘܬ ܠܗܘܢ ܡܢ
ܬܐܪܬܘܗܝ ܕܥܠܡܐ. ܐܡܝܢ ܀

W. WRIGHT.

LONDON.
November, 1864.

ADDITIONS AND CORRECTIONS.

Page ܒ, line 5. After ܐܢܫ ܐܝܟ insert ܠܗܘܢ

.. ܓ, .. 4. For ܢܥܠܠ read ܢܥܘܠ

.. ܗ, .. 2. For ܕܒܣܘܪܬܗ read ܕܒܣܘܪܬܗ

.. .., .. 12. Read ܗܦܟܘ ܡܢ ܐܘܪܚܐ ܠܡܘܬܐ. ܒܣܢܩܘܬܗܘܢ

.. ܙ, .. 20. The word that has been effaced before ܘܠܗܘܢ is doubtless ܢܠܗ. Of ܝܩܘܡ in the next line only the last letter is distinctly legible.

.. .., .. 23. We should probably read ܠܐܘܪܚܬܗܘܢ

.. ܚ, .. 3. Read ܕܡܦܩܐ ܡܦܩܐ ܒܗܘ

.. .., .. 4. Read ܒܥܘܠܗ, and so also in line 5.

.. .., .. 10. Read ܒܝܘܪܐ ܘܩܪܘܒܐ

.. .., .. 12. Read ܘܪܕܝܢ

.. .., .. 23. Read ܠܐܠܗܬܐ

.. ܛ, .. 2. Read ܬܓܠܐ

.. .., .. 5. Read ܚܢܢܐ

.. .., .. 7. Read ܠܐܙܕܢܐ ܢܙܒܢܬܐ. The letters ܢܙܒ are conjectural.

.. .., .. 12. Read ܕܝܢܝܢܘܬܐ

.. .., .. 19—22. In this passage several words and parts of words are merely conjectural, the manuscript being a good deal damaged. In line 19, ܗܘܠܐ is doubtful. In line 20, read in both places ܗܘܘ. In line 21, I have very little doubt that we should substitute ܕܢܚܬ for ܕܒܝܢ (corresponding to ܢܒܝܢ in the next clause); the word is quite illegible in the manuscript.

Page ܘ, line 5. At the beginning, after ܠܐ, insert ܗܘܐ. The words printed ܫܘܪܒܐ and ܐܟܠ are very doubtful.

.. ܝܘ, .. 11. Read ܟܕ ܗܘܐ

.. .., .. 19. Read ܡܣܒܪܬܗ

.. .., .. 23. Read ܕܬ̈ܠܡܐ

.. .., .. 27. Read ܕܫ̈ܢܝ ܗ̈ܘܝ

.. ܝܙ, .. 8. Read ܕܚܠܝܣܡ

.. .., .. 21. Read ܠܦ̈ܠܓܘܬܐ

.. ܝܚ, .. 2. Read ܘܒܥ̈ܕܢܘܗܝ

.. .., .. 14. Read ܥܠܘܗܝ

.. .., .. 19. After ܫܘܬܦ add ܗܘܐ

.. ܝܛ, .. 3. MS. ܘܥܡ ܕܗܘܐ

.. .., .. 13. The ܘ in ܘܬܫܥܒܕܬܐ seems to have been altered into ܕ.

.. ܟ, .. 20. Read ܐܚ̈ܪܢܐ

.. ܟܐ, .. 10. Read ܐܪ̈ܝܘ

.. ܟܒ .. 3. Read ܘܒܟܘܬܗܝ

.. .., .. 21. Read ܐܦ ܚܢܢ

.. ܟܗ, .. 24. In numbering the canons, *letters* have been substituted for the *arithmetical figures* of the manuscript.

.. ܟܘ, .. 4. Read ܘܠܡ ܗܘܐ

.. ܟܙ, .. 12. Read ܟܪܙܬܐ

.. .., .. 24. Read ܠܐ ܬܘܒ

.. .., .. 25. Delete ܗܘܐ after ܘܠܐ

.. ܟܚ .. 6. Delete ܕ before ܬܫܪܝܪ

.. ܟܛ .. 12. Read ܕܡܬܚܪܘܬܐ

.. .., .. 23. Delete ܗܘܘ after ܘܫܡܥܝܢ

.. ܠ .. 4. Read ܘܟܕ ܗܘܘ

.. .., .. 11. Read ܟܬܒܬܐ ܕܗܘܪܢܐ

.. .., .. 20. Read ܘܒܫܘܒܩܢܗ and ܪܫܐ

.. .., .. 23. Read ܘܐܘܟܝܬ

.. .., .. 24. Read ܗܢܘܢ

Page ܟܐ line 2. Add ܗܘܘ after ܕܡܫܠܡ

.. .., .. 7. Read ܕܬܘܕܝܢ

.. .., .. 15. Read ܟܝܢ̈ܬܐ

.. .., .. 19. Read ܗܘܝܢ

.. ܠܒ .. 3. Delete ܗܘܘ after ܘܐܫܠܡܘ

.. .., .. 8. Read ܐܬܐܘܕܥܐ

.. .., .. 11. Read ܫܪܬܐ ܘܟܬܝܒܬܐ

.. ܠܓ .. 9. Read ܘܬܬܦܪܫܘܢ

.. .., .. 20. Instead of ܫܠܘ the manuscript has ܟܡ, which is certainly an error.

.. .., .. 21, Read ܕܒܪܝܬܐ

.. ܠܘ .. 4. The manuscript has ܬܠܡܝܕܘܗܝ. ܘܒܢܝܐ ܗܘ̣

.. ܡ .. 2. Read ܡܢ ܒܪܢܫܐ.

.. .., .. 8. Read ܫܐܠܬ

.. ., .. 12. Delete ܟܐܦܐ

.. .., .. 16. Read ܒܪ̈ܬܐ

.. .., .. 18. The manuscript has ܕܡܘܙ̈ܓܐ

.. .., .. 25. In the manuscript there is a superfluous ܡܕܡ after ܡܬܘܪܐ

.. ܡܐ, .. 10. Read ܘܡܠܠܗ

.. ܡܓ, .. 21. Read ܕܐܝܟ ܗܘܝܐ

.. ܡܕ, .. 1. Read ܕܐܝܟ ܗܘܝܢ

.. .., .. 10. Insert a point after ܕܡܢܝܢܐ

.. ܡܙ, .. 9. Read ܕܥܡܥܡ (for ܕܥܡܥܡ̈ܢ)

.. .., .. 15. Insert a point after ܐܝܬ

.. ܡܛ, .. 14. Read ܫܒܬ ܫܒܘܥܐ

.. ܢܒ, .. 8. Read ܡܫܒܚܐ ܀

.. .., .. 20. Read ܦܠܓܐ

.. ܢܓ, .. 2. Read ܕܟܬܒܬ ܀

.. .., .. 18. The manuscript has ܦܫܝܫ̈ܐ, the points indicating the vocative.

.. ܢܘ, .. 10. Read ܕܦܫܛ ܗܘܢܐ

Page ܢܗ, line 18. ܨܝܡ has been altered in the manuscript into ܨܘܡ
.. ܣ, .. 19. Read ܘܣܘܣ ܟܠ
.. ܣܐ, .. 14. Read ܘܐܬܦܪܘܩ
.. ܣܒ, .. 11. The manuscript has ܕܡܣܬܒܪܘܗ
.. ܣܕ, .. 6. The manuscript has ܘܐܬܚܣܡ, as on p. ܟܛ, line 11.
.. ܣܘ, .. 4. Read ܠܦܪܘܫܠ :
.. ܣܙ, .. 10. The manuscript has incorrectly ܘܐܬܬܦܝܣܘ
.. ܥܕ, .. 12. Read ܕܒܥܘܬܐ ܢܐܡܪ
.. .., .. 13. Read ܕܢܬܒܣܡܘܢ :
.. ܥܗ, .. 11. Insert a point after ܡܠܟܐ
.. ܥܛ, .. 20. The manuscript has ܘܗܘ, the ܘ being a later addition.
.. ܦܐ, .. 18. Read ܬܫܒܚܬܗ
.. ܦܕ, .. 20. The manuscript has ܚܠܘܢܝܬܐ, as if the scribe wished to alter the word into ܚܠܝܢܬܐ
.. ܦܗ, .. 2. Read ܕܢܟܐ
.. .., .. 26. ܡܚܝܠܐ. Here, and in several other places, the point which marks the end of a verse has been placed *under*, instead of *after*, the letters ܐ, ܡ, ܘ, and ܝ.
.. ܦܛ, .. 11. Read ܡܬܠܠܗ, without ܘ
.. ܨܐ, .. 21. Read ܪܪܐ
.. ܨܒ .. 24. Delete the point after ܬܠܡܝܕܐ
.. ܨܓ .. 5. Read ܦܘܪܥܐ
.. .., .. 8. The manuscript has really ܢܘܠܗܘܢ, instead of ܢܠܗܘܢ,
.. .., .. 26. Read ܕܢܠܡ.
.. ܨܕ, .. 9. Read ܕܢܦܠܐ, to distinguish the word from ܕܢܒܠܐ in line 12.
.. ܨܕ, .. 23. Read ܐܬܩܢܗ
.. , .. 25. Read ܗܘܘ.
.. ܨܘ, .. 11. Read ܕܢܗܒ
.. ܨܙ, .. 3. Read ܕܡܬܚܪܪܬܐ

Page ܩܠܒ, .. 8. The word ܠܗܝ, before ܕܬܬܚܫܠ, ought to be deleted.

.. .., .. 22. Read ܕܢ̈ܢܐ

.. ܩܠܛ, .. 24. Read ܘܐܬܥܠܠܘ

.. ܩܢ, .. 14. Read ܕܡܫܬܒܚܢܘܬܐ

. ܩܣ, .. 13. The manuscript has really ܐܘܣܛܘܡܐ

. .., .. 21—25. I fear that this passage is not quite correctly printed, owing to the leaf being slightly torn. In line 21, I believe ܗܘܐ should be inserted after ܥܠ. In line 23, read ܒܪ̈ܘܙܐ. In line 24, place the point after ܕܡܫܬܡܗ instead of ܘܡܫܬܒܪ̈ܢܐ. It is possible that a single word may be wanting after ܕܡܫܬܡܗ, and also after ܕܢ̈ܘܪܬܐ in line 25.

.. ܩܦ, .. 7—17. The following are the variants of Add. 17,193. Line 8, ܕܡܫܝ̈ܚܐ ܠܦܘ̈ܪܫܢܐ. Line 11, ܕܠܐ ܙ̇ ܒܥܬܐ. Line 12, ܕܡܚܠܐ. Line 16, ܠܐ ܡܣܒܝ. ܕܕܠܐ

.. ܩܨ, .. 24. Read ܬܫܒܘܚܬܗ

Page 191, line 23. Like Dr. Cureton, I am ignorant of the meaning of the word ܠܬ̈ܠܡܝ in this passage. It is so written in both MSS. of the Sermons of Mār Jacob Persa (or Aphraates), and can hardly, therefore, be incorrect.

W. WRIGHT.

FROM THE HISTORY OF THE CHURCH.

[BY EUSEBIUS, OF CÆSAREA.]

[CHAPTER] THE THIRTEENTH.

CONCERNING THE KING OF EDESSA.

BUT the history which was about Thaddæus was in this fashion:—When the divine nature of our Saviour and Lord Jesus Christ was published abroad among all men by reason of the wonderful mighty works which he wrought, and myriads, even from countries remote from the land of Judæa, who were afflicted with sicknesses and diseases of every kind, were coming to him in the hope of being healed, King Abgar also, who was renowned for his valour among the nations on the east side of the Euphrates, had his body afflicted with a severe disease, of such a kind as there is no cure for it among men: and when he heard and was informed of the name of Jesus, and about the mighty works that he did, which all men equally testified concerning Him, he sent to him a letter of request by the hand of a man of his own, and entreated him to come and heal him of his disease. Our Saviour, however, at the time that he called him, did not comply with his request: yet he deemed him worthy of a reply; for he promised him that he would send one of his disciples, and would heal his diseases, and give salvation to him and to all who were near to him. Nor was the fulfilment of his promise to him long deferred: but after he was risen from the dead, and was taken up into heaven, Thomas the Apostle, one of the Twelve, as by the instigation of God, sent Thaddæus, who also was numbered among the Seventy disciples of Christ, to Edessa, to be a preacher and Evangelist of the teaching of Christ, and through him the promise of Christ was fulfilled. You have in written documents the evidence of these things, which is taken from (ܒ) the Book of Records which is at Edessa; for at that time the kingdom was still standing. In the documents, therefore, that are there, in which is contained whatever had been done by those of old up to the time of Abgar, these things also are found preserved there up to the present hour. But there is nothing to hinder our hearing the very Letters themselves which are taken by us from the Archives, and have the following form of words which are translated out of the Aramaic into Greek.

Copy of the Letter which was written from King Abgar to Jesus, and sent to him by the hand of Hananias, the Tabularius, to Jerusalem.

"Abgar Uchama, Chief of the country, to Jesus, the good Deliverer, "who has appeared in the country of Jerusalem, Peace. I have heard "about thee, and about the cures which are wrought by thy hands, "without medicines and herbs; for as it is reported, thou makest the "blind to see, and the lame to walk; and thou cleansest the lepers, and "thou castest out unclean spirits and devils, and thou healest those who "are tormented with lingering diseases, and thou raisest the dead. And "when I heard these things about thee, I settled in my mind one "of two things: either that thou art God, who being come down "from heaven, doest these things, or that thou art the Son of God, "and doest these things. On this account, therefore, I have written "to request of thee that thou wouldest trouble thyself to come to "me, and cure this disease which I have: for I have also heard "that the Jews murmur against thee, and wish to do thee harm. But "I have a city, small and beautiful, which is enough for two."

Copy of those things which were written from Jesus by the hand of Hananias, the Tabularius, to Abgar, the Chief of the country.

"Blessed is he that hath believed in me, not having seen me. For "it is written concerning me; that those who see me will not believe "in me, and those who have not seen me, they will believe and be "saved. But touching what thou hast written to me, that I should "come to thee, it is meet (ܠܝ) that I should fulfil here every thing "for the sake of which I have been sent; and after I have ful-"filled *it*, then I shall be taken up to Him that sent me; and when "I have been taken up, I will send to thee one of my disciples, that "he may heal thy disease, and give salvation to thee and to those "who are with thee."

But to these same Letters these things also are appended in the Aramaic tongue: that after Jesus was ascended, Judas Thomas sent to him Thaddæus the Apostle, one of the Seventy: and when he was come, he lodged with Tobias, the son of Tobias. But when it was heard about him they made it known to Abgar, that the Apostle of Jesus is come here, according as he sent thee word. And Thaddæus began to heal every disease and sickness by the power of God, so that all men wondered. But when Abgar heard the great and marvellous cures which he wrought, he supposed that he was the person about whom Jesus sent him word, and said to him, "When I have been taken up, I will send to thee one of my disciples, that he may heal thy disease." Then he sent and called Tobias, with whom he was lodging, and said to him, I have heard that a mighty man is come, and is entered in, and lodges in thy house: bring him up therefore to me. And when Tobias came to Thaddæus he said to him, Abgar the King has sent and called me, and commanded me to take thee up to him, that thou mayest heal him. And Thaddæus said, I will go up, for it is for this purpose that I have been sent to him with power. Tobias therefore rose up early the next day, and took Thaddæus, and came to Abgar. But when they went up, his princes were assembled and standing there. And immediately as he entered in, a great vision appeared to Abgar on the countenance of Thaddæus the Apostle. And when Abgar saw it, he fell down before Thaddæus; and astonishment seized upon all who were standing there, for they had not seen that vision, which appeared to Abgar alone. And he asked Thaddæus, Art thou in truth the disciple of Jesus the Son of God, who said to me, I will send to thee one of my disciples, that he may heal thee (a) and give thee salvation? And Thaddæus answered and said, Because thou hast nobly believed on Him that sent me, therefore have I been sent to thee; and again, if thou wilt believe on Him, thou shalt have the requests of thy heart. And Abgar said to him, thus I have believed on him, so that I have even desired to take an army and lay waste those Jews who crucified him, were it not that I was hindered on account of the dominion of the Romans. And Thaddæus said, Our Lord has fulfilled the will of his Father, and having fulfilled *it*, he has been taken up to his Father. Abgar said to him, I have believed both in Him and in his Father. And Thaddæus said, On this account I lay my hand upon thee in His name. And when he had done this, immediately he was healed of his sickness and of the disease which he had. And Abgar marvelled, because like as he had heard concerning Jesus, so he saw in deeds by the hand of his disciple Thaddæus, that without medicines and herbs he healed him; and not himself only, but also Abdu, son of Abdu, who had the gout; that he too went in, and fell at his feet, and when he prayed over him he was healed. And many other people of their city he healed, and did great works, and preached the word of God.

After these things, Abgar said to him, Thou, Thaddæus, doest these things by the power of God, and we are astonished at them. But in addition to all these things, I entreat thee to relate to me the history of the coming of Christ, and how it was; about his power also, and by what power he did those things which I have heard.

And Thaddæus said, For the present I will be silent; but because I have been sent to preach the word of God, assemble for me to-morrow all the people of thy city, and I will preach before them, and sow amongst them the word of life; also concerning the coming of Jesus, how it took place; and about his mission, for what purpose he was sent by his Father; and about (ꝏ) his power and his deeds, and about the mysteries which he spake in the world, and by what power he did these things, and about his new preaching, and about his abasement and his humiliation, and how he humbled and stripped and abased himself, and was crucified, and descended into hell, and broke through the wall of partition which had never been broken through, and raised up the dead; and descended alone, and ascended with a great multitude to his Father.

Abgar then gave orders that in the morning all the people of his city should assemble, and hear the preaching of Thaddæus. And then he afterwards commanded gold and silver to be given to him; but he received it not, and said to him, If we have forsaken that which was our own, how can we accept that of others?

These things were done in the year three hundred and forty. But that these things might not have been translated in every word out of the Aramaic to no purpose, they are placed here in their order of time.

HERE ENDETH THE FIRST BOOK.

THE DOCTRINE OF ADDÆUS, THE APOSTLE.

* * * * * *

* Addæus [said] to him, Because thou hast so believed, I lay my hand upon thee in the name of Him on whom thou hast so believed; and at the same moment as he laid his hand upon him he was healed from the plague of the disease which he had had a long time. And Abgar was astonished, and wondered, because like as he had heard about Jesus himself, how he acted and healed, so Addæus also, without medicine of any kind, healed in the name of Jesus. And Abdu also, the son of Abdu, had the gout in his feet; and he too brought his feet near to him, and he laid his hand upon them, (ܘ) and healed him, and he had the gout no more. And in all the city also he wrought great cures, and shewed wonderful mighty works in it. Abgar said to him, Now that every man knoweth that thou doest these miracles by the power of Jesus Christ, and behold! we are wondering at thy deeds, I therefore entreat thee to relate to us the history about the coming of Christ, how it was, also about his glorious power, and about the miracles which we have heard that he did, which thou hast seen, together with thy fellow disciples. Addæus said to him, I will not be silent from declaring this, because I have been sent hither for this very purpose, that I might speak and teach every one who, like thee, is willing to believe. Assemble for me to-morrow all the city, and I will sow in it the word of life by the preaching which I will preach before you, about the coming of Christ, how it was, and about Him that sent him, why and how he sent him, and about his power and his marvellous deeds, and about the glorious mysteries of his coming which he spake in the world, and about the certitude of his preaching, and how and for what cause he abased himself, and humbled his exalted godhead by the manhood

which he assumed, and was crucified, and descended to the place of the dead, and broke through the wall of partition which had never been broken through, and gave life to the dead by being slain himself; and descended alone, and ascended with many to his glorious Father, with whom he was from all eternity in one exalted godhead.

And Abgar commanded that they should give to Addæus silver and gold. Addæus said to him, How can we receive any thing which is not our own? for, behold, that which was our own we have forsaken it, as we were commanded by our Lord; because without purses and without scrips, bearing the cross upon our shoulders, we were commanded to preach his Gospel in the whole creation, at whose (1) crucifixion for our sakes, for the deliverance of all men, the whole creation was affected and suffered.

And he related before Abgar the King, before his princes and his nobles, before Augustin, Abgar's mother, and before Shalmath, the daughter of Meherdath, Abgar's wife, the signs of our Lord and his wonders, and the glorious mighty works which he did, and his divine triumphs, and his ascension to his Father: and how they had received power and authority, and at the time when he ascended, by which same power he had healed Abgar and Abdu, the son of Abdu, the second *person* of his kingdom; and how he informed them that he would reveal himself at the end of the times, and at the consummation of all creatures; also the resuscitation and resurrection which is to be hereafter for all men, and the separation which will be between the sheep and the goats, and between the believers and the infidels.

And he said to them, "Because strait is the gate of life, and narrow is the way of truth, for this reason the believers of the truth are few; and through unbelief is Satan's pleasure. On this account there are many liars who lead astray those that behold. For were it not that there is a good end for men who believe, our Lord would not have descended from heaven, and came to the birth, [and the suffering of death; but he is come, and us has he sent * *

* * * * * *

* of the faith which we preach, that God was crucified (for) all men. And if there be any who are not willing to be persuaded by these our words, let them draw near to us, and disclose to us what their mind is, that like as it were a disease, we may apply to their mind healing medicine (ܣܡ), for the recovery of their wounds. For although ye were not present at the time of Christ's passion, nevertheless, from the sun which was darkened, and ye saw *it*, learn ye and understand what great consternation there was at the time of the crucifixion of Him whose Gospel has been spread abroad throughout all the earth by the signs which his Disciples, my fellows, do in all the earth; and those who are Hebrews, and knew only the tongue of the Hebrews, in which they were born, behold, at this day they speak in all tongues, in order that those who are far off, as well as those who are near, may hear and believe that He is the same who confounded the tongues of the rebels, in this region, who were before us, and that it is He who at this day teaches through us the faith of truth and verity, by humble and uncultivated men, who are from Galilee of Palestine. For I myself also, whom ye see, am from Paneas, whence the river Jordan comes out, and I was chosen, together with my fellows, to be a preacher * * * * *

* For I, according as my Lord commanded me, behold, I preach and publish the Gospel; and behold I cast his money upon the table before you, and the seed of his word I sow in the ears of all men: and such as are willing to receive *it*, theirs will be the good reward of the confession; and they who will not believe, against them wipe I off the dust of my feet, as He commanded me. Repent therefore, my beloved, from evil ways and from abominable deeds, and

turn yourselves to him with a good and honest will, as he hath turned himself to you with the favour of his rich mercies; and be not like the generations of old that are passed away, which, because they hardened their heart against the fear of God, have received punishment openly, in order that they might be chastised thereby, and those who come after them may tremble and fear: for the whole object of our Lord's coming into the world was to teach us and to shew us, that at the consummation of the creation (1) there will be a resuscitation of all men; and at that time their acts of conduct will be represented in their own persons, and their bodies will be the volume for the writings of Justice, nor will any one be there who will not know how to read, because every man shall read the writings of his own book * * * * * *

* you that have eyes, inasmuch as ye perceive not, you also are become like those who see not and hear not, and in vain is it to exert your voice which has no effect upon the deaf ear. While they are without blame for not hearing, because they are by nature deaf and dumb, the blame which is justly incurred is yours, because ye are not willing to perceive, not even that which ye do see. For the thick cloud of error which overwhelms your minds suffers you not to obtain that heavenly light, which is the understanding of knowledge. Flee then from things made and created, as I said to you, which are called gods in name only, but are not gods in their nature, and draw near to this who in his own nature is God for ever, and from everlasting; and is not a thing made, like your idols, nor is he a creature and a device, like those images in which ye glory. Because even although he put on this body, still is he God with his Father: for the works of the creation, which trembled at his being slain, and were terrified at his suffering of death, they bear witness that he is God the Creator: for it was not on account of a man, who is of the earth, but on account of Him who

established the earth upon the waters: neither was it on account of a man that the sun became dark in the heavens, but on account of Him who made the great lights: nor was it by a man that the just and righteous were raised to life, but by Him who had granted(a) the power of death from the beginning: nor was it by a man that the vail of the temple of the Jews was rent from the top to the bottom, but by Him who said to them, "Lo, your house is left desolate." For, behold, unless they who crucified him had known that he was the Son of God, they would not have proclaimed the desolation of their city, nor would they have divulged the affliction of their soul in crying Woe! Nor, indeed, even had they been desirous of avoiding this confession, would the terrible commotions which took place at that time have suffered them *to do so.* For, behold, even some of the children of those who crucified *him* are become at this day preachers and evangelists, together with the Apostles, my companions, in all the land of Palestine, and among the Samaritans, and in all the country of the Philistines. The idols also of paganism are despised, and the cross of Christ is honoured, and the peoples and creatures confess God, who became man. If, therefore, while Jesus our Lord was upon earth ye would have believed in him, that he is the Son of God, and, before ye had heard the word of his preaching, would have confessed in him, that he is God, now that he is ascended to his Father, and ye have seen the signs and the wonders which are done in his name, and have heard with your own ears the word of his Gospel, let no man of you doubt in his heart how the promise of his blessing which he sent to you will be established with you— Blessed are ye that have believed in me, not having seen me; and because ye have so believed in me, the city in which ye dwell shall be blessed, and the enemy shall not prevail against it for ever. Turn not aside, therefore, from his faith, for, behold, ye have heard and seen what things bear witness to his faith, that he is the adorable Son and is the glorious God, and he is the invincible King, and he is the power omnipotent; and through faith in him a man is able to acquire the eyes of a true mind, and to perceive that whosoever worshippeth creatures, the wrath of justice will overtake him.

"For every thing which we speak (ܟܠ) before you, as we have received of the gift of our Lord, we speak, and we teach, and we shew, in order that ye may obtain your salvation, and not destroy your spirits through the error of heathenism; because the heavenly Light is arisen over the creation, and He it is that chose the patriarchs of old, and the righteous men, and the prophets, and spake with them by the revelation of the Spirit of Holiness. For He is the God of the Jews who crucified him; the erring heathen also worship Him, even while they know it not, because there is no other God in heaven and in earth; and behold, confession ascendeth up to him from the four quarters of the creation. Behold, therefore, your ears have heard that which was not heard by you *before*, and behold again, your eyes have seen that which was never seen by you *before*. Do no violence, therefore, to that which ye have seen and heard. Put away from you the rebellious heart of your fathers, and free yourselves from the yoke of sin which hath dominion over you in libations and in sacrifices before graven images, and be careful for yourselves about your lives, which are perishable, and the stay of your head, which is frail, and get you a new mind which worships the Maker, and not the things made, in which is represented the image of verity and of truth, of the Father, and of the Son, and of the Spirit of Holiness, while ye believe and are baptized in the triple and glorious names. For this is our doctrine and our preaching. Because it is not in many things that the belief of the truth of Christ consists. And such of you as are willing to be obedient to Christ, ye know that I have many times repeated my words before you, in order that ye might learn and understand what ye hear. And we shall rejoice in this, like the husbandman who rejoiceth in his field which is blessed; God also will be glorified by your repentance towards him. While ye obtain salvation through this, we also, who give you this counsel, shall not be defrauded of the blessed reward of this. And because I am confident that you are a land blessed according to the will of the Lord Christ (ܒܗ), for this reason, instead of the dust of our feet, which it was commanded us that we should wipe off against the city which receiveth not our words, behold I have wiped off to-day at the door of your ears the words of my lips, in which are represented both the coming of Christ which has been, and that which is still to be; and the resurrection also, and the resuscitation of all men, and the separation which is to take place between the believers and the infidels, and the sad punishment which is reserved for those who know not God; and the blessed promise of future joy which they shall receive who have believed in Christ, and worshipped him and his Father most high, and have confessed him and the Spirit of his Godhead. And now it is meet that I conclude my discourse for the present: let those, therefore, who have accepted the word of Christ, and those also who are willing to join with us in prayer, remain with us, and then let them go to their own homes."

And Addæus the Apostle himself rejoiced at this, because he saw that many of the people of the city remained with him, and they were but few who did not remain at that time, while even those few, after not many days, accepted his words, and believed in the Gospel of the preaching of Christ.

And when Addæus the Apostle had spoken these things before the city of Edessa, and King Abgar had seen that all the city rejoiced in his doctrine, men and women equally, and were saying to him, True and faithful is Christ who sent thee to us, he himself also greatly rejoiced at this and praised God; because, like as he had heard from Hanan, his Tabularius, respecting Christ, so he had seen the wonderful mighty works which Addæus the Apostle did in the name of Christ. And Abgar the King also said to him, Like as I sent word to Christ in my letter to him, and like as he sent word to me, and I have received from thee thyself this day, so will I believe all the days of my life, and in the same things will I continue and exult, because I also know that there is no other (ܠܐ) power, in whose name these signs and wonders are done, but by the power of Christ, whom thou preachest in verity and truth. Henceforth, therefore, I will worship him, I and my son Maanu, and Augustin, and Shalmath the Queen. And now, wheresoever thou desirest, build a church, a place of assembly for those who have believed and shall believe thy words; and according as it has been charged thee by thy Lord, so minister thou at *all* times with confidence. Moreover, those who shall be teachers of this Gospel with thee, I am prepared to give to them large gifts, in order that they may have no other work besides the ministry. Whatsoever, also, is required by thee for the expenses of the building, I will give to thee without taking account, and thy word shall be of authority, and prevail in all this city; further, be thou authorized, without any other, to come and enter into my presence, in my royal palace of honor.

And when Abgar went down to his royal palace, he rejoiced, he and his princes with him, Abdu, son of Abdu, and Garmai, and Shemashgram, and Abubai, and Meherdath, together with the rest of their companions, at all that their eyes had seen and their ears had also heard; and in the gladness of their heart they also praised God for having turned their mind to him, and they renounced the paganism in which they stood, and confessed the Gospel of Christ. And when Addæus had built a church, they offered in it vows and oblations, they and the people of the city, and there they offered praises all the days of their life.

And Avida and Barcalba, who were chiefs and rulers, and wore the royal headband, drew near to Addæus, and asked him about the matter of Christ, that he would tell them, how He, being God, had appeared to them like a man: And, How indeed were ye able to look upon him? And he satisfied them all about this, about all that their eyes ([illegible]) had seen, and about every thing which their ears had heard from him. And all that the prophets had spoken concerning him he repeated before them, and they received his words gladly and faithfully, and there was not a man that stood against him, for the glorious acts which he did suffered not any man to withstand him.

But Shavida and Ebednebu, chiefs of the priests of this city, together with Piroz and Diku, their companions, when they had seen the signs which he did, ran and threw down the altars on which they sacrificed before Nebu and Bel, their gods, except the great altar in the midst of the city, and they cried out and said, Truly this is the disciple of that distinguished and glorious Master, of whom we have heard all that he did in the country of Palestine. And Addæus received all those who believed in Christ, and baptized them in the name of the Father, and of the Son, and of the Spirit of Holiness. And those who used to worship stones and stocks sat at his feet, and were recovered from the plague of the foolishness of paganism. Even Jews skilled in the law and the prophets, who traded in silks, they too were convinced, and became disciples, and confessed Christ, that He is the Son of the living God.

But neither did King Abgar nor the Apostle Addæus compel any man by force to believe in Christ, because, without the force of man, the force of the signs constrained many to believe in him. And they received his doctrine with love, all this country of Mesopotamia, and all the regions round about it.

But Aggæus, who made the chains and headbands of the King, and

Palut, and Barshelama, and Barsamya, together with the rest of their companions, clave to Addæus the Apostle, and he received them, and associated them with him in the ministry, while they read in the Old Testament and the New, and the Prophets, (ܗܘ) and the Acts of the Apostles, meditating upon them every day: and he charged them cautiously, to let their bodies be pure and their persons holy, as it is becoming in men who stand before the altar of God, "Be ye indeed also far removed from false swearing, and from wicked murder, and from false witness, which is mixed up with adultery, and from magic arts, which are without mercy, and from soothsaying, and divination, and fortune-tellers; and from fate and nativities, in which the erring Chaldæans boast; and from planets and signs of the Zodiac, on which the foolish trust. And put away from you evil hypocrisy, and bribes, and gifts, by which the innocent are condemned. And besides this ministry to which ye have been called have no other service; for the Lord himself is the service of your ministry all the days of your life. Be also diligent to give the seal of baptism, and love not the superfluities of this world. Listen ye to judgment with justice and with truth, and be not a stumblingblock to the blind, lest through you should be blasphemed the name of Him who opened the eyes of the blind, as we have seen: all therefore who see you will perceive that whatsoever ye preach and teach *to others* you perform yourselves."

And they ministered with him in the church which Addæus had built, at the order and command of King Abgar, and they were furnished from what belonged to the King and to his nobles with some things for the house of God, and others for the supply of the poor. But a large multitude of people assembled day by day, and came to the prayers of the service, and to *the reading of* the Old Testament and the New of Ditonron. They also believed in the revival of the dead, and they buried their departed in the hope of the resurrection. They kept also the festivals of the Church at their proper seasons, and continued every day in the vigils of the Church. And they made visits of almsgiving (ܣܥ) to the sick and to those that were whole, according to the instruction of Addæus to them. Moreover, in the places round about the city, churches were built, and many received from him the Hand of Priesthood: so that the people of the East also, in the guise of merchants, passed over into the country belonging to the Romans, in order that they might see the signs which Addæus did. And those who became disciples received from him the Hand of Priesthood, and in their own country of the Assyrians they taught the sons of their own people, and built houses of prayer there secretly, through danger of the fire-worshippers and the adorers of water.

And Narses, the King of the Assyrians, when he heard of the things which the Apostle Addæus did, sent a message to the same King Abgar: Either send to me the man who doeth these signs before thee, that I may see him and hear his words, or send me word of all that thou hast seen him do in thine own city. And Abgar wrote to Narses, and informed him of all the history of the matter of Addæus from the beginning to the end, and he left nothing which he did not write to him. But when Narses heard those things which were written to him, he was astonished and marvelled.

But Abgar the King, because he was not able to pass over into the country belonging to the Romans, and go to Palestine, and slay the Jews, because they had crucified Christ, wrote a letter and sent it to Tiberius Cæsar, writing in it thus:

"King Abgar to our Lord Tiberius Cæsar: Knowing that nothing is concealed from your Majesty, I write and inform your great and dread Sovereignty that the Jews who are under your hand, and dwell in the country of Palestine, have assembled themselves together, and crucified the Christ, without any fault worthy of death, after he had done before them signs and wonders, and had shewn them great and mighty works, so that he even raised the dead to life for them; and at the time that they crucified him the sun became darkened, and the earth also shook, (ܛ) and all creatures trembled and quaked; and, as if of their accord, at this deed the whole creation quailed, and the inhabiters of the creation. And now your Majesty knoweth what order it is meet for you to give respecting the people of the Jews who have done these things."

And Tiberius Cæsar wrote and sent to King Abgar, and he wrote to him thus:

"The letter of thy Fidelity towards me I have received, and it has been read before me. Touching what the Jews have had the audacity to do with the cross, the Governor Pilate also has written and made known to my Proconsul, Aulbinus, respecting these same things which thou hast written to me. But because the war of the people of Spain, who have rebelled against me, is on foot at this time, for this reason I have not been able to avenge this matter; but I am prepared, when I have leisure, to bring a charge legally against the Jews, who act not according to the law. And on this account Pilate also, who was appointed by me Governor there, I have sent another in his stead, and dismissed him in disgrace, because he exceeded the law, and did the will of the Jews, and, for the gratification of the Jews, crucified Christ who, according to what I hear about him, instead of the cross of death, deserved to be honoured and adored by them, and the more so, because they saw with their own eyes every thing that he did. But thou, according to thy Fidelity towards me, and thine own true compact, and that of thy fathers, hast done well in thus writing to me."

And Abgar the King received Aristides, who had been sent to him by Tiberius Cæsar. And he replied, and sent him back with presents of honor which were suitable for him who sent him to him. And he went from Edessa to Thicuntha, where Claudius, the second from the Emperor, was; and from thence, in the next place, he went to Artica, where ([illegible]) Tiberius Cæsar was. But Caius was watching the regions round about Cæsar. And Aristides himself also related before Tiberius the history of the mighty works which Addæus had done before King Abgar. And when he had leisure from the war, he sent and put to death some of the chiefs of the Jews who were in Palestine. And when King Abgar heard, he was very glad of this, that the Jews had received punishment as it was right.

And some years after the Apostle Addæus had built the church in Edessa, and had furnished it with every thing that was requisite for it, and had converted many of the people of the city, he also built churches in other villages which were far off and near, and completed and ornamented them, and established in them deacons and presbyters, and he taught persons to read the Scriptures in them, and he taught the Ordinances and the Ministry without and within. After all these things, he was seized with that disease of which he departed from this world. And he called for Aggæus before the whole assembly of the Church, and brought him near, and made him Guide and Ruler in his own place. And Palut, who was a deacon, he made him presbyter; and Abshelama, who was a scribe, he made him deacon. And while the Nobles and Chiefs were assembled, and stood near him, Bar Calba, the son of Zati, and Maryhab, the son of Barshemash, and Senac, son of Avida, and Piroz, son of Patric, together with the rest of their companions, the Apostle Addæus said to them, "Ye know and can testify, all of you who hear me, that whatsoever I have preached to you and have taught you, and ye have heard from me, so have I conducted myself among you, and ye have seen it also in practice; because our Lord thus charged us, that whatsoever we preach in words before the people, we should also practise it in deeds before all men. And according to the

Ordinances and Laws which were appointed by the Disciples in Jerusalem, and even the Apostles, my fellows, were guided by them (✝), so likewise you, turn ye not aside from them, nor diminish aught from them: in the same manner as I myself also am guided by them amongst you, and have not turned aside from them to the right or to the left, in order that I might not become a stranger to the promised salvation which is reserved for such as are guided by them. Give heed, therefore, to this ministry which ye hold, and continue in it with fear and trembling, and minister every day. Minister not in it with neglectful habits, but with the discretion of faith: neither let the praises of Christ cease out of your mouth, nor let weariness in the prayer of *stated* times approach you. Give heed to the verity which ye hold, and to the teaching of the truth which ye have received, and to the inheritance of salvation which I commit to you, because before the judgment-seat of Christ will it be required of you, when He maketh reckoning with the pastors and superiors, and when He taketh his money from the traders, with the increase of the profits. For He is the King's Son, and goeth to receive a kingdom, and return; and He will come and make a resurrection of all men, and then He will sit upon the throne of his righteousness, and judge the dead and the living, according as he has told us. Let not the secret eye of your minds from above be blinded, that your offences may not abound in the way which has no offences in it, but error is abominable in its paths. Seek those that are lost, and direct those that err, and rejoice in those that are found; bind up the bruised, and watch over the fatlings; because at your hands will the sheep of Christ be required. Look ye not to honour which passeth away; for the shepherd that looketh to receive honour from his flock, badly, badly stands his flock with respect to him. Let your care over the young lambs be great, because their angels behold the face of the Father which is invisible. Neither be ye stones of offence before the blind, but clearers of the way and of the paths (ܛ) in a difficult country, among the Jews, who crucified Him, and the Pagans who are in error; for with these two sides ye have war, in order that ye might shew the truth of the faith which ye hold: even while ye are quiet, your modest and honourable appearance will fight for you against those who hate the truth and love falsehood. Smite not the poor in the presence of the rich; for their poverty is an infliction bad enough for them. Suffer not yourselves to be beguiled by the abominable deliberations of Satan, lest ye be stripped naked of that faith which ye have put on." * * * *

* * * * * * * *

* * * * * * * *

"Nor will we mingle ourselves with the Jews, who crucified him; nor will we let go this inheritance which we have received from thee, but with it will we depart out of this world; and on the day of our Lord, before the tribunal of his righteous judgment, there will He restore to us this inheritance, according as thou hast told us."

And when these things had been spoken, Abgar the King rose up, he and his Princes, and his Nobles, and he went to his own palace, while they all of them grieved over him because he was dying. And he sent to him honourable and noble apparel, that he might be buried in it. But when Addæus the Apostle saw it, he sent word to him, During my life I have taken nothing from thee, neither will I now at my death take any thing from thee, nor will I belie in myself the word of Christ, which he spake to us, "Accept not any thing from any man, and possess not any thing in this world."

And three days more after these things had been spoken by the Apostle Addæus, and he had heard and received the testimony of the doctrine of their preaching from those belonging to his ministry in the presence of all the Nobles, he departed out of this world; and that day was the fifth of the week, and the fourteenth of the month Iyar. And the whole city was in great mourning and bitter suffering on account of him. Nor was it the Christians (ܒܟܐ) only that grieved over him, but the Jews also, and the Pagans who were in this same city. But Abgar the King grieved over him more than all, he and the Princes of his kingdom. And in the sorrow of his heart he despised and abandoned the honour of his kingdom on that day; and with tears and sighs he wept over him with all men. And all the people of the city that saw him marvelled how greatly he was afflicted on his account. And with great and exceeding honour he conveyed and buried him like one of the Princes when he dies, and he placed him in a large sepulchre of sculpture by the fingers, in which those of the house of Ariu, the ancestors of Abgar the King, were laid: there he laid him compassionately, with sorrow and great grief. And all the people of the Church went from time to time, and offered prayers there diligently; and they celebrated the commemoration his death from year to year, according to the ordinance and instruction which had been committed to them by the Apostle Addæus himself, and according to the word of Aggæus, who himself became Guide and Ruler, and the successor of his chair after him, by the Hand of Priesthood, which he had received from him in the presence of all men.

He, too, by the same Hand that he had received from him, made Priests and Guides in the whole of this country of Mesopotamia. For they also, like the Apostle Addæus, thus held fast his word, and listened and received, as good and faithful heirs of the Apostle of the adorable Christ. But silver and gold accepted he from no man, nor did the gifts of the Princes approach him: for instead of gold and silver, he enriched the Church of Christ with the souls of believers. But the whole state of the men and the women were modest and decorous, and they were holy and pure; because they dwelt in union and modesty without spot, in watchfulness of the ministry decorously, in their carefulness towards the poor, and in their (ܣܥܪ) visitations to the sick: for their ways were full of praise from those who beheld, and their conduct was invested with commendation from strangers, so that even the priests belonging to Nebu and Bel divided the honour with them at all times, by their honourable aspect, by the truth of their words, by the plain speaking which was in their freedom, that was neither subservient to greediness, nor in bondage under blame. For there was no one who saw them that did not run to meet them, that he might greet them honorably, because the very sight of them diffused peace upon the beholders; for their words of peace were spread like a net over the rebellious, while they were entering within the fold of truth and verity. For there was no man who saw them and had any ground to be ashamed of them, because they did any thing which was not just and not becoming: and by these means, their countenances were open, in the preaching of their doctrine towards all men; for whatsoever they said to others and exhorted them *to do*, they themselves exhibited the same in deeds in their own persons, and the hearers, who saw that their actions and words went together, became their disciples without much persuasion, and confessed Christ the King, while they praised God for having turned them to him.

And some years after the death of King Abgar, there arose one of his rebellious sons, who was not obedient to peace, and he sent word to Aggæus, as he was sitting in the Church, Make me a headband of gold, such as thou usest formerly to make for my fathers. Aggæus replied to him, I will not leave the ministry of Christ, which has been committed to me by Christ's disciple, and make the headbands of the evil one. And when he saw that he did not obey him, he sent and brake his legs as he was sitting in the church and expounding. And as he was dying he adjured (ܐܘܡܝ) Palut and Abshelama, Lay me and bury me in this house, for whose truth's sake, behold, I am dying.

And as he had adjured *them*, so they laid him within the centre door of the church, between the men and the women. And there was great and bitter mourning in all the Church, and in all the city, beyond the suffering and mourning which there had been in its interior, like the mourning had been when the Apostle Addæus himself died.

And because he died suddenly and quickly, at the breaking of his legs, he was not able to lay his hand upon Palut, and Palut himself went to Antioch, and received the Hand of Priesthood from Serapion, Bishop of Antioch, which Hand Serapion himself also received from Zephyrinus, Bishop of the city of Rome, from the succession of the Hand of Priesthood of Simon Cephas, who had received it from our Lord, and was bishop there in Rome twenty and five years in the days of that Cæsar who reigned there thirteen years.

And as is the custom in the kingdom of King Abgar, and in all kingdoms, that whatsoever the king orders, and whatsoever is spoken in his presence is committed to writing, and laid up among the records, so also Labubna, son of Senac, son of Ebedshaddai, the king's scribe, wrote these things of Addæus the Apostle from the beginning to the end; while Hanan the Tabularius, the kings' Sharir, set to the hand of witness, and placed it among the records of the kings, where the ordinances and the laws are laid up, and there *the contracts* of the buyers and sellers are kept with care, without any negligence whatever.

Here endeth the Doctrine of the Apostle Addæus, which he preached in Edessa, the faithful city of Abgar, the faithful King.

THE DOCTRINE OF THE APOSTLES.

([illegible]) When Christ ascended to his Father: and how the Apostles received the gift of the Spirit; and the Ordinances and Laws of the Church, and whither each one of the same Apostles went; and from whence the countries belonging to the Romans received the Hand of Priesthood.

In the three hundred and thirty-ninth year of the kingdom of the Greeks, in the month Heziran, on the fourth day of the same, which is the first day of the week, and the completion of Pentecost, on this same day the Disciples came from Nazareth of Galilee, from the place where the conception of our Lord was announced, to the mountain which is called Baith Zaithe, our Lord being with them, but not being visible to them. And at the t[illegible] of the great morning our Lord lifted up his hands, and laid the[illegible] the heads of the Eleven Disciples, and gave to them the gift of the Priesthood; and suddenly a bright cloud received him, and they beheld him as he went up to heaven. And he sat down on the right hand of his Father. And they were praising God because they saw his ascension as he had told them; and they were rejoicing, because they had received the Right Hand of Priesthood of the house of Moses and Aaron. And from thence they went up and proceeded to the upper room, that in which our Lord had celebrated the Passover with them, and in the place where the inquiries had been: Who is it that betrayeth our Lord to the crucifiers? There also were the inquiries, How they should preach his Gospel in the world. And as within that upper room the mystery of His body and blood began, that it might prevail in the world, so also from thence did the teaching of his preaching begin to have authority in the world. And when ([illegible]) the Disciples were thrown into this difficulty, How they should preach his Gospel to strange tongues which they knew not, and they were speaking one to the other after this manner; Although we be confident that Christ will perform by our hands mighty works, and miracles before strange peoples whose tongues we know not, neither are they acquainted with our tongue, who shall teach them and inform them, that it is by the name of Christ, who was crucified, that these mighty works and miracles are done? And while the Disciples were in these deliberations, Simon Cephas rose up and said to them: My brethren, This is not our business, how we shall preach his Gospel, but it is our Lord's; for He knoweth how it is possible for us to preach his Gospel in the world; but we rely upon his care for us, which he promised to us and said; "When I am ascended to my Father I will send to you the Spirit, the Paraclete, that he may teach you every thing which it is meet for you to know, and to make known." And when Simon Cephas had spoken these things to his fellow Apostles, and reminded them, a voice of mystery was heard by them, and a sweet odour, which is strange to the world, was diffused on them, and tongues of fire, between the voice and the odour, came down to them from heaven, and alighted and sat upon every one of them; and according to the tongue which each one of them had received, so he prepared himself to go to the country in which that tongue was spoken and understood. And by the same gift of the Spirit which was given to them on that day, they also appointed Ordinances and Laws which were agreeable with the Gospel of their preaching, and with the true and faithful teaching of their doctrine:

I. The Apostles therefore appointed: Pray ye towards the East, "because as the lightning which lightneth from the east, and is seen even to the west, so shall the coming of the Son of Man be": that by this we may know and understand that He will appear from the East suddenly.

(ܟܘ) II. Again the Apostles appointed, That on the first day of the week there should be service and reading of the Holy Scriptures, and an Oblation. Because on the first day of the week our Lord rose from the place of the dead, and on the first day of the week he manifested himself in the world, and on the first day of the week he ascended up to heaven, and on the first day of the week he will appear in the end with the Angels of heaven.

III. Again the Apostles appointed, That on the fourth day of the week there should be service, because upon it our Lord disclosed to them about his trial and his suffering, and his crucifixion, and his death, and his resurrection. And the Disciples were in this sorrow.

IV. Again the Apostles appointed, That on the sixth day of the week, at the ninth hour, there should be service, because that which had been spoken on the fourth day of the week about the suffering of our Saviour was accomplished on the sixth day of the week, while the worlds and the creatures trembled, and the lights in the heavens were darkened.

V. Again the Apostles appointed, That there should be Presbyters and Deacons like the Levites, and Subdeacons like those who carried the vessels of the hall of the Sanctuary of the Lord, and an Overseer, the same is the Guide of all the people, like Aaron the chief and master of all the priests and Levites of the whole city.

VI. Again the Apostles appointed: Celebrate the day of the Epiphany of our Saviour, which is the chief of the festivals of the Church, on the sixth day of the latter Canun, in the long number of the Greeks.

VII Again the Apostles appointed: Forty days before the day of the Passion of our Saviour fast ye, and then celebrate the day of the Passion, and the day of the Resurrection, because our Lord himself also, the lord of the festival, fasted forty days, and Moses and Elias, who were invested ([illegible]) with this mystery, they also fasted forty days each, and then they were glorified.

VIII. Again the Apostles appointed, That at the conclusion of all the scriptures, the Gospel should be read, as being the seal of all the scriptures; and the people should listen to it standing up on their feet, because it is the glad tidings of Salvation of all men.

IX. Again the Apostles appointed: At the completion of fifty days after his resurrection, make the commemoration of his ascension to his glorious Father.

X. The Apostles appointed, That, except the Old Testament and the Prophets and the Gospel, and the Acts of their own Triumphs, let not any thing be read on the pulpit of the Church.

XI. Again the Apostles appointed, That whosoever is not acquainted with the Faith of the Church, and the Ordinances and Laws which are appointed in it, should not be a Guide and Ruler; and whosoever is acquainted with them and has transgressed them, should not minister any more, because, not being confirmed in his ministry, he acts falsely.

XII. Again the Apostles appointed, That whosoever sweareth, or lieth, or beareth false witness, or goeth amongst sorcerers and soothsayers, and Chaldæans, and putteth faith in fate and nativities, which they hold who know not God, should also, as being a man that knoweth not God, be dismissed from the ministry, and not minister.

XIII. Again the Apostles appointed, If there be any man that doubteth touching the ministry, and it is not confirmed to him, this man should not minister again, because the Lord of the ministry is not confirmed to him, and he deceiveth man, and not God, "before whom no artifices avail."

XIV. Again the Apostles appointed, Whoso lendeth and taketh ([illegible]) usury, and is occupied with merchandise and greediness, he should not minister again, nor continue in the ministry.

XV. Again the Apostles appointed, That he who loveth the Jews like Iscariot, who loved them, or the Pagans, who worship cr atures instead of the Creator, should not enter in amongst them and minister: but if he be already amongst them they should not suffer him, but he should be separated from amongst them, and not minister with them again.

XVI. Again the Apostles appointed, If any one from the Jews or Pagans come and join himself with them, and if, after he has joined himself with them, he turn and go back to the side on which he had stood, if afterwards he return and come to them a second time, he should not be received again, but, like the side on which he had been before, so let those who know him look upon him.

XVII. Again the Apostles appointed, That it is not lawful for the Guide to do the things which pertain to the Church apart from those who minister with him; but with the counsel of them all let him order, and that be done which all of them assent to and object not.

XVIII. Again the Apostles appointed, That all those who dep rt out of this world with the good testimony of the faith of Christ, and with affliction for his name's sake, make ye a commemoration of them on the day on which they were put to death.

XIX. Again the Apostles appointed, In the service of the Church repeat, day by day, David's songs of praise, on account of this: "I will bless the Lord always," and "His praises are always in my mouth," and "In the day and in the night will I meditate and speak, and cause my voice to be heard before thee."

XX. Again the Apostles appointed, Such as divest (ܫܠܚ) themselves of mammon, and run not after the gain of money, let them be chosen and advanced to the ministry of the altar.

XXI. Again the Apostles appointed, The Priest who accidentally bindeth improperly, let him receive the punishment which is just: but let him that has been bound receive the bond as if he had been properly bound.

XXII. Again the Apostles appointed, Those who are accustomed to hear trials, if it appear that they have respect of persons, and condemn the innocent and acquit the guilty, let them not hear another trial, receiving again the rebuke of their hypocrisy as it is fit.

XXIII. Again the Apostles appointed, Such as are high-minded and puffed up with the pride of boasting, let them not be promoted to the ministry, "because that which is exalted among men is abominated before God"; and against them it is said, "I will return the recompense upon those that are proud."

XXIV. Again the Apostles appointed, That there should be a Ruler over the Presbyters who are in the villages, and that he should be acknowledged the chief of them all, at whose hand they should all be required; for Samuel thus went to visit from place to place and ruled.

XXV. Again the Apostles appointed, Those kings who shall hereafter believe in Christ, it shall be lawful for them to go up and stand before the altar together with the Guides of the Church, because David also, and those who were like him, went up and stood before the altar.

XXVI. Again the Apostles appointed, That no man should dare to do any thing by the authority of the Priesthood unjustly and improperly, but with justice, and without the blame of hypocrisy.

(ܐ) XXVII. Again the Apostles appointed, That the bread of the Oblation should be placed upon the altar on the day that it is baked, and not some days after, which is not lawful.

But all these things, it was not for themselves that the Apostles appointed them, but for those who should come after them, for they feared that wolves were about to put on sheeps' clothing: because for themselves, the Spirit, the Paraclete which was in them, was sufficient to conduct them lawfully, according to these Laws which he had appointed by their hands. For they who had received from our Lord power and authority needed not that laws should be appointed for them by others; for Paul also, and Timothy, while they were going about in the country of Syria and Cilicia, committed these same Regulations and Laws of the Apostles and Elders to those who were under the hand of the Apostles, for the churches of the countries in which they were preaching and publishing the Gospel; but the Disciples, after these Ordinances and Laws which they had appointed, ceased not from the preaching of the Gospel, or from wonderful mighty works which our Lord did by their hands. For much people was collected near them every day, who believed on Christ, and they came to them from other cities and hearkened to their words and received them. But Nicodemus and Gamaliel, chiefs of the Synagogue of the Jews, came to the Apostles secretly, consenting to their doctrine. But Judas, and Levi, and Peri, and Joseph, and Justus, the sons of Hananias, and

Caiphas and Alexander the priests, they also came to the Apostles by night, confessing Christ, that he is the Son of God; but they were afraid of disclosing their minds towards the Disciples on account of the sons of their own people. And the Apostles received them with love, saying to them: Destroy not, through the shame and fear of (ܠ) men, your lives before God, and have the blood of Christ required of you, as well as of your fathers who took it upon themselves: for it cannot be accepted before God, that while ye be with those who worship him, ye should go and mingle yourselves with those who slew his adorable son. How do ye expect that your faith should be accepted with those who are true, so long as ye are with those that are false? but it is right that you, as men who believe in Christ, should confess openly this faith which we preach. And when they heard these things from the Disciples, those sons of the priests cried out, all of them equally, before the whole people of the Apostles, We confess and believe in Christ who was crucified, and we confess that he is the Son of God from everlasting; and we renounce those who dared to crucify him; for even the priests of the people confess Christ secretly, but on account of the headship of the people which they love, they are not willing to confess openly, and they have forgotten that which is written that "He is the Lord of knowledge, and artifices avail not before him." But when their fathers had heard these things of their sons, they threatened them greatly, not, indeed, because they had believed on Christ, but because they had declared and spoken openly of the mind of their fathers before the sons of their people. But those who believed clave to the Disciples, and turned not from them, because they saw that whatsoever they taught to the multitudes, they fulfilled the same themselves in deeds before all men. And whenever affliction and persecution arose against the Disciples, they rejoiced in being afflicted with them, and they received stripes and imprisonment with gladness, in the confession of their faith in Christ; and all the days of their life they preached Christ before the Jews and the Samaritans. And after the death of the Apostles there were Guides and Rulers in the churches, and whatsoever (ܠܟ) the Apostles had committed to them, and they had received from them, they taught to the multitudes all the time of their lives. They again, at their deaths also committed and delivered to their disciples after them every thing which they had received from the Apostles; also what James had written from Jerusalem, and Simon from the city of Rome, and John from Ephesus, and Mark from the great Alexandria, and Andrew from Phrygia, and Luke from Macedonia, and Judas Thomas from India; that the epistles of an Apostle might be received and read in the Churches, in every place, like those Triumphs of their Acts, which Luke wrote, are read, that by this the Apostles might be known, and the Prophets, and the Old Testament and the New; that one truth was preached by them all, that one Spirit spake in them all from one God, whom they had all worshipped and had all preached. And the countries received their doctrine. Every thing, therefore, which had been spoken of our Lord by the hand of the Apostles, and the Apostles had delivered to their disciples, was believed and received in every country, by the intimation of our Lord, who said to them, "I am with you, even till the world ends:" while the Guides were disputing with the Jews from the books of the Prophets, and contending against the erring Pagans with the terrible mighty works which they did in the name of Christ: for all the peoples, even those who dwelt in other countries, were quiet and silent at the Gospel of Christ; and those who confessed cried out under the persecution, "This persecution of us to-day shall be an advocate for us because we were formerly persecutors." For there were some of them against whom death by the sword was decreed, and some of them from whom they took away whatsoever they possessed and dismissed them; and as often as affliction arose against them, their congregations became enriched and increased (ܠܐ), and with gladness of their heart they received death of every kind. And by the Hand of Priesthood, which the Apostles themselves had received from our Lord, their Gospel was spread abroad in the four quarters of the world rapidly. And while they visited one another, they ministered to each other.

Jerusalem received the Hand of Priesthood, and all the country of Palestine, and the parts of the Samaritans and the Philistines, and the country of the Arabians, and of Phœnicia, and the people of Cæsarea, from James, who was Ruler and Guide in the Church of the Apostles, which had been built in Sion.

The great Alexandria and Thebais, and the whole of Inner Egypt, and all the country of Pelusium, and even to the borders of the Indians, received the Apostles' Hand of Priesthood from Mark, the Evangelist, who was Ruler and Guide there in the church which he had built there, and ministered.

India, and all its own countries, and those bordering on it, even to the farthest sea, received the Apostles' Hand of Priesthood from Judas Thomas, who was Guide and Ruler in the church which he built there, and ministered there.

Antioch, and Syria, and Cilicia, and Galatia, even to Pontus, received the Apostles' Hand of Priesthood from Simon Cephas, who himself laid the foundation of the church there, and was Priest, and ministered there up to the time when he went up from thence to Rome, on account of Simon the Sorcerer, who was deceiving the people of Rome by his sorceries.

(ܠܒ) The city of Rome, and all Italy, and Spain, and Britain, and Gaul, together with the other remaining countries which bordered on them, received the Apostles' Hand of Priesthood from Simon Cephas, who went up from Antioch, and became Ruler and Guide there in the Church which he built there and in its environs.

Ephesus, and Thessalonica, and all Asia, and all the country of the Corinthians, and of all Achaia and its environs, received the Apostles' Hand of Priesthood from John the Evangelist, who had leaned upon the bosom of our Lord, who built a Church there, and ministered there in his office of Guide there.

Nicæa, and Nicomedia, and all the country of Bithynia, and of Gothia, and of the regions round about it, received the Apostles' Hand of Priesthood from Andrew, the brother of Simon Cephas, who was Guide and Ruler in the Church which he built there, and was Priest and ministered there.

Byzantium, and all the country of Thrace, and its environs, even to the great river, the border which separates between the Barbarians, received the Apostles' Hand of Priesthood from Luke the Apostle, who built a Church there, and ministered there in his office of Ruler and Guide there.

Edessa, and all its environs which were on all sides of it, and Soba, and Arabia, and all the North, and the regions round about it, and the South, and all the places of the borders of Mesopotamia, received the Apostles' Hand of Priesthood from Addæus, the Apostle, one of the Seventy two Apostles, who taught there, and built a Church there, and was Priest and ministered there in his office of Guide there.

The whole of Persia of the Assyrians and Armenians and Medians, and of the countries round about Babylon, the Huzites and the Gelæ, even to the borders of the Indians, and even to the country (ܠܗ) of Gog and Magog, and again all the countries from all sides, received the Apostles' Hand of Priesthood from Aggæus, a maker of *golden* chains, the disciple of Addæus the Apostle.

But the rest of the other fellows of the Apostles went to the distant countries of the Barbarians, and taught from place to place, and passed on, and there they ministered with their preaching; there also was their departure out of this world, while their disciples after them continued to go on up to the present day. And there was no change or addition made by them to what they preached.

But Luke the Evangelist had this diligence, and wrote the Triumphs of the Acts of the Apostles, and the Ordinances and Laws of the ministry of their Priesthood, and whither each one of them went. By his diligence, therefore, Luke wrote these things, and more than these, and he placed them in the hand of Priscus and Acquilas, his disciples; and they accompanied him even up to the day of his death: like as Timothy and Erastus, of Lystra and Menaus, the first disciples of the Apostles, accompanied Paul until he went up to the city of Rome, because he had withstood the orator Tertullus. And Nero the Emperor slew him with the sword, and Simon Cephas, in the city of Rome.

DOCTRINE OF SIMON CEPHAS, IN THE CITY OF ROME.

In the third year of Claudius Cæsar, Simon Cephas departed from Antioch to go to Rome. And as he passed on he preached in the countries the word of our Lord. And when he drew nigh to enter in there, many had heard and they went out to meet him, and the whole Church received him with great joy. And some of the princes of the city who (ܠܗ) wore the headbands of kings came out to him that they might see him and hear his word; and when the whole city was gathered together near him, he stood up to speak with them, and to shew them the preaching of his teaching how it was; and he began to speak to them thus: Men, sons of Rome, saints of all Italy, hearken to what I say to you. To-day I preach and proclaim Jesus the Son of God, who came down from heaven, and was made man, and was amongst us like ourselves, and wrought marvellous mighty works and signs and wonders before us, and before all the Jews who are in the land of Palestine. And you also have heard of those things which he did, because they came to him also from other countries on account of the fame of his healing, and on the report of his marvellous helps. And every one that came near to him was healed by his word. And because he was God, at the same time as he healed he also forgave sins: for his healing which was manifest bare witness to his secret forgiveness, that it is true and to be believed. For this Jesus the prophets preached in their mysteries, while they waited to see him, and to hear his words: that he who was with his Father for ever and from everlasting, is God, who was hidden in the height, and is appeared in the depth, the glorious Son, who is of his Father, and is glorified together with his Father and with the Spirit of his Godhead, and the terrible power of his majesty. He also was crucified of his own will by the hands of sinners, and was taken up to his Father, while I and my companions beheld, and he will come again in his own glory and that of all his holy angels, as we have heard him say to us. For we are not able to speak any thing which has not been heard by us from him, nor do we write in the book of his Gospel any thing which he has not spoken to us, because (ܠ) this word is spoken that the mouth of the liars may be stopped, on the day that the sons of men shall give an account of their idle words at the place of Judgment. But because we were catchers of fish, and not skilled in books, on this account he said to us, 'I will send you the Spirit, the Paraclete, that he may teach you what ye do not know;' for by his gift we speak these things which ye hear. And further by it we bring aid to the sick and healing to the deceased; that by the hearing of his word, and by the aid of his power, e may believe in Christ, that he is

God, the Son of God, may be delivered from the service of bondage and may worship him and his Father, and glorify the Spirit of of his Godhead. For when we glorify the Father we also glorify his Son with him, and when we worship the Son we also worship the Father with him; and when we confess the Spirit we also confess the Father and the Son, because in the name of the Father, and the Son, and the Spirit, were we commanded to baptize those who believe, that they might live for ever."

"Flee therefore from the words of the wisdom of this world, in which there is no profit, and draw near to those which are true and faithful, and accepted before God; and their reward is reserved, and their recompense abideth. And now that the light is arisen upon the creation, the world also has obtained the eyes of the mind, that every man might see and understand that it is not right that creatures should be worshipped instead of the Creator, neither together with the Creator, because every thing which is creature ought to be a worshipper of its maker, and is not to be worshipped like its creator. But this one who came to us is God, the Son of God, in his own nature, although he mingled his godhead with our manhood, in order that he might renew our manhood by the aid of his godhead. And on this account it is just that we should worship him, because he is to be worshipped together with his Father, and that we should not worship creatures, which were created for the worship of the Creator. For he is the God of Truth (ܫܪܪܐ) and of Verity: it is he who was before the worlds and things created: he is the Son of Truth, and the glorious fruit who is of the Father most high. But ye see the wonderful deeds which accompany and follow these words: one would hardly believe the short time since he ascended to his Father, and see how his Gospel is spread abroad through the whole creation, that by this it may be known and believed that he is the creator of the creatures, and by his assent the creatures subsist. And inasmuch as ye saw the sun become darkened at his death, ye yourselves also are witnesses. But the earth shook when he was slain, and the vail was rent at his death: and touching these things the Governor Pilate also was witness, for he sent and made them known to Cæsar, and these things, and more than these, were read before him and before the princes of your city. And on this account Cæsar was angry against Pilate, because he had unjustly been persuaded by the Jews, and for this reason he sent and took away from him the authority which he had given to him. And this same thing was published abroad and made known in all the dominion of the Romans. What, therefore, Pilate saw and made known to Cæsar and to your honourable Senate, the same I preach and declare, and my fellow-Apostles. And ye know that Pilate could not have written to the Government any thing which did not take place and he saw with his own eyes: but that which did take place and was done in reality, the same he wrote and made known. And those who watched the sepulchre were witnesses also of those things which took place there; they became like dead men: and when those watchers were questioned by Pilate, they confessed before him how large a bribe the chief priests of the Jews had given to them, in order that they might say that we, his disciples, stole away the body of Christ. Behold, therefore, ye have heard many things, but if ye be not willing to be convinced by those things which ye have heard, nevertheless be convinced by the mighty works that ye see, (ܠܕ) which are done in his name. Let not Simon the Sorcerer deceive you, by semblances that are not real which he exhibits to you; like as to men without understanding, who know not how to discern what they see and hear. Send, therefore, and bring him where your whole city is assembled together, and choose for you some sign for us to do before you, and the one whom ye see perform that same sign, your part will be to believe in him."

And in the same hour they sent and fetched Simon the Sorcerer, and the men who were of his opinions said to him: As a man, in whom we are confident that there is power in thee to perform any thing, perform thou some sign before us all, and this Simon the Galilæan, who preacheth Christ, shall see. And as they were thus speaking to him a dead man happened to be passing by, the son of one of the chiefs, and well known and illustrious among them. And all of them being assembled together said to him: The one of you that shall restore to life this dead man, he is true, and to be believed and accepted, and we will all follow him in every thing that he saith to us. And they said to Simon the Sorcerer, Because thou hast been here before Simon the Galilæan, and we have known thee before him, exhibit thou first the power which accompanieth thee. But Simon hesitatingly drew near to the dead man, and they set down the bier before him; and he looked to the right hand and to the left, and gazed up to heaven, saying many words: some of them he spake aloud, and some of them secretly and not aloud. And he waited a long while and nothing took place, and nothing was done, and the dead man was lying upon his bier. And in the same hour Simon Cephas drew near to him that was dead with confidence, and cried aloud before all the assembly which was standing there: In the name of Jesus Christ, whom the Jews crucified at Jerusalem, and whom we preach, rise up from thence; (ܩܘܡ) and immediately, as the word of Simon was spoken, he that was dead revived and rose up from the bier. And all the people saw and marvelled. And they said to Simon: Christ, whom thou preachest, is true: and many cried out and said, Let Simon the Sorcerer and deceiver of us all be stoned. But Simon, by reason that every one was running to see the dead man who was come to life again, escaped from them from one street to another, and from house to house, and fell not into their hands on that day.

But the whole city took Simon Cephas and they received him gladly, and with love: and he ceased not to perform signs and wonders in the name of Christ, and many believed in him. But Cuprinus, the father of him who was restored to life conducted Simon Cephas with him to his house, and received him in a proper manner, while he and all his household believed in Christ, that he is the son of the living God. And many of the Jews and of the Pagans became disciples there. And when there was great rejoicing at his doctrine, he built a church there in Rome and in the neighbouring cities, and in all the villages of the people of Italy; and he ministered there in the office of Guide and Ruler twenty-five years.

And after these years Nero Cæsar seized him, and bound him in prison: and he knew that he would crucify him, so he called Ansus, [*Linus*] the Deacon, and made him Bishop in his own stead in Rome. And these things Simon himself spake, and the other remaining things also which he had, he commanded Ansus [*Linus*] to teach before the people, saying to him, Besides the New Testament and the Old, let there not be read any thing else before the people, which is not right. When therefore Cæsar had given orders that Simon should be crucified with his head downwards, as he had himself requested of Cæsar, and that Paul's head (ܪܫܐ) should be taken off, there was great trouble among the people, and bitter grief in all the Church, because they had been deprived of the sight of the Apostles. And Isus [*Linus*] the Guide arose and took up their bodies by night and buried them with great honour, and a house of assembly for many was made there. And at that time, as if by the judgment of righteousness, Nero abandoned his empire and fled, and there was a short cessation from the persecution which Nero Cæsar had raised against them. And many years after the great crowning of the Apostles who had departed out of the world, while the Hand of Priesthood was proceeding in all Rome and in all Italy, it happened then that there was a great famine in the city of Rome.

HERE ENDETH THE DOCTRINE OF SIMON CEPHAS.

THE ACTS OF SHARBIL, WHO HAD BEEN THE HIGH PRIEST OF IDOLS, AND WAS CONVERTED TO THE CONFESSION OF THE CHRISTIAN RELIGION IN CHRIST.

In the fifteenth year of the Autocrat Trajan Cæsar, and in the third year of the reign of King Abgar the seventh, which is the year four hundred and sixteen of the kingdom of Alexander, King of the Greeks, and during the high-priesthood of Sharbil and of Barsamya, Trajan Cæsar gave command to the Governors of the countries of his dominions, that sacrifices and libations should be increased in all the cities of their administration, and that those who did not sacrifice should be arrested and be delivered over to stripes and lacerations, and to bitter inflictions of all kinds of tortures, and should afterwards receive the sentence of death by the sword. And when this edict arrived at the city of Edessa of the Parthians, it was the great (ܘܒܝ) festival on the eighth of Nisan, on the third day of the week. The whole city was assembled together near the great altar which is in the middle of the city opposite the office of records, all the gods having been brought together, and been decorated, and set up in honor, both Nebu and Bel together with their companions. And all the high-priests were offering sweet incense and libations, and the odour of the sacrifices was diffusing itself, and sheep and oxen were being slaughtered, and the voice of the harp and the tabor was heard in the whole of the city. But Sharbil was the chief and ruler of all the priests, and he was greatly honoured above all his fellows, and he was clad in splendid and magnificent vestments, and a headband which was embossed with figures of gold was set upon his head, and at the intimation of his word every thing that he ordered was done. And Abgar the king, son of the gods, was standing at the head of the people; and they were obedient to Sharbil, because he drew nearer to all the gods than any of his fellows, as being also the one who returned an answer to every man according to what he heard from the gods. And while these things were being done by the command of the king, Barsamya, the Bishop of the Christians, went up to Sharbil, he and Tiridath the presbyter and Shalula the deacon, and he said to Sharbil, the great high-priest: Christ the King, to whom belong heaven and earth, will require at thy hands all these souls against which thou sinnest and leadest them astray, and turnest them away from the God of verity and truth, to idols which are made and deceitful, that are not able to do any thing with their hands. Neither dost thou spare thine own soul which is perishing from the true life of God; and thou declarest to this same people that the dumb idols talk with thee, and thou approachest thine ear to them one after another, as if thou heardest something from them, and sayest to this (ܥܡܐ) people: The God Nebu commanded me to say to you, 'On account of your sacrifices and your oblations I cause peace in this your country.' And Bel saith, 'I cause great plenty in your land,' and those who listen to thee do not discern that thou art deceiving them greatly, because "they have a mouth and they speak not, and eyes have they and they see not with them," which same you support, and it is not they which support you, as ye suppose; you also set tables before them, and it is not they which supply you. Now therefore be persuaded by me as to what I say to thee and advise thee. If thou be willing to hear me, abandon idols which are made, and worship God the Maker *of all things*, and his Son Jesus Christ. Let it not be that thou be ashamed of him, and worship him not, because he took upon him flesh, was made man, and was stretched out upon the cross of death: for all these things which he endured, it was for the sake of the salvation of men, and for the sake of their deliverance. For he who put on flesh is God, the Son of God, Son of the essence of his Father, and Son of the nature of him who begat him; for he is the adorable brightness of his Godhead and the glorious manifestation of his majesty, he also has existed with his Father from eternity and for ever, his arm, and his right hand, and his power, and his wisdom, and his might; and the living Spirit, which is from him, the propitiator and sanctifier of all who worship him. Which things Palut taught us, whom thy reverence is acquainted with, and thou knowest that Palut was the disciple of Addæus the Apostle. King Abgar also, who was older than this Abgar, who worshippeth idols as well as thou, he too believed in Christ the King, the Son of him whom thou callest Lord of all the gods. For it is commanded to Christians that they should not worship any thing that is made and is a creature and in its nature is not God: like as ye worship idols made by men, who themselves (ܗܢܘܢ) also are made and are creatures. Be persuaded, therefore, by these things which I have said to thee, because they are the faith of the Church; for I know that all this people looketh up to thee, and I am certain that if thou be persuaded, many also will be persuaded with thee.

Sharbil said to him, Very acceptable unto me are these words of thine which thou hast spoken before me, and they are greatly accepted by me. But I know that I am lost from all these things, and there is no longer for me any remedy; and now that hope is cut off from me, why weariest thou thyself about an obscure dead man, for whose death there is no hope of resurrection: for I have been slain by paganism and am become a dead corpse of the evil one: in sacrifices and libations of deceit have I consumed all the days of my life.

And when Barsamya the Bishop heard these things, he fell down at his feet and said to him, There is hope for the penitent, and healing for those that are wounded. I will be surety to thee for the abundant mercies of the Son Christ, that he will forgive thee all that thou hast sinned against him, in that thou hast worshipped and honoured his creatures instead of himself; for that gracious one who extended himself upon the cross of death, will not withhold his grace from souls which are convinced and flee for succour to his favour which is over us: like as he did towards the thief, he is able to do towards thee, and also towards those who are like thee. Sharbil said, Thou, like a skilful physician, who suffers pain himself at the pain of the afflicted, hast done well in being careful about me. But now, because it is the festival to day of this people—of every one—I am not able to go down with thee to day to the church; depart, go thou down with honour, and to morrow at night I will come down to thee. Henceforth I have renounced for myself the gods which are made, and I will confess the Lord Christ, the maker of all men.

And the day after, Sharbil arose and went down (ܢܚܬ) to Barsamya by night, he and his sister Babai, and he was received by the whole Church: and he said to them, Offer prayers and supplications for me, that Christ may forgive me all that I have sinned against him, during all this long period of years. And because they were afraid of the persecutors, they gave him the seal of salvation, as he made his confession of belief in the Father, and in the Son, and in the Spirit of holiness.

And when the whole city had heard that he was gone down to the church, there began to be a commotion among the multitude, and they arose and went down to him, and saw him clad in the fashion of the Christians. And he said to them, May the Son Christ forgive me all the sins that I have sinned against you, and all which I have declared to you that the gods spake to me, when they did not speak: and inasmuch I have been to you an abominable cause, may I be to you now a good cause;

instead of the idols made *with hands* which ye once did worship, may ye henceforth worship God the maker *of all things*. And when they had heard these things, there remained with him a great multitude of men and of women, and Labu also, and Hafsai, and Barcalba, and Avida, chief persons of the city, they said to Sharbil all of them, Henceforth we also renounce whatsoever thou hast renounced, and we confess Christ the King, whom thou hast confessed.

But Lysanias, the judge of the country, when he had heard that Sharbil had done this, sent by night, and took him away from the Church, and many Christians went up with him; and he sat down to hear him and to judge him, before the altar which is in the middle of the city, where he was sacrificing to the gods; and he said to him, Wherefore hast thou renounced the gods whom thou formerly didst worship and offer sacrifice to them, and hadst been made high priest to them, and behold, to-day thou confessest Christ, whom thou didst deny of old. For see how those Christians, to whom (ܥܡܗ) thou art gone, renounce not any thing in which they stand, like as thou hast renounced that in which wast born. If thou believe the gods to be true, why hast thou renounced them to-day? but if thou believe them not, as thou declarest respecting them, why didst thou sacrifice to them and worship them? Sharbil said, When I was blind in my mind, I worshipped that which I knew not; but to-day, because I have obtained the clear eyes of the mind, there is no ground for me henceforth to stumble at carved stones, or that I should any longer be the cause of stumbling to others. For to him whose eyes be open, it is a great disgrace to go and fall into the pit of destruction. The judge said, Because thou hast been high priest of the gods who ought to be honoured, and hast been partaker of the mystery of those, whom the mighty emperors worship, I will have patience with thee, in order that thou mayest be persuaded by me not to turn away from the service of the gods; but if thou wilt not be persuaded by me, I swear by the samo gods whom thou hast renounced, that I will punish thee in the same manner as a man guilty of murder, and will take vengeance on thee for the violence done to the gods, against whom thou hast rebelled and renounced them, as well as for the insult with which thou hast insulted them, nor will I omit to inflict upon thee every kind of torture; and like as thy honour formerly was great, so also will I make thy disgrace great this day.

Sharbil said, Neither shall I be content for thee to look upon me as of old, when I worshipped gods made *with hands*. But look thou upon me to-day, and interrogate me as a Christian man, who renounceth idols, and confesseth Christ the King. The judge said, How is it that thou art not afraid of the emperors, nor ashamed of saying before those who are listening to thy trial, 'I am a Christian?' But confess that thou wilt sacrifice to the gods according to thy former custom, so that thy honour may be great (ܪܒܐ) like it formerly was: lest I make all those, who have believed like thyself, to tremble at thee. Sharbil said, I fear the King of kings, but of any king of earth I am not afraid, nor of thy threats regarding me, which lo! thou denouncest against the worshippers of Christ, in whom I made my confession yesterday, and lo, to-day for his sake I am tried, like as he also was brought to judgment for the sake of sinners who resemble me. The judge said, Even although thou wilt not spare thyself, still I spare thee, by refraining from cutting off those hands of thine, with which thou hast placed incense before the gods, and from stopping with thy blood those ears of thine with which thou hast heard their mysteries, and that tongue of thine which has declared and explained to us their secret things. Behold I fear them and spare thee; but if thou continue thus, may those gods be witness against me, that I will not spare thee.

Sharbil said, Thou, as a man who fearest the emperors and art afraid of idols, spare thou me not. For I know not what thou sayest: on this account also my mind is not moved nor troubled by these things which thou sayest, for through thy judgments shall all those, who will not worship any thing which is not god in its own nature, escape the judgment to come. The judge said, Let him be scourged with thongs, because he has had the daring to answer me thus, and has withstood the edict of the emperors, nor has he regarded the honour with which the gods honoured him, because, lo, he has renounced them. And he was scourged of ten, who seized him according to the command of the judge.

Sharbil said, Thou art not aware of the torment of the justice of the world to come: for thou must cease, and thy judgments also will pass away, but justice will not pass away, nor will its vengeance end. The judge said, Thou art so drunken with this same Christianity, that thou dost not even know before whom thou art being judged, and by whom thou art scourged,—by those who formerly honoured thee, and paid adoration to thy office of high-priest (ܟܘܡܪܐ) to the gods. Why dost thou hate honour and love this disgrace? For although thou speakest unlawfully, nevertheless I am not able to turn aside from the emperor's laws. Sharbil said, As thou lookest that thou mayest not transgress the laws of the emperors, and if indeed thou do transgress, thou knowest what order they will give against thee, so I also look that I may not turn aside from the law of Him who said, 'Thou shalt not worship any image, nor any similitude,' and on this account I will not sacrifice to made idols. For sufficient is the period that I sacrificed to them when I was in ignorance. The judge said, Bring not upon thyself judgment in addition to that judgment in which thou already standest: it is sufficient for thee that thou hast said, 'I will not sacrifice.' Be not audacious and insult the gods by calling them made idols, whom even the emperors honour. Sharbil said, If, on behalf of the emperors who are far away, and are not near, nor aware of those who slight their commands, thou biddest me to sacrifice; why biddest thou me to sacrifice on behalf of idols who are present and are seen, but themselves see not? And by this thou hast declared before all thy Officials, that because 'they have mouths and they speak not,' thou art become an advocate on their behalf, which 'they who made them will be like to them; and every one who trusteth upon them,' like thee. The judge said, It was not for this purpose that thou wast called before me, that instead of the honour which is due, thou shouldest insult the emperors; yet draw near to the gods and sacrifice, and spare thyself, oh self-reviler.

Sharbil said, Why is it requisite that thou shouldest ask me many questions after that which I have said to thee—'I will not sacrifice,' and thou hast called me a self-reviler? Would indeed that from my childhood I had had this mind, and had thus reviled my own soul which was perishing. The judge said, (ܡܬܚ) Hang him up and tear his sides with combs. And when he was thus torn, he cried out and said, For Christ's sake, who has caused his light to shine secretly into the darkness of my mind.—And after he had thus spoken, the judge again commanded him to be torn with the combs, on his face.

Sharbil said, It is better that thou shouldest torture me *here* because I will not sacrifice, than that I should be condemned there for having sacrificed to the work of men's hands. The judge said, Let his body be bent backwards, and let straps be bound upon his hands and his feet, and when he has been bent backwards, let him be scourged upon his belly. And they scourged him in this manner according to the command of the judge. Then he ordered him to be taken up to the prison and cast into a dark pit. And the executioners and the Christians who came up with him from the church, carried him, because he was not able to walk upon his feet, on account of his being bent backwards; and he was in the prison many days.

But on the second of Ilul, on the third day of the week, the judge arose and went down to his judgment-hall by night, and all his Officials were with him, and he commanded the keeper of the prison, and they brought him before him, and the judge said to him, Thou hast been in the prison this length of time, what is thy determination touching those things about which thou hast been interrogated before me? art thou persuaded to minister to the gods according to thy former custom, agreeably to the edict of the emperors? Sharbil said, This has been my determination in the prison, that what I had begun before thee, the same will I complete even to the end; nor will I belie my word, for I will never again confess the idols, which I have renounced, nor will I renounce Christ the King, whom I have confessed. The judge said, Hang him up by his right hand, because he has withdrawn it from the gods, that he may not again offer incense with it, until (a) his hand with which he ministered to the gods be disjointed, because he persists in that one saying of his. And while he was hanging by his hand they questioned him and said to him Wilt thou comply and sacrifice to the gods? But he was not able to return them an answer, on account of the dislocation of his arm Then the judge gave orders, and they loosed him and took him down. But he was not able to bring his arm up to his side until the executioners had pressed it and brought it up to his side.

The judge said, Put on incense, and go whither thou desirest, and no one shall compel thee to become high-priest again. But if thou wilt not *do so*, I will shew thee bitterer tortures than these. Sharbil said, Gods, which made not the heaven and earth, may they perish from under these heavens. But thou, menace not with words of threatening, but, instead of words, shew upon me the deeds of threats, so that I may not hear thee again make mention of the name of gods accursed. The judge said, Let him be burnt with the cautery of bitter fire between his eyes and upon his cheeks. And the executioners did so until the stench of the cautery rose in smoke in the midst of the judgment hall, but he would not sacrifice.

Sharbil said, Thou hast thyself heard from me what I said to thee; that thou art not aware of the smoke of the tribulation of the fire which is prepared for those who, like thee, confess idols made *by hands*, and deny the living God, after thy fashion. The judge said, Who taught thee to say all these things before me in this manner—a man who wast once a friend of the gods and an enemy of Christ? for lo, now thou art become his advocate. Sharbil said, Christ in whom I have confessed, he it is that taught me to speak thus, for he needeth not that I should be his advocate, because his mercies are eloquent advocates for guilty men such as I am, they also are availing to plead on my behalf, at that day on which the eternal sentences will be passed. The judge said, Let him be hanged up (ܒܐ), and let him be torn with combs upon his former wounds; let also salt and vinegar be rubbed into the wounds upon his sides. Then he said to him, Renounce not the gods in whom thou once confessedst. Sharbil said, Spare me again from saying that there be gods, and powers, and fates, and nativities; but I confess one God who made the heaven and earth, and the seas, and every thing that therein is; and the Son, who of him is Christ the King. The judge said, It is not about this thou art interrogated before me, as to what is the belief of the Christians, in which thou hast confessed, but about that which I spake to thee, that thou shouldest not renounce those gods to whom thou wast made high-priest.

Sharbil said, Where is thy wisdom, and that of the emperors in whom thou pridest thyself? because ye worship the work of the hands of artificers and confess them, but the artificers themselves, who made these idols, ye insult by the burdens and the imposts which ye lay upon them. The artificer standeth up in thy presence to do honour to thee, and thou standest up before the artificer's work and doest honour to it, and bowest down to it. The judge said, Thou art not the person to inquire into these things, but art thyself to be strictly inquired into, as to the cause why thou hast renounced the gods, and refusest to offer incense to them like thy fellow high-priests. Sharbil said, Death on account of this is true life, for those who confess Christ the King; them also will he confess before his glorious Father. The judge said, Let candles of fire be brought, and let them be passed round about his face and the sides of his wounds; and they did so a great while. Sharbil said, It is well that thou burnest me with this fire, in order that I may escape "from that fire which is not quenched, and the worm that dieth not," which is denounced against those [who worship things made instead of the Maker; for it is commanded to the Christians not to honour and worship any thing except Him who, in his own nature, is God most high ([illegible]); for whatsoever is made and created ought to worship its maker, and is not to be worshipped together with its creator as thou supposest. The governor said, This is not what the emperors commanded me to inquire at thy hands, whether there be judgment and vengeance after the death of men; nor do I care about this, whether that which is made is to be honoured or not to be honoured: as for myself, what the emperors commanded me is this: that whosoever will not sacrifice to the gods, and offer incense to them, I should employ against him stripes, and combs, and keen edged swords.

Sharbil said, The kings of this world have perception of this world only, but the King of all kings, he hath revealed and shewn to us that there is another world, and a future judgment, in which a recompense will be made between those who have served God, and those who have not served him nor confessed him: for this reason I cry aloud, that I will not sacrifice to idols again, and I will not offer oblations to devils, and I will not honour evil spirits. The judge said, Let nails of iron be driven in between the eyes of the rebel, and let him go to that world which he is looking for, like one that dealeth in fables. And the executioners did so to him while the sound of the knocking of the nails was heard which were driven into him sharply.

Sharbil said, Thou hast driven in nails between my eyes, in the same manner as nails were driven into the hands of that glorious architect of the creation, and on account of this all natures of the creation trembled and quaked at that time. For these tortures, which, lo! thou art inflicting upon me are nothing with respect to that future judgment: for "they whose ways are always loose, because they have not the judgment of God before their eyes," on this account do not even confess that there is a God, neither will he confess them. The judge said, Thou sayest in words, (ܠܐ) that there is a judgment but I will shew to thee in deeds, that instead of that judgment which is to come, thou mayest tremble and be afraid of this which is before thine eyes, in which, behold, thou now standest, and mayest not multiply thy speech before me. Sharbil said, He who desireth to set God before his eyes in secret, God himself is at his right hand, I, also, am not afraid of thy threats of torture with which thou menacest me and triest to terrify me. The judge said, Let Christ, whom thou hast confessed, deliver thee from all the tortures which I have inflicted upon thee, and am about still to inflict on thee, and let him shew his deliverance towards thee openly, and save thee out of my hands. Sharbil said, The true deliverance of Christ towards me is this,—the secret power which he has bestowed upon me to endure whatsoever tortures thou hast inflicted upon me, and whatsoever thou hast settled in thy mind to inflict upon me further; and although thou hast well seen this, thou hast not been willing to believe my word. The judge said, Take him away from my presence, and let him be hanged upon a tree, turned with his head downwards, and let him be beaten with whips while he is hanging; and the executioners did so at the door of the judgment hall.

Then the governor commanded, and they brought him up before him and he said to him, Offer sacrifice to the gods, and perform the will of the emperors, thou high-priest, that hatest honour and lovest disgrace instead. Sharbil said, Why dost thou repeat thy words again, and command me to sacrifice, after having oftentimes heard from me that I will never sacrifice again? For it was not any force of the Christians that withheld me from sacrifices, but their truth; this has delivered me from the error of paganism. The judge said, Let him be thrown into a chest of iron like a murderer, and let him be scourged with thongs like a malefactor; and the executioners did so, until there remained not a sound place on him.

Sharbil said, These tortures, which thou supposest to be bitter, out of the midst of their bitterness (ܢܐ) spring up for me fountains of deliverance and mercies on the day of the eternal sentences. The governor said, Let small and round pieces of wood be placed between the fingers of his hands, and let them squeeze upon them bitterly; and they did so to him, until the blood came out [from under the nails] of his fingers.

Sharbil said, If thine eye be not yet satisfied with the tortures of my body, add still to its tortures whatsoever thou desirest The judge said, Let the fingers of his hands be loosed, and make him sit upon the ground, and bind his hands upon his knees, and place a piece of wood under his knees, and let it pass over the bands of his hands, and hang him up by his feet, when bent, with his head downwards; and let him be scourged with thongs; and they did so to him.

Sharbil said, Those who fight against God cannot be victorious, neither can they be condemned whose confidence is God; and for this reason I say that "neither fire, nor sword, nor death, nor life, nor height, nor depth, are able to separate my heart from the love of God which is in our Lord Jesus Christ." The judge said, Make hot a ball of lead and brass, and place it under his armpits; and they did so, even till the top of his ribs became visible.

Sharbil said, These tortures of thine against me are too little for thy rage against me, unless thy rage were little and thy tortures were great. The judge said, Thou wilt not hurry me by these things which thou sayest, for I have room in my mind [to have patience with thee, and to see every evil, and hateful, and bitter thing that I shall exhibit in the torture of thy body, because thou wilt not comply and sacrifice to the gods whom thou once didst worship. Sharbil said, Those things which I have said and repeated before thee thou knowest not in thine unbelief, how] to hearken to them, how then supposest thou that thou knowest what things are in my mind? The judge said, The changes of words (ܙܢܡ) which thou utterest will not help thee, but will rather increase the afflictions upon thee manifold. Sharbil said, If one of the stories of one of thy gods be believed by thee, it is a shame to say how it is; for one had intercourse with boys, which is not right, and another fell in love with a virgin who took refuge in a tree, as your shameful stories tell. The judge said, This fellow, who formerly honoured the gods, but now is turned and has reviled them, and has not been afraid, who likewise has despised the edict of the emperors and not trembled, set him to stand upon a gridiron heated with fire; and the executioners did so, until the under part of his feet was burnt.

Sharbil said, If thy rage is excited at the mention of the abominable and indecent stories of thy gods, how much more oughtest thou to be ashamed of their acts? For, behold, were a man to do what one of thy gods doeth, and they were to bring him before thee, thou wouldest pass sentence of death upon him. The judge said, I will take vengeance upon thee to-day for thy blasphemy against the gods, and thine audacity in insulting even the emperors, nor will I leave thee alone until thou [offer incense to them, according to thy former custom.

Sharbil said, Stand therefore by thy threats and belie not thyself, but shew towards me in deeds that power which the emperors have given to thee, nor disgrace the emperors by thine own falsehood, and be also despised thyself] in the eyes of thine own Officials. The judge said, Thy blasphemy against the gods, and thine insolence towards the Emperors, have brought upon thee these tortures in which thou now standest; and if thou add further to thine insolence, afflictions which are bitterer than these shall be further added upon thee. Sharbil said, Thou hast the authority as judge to do whatsoever thou wishest, and spare not. The judge said, He that hath not spared his own body from enduring these tortures, how can he be afraid or be ashamed (ܒܗܬ) of obeying the command of the emperors? Sharbil said, Thou hast well said that I am not ashamed, because near at hand is he that justifieth me, and my whole mind is caught up in rapture towards him. For because I formerly offended him by the sacrifices of idols, I am trying to appease him to-day by the afflictions of my own person; for my mind is carried away captive to God who became man. The judge said, It is a captive, then, that I am interrogating, and a madman without sense, and, lo, I am talking with a dead man who is burnt already. Sharbil said, If thou believe that I am mad, question me no further, for it is a madman that is interrogated, for, rather, I am a dead man who is burnt, as thou hast said. The judge said, How can I count thee a dead man, for lo! thou hast just cried aloud, I will not offer sacrifice. Sharbil said, Even I know not how to return an answer to thee who hast called me a dead man, and comest back and interrogatest me like one that is alive. The judge said, Rightly I have called thee a dead man, because thy feet are burnt and thou carest not for it; and thy face is scorched and thou holdest thy peace; and nails are knocked in between thine eyes and thou takest no account of it; thy ribs also are seen between the wounds and thou revilest the emperors; and thy whole body is torn to pieces and wounded with stripes, and still thou blasphemest the gods; and because thou hatest thy body, lo! thou sayest whatsoever pleaseth thee. Sharbil said, If thou call me audacious because I have endured these things, for thyself who hast inflicted them upon me, it is right that thou shouldest be called a murderer in thy acts and a blasphemer in thy words. The judge said, Behold, thou hast insulted the emperors and the gods as well, and, lo! now thou insultest me too, in order that I may doom thee to death speedily; but instead of this which thou lookest for, I am ready to inflict upon thee yet bitter and severe tortures. Sharbil said, Thou knowest that which I have said to thee many times; Instead of denunciations and threats, exhibit upon me the act of the threat (ܠܐ) in order that thou mayest be known to do the will of the emperors. The judge said, Let him be torn with the combs upon his legs and the sides of his thighs; and the executioners did so until his blood ran down and fell upon the ground.

Sharbil said, Well is it that thou treatest me thus, because I have heard that one of the Doctors of the Church has said, "The scars, indeed, of my body—that I may come to the resurrection from the dead:" and I, who was an obscure dead man, lo! thy tortures raise me up again. The judge said, Let him be torn on his face; because he is not ashamed of the nails which are driven in between his eyes, and they tare him upon his cheeks, and between the nails which were driven into them.

Sharbil said, I will not obey the emperors, who command that to be worshipped and honoured which is not of its own nature, God; neither is God in its nature, but is the work of him that made it. The judge said, Like as the emperors worship, so also worship thou; and as the judges honour, so also honour thou.

Sharbil said, Even although I insult that which, being the work of men, has no sense or perception of any thing, yet insult not thou God, the maker of all things, and worship together with him that which is not of him, and is foreign to his nature. The judge said, Does your doctrine teach you thus, that you shall insult even the luminaries which give light to all sides of the earth? Sharbil said, Although it be not written for us that we shall insult them, still it is written for us that we should not worship them nor honour them, because they are things made: for this were a bitter evil that any thing made should be worshipped together with its maker; it is also an insult to the Maker that his creatures should be honoured together with himself. The judge said, Christ, whom thou confessest, was hanged on a tree; upon a tree also I will hang thee like thy master. And they hanged him upon a tree a long while.

Sharbil said, Christ, whom, lo! thou mockest, see (ܚܙܝ) how thy many gods stood not before him: for behold! they are despised and neglected and are made a laughing-stock and a jest to those who formerly bowed down to them. The judge said, How is it that thou renouncest the gods and confessest Christ, who was hanged on a tree? Sharbil said, The great glory of Christians is the cross of Christ; because through it was effected deliverance of salvation for all those who worship him, and through it they have acquired that clear sight, which keeps them from worshipping creatures together with the Creator. The governor said, Let thy glorying in the cross be kept within thy heart, and by thy hands let incense be offered to the gods. Sharbil said, Those who have obtained deliverance through the cross cannot any more worship the idols of error which are made *with hands;* for creature cannot worship creature, because it also ought to worship him who made it, and it is an insult to its maker that it should be worshipped together with its maker, as I have said before. The Governor said, Let thy books alone which have taught thee this, and do thou the commandment of the emperors, that thou die not by the emperors' law. Sharbil said, Is this the righteousness of the emperors in whom thou pridest thyself, that we should abandon the law of God and keep their laws? The governor said, The citation of the books in which thou believest, and from which thou hast quoted, these have placed thee in these afflictions; for if thou hadst offered incense to the gods, great would have been thine honour, like it formerly was, as being high-priest of the gods. Sharbil said, To thine infidel heart these things seem as if they were afflictions, but to the true heart affliction begetteth patience, and from the same is experience, and from experience is the hope of confession. The Governor said, Hang him up and tear him with combs upon his former wounds. And through the fury of the judge towards the executioners, his bowels (ܪܠ) were near being seen; and in order that he might not die under the combs, and escape from still further tortures, he gave orders, and they took him down.

And when the judge saw that he was become silent, and was not able to return him any further answer, he refrained from him a little, until his soul returned unto him again. Sharbil said, Why hast thou spared me even this little time, and deprived me of the gain of martyrdom? The governor said, I have not spared thee at all, but I have refrained a little because thy silence made me cease awhile; and if I were able to exceed the laws of the emperors, I should be pleased to torture thee, in order that I may further take vengeance upon thee for thine insult towards the gods; for in despising me thou hast despised the gods, and I also have endured thee and tortured thee thus, like a man who so deserves it.

And the judge gave orders, and the curtain fell suddenly before him for a short time, and he made ready and settled the sentence which he was to give against him publicly. And suddenly the curtain was opened again, and the judge cried aloud and said, This Sharbil, who was formerly high-priest of the gods, but has turned, and this day renounced the gods, and cried aloud, I am a Christian, and has not been afraid of the gods, but has insulted them, and further, has had no fear of the emperors' edict, whom I commanded to offer sacrifice to the gods according to his former practice, and he has not offered sacrifice, but also *has greatly* insulted them: I have looked and seen that a man who doeth these things, it is right that no mercy should be shewed towards him, even were he to sacrifice: and it is not right that he should any longer behold his lords' sun, because he has slighted their laws; I have order that, according to the law of the emperors, a strap be cast into the mouth of this insulter, as if it were the mouth of a murderer, and that he should be taken outside the city of the Emperors with haste, like one who has insulted the lords of the city and the gods who preside over it: I give sentence that he be sawn with a saw of wood, and when (ܣ) he is near to die, then his head be taken off by the sword of the slayers.

And at the same moment the strap was suddenly thrust into his mouth, and the executioners seized him, made him run quickly upon his feet which had been burnt, and they took him outside the city, while the people were running after him. They also had stood and looked on at his trial all day, and wondered how he had had no suffering under his afflictions: for his countenance, which was cheerful, testified to the joy of his heart. And when the executioners arrived at the place where he was to receive the punishment of death, the people of the city also were with them to see if they did according as the judge had ordered, and to hear what Sharbil might say at that time, in order that they might inform the judge of the country.

And they gave him wine to drink, as is the custom for the murderers to drink, and he said to them, I will not drink, because I desire to feel the saw with which ye saw me, as well as the sword which ye pass over my neck; but instead of this wine which will not help me, grant me a little time to pray while ye stand. And he stood up and looked towards the east, and lifted up his voice and said, Forgive me, O Christ, all that I have sinned against thee, all by which I have made thee angry in the polluted sacrifices of dead idols; spare also all my life, and deliver me from the judgment to come, and be merciful to me as thou wast merciful to the thief, receive me also like those penitents who repent and are turned to thee, and thou art turned to them: and because I entered into thy vineyard at the eleventh hour, instead of judgment, deliver me from justice: let thy death for the sake of sinners, raise up my dead body on the day of thy coming.

And when the Sharirs of the city heard these things, they were angry against the executioners for having given him leave to pray. And while the nails were standing which had been driven in between his eyes, and his ribs were to be seen between the wounds of the combs; and from his burnt sides and ([illegible]) the soles of his feet which were scorched and burnt, as well as from the wounds of his face, and his sides, and his thighs, and his legs, the blood was running and dropping down on the ground; they brought the carpenter's instruments, and thrust him into a wooden vice, and pressed it upon him until the bones of his joints creaked from the pressure: then they put upon him a saw of iron and began to saw him asunder: and when he was at the point to die, because the saw had nearly reached his mouth, they smote him with the sword and took off his head while he was still squeezed down in the vice.

And his sister Babai drew near and spread out her skirts and caught his blood, and she said to him, May my spirit be united with thy spirit near Christ whom thou hast known and believed. And the Sharirs of the city ran and went up and made known to the judge what things Sharbil had uttered in his prayer, and how his sister had caught his blood; and the judge commanded them to return and tell the executioners, that in the same place in which she had caught the blood of her brother, she also should receive the punishment of death. And the executioners laid hold upon her, and every one of them on his own part tortured her; and while she was carrying her brother's blood, her soul took its flight from her, and they mingled her blood with his. And when the executioners were entered into the city, the brethren and some young men ran and stole away the dead bodies of them both, and they laid them in the sepulchre of the father of Abshelama the bishop, on the fifth of Ilul, and on the sixth day of the week.

I wrote these acts on paper, I, Marinus, and Anatolus, the notaries; and we placed them in the archives of the city, where the charters of the kings are placed.

But this Barsamya, the bishop, converted Sharbil the high-priest. But he lived in the days of Binus, [Fabianus] bishop of Rome, in whose days the whole (ܥܡܐ) people of Rome assembled themselves together and cried out to the Prætor of their city, and said to him, There are too many strangers in this our city, and they cause the famine and the dearer price of every thing: we therefore intreat thee to order them to depart out of the city. And when he had given the order for them to depart out of the city, these strangers assembled themselves together and said to the Prætor, We beseech thee, my lord, command also that the bones of our dead may also go out with us; and he commanded them to take the bones of their dead, and to depart; and all the strangers assembled themselves together to take the bones of Simon Cephas and of Paul, the Apostles; and the people of Rome said to them, We will not give you the bones of the Apostles: and the strangers said to them, Learn and see that Simon, who is called Cephas, is of Bethsaida of Galilee, and Paul, the Apostle, is of Tarsus, a city of Cilicia. And when the people of Rome knew that the matter was so, then they let them alone. And when they took them up and were removing them from their places, at the same moment there was a great earthquake, and the walls of the city were near falling down, and the city near to be overthrown; and when the people of Rome beheld it, they turned and intreated the strangers to remain in their city, and that the bones might be laid in their places again. And when the bones of the Apostles were returned to their places, there was a calm, and the earthquakes ceased, and the winds became quiet, and the air became bright, and the whole city was cheerful. And when the Jews and Pagans saw, they ran and fell at the feet of Fabianus, the bishop of their city, while the Jews cried out, We confess Christ whom we crucified: He is the son of the living God, of whom the prophets spoke in their mysteries. And the Pagans also cried out and said to him, We renounce idols and graven images, because there is no use in them, ([illegible]) and we believe in Jesus the King, the Son of God, who is come and is about to come again; and if there were any other doctrines in Rome and in the whole of Italy, they also renounced their doctrines, like as the Pagans had renounced, and confessed the Gospel of the Apostles, which was preached in the Church.

HERE END THE ACTS OF SHARBIL THE CONFESSOR.

MARTYRDOM OF BARSAMYA, THE BISHOP OF THE BLESSED CITY EDESSA.

In the year four hundred and sixteen of the kingdom of the Greeks, which is the fifteenth year of the reign of the Autocrat, our lord, Trajan Cæsar, in the consulship of Commodus and Cyrillus, in the month Ilul, on the fifth day of the same, the day after Lysinas, the judge of the country, had heard Sharbil the high-priest; while the judge was sitting at his seat of judgment, the Sharirs of the city entered into his presence, and said to him, We give information before your lordship respecting Barsamya, the Guide of the Christians, that he went up to Sharbil, the high-priest, as he was standing and ministering before the gods, who are to be honoured, and sent and called him to him secretly: and he spake to him out of the books which he reads in the church of their place of assembly, and he repeated to him the faith of the Christians, and said to him, It is not right for thee to worship many gods, but rather one (ܚܕ) God only, and his son Jesus Christ: until he converted, and made him renounce the gods which he had formerly worshipped; and by the means of Sharbil himself many also have been converted, and are gone down to the church, and lo! this day they confess Christ; Avida also, and Nebo, and Barcalba, and Hafsai, honourable and chief persons of the city, have yielded to Sharbil in this; we, therefore, as being the Sharirs of the city, make this known before your lordship, in order that we may not subject ourselves to punishment, as offenders, because we had not made known before your lordship what things had been spoken in secret to Sharbil by Barsamya the Guide of the Church. Now, therefore, your lordship knoweth what is right to command respecting this same thing.

And in the same hour as the judge heard these things, he sent the Sharirs of the city and some of the Officials with them, to go down to the church and bring up Barsamya from the church. And they took him and brought him up to the judgment-hall of the judge; and many Christians went up with him, saying, We also will die together with Barsamya, because we also agree with him in the discipleship to which he has also converted Sharbil, and in whatever he has spoken to him, and in whatever he received from him and was persuaded by him, and was ready to die for the sake of what he heard from him. And the Sharirs of the city went in and told the judge:—Barsamya, as thy lordship gave orders, lo! he standeth at the door of the judgment-hall of thy authority; and honourable chief persons of the city, who have been converted as well as Sharbil, behold! they are standing by Barsamya and crying out, We all will die with Barsamya, who is our instructor and our guide!

And when the judge heard these things which the Sharirs of the city said to him, he commanded them to go out and write down ([illegible]) the names of the men who were crying out, We will die with Barsamya. And when they went out to write down these men, they who so cried out were too many for them, and they were not able to write down their names, because they were too many for them; because the cry came to them from all sides, that they would die with Barsamya for Christ's sake. And when the tumult of the people became great, the Sharirs of the city turned back and went in to the judge, and said to him, We are not able to write down the names of the men who are crying aloud outside, because they are very many, and cannot be numbered. And the judge commanded that Barsamya should be taken up to the prison, in order that the people might be dispersed which was collected together about him, lest through the tumult of many people, there might be some trouble in the city. And when he went up to the prison those remained with him who had become disciples together with Sharbil.

And when many days were passed, the judge rose up in the morning and went down to his court of justice, in order that he might try Barsamya; and the judge gave orders, and they brought him from the prison; and he went up and stood before him; and the staff said, Behold, he standeth before your lordship. The judge said, Art thou Barsamya who hast been made Ruler and Guide of the people of the Christians, and hast converted Sharbil, who was great high-priest of the gods and worshipped them? Barsamya said, It is I who have done this, and I do not deny it: I am also ready to die for the sake of the truth of this. The judge said, How wast thou not afraid of the emperors' edict, that when the emperors give command that every one should offer sacrifice thou hast made Sharbil the high-priest, while he was standing and sacrificing to the gods, and offering them incense, to renounce that which he confessed, and to confess Christ whom he denied? (ܣܘ) Barsamya said, Inasmuch as I am become entirely a pastor of men, it was not for the sake of those only who are found, but also for the sake of those who have strayed from the fold of truth, who are made a prey for the wolves of paganism: and had I not instructed Sharbil, his blood would have been required at mine own hands, and had he not listened to me I should have been innocent of his blood. The judge said, But now that thou hast confessed that it was thou who madest Sharbil a disciple, at thine own hands will I require his death; and on this account it is right that thou shouldest be condemned before me rather than he, because through means of thee he has been put to death by the sad deaths of severe tortures, for having left the edict of the emperors and having obeyed thy words. Barsamya said, Not to my words was Sharbil converted, but to the word of God which he spake: "Thou shalt not bow down to images and the similitudes of men." And not I alone am content to die the death of Sharbil for his confession in Christ, but also all the Christians, children of the Church, likewise desire this, because they know that by this they will find their salvation before God. The judge said, Answer me not in this manner, like thy disciple Sharbil, lest thine own tortures be even worse than his: but promise that thou wilt sacrifice before the gods on his behalf. Barsamya said, Sharbil, who knew not God, I taught him to know him, but me, who know God from my youth, biddest thou me renounce God? God forbid that I should do this thing. The judge said, You have converted the whole creation to this teaching of Christ, and lo, they renounce the many gods whom the many worshipped. Pass on from this mind, lest I make those who are near to tremble while they look on at thee to-day, and those that are far off, who shall hear of the tortures of thy trials. Barsamya said, If God be the help ([illegible]) of those who call upon him who is able to oppress them? or what is the power that can prevail against them? or thine own threats, what can they do to those who, before thou give order against them that they should die, have set their death before their eyes, and are expecting it every day. The judge said, Bring not the matter of Christ before my judgment-seat; but instead of this, obey the edict of the emperors, who command to offer sacrifice to the gods. Barsamya said, Even when we do not bring the matter of Christ before thee, Christ's passion is pourtrayed and fixed in those who worship Christ; and more than thou hearkenest to the commands of the emperors: we Christians hearken to Christ the King of kings. The judge said, Lo thou hast obeyed Christ and worshipped him up to-day; henceforth obey the emperors themselves, and worship the gods which the emperors worship. Barsamya said, How biddest thou me to renounce that in which I was born, when, lo, thou didst require it at the hand of Sharbil, and saidest to him, Why hast thou renounced the paganism in which thou wast born and confessed the Christian religion to which thou wast a stranger; for, behold, even before I came into thy presence thou hast given testimony beforehand, and said to Sharbil, The Christians, to whom thou art gone, renounce not that in which they were born, and in which they stand: abide, therefore, by thy word which thou hast spoken. The judge said, Let Barsamya be scourged, because he has rebelled against the edict of the emperors, and has caused also to rebel with him those who were obedient to the emperors.

And when he had been scourged of five he said to him, Reject not the emperors' edict, nor insult the gods of the emperors. Barsamya said, Thy mind is greatly blinded, oh Judge! and also that of the emperors who gave thee authority; neither are the things which are false perceived by you: nor do ye understand that the whole creation, (ܗܐ) behold, it has worshipped Christ; and to me, sayest thou to me, Worship him not, as if I alone worshipped him whom the angels above worship in the height. The judge said, And if ye have taught men to worship Christ, who is it that has persuaded those above that they should worship Christ? Barsamya said, Those above themselves have declared and taught those who are below about the living worship of Christ the King, which they pay to him and to his Father together with the Spirit of his godhead. The judge said, Let alone these things which are written for you, and which ye also teach to others, and comply with those things which the emperors have commanded, and reject not their laws, lest ye be rejected by means of the sword from the light of this honoured sun. Barsamya said, The light, which passeth away and abideth not, it is not that true light, but it is the similitude of that true light, whose rays darkness approacheth not, which is reserved and standeth fast for the true worshippers of Christ. The judge said, Speak not in my presence of any thing else, but of that about which I have asked thee, lest I cast thee out from life to death, because thou hast renounced this light which is seen, and confessest that which is not seen. Barsamya said, I have not the power to neglect that about which thou askest me, and to speak about what thou dost not question me. It is thou that spakest to me about the light of the sun, and I said before thee that there is a light in the height which is superior in its light to this of the sun which thou worshippest and honourest; for it will be required of thee touching this, why thou hast worshipped thy fellow-creature instead of God thy creator. The judge said, Insult not even the sun, the light of the creation, nor slight the emperors' commandment, and stand in contention against the lords of the country, who have the authority over it. Barsamya said, What help does the light (ܦܛ) of the sun afford to a blind man who cannot see it, for without the eyes of the body it is not possible for its rays to be seen; so that by this thou mayest know that it is the work of God, because it is not able to shew its light to the blind.

The judge said, After I have tortured thee, as thou deservest, then I will write against thee to the government what insult thou hast done to the gods, in that thou hast converted Sharbil the high-priest who honoured the gods, and that ye despise the laws of the emperors, and that ye make no account of the judges of the country, and ye are living in the dominions of the Romans like barbarians. Barsamya said, Thou dost not terrify me by these things which thou sayest. Although I be not near to the emperors to-day, still, behold, I am now standing before the authority which the emperors have given to thee, and am being tried, because I have said, I will renounce not God, to whom belong heaven and earth, nor his son Jesus Christ, the King of all the earth. The judge said, If thou be sure of this, that thou art standing before the authority of the Emperors and being tried, obey their commands, and rebel not against their laws, lest thou receive the punishment of death like rebels. Barsamya said, Even if those who rebel against the Emperors, when they righteously rebel, are condemned to death, as thou sayest; such as rebel against God, the King of kings, even the punishment of death by the sword is too little for them. The judge said, It was not that thou shouldest expound in my judgment-hall that thou camest in before me, because the trial in which thou standest is far removed from expounding and near to the punishment of death, for such as insult the Emperors and comply not with their laws. Barsamya said, Because God is not before your eyes, neither are ye willing to listen to the word of God: but carved images that have no sense, "which have a mouth and speak not," ([illegible]) are reckoned by you as though they spake, because your intellect is blinded by the darkness of heathenism in which ye stand. The judge said, Let alone these things of which thou speakest, because they will not help thee at all; and worship the gods, before bitter combs and severe tortures come upon thee. Barsamya said, Do thou let alone these many questions with which, behold, thou interrogatest me, and give orders for the stripes and the combs with which thou threatenest me, for thy words will not help thee so much as thy inflictions help me. The judge said, Let Barsamya be hanged up and be torn with combs.

And at that moment letters came to him from Alusis [*Lusius*] the chief Proconsul, father of Emperors. And he gave command, and they took down Barsamya, and he was not torn with combs, and they took him outside the judgment hall. And the judge commanded that the nobles, and the chief persons, and the princes, and the honourable persons of the city, should come into his presence in order that he might hear what was the order which was issued by the Emperors, through the Proconsuls, who were the rulers of the countries of the dominion of the Romans. And it was found that the Emperors had written by the hand of the Proconsuls to the judges of the countries,—Since our Majesty gave orders that there should be a persecution against the people of the Christians, we have heard and learned from our Sharirs, which we have in the countries of the dominion of our Majesty, that the people of the Christians are men who avoid murder, and sorcery, and adultery, and theft, and bribery, and fraud, and those things for which even the laws of our Majesty require punishment from such as do them: we therefore, by the justice of our Rectitude, have given command, that on account of these things the persecution of the sword should cease from them, and that there shall be rest and quietness in all our dominions, they continuing to minister according to their custom, and that no man should hinder them. But it is not that we shew affection towards them, but towards their laws, which agree with the laws (ܢܡܘܣܐ) of our Majesty; and if any man hinder them after this our decree, that sword which is ordered by us to pass upon those who neglect our decree, the same have we ordered to pass upon those who slight this decree of our Clemency.

And when this decree of the Emperors' Clemency was read, the whole city rejoiced that there was quietness and rest for every man. And the judge gave orders, and they released Barsamya, that he might go down to his church. And the Christians went up in great numbers to the judgment hall, and a vast multitude of the people of the city, and they received Barsamya with great and exceeding honour, repeating psalms before him, according to their custom, with the women of the chiefs of the wise men, and they thronged upon him and saluted him, and they called him Persecuted Confessor, friend of Sharbil the

Martyr. And he said to them, Persecuted I am like yourselves, but from the tortures of Sharbil and his fellows I am far removed. And they said to him, We have heard from thee that a doctor of the church has said, "The will, according to what it is, so is it accepted." And when he was entered into the Church, he and all the people that were with him, he stood up and prayed, and blessed them and dismissed them to go to their own houses, rejoicing and praising God for the deliverance which he had wrought for them and for the church. And the day after Lysinas the judge of the country had set his hand to these Acts, he was dismissed from his authority.

But I, Zenophilus and Patrophilus, are the notaries who wrote these things, Diodorus and Euterpes, Sharirs of the city, bearing witness with us by setting to their hand, as the antient laws of the antient kings prescribe.

But this Barsamya, the Bishop of Edessa, who converted Sharbil, the highpriest of the same city, lived in the days of Fabianus, the Bishop ([illegible]) of the city of Rome. And the hand of priesthood was received by this same Barsamya, from Abshelama, who was Bishop in Edessa; and Abshelama, the hand was received by him from Palut the former; and Palut, the hand was received by him from Serapion, Bishop of Antioch; and Serapion, the hand was received by him from Zephyrinus, Bishop of Rome; and Zephyrinus of Rome received the hand from Victor, of the same place of Rome; and Victor received the hand from Eleutherius; and Eleutherius received from Soter; and Soter received from Anicetus; and Anicetus received it from Dapius [*Pius*]; and Dapius received from Telesphorus; and Telesphorus received from Xystus; and Xystus received from Alexander; and Alexander received from Erastus; and Erastus received from Cletus; and Cletus received from Anus [*Linus*]; and Anus received from Simon Cephasi; and Simon Cephas received from our Lord, together with his fellow Apostles, on the first day of the week of the ascension of our Lord to his glorious Father, which is the fourth day of Heziran, which is the nineteenth year of the reign of Tiberius Cæsar, in the consulate of Rufus and Rubelinus, which year is the year three hundred and forty one: for in the year three hundred and nine was the manifestation of our Saviour in the world, according to the testimony which we have found in a correct volume of the Archives, which errs not at all in whatever it declares.

HERE ENDETH THE MARTYRDOM OF BARSAMYA, BISHOP OF EDESSA.

MARTYRDOM OF HABIB THE DEACON.

(ܥܒ) In the month Ab, of the year six hundred and twenty of the kingdom of Alexander of Macedon, in the consulate of Licinius and Constantine, which is the year in which he was born, in the rule of Julius and Barak, in the days of Cona, Bishop of Edessa, Licinius made a persecution against the church and all the people of the Christians, after that first persecution which the Emperor Diocletian had made. And the Emperor Licinius gave orders that there should be sacrifices and libations, and that the altars should be repaired in every place, that they should burn perfumes and frankincense before Jupiter. And when many were being persecuted they cried out of their own free will, We are Christians, and they were not afraid of the perseuction, because those who were persecuted were more numerous than those who persecuted them. But Habib, who was of the village Telzeha, and had been made a deacon, both went about to the churches in the villages secretly, and read the scriptures, and encouraged and strengthened many by his words, and admonished them to stand fast in the truth of their faith, and not to be afraid of the persecutors, and he gave them instructions. And when many were confirmed by his words, and received what he said affectionately, being cautioned not to renounce that position in which they stood, and when the Sharirs of the city, who had been appointed for this same purpose, had heard, they went in and made known to Lysanias the governor, that was in the city of Edessa, and said to him, That Habib, who is a deacon in the village Telzeha, goeth about, and ministers (ܫܡܫ) secretly in every place, and he withstandeth the Emperor's command, and is not afraid. When, therefore, the governor heard these things, he was filled with rage against Habib; and he made a report, and sent and made known to Licinius the Emperor all that Habib had done, both that he might learn and see what command would be given respecting him and those who would not sacrifice: for although an edict had been promulgated that every man should sacrifice, still it had not been ordered what was to be done to those who would not sacrifice; because they had heard that Constantine, in Gaul and Spain, was become Christian, and did not sacrifice. And Licinius the Emperor gave orders to Lysanias the governor, Whosoever thus dares to transgress our command, our Majesty has decreed, that he should be put to death by fire: and that the rest who do not comply and sacrifice, should be put to death by the sword.

And when this command came to the city of Edessa, Habib, the same on whose account the report had been made, was gone over to the country of the people of Zeugma, in order that he might also minister there secretly. And when the governor sent and inquired for him in his own village, and in all the surrounding country, and he could not be found, he commanded that all his family should be arrested, and the inhabitants of his village, and they arrested them and put them into irons, his mother and the rest of his family, and also some of the people of his village and they brought them to the city, and bound them in prison. And when Habib heard of this which had taken place, he considered in his mind, and meditated in his thoughts, It is expedient for me that I go and appear before the judge of the country, rather than that I should remain in secret, and others go up and be crowned on my account, and I should find myself in great shame. For what benefit will the name of Christian confer upon him who fleeth from the confession of Christianity. (ܗܐ) Behold, if he escape this, the death of nature is before him whithersoever he goeth, and he is not able to flee from it, because this is decreed against all the children of Adam.

Then Habib arose and went to Edessa secretly, having prepared his back for the stripes, and his sides for the tearing of the combs, and his body for the burning of fire. And he went alone to Theotecna, a veteran, who was the chief of the governor's band, and he said to him, I am Habib of Telzeha, whom ye are seeking. And Theotecna said to him, If it be that no man saw thee when thou camest to me, obey what I say to thee, and depart and go to the place where thou wast before, and be there at this time, and let no man know or be aware of this, that thou camest to me and spakest with me, and that I gave thee this advice; neither be thou at all anxious about thy family and the inhabitants of thy village, for no man will hurt them in any thing, but they will remain a few days in prison, and the governor will then dismiss them, because the Emperors have not ordered any thing bad or dreadful touching them: if, therefore, thou wilt not obey me in these things which I have said to thee, I am free of thy blood, because if it be that thou appear before the judge of the country, thou wilt not escape from death by fire, according to the command of the Emperors, which they have given respecting thee.

Habib said to Theotecna, I am not anxious about my family and the inhabitants of my village, but about my own salvation, lest it should be lost. Also I am much grieved about this, that I did not happen to be in my village on the day that the governor inquired for me, and behold many are thrown into irons on my account, and I have been suspected by him as a fugitive. Wherefore, if thou wilt not comply and take me up before the governor, I will go alone and make my appearance before him. And when Theotecna heard him speak thus to him, he laid hold upon him firmly, ([illegible]) and delivered him up to his domestics, and they conducted him with him to the judgment hall of the governor. And Theotecna went in and made it known to the governor, and said to him, Habib of Telzeha, whom thy lordship was searching after, is come. And the governor said, Who is it that has brought him? and where did they find him? and what was he doing where he was? Theotecna said to him, He came hither of his own free will, and without the constraint of any one, for no one was aware of him.

And when the governor had heard this, he was embittered against him greatly, and spake thus. This fellow, who has so acted, has shewn great contempt towards me and has despised me, and has accounted me as no judge; even because he has so done, it is not right that any mercy be shewed towards him, neither that I should be in a hurry to pass sentence of death against him, according to the command issued against him by the Emperors; but it is right for me to have patience with him, in order that his tortures and bitter judgments may be the more increased, and through him I may terrify many from daring again to flee. And when many people were collected together and standing by him at the door of the judgment hall, some of them being his own Officials and others being the people of the city, there were some of them that said, Thou hast done badly in coming and shewing thyself to those who were searching for thee, without being compelled by the judge: and there were others again who said to him, Thou hast done well in coming and making thy appearance of thine own free will, rather than that the compulsion of the judge should bring thee: for now is thy confession in Christ known to be of thine own will, and not by the compulsion of men.

But these things, which the Sharirs of the city had heard from those who were speaking to him, while they were standing at the door of the judgment hall, and that also, which had been told to the Sharirs of the city, that he had gone secretly to Theotecna, and that he had not wished (ܨܒܐ) to denounce him, they made known to the judge, every thing that they had heard. And the judge was angry against those who had been saying to Habib, Wherefore didst thou come and shew thyself to the judge, without being compelled by the judge himself? And he said to Theotecna, It was not right for a man, who has been made the chief of his fellows, to act so deceitfully towards his own ruler, and frustrate the Emperors' edict, which they denounced against the rebel Habib, that he should be burned with fire. Theotecna said, I have not acted deceitfully towards my fellows, neither have I looked to frustrate the edict which the Emperors promulgated; for what am I before thy lordship, that I should have dared to do this thing? I strictly questioned him as to that which thy lordship also inquired at my hands, in order that I might know and see if it was of his own free will that he came hither, or whether the compulsion of thy lordship had brought him by the hand of others; and when I had heard from him that he came of his own will, I carefully brought him to the honourable door of the judgment hall of thy rectitude.

And the governor gave orders on a sudden, and they brought Habib into his presence. The band said, Behold he standeth before thy lordship. And he began to interrogate him thus, and said to him, How is thy name? and whence art thou? and what art thou? He said to him, My name is Habib, and I am from the village Tẹlzeha, and I have been made a deacon. The governor said, Wherefore hast thou transgressed the edict of the Emperors, and dost minister in thine office, which is forbidden to thee by the Emperors, and art not willing to sacrifice to Jupiter, whom the Emperors worship? Habib said, We are Christians. We do not worship the works of men, who are nothing, neither are their works any thing; but we worship God who made ([illegible]) the men themselves. The governor said, Stand not with that bold heart with which thou art come before me, and insult not Jupiter the great glory of the Emperors. Habib said, But Jupiter is this idol, the work of men: thou hast said well, that I insult him. But if the carving of him out of wood and fixing of him with nails proclaim aloud respecting him that he is a thing made, how sayest thou to me that I insult him, for lo, his insult is from himself and against himself. The governor said, By this very thing that thou art not willing to worship him, thou insultest him. Habib said, If, because I do not worship him, I insult him, how great an insult then has the carpenter inflicted on him, who carved him out with an axe of iron, and the smith, who struck him and fixed him up with nails. And when the governor heard that he spake thus, he commanded him to be scourged unsparingly. And when he had been scourged of five, he said to him, Wilt thou now obey the Emperors? but if thou wilt not obey, I will tear thee severely with combs, and I will torture thee with all kinds of torture, and then at last I will give orders against thee, that thou be burnt with fire.

Habib said, These threats, which, lo, thou art now threatening me with, are much less and smaller than those which I had already made up my mind to endure; therefore I came and made my appearance before thee. The judge said, Cast him into the iron cage of murderers, and let him be scourged as he deserves: and when he had been scourged they said to him, Offer sacrifice to the gods; and he cried aloud and said, Accursed are your idols, and so are they who, with you, worship them like you. And the governor gave orders, and they took him up to the prison, but they did not give him permission to speak with his own family, nor with the inhabitants of his village, according to the command of the judge. But that day was the Emperors' festival.

And on the second (ܒ) of Ilul, the governor gave orders, and they brought him from the prison, and he said to him, Renounce that in which thou standest, and obey the edict which the Emperors have promulgated. But if thou wilt not obey, I will make thee obey them by bitter tearings of combs. Habib said, I have not obeyed them, and I am also determined in my mind that I will not obey them, not even if thou condemn me with judgments which are also worse than those which the Emperors have decreed. The governor said, By the gods I swear, that unless thou offer sacrifice, I will not omit any severe and bitter torture that I will not inflict upon thee: and we shall see if Christ, whom thou worshippest, will deliver thee. Habib said, All those who worship Christ, are delivered by Christ, because they have not worshipped creatures together with the Creator of the creatures. The governor said, Let him be stretched out and be scourged with whips, until there remain not a place in his body, on which he has not been scourged. Habib said, These inflictions, which thou supposest to be bitter in their scourgings, of them are platted crowns of victory for those who endure them. The governor said, How can ye call afflictions ease, and account the tortures of your bodies a crown of victory? Habib said, It pertaineth not to thee to ask me concerning these things, because thine unbelief is not worthy to hear the persuasion of these things. That I will not sacrifice, I have already said, and still say. The governor said, Because thou deservest these judgments, thou art set in them. I will put out those eyes of thine, which look upon this Jupiter, and are not afraid of him; and I will stop thine ears, which hear the laws of the Emperors, and are not terrified. Habib said, God, whom thou deniest here, hath another world (a), but there thou wilt confess him with scourgings, after thou hast further denied him. The governor said, Let that world alone about which thou hast spoken, and attend now to this trial in which, behold, thou standest, for there is no one who is able to deliver thee from it, unless the gods deliver thee if thou sacrifice to them. Habib said, Those who die for the sake of Christ's name, and worship not things made and creatures, will find their lives in the presence of God: and those who love the life of this present time more than that, their torment will be for ever.

And the governor gave order, and they hanged him up and tare him with combs, and as they were tearing him with the combs they pushed him about: and he was hanging a long time, until the shoulder-blades of his arms creaked. The governor said to him, Wilt thou comply even now, and place incense before this Jupiter. Habib said, Before these sufferings I would not comply with thee, and now that I have suffered, how thinkest thou that I should comply with thee, and lose thereby that which I have gained by them. The governor said, By judgments fiercer and bitterer than these I am prepared to make thee obey, according to the Emperor's edict, until thou do their pleasure. Habib said, Thou art judging me for not having obeyed the decree of the Emperors, when, behold, even thou, whom the Emperors have elevated and made thee a judge, hast transgressed their decree, in that thou hast not done to me, what the Emperors commanded thee. The governor said, Thou sayest thus, like a man who prefers an accusation, because I have had patience with thee. Habib said, If thou hadst not scourged me, and bound me, and torn me with combs, and put my feet into the st cks, it might have been supposed that thou hadst had patience with me: but if these things have intervened, where is thy patience towards me of which thou hast spoken? The governor said, These things which thou hast said will not help thee, because ([illegible]) they are all of them against thee, and they will bring upon thee afflictions which are even bitterer than those which the Emperors have decreed against thee. Habib said, If I had not been aware that they will help me, I should not have spoken a word about them before thee. The Governor said, I will silence these words of thine, and at the same time appease the gods by thee for thy not having worshipped them, and I will satisfy the Emperors on account of thee, because thou hast rebelled against their decrees. Habib said, I am not afraid of the death with which thou threatenest me, for had I been afraid of it, I should not have gone about from house to house, and ministered; for its sake it was that I did so minister.

The governor said, How is it that thou worshippest and adorest a man, but art not willing to worship and adore this Jupiter? Habib said, A man I worship not, because it is written for me, "Cursed is every one that putteth his trust in man;" but God, who took upon him flesh and became man, I worship and glorify. The governor said, Do thou what the Emperors have commanded; and as to what is in thy mind, if thou be willing to let it alone, *well*, but if thou be not willing, then let it not alone. Habib said, Both these things cannot be, because falsehood is contrary to truth, nor is it possible for that to be taken away from my thoughts which is firmly fixed in my mind. The governor said, By bitterer and severer tortures, I will make thee put away from thy thoughts, that of which thou saidest, It is firmly fixed in my mind. Habib said, These inflictions respecting which thou supposest that by them it will be rooted up from my mind, by these it is that it groweth in the midst of my heart like a tree which beareth fruit. The governor saith, What help can stripes and tearing of combs give to this tree of thine? and more especially at the time that I order fire against it, to burn it unsparingly. Habib said, ([illegible]) It is not to those things which thou lookest to, that I look, because I contemplate the things which are not seen, and on this account I do the will of God the maker *of all things*, and not that of a made idol, which cannot even perceive any thing whatever. The governor said, Because he thus denies the gods whom the Emperors worship, let additional tearing of combs be laid upon his former wounds; for in the multitude of questions which I have had the patience with him to ask him, he has forgotten his former tearings of combs. And while they were tearing him he cried aloud, and said, "The sufferings of this time are not equal to that glory which is about to be revealed in those who love Christ."

And when the governor saw that even under these afflictions he would not sacrifice, he said to him, Does your doctrine teach you thus, that you should hate your own bodies? Habib said, It is not that we hate our bodies, but in the scriptures it is written for us: "Whosoever will lose his life shall find it;" and another thing also is written for us, "that we should not give that which is holy to dogs, and that we should not cast pearls before swine." The governor said, I know that all which thou thus speakest is in order that my rage and the anger of my mind may be excited, and that I should give sentence of death against thee speedily. I will not therefore be hurried on to that which thou desirest, but I will have patience; not, indeed, for thy ease, but in order that the infliction of thy tortures may be increased, and that thou mayest see thy flesh falling off before thee from the combs which are passing over thy sides. Ḥabib said, I also am looking to this, that thou shouldest multiply thy tortures upon me as thou hast said. The governor said, Comply with the desire of the Emperors, because they have power to do whatsoever they will. Habib said, It does not belong to men to do whatsoever they will, but to God, who has the power in heaven, and over all the inhabitants of the earth; (ܠܗ) nor is there any one that can rebuke him and say, What doest thou?

The governor said, Death by the sword is too little for this insolence of thine: I am therefore prepared to pass against thee a sentence of death, which is bitterer than that of the sword. Habib said, But I look for a death more lingering than that of the sword, which thou wilt decree against me at the time that thou wishest.

And afterwards the governor began to give the sentence of death against him; and he called out aloud before his Officials, while they were listening, and the nobles of the city also, This Habib, who has denied the gods, as ye also have heard from him, and has likewise insulted the Emperors, it is right that life also should be denied to him from under this honoured sun, and that he should no longer behold this luminary, the associate of gods; and were it not that it has been decreed by former Emperors that the corpses of murderers should be buried, it would be right that the body of this fellow should not be buried, because he has been so insolent. I give sentence therefore, that a strap be cast into his mouth as into the mouth of a murderer, and that he be burned by a slow lingering fire, in order that the torture of his death may be increased.

And he went out from the presence of the governor with the strap thrust into his mouth, and a multitude of the people of the city ran after him. And the Christians were rejoicing because he had not turned aside nor abandoned his position, and the Pagans were threatening him because he would not sacrifice. And they took him out by the western door of the arches over against the cemetery, which was built for Abshelama, Abgar's son.

But his mother was clad in white, and she went out with him. And when he was arrived at the place where they were going to burn him, he stood up and prayed, and all those who came with him, and he said, Oh King Christ, for thine is this world and thine is the world ([illegible]) to come, behold, and see, that while I might have been able to flee from these afflictions, I did not flee, in order that I might not fall into the hands of thy justice: let therefore this fire, in which I am to be burned, be to me for a recompense before thee, so that I may be delivered from that fire which is not quenched. And receive thou my spirit into thy presence, through the spirit of thy Godhead, oh glorious Son of the adorable Father. And when he had prayed, he turned and blessed them, and they gave him the salutation as they wept, men and women, and they said to him, Pray for us in the presence of thy Lord, that he would cause peace for his people, and the renewal of his churches which are cast down.

And while Habib was standing they dug a place, and took him and set him in the midst of it, and they fixed up by him a stake. And they came to bind him to the stake, and he said to them, I will not stir from this place in which ye are going to burn me. And they brought faggots and set them in order, and placed them on all sides of him: and when the fire burnt up and the flames ascended fiercely they called out to him, Open thy mouth. And the moment he opened his mouth his soul mounted up; and they cried out, both men and women, with the voice of weeping. And they drew him and took him up out of the fire, and they threw over him fine linen and choice unguents and spices, and they seized upon some of the faggots for burning him, and the brethren carried him and some laics. And they wound him up and buried him by Guria and Shamuna the martyrs, in the same grave in which they were placed, on the hill which is called Baith Allah Cucla, repeating over him psalms and hymns: and they conducted his body, which was burnt, in an affectionate and honourable manner.

And even some Jews and Pagans took part with the Christian brethren in winding up and burying his body. And at the time when he was burned, and also at the time when they buried him, there was one spectacle of grief spread over those within and those without, and tears were running down ([illegible]) from all eyes, while every one gave glory to God, because he had given his body the burning of fire for his name's sake.

But the day on which he was buried was the sixth day of the week, the second of the month Ilul; on the day that it was heard how Constantine the Great had begun to depart from the interior of Spain, in order to proceed to Rome, the city of Italy, that he might carry on the war against Licinius, who at this day has the dominion over the Eastern parts which pertain to the Romans; and, lo, the countries are in commotion on all sides, because no man knoweth which of them will be victorious and continue in the power of the empire. But the Notaries wrote down every thing that they had heard from the judge: and the Sharirs of the city wrote the rest of the things which were spoken outside the door of the judgment hall, and, as is the custom, they make known to the judge all that they heard and saw, and their sentences are recorded in their Acts.

But I, Theophilus, who had renounced the evil inheritance of my fathers, and made my confession in Christ, gave diligence and wrote a copy of these Acts of Habib, as I had also formerly written of Shamuna and Guria, his fellow martyrs; and inasmuch as he had felicitated them upon their death by the sword, he resembled them himself also in his being crowned by the burning of fire. Moreover I have written the year, and the month, and the day of their being crowned as martyrs, not indeed for the sake of those who saw the deed as I did, but in order that they who come after us might learn what was the time of these Martyrs, and what kind of men they were; and also from the Acts of the former Martyrs, who *lived* in the days of the Emperor Domitianus, and of the rest of the Emperors who also raised a persecution against the church, and likewise put many to death, by stripes and lacerations, and by bitter inflictions ([illegible]), and by keen edged swords, and by burning fire, and by the terrible sea, and in the merciless mines. Both all these things, and things like them, they *suffered*, for the hope of the future reward.

Now the afflictions of these Martyrs, and of those whom I had heard of, opened the eyes of me, Theophilus, and enlightened my mind, and I confessed Christ, that he is the Son of God, and that he is God. And may the dust of these Martyrs' feet, which I received as I ran after them at the time of their departure and reception of their crown, procure me pardon for having denied Him, and may He confess me before those who worship him, because I have now confessed him.

And after the twenty-seven interrogatories, which the judge put to Habib, he gave against him sentence of death to be burned with fire.

HERE ENDETH THE MARTYRDOM OF HABIB THE DEACON.

ORATION ON HABIB THE MARTYR, COMPOSED BY MAR JACOB.

Habib the Martyr, clad in flames, hath called to me out of the fire, that also for him I should form an image of beauties among the glorious. Companion of the victorious, lo, he beckoneth to me out of the burning, that for his Lord's glory I should sing of him. In the midst of glowing coals stands the man, and, lo, he calleth to me to form his image, but the flame permits me not. His love is fervent, also warm his faith, his fire too burneth; and who is able to recount his love? But with that love which placed the martyr in fire, no man is able to describe his godly beauties ([illegible]). For who could dare approach and see in the flame, whom he resembleth, and how he is to be represented with the glorious? Shall I form his image by the side of the Children of the Furnace? With Hananiah, shall I reckon Habib? I know not. Lo, they were not burned there; how then does he resemble them, for he was burned and the Children not? Which then more comely, Habib the martyr, or Azariah? The image is difficult for me: how to view it I know not. Lo, Mishael was not burned by the flame; but Habib was burned: then which more comely to him that looketh on? Who would dare to say this less lovely is than that, or not so comely this as that, to him who seeth him? Three in the fire, and the flame toucheth them not. But the one was burned. And how am I able to tell what is the Fourth's, who went down into the midst of the furnace, to form an image for Habib there, together with the Three? He gave to him a place in the fire, to him who was burned, that he might be instead of him the fourth with the victorious. If then, the beauties of the Three be glorious although they were not burned, how shall not this, who was burned, be mingled with the glorious? If a man have the power either to be burned or not be burned, he that was burned, more exalted is his beauty than that of the Three. But because the disposal is of the Lord, glorified is He to be where he rescues and where he delivers up. But the will also of the Three who were not burned, and of him who was burned, was one and the same, here and there. And had the Lord of the fire commanded it to burn them, burned had been the Three, so far as pertained to them; if, too, to it he had intimated not to burn that one, burned had he not been; nor was it of himself that he was rescued. It was of their own will to go into the fire when they went in; but that they were not burned, the Lord of the fire willed and ordered it. Therefore one equal beauty is that of him who was burned, and of him who was not burned, because the will was also equal.

Beloved martyr, exalted is thy beauty; high is thy degree; becoming too thy crown ([illegible]); and thy story associated with that of the glorious! Choice gold art thou, the fire, too, hath tried thee, and thy beauty shineth bright. And, lo, into the King's crown art thou wrought, together with the victorious! Good labourer, who, in the doctrine of the Son of God, runneth his course like a prosperous man, on account of the beauty of his faith! Habib the martyr was a doctor of the truth; a preacher, too, whose mouth was filled with faith. Watchful he was and prompt, and with his doctrine encouraged by his faith the household of the house of God. Full of light he was, and contended against the darkness which covered the country from the paganism which had obscured it. The Gospel of the Son filled his mouth in the congregations; and as a leader he became to the villages at that time when he arrived. Zealous he was because he was anxious about the doctrine divine, that he might establish the party of the faith. At the time when blew the winds of the heathen he was a lamp, and blazed forth when they blew upon him; and was not quenched. Ardent was he, and full of his Lord's love, and careful for his sake, that he might speak of him without dismay.

The thorns of error sprang up in the place from paganism, and so far as he could he rooted them up by his diligence. He taught, admonished, and confirmed in faith the Christians who by persecutors were oppressed. Against the sword and fire contended he, with love hot as the flame, nor did he fear. Like a two-edged scimetar, keen was his faith, and against error did he contend. He became leaven in this country, which was sunken through the love of vanity's idols, that error had introduced. Like salt was he in savoury doctrine to this clime, which was become insipid through unbelief. A deacon was he, and filled the chief-priest's place, by preaching and by teaching of the truth. He was a good shepherd to the flock while he was superintendant; and his life he laid down for the flock while he tended it (ܗܠ). He drove away the wolf, and thrust back from it beasts of prey. The fissures he stopped up, and carried the lambs into their folds. He went out secretly and encouraged the congregations: he strengthened and admonished them, and made them to lie down. Armour of faith he forged, and put on them, that they might not be despised by paganism, which was rife. The flocks of the fold of the Son of God were being laid waste by persecutors, and he encouraged the lambs and ewes.

He was an advocate for the children of the house of faith. Them, too, he taught not to be alarmed by persecutors; them he taught to run to meet death, without being afraid either of sword or fire. In the doctrine of the Son of God he prospered, so that faith ran without being terrified. Then Error grew envious, furious, and maddened on account of him. Out after him she went to shed on the earth innocent blood. The Calumniator, who hates the race of man, laid snares for him, to rid the place of his society. The Hater of truth went out after him to put him to death, that his voice might cease from the teaching of the house of God. Error strove that Habib might die, because she hated him; and pain stimulated her, and she sought him to draw out his soul. His story, too, was agitated before the country's pagan judge; and the report of him reached the king:. incited by great rage, and because the diadem was interwoven with paganism, he decreed death on Habib's account, because he was full of faith. And when the edict reached the judge, he armed himself with rage and fury; so with a mind thirsting for blood, and, like hunters, which throw nets for the young stag, they went out after Habib to hunt. But this man was a preacher of the faith, who, in the highway of the cross, had prospered. And by his doctrine his people's children to help, his labour had embraced the countries round. But when after him Error went out, she found him not;—not that he was fled, but was gone out to preach. And because the pagans' fury transgressed (ܟ) all right, his kindred and his mother they seized on his account.

Blessed art thou, oh woman, because thou art the martyr's mother; on his account they seized and bound thee wickedly. What seek they of thee, oh thou full of beauty? why did they search for thee? Behold, they seek thee, that thou mayest bring the martyr to be a sacrifice. Bring, bring to the place of offering thy sweet fruit, whose savour fragrant is, that it may incense be to the Deity. Graceful shoot, thy cluster bring whence it is, that its wine may become libation of sweet taste.

The lamb heard that they were seeking him to be a sacrifice, and walked and came rejoicing to the sacrificers. That others on his account oppressed were he heard, and his own pain in many's stead came to bear. The lot fell on him to be alone a sacrifice; and the fire that was to offer him up beheld at him as he came. Of many who were imprisoned on his account, not even one was seized to die, except himself alone. Worthy was he; and martyrdom was reserved for him; nor is man able to snatch the martyr's place. Therefore, of his own free-will, he came to be arrested by the judge and die for Jesus' sake. He heard that they were seeking him; and came to be arrested, while they sought for him. And he went in before the judge, with open countenance. Himself he hid not, nor wished to escape the judge; for he was full of light, and from the darkness fled not. No thief was he, nor murderer, nor robber, nor child of night, for in the day was all his race. To whom from his fold should the good shepherd flee, and leave his flock to be devoured by thieves? To whom the physician flee, who goes out wounds to heal, and cure souls by the blood of the Son of God? Openness of countenance and a large heart the man possessed; and to meet death marched on, rejoicing for Jesus' sake. He went in, and stood before the judge, and said to him, I am Habib, (ܚܒܝܒ) whom ye did seek: lo! here I stand. And the pagan shook, and wonder seized him, and he marvelled at him—at the man who neither feared sword nor fire. When he supposed that fleeing he would flee, he entered in and laughed at him. And the judge shook, because he him beheld courageous against death. A disciple was he of that Son of God, who said, Rise, come, let us go, for lo, he that betrayeth me is at hand. And to the crucifiers again he said, Whom seek ye? They say, Jesus. And he said to them, I am he. The Son of God, of his own free will, approached the cross; and to Him the martyr looked, and offered himself before the judge. On him the pagan looked, and was disturbed, and was embittered, and his rage arose, and in his fury questions he began to moot; and, as if he were a man who had shed on the ground blood of the slain, that holy man he questioned, nor was ashamed, threatening, and terrifying, and frightening him, and telling over sufferings which he had prepared on his account. But Habib, when questioned, feared not; ashamed he was not, nor was he frightened by his threats. Lifting up his voice, he confessed Jesus God's Son, that he his servant was, and was his priest, and minister. While the pagans' fury roared at him like a lion, he was not shaken to withhold his confession of the Son of God. Scourged he was, and greatly dear to him the scourges were, because a little of God's Son's stripes he bare. He put on bonds, and looked up to his Lord, whom also they had bound: his heart rejoiced, too, that he had now begun to go along the path of his sufferings. He was raised on the tree, and they tare him, but his soul was bright, because he was worthy that on him should come the agony of crucifixion's pains. He set his face to walk along the way of death; and what desired he to find in it but sufferings? The fire of sacrifice was betrothed to him, and to her he looked; but she to him sent combs and stripes and wounds that he might taste. While she was coming, sufferings to him she sent, that by their means he might prepared be (ܢܒ); so that she might not trouble him when they met. Sufferings purged him, so that when the flame proved him, no dross in his choice gold might then be found. And he endured all pains that fell upon him, that he might be experienced, and in the fire stand like one excellent. And he received with joy the sufferings he endured, because he knew that at the end of them he should find death. Neither of death was he afraid nor sufferings, because with crucifixion's wine his heart was drunk. His body, while dragged by persecutors, he disregarded; his limbs, too, while they bitterly were torn. Stripes on his loins, combs on his sides, upon his feet the stocks, fire, too, before him, still was he brave and faithful.

They mocked him, Lo, thou worshippest a man. But he replied, A man I worship not, but God, who took upon him flesh and became man, him worship I, because, together with his Father, he is God. The martyr Habib's faith was full of light, and by it was enlightened Edessa full of faith. The daughter of Abgar, whom Addæus to the cross betrothed, her light is in him, in him her truth, her faith also: of it her king is, her martyrs of it, her truth of it, the teachers of her faith are of it also. Abgar believed that Thou art God, the Son of God; and received a blessing for his faith's excellence. Sharbil the martyr, son of the Edessæans, likewise said, My heart is captive with God who became man. Habib the martyr, also at Edessa crowned, confessed the same, that He took upon him flesh and became man; that He is the Son of God, and God, and became man. Edessa learned from teachers of the truth: her king taught her the faith, her martyrs taught her, but to others, teachers of error, she would not obey. Habib the martyr, out of the midst of fire, in Edessa's ear thus cried, Man I worship not; for God, (ܗܘ) who took a body and became man, him I worship, confessed the martyr, with uplifted voice. From confessors, lacerated, burnt, uplifted, slain, and from a righteous king, Edessa learned the faith, and knows our Lord, that He is even God, the Son of God: she also learned and believed that He took flesh and became man. Nor learned she from common scribes the faith: her king taught her, her martyrs taught her, and she believed them: and if she ever be accused of worshipping man, she shews her martyrs who died to prove, That He is God. Man, indeed, I worship not, Habib said, for it is written, "Cursed is he that putteth his trust in man." Because He is God I worship him, and honour him, nor on his account will I renounce his faith. This truth Edessa from her youth maintained, nor, daughter of the poor, in her old age, changed she it. Her righteous king to her became a scribe, and of him she learned about our Lrod, that He is the son of God, and God. Addæus, who brought the bridegroom's ring and placed it on her hand, betrothed her thus to the Son of God, his only Son. Sharbil, the priest, who tried and proved all gods, died, as he said, for God's sake, who became man. Shamuna and Guria, for the sake of the only Son, stretched out their necks and died for him, because he is God; Habib the martyr, the congregations' teacher, preached of him, that He took upon him flesh and became man. For a man's sake the martyr would not have been burned in fire, but burned he was for God's sake, who became man. And witness Edessa is that, in the fire, he thus confessed; and from the confession of a martyr that was burned who will flee? All hearts faith puts to silence and convicts, being full of light: nor stoopeth down to shades: him it condemneth who maligns the Son, by saying, He is not God; him also that saith, He took not on him flesh, and became man. Faithful in truth upon the fire he stood, (ܩܡ) and became incense, whose perfume appeased the Son of God. In all afflictions, tortures, and sufferings, thus did he confess, and thus also the blessed *city* taught. And this truth Edessa held touching our Lord; both that He is God, and of Mary was made man. And him who denies his Godhead the bride hates, and condemns and despiseth him who speaks against his manhood; but Him in Godhead and in manhood she knows as one, the only Son, whose body is not separated from him. And thus to believe the daughter of the Parthians learned, thus she affirmed, and thus she teaches all who listen to her.

The heathen judge then issued his command that the martyr

should be taken out and burned in the fire which was reserved for him. Forthwith a strap was thrust into hi mouth, as though he were a murderer, while in his heart was kept his confession with God: and him they seized, and from the judgment hall he went out with joy, because the hour was near that his faith's crown should come. And crowds of men with him went out, to bear him company; nor looked they on him carried forth as a dead man, but as a man who went to be a bridegroom through fire; and to receive the crown for him reserved of righteousness. They looked upon him as one who went to battle, and spears, and lances, and swords, surrounded him, but them he vanquished. Him they beheld go up, like a champion from the contest; and chaplets for his victory were brought to him by those who beheld. Him they beheld conquer dominions and powers which all made war on him: them he put to shame. In him rejoiced the whole Christian crowd, because he raised up the side of faith by sufferings which he endured. The Church with him went out, like a bride full of light; and her face was beaming at the beloved martyr joined to her.

His mother, then, for it was her son's marriage feast, in garments nobler than her wont, adorned herself; since sordid raiment suits not the banquet hall, all tastefully she clad herself in white. Here to the battle love came down to fight, within the mother's soul, the love of nature and the love of God ([illegible]). She saw her son dragged to be thrown in flames; yet, having in her the Lord's love, she grieved not. The mother's yearning womb cried out on its fruit's behalf, but faith put it to silence, so that its tumult ceased. Nature yelled aloud over her severed limb, but the Lord's love made the soul drunken, so that it perceived it not. Nature loved, but in the strife the Lord's love prevailed within the mother's soul, so that she murmured not for her beloved. Instead of pain, her heart was all full of joy; and instead of mourning, she went out in gay array. When he went to be burned she followed him, and was elate, because the Lord's love nature's vanquished. And in white garments, as for a bridegroom, she made a feast, and the martyr's mother was cheerful on his behalf. Shamuni the second may we this blessed woman call; because, had seven been burned instead of one, she would have been content. One only had she, and gave him up to be the fire's food; and like that one, had she had seven she would have given them. Into the fire he was cast, and the flame surrounded him. His mother looked on, and grieved not at his being burned. There is another eye that looketh to the things not seen. Dear to her soul was he, therefore rejoiced she when he was burned. She looked for jewels of light, which are in martyrs' crowns; and glory reserved for them after their pains; and promised blessings which they inherit there through their afflictions; and the Son of God, who doth invest their limbs in robes of light; and to the varied beauties of that kingdom which will not perish; and that great door which is open for them to enter in to God. To these the martyr's mother looked while he was burned, so she rejoiced, exulted, and accompanied him in white. She looked upon him while the fire consumed his body; and grieved not because his crown was very great. Into the fire, upon the coals, the sweet root fell, and became incense, and cleansed the air from filth. With sacrifice's smoke the air was foul become, (ܥܘ) but, by this martyr's burning, it was purified. The sky was fetid from altar's sacrifices, but the martyr's sweet perfume mounted up, and it grew sweet. Then ceased the sacrifices, and in the congregations there was peace. The sword was sheathed, nor Christians any more laid waste. With Sharbil it began, with Habib ended in our land. From that time, and until now, not one has it slain: since he was burned, Constantine, the chief of victors, reigns;

and now the Cross the emperor's diadem surmounts, and is set upon his head. Idolatry's lofty horn is crushed, and since the martyr's burning, and until now, it has not pierced one. His smoke arose, and incense to the Deity became; and the air was purified, which paganism had infected. By his burning, too, the country was entirely cleansed. Blessed be he that gave to him a crown and glory, and a good name.

HERE ENDETH THE ORATION ON HABIB, COMPOSED BY MAR JACOB.

AN ORATION ON SHAMUNA AND GURIA, COMPOSED BY MAR JACOB.

SHAMUNA and Guria, martyrs who triumphed in their afflictions, have asked me, in love, to tell of their exploits. To faith's combatants the doctrine calleth me, to go and see their contests and their crowns. Children of the right hand, who with the left have battle done, to-day have called me to recount the wonder of their struggles: simple old men, who entered (ܥܠ) the battle like the mighty, and in the war of blood became richly victorious. These were their country's salt, and it was glad of it, for it restored its flavour, which was grown tasteless through unbelief. Lamps of gold, full of crucifixion's oil, were they, from which was lighted up all our quarter, then grown dark. Two lamps, whose lights were not put out when all the winds of every error blew. Good labourers, who laboured from the dawn of day in the blessed vineyard of God's house righteously. Walls of our country, which became for us a shelter from all robbers, in all the surrounding wars. Havens of peace, homes of refuge, too, for all who are distressed; and place to lay the head for every one in need of help. Two precious pearls, which were the ornament of my lord Abgar's bride, Aramæan's son. Doctors they were, who practised their doctrine in their blood; whose faith by their own sufferings was known. On their own bodies, in frequent wounds and stripes, the story of the Son of God they wrote. Their love they shewed not only by words of mouth, but by tortures, and the dislocations of their limbs. For love of God's Son's sake, their bodies they gave up, because the lover it behoves for his love himself to give. Fire and sword had proved their love, how firm and true it was. And more than silver tried in earth, their necks were beautiful. They looked to God, and because they saw his beauties high above, therefore their sufferings for his sake were able to despise. The Sun of righteousness above was risen within their hearts: by which they were enlightened, and with light the darkness chased. Vanity's idols, by error brought, they mocked at in the faith of the blessed Son of God, which is full of light. As a fire within their hearts the Lord's love became, nor could the thorns of unbelief at all withstand its force. Captive with God was bound their love, which will not ever change ([illegible]): therefore they could despise the sword which was athirst for blood. With harmlessness and wisdom at the judgment-seat they stood, as they commandment had received from him who taught the truth. When they despised and gave up kindred and family, harmless they were, for possessions and wealth were lightly esteemed by them: yet prudent in the judgment-hall, with serpents' wisdom wise, cautiously they watched o'er the faith of God's house. When seized a serpent is and struck, his head he always guards; but yielding, giveth up his body to those who seize upon him. So long as guarded is his head, his life abideth in him; but if his head be smitten, then his life to destruction goes. The soul's head is the faith of men: if this then be preserved, in it also their salvation is kept unhurt: be the whole body bruised with strokes, so long as faith be kept, the soul still lives. But should the faith by unbelief be smitten and struck down, lost is the soul, and perisheth the salvation of men. Shamuna and Guria guarded the faith as men, that it might not be beaten down by persecutors, for well they knew if faith preserved be, safe from destruction soul and body are. Therefore they were careful of their faith, that it might not be smitten, for in it was their salvation hidden. Their bodies they gave up to blows and dislocation, and every torture, that their faith might not be smitten. Like as the serpent also hides his head from blows, so they their faith concealed in the centre of their hearts. Smitten was the body, endured stripes, and sufferings sustained, but yet within their hearts the faith was not smitten down. By speaking, the mouth to death gives up the soul, and like a sword, makes slaughter with the tongue; from which spring up both life and death for men. He that denieth dies; confesseth lives, possessing the power: denial is death, but in confession of the soul is life. Over both, the mouth hath power too, even like a judge. The word of mouth (ܡܠܬܐ) opens the door for death to enter in: it also bids salvation rise upon the sons of man. The Thief, too, by one word of faith, the kingdom of heaven gained, and Paradise inherited, of every blessing full. The wicked judges required the martyrs, sons of the right-hand, only by word of mouth to utter blasphemy; but like true men holding fast the faith, no word they gave which might serve unbelief.

Shamuna, beauty of our faith, who can suffice for thee? because too weak and feeble is my mouth to tell thy praise: thy truth thy beauty is, thy crown thy sufferings, thy wealth thy stripes: and by thy blows illustrious the glory of thy combat. Proud of thee our country is, as of a treasure full of gold; for thou to us art riches, and an envied treasure not to be stolen.

Guria, martyr, mighty champion of our faith, who, to recount thy godly beauties is sufficient? Lo, tortures on thy body are like beryl set, and on thy neck the sword, like a chain of choice gold. Thy blood upon thy body a glorious splendid robe, and thy loins' scourging like raiment the sun cannot compare with. Adorned thou art and beautified by these, thy many sufferings; and glorious are thy beauties, from the wounds severe upon thee.

Shamuna, our riches, thou art richer than the wealthy, for lo, at thy door the wealthy stand that thou mayest make them sit. Small is thy village, thy country poor, yet who has granted thee, that lords of villages and towns should try to do thee pleasure? Lo, judges in their robes and garbs take from thy threshold dust, as if it were the medicine that would ensure them life. Rich is the cross, and addeth wealth to those who fall before it, but still its poverty rejects all the riches of the world.

Shamuna and Guria, sons of the poor, lo, at your doors bow down the rich, to gather up from you their own necessities. The Son of God in poverty and need shewed to the world that all its riches nothing be ([illegible]). All fishermen, all poor, all weak, all those of little note, became victorious by his faith. One fisherman, whose village, was Baithsaida, him chief made He and steward of the twelve. One tentmaker, who before had been a persecutor, him took He and caused to become a chosen vessel of faith.

Shamuna and Guria, arose from villages not wealthy, and lo, in a mighty city became lords, at whose doors chiefs and judges stand, and from them ask compassion their need to satisfy. By confession of faith in God's Son, these blessed men uncounted wealth obtained. Poor He became, and made rich the poor; and lo, the whole creation, through his poverty, grows rich. Chosen martyrs! against error they waged war, and by confession of God's Son as brave men they stood. In went they, and before the judge they confessed Him with open face, that he might them, as they had him, confess, before his Father. The war of pagans assailed them like a storm, but their pilot was the cross, and onward steered them. Required they were to sacrifice to idols without life, yet ceased they not from their confession of the Son of God. Blasts of idolatry blew full against their face, but firm were they as rocks against the raging storm. Like a swift whirlwind, error snatched at them; but because they were protected, it could not injure them. The wicked one set on his dogs to bark and bite at them, but having for a staff the cross, they drave them all to flight. And who sufficient is to tell their struggles, their sufferings, or their dislocated limbs? or who is able to pourtray their crowns, how they returned victorious from the fight? To judgment they went up, but of the judge thought not, nor careful were when questioned what to speak. The threatening judge spake much in threats, and of all tortures told, and (ܦܐ) suffering; that he might frighten them: His words he magnified in menaces and threats; that he by terror might compel them to offer sacrifice. His threats the combatants despised, his menaces, and doom, and all corporeal deaths. For insults they prepared themselves, for stripes and provocation, for blows, and to be dragged and burned, and for imprisonment; for bonds and every evil thing, for torture and all pains, being full of joy. They were not terrified, nor frightened, nor disturbed, nor did the tortures' violence bend them to sacrifice. Their body they despised, and counted as earth's dung, because they knew the more it suffered, its beauty would greater be. The more the judge, to frighten them, increased his menaces, him so much the more did they despise, nor fear his threats. To them told he how many tortures he had prepared for them, to him they told about Geh· nna, which was reserved for him. By what he spake he tried to make them sacrifice; to him spake they of that dread judgment there. Truth is much wiser than the words of wisdom; but very odious, however adorned, a lie. Shamuna and Guria persisted in speaking truth, and still the judge made use of lying words. Therefore his threatening they feared not, for all his menaces failed against the truth. The world's life they contemned, despised, abandoned, and neglected it; nor did they wish to enter it again. From the tribunal they set their face to go to the promised place of life in the new world. They thought not of possessions, nor of houses, nor of the superfluities of this world full of evil. In the world of light with God was their heart bound, and to that same place set they their face to go. To the sword they looked, to come and be a bridge, to pass them over to God, in whom they hoped. This world they counted as a (ܡܛܠܐ) tabernacle, but that world yonder a city full of beauties. They hastened to depart hence by the sword to the place full of light and of blessings for the worthy. The judge commanded to hang them by their arms, and without mercy they bitterly stretched them out. A demon's fury breathed rage in the judge's heart, and embittered him to crush those faithful ones. Between the height and depth he stretched them out, that he might torture them. And they became a wonder to both sides, how much they suffered. Heaven was astonished and earth at these old men's frame, how great suffering it endured, nor begged for help from pain. Their feeble bodies were hung and dragged by their arms, yet there was silence deep, nor cry for help nor murmur. All those who saw their contests marvelled how their extended bodies the pains endured. Astonished, too, was Satan at their chaste frames, what weight of grief they bare without a groan. The angels, too, rejoiced at their patience, how it endured that fearful contest then. But combatants who waited for their crown, into their hearts entered no weariness. The judge, however, weary grew, and wondered; but these brave men by afflictions were not wearied. Them asked he, were they willing to sacrifice: the mouth from pain no utterance could give. And, so, their persecutors increased their pains until they left the word no place to speak. Silent was the mouth, under their limbs' afflictions, but like a hero, the will was vigorous with its own. Alas for persecutors! how are they cut off from righteousness; but children of light, how are they clad in faith? Speech they required when there was no place to speak, for the mouth's utterance was cut off by pain. Fast bound the body was and silent the mouth, nor could it give the word when questioned wickedly (ܥܘܠ). And what could the martyr do who had no strength to say, when asked, he would not sacrifice. Quite silent were these old men full of faith, nor were they able to speak out from pain; yet they were questioned: how then, if one speak not when questioned, does he assent to what is said? That these old men be not thought to assent, they show, by beckoning, the word too hard to speak: they moved their heads, and by a nod for speech disclosed the will of the new man within. Their heads hung down while in their pains they beckoned that they would not sacrifice, and all men knew their minds. While there was place for speech in them, they confessed with speech, but when this was taken away by pain, they spake by a nod. Faith with and without the voice they spake, so that both speaking and when silent they were true. Who would not wonder how narrow life's path is; how strait, likewise, to such as walk therein? Who will not marvel how to the watchful will and prompt, it is very broad and full of light for such as go therein? Around the way are ditches; it is also full of pits: and if one turn aside a little from it a pit receiveth him. Between the right and left there is but a nod: on Yes and No stands sin and righteousness. By a nod only these blessed men refused to sacrifice, and by a nod only the way led them to Eden. But had this same nod inclined and turned a little towards the depth, their way had been down to hell. Upwards they nodded, prepared upwards to go: and by that nod they rose and mixed with the heavenly ones. Between nod and nod was Paradise and hell: they beckoned dissent to sacrifice, and the kingdom's heirs became. Even silent for God's Son advocates they were, for faith consisteth not in many words. (ܣܙ) Confession full of voice their patience was, as, though with open mouth, they beckoned faith's assent; and all knew what they said when silent. And the faith of God's house grew rich, increased; and error was ashamed, because two old men, that, while they even spake not, vanquished her: silent they were, and their own faith stood fast. And when troubled voices from the judge were heard, and the emperor's edicts dreadful were and fierce, and paganism had its face uncovered, its mouth, too, open, and its voice was high, yet the old men were quiet under pain; then was the edict null, and the judge's voice grew cold, and the martyrs' voiceless sign bare off the palm. Voices and tumult and sound of stripes on the left, but on the right great calm and suffering stood. And by one nod, which these old men upwards raised, faith's head was elevated, and error put to shame. Condemned were they who spake, and the silent had victory, for without voice they beckoned the word of faith.

When they by silence triumphed, they took them down, and bound them, threatening still to vanquish them. Prison for the martyrs, and a pit void of light; and yet by them esteemed as light interminable. No bread, no water, no light, yet them it pleased for the love's sake of the Son of God. The judge commanded to hang them by their legs with downward heads, by a sentence far from just. Hanged, with head downward, Shamuna was, and prayed; prayer innocent and strained clear from pain. Sweet fruit hung on the tree in that judgment hall; whose taste and fragrance made even the angels marvel. Oppressed his body was, but his faith was sound. Bound was his body, but his prayer was loose over his work: for even nothing can prayer impede, nor either sword or fire hinder it. His body was subverted, but his prayer abounds; and straight his way ([illegible]) up thither to the angels' place. The more affliction on this choice martyr grew, the more confession from his lips was heard. For the keen sword the martyrs dearly longed: they sought it like a treasure full of wealth. A new work in the world God's Son has wrought, that dreadful death by many should be beloved. Never was it heard that men ran to meet the sword, excepting those whom Jesus enlisted by his cross. That death is bitter all men know, lo, from eternity. To martyrs alone, when slain, it is not bitter. At the keen sword they laughed when they saw it, and in it rejoiced, for it gained them their crowns. They let the body be smitten as something hated: nor, had they loved it, would have held it back from pain. The sword they looked for, and the sword out went and crowned them. Because for it they looked, it met them as they desired. By his crucifixion the Son of God slew death; and because death was slain the martyrs it distressed not. With a crushed serpent one playeth without fear; a coward, too, will drag at a dead lion. Our Lord crushed the great serpent by his cross, and by his passion the dread lion God's Son slew. Death bound He, and cast him down and trode upon him at hell's door; and all who wish may now draw near and mock him because he is slain. Shamuna and Guria, old men, mocked at death; especially at that lion by God's Son slain. That great serpent, which slew Adam among the trees, who that has not drunk of the cross's blood could seize? By his cross the Son of God the dragon crushed; and, lo, that bruised serpent now boys and old men mock at. Pierced is that lion by the lance of God's Son's side, and every one that wishes now tramples, despises, mocks him. The cause of all (ܟܠ) good things is the Son of God himself; Him, therefore, ought all mouths duly to celebrate. With blood which ran down from his wounds he did espouse the bride: and from the necks' of his bridegroom friends the spear demanded blood. The Lord of the feast hung nakedly on the cross, and cast his blood on every one who came to be a guest. Shamuna and Guria for his sake gave up their bodies to sufferings, and to torture, and to every kind of woe. Him they looked to while mocked at by wicked men, and so endured without murmur the mockery of themselves. By your deaths, oh ye blessed men, Edessa waxed rich, for well ye ornamented her with your crown and suffering. Ye are her beauty, her bulwark ye, her salt ye are likewise; her wealth, her store, her boast, and all her treasury. Ye are the stewards of her faith; for by your suffering the bride ye did array with beauty. Parthians' daughter, spouse of the cross, she boasts herself of you, for, lo, she was enlightened by your teaching. Her advocates are ye, teachers, who by silence conquered error, which lifted up on high its voice in unbelief. The old men of the Hebrews' daughter were sons of the evil one; lying witnesses who killed Naboth, being mad. Her Edessa surpassed by two excellent old men, who became witnesses of the Son of God, and like Naboth died. Two aged men were there, and here also two, and these and those were both alike called witnesses. Now, let us see which of these were witnesses of God's choice, which city also is beloved for its good old men's sake. Lo, the sons of the evil one, who did Naboth slay, are witnesses: and here again are witnesses Shamuna and Guria. Now let us see which witnesses, which old men, which city have open countenance with God. That harlot's witnesses were sons of the evil one, and lo! in their very names their shame is all pourtrayed. Edessa's aged witnesses righteous were and just, and resemble Naboth, who was slain for righteousness, ([illegible]). They were not two false liars, like the sons of the evil one: nor does Edessa resemble Sion, which nailed Him on the cross. Her old men, lying like herself, dared wickedly to shed on the ground innocent blood. By the witnesses of this place, behold, the truth was told. Blessed be He who gave to us the treasure of their crowns.

HERE ENDETH THE ORATION ON GURIA AND SHAMUNA.

CANTICLE OF MAR JACOB THE DOCTOR, UPON EDESSA, WHEN SHE SENT TO OUR LORD TO COME TO HER.

Edessa sent to Christ, by an epistle, to come to her and enlighten her. For all Gentiles she to Him made intercession that he would quit Sion which hated him, and come to the Gentiles who loved him.

She sent to him and besought him that he would enter into friendship with her. By her righteous king she made intercession to him, that he would leave the People and towards the Gentiles direct his burden.

From among all kings, one wise king the daughter of the Gentiles found: him she made ambassador, by him to her Lord she sent.—Come to me; in thee will I forget idols and all graven images.—

The harlot that was standing in the market-place heard of his fame from afar, as she was erring with idols, playing the girl with graven images. She loved, she desired him while he was far away, and begged him to admit her into his chamber.

Let the beloved bridegroom kiss me; with the kisses of his mouth shall I be blessed. I have heard of him from afar; may I see him from near; and may I place my lips upon his, and delight mine eyes with the sight of him.

Thy teats are better to me than wine, for the scent of thy sweetness is eternal life. I will nourish myself with thy milk; with thy scent will I make myself sweet from the smoke of idols, which, with its fetid odour, did make me stink.

Draw me after thee into thy fold ([illegible]); because I am a sheep gone astray in the world. After thee I run, and thy voice do I seek, that the number a hundred by me may be made complete, by a lost one which is found.

Let Gabriel rejoice and be glad with all the angels' host in thee, the good shepherd, who the wounded sheep didst carry on thy shoulders, that the number a hundred might be preserved.

Thy love is better than wine, and thy affection than the countenance of the upright. In wine let us remember thee, how by the cup of thy blood thou hast obtained for us new life; and the upright praised thy love.

I am a church of the Gentiles, and I have loved the only Son, who has been sent. Because his betrothed hated him I have loved him; and through Abgar the Black have I entreated him to come and visit me.

I am black and comely: ye daughters of Sion, pure is your envy, because the son of the glorious one has espoused me to make me enter into his chamber. When I was odious he loved me, because he is able to make me clearer than water.

Black was I in sins, and comely am I become, because I have turned and repented: I have cast away in baptism all that odious colour, because the Saviour of all creatures has washed me clean in his pure blood.

HERE END THE EXTRACTS FROM THE CANTICLE ON EDESSA.

EXTRACTS FROM VARIOUS BOOKS, RELATING TO ABGAR THE KING AND ADDÆUS THE APOSTLE.

I.

OF THE BLESSED ADDÆUS THE APOSTLE. FROM HIS DOCTRINE WHICH HE DELIVERED IN EDESSA BEFORE ABGAR THE KING AND THE ASSEMBLY OF THE CITY.

AND when he entered the sepulchre, he rose again and came out of the sepulchre together with many; and those who were watching the sepulchre saw not how he came out of the sepulchre: and the Watchers from on high, they were the proclaimers and announcers of his resurrection. For, had he not willed he had not died, because he is the Lord of death, the exit; nor (ܦܠ) had it not pleased him, would he have put on the body, inasmuch as he is himself the creator of the body: for that will which caused him to stoop to the birth from the virgin, the same again humbled him to the suffering of death. *And after a few words,* For although his appearance was that of men, nevertheless his power, and his knowledge, and his authority, was that of God.

II.

FROM THE DOCTRINE OF ADDÆUS THE APOSTLE, WHICH WAS SPOKEN IN THE CITY EDESSA.

YE know that I said to you, that all the souls which go out of the bodies of men are not under death, but live and subsist; and there are for them mansions and abodes of rest. For the thought of the soul does not cease, nor the knowledge, because it is the image of the immortal God. For it is not devoid of perception like the body, which has no perception of its corruption which hath dominion over it. But recompense and reward it will not receive apart from its body, because the passion is not of itself alone, but of the body also in which it dwelt for a time. But those who believe not, because they knew not God, are without advantage, then they repent.

III

From the Epistle of Addæus the Apostle, which he spake in the city of Edessa.

Give heed, therefore, to this ministry which ye hold, and continue in it with fear and trembling, and minister every day. Minister ye not in it with neglectful habits, but with the discretion of faith; neither let the praises of Christ cease from your mouths, nor let weariness in the time of prayers approach you. Give heed to the verity which ye hold, and to the teaching (ܦ) of the truth which ye have received, and to the teaching of salvation which I commit to you. Because before the judgment seat of Christ will it be required of you, when he maketh reckoning with the pastors and superintendants, and when he taketh his money from the traders with the increase of the doctrines. For he is the King's Son, and goeth to receive a kingdom, and he will return, and come and make a resurrection of all men.

IV.

Addæus preached at Edessa and in Mesopotamia, but he was from Paneus, in the days of Abgar the king. And when he was among the Zophenians, Severus, the son of Abgar, sent and slew him at Agel Hasna, and a young man his disciple.

V.

71. And Narcissus. For they did not suffer the selection of the

Seventy-two to fail, as neither that of the Twelve. But he was of the Seventy-two: perhaps he was a disciple of Addæus the Apostle.

VI

From the exit of my Lady Mary from the world, and the birth and childhood of our Lord Jesus Christ.

Book the Second.

In the year three hundred and forty-five, in the month Tishrin the latter, my Lady Mary went out from her house, and went to the sepulchre of Christ, because she used to go every day and weep there. But the Jews, immediately after the death of Christ, seized the sepulchre and heaped great stones at the door of it. And they set men to watch over the sepulchre and Golgotha, and charged them, that if any one should go and pray by the sepulchre or by Golgotha, he should forthwith be put to death. And the Jews took away the cross of our Lord and those two other crosses, and that spear with which our Saviour was struck, and those nails which they had fixed in his hands (ܦܣܐ) and his feet, and those robes of mockery in which he had been clad, and they hid them, because they were afraid lest any one of the kings or the chief persons should come and inquire about the death of Christ.

And those that kept watch went in and told to the priests that Mary cometh evening and morning, and prayeth there. And there was a tumult in Jerusalem on account of my Lady Mary. And the priests went to the judge, and said to him, My lord, send and command Mary that she go not and pray at the sepulchre and at Golgotha. And while they were considering, lo, letters came from Abgar, the king of the city Edessa, to Sabina, the governor, who had been appointed by the Emperor Tiberius, and even as far as to the river Euphrates the governor Sabina had authority. And because the Apostle Addæus, one of the Seventy-two Apostles, was gone down and had built a church at Edessa, and had cured the disease which king Abgar had; for king Abgar loved Jesus Christ, and was always inquiring about him; and when Christ was put to death, and Abgar the king heard that the Jews had slain him on the cross, he was greatly grieved. And Abgar arose and rode until he came to the river Euphrates, because he desired to go up against Jerusalem and lay it waste. And when Abgar came and was arrived at the river Euphrates, he considered in his mind, that if I pass over, there will be enmity between me and the Emperor Tiberius. So Abgar wrote letters and sent to Sabina the governor, and Sabina sent them to Tiberius the Emperor. For after this manner wrote Abgar to the Emperor Tiberius.

From Abgar the king of the city Edessa. Much peace to thy Majesty, our Lord Tiberius. In order that thy Majesty might not be offended at me, I have not crossed the river Euphrates, for I wished to go up to Jerusalem and lay her waste, because she had slain Christ, a wise physician. But thou, inasmuch as thou art a great king, and hast authority over all the earth and over us, send and do me judgment upon the people of Jerusalem. For let thy majesty know that I desire that thou do me judgment upon those crucifiers.

And Sabina received the letters, and sent them to the Emperor Tiberius. And when he read them, the Emperor Tiberius was greatly incensed, and he desired to destroy and slay all the Jews. And the people of Jerusalem heard and were troubled. And the priests went to the governor, and said to him, My lord, send and command Mary that she go not and pray near the sepulchre and Golgotha. The judge said to the priests, Go ye, charge and caution her what ye desire.

VII.

From the Oration composed by my Lord Jacob, the Doctor, on the fall of Idols.

He turned to Edessa and found in it a great work, that the king was become a labourer for the church, and was building it. The Apostle Addæus stood in it like a builder, and king Abgar laid aside his diadem and builded with him. An Apostle and a king, when they agree the one with the other, what idol must not fall before them? Satan fled from the disciples to the land of Babylon: and the story of the crucifixion had gone before him to the Chaldæans. He saw, when they were laughing at the signs of the Zodiac, that he was nothing. .

VIII.

From the Oration about the city of Antioch.

To Simon Rome, and to John fell Ephesus; to Thomas India, and to Addæus the country of the Assyrians. And when they were sent each one to the country which fell to him, they set their faces to convert the countries.

MARTYRIUM SANCTORUM CONFESSORUM SAMONÆ, GURIÆ ET ABIBI, EX SIMEONE METAPHRASTE.

Agebatur quidem sexcentesimus annus ab imperio Alexandri Macedonis: novem autem annos jam transegerat Diocletianus, sceptra tenens Romanorum: et sextum jam consultatum obtinebat Maximianus: Augarus autem Zoaræ filius, his temporibus erat Prætor, et Cognatus erat Episcopus Edessenorum, et magna excitabatur persecutio adversus ecclesias omnibus, qui erant sub ditione Romanorum. Et nomen quidem Christianorum, tanquam nefarium, probris appetebatur et exagitabatur: sacerdotes autem et monachi, propter firmam fidem et inexpugnabilem, miserabilibus tradebantur suppliciis, desiderioque et metu distrahebantur pii. Nam cum libere eloqui veritatem propter Christi vellent desiderium, refugiebant rursus metu suppliciorum. Nam ii quidem, qui se armabant adversus pietatem, studebant ut Christiani Christianismum abjurarent, Saturnoque et Rheæ se adjungerent: contra autem fideles, ut nihil esse ostenderent ea, quæ ab illis colebantur.

Illo ergo tempore Gurias et Samonas apud Judicem accusantur, quorum ille quidem ex Sarcigitua, hic autem ex vico Ganade erat ortus, ambo educati Edessæ, quam vocant Mesopotamiam, quod sit media inter Euphratem et Tigridem, et antea quidem ejus fama ad paucos pervaserat: post martyrum autem certamina erat omnium sermone celebrata. Atque sancti quidem nequaquam versabantur in civitate: sed procul ab ea remoti, ut qui vellent procul abesse ab ejus tumultibus, studebant esse Deo soli manifesti. Et Guriæ quidem continentia et charitas, erat bona et honesta possessio, et ex illius studio cognomen est ei impositum, adeo ut ex nomine eum non cognoveris, nisi prius dixeris continentem. Samonæ autem erat in Deum corpus et animus juvenilis et alacris, et cum Guria virtute contendebat. Ii ergo accusantur ad Judicem, quod non solum omnem finitimam Edessæ regionem sua doctrina confirmarent, et ut suæ adhærerent fidei, animum adderent: sed etiam efficerent, ut despicerent persecutores, et ut illorum impietatem omnino nihil facerent, docerent, convenienter ei, quod scriptum est: Nolite confidere in principibus, in filiis hominum, in quibus non est salus. Quibus Judex ad magnam accensus insaniam, jubet omnes, qui habent in honore religionem Christianam, sequentes doctri[illegible] Guriæ et Samonæ, simul cum iis, qui eos ad id inducebant, comprehensos, in tuta includi custodia. Jussus autem ad effectum est deductus, et capta occasione, cum aliis quidem ex his plagas imposuisset, alios autem aliis tormentis subjecisset, et ut Imperatoris decreto parerent, suasisset: tanquam qui benigne et clementer se gereret, alios quidem sinit domum abire: sanctos autem ut primos, et qui pietatem aliis impertiissent, jussit adhuc affligi in carcere, qui ipsi quoque martyrii gaudebant societate. Audiebant enim in aliis provinciis multos idem, quod ipsi, certamen suscepisse: ex quibus erat Epiphanius et Petrus, et sacrosanctus Pamphilus cum multis aliis in Cæsarea Palestinæ, Timotheus Gazæ, in magna Alexandria Timotheus, Agapetus Thessalonicæ, Hesychius Nicomediæ, Philippus Adrianopoli, Melitinæ Petrus, Hermes, et ejus socii in confiniis Martyropolis: qui fuerunt etiam redimiti corona martyrii a Duce Heracliano cum aliis confessoribus, quorum est major numerus, quam ut possit ad nostram venire cognitionem. Sed redeundum est ad ea, de quibus prius dicebamus.

Antonius ergo Præses Edessæ, cum concessisset aliis, ut domum reverterentur, ei in altum erecto tribunali, jubet ad se adduci martyres: et cum fecissent, quod jussi fuerant apparitores, sanctis dicit Præses: Divinissimus noster Imperator hæc jubet, ut et a Christianismo deficiatis, quem sequimini, et imagini Jovis cultum divinum tribuatis, thus in ara sacrificantes. Ad hæc Samonas: Absit, inquit, ut vera fide relicta, propter quam speramus fore, ut vitam assequamur immortalem, manuum opus et figmentum colamus: Præses autem: Imperatoris, inquit, jussa omnino sunt implenda. Respondit Gurias: Puram et divinam nostram fidem nunquam inficiabimur, sequentes voluntatem hominum, in quos cadit interitus. Habemus enim patrem in cælis, cujus sequimur voluntatem, qui dicit: Qui me confessus fuerit coram hominibus, ego quoque eum confitebor coram patre meo, qui est in cælis. Qui me autem negaverit coram hominibus, ego quoque eum negabo coram patre meo, et Angelis ejus. Judex autem: Non vultis ergo, inquit, parere voluntati Imperatoris? Quomodo vero non fuerit absurdum, ea quidem, quæ visa fuerint hominibus, iisque qui non multum et quantum vos, possunt, reipsa ad effectum deduci: eorum autem, qui rerum potiuntur, jussa fieri irrita? Qui Regis regum, inquiunt sancti, faciunt voluntatem, carnis voluntatem respuunt ac rejiciunt. Deinde cum Præses minatus esset mortem, nisi parerent: Samonas, Non moriemur, inquit, ô Tyranne, si creatoris sequamur voluntatem: imo vero vivemus potius. Sed si ea secuti fuerimus, quæ jubet vester Imperator, scias, quod etiamsi tu nos interemeris, nos tamen male peribimus.

Postquam hæc audivit Præses, jubet Anovito commentariensi eos in tutissimam conjicere custodiam. Veritatem enim ægre fert animus, qui sua sponte est ad malum propensus: ut, qui ægrotant oculi, splendorem solis. Postquam autem ille fecit, quod ei fuerat imperatum, et martyres fuerunt in carcere, in quo etiam multi alii sancti prius inclusi fuerant a militibus, Imperator quidem Diocletianus, accersito Musonio Præside Antiochiæ, jubet eum venire Edessam, et Christianos, qui in ea erant inclusi, sive erant communis, sive sacrati ordinis, de sua interrogare religione, et eis finem dare convenientem. Cum is ergo venisset Edessam, et Samonam et Guriam primos curâsset sistendos ad tribunal judiciale, dicit eis: Domini hic est orbis terræ, hic est jussus, ut vos aræ Jovis vinum libetis, et thus imponatis. Sin minus, ego vos variis consumam suppliciis. Corpus enim flagris lacerabo, donec perveniam usque ad ipsa viscera: plumbum autem fervens non prius cessabo vestris axillis infundere, quam id pervaserit usque ad intestina. Deinde nunc quidem manibus, nunc vero pedibus suspendam, et efficiam, ut solvantur compages articulorum: novaque et inaudita excogitabo supplicia, quæ nec omnino quidem ferre poteritis.

Respondit autem Samonas: Vermem, cujus minæ sunt intentatæ iis, qui negant Dominum, et ignem, qui non extinguitur, magis, quam ea, quæ tu enumerâsti, tormenta formidamus. Ipse enim, cui cultum offerimus rationalem, primum quidem nos corroboratos adversus varia hæc tormenta, eripiet a tuis manibus. Deinde etiam in tuto collocabit, ubi est habitaculum omnium lætantium. Alioqui autem omnino adversus solum corpus armaris: Quid enim animam potueris lædere? Quæ quandiu quidem habitat in corpore, tormentis evadit præclarior: ea autem recedente, nullus est omnino sensus corpori. Quo magis enim homo noster externus corrumpitur, eo magis internus renovatur in dies: per patientiam enim hoc propositum certamen peragimus. Præses autem rursus veluti protestans, ut, si non parerent, puniret justius: Discedite ab errore, inquit, vobis consulo, et cedite jussui Imperatoris. Non poteritis enim ferre tormenta. Cui sanctus Gurias, Neque errori, ut tu dicis, servimus, respondit: nec Imperatoris jussui unquam paruerimus: absit ut tam pusilli animi simus, et tam amentes. Sumus enim illius discipuli, qui animam suam pro nobis posuit, divitias benignitatis et suam in nos ostendens charitatem. Resistemus ergo peccato usque ad mortem, neque quicquid acciderit, supplantabimur a machinis adversarii, quibus primus homo captus, decerpsit mortem per ligni inobedientiam: et Cain persuasus, fratris quidem sanguine manus polluit: gemere autem et tremere, invenit præmia peccati. Sed nos

Christi verbis mentem adhibentes, non timebimus eos, qui occidun corpus, animam autem non possunt occidere: illum potius timebimus, qui nostram animam et corpus potest perdere. Tyrannus autem, Non ut, inquit, vestras percurrentes scripturas, possitis refellere, quæ a nobis objiciuntur, ideo ira non moveor, et me præbeo patientem; sed ut jussum Imperatoris exequentes, cum pace domum revertamini.

Hæc oratio nihil flexit martyres, sed propius accedentes: Quid nostra, aiunt, refert, si irasceris, et es ad iram propensus, et tanquam nives pluis tormenta? Tunc enim nobis magis benefacies, clariorem reddens nostram probationem patientiæ, et concilians majores remunerationes. Hæc est enim summa nostræ spei, hunc incolatum, qui est ad tempus, relinquere, et migrare ad æternum. Habemus enim tabernaculum non manu factum in cælis, quod etiam sinum Abrahæ scriptura, propterea quod is esset familiaritate Deo conjunctus, solet vocare. Cum itaque vidisset Præses immutabilem eorum constantiam, statim mittens dicere, processit ad castigandum, et jubet Anuino Commentariensi utrunque una manu suspendi, et eis toto pondere corporis divulsis, adhuc eorum pedibus gravem suspendere lapidem, ad sensum acrioris doloris. Atque hoc quidem ita se habebat, et ab hora tertia usque ad octavam tale tormentum forti animo tolerabant, non vocem emittentes, non gemitum, non aliquid aliud ostendentes, quod esset pusilli et abjecti animi. Dixisses eos pati in alieno corpore, aut aliis patientibus, ipsos solum esse spectatores eorum, quæ fiebant.

Interim autem, dum ii penderent manibus, occupatus erat Præses in aliis audiendis. Deinde cum ab eis quievisset, jubet Commentariensem interrogare sanctos, an jussui, Imperatoris vellent parere, ut liberarentur a tormento: et cum ille quidem interrogaret, hi vero non possent, aut non vellent respondere, jubet eos includi in interiore custodia, in lacu tenebroso et nomine et re ipsa, et pedes usque ad diem sequentem affixos esse ligno. Die autem jam apparente, a ligni quidem vinculis pedes sunt relaxati: carceris autem aditus fuit obstructus, ut nec solaris quidem radius posset subire: edictum autem fuit custodibus, non frustum panis, nec parvam quidem guttam aquæ tres totos dies eis præbere. Quamobrem decætero tenebrosus carcer et longa inedia erat condemnatio martyribus. Cum autem adesset tertius dies circa principium mensis Augusti, apertus quidem fuit aditus carceris: illi autem in eo retenti sunt usque ad decimum Novembris. Deinde Judex eos curat sistendos pro suo tribunali. Et nec tantum, inquit, tempus vobis præbuit, ut mutati aliquod salutare caperetis consilium? Illi autem respondent: Quod nobis videtur, tibi jam sæpius ostendimus: tu autem fac ea, quæ tibi fuerunt imperata. Præses autem statim jubet Samonam altero pede in genu inclinari, et ferreum vinculum injici ejus genui. Quod cum factum esset, eum quidem suspendit præcipitem a pede, quem inclinaverat, alterum deorsum trahens pondere ferri, quod verbis non potest explicari: et sic athletam moliens discerpere. Quo quidem tempore cum coxæ acetabulum per vim sedem suam reliquisset, effectum est, ut Samonas claudicaret: Guriam autem, quod esset imbecillus et subpallidus, sinebat impunitum, non quod eum benignis adspexisset oculis, non quod esset misertus ejus imbecillitatis: sed ut qui, quod eum punire cuperet, potius pepercisset. Ne forte, aiebat, nobis imprudentibus consumeretur ante cruciatus.

Et jam erant quidem duæ horæ diei, ex quo suspensus erat Samonas: hora autem quinta jam aderat, et is adhuc pendebat sublime: et qui circumsistebant milites, movebantur misericordia, et hortabantur ut Imperatoris pareret imperio. Sed peccatorum misericordia caput sancti non pinguefecit. Ille enim etsi acerbe premeretur a tormento, ipsos ne ullo quidem dignabatur responso, sinens eos lugere, et se potius, non illum dignum censere misericordia. In cælum autem tollens oculos, precabatur Deum ex profundo cordis, et ei revocabat in memoriam miracula, quæ a seculo facta sunt: Domine Deus, dicens, sine quo nec passerculus quidem cadet in laqueum: qui Davidi dilatâsti cor in afflictionibus: Qui Prophetæ Danieli vim dedisti etiam contra leones: Qui pueros Abramiæos et Tiranni et flammæ victores effecisti; tu quoque nunc Domine adspice ad bellum, quod contra nos geritur, qui nostræ naturæ nôsti imbecillitatem. Conatur enim inimicus figmentum tuæ dexteræ avertere ab ea, quæ est apud te, gloria. Sed tu benignis tuis nos intuens oculis, conserva in nobis, qui extingui non potest, lucernam tuorum mandatorum: tua autem luce dirige nostras semitas, et dignare nos frui ea, quæ est in te, beatitudine: Quoniam es benedictus in sæcula sæculorum. Atque ille quidem Agonothetæ emittebat hanc gratiarum actionem: quidam autem scriba, qui aderat, literis mandavit quæ dicta sunt.

Jussit autem Præses Commentariensi eum solvere a supplicio. Ille vero cum sic fecisset, et portâsset cum iis, qui aderant, jam doloribus defessum et confectum, in priorem ferentes custodiam, deponunt juxta sanctum Guriam. Cum autem esset Novembris decimusquintus, noctu circiter galli cantum surrexit Iudex: eum vero precedebant lampades et satellites: et cum ad basilicam venisset, quæ dicitur, ubi erat judicium, cum magno fastu sedet pro tribunali: et accersit athletas Guriam et Samonam. Et hic quidem venit ambulans in medio duorum, et fultus utriusque manibus. Nam et premebat inedia, et gravabat senectus, bona spe solummodo eum refrigerante. Gurias autem ipse quoque portatus ducitur, ut qui nec posset omnino ingredi, utpote quod pes ei fuisset graviter a vinculo sauciatus. Ad quos defensor impietatis: Cum data, inquit, fuerit vobis potestas, de eo, quod est vobis conducibile, simul deliberâstis. Dicite ergo, an novi aliquid sit a vobis consideratum: et an priorum vos aliqua subierit pœnitentia: et parete jussui divinissimi. Sic enim vestris opibus et possessionibus, quinetiam hac suavissima quoque luce fruemini. Ad hæc martyres: Nemo, inquiunt, qui sapit, magnifecerit parum manere in iis, quæ fluunt. Sufficit enim nobis tempus, quod præcessit, ad usus eorum et adspectum: nec eorum aliquid desideramus. Quam autem mortem nunc nobis intentas, ea nos ad immortalia transmittit tabernacula, et efficiet, ut simus participes ejus, quæ est illic, beatitudinis.

Præses autem: Quæ a vobis, inquit, dicta sunt, nostras aures magna affecerunt tristitia. Ego autem paucis exponam id, quod videtur. Nam si aræ quidem thus imponitis, et imagini Jovis sacrificatis, recte se habuerit: et unusquisque vestrûm domum abibit. Sin vero adhuc pergitis Imperatoris jussui non parere, amputabuntur vobis omnino capita, hoc enim vult et statuit magnus Imperator. Ad quæ respondens generosissimus Samonas: Si nos, inquit, tanto affeceris beneficio, ut liberemur quidem ab iis, quæ hic sunt, molestiis: transmittamur autem ad eam, quæ est illic, beatitudinem, quantum in nobis quidem situm est, tibi reddetur merces ab eo, qui nostra dispensat ad id, quod est utile. Ad hæc cum respondisset Præses, ut videbatur, benignius, et dixisset: Ego toleranter hucusque tuli, longas illas sustinens orationes, ut mora temporis mutati, traduceremini ad id quod est utile, et supplicium mortis non subiretis. Qui morti, quæ est ad tempus, inquit, se tradunt propter Christum, clarum est fore, ut ii liberentur ab æterna. Qui enim mundo moriuntur, vivunt in Christo. Nam Petrus quoque, qui resplendet in choro Apostolorum, cruce fuit condemnatus et morte: et filius tonitrui Jacobus, ab Herode Agrippa fuit interfectus gladio. Quinetiam Stephanus quoque fuit appetitus lapidibus, qui primus percurrit stadium martyrii. Quid autem dixeris de Johanne? an ne ejus quidem admittes egregiam illam constantiam, et loquendi libertatem, quod mori maluerit, quam cubilis tacere impudicitiam: adultera vero ejus caput acceperit præmium saltationis?

Rursus autem Præses: Non ut vestros, quos dicitis, sanctos enumeretis, vos fero toleranter: sed ut mutato consilio, jussis cedentes

Imperatoris, ab acerbissima morte liberemini. Si enim sitis nimium audaces et insolentes, quid aliud, quam vos majora excipient supplicia, quibus oppressi, vel inviti facietis id, quod nos exigimus: quo tempore nec omnino quidem poteritis refugium habere ad misericordiam? Nam quod sit per vim, ne potest quidem provocare ad commiserationem: quomodo contra quod sponte sit, est dignum misericordia. Christi autem confessores et martyres dixerunt: Non opus est multis verbis. Ecce enim nos sumus tibi præsto ad omnia subeunda supplicia. Quod ergo tibi fuit imperatum, ne differas exequi. Nos enim Christi veri Dei sumus adoratores, et rursus dicimus: Cujus regni non erit finis. Qui etiam potest solus vicissim glorificare eos, qui ejus nomen glorificant. Interim autem dum hæc dicerentur a sanctis, Præses tulit in eos sententiam, ut mortem subirent gladio. Illi vero lætitia, quæ verbis non potest explicari, affecti: Te vere decet gloria et laudatio, qui es Deus universorum, clamabant: quod tibi placuerit, ut susceptum certamen perageremus, ut a te quoque immortalem splendorem assequamur.

Cum ergo vidisset Præses immutabilem eorum constantiam, et quemadmodum in animæ exultatione extremam accepissent sententiam, sanctis quidem, Deus, inquit, eorum, quæ fiunt, sit inspector, quod non per me volebam vos vitæ finem accipere; sed inexorabilis jussus me ad id cogit Imperatoris. Spiculatori autem jubet accipere martyres, et in curru imponere, et procul a civitate abducere cum militibus, et eis illic finem afferre gladio. Ille autem cum per portam Romanensem sanctos noctu eduxisset, cum altus sopor teneret cives, ad septentrionalem partem civitatis abducit in montem Bethelabicla. Illi vero cum fuissent in eo loco, et in lætitia cordis et magna animi constantia e vehiculo descendissent, a spiculatore et iis, qui sub eo erant, tempus ad orationem petiêrunt, et acceperunt. Perinde enim, acsi non sufficerent tormenta et sanguis ad intercedendum pro eis, propter summam modestiam adhuc etiam opus habebant precatione. Cum itaque oculos in cælum sustulissent, et intense precati essent, Deus et pater Domini nostri Jesu Christi, suscipe in pace spiritus nostros, postremo dixerunt. Samonas autem conversus ad spiculatorem, Exequere, inquit, id quod est tibi imperatum: cumque genu simul inclinasset cum Guria, eis amputantur capita decimoquinto Novembris. Atque hoc modo quidem se habuerunt res martyrum.

Cum autem tertium quoque quæreret numerus, ut in his glorificaretur Trinitas, invenit (ô optimam providentiam) tempore quidem postea Abibum, qui autem idem cum iis, qui præcesserant, iter ingredi constituerat, et illo ipso martyrii die fuit consummatus. Magnus ergo inter martyres Abibus, ex eadem quidem, ex qua illi patria, nempe ex Thelsæa vico erat ortus: sacro autem diaconatûs fuerat honoratus chrismate. Cum vero Licinius teneret sceptra imperii Romanorum, et Lysanias creatus fuisset Præses Edessæ, excitata rursus erat persecutio adversus Christianos, et Abibo universum imminebat periculum. Is enim obibat civitatem, divinas cunctos docens scripturas, et magno animo confirmans ad pietatem. Cum autem hæc venissent ad aures Lysaniæ, ea Licinio Imperatori ab eo significantur. Studebat enim, ut ipse ei committeret quæstionem habendam de Christianis, et maxime de Abibo. Neque enim fuerat ei prius commissa. Ille vero literis datis, jubet ut morte Abibum afficiat. Literis ergo redditis Lysaniæ, quæritur ubique Abibus. Ipse autem degebat in quadam parte civitatis, propter statum Ecclesiasticum: mater vero et quidam ex iis, qui ad eum genere attinebant, cum eo versabantur. Ille autem cum rem rescivisset, ne daret pœnas,quod martyrii deseruisset ordines, cuidam, qui erat ex primis cohortis (is autem vocabatur Theotecnus) seipsum indicat: et tandem, Quem quæritis, inquit, Abibum? ipse sum, inquit. Ille vero benigne eum intuens: Nemo, inquit, adhuc novit te ad nos venisse, ô homo. Abi ergo, et servare: nec sis solicitus de matre, nec de iis, qui genere ad te attinent. Nullus enim eos potuerit omnino afficere molestia. Et hæc quidem Theotecnus.

Abibus autem, cum tempus vocaret ad martyrium, nolebat pusillo et abjecto animo suffurari salutem. Ei itaque dicit : Non propter charam matrem, nec propter cognatos me reddo manifestum : sed adsum propter Christi confessionem. Ecce enim vel te nolente apparebo coram Præside, et meum Christum prædicabo coram principibus et regibus. Theotecnus itaque veritus, ne sua sponte veniret ad Præsidem, et ea de causa ei afferretur periculum, ut qui eum non fecisset manifestum, assumit Abibum, et eum adducit ad Præsidem : Hic ille est, inquit, qui quæritur Abibus. Cum autem Lysanias audiisset Abibum sua sponte adiisse ad certamina, arbitratus eam rem esse contemptus et audaciæ, ut qui parvifecisset austeritatem tribunalis, eum statim curat ducendum in judicium : conditionemque ab eo petit, et nomen, et patriam. Cum vero respondisset se quidem esse ortum e vico Thelsæa, significasset autem, se esse Christi ministrum, statim martyrem est criminatus Præses, quod non obtemperâsset jussis Imperatoris. Hujus autem rei apertum esse dicebat indicium quod Iovi thus non sacrificaret. Ad hæc, se quidem Christianum esse, dicebat Abibus, et non posse verum Deum relinquere, sacrificare autem inanimis et nullo sensu præditis operibus manuum. Præses vero, eum brachia vinctum funibus, jussit in ligno sublimem extolli, et ferreis unguibus lacerari. Erat autem suspensio longe violentior, quam laceratio. Veniebat enim in periculum, ne discerperetur, cum violenta extensione ei divellerentur brachia.

Interim dum is penderet sublimis, conversus est Præses ad blanditias, et fingebat se esse patientem. Minabatur autem etiam graviora, si non mutaret propositum : Ille autem : Nemo, inquit, me abducet a fide : neque persuadebit, ut adorem dæmones, etiamsi plura tormenta inferat et majora. Cum autem vellet scire Præses, quamnam ei utilitatem tormenta conciliarent, quæ corpus solum consumunt, Christi martyr Abibus: Non ad præsens usque tempus, inquit, nostra consistunt: nec ea solum sequimur, quæ cernuntur. Quod si tu quoque volueris adspicere ad spem et promissam nobis remunerationem, forte etiam dices cum Paulo: Non sunt condignæ passiones hujus temporis ad gloriam, quæ est revelanda in nobis. Cum autem Præses ea, quæ dicebantur, damnaret stultitiæ: et nunc quidem blandiens et subiens personam patientiæ, nunc vero minans et acerbam ei mortem intentans, neutri eorum eum videret cedere: Non tibi repentinum et totum simul vitæ finem afferam, sententiam ei pronunciavit: sed te lento igne paulatim liquefactum, efficiam immitem et implacabilem animam deponere. Dixit, et cum versus septentrionem extra civitatem collecta fuisset materia, ducebatur ad rogam, sequente quidem matre, sequentibus autem iis quoque, qui aliâs cognatione ad eum attinebant. Ille vero postquam esset precatus, et bene dixisset omnibus, et eis osculum dedisset in Domino, accensa autem esset materia ab iis, qui ad id serviebant, in ignem injicitur: et cum aperto ore flammam accepisset, apud eum, qui dederat, spiritum deposuit. Deinde cum ignis esset sedatus, qui ad eum attinebant, precioso linteo eum circundederunt, et unguentis unxerunt: cumque psalmos et hymnos, ut par erat, cecinissent, prope Samonam et Guriam eum deposuerunt, ad gloriam Patris et Filii et Spiritûs Sancti, quæ est divina Trinitas, et in quam non cadit divisio. Quam decet honor et adoratio nunc et semper, et in sæcula sæculorum, Amen. Talem quidem vitæ finem invenit martyr Abibus tempore Licinii, et talem cum sanctis nactus fuit depositionem, et sic piis attulit requiem a persecutionibus. Nam deinceps quidem Licinio fuit diminuta potentia: Constantino autem floruit dominatio, et creverunt ei sceptra Romanorum: qui primus inter Imperatores libere professus est pietatem, et Christianis concessit vivere ut Christianos. *—From SURIUS; De Probatis Sanctorum Vitis, 4 vol. fol. Colon. Agrip.* 1618. *Nov. 15th, p.* 339.

MOÏSE DE KHORÈNE

HISTOIRE D'ARMÉNIE.

LIVRE SECOND. CHAPITRE XXVI.

Règne d'Abgar.—L'Arménie est entièrement soumise au tribut des Romains.—Guerre avec les Troupes d'Hérode.—Le Fils de son Frère, Joseph, est tué.

Abgar, fils d'Archam, monte sur le trône la vingtième année d'Archavir, roi des Perses. Cet Abgar était appelé Avak-aïr (grand homme), à cause de sa grande mansuétude et de sa sagesse, et de plus, à cause de sa taille. Ne pouvant bien prononcer, les Grecs et les Syriens l'appelèrent Abgar. La deuxième année de son règne, toutes les contrées de l'Arménie deviennent tributaires des Romains. Ordre est donné par l'empereur Auguste, comme il est dit dans l'Évangile de saint Luc, de faire un dénombrement en tous lieux : pour cela envoyés en Arménie, des commissaires romains y apportèrent la statue de l'empereur Auguste, et l'érigèrent dans tous les temples. En ce même temps, vient au monde notre sauveur Jésus-Christ, fils de Dieu. A la même époque il y a trouble entre Abgar et Hérode ; car Hérode voulait que sa statue fût érigée auprès de la statue de César, dans les temples de l'Arménie : Abgar se refuse à cette prétention. D'ailleurs, Hérode ne cherchait qu'un prétexte pour fondre sur Abgar ; il envoie une armée de Thraces et de Germains faire incursion dans le pays des Perses, avec ordre de passer sur les terres d'Abgar.

Mais Abgar loin de consentir, s'y oppose, disant que l'ordre de l'empereur est de faire passer les troupes en Perse par le désert. Hérode, indigné, et ne pouvant pas agir par lui-même, accablé de douleurs; en punition de sa coupable conduite envers le Christ, comme le rapporte Joseph, envoie son neveu, à qui il avait donné sa fille, mariée d'abord à Phéror, son frère. Le lieutenant d'Hérode, à la tête d'une armée considérable, se hâte d'arriver en Mésopotamie, rencontre Abgar au camp de la province Pouknan, périt dans le combat, et ses troupes sont mises en fuite. Bientôt après, Hérode meurt: Archélaüs, son fils, est établi par Auguste ethnarque de la Judée.

XXVII.

Fondation de la Ville D'Édesse. — Notice abrégée sur la race de notre Illuminateur.

Peu te temps après, Auguste meurt, et Tibère en sa place est empereur des Romains. Germanicus, devenu César, trainant à sa suite les princes du royaume d'Archavir et d'Abgar envoyés à Rome, triomphe, au sujet de leur guerre, dans laquelle ces princes avaient tué le neveu d'Hérode. Abgar, indigné, médite des projets de révolte, et se prépare aux combats. Il bâtit une ville sur le terrain occupé par l'armée arménienne d'observation, là où précédemment on gardait l'Euphrate contre les entreprises de Cassius; cette nouvelle ville est appelé Édesse. Abgar y transporta sa cour, qui était à Medzpine, tous ses dieux, Naboc, Bel, Patnicagh et Tarata, les livres des écoles attachées aux temples, et même les archives royales.

Après quoi Archavir étant mort, Ardachès, son fils, règne sur les Perses. Quoique ce ne soit pas l'ordre de l'histoire quant aux temps, ni même l'ordre selon lequel nous avons entrepris ces annales, mais comme il s'agit des descendans du roi Archavir, du sang même d'Ardachès, son fils, nous allons, pour faire honneur à ces princes, les placer, par anticipation de temps, près d'Ardachès, afin que le lecteur sache qu'ils sont bien de la même race, de la race du brave Archag; puis nous signalerons le temps de l'arrivée de leurs pères en Arménie, les Garénian et les Sourénian de qui descendent saint Grégoire et les Gamsarian, lorsque, suivant l'ordre des événemens, nous arriverons au règne du roi sous lequel ils parurent.

Abgar ne réussit pas dans ses projets de révolte; car, des troubles étant survenus entre ses parens du royaume de Perse, il partit à la tête d'une armée pour apaiser et faire cesser la discorde.

XXVIII.

Abgar vient en orient, maintient Ardachès sur le Trône de Perse.— Concilie ses frères, de qui descendent notre Illuminateur et ses parens.

Abgar, étant allé en orient, trouve sur le trône de Perse Ardachès, fils d'Archavir, et les frères d'Ardachès en lutte avec lui; car ce prince pensait à régner sur eux dans sa postérité, et eux ne voulaient pas y consentir. C'est pourquoi Ardachès les cerne de toutes parts, suspend sur leur tête le glaive de la mort; les déchiremens, la discorde étaient entre leurs troupes et leurs autres parens et alliés; car le roi Archavir avait trois fils et une fille: le premier de ces fils était le roi Ardachès lui-même, le second Garène, le troisième Sourène; leur sœur nommée Gochm, était femme du général de tous les Arik, général choisi par leur père Archavir.

Abgar persuade aux fils d'Archavir de faire la paix; il en fixe entr'eux les conditions et stipulations: Ardachès règnera avec sa postérité comme il méditait, et ses frères seront appelés Bahlav, du nom de leur ville et de leur vaste et fertile pays, de manière que leurs satrapies soient les premières, plus élevées en rang que toutes les satrapies de Perse, comme vraiment race de rois. Des traités, des sermens stipulent que, en cas d'extinction d'enfans mâles d'Ardachès, ses frerès arriveront au trône ; après la race régnante d'Ardachès ses frères sont distingués en trois races ainsi dénommées: la race de Garène Bahlav, la race de Sourène Bahlav, et la race de leur sœur, la race Asbahabied Bahlav, race ainsi appelée du nom de la seigneurie de son mari.

On dit saint Grégoire issu de la race Sourène Bahlav, et les Gamsarian de la race Garène Bahlav. Nous rapporterons dans la suite les circonstances de l'arrivée de ces personnages, signalant seulement ici leurs noms auprès d'Ardachès, afin que tu saches que ces grandes races sont bien le sang de Vagharchag, c'est-à-dire la postérité du grand Archag, frère de Vagharchag.

Tout étant ainsi réglé, Abgar prend avec lui la lettre des traités, et retourne dans ses états, non en parfaite santé, mais en proie à de vives douleurs.

XXIX.

Abgar revient d'orient.—Il prête secours à Arète, en guerre contre Hérode Tétrarque.

Quand Abgar fut revenu d'orient, il apprit que les Romains le soupçonnaient d'y être allé pour lever des troupes ; en conséquence, il fait parvenir aux commissaires des Romains la connaissance des causes de son voyage en Perse, ainsi que le traité conclu entre Ardachès et ses frères, mais on n'ajouta aucune croyance à ses rapports ; car il était chargé par ses ennemis Pilate, Hérode le Tétrarque, Lysanias et Philippe. Abgar s'étant rendu dans sa ville d'Édesse, se ligua avec Arète, roi de Pétra, et lui donna des troupes auxiliaires, sous la conduite de Khosran Ardzrouni, pour faire la guerre à Hérode. Hérode avait d'abord épousé la fille d'Arète, puis l'avait répudiée, pris ensuite Hérodiade du vivant même de son mari, circonstance pour la quelle il avait fait périr Jean-Baptiste. Ainsi il y eut guerre entre Hérode et Arète en raison de l'injure faite à la fille d'Arète. Vivement attaquées, les troupes d'Hérode furent défaites, grâce au secours des braves Arméniens; comme si, par la Providence divine, vengeance était tirée de la mort de Jean-Baptiste.

XXX.

Abgar envoie des Princes à Marinus.—Ces députés voient notre Sauveur le Christ.—Commencement de la Conversion d'Abgar.

A cette époque, fut élevé par l'empereur au commandement de la Phénicie, de la Palestine, de la Syrie et de la Mésopotamie, Marinus, fils de Storoge. Abgar lui envoya deux de ses principaux officiers, Mar-Ihap prince d'Aghtznik et Chamchacram, chef de la maison des Abahouni, ainsi qu'Anan, son confident. Les envoyés se rendent dans la ville de Petkoupine pour faire connaître à Marinus les causes du voyage d'Abgar en orient, en lui montrant le traité conclu entre Ardachès et ses frères, et, en même temps, pour invoquer l'appui de Marinus. Les députés trouvèrent à Eleuthéropole le gouverneur romain; celui-ci les reçoit avec amitié et distinction, et fait cette réponse à Abgar: "Ne crains rien pour cela de la part de l'empereur, pourvu que tu aies bien soin d'acquitter entièrement le tribut."

A leur retour, les députés arméniens allèrent à Jérusalem voir notre Sauveur, le Christ, attirés par le bruit de ses miracles. Devenus eux-mêmes témoins oculaires de ces prodiges, ils les rapportèrent à Abgar. Ce prince, saisi d'admiration, crut véritablement que Jésus était bien le fils de Dieu, et dit: "Ces prodiges ne sont pas d'un homme, mais d'un Dieu. Non, il n'est personne d'entre les hommes qui puisse ressusciter les morts, Dieu seul a ce pouvoir." Abgar éprouvait dans tout son corps des douleurs aiguës qu'il avait gagnées en Perse, plus de sept années auparavant; des hommes il n'avait reçu aucun remède à ses maux; Abgar fit porter une lettre de supplication à Jésus, il le conjurait de venir le guérir de ses douleurs. Voici cette lettre.

XXXI.

Lettre d'Abgar au Sauveur Jésus-Christ.

"Abgar fils d'Archam, prince de la terre, à Jésus, sauveur et bienfaiteur des hommes, qui as apparu dans la contrée de Jérusalem, salut:

"J'ai ouï parler de toi et des cures opérées par tes mains, sans remèdes, sans plantes; car, comme il est dit, tu fais que les aveugles voient, que les boiteux marchent, que les lépreux sont guéris; tu chasses les esprits immondes, tu guéris les malheureux affligés de maladies longues et invétérées; tu ressuscites même les morts. Comme j'ai ouï parler de tous ces prodiges opérés par toi, j'en ai conclu ou que tu es Dieu, descendu du ciel pour faire de si grandes choses, ou que tu es fils de Dieu, toi qui produis ces miracles. En conséquence je t'ai donc écrit, te priant de daigner venir vers moi et de me guérir des maux qui m'affligent. J'ai ouï dire aussi que les Juifs murmurent contre toi et veulent te livrer aux tourmens: j'ai une ville, petite mais agréable, elle peut nous suffire à tous deux."

Les messagers, porteurs de cette lettre, rencontrèrent Jésus à Jérusalem, fait confirmé par ces paroles de l'Évangile: "Quelques uns d'entre les païens vinrent trouver Jésus; mais ceux qui les entendirent, n'osant rapporter à Jésus ce qu'ils ont entendu, le disent à Philippe et à André qui redisent tout à leur maître." Le Sauveur n'accepta pas alors l'invitation qui lui était faite, mais il voulut bien honorer Abgar d'une réponse ainsi conçue :

XXXII.

Réponse à la Lettre d'Abgar, réponse que l'Apôtre Thomas écrivit à ce prince par ordre du Sauveur.

" Heureux celui qui croit en moi sans m'avoir vu ! Car il est écrit de moi : " Ceux que me voient, ne croiront point en moi, et ceux qui ne me voient point, croiront et vivront." Quant à ce que tu m'as écrit, de venir près de toi ; il me faut accomplir ici tout ce pourquoi j'ai été envoyé, et lorsque j'aurai tout accompli, je monterai vers celui qui m'a envoyé ; et quand je m'en irai, j'enverrai un de mes disciples, qui guérira tes maux, te donnera la vie à toi et à tous ceux qui sont avec toi."

Anan, courrier d'Abgar, lui apporta cette lettre, ainsi que le portrait du Sauveur, image qui se trouve encore aujourd'hui dans la ville d'Édesse.

XXXIII.

Prédication à Édesse de l'Apôtre Thadée.—Copie de Cinq lettres.

Après l'ascension de notre Sauveur, l'apôtre Thomas, l'un des douze, envoie un d'entre les soixante-dix disciples, Thadée, dans la ville d'Édesse, pour guérir Abgar et évangéliser, selon la parole du Seigneur. Thadée vient dans la maison de Tobie, prince juif, qu'on dit être de la race des Pacradouni. Tobie, ayant quitté Archam, n'abjura point, avec ses autres parens le judaïsme, mais en suivit les lois jusqu'au moment où il crut au Christ. Bientôt le nom de Thadée se répand dans toute la ville. Abgar, en apprenant son arrivée, dit : " C'est bien celui au sujet duquel Jésus m'a écrit ;" et aussitôt Abgar manda l'apôtre. Lorsque Thadée entra, une apparition merveilleuse se peignit aux yeux d'Abgar sur le visage de l'apôtre ; le roi s'étant levé de son trône, tomba la face contre terre et se prosterna devant Thadée. Ce spectacle surprit fort tous les princes assistans, car ils ignoraient le fait de la vision. " Es-tu vraiment, dit Abgar à Thadée, es-tu disciple de Jésus à jamais béni ? es-tu celui qu'il m'a promis de m'envoyer, et peux-tu guérir mes maux ?"—" Oui," répondit Thadée, " si tu crois en Jésus-Christ, fils de Dieu, les vœux de ton cœur seront exaucés."— " J'ai cru en Jésus," dit Abgar, " j'ai cru en son père ; c'est pourquoi je voulais aller à la tête de mes troupes exterminer les Juifs qui ont crucifié Jésus, si je n'avais été empêché à cause de la puissance des Romains."

Dès lors Thadée se mit à évangéliser le roi et sa ville ; posant les mains sur Abgar, il le guérit ; il guérit aussi un podagre, Abdiou, prince de la ville, très honoré dans toute la maison du roi. Il guérit encore tous les malades et les infirmes de la ville, et tous crurent en Jésus-Christ. Abgar fut baptisé et toute la ville avec lui, et les temples des faux dieux furent fermés, et toutes les statues des idoles placées sur les autels et les colonnes furent cachées, voilées avec des roseaux. Abgar n'obligeait personne par la force d'embrasser la foi, mais de jour en jour le nombre des croyans se multipliait.

L'apôtre Thadée baptise un fabricant de coiffures de soie, appelé Attée, le consacre, l'établit à Édesse et le laisse au roi en sa place. Thadée, après avoir reçu des lettres patentes d'Abgar, qui veut que tous écoutent l'Évangile du Christ, s'en va trouver Sanadroug, fils de la sœur d'Abgar, que ce prince avait établi sur le pays et sur l'armée. Abgar se plut à écrire à l'empereur Tibère une lettre ainsi conçue :

Lettre d'Abgar à Tibère.

"Abgar, roi d'Arménie, à mon seigneur Tibère, empereur des Romains, salut:

"Je sais, que rien n'est ignoré de ta majesté; mais comme ton ami, je te ferai encore mieux connaître les faits par écrit. Les Juifs, qui habitent dans les cantons de la Palestine, ont crucifié Jésus. Jésus sans péché, Jésus après tant de bienfaits, tant de prodiges et de miracles accomplis en leur faveur, jusqu'à ressusciter les mort. Sache bien que ce n'est pas là les effets de la puissance d'un simple mortel, mais de Dieu. Pendant le temps qu'ils l'ont crucifié, le soleil s'obscurcit, la terre fut agitée, ébranlée; Jésus lui-même, trois jours après, ressuscita d'entre les morts et apparut à plusieurs. Aujourd'hui, en tous lieux, son nom seul, invoqué par ses disciples, produit les plus grands miracles: ce qui m'est arrivé à moi-même en est la preuve la plus évidente. Ton auguste majesté sait désormais ce qu'elle doit ordonner à l'égard du peuple juif, qui a commis ce forfait; elle sait si elle doit faire publier par tout l'univers l'ordre d'adorer le Christ comme vrai Dieu. Salut et santé."

Réponse de Tibère à la Lettre d'Abgar.

"Tibère, empereur des Romains, à Abgar, roi des Arméniens, salut:

"On a lu devant moi ta gracieuse lettre, et je veux que remercîment t'en soit fait de ma part. Quoique nous eussions déjà de plusieurs ouï raconter ces faits, Pilate nous a informé officiellement des miracles de Jésus. Il nous a certifié qu'après sa résurrection d'entre les morts, il a été reconnu par plusieurs pour être Dieu. En conséquence j'ai voulu, moi aussi, faire ce que tu proposes; mais comme c'est la coutume des Romains, de ne pas admettre un dieu seulement d'après l'ordre du souverain, tant que l'admission n'a pas été discutée, examinée en plein sénat, j'ai donc dû proposer l'affaire au sénat, et lé sénat l'a rejetée avec mépris, sans doute, parce qu'elle n'avait pas été examinée d'abord par lui. Mais nous avons donné ordre que tous ceux à qui Jésus conviendra, le reçoivent parmi les dieux. Nous avons menacé de mort quiconque parlerait mal des chrétiens. Quant au peuple juif, qui a osé crucifier Jésus, lequel, comme je l'entends dire, loin de mériter la croix et la mort, était digne d'honneur, digne de l'adoration des hommes; lorsque je serai débarrassé de la guerre contre l'Hispanie révoltée, j'examinerai l'affaire, et je traiterai les Juifs comme ils le méritent."

Abgar écrit encore une lettre à Tibère.

"Abgar roi des Arméniens, à mon seigneur Tibère empereur des Romains, salut:

"J'ai reçu la lettre écrite de la part de ton auguste majesté, et j'ai applaudi aux ordres émanés de ta sagesse. Si tu te ne fâches pas contre moi, je dirai que la conduite du sénat est extrêmement ridicule et absurde; car, pour les sénateurs, c'est d'après l'examen et par le suffrage des hommes que peut être donnée la divinité. Ainsi donc, si Dieu ne convient point à l'homme, il ne peut être Dieu, puisqu'il faut que Dieu soit jugé, justifié par l'homme. Il paraîtra sans doute juste à mon seigneur et maître, d'envoyer un autre gouverneur à Jérusalem en place de Pilate, qui doit être ignominieusement chassé du poste puissant où tu l'avais mis, car il a fait la volonté des Juifs, il a crucifié le Christ injustement, sans ton ordre. Porte toi bien, je le désire."

Abgar ayant écrit cette lettre, en déposa copie, ainsi que copie des autres lettres, dans ses archives. Il écrivit aussi au jeune Nerseh, roi d'Assyrie, à Babylone.

Lettre d'Abgar à Nerseh.

" Abgar, roi des Arméniens, à mon fils Nerseh, salut :

" J'ai reçu ta lettre et tes hommages ; j'ai déchargé Béroze de ses fers, et lui ai remis ses offenses ; si cela te fait plaisir, donne lui le gouvernement de Ninive. Mais quant à ce que tu m'écris de t'envoyer ce médecin qui fait des miracles et prêche un autre Dieu supérieur au feu et à l'eau, afin que tu puisses le voir et l'entendre, je te dirai : Ce n'était point un médecin selon l'art des hommes, c'était un disciple du fils de Dieu, créateur du feu et de l'eau ; il a été destiné, envoyé aux contrées de l'Arménie. Mais un de ses principaux compagnons, nommé Simon, est envoyé dans les contrées de la Perse. Cherche le et tu l'ententendras, toi, ainsi que ton père Ardachès. Il guérira tous vos maux et vous montrera le chemin de la vie."

Abgar écrit aussi à Ardachès, roi des Perses, la lettre qui suit :

Lettre d'Abgar à Ardachès.

" Abgar, roi des Arméniens, à Ardachès, mon frère, roi des Perses, salut :

" Je sais que tu as ouï parler de Jésus-Christ, fils de Dieu, que les Juifs ont crucifié, de Jésus qui est ressuscité d'entre les morts, et a envoyé ses disciples par tout l'univers pour instruire les hommes. L'un de ses principaux disciples, nommé Simon, se trouve dans les états de ta majesté. Cherche le, tu le trouveras et il vous guérira de toutes vos maladies, et il vous montrera le chemin de la vie, et tu croiras à ses paroles, toi, tes frères et tous ceux qui t'obéissent volontairement.

Il m'est bien doux de penser que mes parens, selon la chair, seront aussi mes parens, mes amis, selon l'esprit."

Abgar n'avait pas encore reçu réponse à ces lettres, lorsqu'il meurt, ayant régné trente-huit ans.

XXXIV.

Martyre de nos Apôtres.

Après la mort d'Abgar, le royaume d'Arménie est divisé en deux : Ananoun, fils d'Abgar, règne à Édesse, et le fils de sa sœur, Sanadroug, en Arménie. Ce qui se passa de leur temps, a été décrit par d'autres antérieurement : l'arrivée de l'apôtre en Arménie, et la conversion de Sanadroug, et son apostasie par crainte de satrapes arméniens, et le martyre de l'apôtre et de ses compagnons au canton Chavarchan, appelé aujourd'hui Ardaz, et le pierre s'entrouvrant pour recevoir le corps de l'apôtre, et, l'enlèvement de ce corps par ses disciples, son inhumation dans la plaine, et le martyre de la fille du roi, de Santoukhd près du chemin, et l'apparition des reliques des deux saints, et leur translation dans les rocailles ; toutes circonstances rapportées par d'autres, comme nous l'avons dit, long-temps avant nous : nous n'avons pas cru important de les répéter ici. De même aussi ce qui se rapporte au martyre d'Attée, disciple de l'apôtre, à Édesse martyre ordonné par le fils d'Abgar, se trouve rapporté par d'autres avant nous.

Le prince qui régna après la mort de son père, ne fut pas l'héritier des vertus paternelles ; il ouvrit les temples des idoles, embrassa le culte des païens. Il envoie dire à Attée : "Fais moi une coiffure en toile tissée d'or, comme celles que tu faisais autrefois pour mon père." Il reçut cette réponse d'Attée : "Mes mains ne feront point de coiffure pour un prince indigne, qui n'adore pas le Christ Dieu vivant." Aussitôt, le roi d'ordonner à un de ses gens d'armes de couper les pieds à Attée. Le soldat étant allé et ayant vu le saint personnage assis dans la chaire doctorale, avec son glaive lui coupa les jambes, et aussitôt le saint rendit l'esprit. Nous mentionnons ce fait sommairement, comme un fait rapporté par d'autres depuis longtemps.

Vint ensuite en Arménie l'apôtre Barthélemi qui fut martyrisé chez nous, en la ville d'Arépan. Quant à Simon, envoyé en Perse, je ne puis pas rapporter avec certitude ce qu'il fait, ni où il souffre le martyre. On raconte qu'un Simon apôtre est martyrisé à Vériospore. Le fait est-il vrai, ou pourquoi la venue du saint en ce lieu? je ne sais; j'ai seulement signalé cette circonstance afin que tu saches bien que je n'épargne aucun soin, pour te rapporter tout ce qui est nécessaire.

XXXV-

Règne de Sanadroug.—Meurtre des Enfans d'Abgar.—La Princesse Hélène.

Sanadroug étant sur le trône, lève des troupes avec le secours des braves Pacradouni et Ardzrouni, qui l'ont élevé, et va faire la guerre aux enfans d'Abgar, pour se rendre maître de tout le royaume. Pendant que Sanadroug était occupé de ces affaires, comme par un effet de la Providence divine, vengeance est tirée de la mort d'Attée; car une colonne de marbre que le fils d'Abgar faisait élever à Édesse, sur le comble de son palais, comme il était dessous pour ordonner le travail, échappa des mains des ouvriers, tomba sur lui et lui écrasa les pieds.

Aussitôt de la part des habitans de la ville vint à Sanadroug un message, pour lui demander un traité par lequel il s'engageât à ne pas les troubler dans l'exercice du christianisme, moyennant quoi ils livreront la ville et les trésors du roi. Sanadroug promit, mais dans la suite viola son serment; Sanadroug passa au fil de l'épée tous les enfans de la maison d'Abgar, à l'exception des filles, qu'il retira de la ville pour les établir au canton de Hachdiank. Quant à la première des femmes d'Abgar, appelée Hélène, il l'envoya dans sa ville à Kharan, et lui laissa la souveraineté de toute la Mésopotamie, en souvenir des bienfaits qu'il avait reçus d'Abgar par le moyen d'Hélène.

Hélène, pieuse comme son mari Abgar, ne voulut pas habiter au milieu des idolâtres; elle s'en alla à Jérusalem du temps de Claude, durant la famine qu'avait prédite Agabus; elle acheta en Égypte, avec tous ses trésors, une immense quantité de blé qu'elle distribua aux indigens, fait dont témoigne Joseph. Le tombeau d'Hélène, tombeau vraiment remarquable, se voit encore aujourd'hui devant la porte de Jérusalem.

XXXVI.

Restauration de la Ville de Medzpine. — Dénomination de Sanadroug. — Sa Mort.

De tous les faits et gestes de Sanadroug, nous de jugeons digne de souvenir que la construction de la ville de Medzpine; car cette ville ayant été ébranlée par un tremblement de terre, Sanadroug la démolit, la reconstruisit plus magnifique, la ceignit de doubles murailles et de remparts. Sanadroug fit élever au milieu de la ville sa statue tenant à la maine une seule pièce de monnaie, ce qui signifie: "Tous mes trésors ont été employés à construire la ville, et ne m'est plus resté que cette seule pièce de monnaie."

Mais pourquoi ce prince fut-il appelé Sanadroug? nous dirons: C'est que, voyageant pendant l'hiver en Arménie, la sœur d'Abgar, Otée, fut assaillie par un tourbillon de neige dans les monts Gortcuk; la tourmente a dispersé tout le monde, au point que le compagnon ne sait pas où a été poussé son compagnon. La nourrice du prince,

Sanod, sœur de Piourad Pacradouni, femme de Khosran Ardzrouni, ayant pris le royal enfant, car Sanadroug était encore au berceau, le mit sur son sein et resta avec lui sous la neige trois jours et trois nuits. La fable s'est emparée de ce fait; elle raconte qu'un animal, espèce nouvelle, merveilleux, d'une grande blancheur, envoyé par les dieux, gardait l'enfant. Mais, autant que nous en avons été informés, voici le fait: un chien blanc, qui se trouvait au milieu des hommes envoyés à la recherche, rencontra l'enfant et sa nourrice; le prince fut donc appelé Sanadroug, dénomination tirée du nom de sa nourrice, (et du mon arménien *dourk* don,) comme, pour signifier don de Sanod.

Sanadroug, monté sur le trône la douzième année d'Ardachès, roi des Perses, ayant vécu trente ans, mourut à la chasse d'un trait qui lui perça les entrailles, comme en punition des tourmens qu'il avait fait souffrir à sa sainte fille. Ghéroupna, fils de l'écrivain Apchatar, a recueilli tous ces faits, arrivés du temps d'Abgar et de Sanadroug, et les a déposés dans les archives d'Édesse.

The above extract is taken from the edition, in two vols, printed at Paris, of which the following is the title: MOÏSE DE KHORÈNE AUTEUR DU Ve SIECLE HISTOIRE D'ARMÉNIE TEXTE ARMÉNIEN ET TRADUCTION FRANÇAISE avec notes explicatives et précis historiques sur l'arménie par P. E. LE VAILLANT DE FLORIVAL.

NOTES.

PAGE 1.—The MS. from which this extract from Eusebius' Ecclesiastical History is taken is one of those found in the Nitrian Cloister and now in the British Museum, *Cod. Add.* 14,639. fol. 15 b. See a description of this MS. *Corpus Ignatianum*, p. 350. It is only the first volume: the second, I believe, is in the Imperial Library at St. Petersburgh.

Line 6.—*Abgar.* This seems to have been a title common to many of the Kings or Toparchs of Edessa. J. S. Assemani says that all bore it: " ܐܒܓܪ: Hoc prænomine omnes Toparchæ Edesseni appellabantur, non secus atque Imperatores Romani *Cæsares*, Reges Ægypti *Pharones* vel *Ptolemæi*, et Reges Syriæ *Antiochi*. *Abgar* autem Syriace *Claudum* sonat." See *Bibliotheca Orientalis Clementina-Vaticana*, Vol. I., p. 261. Spanheim and Valesius thought the word should be written *Acbar*, as if from the Arabic اكبر, signifying the *greatest*. See Assemani, *ibid;* Theop. Sigf. Bayer, *Historia Osrhoena*, p. 73; and Fabricius *Codex Apocryphus, N. T.*, p. 316. The more probable signification seems to be that given by Moses Chorenensis, Book II. c. xxvi. "Cet Abgar était appelé *Avak-aïr* (grand homme) à cause de sa grande mansuétude et de sa sagesse, et de plus, à cause de sa taille. Ne pouvant bien prononcer, les Grecs et les Syriens l'appelèrent *Abgar.*" See p. 125. Assemani gives a series of the Kings of Edessa from the *Chronicon Edessenum* and other sources: in *Bibl. Orient.* Vol. I. p. 387—423. See also Bayer's *Historia Osrhoena*, and T. Wise, *Historia de Nummo Abgari Regis*, p. 4. A list of those who bore the name of Abgar, as gathered from Greek and Latin authors, is given by J. E. Grabe in *Spicilegium SS. Patrum*, Vol. I., p. 314.

l. 8.—*A severe disease.* See respecting this disease which Abgar took in Persia, Moses Chor. B. II. c. 28, 30, p. above 128, 129. Procopius, *De bello Persico*, B. II. c. 12, says that Abgar suffered from gout, probably from confounding his disease with that of Abdu mentioned below: Cedrenus says it was the black leprosy: see Fabricius, *Cod. Apoc. N. T.* p. 318, and Grabe *Spicilegium*, Vol. I. p. 315.

l. 12.—*A man of his own.* Greek δι' επιστοληφορου. The rest of this passage is not very closely rendered in Syriac from the Greek.

l. 13.—*Our Saviour.* Not in the Greek.

l. 17.—*Who were near to him.* ܩܪܝܒܘܗܝ: those who were connected with him or belonged to him, Gr. των προσηκοντων.

l. 19.—*Thomas the Apostle.* His real name was Judas or Jude, see p. 3, line 14; the appellation *Thomas*, meaning a *Twin*, being added to distinguish him from others bearing the name Judas: see Preface to *Remains of a very antient Recension of the Four Gospels in Syriac*, p. L, and the authorities given there. Besides the Greek Acts of Thomas, published by Thilo, *Acta S. Thomæ Apostoli*, 8vo. Lips. 1832. There is also a copy of Acts in Syriac more extended than the Greek, which ought to be published, in the British Museum, Cod. Add. 14,645, fol. 1. In addition to the work of Thilo just spoken of, those who wish to know more of St. Thomas and his preaching in India may consult Fabricius, *Cod. Apoc. N. T.* p. 688; Assemani *Bibl. Orient.* Vol. III. Part II. pp. 25, 435; Buchanan, *Christian Researches in Asia*, 8vo. 1812; Swanston, *Memoir of the Primitive Church*, in the Journal of the Asiatic Society, Vol. I. p. 171, 1834, and Vol. II. p. 51, 1835; Ritter, *Erdkunde*, Vol. V. pp. 601, 945. There was a church dedicated to Thomas at Edessa, and his body is said to have been translated there, A. D. 394: see Assemani, *Bibl. Orient.* Vol. I. pp. 49, 399, and Vol. II. p. 387.

PAGE 2. *l.* 1.—*Thaddæus:* so in this place translated from the Greek of Eusebius, but in the original Syriac treatises he is called *Addæus:* see *below*, passim.

l. 2.—*The Seventy.* In *Doctrine of the Apostles*, p. 34, he is said to be one of the *Seventy-Two Apostles.* Their names are given in Cod. Add. 14,601, fol. 164; and also by Assemani from the work called ܕܒܘܪܝܬܐ or *The Bee*, in *Bibl. Orient.* Vol. III. p. 319. Jerome supposed him to be the Apostle Jude. "Thaddæum Apostolum Ecclesiastica tradit Historia missum Edessam ad Abagarum Regem Chosdroenæ, qui ab Evangelista Luca Judas Jacobi dicitur, et alibi appellatur Lebœus, quod interpretatur corculum. Credendumque est eum fuisse trinomium, sicut Simon Petrus, et filii Zebedæi Boanerges ex firmitate et magnitudine fidei nominati sunt." See *Com. in Matt.* c. 10. His real name, like that of Thomas, seems to have been the very common one, Judas. *Edessa—fulfilled.* In the book ascribed to Abdias, *Historia Certaminis Apostolici*, this is mentioned in the Life of Thomas: — "Acceptoque Spiritus Sancti dono, Thaddæum unum ex septuaginta discipulis, ad Abgarum regem Edessenæ civitatis transmisit, ut eum ab infirmitate curaret, juxta verbum quod ei a Domino scriptum erat: see Fabricius, *Cod. Apoc.* N. T. p. 688.

l. 5.—*The Book of Records which is at Edessa.* These were kept in the archives of the kingdom, which were transferred by Abgar from Nisibis to Edessa when he made it the capital of his dominions. See Moses Chor. B. II. c. xxvii. p. 126, *above.* At a later period, under Vespasian and Titus, we read, "Les fonctionnaires de Romains, après avoir restauré magnifiquement la ville d'Édesse, y établissent des trésoreries destinées à recevoir les impôts perçus sur l'Arménie, la Mésopotamie, l'Assyrie. Ils rassemblent a Édesse toutes les Archives, organisent deux écoles, l' une pour la langue du pays, le syrien, et l'autre pour le grec; ils transportent à Édesse les Archives relatives au tributs et aux temples, Archives qui étaient à Sinope, ville du Pont:" B. II. c. xxxviii. The same writer also refers to ancient archives, B. I. c. 9, 19, 21. B. II. c. 10. See the extract from the *Chronicon Edessenum*, cited p. 143: see also p. 61, line 15. The archives appear to have been still kept at Edessa A. D. 550. See Assemani, *Bibl. Orient.* Vol. I., p. 387.

l. 6.—*For the kingdom was still standing.* Gr. *τοτηνικαυτα βασιλευομενομενην πολιν*, which Rufinus has rendered thus: "In qua tunc supradictus Abgar regnabat." These words appear to be an addition by Eusebius, and to confirm the conjecture of Grabe, that this extract from the Archives of Edessa was not made by Eusebius himself, but by Sextus Julius Africanus, and copied from his Chronographia into the Ecclesiastical History. See *Spicilegium*, Vol. I. p. 314. The kingdom of Edessa was brought to an end and entirely subjected to the Romans, A. D. 217 or 218. See Assemani, *Bibl. Orient.* Vol. I. p. 388; Bayer, *Hist. Osrh.* p. 177. This was precisely the time when Africanus was in these parts. See M. Routh, *Reliquiæ Sacræ*, Vol. II. p. 221, 2nd Edit.; Fabricius, *Bibl. Græc.* Vol. v. p. 270. A few years later, in the 9th year of Diocletian, we find Abgar no longer called *King*, but *Prætor.* See *Martyrium S. S. Confess. Samonæ.* p. 123. The fact of Eusebius having followed Africanus is also confirmed by Moses Chor., who writes thus, B. II. c. 10: "Nous commencerons à te faire le récit des événements d'après le cinquième livre d'Africanus le chronologiste, dont le témoignage est confirmé par Joseph, Hippolyte, et beaucoup d'autres grecs; car Africanus a extrait des cartularies et des Archives d'Édesse, est-à-dire Ourha, tout ce qui était de l' histoire de nos rois: ces livres avaient été apportés de Medzpine; Africanus se servit aussi des histoires des temples de Sinope du Pont; que personne n'en doute, car nous avons vu nous mêmes de nos propres yeux ces archives. En témoinage et garantie te vient encore l' histoire ecclésiastique d'Eusèbe de Césarée, que le bienheureux docteur Machdotz fit traduire en Arménien ; cherche a Kéghacouni, au canton de Sunik, et tu trouveras, première rapsodie N°. treize, l'assurance que dans les archives d'Édesse est l'histoire de tous les faits et gestes de nos derniers rois jusqu'à Abgar, et après Abgar jusqu'à Érouant ; documents qui, je pense, se trouvent encore conservés dans cette ville." *Julius Africanus* is said not only to have translated Abdias into Latin, but also to have written *Narratio de iis quæ in Perside domino Jesu Christo nato acciderint.* This is published in *Beyträge zur Geschichte und Literatur.* 1804, Part IV. p. 49. This appears to be fabulous and worthless.

l. 10.—*Nothing to hinder*: Gr. ουδεν δε οἶον.

l. 13.—*King Abgar.* Gr. τοπαρχου. Rufinus *Regé Abgaro vel Toparcho.*

l. 14.—*Hananias.* This form seems to be taken from the Greek here. In the original Syriac document it is written *Hanan*, see p. 23; and so in Moses Choren., see p. 131. *Tabularius*: the Greek, has ταχυδρομον, and Rufinus *Cursorem.* This seems to have been an error. Galanus from the Armenian calls him *Tabellarius*: see *Concil. Ecc. Arm. cum. Rom.* Vol. I. p. 7. The post which Hananias filled must have been one of much more dignity and trust than that of *Cursor.* The office which Hananias held seems to have been that of a Secretary of State: see Moses Chor. B. II. c. 29 and 30; where, in the translation of L. Vaillant de Florival, he is called Abgar's *Confident*, which corresponds with *Sharir*, as he is styled in these Acts: see p. 23. The Sharirs had the custody of the archives, as we learn from the Chronicle of Edessa: ܡܪܝܗܒ ܒܪ ܫܡܫ. ܘܩܝܘܡܐ ܒܪ ܡܓܪܛܛ ܣܦܪ̈ܐ ܕܐܘܪܗܝ، ܗܢܘܢ ܟܬܒܘܗ، ܠܬܫܥܝܬܐ ܗܕܐ ܘܠܦܘܩܕܢܐ ܕܐܒܓܪ ܡܠܟܐ. ܘܒܪܕܝܢ ܘܒܘܠܝܕ ܗܠܝܢ ܕܗܢܘܢ ܣܝܡܝܢ ܗܘܘ ܥܠ ܐܪ̈ܟܝܘܢ ܕܐܘܪܗܝ، ܗܢܘܢ ܩܒܠܘ ܗܘܘ ܘܣܡܘܗ ܠܗ ܒܝܬ ܓܙܝܗܘܢ ܐܝܟ ܫܪ̈ܝܪܐ ܕܗܝܡܢܘܬܐ. : which Assemani translates thus: "Hæc Acta, Regisque Abgari Edictum conscripsere Mar-Jabus Bar Semes et Kajumas Bar-Magartat, Notarii Edesseni; eaque in Archivum Edessenum intulere Bardinus et Bulidus ejusdem Archivi Præfecti, utpote publicæ fidei testes (*Sharir*)." See *Bibl. Orient.* Vol. I. p. 393; see also p. 84. The Latin term *Tabularius* was well known in those parts certainly before this extract from the archives of Edessa was used by Eusebius. Julius Capitolinus tells us that Marcus Antoninus established *Tabularii* in all the provinces, in the chapter in which he is writing of these parts, c. 9; and Abdias, in the life of St. Simon and St. Jude, speaks of the *Tabularii pxci* in these countries: see Fabricius, *Cod. Apoc.* N. T. p. 616; and Eusebius, in *Hist. Ecc. Martt. Palest.* c. 9. The Latin term was *Notarius*: see Ammianus Marcellinus Vol. III., *Edit. Lips.* 1808. p. 464. Respecting the Tabularii, see Jacob Gothofridus *ad Cod. Theodos,* VIII. t. ii. Vol. II. p. 475., and Pancirolus *Notitia Dignitatum,* p. 126.

l. 16.—*Abgar Uchama.* Gr. Αβγαρος only, with the exception of one copy, which adds Ουχανιης υιος: see Burton's Edition. Rufinus, who followed the earliest editions of Eusebius, has also *Uchaniæ filius.* The Greek transcribers seem to have been ignorant of the meaning of *Uchama,* which signifies *dark,* and was an epithet peculiar to this king Abgar: see Assemani *Bibl. Orient.* Vol. I. p. 420. He was the 14th King: the 11th was called Abgar *Sumaca,* or the *red*: see Bayer, *Hist. Osrh.* p. 91. *Chief of the Country.* Gr. τοπαρχης: the later copies of the Greek add Εδεσσης, which is omitted in Rufinus.

l. 17.—*Peace.* The Gr. has χαιρειν. Rufinus *salutem.* *I have heard.* St. Matthew, iv. 24, tells us, "and his fame went throughout all Syria; and they brought unto him all sick people that were taken with divers diseases and torments, and those which were possessed with devils, and those which were lunatics, and those that had the palsy; and he healed them." Abgar therefore might easily have heard at Edessa of Christ, by common report. Another reason, however, for this account reaching Abgar is given by Moses Chor. see p. 129 *above,* and *note on that place below.*

l. 23.—*I settled in my mind.* See a conclusion similar to this of Abgar by the people of Lystra, &c., *Acts* xiv. 11, and the people of Melita, *ibid.* xxviii. 6. So also by the Centurion, *Mark* xv. 39; and by Nicodemus, *John* iii. 2.

l. 30.—At the end of this letter a passage is added in several Greek copies: "Thus wrote Abgarus, as then but little enlightened from above. It is also worth while to hear the answer of Jesus returned to him by the same courier. Short indeed it is, but it has much power and efficacy in it." *English Trans.* Valesius was convinced that these words were not written by Eusebius: see Fabricius, *Cod. Apoc.* p. 318. Burton omits them in his edition: see note on this place. Neither are they found in Rufinus.

Page 3. *l.* 1.—*Copy of those things which were written.* Gr. τα αντιγραφεντα. Rufinus, *Exemplum rescripti.*

l. 3.—*Blessed is he.* ܛܘܒܘܗܝ ܠܐܢܫܐ: the other copy ܛܘܒܐ. The Gr. Editt. have μακαριος ει, though several MSS. have μακαριος ὁ: see

Burton's Edit. Valesius has the following note on this place: "In what part of the *Old Testament* these words occur I am yet to seek. Indeed, in the Gospel of St. John, c. xx. v. 29, it is writt n that our Lord said to Thomas after his resurrection, *Blessed are they that have not seen, and yet have believed.* But this Epistle of Christ to King Abgarus, if it be genuine, preceded that reprehension of the Apostle Thomas some years." *English Trans.* p. 14. There seems to be no ground whatever for this assertion of Valesius. The period of time intervening between the two events must have been short, as, indeed, Valesius himself shews in the Note cited by me on the next page. Fabricius compares these words, cited as being *written*, with Isai. vi. 9, Lii. 15, and observes, "Sane cum his Prophetæ locis sensui Epistolæ magis convenit quam cum loco quem plerique hic respici putant:" see *Cod. Apoc. N. T.* p. 318.

l. 26.—*A mighty man.* ܓܒܪܐ ܫܠܝܛܐ. Gr. ανηρ τις δυναστης. Rufinus, *vir quidam potens.*

l. 28.—*The king.* Gr. τοπαρχος. Rufinus *toparcha.*

Page 4, *l.* 7.—*There* ܬܡܢ. The other MS. has ܩܕܡܘܗܝ *before him.*

l. 12.—*Nobly.* ܪܘܪܒܐܝܬ Gr. μεγαλως. Rufinus *magnifice.*

l. 15.—*So that—Romans.* Compare the letters of Abgar and Tiberius, p. 16 below; see also p. 111.

l. 18.—*Our Lord.* Some Gr. MSS. add Ιησους. Rufinus as here.

l. 25.—*Abdu, son of Abdu.* This same person is mentioned at p. 7, below, where he is called ܬܪܝܢܐ ܕܡܠܟܘܬܐ: which I have translated *the second person* of his kingdom. It probably means one of the second rank in the kingdom. Tacitus mentions a person of this name, who must have been cotemporary, if not the same—"Sed Parthis mittendis secretos nuntios validissimus auctor fuit Sinnaces, insigni familia, ac perinde opibus, et proximus huic Abdus, ademptæ virilitatis: non despectum id apud barbaros, ultroque potentiam habet. See *Annal.* vi. 31 and 32.

l. 26.—*He too went in and fell at his feet.* ܐܦ ܗܘ ܥܠ ܘܢܦܠ ܥܠ ܪ̈ܓܠܘܗܝ like the Gr. ος και αυτος προσελθων υπο τους ποδας αυτου επεσεν: ευχας τε δια χειρος λαβων εθεραπευθη; but the original Syriac at p. 6. ܐܦ ܗܘ ܩܪܒ ܗܘܐ ܠܗ ܪ̈ܓܠܘܗܝ ܘܣܡ ܗܘ ܐܝܕܐ ܥܠܝܗܘܢ ܘܐܣܝܗ ܗܘܐ: *He too brought his feet near to him, and he laid his hands upon them and healed him*, the variation, probably, having arisen from the translation into Greek and the re-translation into Syriac.

Page 5, *l.* 3.—*Christ.* Gr. Ιησου.

l. 5.—*For the present I will be silent.* ܗܫܐ ܫܬܩ ܐܢܐ. The original

Syriac at p. 6: ܡܢ ܗܕܐ ܠܐ ܫܬܩ ܐܢܐ: *I will not be silent from declaring this.*

l. 12.—*His new preaching.* ܟܪܘܙܘܬܗ ܚܕܬܐ. In the original Syriac, p. 6. ܚܦܝܛܘܬܐ ܕܟܪܘܙܘܬܗ: *the certitude of his preaching.* The Greek translator seems to have confounded ܚܦܝܛܘܬܐ, *diligentia, sedulitas, certitudo,* with ܚܕܬܐ: *nova,* an error which could hardly have happened in translating from Greek into Syriac.

l. 15.—*Hell.* ܠܫܝܘܠ. Greek ᾳδην. The original Syriac, p. 6 ܠܒܝܬ ܡܝ̈ܬܐ *the place of the dead*; and so we find it in the DOCTRINE OF THE APOSTLES, p. 26 below. *And brake through the wall of partition*: compare St. Paul *Ephes.* ii. 14, "and hath broken down the middle wall of partition."

l. 16.—*And descended alone and ascended with a great multitude to his Father.* In the longer Recension of the Ignatian Epistles, cix. of that to the Trallians, we read almost the same words. *και κατηλθεν εις ᾳδην μονος, ανηλθε δε μετα πληθους· και εσχισε τον απ' αιωνος φραγμον, και το μεσοτοιχον αυτου ελυσε.* The same thing is also referred to by Mar Jacob, the Persian, in his sermon on ܚ̈ܠܘ ܡܫܝܚܐ, Cod. 14,614, fol. 40. ܘܦܪܘܩܢ ܟܕ ܢܚܬ ܠܒܝܬ ܡܝ̈ܬܐ ܐܚܝ، ܠܣܓܝ̈ܐܐ ܘܐܩܝܡ ܐܢܘܢ *And our Saviour, when he descended to the place of the dead, gave life to many and raised them up.* Archbishop Usher in his Notes upon this passage of the Epistle to the Trallians cites words of Macarius of Jerusalem and of Cyril of Jerusalem to the same effect: see his Notes on Polycarp's and Ignatius' Epistles, p. 26. We read also, *Matt.* xxvii. 52, "And the graves were opened, and many bodies of the saints which slept arose, and came out of the graves after his resurrection, and went into the holy city, and appeared unto many."

l. 20.—*Silver.* The Gr. has *ασημον*, which this has imitated by using ܐܣܝܡܐ. The original Syriac at p. 7 has ܟܣܦܐ.

l. 23.—*The year three hundred and forty.* Valesius has the following note on this place: "This three hundredth and fortieth year, according to the account of the *Edessens*, falleth with the first year of the 202nd Olympiad. For the Edessens numbered their years from the 117th Olympiad, fixing their era upon the first year of Seleucus his reign in Asia (as Eusebius writes in his Chronicon), from which time to the beginning of the 202nd Olympiad there are just 340 years. Now the beginning of the 202nd Olympiad falleth with the 15th year of Tiberius, in which year as many of the Ancients believed our blessed Saviour suffered and ascended. So that this account falls right, placing Thaddæus his coming to Edessa and his curing King Abgarus on the same year in which our blessed Saviour suffered." *Eng. Trans.*, p. 15. In the *Doctrine of the Apostles*, our Lord's ascension is said to have been in the year 339: see p. 24. Ebediesu says Christ was baptized in the 15th year of Tiberius, and the 341 of Alexander: see Mai, *Scriptt. Vett. Nov. Col.* Vol. X. p. 325. In the *Bee*, Ch. 52, Augustus is said to have reigned 57 years. In the 43rd year of his reign Christ was born. Tiberius reigned 23 years: in the 15th Christ was baptized, and in the 17th crucified. Orosius says Christ was crucified in the 17th year of Tiberius: see Lipomanus, *Sanct. Hist.*, Part I. p. 155. The Chronicon Edessenum places the birth of Christ in the year 309, and so does Barhebræus; see Assemani, *Bibl. Orient.* Vol. I. p. 389. According to these authorities, therefore, Abgar's conversion would have been in the 31st year from the birth of our Lord.

Page 6.—DOCTRINE OF ADDÆUS THE APOSTLE. The MS. from which the following fragment is taken is also from the Nitrian collection in the British Museum, No. 14,654, at fol. 33. It is contained on one leaf only, with the above inscription in red letters at the top of the page. The volume, as it is now bound, consists of several fragments of MS. of great antiquity, written in two columns, and contains chiefly Acts of Martyrs: its age appears to be certainly not later than the beginning of the fifth century. It is probably the same as that which Assemani saw at Scete, and describes as *pervetustus*, which contained the Acts of Addæus, Sharbil, &c.: see *Bibl. Orient.* Vol. III. p. 19. *Doctrine of Addæus.* At page 109, where I have given an extract from this, cited by another writer, it is called ܐܓܪܬܐ ܕܐܕܝ, *Epistle* or *Treatise* of Addæus.

l. 1.—*Because thou hast so believed.* The part comprised in this fragment corresponds with that given by Eusebius, from p. 4. line 20, to p. 5. line 22. It will be seen, that although the two are identical, this is the fuller. The extract in Eusebius seems to be abridged. There are also other slight variations, such as we may expect to find in the original language, and in a retranslation from the Greek into Syriac. Some of these have been already remarked upon, and I shall notice a few more. The other variations the reader will observe for himself.

l. 4.—*The plague of the disease.* ܡܢ ܟܘܪܗܢܐ ܕܡܟܐܒܘܬܐ: in the translation from Eusebius, p. 4 ܡܢ ܟܘܪܗܢܗ ܘܡܢ ܡܟܐܒܘܬܐ: *of his sickness and of the disease.* A variation which has evidently arisen from confounding ܕ and ܘ, which is not unfrequent. *A long time*, not in Eusebius. According to Moses Chor. he had been suffering for seven years from a disease which he caught in Persia: see B. II. c. xxx. p. 130.

l. 7.—*Abdu, son of Abdu.* Le Vaillant de Florival writes the name *Abdion*: see p. 132, where Moses Chor. calls him "Prince de la ville, très honoré dans toute la maison du roi." Compare what Tacitus says of him cited at p. 145 *above.* In the account of Constantine Porphyrogenitus, as given by Simeon Metaphrastes, he is said to have been the person who brought to Abgar information of Addæus' arrival at Edessa: "Quamobrem cum fama cito pervasisset, pervenit etiam ad Abgarum per quendam ex ejus proceribus, qui vocabatur Abdu, illic scilicet esse Christi Apostolum, &c.;" see Lipomanus, *Sanctorum Historia,* Part I. p. 189. The following also relates to him, but whether it refers to the fact just stated, or to his having been one of Abgar's envoys, who passed through Palestine (see p. 129 and the Notes on that paragraph), I know not: "Cum itaque multa prius effecerit miracula Domini Apostolus, et omnes curasset a morbis suis, inter quos is erat etiam, qui primus de eo famam retulit ad Barbarum (perhaps it should be read Abagarum) quem liberavit a podagra." *Ibid,* p. 190.

l. 8.—*Gout.* Here we have ܦܠܓܪܐ: but in the translation ܦܘܕܓܪܐ nearer to the Greek ποδαγρα.

l. 22.—*Him that sent him,* or *his sender.* ܫܠܘܚܗ: in the Greek της αποστολης αυτου; and therefore retranslated p. 5 ܫܠܝܚܘܬܗ.

Page 7. *l.* 11. — *The whole creation.* The same as *Mark* xvi. 15. πασῃ τῃ κτισει. This is an Aramaism not unfrequently used by St. Paul, rendered in our English version, *Rom.* viii. 22, *the whole creation groaneth and travaileth in pain together until now.* It occurs several times in these pages. Compare Sharbil's words, p. 52.

l. 14.—*His princes and his nobles.* ܪ̈ܘܪܒܢܘܗܝ ܘܚܐܪ̈ܘܗܝ. It is difficult to know what is the exact political position of these two orders. The latter more literally would be *his free-men,* free citizens, in contradistinction to serfs and slaves.

l. 15.—*Shalmath.* I have no authority for the pronunciation of this word, there being no vowels. This observation will apply to almost all the proper names occurring in my translation. Any one, therefore, if he have better grounds, may supply other vowels, and a more accurate orthography. Referring, however, to Josephus, *Antiq. Jud.* B. XVIII. c. vii., I read the name of the wife of Phasaelus, Σαλαμψιω, which, if it be the same name as this, the name would be *Shalamtho* ܫܠܡܬܐ. *Daughter of Meherdath.* Who this Meherdath was does not appear. He may be the person mentioned at p. 13. He might also have been some connexion of Meherdates, the King of the Parthians, whom Tacitus mentions, *Annal.* B. xii. c. 12, and says that he was entertained at Edessa by Abgar, "qui juvenem ignarum, et summam fortunam in luxu ratum, multos per dies adtinuit apud oppidum Edessam:" see Assemani, *Bibl. Or.* Vol. I. p. 421. Moses Chor. B. II. c. xxxv. says that the first or chief wife of Abgar was *Helena*: see p. 138.

Page 8. *l.* 4.—*Of the faith.* The remaining part of the DOCTRINE OF ADDÆUS, from this place to the end, is taken from a MS. of the Nitrian collection now in the British Museum. Cod Add. 14,644. Dr. Land has given a description of this MS. in his *Anecdota Syriaca*, p. 19. I regret that the same want of knowledge or of attention, which characterizes all Dr. Land's publications,* which I have seen, should have rendered it necessary for me to furnish another description. The MS. is in 8vo., and consists at present of ninety-three leaves; two or three apparently are lost from the beginning, and a few others in the body of the volume. It was one of those MSS. procured in the year of the Greeks 1243, A.D 931, by the abbot Moses during his visit to Bagdad, who has written on the last leaf the same inscription as that given by me in the Preface to *Festal Letters of Athanasius*, p. xxv., which is also found in many of these volumes. It appears to be of the sixth century. The original contents of the volume are thus stated in red ink at the end of the volume, fol. 92 vers.

ܐܬܬܣܝܡ ܕܝܢ ܒܟܬܒܬܐ ܗܕܐ ܫܠܝ̈ܚܘܬܐ ܘܣܗܕ̈ܘܬܐ ܬܫܒ̈ܚܬܐ
ܚܕܐ. ܕܐܒܓܪ ܡܠܟܐ. ܘܡܠܦܢܘܬܐ ܕܐܕܝ ܫܠܝܚܐ. ܘܬܫܥܝܬܗ
ܕܫܪܒܝܠ. ܘܬܫܥܝܬܗ ܕܫܪܒܝܠ ܕܐܬܬܝܡ ܩܕ̈ܝܫܝܢ. ܘܣܗܕܘܬܗ
ܕܫܪܒܝܠ ܘܒܪܣܡܝܐ ܐܦܣܩܘܦܐ. ܘܡܠܦܢܘܬܗ ܕܫܡܥܘܢ
ܟܐܦܐ. ܘܡܠܦܢܘܬܐ ܕܫܠܝ̈ܚܐ. ܘܬܫܥܝܬܗ ܕܡܪܝ، ܐܒܪܗܡ
ܩܕܘܫܐ. ܘܢܨܚܢܗ ܕܫܪܒܝܠ ܡܪܝ، ܗܒܝܒ ܡܠܝܟܐ.
ܘܣܗܕܘܬܐ ܕܫܡܘܢܐ ܘܓܘܪܝܐ ܬܠܬ ܐܦܣܩܘܦ ܘܡܠܦܢ
ܘܐܦ ܠܥܠܡ. ܘܣܗܕܘܬܗ ܕܗܒܝܒ ܡܫܡܫܢܐ. ܘܣܗܕܘܬܗ ܕܡܪܝ،

. . . .

* It is with pain that I have to speak in such terms of the works of a gentleman who has shewn himself anxious to acquire distinction by pursuing these difficult and laborious studies; but when such an one, being a foreigner with no great knowledge of the English language, presumes to accuse the Version of the venerable Translators of our Authorized Translation of the Bible both of ignorance of the English tongue and of want of knowledge of the geography of the Holy Land, it shows a degree of hasty self-reliance which could not fail to lead him often into error, and to mislead others who have not the opportunity of bringing the accuracy of his writings to the test. See *Journal of Sacred Literature*, 1858.

ܫܪܒܝܠ. ܘܗܘܦܘܡܢܡܛܐ ܕܡܪܝ ܩܘܣܡܐ ܘܕܡܪܝ ܕܡܝܢܐ ܐܚܘܗܝ، ܐܣܘܬܐ ܫܪܝܪܐ. ܘܬܫܥܝܬܐ ܕܥܠ ܓܒܪܐ ܕܐܠܗܐ. ܕܗܘܝܢ ܒܡܢܝܢܐ ܐܪܒܥܣܪ "There are arranged, then, in this volume, Select Narratives and Martyrdoms. One of Abgar the King, (No. 1); and the Doctrine of Addæus the Apostle (2); and the Invention of the Cross (3); and the Invention of the Cross the second time (4); and the Martyrdom of the blessed Cyriacus, the Bishop (5); and the Doctrine of Simon Cephas (6); and the Doctrine of the Apostles (7); and the Narrative of Mari Abraham of Cheduna (8); and the Triumphs of Mari Saba Julianus (9); and the Martyrdom of Sophia and her three daughters, Pistis, Helpis, and Agape (10); and the Martyrdom of Jacob, who was cut to pieces (11); and the Martyrdom of Mari Sharbil (12); and the Hypomnemata of Mari Cosmas and Mari Damianus, his brother, true physicians (13); and the Narrative touching the Man of God (14); which are in number fourteen."

Of these fourteen, No. 1 is altogether lost. No. 2, printed in this volume, is imperfect, and is contained in the nine first folios. The order is then inverted. On folio 10 commences No. 7 to fol. 18. No. 3 begins on fol. 18, and comprises also No. 4, which is rather the Invention of the nails of the Cross, to fol. 23, vers. No. 5 follows. This Cyriacus was a Jew named Judas who found the Cross at the Empress Helena's instigation, and afterwards became converted to Christianity, and was ordained bishop by Sylvester, Bishop of Rome; from fol. 23 to fol. 27. The next is No. 8, fol. 28—43: it is imperfect at the end, about two lines wanted, as appears by comparison of Cod. Add. 12,160, fol. 116. No 11 comes next, imperfect at the beginning, two leaves supplied in a much later hand: it extends to fol. 53 vers., on which page is No. 9 to fol. 63, imperfect, several leaves missing. Next to this is No. 10, from fol. 63 vers. to fol. 72. Then comes No. 12, fol. 72 vers. to fol. 84 vers., printed in this volume. The next is No. 13, imperfect, wanting some leaves in the middle, fol. 84 vers.—fol. 87. And last, No. 14, from fol. 87 vers. to the end. Dr. Land did not observe the following rubric at the bottom of fol. 87 ܫܠܡܬ ܣܗܕܘܬܐ ܕܡܪܝ ܩܘܣܡܐ ܘܕܡܪܝ ܕܡܝܢܐ ܐܚܐ ܢܨܝܚܐ ܘܡܫܒܚܐ. "Here endeth the Martyrdom of Mari Cosmas and of Mari Damianus, glorious and triumphant brothers." He also overlooked the rubric on the other side of the leaf, at the top, ܬܫܥܝܬܐ ܕܥܠ ܓܒܪܐ ܕܐܠܗܐ ܕܗܘܐ ܡܢ ܪܗܘܡܐ. "The Narrative touching the man of God who was from Rome;" but seeing a blank leaf of vellum bound in between fol. 86 and 87, to show that something was missing, he has written "Inter fol. 86 et 87 initium Historiæ quatuordecim virorum Dei ex urbe Roma." The blunder, which, against sense and grammar, he has committed by confounding the number of works in the volume with the *Man of God from Rome*, and multiplying him by fourteen, has been already pointed out by Dr. W. Wright.

l. 10.—*The sun which was darkened.* See the same argument in *Doctrine of Simon Cephas*, p. 38.

l. 13.—*His disciples—knew only the Hebrew tongue.* See *Doctrine of the Apostles*, p. 25, and *Doctrine of Simon Cephas*, p. 36. Respecting the Apostles' ignorance of other tongues besides the *Syriac*, see Eusebius, *Theophania*, B. IV. c. 6, 8; B. V. c. 26; and Lee's Translation, pp. 217, 226, 309.

l. 18.—*The rebels in this region.* That is, "the whole of the country of Mesopotamia," as it is called *below*, p. 21; referring to the confusion of tongues at the Tower of Babel.

l. 21.—*From Paneas. Paneas*, otherwise *Cæsarea Philippi*: see Eusebius, *Hist. Ec.* B. VII. c. 17, and Valesuis' Note. Josephus, *Antiq. Jud.* B. XVIII. c. ii. 1. This is referred to in the Extract No. IV. p. 109.

l. 25.—*I cast his money upon the table.* Compare *Matt.* xxv. 27. Compare also the celebrated saying attributed to Christ, Γινεσθε τραπεζιται δοκιμοι. See Fabricius, *Cod. Apoc. N. T.*, p. 320. Grabe *Spicilegium*, p. 13. In the *Didascalia Apostolorum*, edited by Lagarde, in Syriac, this is given

ܗܘܘ ܡܦܪ̈ܫܢܐ ܒܚܝܪ̈ܐ ܡܬܒܥܐ ܗܘ ܠܗ ܡܟܝܠ ܠܐܦܝܣܩܘܦܐ
ܐܝܟ ܒܚܘܪܐ ܕܟܣܦܐ ܕܢܗܘܐ ܡܦܪܫܢܐ ܒܝ̈ܫܐ ܡܢ ܛܒ̈ܐ.

"Be expert discerners (or money-changers). It is requisite, therefore, that a Bishop, like a trier of silver, should be a discerner of the bad and the good," p. 42.

Page 9. *l.* 9.—*At that time—his own book.* See *Rev.* xx. 12. Compare also Mar Jacob, *On their own bodies*, &c., p. 97. A few lines are missing here in the MS.

l. 27.—*For the works of the Creation*, &c. Compare *Doctrine of the Apostles*, p. 26; *Doctrine of Simon Cephas*, p. 36; *Acts of Sharbil*, p. 52.

Page 10. *l.* 5.—See Josephus' account of the magnificence of the Vail of the Temple. *Wars of the Jews*, B. V. c. 5. sec. 4.

l. 7.—*For behold—in crying Woe.* This passage seems to accord with what is said in the antient Syriac Gospel of St. Luke, xxiii. 48: "And all those which were assembled there, and saw that which was done, were smiting upon their breast, and saying, Woe to us, what is this? Woe to us from our sins." See *Remains of a very antient Recension of the Four Gospels in Syriac*, p. 85. In our received text, instead of these last words, we have "Smote upon their breasts, and returned."

l. 26.—"*Blessed are ye that have believed in me, not having seen me; and because ye have so believed in me, the city in which ye dwell shall be blessed, and the enemy shall not prevail against it for ever.*" These words are not in the Epistle of our Lord to King Abgar, although the first part is similar to the beginning of that Epistle. They must, therefore, either have been a message brought by Addæus himself, as Ephraem Syrus seems to intimate in the passage quoted from his *Testament* below; or, what seems much more probable, they are a later amplification or interpolation, although anterior to the time of Ephraem. This is confirmed by Procopius:—*Φασι δε και τουτο αυτον επειπειν, ως ουδε η πολις ποτε βαρβαροις αλωσιμος εσται.* Τουτο *της επιστολης το ακροτελευτιον οι μεν εκεινου του χρονου την ιστοριαν ξυνγραψαντες, ουδαμη εγνωσαν· ου γαρ ουν ουδεπη αυτου εμνησθησαν.* Εδεσηνοι *δε αυτο ξυν επιστολη ευρεσθαι φασιν· ως τε αμελει και αναγραπτον ουτω την επιστολην αντ' αλλου του φυλακτηριου εν ταις της πολεως πεποιηνται πυλαις.* "Hoc enim subjunxisse aiunt, urbem semper inexpugnabilem fore Barbaris. Quod postremum epistolæ caput eos, qui historiam scripserunt illius temporis latuit: nusquam enim mentionem ejus fecerunt. Edesseni vero id literis annexum reperiri perhibent, adeo ut epistolam eo modo exscriptam in portis urbis pro quovis alio munimento posuerunt:" quoted by Grabe in his *Spicilegium*, Vol. I. p. 313. Respecting this, Evagrius writes in his Ecclesiastical History, Book IV. c. 27, "The same Procopius records what has been related by the antients concerning Edessa and Abgarus, and how Christ wrote to Abgarus. Further, also, how in another incursion Chosroes resolved upon a seige of the Edessens, supposing he should enervate what had been divulged to the faithful, to wit, that Edessa should never be subdued by an enemy. Which thing is not, indeed, extant in that letter sent from Christ our God to Abgarus, as may be gathered by the studious, from what has been related by Eusebius Pamphilus, who has inserted that letter word for word into his History. Nevertheless, it is both divulged and believed amongst the Faithful, and the event itself declared the truth, faith bringing the prediction to effect, &c." *English Trans.*, p. 488. In the Epistle of Christ to Abgar, edited by the Emperor Constantine Porphyrogenitus, the words *και ποιησει τη πολει σου το ικανον, προς το μηδενα των εχθρων κατισχυσαι αυτη*: cited by Bayer,

Hist. Osrh. p. 107. This is translated by Lipomanus, "Et tuæ civitati cavebit ut nullus eam possit superare inimicus." Part I. p. 188. The first words of this are given by Cedrenus thus: και τη πολει σου γενησεται το ικανον: see Grabe *Ibid*, p. 8, and Fabricius, *Cod. Apoc. N. T*, p. 319. Constantine Porphyrogenitus' account of the conversion of Abgar, &c., is given by Simeon Metaphrastes, and printed in Greek by Combefis in his *Origg. Constantipoll. Manip.*, Paris, 1664. p. 75—101; and in Latin by Lipomanus, in *Sanctorum Hist.*, Part I., p. 187, *Constantini, cognomento Porphyrogeniti, Narratio collecta ex diversis historiis de non manu facta Christi Dei nostri imagine, missa ad Abagarum, et ex Edessa translata in hanc beatissimam urbium Reginam Constantinopolim.* (A. C. 944.) Also given by Surius, August 16th. See an account of this in Arabic, by Macarius of Antioch, *Cod. Add.* 9965, f. 33 vers.

In the Testament of Ephraem, as published by Vossius, we read, "Et benedicta vestra sit civitas, in qua habitatis. Ipsa enim sapientum est civitas, et mater, Edessa: quæ quidem etiam palam atque manifeste ex ore Christi Domini benedicta est per suos discipulos, nostros vero Apostolos. Nam quando Rex Abagarus, qui hanc civitatem extruxit, rogabat, exciperet eum qui peregrinus in terris apparuerat, Salvatorem inquam universorum, et Dominum Christum, dicebat: "Omnia audivi, quæ a te facta sunt, et quæcumque a reprobis et aspernantibus te Judæis passus es. Veni igitur huc, et nobiscum habita: habeo enim mihi civitatem hanc exiguam, quæ tibi et mihi sufficiet." Cujus etiam fidem admiratus Dominus, mittens ei per nuntios, perpetuò civitati illi benedixit, firmans ipsius fundamenta: benedictioque illa inhabitans in ea permanebit, donec Sanctus e cælo apparebit Jesus Christus Filius Dei, et Deus ex Deo:" see Ephraem Syrus, *Opera Omnia*, a Ger. Vossio, 3rd edit., p. 788. Assemani, upon comparing the original Syriac with both the Greek edition and the Latin, having observed that the Greek interpreter had added many things of his own, gives the original Syriac of the above passage, which he renders thus: "Benedicta civitas, in qua habitatis, Edessa sapientum mater, quæ ex vivo Filii ore benedictionem per ejus Discipulum accepit. Illa igitur benedictio in ea maneat donec Sanctus apparuerit." *Bibl. Orient.*, Vol. I. p. 141. This *Testament* is printed entire in Syriac with a Latin translation, with only three verbal variations from this cited here, in Ephraem Syrus, *Opera Omnia*, Rome, Vol. II. p. 395. Darius Comes, in Epist. ad Augustinum, also mentions this: "Affuit Deus Regi, et amplifi cato petitionis munere per Epistolam, non modo salutem ut supplici, sed etiam securitatem ut Regi transmisit. Jussit insuper et urbem ab hostibus in perpetuum esse ac semper immunem :" cited by Fabricius, *Cod. Apoc. N. T.*, p. 319.

This notion of the immunity of the City of Edessa is referred to by several Syriac writers. Thus Joshua Stylites cites the passage ܡܕܝܢܬܟ ܬܗܘܐ ܒܪܝܟܐ: ܘܒܥܠܕܒܒܐ ܠܐ ܢܬܚܝܠ ܒܗ ܠܥܠܡ. "And thy city shall be blessed, and the enemy shall not prevail against it for ever :" see Assemani, *Bibl. Orient.* Vol. I. p. 261. So Mar Jacob, in his Epistle to the Homerites: ܐܓܪܬܐ ܕܟܬܒ ܡܪܢ ܡܫܝܚܐ ܠܘܬ ܐܒܓܪ: writes ܘܥܡ ܗܠܝܢ ܐܫܬܘܕܝ ܐܠܗܐ ܠܐܒܓܪ ܡܠܟܐ ܡܗܝܡܢܐ ܕܥܠ ܡܕܝܢܬܗ ܠܐ ܢܬܚܝܠ ܒܥܠܕܒܒܐ ܠܥܠܡ. "Moreover God promised to King Abgar the Faithful, that the enemy should not prevail against his city for ever :" see *Cod. Add.* 14,587, fol. 47 vers., see also fol. 48 rect.

Nor did the belief in the protecting power of this Letter of our Lord prevail in the East only, for we find, at a very early period also, that it obtained even in our own British Isles. In a very antient MS. in the British Museum, *Royal MS.*, 2 A. xx. f. 12, containing a Service Book of the Saxon times, we find this Epistle in the Latin version of Rufinus, immediately following the Lord's Prayer and the Apostle's Creed. "In nomine Patris et filii et Spiritus Sancti : *Incipit Epistola Salvatoris omnium Ihesu Christi ad Abagarum regem, quam Dominus manu scripsit et dixit.* "Beatus es qui me non vidisti et credidisti in me. Scriptum est enim de me, quia hi qui vident me, non credent in me : et qui me non vident, ipsi in me credent et vivent. De eo autem quod scripsisti mihi ut venirem ad te, oportet me omnia propter quæ missus sum hic explere ; et postea quam complevero recipi me ad eum, a quo missus sum. Cum ergo fuero adsumptus, mittam tibi aliquem ex discipulis meis, ut curet egritudinem tuam, et vitam tibi, ac his qui tecum sunt præstet, et salvus eris, sicut scriptum, Qui credit in me salvus erit." *Sive in domu tua, sive in civitate tva, sive in omni loco nemo inimicorum tuorum dominabit. Et insidias diaboli ne timeas, et carmina inimicorum tuorum distruuntur* (sic), *et omnes inimici tui expellentur a te : sive a grandine, sive a tonitrua* (sic) *non noceberis, et ab omni periculo liberaberis : sive in mare, sive in terra, sive in die, sive in nocte, sive in locis obscuris. 'Si quis hanc epistolam secum habuerit, securus ambulet in pace,"* fol. 12. In this MS. p. 18 b, Thaddæus is called Tatheus, as in the first edition of Rufinus. Those who are curious may read the Story of Abgar in Anglo-Saxon, published by L. C. Müller, from a Cotton M.S., in *Collect. Anglo-*

Saxon, Havniæ, 1835; and "Abgarus Legenden paa Old-Engelsk," with an English translation by G. Stephens, Copenhagen, 1853.

The practice of keeping this letter as a phylactery prevailed in England till the last century, as I find from Jeremiah Jones. "The common people in England have had it in their houses in many places in a frame with a picture before it, and they generally, with much honesty and devotion, regard it as the word of God, and the genuine epistle of Christ." See his *New and Full Method*, Oxford, 1798, Vol. II. p. 6. I have a recollection of having seen the same thing in cottages in Shropshire.

Page 11, *l.* 2.—*The eyes of the true mind.* Compare p. 19, line 21: *The secret eye of your mind*; p. 37, line 13: *The eyes of the mind*; p. 45, line 23: *The clear eyes of the mind.* See also St. Paul *Ephes.* i. 18: τους οφθαλμους της διανοιας: and Clement. *Epist. ad Corinth*, 36; and *Epist. Smyrn. de Polycarpi Mart.* 2, τοις της καρδιας οφθαλμοις.

l. 23.—*The stay of your head.* ܡܣܡܟ ܪܝܫܟܘܢ This word is not in the dictionaries, but its derivative and form are known. Mar Jacob, p. 97, line 10, has ܘܣܡܘܟܝܗ ܪܝܫܐ ܕܟܠ ܡܢ ܕܗܘܝܢ ܥܠ ܗܝܡܢܘܬܐ. In *Cod. Add.* 14,484 fol. 63, rect. we read ܗܘ ܡܠܟܐ ܡܣܡܟ ܗܘܐ ܪܝܫܗ.

l. 27.—*Because it is not in many things that the belief of the truth of Christ consists.* This is alluded to by Mar Jacob—*For faith consisteth not in many words*, p. 103, line 9.

Page 12, *l.* 24. — *Accepted his words.* We might have expected here ܡܩܒܠܘ ܗܘܘ but the text has ܗܘܐ as the MS. reads it.

Page 13, *l.* 10.—*My son Maanu.* Abgar had two sons of the name. This is probably the elder, who succeeded his father at Edessa, and reigned seven years: see Assemani, *Bibl. Orient.* Vol. I. p. 421. Bayer makes him the 15th King of Edessa. "Maanu bar Abgar. Dionysius Telmariensis scribit, eum anno 2061. mortuo patri successisse et septem annos regnasse. Secundum nostras rationes regnare cœpit Edessæ A. Abrahæ 2060. Martis mense A. V. C. 798. a Christo nato 45. Moses Chorenensis Ananum vocat, quod non longe recedit a Syriaco nomine: *Hist. Osrh.* p. 125. Le Vaillant de Florival writes the name *Ananoun*: see p. 136. *Augustin*: she was Abgar's mother, as we have seen above, p. 7.

l. 23.—*Shemashgram.* I have written this name according to the vowels in the treatise of Bardesan. See, respecting this and the Greek forms of the word, Notes to my *Spicilegium Syriacum*, p. 77. Whiston, from the Armenian form, writes the name "*Samsagramum*, Apahuniæ gentis principem;"

and Le Vaillant de Florival, "*Chamchacram*, chef de la maison des Abahouni :" see B. II. c. 30. He was sent, together with Hanan and Maryhab, as envoy to Marinus: see *Ibid*, p. 129. *Meherdath* seems to be the person mentioned by Tacitus in connexion with Abdu: see note *above*, p. 145.

PAGE 14, *l.* 1.—*Avida.* The MS. reads distinctly here ܚܘܒܕܐ; but it is doubtless a mistake: Avida occurs several times in connexion with Barcalba: see pp. 18, 45, 63. The name Avida also occurs in Bardesan: see *Spicil. Syr.*, pp. 1, 77. *Barcalba*, he was the son of Zati, as we learn from p. 18.

l. 2.—*Royal headband.* ܠܒ̈ܫܝ ܚܘ̈ܪܐ ܕܡܠܟܘܬܐ: at line 30 we also read ܐܣܛܠ̈ܐ ܘܚܘ̈ܪܐ ܕܡܠܟܘܬܐ, but in the *Doctrine of Simon Cephas*, p. 36, line 1, ܠܒܫܝ ܚܘ̈ܪܐ ܕܡܠܟܘܬܐ, where I have translated it "headbands of the Kings," assuming that the true reading should be as here; but in the Peshito *Acts* x. 30, we have ܠܒܝܫ ܚܘ̈ܪܐ "indutus albis." Compare חוּרָי *Is.* xix. 9: ארגים חורי "weavers of white" (linen or silk). In either case the meaning would be to denote some mark of great distinction or nobility. Plutarch calls the "candida fascia" διαδημα βασιλικον: see Note on Suetonius, c. 79. p. 156, *edit. Varr.*, *Lond.* 1826.

l. 12.—*Piroz.* This may, perhaps, have been the same as the person mentioned by Abgar in his letter to Narses: see Moses Chor, p. 135. It is the same name as the Greek and Latin Berosus, and as the Persian فیروز of the present day.

l. 14.—*Nebu and Bel.* These were the chief gods of Edessa, of which the former represented the *Sun* and the latter the *Moon*: see Mar Jacob of Sarug in Assemani, *Bibl. Orient.* Vol. I. p. 327; Bayer, *Hist. Osrh.* p. 139.

l. 22.—*Jews—who traded in silk.* ܕܐܒܪ̈ܝܫܡܐ ܡܬܓܪܝܢ These seem to have been Jews residing at Edessa for the purpose of carrying on traffic with the countries to the East. Batne, in the province of Osrhoene, about a day's journey from Edessa, which Ammianus Marcellinus calls, "Municipium Osdroenæ," B. XXIII. c. ii. 7, was the celebrated mart where the Indians and the Seres came to trade at a fair held at the beginning of September, "refertum mercatoribus opulentis: ubi annua sollemnitate, prope Septembris initium mensis, ad nundinas magna promiscuæ fortunæ convenit multitudo, ad commercanda, quæ Indi mittunt et Seres, aliaque plurima vehi terra marique consueta:" *Ibid*, B. XIV. c. iii. 3. See Huet, *Hist. du Commerce et de la Navigation des Anciens*, p. 370. These *Seres*, as Ammianus Marcellinus, as well as other writers, tells us, manufactured *Sericum*. "Nentesque subtemina, conficiunt sericum, ad usus antehac nobilium, nunc etiam infimorum sine ulla discretione proficiens," *Ibid.* B. XXIII, c. vi. 67. The reader will recollect Virgil's verse, Geor. ii. 121, "Velleraque ut foliis depectunt tenuia Seres." This seems to be the ܪ̈ܟܝܟܐ in which the Jews in this country traded. We find this word, which, as an epithet, means *mollis, tenuis, lenis,* used as a noun substantive, as it is here, in the *Ancient Recension of the Four Gospels in Syriac,* Matt. xi. 8. ܪ̈ܟܝܟܐ ܠܒܝܫ: and in the Greek Gospel of Matthew, following the original Hebrew, *εν μαλακοις ημφιεσμενον*; while St. Luke adds *ιματιοις* after *μαλακοις*. Yet both state that *μαλακοις* was the dress of the nobles, "they that wear soft *clothing* are in kings' houses;" identifying *μαλακα* with "Sericum ad usus antehac nobilium" of Ammianus Marcellinus. Although I have rendered it silk, it would appear, from the accounts given, to be cotton or muslin, *lana xylina,* not *bombycina*: see Plinius, *Hist. Nat.* vi. 20.

l. 30. — *Chains.* The word ܫܐܪ̈ܝܐ, which I have translated *chains,* upon the authority of Castel, (compare also Buxtorf. Lex. Chald. et Syr. ad שיר), would perhaps be more correctly rendered *silks* or *muslins.* Thus, in a passage cited by Assemani *Bibl. Orient.* Vol. I. p. 186, we find ܫܕܪ ܠܗ ܚܘܠܐ ܕܫܐܪ̈ܝܐ ܕܠܐ ܒܚܘܣܪ, "which he translates "non modicam quantitatem *fili serici* transmisit." In the *Doctrine of the Apostles,* at p. ܠܗ line 2, Aggæus is called ܥܒܕ ܫܐܪ̈ܝܐ, which I have there translated, "maker of *golden* chains," having reference to p. 22, line 23. Here C. reads ܫܝܪ̈ܝܐ, which Castel also renders "sericum." Moreover, in the account of Aggæus by Moses Choren., he is called "un fabricant de coiffures de soie," in the translation of Le Vaillant de Florival; and "quendam serici opificem," in that of Whiston: see B. II. c. xxxiii. p. 131. *Whiston's edit.* p. 137. *Headbands of the king,* or diadems. These seem to have been made of silk or muslin scarves, such as form the turbans of orientals at the present day, interwoven with gold, and with figures and devices upon them. Such, at any rate, was that worn by the high-priest of Bel and Nebu. See *Acts of Sharbil,* p. 41.

Page 15, *l.* 3.—*Old Testament and the New.* It is plain that these terms could only have been used here in the sense of the Law of Moses and the Gospel, and not in the full sense which we now give. If by the "Acts [or Visitations] of the Apostles," ܣܘܥܪ̈ܢܝܗܘܢ ܕܫܠܝ̈ܚܐ, we are to understand those written by St. Luke, this passage seems to shew that the compiler of these Acts of Addæus, wrote some years subsequently to the events which he relates, or that it has been added by an interpolator still later. For at the earlier period of Addæus' ministry, no other part of the New

Testament was written than the original Hebrew Gospel of St. Matthew, which, as giving an account of the new dispensation of Jesus Christ, might have been called the New Testament or Covenant. The Acts of the Apostles, in the Peshito, is ܟܬܒܐ ܕܦܪܟܣܝܣ ܗܘ ܕܝܢ ܬܫܥܝܬܗܘܢ ܕܫܠܝܚܐ ܛܘܒܢܐ "The Book of πραξεις, that is, Stories of the Blessed Apostles." Compare *Doctrine of the Apostles*, pp. 27, 32, where those by Luke are called "Triumphs of the Apostles," and *Doctrine of Simon Cephas*, p. 40.

l. 29.—*Ditornon.* The reading of the MS. here is not quite clear. I am disposed to consider that the word ought to be *Diatessaron*, which Tatian, the Syrian, compiled from the Four Gospels about the middle of the second century. This we know to have been in general use at Edessa up to the fourth century, and to have had a commentary written upon it by Ephraem Syrus. See Assemani *Bibl. Orient.* Vol. I. p. 517. Theodoretus states, *Hæret. Fab.* B. I c. 20, that he found more than 200 copies of this work received in the churches in his own diocese, which he caused to be removed, and substituted copies of the Four Gospels in their stead. See Fabricius, *Cod. Apoc. N. T.* p. 377. Ebediesu writes thus of Tatian in the Preface to his Collection of Canons: "Tatianus quidam philosophus cum Evangelistarum loquentium sensum suo intellectu cepisset, et scopum scriptionis illorum divinæ in mente sua fixisset, unum ex quatuor illis admirabile collegit evangelium, quod et Diatessaron nominavit, in quo cum cautissime seriem rectam eorum, quæ a Salvatore dicta ac gesta fuere, servasset, ne unam quidem dictionem e suo addidit." See Card. Mai, *Scriptt. Vet. Nov. Coll.* Vol. X. p. 23. If this be so, there is here a later interpolation. It is stated by Bar Hebræus that some of the books of the Old Testament and the New were translated at Edessa in the time of Abgar and Addæus: see Assemani, *Bibl. Orient.* Vol. II. p. 279; Walton, *Proleg. ad Bibl. Polyglot*, p. 89. There is also a record preserved of a very antient copy of a Gospel written by the hand of Aggæus himself, the disciple and successor of Addæus, in the year of the Greeks 389, or A.D. 78: see Assemani *Bibl. Orient.* Vol. II. p. 486, and *Preface to Remains of a very antient Recension of the Four Gospels in Syriac*, p. lxxvii. This seems to derive some confirmation from the fact of Addæus having established deacons and presbyters in the churches, and taught persons to read the Scriptures in them: see p. 18.

PAGE 16, *l.* 11.—*Fire worshippers and adorers of water*: see Strabo *de Persis*, c. xv. διαφεροντως δε τῳ πυρι και τῳ υδατι θυουσι; see also Abdias *Hist. Cert. Apost.*, B. VI. c. 7, "Solem et lunam deorum numero applicantes, aquam simul deitatem habere docebant:" Fabricius, *Cod. Apoc. N. T.* p. 609, and his Notes there; see also Assemani, *Bibl. Orient.* Vol. I. p. 191, and Sim. A. Assemani, *Acta Martyr.* Vol. I. pp. 40, 113, 227. Mar Jacob of Sarug, in his sermon on the Fall of Idols, Cod. Add. 14,624, fol. 12, writes ܠܫܡܫܐ ܘܣܗܪܐ ܘܠܟܘܟܒܬܐ ܘܠܢܗܝܪܐ: ܘܠܢܘܪܐ ܘܡܝܐ ܘܠܚܝܘܬܐ ܐܣܓܕ ܐܢܘܢ. "He made them worship the sun, and the moon, and the stars, and the lights, and fire, and water, and living creatures."

l. 17.—*And Abgar wrote to Narses.* This Letter is given by Moses Chor., see p. 135.

l. 22.—*Because he was not able to pass over into the country belonging to the Romans.* In consequence of the treaties by which the limits of the Roman Empire, fixed by Augustus, extended to the Euphrates: see Tillemont *Hist. des Empereurs*, Vol. I. p. 37.; see also Extr. vi. p. 111, Dio Cassius, liv. 8. *ο Σεβαστος εστησεν ορια τῃ Ρωμαιων αρχῃ Τιγριν τε και Ευφρατην.*

l. 24.—*Wrote a letter and sent it to Tiberius.* This letter, and the answer of Tiberius, are given by Moses Chor., with a few variations, which the reader will observe, p. 133. See, respecting this letter to Tiberius, Henke, Proleg. *De Pontii Pilati Actis in causa Domini Nostri ad Imp. Tiberium missis probabilia*, p. xxiii., Helmstad, 1784. Bar Hebræus mentions these Epistles, *Chron. Syriac.* text, p. 52.

PAGE 17, *l.* 13.—*Pilate also has written.* There can be no doubt that Pontius Pilate sent an account to the Roman Government of what took place with respect to Jesus, which it was his duty to do as governor of Judea. This is mentioned by Justin Martyr, Tertullian, Eusebius, Epiphanius, Chrysostom, &c., as well as in various Apocryphal writers. A full notice of all this has been given by Fabricius, *Cod. Apoc. N. T.* p. 24; Walchius, *Hist. Eccl.* p. 174; Baronius, *Annal.* A. 34. ccxxii.—viii. Tischendorf de antiquis Pilati Actis Cæsari distinctis, in *Proleg. ad Evangelia Apocrypha*, p. lxii. Bishop Pearson's Lectiones in Acta Apostolorum, in his *Opera Posthuma*, pp. 50, 63. To these I would add the early testimony given in the *Doctrine of Simon Cephas*, p. 38, already given.

l. 14.—*My proconsul Aulbinus.* There is evidently an error in this Syriac name, such as most frequently occurs in proper names in Syriac, both on account of their being foreign to the transcribers, and of the total omission of the vowels. The name may perhaps have been confounded with that of Albinus, who was made governor of Judea by Nero, A.D. 62: see Tillemont *Hist. des Empereurs*, Vol. I. p. 561; Eusebius, *Hist. Ecc.* B. II. c. 23: see Valesius' Note, p. 28, *English Trans.* In the Apocryphal work, p. 111, the name is also given "Sabinus, the governor who had been appointed by the Emperor Tiberius, and even as far as the River Euphrates the governor Sabinus had authority." Mention of this person is altogether omitted by Moses Chor. in his history, probably because he did not know how to give the name correctly: see p. 133. The person intended could be no other than Vitellius, who was then governor of Syria, and removed Pilate from the administration of Judea, sending Marcellus in his stead, and ordered him to appear before Tiberius at Rome. The Emperor died before he reached Rome: see Tillemont, *Hist. des Empereurs*, Vol. I. pp 129, 682; *Ibid*, p. 420. See Josephus, *Antiq. Jud.* B. XVIII. c. iv. 2.

l. 15.—*People of Spain.* The letter of Tiberius, as it is read in Moses Chor., differs a good deal from this, and the reference to Spain is found near the end: see p. 134. Whiston has the following Note on this place: "Tametsi bellum hoc Hispanicum nusquam forsan alibi disertè memoretur, tamen non desunt scriptorum testimonia, ex quibus conjectura in eam rem duci potest. Nam Tiberius Hispaniarum principes olim vexaverat, atque etiam hoc ipso tempore provinciam eam plane neglexit; adeò ut tum Hispanos ad rebellandum provocaverit, tum etiam ejus faciendi opportunitatem idoneam dederit: *Regressus in Insulam, Reipublicæ quidem curam usque adeò abjecit, ut postea non decurias equitum unquam supplèrit, non tribunos militum præfectosque, non provinciarum præsides ullos mutaverit:* Hispaniam *et Syriam per aliquot annos sine consularibus legatis habuerit.* Suet. in Tiberium, c. 41. *Præterea Galliarum et Hispaniarum, Syriæque et Græciæ principes confiscatos:—Plurimis etiam civitatibus et privatis veteres communitates et jus metallorum* (quod ad Hispaniam præcipuè spectabat) *ac vectigalium adempta*, Ibid. c. 49. Vide etiam Tacit. Annal. vi. 27. Cæterum non omnino præteriri debet Vellei Paterculi locus, qui, nisi in eo non vana mendi suspicio subesset, rem totam clarè confirmaret. *At Tiberius Cæsar, quum certam Hispanis parendi confessionem extorserat, parem Illyriis Dalmatisque extorsit*, L. ii. c. 39." We know, however, that about the very time at which this letter of Tiberius must have been written, Vitellius was mixed up with the wars of the Parthians and Hiberians: see Tillemont, *Hist. des Empereurs*, Vol. I. p. 131; and as Hiberi is a name common to Spaniards, as well as Hiberians, the difference might have arisen in translating Tiberius' Epistle out of Latin into Syriac: or, indeed, Tiberius, with his usual dissimulation, might have used this word to conceal some ulterior designs. See Amm. Marcell. "Itidem Hiberia ex Hibero, nunc Hispania," B. XXIII. c. 21.

l. 21.—*Because he exceeded the law.* Baronius says that there ought to have been a delay of ten days before the sentence was carried into execution, and that in this manner Pilate violated the law of the Roman Emperor by crucifying our Lord so soon after sentence had been passed: "recens quippe erat Senatusconsultum Tiberianum, sic dictum, quod Tiberio Imperatore, a quo ipse Præses in Judæam est missus, factum erat ante annos duodecim, ipso Tiberio quartum et Druso Coss., quo cautum fuerat, ut supplicia damnatorum in decimum usque diem differrentur, ut Suetonius, Dio et alii testantur:" see *Annal.* 34, sec. 92.

l. 24.—*Deserve to be honoured and adored.* Tiberius is said by Tertullian to have referred to the Senate the question of admitting Christ among the Gods. "Tiberius ergo, cujus tempore nomen Christianum in sæculum introivit, annunciata sibi ex Syria Palæstina, quæ illic veritatem istius divini revelârant, detulit ad Senatum cum prærogativa suffragii sui. Senatus quia non ipse in se probaverat, respuit. Cæsar in sententia mansit, comminatus periculum accusatoribus Christianorum." *Apol.* c. 5. Mentioned also by Eusebius, *Hist. Ecc.* B. II. c. ii.; Baronius, *Ibid.* sec. 222, &c.; Bishop Pearson, Lect. in Act. Apost. *Opera Posth.*, p. 63.: see Mosheim, *Diss. ad Hist. Ecc.*, Vol. I. p. 357; Steph. Le Moyne, *Varia Sacra*, Vol. II. p. 145. This has also been interpolated into the Epistle of Tiberius to Abgar as it is found in Moses Chor., see p. 135. There is also given by the same Moses another letter of Abgar to Tiberius, in reply to this: see *Ibid.*

l. 28—*Aristides.* There is no mention of this person in Moses. Chor.; nor of the presents with which he returned to Tiberius. He, however, gives an Epistle which Abgar is said to have written in reply, of which there is no indication here.

Page 18, *l.* 1.—*Thicuntha.* This word has been so much distorted and disfigured by the transcribers that I am not able to recognise what is the place intended. The same may be said of *Artica* in the next line. This, however, may, be pronounced *Ortyka*, and be intended for *Ortygia* near Syracuse, which was not very far distant from the Island Capreæ, where we know that Tiberius at this time resided, seldom leaving it to go further than to the neighbouring coast of Campania: see Tacitus, *Annal.* B. IV. c. 67; Suetonius, *Tib.* c. 40; Josephus, *Antiq.* B. XVIII. c. vi; Tillemont, *Hist. des Empereurs*, p. 93.

l. 19.—*Guide and Ruler.* It is plain from the context here, as well as wherever it occurs in these early Syriac documents, that this title is precisely the same as that of Bishop, although the Greek word Επισκοπος had not yet obtained in the East. The first mention which we find of the title *Bishop* is in the *Acts of Sharbil*, p. 65, about A.D. 105—112, where Barsamya is called the *Bishop of the Christians*, although more generally designated as here.

The occurrence of the word at p. 23 in these *Acts of Addæus* is in a passage evidently interpolated at a much later period: see Note p. 165 *below*. It is also found in the *Doctrine of Simon Cephas*, p. 40, which seems to have been written very early in the second century, or even at the end of the first.

l. 20.—*Palut.* If this word be not of Syriac origin, it may be an abbreviation from the Greek Φιλωτας, as Patric, four lines below, is from the Latin *Patricius.*

l. 23.—*Zati.* This is perhaps the same name as Izates: see Josephus, *Antiq. Jud.*, B. XX. c. ii. 1, 4; Tacitus *Ann.* B. XII. c. 14. See also Assemani, *Bibl. Orient.* Vol. I. p. 421. *Maryhab*, seems to be the same person that is spoken of by Moses. Chor. as having been sent by Abgar as one of the envoys to Marinus. "Mar-Ihap, prince d'Aghtznik:" see p. 129 *above.*

l. 24.—*Senac.* Tacitus writes this name Sinnaces: see Note on p. 145.

PAGE 19, *l.* 1.—*Ordinances and Laws which were appointed by the disciples at Jerusalem.* These are given in the *Doctrine of the Apostles*, see p. 25.

l. 7–19.—*Give heed—resurrection of all men.* This passage is cited in the extract given at p. 109.

PAGE 20, *l.* 10.—One leaf apparently is lost from the MS. in this place.

l. 25.—*Accept not any thing from any man, and possess not any thing in this world.* These words of our Lord are not found in this form in any of the Gospels; they are, however, tantamount to the instruction given by him to the Twelve when he sent them forth. *Matt.* x. 7—10.

PAGE 21, *l.* 2.—*Fourteenth of the month Iyar* (*May*). This date is not only confirmed by Amru, the historian cited by Assemani, *Bibl. Orient.*, Vol. II. p. 392, but also by a very antient Syriac Calendar. Bar Hebræus, therefore, is mistaken, not only in giving the day as the 30th of July, but also in saying that he was put to death: he has evidently confounded Addæus with his immediate successor Aggæus; like as Moses Chor. has mistaken the name, see p. 136. Bar Hebræus also confounds the places of their burial, saying that Addæus was buried in a church which he had built at Edessa: see Assemani, *Bibl. Orient.* Vol. II. p. 392. Addæus was buried by Abgar in the sepulchre of his ancestors, p. 21, and Aggæus in the church which he had built, p. 23. The death of Addæus took place before that of Abgar, which happened A.D. 45: see *Ibid*, Vol. I. p. 420; Bayer, *Hist. Osrh.*, p. 125. It would, therefore, appear that his ministry at Edessa was of about ten or eleven years duration.

l. 12.—*Those of the house of Ariu, the ancestors of Abgar the King.* See Moses Chor., B. II. c. xiv., and Abgar's descent from Arsaces: Bayer, *Hist. Osrh.* p. 97.

l. 17.—*The ordinance and instruction—by the Apostle Addæus.* Compare *Doctrine of the Apostles*, XVIII. p. 28.

l. 19.—*Aggæus who himself became Guide and Ruler and the successor of his Chair after him.* See *Doctrine of the Apostles*, pp. 32, 34 *below*; see Assemani, *Bibl. Orient.* Vol. II. p. 392; Vol. III. p. 611.

l. 28.—*The whole state* ܩܠܝܪܘܣ: this seems to apply to those who especially belonged to the ministry of the church; thus ܒܢܝ ܩܠܝܪܘܣ is used for "clerici," in contradistinction to ܒܢܝ ܥܠܡܐ "laici:" see Assemani, *Bibl. Orient.* Vol. I. p. 189, &c.

Page 22, *l.* 11.—*Like a net.* Alluding to our Lord's words, *Matt.* xix. 1, "I will make you fishers of men." Compare with this τῃ σαγηνῃ του ευαγγελιου ζωγρησαι, used by Nicephorus, as applied to this Addæus. *Hist. Eccl.* B. II. c. 40.

l. 14.—*One of his rebellious sons.* This would seem to be the second son of Abgar called Maanu, who succeeded his brother Maanu, and reigned fourteen years, that is, from A.D. 52 to A.D. 65, according to Dionysius, cited by Assemani, *Bibl. Orient.* Vol. I. p. 421; see also Bayer, *Hist. Osrh.* p. 130. Moses Chor., who evidently copied from this document, does not give the name of the king; unless, indeed, the words "Le prince, qui régna après la mort de son père" are to be referred to "Ananoun fils d'Abgar règne à Édesse" at the beginning of the chapter: see p. 136. Clem. Galanus also writes: "Secundus Rex post Abagarum fuit filius quidam ejus anonymus, qui Christianam Patris religionem aspernatus, fideles atrociter insectatus est; ac misere vitam complevit. Tertius fuit Sanatrughus, filius sororis Abgari, cujus imperio Sanctos Apostolos Bartholomæum et Thaddæum in regionibus illis interfectos fuisse narrant Armenii:" see *Conciliatio Ecc. Arm. cum Rom.* p. 9; see Assemani, *Ibid.* In the extract given at p. 109, *Severus*, son of Abgar, is stated to have slain Addæus. This is most probably a mistake in substituting Addæus for Aggæus, such as Moses Chor. has made: see Note p. 162, above. In the book called *The Bee*, by Solomon Bishop of Bassora, about A.D. 1222, (concerning which see Assemani *Bibl. Orient.* Vol. III. p. 309), in the 49th chapter, Touching the Apostles, and the places of each one of them, and of their deaths, we find the following ܐܕܝ، ܡܢ ܦܢܝܣ ܐܝܬܘܗܝ ܗܘܐ. ܘܐܚܪܝ ܒܐܘܪܗܝ، ܕܒܝܬ ܢܗܪܝܢ ܡܥܢܘ ܐܒܓܪ. ܩܛܠܗ ܕܝܢ ܣܘܪܘܣ ܒܪܗ ܕܐܒܓܪ ܠܘܬ ܚܣܢܐ ܕܐܓܠ. ܘܐܫܬܟܚ ܦܓܪܗ ܠܒܪ ܘܐܣܬܠܩܘ ܠܪܗܘܡܐ. ܘܐܝܬ ܕܐܡܪܝܢ ܕܒܗ ܒܐܘܪܗܝ، ܐܬܬܣܝܡ. ܐܝܟ ܬܠܡܝܕܗ ܐܝܬܘܗܝ، ܗܘܐ ܠܗܘܕ ܒܒܗ

ܫܝܪ̈ܝܩܐ ܕܐܒܓܪ ܘܐܬܬܠܡܕ. ܘܒܬܪ ܡܘܬܗ ܕܐܒܓܪ ܐܡܠܟ
ܒܪܗ ܚܠܦܘܗܝ. ܘܬܒܥ ܡܢ ܐܓܝ ܕܢܙܩܘܪ ܠܗ ܫܝܪ̈ܝܩܐ. ܘܟܕ
ܠܐ ܐܬܛܦܝܣ ܒܕ ܐܡܪ ܕܠܐ ܡܫܟܚ ܐܢܐ ܕܐܫܒܘܩ ܬܘܠܡܕܐ
ܕܟܪܘܙܘܬܐ ܘܐܗܦܘܟ ܠܙܩܘܪܘܬܐ. ܡܚܝܗܝ ܒܚܘܛܪܐ ܥܠ
ܫܩ̈ܘܗܝ ܘܬܒܪ ܐܢܝܢ ܘܡܝܬ. ܬܕܝ ܗܘܐ ܚܠܦܘܗܝ ܒܐܘܪܗܝ.
ܘܩܛܠܗ ܐܦ ܠܗ ܗܘ ܗܪܘܕܣ ܒܪܗ ܕܐܒܓܪ ܘܐܬܬܩܒܪ ܒܐܘܪܗܝ.

"Addæus was from Paneas, and he preached in Edessa of Mesopotamia in the days of Abgar. But Herodes, the son of Abgar, slew him at the Castle of Agel; and his body was afterwards taken up, and they brought it to Rome. There are some who have said that it was deposited at Edessa. *Aggæus*, his disciple, was formerly a maker of silks for Abgar, and he became converted. And after the death of Abgar, his son reigned in his stead, and he required of Aggæus to weave him silk. And when he did not comply, saying, I cannot give up the teaching of preaching and turn to weaving, he struck him upon the legs with a club and brake them, and he died. *Thaddæus* succeeded him in Edessa, but the same Herodes, the son of Abgar, slew him, and he was buried at Edessa." This is from a MS. in my possession. It is easy to see here that errors have arisen from the confusion of the name of *Addæus*, *Aggæus*, and *Thaddæus;* and that the *Herodes* here is the same as *Severus* in the extract at p. 109. Cedrenus, cited by Assemani *Bibl. Orient.* Vol. I. p. 421, writes: "Huic pio instituto obtemperatum est, quamdiu Abgarus, atque post hunc filius vixerunt. Nepos autem, quum in avi locum et regnum successisset, abjecta pietate, ad simulacrorum cultum descivit: statuitque, sublata Christi imagine, statuam dæmonis reponere." In the account of Constantine Porphyrogenitus, as given by Simeon Metaphrastes, we read, "Itaque conservatum est hoc hujus viri pietatis expressum monumentum et Deo dicatum donarium, donec in hoc vitæ incolatu mansit Abagarus, et ejus filius qui regni simul et pietatis paternæ fuit successor. Cæterum eorum filius et nepos fuit quidem successor paterni et aviti imperii, non fuit autem hæres etiam pietatis. Sed in pietatem calcibus, ut ita dicam, insultavit et ad dæmones et idola transfugit:" Lipomanus, *Sanct. Hist.* Par. I. p. 190. If, therefore, we assume that it was Abgar's grandson, Abgar, son of Maanu, as given by Dionysius, (whose reign of twenty years was extended from A.D. 65 to A.D. 86, see Bayer, *Hist. Osrh.* pp. 130, 147,) who caused Aggæus to be put to death, this would be perfectly consistent with the fact of a copy of the Gospels having been transcribed by Aggæus, A.D. 78, or eight years before the death of this king: see Note, page 158 *above*.

l. 27.—*And brake his legs.* This ignominious mode of execution, which put an end to the sufferings of the two Thieves on the cross, seems to have been of Roman rather than of oriental origin. Seneca *De ira*, B. III. c. 32, writes, "Magnam rem sine dubio fecerimus, si servulum infelicem in ergastulum miserimus. Quid properamus verberare statim, crura protinus frangere?" It was in use in the time of Plautus, "Crura hercle effringentur." Suetonius has "Thallo a manu, quod pro epistola prodita denarios quingentos accepisset, crura fregit." *Octavius*, c. 67. On which passage Casaubon has the following note: "Crurifragium olim servorum et ancillarum pœna erat, meminit iterum Suetonius, Lib. iii. c. 44. Fuit et publicum maleficorum hominum supplicium: ut delatorum sub Commodo. Eusebius Lib. v. δειλαιος παρα καιρον την δικην εισελθων, αυτικα καταγνυνται τα σκελη. Vide etiam Agathiam L. iv. Sed exempla in Martyrologiis, et apud alios etiam scriptores passim." The object of the king in putting this early martyr to this kind of death seems to have been to degrade and disgrace him.

PAGE 23. *l.* 6—13. *And because he died—thirteen years.* This passage is a barefaced interpolation by some ignorant person much later, who evidently is also responsible for the interpolated passages in the Martyrdom of Sharbil, p. 61, and in that of Barsamya p. 72. For this Palut was made *Presbyter* by Addæus himself, when Aggæus was appointed *Bishop*, or *Guide and Ruler*, see p. 18. This took place before the death of Abgar himself, who died A.D. 45, as we have seen above. How then could he have been made Bishop by Serapion of Antioch, who did not succeed to that episcopal throne before the beginning of the third century, if, as is here stated, he was consecrated Bishop by Zephyrinus of Rome, who did not become Pope till A.D. 201? See H. Dodwell, *Diss. Sing. de Pontt. Rom. Primæva Successione*, p. 83.

l. 12.—*In the days of that Cæsar who reigned there thirteen years.* He seems to mean Claudius, although the twenty-five years of Peter's episcopate extended through his reign and that of Nero: the duration of each was about thirteen years: see *Ibid.* p. 77.

l. 17.—*Labubna.* Moses Chor. refers to this author, B. II. c. 36: "Ghéroupna, fils de l'écrivain Apchatar, a recueilli tous ces faits, arrivés du temps d'Abgar et de Sanadroug, et les a déposés dans les archives d'Édesse:" translation of Le Vaillant de Florival. Whiston writes the name "Lerubnas, Apsadari Scribæ filius:" Apsadar, of the one, and Apchatar of the other, are evidently corruptions in the Armenian from Abdshaddai or Ebedshaddai of the Syriac. The variation in the orthography of the names arises simply from the different way in which the first letter may be enunciated. On the interchange of the letter G, L, and R, see St. Martin, *Mémoires Historiques et Geographique sur l'Arménie*, Vol. I. p. 215. Guis. Çappellotti, in his Italian translation of Moses Choren. *Storico Armeno del quinto seçolo*, Venez. 1841, writes the names "Lerubnase figlio de Afsadari." In a letter to me, dated St. Lazare, Venise, 23 Janvier 1863, the learned Dr. Alishan writes thus: "Vous vous rappelerez peutêtre, que notre historien Moïse de Khorène, traduit en plusieurs langues, fait mention d'un ecrivain nommé Ghérubna, qui vivait sous le règne d'Abgar, et qui ecrivit l'histoire de ce même roi ou les événements de cette époque. Or j'ai découvert dans un manuscrit probablement de XIIme. siècle une histoire d'Abgar et de Thaddé dont l'auteur, y est-il-dit, est un certain Ghérubnia, qui l'aura écrit avec l'aide d'Anané, confident du roi Abgar. Je suis porté a croire que c'est la traduction de l'original, que vous avez découvert en langue Syriaque. L'Arménien est complait: et bien que rédigé sous le roi Abgar, il y a eut beaucoup d'interpolations, selon moi, dans cet histoire, tout ou en partie, au commencement du siècle IIIme. Nous pensons aussi a publier cet histoire: en attendant nous serons heureux de vous voir, Monsieur, nous devancer. Il se trouve aussi dans nos Ménologues une biographie ou les Acts de Saints Barsémi et Sabylle, mais en abrégé. Je me réjouis avec vous de la découverte, que vous venez de faire, des ouvrages de St. Jaques de Nisibe, dont nous n'avons pas en Arménien d'exemplaires assez anciens."

PAGE 24.—DOCTRINE OF THE APOSTLES. This work is taken from the same MS. as the preceding, Cod. Add. 14,644, fol. 10, and is printed verbatim from it. It is also found in Cod. Add. 14,531, fol. 109. It has been already printed entire by A. P. de Lagarde in his *Reliquiæ Juris Ecclesiastici Antiquissimæ*, Vienna, 1856, p. ܠܐ It is there attributed to *Addæus*

ܬܘܒ ܡܢ ܡܟܬܒܢܘܬܐ ܕܡܠܦܢܘܬܐ ܕܐܕܝ ܫܠܝܚܐ: ܗܘ ܕܬܠܡܕ
ܘܐܠܦ ܠܐܘܪܗܝܐ ܘܠܟܠܗܘܢ ܗܢܘܢ ܕܒܐܬܪܐ ܕܒܝܬ ܢܗܪܝܢ

"Again from the Treatise of the *Doctrine of Addæus the Apostle*, who taught and instructed the people of Edessa, and all those who were in the region of Mesopotamia." And at the end of it is written, "Here endeth the Treatise of Addæus the Apostle." Dr. Land, in his *Anecdota Syriaca*, p. 19, in the imperfect description which he has given of the MS. 14,644, writes, "F. 10. r. sqq., Doctrina Apostolorum. Edidit de Lagarde e codice Sanctogermanensi 38 bibl. Imp. Paris. Lipsiæ anno 1854." It is plain that Dr. Land could never have compared the two. The book in which he says this treatise is published is altogether another work, was printed at a different place, with different type, and two years earlier: and its title is *Didascalia Apostolorum Syriace, Lipsiæ*, 1854.

It is well known that we owe the publication of the *Didascalia* to De Lagarde; although his name does not appear: indeed, the author in his preface gives the reason for withholding his name. This treatise had also been printed before, omitting the beginning, and commencing with the first Ordinance or Canon, in Syriac, in the 10th volume of the *Scriptorum Veterum Nova Collec.*, by the Cardinal Mai, with a Latin translation by A. Assemani, pp. 3—8; and Text, pp. 169—175. "Ebediesu Metropolitæ Sobæ et Armeniæ Collectio Canonum Synodicorum, ex Chaldaicis Bibliothecæ Vaticanæ codicibus sumpta, et in Linguam Latinam translata ab Aloysio Assemani. Præcedit Epitome Canonum Apostolicorum, auctore eodem Ebediesu." By Ebediesu this work is called ܩܢܘܢܐ ܕܢܡܘܣܐ ܘܬܘܩܢܐ ܕܣܡܘ ܫܠܝܚܐ: "Canones rituum et legum quos constituerunt Apostoli." And at the end ܫܠܡܬ ܣܘܢܗܕܘܣ ܩܕܡܝܬܐ ܕܫܠܝܚܐ "Explicit Synodus I. Apostolorum." It is cited by Bar Hebræus in his "Nomocanon," translated by J. A. Assemani, and printed by Cardinal Mai in the same Vol. X. Par. ii. p. 31, *Didascalia Adæi Apostoli unius e* 70. I also have found it quoted in Cod. Add. 14,173, fol. 37, as ܩܢܘܢܐ ܕܫܠܝܚܐ: "Canons of the Apostles." It was likewise known to Johannes Damascenus: see *Opera*, edit. Le Quien, Vol. I. p. 266. The text of the *Doctrine of the Apostles* I have printed exactly as I found it in 14,644. I have, however, carefully compared it with 14,531, and with that edited by De Lagarde, and made use of this collation in the English translation. Wherever I have had occasion to refer to these texts in the Notes, they are designated A. B. C. respectively.

l. 10.—*The three hundred and.* These words have been omitted in A. I have supplied them from B., which adds ܬܠܬܡܐܐ. C. reads ܫܡܒ or 342. Bar Hebræus, in his *Nomocanon*, has the following reference to this passage, "*Ex Didascalia Adæi Apostoli unius e* 70, Anno 339. Græcorum, die 4 Junii in complemento Pentecostes, cum glorificarent Apostoli Deum in cœnaculo, ubi fecerant Pascha, descendit super eos Spiritus Sanctus, et docuit eos ordines et leges, et ipsi imposuerunt eas illis, qui consenserunt prædicationi ipsorum." In a Note on this J. A. Assemani adds "In margine legitur 'Didascalia Adæi ad Edessanos et reliquos, anno Græcorum 342. die 14. mensis Junii." See Mai, *Scriptt. Vet. Nova Coll.* Vol. X. Par. ii. p. 31.

l. 11.—*Fourth day* ܐܪܒܥܬܐ: B. reads ܐܪܒܥܐ, but C. ܐܪܒܥܣܪܐ "fourteenth."

l. 12.—*Pentecost.* The Ascension of our Lord and the day of Pentecost seem to be confounded here.

l. 15.—*Baith Zaithe,* that is, the Mount of Olives. Luke in his Gospel, xxiv. 50, says that "he led them out as far as Bethany, and he lifted up his hands, and blessed them;" but says nothing about his conferring upon them the gift of the priesthood, as we find here. In the Acts, i. 12, he says after the Ascension, "then returned they unto Jerusalem from the mount called Olivet;" but omits there all mention of our Lord lifting up his hands and blessing them.

l. 24.—*Upper Room.* ὑπερῷον: see Bishop Pearson, *Lectiones in Acta Apostolorum,* pp. 30, 31, and Whiston's, *Essay on the Apostolic Constitutiones,* p. 20.

PAGE 25, *l.* 12.—*When I am ascended to my Father I will send to you the Spirit, the Paraclete, that he may teach you every thing which it is meet for you to know and to make known.* We find this promise, but not in the same words, in St. John xiv. 26, "But the Comforter (ὁ παρακλητος), *which is* the Holy Ghost, whom the Father will send in my name, he shall teach you all things, and bring all things to your remembrance, whatsoever I have said to you."

l. 17.—*A sweet odour, which is strange to the world.* There is no mention of this in the Acts. *Odour* ܪܐܝܚܐ; B. C. reads ܪܣܡܐ *Was diffused* ܦܗܡ, both B. and C. read ܦܐܫ, which seems to be more correct.

l. 19.—*From heaven.* ܡܢ ܫܡܝܐ: B. reads ܡܢ ܫܠܝܐ "suddenly."

l. 20.—*According to the tongue,* &c.: this leaves no doubt whatever as to the meaning which was from the first attached to the gift of tongues by the oriental Christians who used this.

l. 26.—*The Apostles.* Ebediesu adds *holy* all through.

l. 27.—*As the lightning, &c.* *Matt.* xxiv. 27.

l. 30.—*Suddenly.* ܡܢ ܫܠܝܐ. B. C. read ܒܚܪܬܐ "at the last." Ebediesu ܡܢ ܫܡܝܐ "de cœlo." This first Canon is cited by Bar Hebræus, in his *Nomocanon.* "*Adæi.* 1. Constituerunt itaque Apostoli—ad orientem orate—quia ab oriente apparebit Dominus in fine." Card. Mai, *Scriptt. Vet.* Vol X. Par. ii. p. 33; and by Johannes Damascenus. It is also found in Cod. Add. 17,193, fol. 37, with Nos. 2, 3, 4, and 14, where they are called ܩܢܘܢܐ ܕܫܠܝܚܐ "Canons of the Apostles." Respecting "praying towards the East:" compare *Apostolic Constitutions,* B. II. c. 57, VII. c. 44, and Tertullian, *Apol.* c. 16.

Page 26, *l.* 1.—II. Compare this Canon with *Apostolic Constitutions*, B. II. c. 59; compare also for this and the three following Canons, *Compendiaria Fidei Expositio*, cited by Grabe, *Spicilegium*, Vol. I. p. 53.

l. 7.—*Angels of heaven.* C. reads ܡܠܐܟܘܗܝ ܩܕܝܫܐ "His holy angels."

l. 9.—III. Compare *Apostolic Constitutions*, B. V. c. 13—15.

l. 11.—*His trial*, ܢܣܝܢܗ. B. reads ܕܢܚܗ "his manifestation."

l. 13.—*This sorrow.* C. has ܡܛܠ ܗܕܐ ܒܟܪܝܘܬܐ "on account of this in sorrow."

l. 20.—V. See *Apostolic Constitutions*, B. II. c. 25.

l. 23.—*Overseer, the same is the Guide*, ܕܘܩܐ. This does not correspond with the Greek επισκοπος, but with σκοπος, as we find upon comparing the Syriac Didascalia, edit. De Lagarde, p. 13, ܘܐܢܬ ܒܪܢܫܐ ܕܘܩܐ ܗܘ ܝܗܒܬܟ ܠܒܝܬ ܐܝܣܪܝܠ ܕܬܫܡܥ ܡܢ ܦܘܡܝ ܡܠܬܐ which corresponds with the Greek of the Constitutiones Apost., B. II. c. 6. sec. 2. Υιε ανθρωπου, σκοπον δεδωκα σε τῳ οικῳ Ισραηλ, και ακουσῃ εκ στοματος μου λογον: *Ezek.* xxxiii. 7; where in our English version, it is rendered *watchman*, "Lo thou, O son of man, I have set thee a watchman unto the house of Israel."

l. 24.—*The people.* ܥܡܐ. For this B. reads ܥܠܡܐ "world."

l. 25.—*City.* B. reads ܡܫܪܝܬܐ "camp."

l. 26.—*Celebrate.* Ebediesu adds here ܘܥܐܕܐ ܕܒܝܬ ܝܠܕܗ ܕܡܪܢ ܒܥܣܪܝܢ ܘܚܡܫܐ ܒܟܢܘܢ ܩܕܡܝܐ. : "Celebrate diem Nativitatis Domini nostri die 25. Decembris, quia hoc est caput omnium Festorum: et Festum Epiphaniæ die 6. Januarii in supputatione extensa Græcorum." This is evidently an interpolation by a much later hand: for we learn from Dionysius Bar Salibi, a writer of the 12th century, that in antient times these two festivals were kept on the same day, the 6th of January. Quoting Jacob of Edessa, he writes, "Sanctus Eusebius, anno, inquit, 312. Græcorum, qui est annus quadragesimus tertius Augusti, et 33. Herodis, quo tempore missus est in Syriam Cyrinus, Christus natus est. Jacobus Edessenus, quem nos sequimur: anno 309. Græcorum qui est annus 41. Augusti et 31. Herodis: ejusdem autem passio anno 21. Tiberii. . . . . . . S. Ephraem in quodam sermone scribit: 'Die decima (Martii) accidit ejus conceptio, et sexta (Januarii) ejus nativitas:' Jacobus vero Edessenus; Epist. ad Mosem Tur-Abdinensem: Nemo exactè novit diem nativitatis Domini: hoc dumtaxat indubitabile est, eum noctu natum fuisse, ex his quæ scribit Lucas. Et in provinciis quidem orientalibus, et quæ ad septentrionem vergunt, usque ad tempora Arcadii Imperatoris et S. Johannis, die 6. Januarii hoc festum agebant, illudque appellabant festum Nativitatis, hoc est, Epiphaniæ, quemadmodum in S. Theologi Oratione de Nativitate vocabatur." And an anonymous Syriac writer, also cited by Assemani, states: "Mense Januario natus est Dominus, eodem die quo Epiphaniam celebramus, quia veteres uno eodemque die festum Nativitatis et Epiphaniæ peragebant." *Bibl. Orient.* Vol. II. pp. 163, 164.

The following is also a Note of Assemani on this subject, *Ibid*, Vol. III. p. 87: "In Ægypto et reliquis Orientalibus Ecclesiis Festum Nativitatis et Epiphaniæ Domini usque ad tempora S. Johannis Chrysostomi simul celebratum fuit, ut idem Chrysostomus, Homil 72. tom. 5. quæ est *In Natalem Diem Salvatoris Nostri*, testatur, affirmans, quum illam recitasset Orationem, nondum decem elapsos fuisse annos, quum primum dies ille, Nativitatis nimirum, innotuisset Ecclesiæ Orientali."

l. 30.—VII. Compare *Apostolic Constitutions*, B. V. c. 13.

PAGE 27, *l.* 7.—VIII. This is No. X. in Ebediesu. It is cited by Bar Hebræus in his Nomocanon. "*Adæi Apostoli*, 8. In fine omnium librorum Evangelium legatur, tanquam coronis quædam, et populus stans illud audiat." Card. Mai, *Scrip. Vett.*, Vol. X. Par. II. p. 52. Compare *Apost. Constit.*, B. II. c. 57.

l. 12.—IX. This is No. VIII. in Ebediesu. *Fifty days.* C. reads ܐܪ̈ܒܥܝܢ "forty."

l. 15.—X. This is No. IX. in Ebediesu. It is cited on the margin of Cod. Add. 14,609, fol. 123. *Except the Old Testament, &c.* Compare *Doctrine of Simon Cephas*, p. 40; *Apost. Constit.*, B. II. c. 57. Philastrius, hæresi lxxxvii, quotes this with some additions, "Propter quod statutum est ab Apostolis et eorum successoribus, non aliud legi in Ecclesia debere Catholica, nisi Legem, et Prophetas, et Evangelia, et Actus Apostolorum, et Pauli tredecim Epistolas, et septem alias, Petri duas, Johannis tres, Judæ unam, et unam Jacobi, quæ septem Actibus Apostolorum conjunctæ sunt." Cited by Fabricius, *Cod. Apoc. N. T.*, p. 749.

l. 25.—*Or lieth.* ܐܘ ܡܣܬܒܠ. B. C. and Ebediesu read ܘܡܣܬܒܠ "and lieth."

PAGE 28, *l.* 5.—"*Before whom no artifices avail.*" 1 *Sam.* ii. 3, as in the Peshito: our English version has followed the קְרִי, substituting ולו for ולא, "and by him actions are weighed." The Septuagint has και θεος ετοιμαζων επιτηδευματα αυτου.

l. 28.—XVIII. This is cited by Gregory Bar Hebræus in his Nomocanon, translated by J. A. Assemani. "*Adæi.* Constituerunt Apostoli, ut illorum, qui exeunt ex hoc sæculo cum testimonio bono, et tribulationes passi sunt propter nomen Domini nostri, memoriam agatis, in die interfectionis eorum." See Mai, *Scrip. Vett. Nova Coll.* Vol. X. Par. II. p. 36. We find this carried out by the Church of Smyrna, as is testified by their letter respecting the Martyrdom of Polycarp, "The Lord grant we may with joy and gladness celebrate the birth-day of his martyrdom, both in memory of those who have hitherto undergone and been victorious in the glorious conflict, and also for the instruction and preparation of such as shall hereafter be exercised therein :" see Eusebius, *Hist. Eccl.* B. IV. c. 15. *English Trans.* p. 59.

Page 29, *l.* 13.—XXII. Compare this with *Doctrine of Addæus*, p. 15 ; *Apost. Constit.*, B. II. c. 45.

l. 29.—XXV. This is cited by Gregory Bar Hebræus in his Nomocanon. "Adaei. Reges, qui credituri sunt, poterunt ascendere ad altare una cum sacerdotibus, quoniam David quoque, et alii, qui instar ejus, ascendebant :" *Scrip. Vett.*, Vol. X., Part. II. p. 8.

Page 30, *l.* 8.—XXVII. This is also cited by Gregory Bar Hebræus, "*Adæi Apostoli*, 26. Panis oblationis in illa die, qua coquitur, ascendat ad altare, et non post aliquot dies, quod fieri non licet :" *Ibid*, p. 19. This is likewise quoted by Dionysius Bar Salibi in his *Expositio Missæ*, as given by Assemani, without the name of Addæus, but referring it to the Apostles, "Statuerunt Apostoli, sicut in Canone," &c., *Bibl. Orient.* Vol. I. page 183.

l. 19.—*For Paul also and Timothy*, &c. Compare *Acts* xv.

Page 31, *l.* 1.—*Caiphas.* There prevailed a common belief among the Jacobites that Caiphas, whose name was also Joseph (see Tillemont, *Mem. pour servir a l'Hist. Eccl.*, Vol. I. p. 14), was the same person as Josephus the historian, and that he was converted to Christianity : see Assemani, *Bibl. Orient.* Vol. II. p. 165. In the *Bee*, ch. 44, I read ܩܝܦܐ ܕܝܢ ܕܚܝܒ ܠܡܪܢ ܗܘܝܘ ܝܘܣܦܘܣ ܘܫܡܗ ܕܝܢ ܕܒܪܐܒܐ ܝܫܘܥ ܡܬܩܪܐ "But Caiphas, who condemned our Lord, the same is Josephus. And the name of Barabbas was called Jesus."

l. 27 —*Whatsoever they taught the multitudes, they fulfilled the same themselves in deeds before all men.* Compare *Doctrine of Addæus*, "Whatsoever they said to others and exhorted them to do, they themselves exhibited the same in deeds in their own persons," p. 22.

Page 32, *l.* 3.—*After the death of the Apostles there were Guides and Rulers in the church.* It would appear from this passage that this treatise must have been written anterior to the time when the title of Bishop, as especially appropriated to those who succeeded to the apostolic office, had generally obtained in the East.

l. 10.—*Andrew from Phrygia—Thomas from India.* From this it appears that there were Epistles, or other writings, both of Andrew and Thomas, acknowledged at this time in the church in the East. There still exists a writing, Πραξεις και μαρτυριον του αγιου αποστολου Ανδρεου, which was first published by Car. Christ. Woog, with the title "Presbyterum et diaconorum Achaiæ de Martyrio S. Andreæ Apostoli epistola encyclica." *Lipsiæ*, 1749. This has been reprinted with emendations by Const. Tischendorf, in *Acta Apostolorum Apocrypha*, p. 106. It is also given in Latin by Surius, at Novemb. 30. Several learned men have held it to be genuine. See Tillemont, *Mem. p. s. a l'Hist. Ecc.*, Vol. I. p. 589. Tischendorf, *Prolegomena.* The Acts of St. Andrew are twice mentioned by Epiphanius, in connection with those of St. Thomas, *Hæres.* 42, 61: see Fabricius, *Cod. Apoc. N. T.* p. 747. Respecting the Acts of St. Thomas, see p. 141 above. Although, perhaps, interpolated and changed, these Acts, which were then received and read in the Eastern churches, are, doubtless, very antient, and contain some germ of truth. There is no mention here of the Epistles of St. Paul. At this early period they might not have been collected together and become generally known in the East. The Epistle of Jude, likewise, is omitted here, but it was never received into the Syriac Canon: see De Wette, *Einleitung*, 6th edit. p. 342.

l. 14.—*Apostles—the Old Testament and the New.* It is plain that the Epistles were not at that time considered as a part of what was called the *New Testament*, nor the Prophets of the *Old*: see *Note*, p. 157.

Page 33, *l.* 14. — *Pelusium.* ܦܠܘܣܝܢ. B. ܦܠܘܣܝܡ. C. reads ܦܢܛܐܦܘܠܝܣ "Pentapolis." *Indians.* ܗܢܕܘܝܐ. B. reads ܗܢܕܘ. C. ܟܘܫܝܐ, "Ethiopians."

l. 24. — *The church there.* C. adds after this ܘܒܢܐ ܥܕܬܐ ܒܐܢܛܝܘܟܝܐ "and he built a church at Antioch."

l. 28.—*And Britain,* ܒܪܘܛܢܝܐ. B. reads ܒܪܝܛܢܝܐ. C. ܒܪܛܢܝܐ. A. Assemani has wrongly rendered it "Bithynia:" see Card. Mai, *Scrip. Vett. Nova Coll.* Vol. X. p. 7.

Page 34, *l.* 9.—*Gothia.* C. reads ܓܠܛܝܐ ܓܘܝܬܐ "Inner Galatia."

l. 14.—*The great River.* C. reads ܕܢܘܒܝܣ: "the Danube."

l. 17.—*Soba.* This is the same as Nisibis: see Assemani, Diss. de Syris Nest. *Bibl. Orient.* Vol. III. Par. II. p. dcclxviii.

l. 22.—*The Seventy-two Apostles.* See Walchius, *Hist. Eccl.* p. 302, and Tillemont, Note sur les 72 Disciples, *Mem. Hist. Eccl.* Vol. I. p. 436: "Le texte grec de St. Luc ne conte que 70 Disciples; le latin en met 72. L'auteur des Recognitions, qui en met 72, aussibien que celui des Constitutions apostoliques, dit que J. C. les choisit en ce nombre a l'imitation de ceux de Moyse. D'autres anciens disent le mesme chose, ou d'autres equivalents. Baronius cite plusieurs anciens grecs et latins, qu'il dit avoir lu 72. . . . . Mr. Cotelier remarque fort judicieusement que l'usage aura plus aisément fait 70 de 72, que 72 de 70."

l. 24.—*Huzzites.* See, respecting these, Assemani, *Bibl. Orient.* Vol. III. Par. II. p. 419—421.

l. 25.—*Gog and Magog.* See Assemani, *Acta Martt.* Vol. I. p. 36.

l. 27.—*The chainmaker.* See Note, p. 157 *above*.

Page 35, *l.* 9.—*Priscus.* B. reads ܦܪܝܣܩܠܐ: "Priscilla." C. ܦܪܝܣܩܠܐܣ "Priscillas." In 2 *Tim.* iv. 19 the name is written Prisca; but *Acts* xviii. 2, and *Rom.* xvi. 3, Priscilla. Correct here a misprint, and read Aquilas.

l. 11.—*Timothy and Erastus of Lystra.* We find from *Acts* xvi. 1, that Timothy was of Lystra, and at xix. 22 he and Erastus are mentioned together. *Meneas*, C. reads ܡܝܠܝܛܘܣ "Miletus;" but the last three letters are in a more recent hand. It is probably the same as Manaen, whom, *Acts* xiii. 1, we find to be associated with Saul at Antioch. The name is there written in the Peshito *Manael.* Salomon of Bassora, in the *Bee*, mentions one of the Seventy of this name, ܡܢܐܘܣ, *Menaus*: see Assemani, *Bibl. Orient.* Vol. III. p. 319; and the same in a copy in my hands. In a list of the 72 given in Cod. Add. 14,601 fol. 164, the name is ܡܢܐ, *Mena* or Menas.

l. 14.—*The city of Rome.* After this C. adds ܟܕ ܙܩܦܘܗܝ ܥܠ ܙܩܝܦܐ "Crucifying him on the cross." C. also adds ܫܠܡ ܡܟܬܒܢܘܬܐ ܕܐܕܝ ܫܠܝܚܐ "Here endeth the Treatise of Addæus the Apostle."

l. 19.—Doctrine of Simon Cephas. This is found in the same MS. as the preceding, Cod. Add. 14,644, fol. 15, which I denote by A. There is also another copy of it, B., in Cod. Add. 14,609. This MS. B. is written in two columns quarto, and is imperfect, several leaves having been lost in the body of the volume. The Rubric on the first page is ܡܠܦܢܘܬܐ ܕܫܡܥܘܢ ܟܐܦܐ

ܕܟܠ ܓܢܣ : "Table of Treatises of all kinds." It contains an Epistle of John the Monk to Hesychius the Monk; Stories of the Triumphs of Mar Jacob the Bishop; of Mari Abraham, Bishop of Haran. This *Doctrine of Peter*, fol. 16 rect. to 19 rect.; Triumphs of St. Anthony, by Athanasius; Story of Brethren Monks in Egypt, which are separately enumerated, apparently by Palladius; a Letter of Herod to Pilate, and of Pilate to Herod; an Epistle of Cyril of Jerusalem; and the Story of Clement who followed Simon Cephas: which last work has been published by De Lagarde from Cod. Add. 12,150, collated with this, under the title "Clementis Romani Recognitiones Syriace, Lipsiæ, 1861."

l. 19.—*Simon Cephas.* B. reads ܦܛܪܘܣ ܫܠܝܚܐ, "the Apostle Peter."

l. 20.—*In the third year.* The MS. reads ܬܠܬܝܢ: evidently an error. Tillemont says that St. Peter went to Rome in the second year of Claudius: "Il y vint sous l'Empire de Claude, en la deuxieme année de son règne selon quelques anciens, qui est la 42ᵉ de J. C., lorsque ce prince mesme estoit Consul avec C. Cæcina Largus, et en la deuxieme aussi de la 205ᵉ Olympiade. C'estoit environ 25 ans avant sa mort, qui est le temps que l'Eglise Romaine donnait à son episcopat;" *Memm. Hist. Eccl.*, Vol. I. p. 162. Eusebius tells us that he went to Rome under Claudius: *Hist. Eccl.*, B. II. c. 14.

l. 23.—*There*: from this place to "that the light," Page 37, line 12, is lost in A., and the text supplied from B.

l. 25.—*Wore headbands of kings.* If the reading ܦܘܪ̈ܐ is to be retained, it should be rendered "were clad in white:" see Note, p. 156.

PAGE 36, *l.* 21.—*Nor do we write in the book of his Gospel.* No reference to any particular Gospel, perhaps, is intended by these words. St. Peter could hardly have referred to the Gospel of St. Mark, which is said to have been composed under his own direction; nor, indeed, to that of St. Matthew or St. Luke, which do not appear to have been written so early as the third year of Claudius, A.D. 42, still less to the Apocryphal Gospel attributed to him. See Grabe, *Spicilegium*, Vol. I. p. 56; Fabricius, *Cod. Add. N. T.* pp. 374, 375.

l. 26.—*I will send you the Paraclete, that he may teach you that which ye do not know.* These words are similar to *John* xiv. 26, "The Comforter (Paraclete), he shall teach you all things:" see Note on page 25, line 12.

l. 27.—*For it is by his gift, &c.* Compare Peter's speeches in *Acts* iii. and iv.

PAGE 37, *l.* 19.—*Mingled his godhead with our manhood.* ܡܙܓ. The word is much effaced in B., but it seems to be ܡܟܝܟ: "humbled" his Godhead, ܡܛܠ ܐܢܫܘܬܢ "on account of our manhood," which would be, perhaps, a more appropriate reading. Respecting the word ܫܠܛ, which was supposed to countenance the Eutychian Heresy, see Assemani, *Bibl. Orient.* Vol. I. p. 81.

PAGE 38, *l.* 4.—*The Governor Pilate also was witness.* See Note, p. 159 above.

l. 10.—*Dominion.* ܐܘܚܕܢܐ. B. reads ܫܘܠܛܢܐ.

PAGE 39, *l.* 3.—*To perform any thing*: from this place to an "assembly," page 40 line 25, is lost in A.

l. 6.—*The son of one of the chiefs.* This story of Peter's raising a young man to life at Rome is also told by Abdias in his *Historia Apostolica*, de S. Petro, B. 1. c. xvi., where he is called "adolescens nobilis, propinquus Cæsaris:" see Fabricius, *Cod. Apoc. N. T.* p. 431. In the Life of SS. Peter and Paul, attributed to Hegesippus, and printed by Lipomanus, he is also called "adolescens nobilis, propinquus Cæsaris:" see *Sanct. Hist.* Par. I. p. 295. The story of a contest between Simon Cephas and Simon the Sorcerer at Rome, after the former had driven away the latter from Cæsarea, is told, as by St. Peter himself, in the Apostolic Constitutions, but differently from this: see *Apost. Const.*, B. VI. c. 8. It is referred to in a very antient copy of Acts of Eleutherius, Codd. Add. 14,654, fol. 18, in the following terms:
ܘܫܪܝ܂ ܕܢܐܡܪ. ܓܒܪ̈ܐ ܪ̈ܗܘܡܝܐ ܪܒ ܗܘ ܐܠܗܐ ܗ̇ܘ ܕܬܢܢ ܐܟܪܙܘܗ ܦܛܪܘܣ ܘܦܘܠܘܣ ܗ̇ܘ. ܕܒܫܡܗ ܥܒܕܘ ܗܘܘ ܗܪܟܐ ܬܗܪ̈ܬܐ ܘܐܬ̈ܘܬܐ. ܕܠܗ̇ܘ ܪܫܐ ܕܫܐ̈ܕܐ ܫܡܥܘܢ ܚܪܫܐ. ܗ̇ܘ ܕܦܠܚ ܗܘܐ ܠܗܠܝܢ ܛܠܠ̈ܝܬܐ. ܐܝܠܝܢ ܕܡܝܩܪܢܐ ܡܝܩܪ ܗܕܪܝܢܘܣ ܐܝܩܪܗܘ. ܘܝܘܡܢ ܚܙܘ ܘܚܙܘ ܐܝܢܐ ܚܝܠܐ ܡܚܘܐ ܐܠܗܐ ܒܐܝܠܝܢ ܕܡܚܒܝܢ ܠܗ "And he began to speak, Men of Rome, great is that God whom Peter and Paul preached here, in whose name they performed here those miracles and signs which put to shame that chief of devils, Simon the Sorcerer, who served these shadows which Hadrian honours this day. To-day, also, behold and see what power God shews forth in those that love him." These acts at the beginning state that what is there told took place in the 21st year of the reign of Hadrian, when he was returned from the East to Rome, ܕܗܕܪܝܢܘܣ ܡܠܟܐ ܒܫܢܬ ܥܣܪܝܢ ܘܚܕܐ ܕܡܠܟܘܬܗ. ܟܕ ܕܥܒܪ ܡܢ ܡܕܢܚܐ ܠܪܗܘܡܐ.

PAGE 40, *l.* 3.—*Cuprinus.* This should, perhaps, be Cyprianus, a name well known, and which I have seen written in Syriac exactly in the same manner as here, when there could be no doubt of Cyprianus being meant. I find no mention elsewhere of such a person being connected with St. Peter at Rome. Pudens is the name of the Roman, said also to have been a Senator, who is supposed to have received St. Peter in his house: see Baronius, *Annal.* 44, § 61; Tillemont, *Mem. Hist. Ecc.*, Vol. I. p. 163.

l. 11. — *Twenty-five years.* This is the time usually allotted to St. Peter's Episcopate at Rome; although it is certain that he did not constantly reside there during that period. We find him the year after at Jerusalem: see *Ibid*, p. 165.

l. 13.—*Anus.* ܐܢܘܣ, at line 24 on the same page "Isus," ܐܝܣܘܣ, where B. has ܠܐܢܘܣ "*Lainus*;" and so likewise in an extract from this, found on the margin of Cod. Add. 14,609, fol. 123 rect. In the interpolated passage at the end of the Acts of Barsamya p. 71, line 29, we have "Anus," ܐܢܘܣ. The error can be chiefly traced to the scribe having mistaken ܠ for a prefix, instead of a part of the word. The person meant is undoubtedly *Linus.* In the *Bee* we find "Milus," which Assemani says is a mistake for "*Linus*:" see *Bibl. Orient.* Vol. III. pp. 3, 19. In the Apostolic Constitutions, B. VII, c. 46, we read "Of the church of Rome, Linus, the son of Claudia, was the first ordained by Paul, and after Linus' death, the second ordained by me, Peter." In Abdias, Peter is said to have ordained Clement shortly before his death. "Post hæc autem Petrus Romam veniens, in ipsis diebus sibi finem vitæ imminere præsensit. In conventu ergo fratrum positus, apprehensa Clementis manu, repente consurgens in auribus totius Ecclesiæ hæc protulit verba, Audite me fratres . . . . Clementem hunc episcopum vobis ordinabo, &c." De Petro, c. xv. This is, however, taken from the Epistle of Clement to James, as Fabricius observes, see *Cod. Apoc. N. T.*, p. 429; Tertullian also says that Clement was ordained by Peter, *De Præscript*, c. 22; see Bishop Pearson, *De Serie et Succes. Rom. Epis.* dis ii. c. 2, p. 154; and Dodwell, *Diss. Sing. de Rom. Pont.* p. 103. Linus is said, by Sigebertus Gemblacensis, and by an anonymous author of the Life of Nerius, given by Surius and Henschenius, in *Actt. Sanctt.*, to have written an account of the Martyrdom of Peter and Paul. This is consistent with the account given here in the *Doctrine of Peter*, which the Apostolic Constitutions, just cited, seem rather to contradict: see Fabricius, *Cod. Apoc. N. T.* page 775.

l. 17.—*Besides the New Testament and the Old, let there not be read before the people any thing else.* This agrees with the 10th Canon in the *Doctrine of the Apostles*, p. 27, see Note on that above. *Before the people.* In the Canon just referred to, it is said "in the pulpit of the church;" and in the Doctrine of Addæus it is stated "that a large multitude of the people assembled for the reading of the Old Testament and the New." It would seem, therefore, that this inhibition related only to public reading of other writings. The following from Philastrius, *Hæres.* 87, illustrates perhaps what is meant: "Hæresis est etiam quæ Apocrypha, id est secreta dicitur, quæ solum Prophetas et Apostolos accipit, non Scripturas Canonicas, id est, Legem et Prophetas, Vetus scilicet et Novum Testamentum. Et cum volunt solum illa Apocrypha legere studiose, contraria Scripturis Canonicis sentiunt, atque paulatim dogmatizant, contra eos dantes sententias, contra Legem et Prophetas, contraque dispositiones beatissimorum Apostolorum consulta ponentes. Ex quibus sunt maxime Manichæi, Gnostici, Nicolaitæ, Valentiniani, et alii quam plurimi, qui Apocrypha Prophetarum et Apostolorum, *i.e.* Actus separatos habentes, Canonicas legere Scripturas contemnunt. Propter quod statutum est ab Apostolis et eorum successoribus, non aliud legi in Ecclesia debere Catholica, nisi Legem et Prophetas, et Evangelia et Actus Apostolorum et Pauli tredecim Epistolas, et septem alias, Petri duas, Johannis tres, Judæ unam, et unam Jacobi, quæ septem Actibus Apostolorum conjunctæ sunt. Scripturæ autem absconditæ, id est Apocrypha, etsi legi debent morum causa a perfectis, non ab omnibus legi debent, quia non intelligentes multa addiderunt et tulerunt quæ voluerunt hæretici." *Cod. Apoc. N. T.* p. 749.

l. 29.—*The great crowning of the Apostles,* which would mean their martyrdom; but instead of ܟܘܠܠܗܘܢ, B. has ܕܥܡܠܗܘܢ "of their labour;" and on the margin of Cod. Add. 14,609, fol. 123 ܕܥܡܠܘ ܒܣܒܪܬܐ "that they had laboured in the Gospel."

Page 41, *l.* 1.—*It happened that there was a great famine in the city of Rome.* This abrupt termination seems to indicate that there was originally something more which followed. The famine referred to seems to be the same as that mentioned in the interpolated passage at the end of the Acts of Sharbil, p. 61, which doubtless is by the same hand as the interpolation in this place.

l. 6.—Acts of Sharbil.—There are two copies from which these *Acts of Sharbil* have been printed. The one which I have chiefly followed, is found in the same MS. as the preceding Cod. Add. 14,644, fol. 72 vers. The text of this has been printed exactly as it occurs, correcting one or two evident errors by the other MS., and also supplying from it the deficiencies. This is represented by A. in these Notes. The other copy, Cod. Add. 14,645, which also belongs to the collection from Nitria, is some three or four centuries later, and is a large thick quarto volume, written in two columns. It contains various Acts of Martyrdom, and is designated in these Notes as B. I have carefully collated it with A., but have not thought it necessary to notice all the variations. It contains several additional and enlarged passages, which seem to have been interpolated in the interval between the period of the transcription of the two copies. I may remark here, that I have almost invariably found in these Syriac MSS. that the older are the shorter, and that subsequent editors or transcribers felt themselves at liberty to add occasionally or paraphrase the earlier copies which they used. The *Acts of Sharbil* commence, fol. 221, rect. thus: ܥܠ ܣܒܪܐ ܕܐܠܗܐ ܫܪܝܢܢ ܠܡܟܬܒ ܗܘܦܡܢܡܛܐ ܡܓܒܝܬܐ. ܣܗܕܘܬܐ ܩܕܡܝܬܐ: ܕܫܪܒܝܠ ܟܘܡܪܐ ܪܒܐ ܘܕܒܒܝ ܚܬܗ ܕܣܗܕܘ ܒܐܘܪܗܝ، ܡܕܝܢܬܐ ܡܒܪܟܬܐ: "In the hope of God we begin to transcribe Select Martyrdoms. Martyrdom the First, of Sharbil the High Priest, and of Babai, his sister, who suffered martyrdom in the blessed city of Edessa." In the *Martyrologium Romanum*, Januar. 29. the following short notice is given: "Edessæ in Syria Sanctorum Martyrum Sarbelii et Barbeæ Sororis ejus, qui a Beato Barsimæo Episcopo baptizati, in persecutione Trajani sub Lysia Præside coronati sunt." And in the *Menologium Græcum*, on the 15th of September: "Sarbelius, idolorum sacerdos, unacum Sorore Barbæa conversus est ad fidem Christi per Barsimæum Edessæ Episcopum, et ambo tenti; post gravissima tormenta Sarbelius inter duo ligna sectus est; soror autem capite truncata." Assemani, *Bilb. Orient.* Vol. I. p. 331; see also the Bollandists at January 29.

Acts: the Greek word Υπομνηματα is retained here. From this and the occurrence of other Greek words it seems plain that these Acts were originally written in that language. The Greek Υπομνηματα corresponds with the Latin *Acta.* They were taken down by notaries called in Greek ταχυγραφοι: see Grabe, *Spicilegium*, Vol. I. p. 319, and in Latin *Exceptores.* They were then arranged in proper order by persons called Υπομνηματογραφοι, and by the Latins *Ab actis*, from notes taken down by the Exceptores, or Notarii: see below, p. 71. Valesius, in his notes to Eusebius, *Hist. Ecc.* B. I. c. 9. n. b. writes, "Acts were Books wherein the Scribes that belonged to the several places of judicature recorded the sentences pronounced by the Judges. See Calvin's Lex.

Jurid., the word Acta." And again, on B. VII. c. xi. n. d., "For the Greeks use Υπομνηματα in the same sense as the Latins use their word *Acta.* Those which wrote these, the Υπομνηματογραφοι, the Latins call *Ab actis.*" Bishop Pearson writes thus: "Ut enim actus Senatus et acta diurna Populi Romani conficiebantur; sic et in Provinciis Romanis idem a Presidibus et Cæsarum Procuratoribus factum est; qui ad Imperatores sæpissime de rebus alicujus momenti Epistolas scripserunt, ut passim observare est in historiis Romanis. *Lect. in Act. Apost.* p. 50. See the account of the writing of the Acts of Barsamya, p. 61, and of Habib, p. 84; and *Notes* thereon: see also Baronius, *ad Ann.* 238; Victor Le Clerc, *Des Journaux chez les Romains.* Thilo. *Cod. Apoc. N. T.* p. 489.

l. 9.—*The fifteenth year of the Emperor Trajan*; that is, A.D. 112. But A.G. commences 311, or 312 before Christ; and therefore A.G. 416 would answer to A.D. 105. There is, therefore, apparently some error in the dates.

l. 10.—*King Abgar the Seventh.* This should be the King who was reigning in the 15th year of Trajan, that is, Maanu Bar Ajazath, who was the seventh King of Edessa after Abgar Uchama: see Bayer, *Hist. Osrh.* p. 149, and Assemani, *Bibl. Orient.* Vol. I. p. 422.

l. 12.—*The high-priesthood of Sharbil and Barsamya.* Hence it would appear that Christianity and Paganism were both tolerated together in Edessa at this time, and equal honour attributed to the head of each religious party, agreeably to what is stated in the *Doctrine of Addæus*, p. 14, "Neither did King Abgar compel any man by force to believe in Christ."

l. 21.—*The great altar.* This we see was not overthrown when the other altars to Bel and Nebu were thrown down in Abgar's time: see *Ibid.*

l. 22.—*Office of records,* ܒܝܬ ܟܬܒܐ. This, perhaps, is the same as ܒܝܬ ܐܪܟܐ at p. 2.

l. 24.—*Their companions.* See, respecting these, Bayer, *Hist. Osrh.* p. 139, and *Note*, p. 156.

l. 25.—*And libations.* B. adds "before the god Jupiter;" ܩܕܡ ܙܘܣ ܐܠܗܐ.

l. 27.—*Sharbil.* The etymology of this word, as given by Dr. Land in his *Anecdota Syriacá*, p. 20, is unquestionably erroneous. He writes, "ܫܪܒܝܠ est 'progenies Dei;' contrahitur e ܫܪܒ (cæteroquin adhiberi solet forma fem. ܫܪܒܬܐ, sed vide Ewaldum in Gramm. Hebr. edit. VI. p. 326 init.) et ܐܠ, cum vocali copulente." The last syllable is ܒܠ, Bel, the same as we find used in Hebrew, in the compound of proper names, for Baal, whose

High Priest Sharbil was. The compounds in ܐܝܠ. Hebrew אֵל, refer to the God of the Israelites, the true God, and not to the Chaldæans, worshippers of Baal. The analogy, therefore, of ܐܟܒܝܠ and جبريل is not applicable. He might have found an analogy in ܒܥܐܒܝܠ; see Assemani, *Bibl. Orient.* Vol. II. page 222.

Page 42, *l.* 2.—*Abgar the King, son of the gods.* The Kings of Edessa, like other oriental sovereigns, seem to have arrogated to themselves this title. We find Sapor, King of Persia, in the Acts of Sapor and Isaac putting this question, ܠܐ ܝܕܥܬܘܢ ܕܡܢ ܙܪܥܐ ܐܢܐ ܕܐܠܗ̈ܐ: "Know ye not that I am of the seed of the gods?" see Assemani, *Act. Mart.* Vol. I. page 227.

l. 25.—*Which supply you.* B. adds here ܘܒܟܠܗܝܢ ܗܠܝܢ ܛܥܝܬ ܠܐܠܗܐ ܥܒܘܕܐ ܕܒܢ̈ܝܢܫܐ ܟܠܗܘܢ. ܘܡܛܠ ܢܓܝܪܘܬ ܪܘܚܗ ܗܘܐ ܡܬܥܠܝܬ ܥܠ ܡܪܚܡܢܘܬܗ. ܘܠܐ ܨܒܝܬ ܕܬܬܦܢܐ ܠܘܬܗ. ܐܝܟ ܕܢܬܦܢܐ ܗܘ ܠܘܬܟ. ܘܢܦܪܩܟ ܡܢ ܛܥܝܘܬܐ ܗܕܐ ܕܩܐܡ ܐܢܬ ܒܗ. "And in all these things thou hast forgotten God, the maker of all men, and because of his long-suffering hast exalted thyself against his mercy, and hast not been willing to turn to him, so that he might turn to thee and deliver thee from this error, in which thou standest."

l. 29.—*And was stretched out,* ܐܬܦܫܛ. B. ܘܐܬܦܫܛܬ.

Page 43, *l.* 11.—*King Abgar also, who was older than this Abgar, that worshippeth Idols as well as thou, he also believed in the King Christ, the Son of him whom thou callest the Lord of all Gods.* Instead of this, B. reads, ܐܒܓܪ ܡܠܟܐ: ܐܒܐ ܕܐܒܘܗܝ ܕܗܢܐ ܐܒܓܪ ܡܠܟܐ. ܕܗܐ ܥܕܡܐ ܠܝܘܡܢܐ ܦܠܚ ܠܦܬܟܖ̈ܐ ܡܝ̈ܬܐ. ܗܘ ܐܝܟܘܬܟ. ܡܘܕܐ ܗܘܐ ܣܓܝܐܐ ܒܡܫܝܚܐ ܒܪܗ ܕܐܠܗܐ. ܗܘ ܕܩܪܝܬ ܠܗ ܡܪܐ ܕܟܠܗܘܢ ܐܠܗ̈ܐ. "King Abgar, father of the father of this King Abgar, who to this day worshippeth dead idols as well as thou, he abundantly confessed in Christ, the Son of that God whom thou callest the Lord of all Gods." In the Peshito of the New Testament, where the Greek has Ζευς, we find ܡܪܐ ܐܠܗ̈ܐ. *Acts*, xiv. 12.

l. 16.—*Idols made by men.* B has ܠܥܒܕ ܐܝ̈ܕܝܐ ܕܒܢ̈ܝܢܫܐ: "the work of men's hands."

l. 21.—*Persuaded with thee—remedy for me.* B. has this passage as follows: I omit the text, and give only the translation; "But if thou wilt not be persuaded by me, thy blood is upon thine own head, and I am clear of thy death. Sharbil answered and said to Barsamya, I did not know that the Christians teach according to what thou hast now spoken before me, because I am a High-Priest, the son of high priests, and I did not know that Jesus Christ, whom ye worship, is God and the Son of God, but I supposed that he was an ordinary man. Neither, again, did I know that he was crucified of his own free will, for I supposed that the Jews crucified him by force of themselves. But now having learned that he himself, of his own free will, gave himself up to be crucified for the salvation of man, although these words, which thou hast spoken to me, be very acceptable to me, still am I lost from all these things which I have heard from thee and for me there is no more any remedy."

l. 30.—*And when Barsamya, the Bishop, heard these things.* B. adds, "from Sharbil, his tears flowed and he wept."

PAGE 44, *l.* 22.—*The seal of salvation.* See Abdias, *Apost. Hist.*, de St. Thoma, where it is called "signum salutis," in Græco est σφραγις: see Fabricius, *Cod. Apoc. N. T.* pp. 537, 700, 701, 822. B. adds, "of baptism, baptizing him."

l. 26.—*Of the Christians.* B. adds here, "and he sat and listened to the Scriptures of the church, and the testimonies which are spoken in them, touching the birth, and the passion, and the resurrection, and the ascension of Christ, and when he saw those that came down to him."

PAGE 45, *l.* 8.—*Lysinias, the Judge of the country.* In B., in a passage added below, he is styled ܠܘܣܝܢܐ "Lysinas," and in the Martyrdom of Barsamya p. 63 ܠܘܣܝܢܘܣ; "Lysinus or Lusinus." In the Martyrologium Romanum he is called "Lysias præses:" see Assemani, *Bibl. Orient.* Vol. I. p. 331. Tillemont supposes him to be the same person as Lusius Quietus: "Nous aurons une preuve plus formelle que le persecution de Trajan a continué jusqu' à la fin du regne de ce Prince, si nous recevons, ce que on dit de la confession de S. Barsimée Evesque d'Edesse, honoré le 30. de Janvier, et de S. Sarbele honoré avec sainte Barbée ou Babée sa sœur le 29. du mesme mois. Car on met tout cela sous Trajan, et sous Lysias son Lieutenant. Ainsi ce ne peut estre qu'en l'an 116. auquel Lusius Quietus prit et brula la ville d'Edesse, un an avant la mort de Trajan." *Hist. des Emper.* Vol. II. p. 238. Bayer adopted the same view. 'Res igitur in Ægypto et Cypro gessit Lusius A. C. 117, quo anno, decima die Augusti Trajanus decessit, et anno ante Edessa gravem sensit iracundiam victoris. Videtur autem Lusius is esse, quem Menologium Basilii Porphyrogennetæ vocavit Λυσιαν ηγεμονα, sub quo Barsimæus Episcopus Edessæ et Sarbelus, ejus quoque soror Babaea passi sunt martyrium:" see *Hist. Osrh.* p. 154. The time, however, does not agree. This martyrdom took place, at the latest, in the 15th year of Trajan, but the capture of Edessa under Lusius Quietus was four years later, in the 19th of Trajan. *Had heard.* B. adds here. "from the Sharirs of the city."

l. 9.—*Sharbil had done this.* B. adds here, "He wrote a letter and made known to the chief Præfect; and he sent to the city where the Emperor was staying, and informed him of the matter of Sharbil, the Chief Priest, who was become Christian; and inquired what he should do with him, for he feared to scourge and tear him, if he were to refuse to sacrifice according to his former custom, being in dread of this, because it had been ordered by the Emperors that the High Priests, who ministered to the gods should be duly honoured by the Judges of the countries. The Præfect then wrote to Lysinas, the Judge of the country, As it hath been ordered by the Emperors, so do to every one who will not sacrifice to the gods. And when Lysinas, the Judge of the country, received this command." *By night.* B. adds, "the Sharirs of the city."

Page 47, *l.* 5.—*With thongs.* The Syriac is ܒܠܘܪܝܣ, which is a foreign word. I suspect it to be the Latin *Loris*, which the Syriac translator, not understanding, or not knowing the exact equivalent, might have written ܒܠܘܪܝܣ, and a subsequent transcriber, have changed it into ܒܠܘܪܝܣ. It seems plain that the still later copyist to whom the text B. is due, did not know what it meant; and therefore omitted the word altogether, substituting "Sharbil" in its place.

l. 13.—*The Judge.* B. reads here ܗܓܡܘܢܐ "Governor," and so generally in the corresponding places below.

l. 14.—*Know.* B. ܬܦܪܘܫ: "discern."

Page 48, *l.* 4.—*Officials.* The Latin word retained. The Greek word was ταξις, used below, p. 77. These were the officers that attended upon the Presidents and chief Magistrates: "Officii nomine designantur publici ministri, qui Proconsulibus, Præsidibus et Magistratibus in publicis muniis inserviebant; hinc Officiales. De his quoque erudite disserit Baronius in notis ad diem 27 Mai": see Ruinart, *Acta Martyr.* p. 384.

l. 15.—*Hang him up and tear his sides with combs.* Compare Acta SS.

Saturnini et Dativi. "Statimque jubetur Officium eundem in equuleum sublevare, extensumque ungulis præcidi. Sed cum carnifices jussa crudelia atroci velocitate complerent, starentque sævientes in dictis, et denudatis ad vulnera martyris lateribus, erectis ungulis imminerent, &c." *Acta Martyr. Ibid.*

l. 26.—*The executioners.* ܩܘܐܣܛܝܘܢܪܐ: "Quæstionarii." See Ruinart, *Ibid*, p. 167, and Note p. 168: "Quæstionarii dicti sunt carnifices, qui reos cruciabant ut veritatem ab eis extorquerent. Vide append. Cod. Theodos. Const. 3. Aliquando etiam isti a Græcis dicti sunt χουεστιοναριοι, ut notat eruditiss. Canguius in Glossar. Latino." At pp. 242, 244 *Ibid.* they are called δημιοι.

Page 49, *l.* 26. —*Gods which made not—under the heavens. Jer.* x. 11. We find the same words in the mouth of Charitne the Martyr, about A.D. 290, "Dii, qui cœlum et terram non fecerunt, pereant:" see Surius, *October* 5, p. 85.

Page 50, *l.* 2.—*The stench of the burning.* The same thing is told of the martyr Attalus in the Epistle of the Church of Lyons. Eusebius, Hist. Ecc. B. V. c. 1: "But Attalus, when he was set in the iron chair and scorched all over, when the savour of his burnt flesh ascended from his body, said to the multitude in the Roman tongue." *English Trans.* p. 73. The *iron chair* mentioned here is the τηγανον.

Page 51, *l.* 12.—*Denounced against those.* The passage from this place to "in the eyes," page 55, line 8, is lost in A. and supplied from B.

l. 15.—*Vinegar and Salt.* Sometimes vinegar and salt were put up the nostrils of the martyrs: see Martyrdom of Tarachus, Ruinart, *Acta Mart.* page 429.

Page 52, *l.* 2.—*Like one that dealeth in fables.* I am by no means sure that this is the meaning of ܦܒܘܠܪܐ, which is a foreign word; or that "Fabularius" be the Latin word intended: it may be a Greek form, though apparently corrupted.

l. 7.—*The glorious architect of the creation.* We find a similar expression to this in Mar Jacob's Sermon on the Fall of Idols.

Page 53, *l.* 17.—*Small and round pieces of wood.* These seem to be the Obelisci. The Martyr Minias, about A.D. 240, had the same torture inflicted on him, "sed deposito de eculeo, ligneisque verubus præacutis sub ungues ejus infixis, omnes digitos ejus præcepit pertundi:" see Surius, *Sanctt. Vit.*, October 25, p. 384.

Page 54, *l.* 9.—This passage inclosed in brackets thus [ ], has been torn out in A., and is supplied from B., and so likewise in the following passages.

l. 24. *Gridiron.* ܛܪܛܠܐ. This seems to be a corruption from the Latin *Craticula* ܩܪܛܠܐ; see Eusebius, B. V. c. 1, where the Greek is τηγανον. On this Valesius has the following note, "τηγανον is the Greek term; which Rufinus translates *craticulam, i.e.* a gridiron. It is the same, which before is called the *iron chair*, on the which the martyrs, being set, were broiled, as it were on a gridiron:" see *English Trans.* p. 73.

Page 58, *l.* 16.—*His bowels were near being seen.* Compare the Epistle of the Smyrnæans touching the Martyrdom of Polycarp, *οι μαστιξι μεν καταξανθεντες, ωστε μεχρι των εσω φλεβων και αρτηριων την της σαρκος οικονομιαν θεωρεισθαι υπεμειναν*: see *Patres Apost. Jacobson, Edit.* IV. p. 608.

l. 30.—*The curtain.* ܘܠܐ, Latin "velum" or "vela." We find this Latin word also retained in Greek, *βηλον*, in the Martyrdom of Euplus, published by J. B. Cotelerius in *Eccles. Græc. Monumenta*, Vol. I. p. 192, *εν σικρεταριῳ προ βηλου.* The note of Cotelerius thereon, *Ibid.* p. 752, will illustrate the passage before us: "Assentior viris doctis, qui secretaria judicum interpretantur tribunalia, conclavia, loca in quibus jus reddebant, et reorum causas expendebant. . . . . Glossæ Nomicæ Σεκρετον· δικαστηριον. Rationem nominis reddit S. Augustinus libro de ovibus, cap. 3. *Ultimam* inquit *sententiam, quam dictaturus est judex, in tabella descripturus manu sua, ultra quam sententiam nihil jam judicaturus est, partes non audiunt. Illis foras exeuntibus scribitur: attonitæ sunt ambæ partes atque suspensæ, contra quam vel pro qua sententia illius procedat. Magnum secretum judicis; unde secretarium nominatur.*" See also Ruinart, *Acta Martyr.* p. 407: "Calvisianus intra velum interius ingrediens, sententiam dictavit. Et foras egressus afferens tabellam, legit: Euplium Christianum, edicta Principum contemnentem, deos blasphemantem, nec resipiscentem, gladio animadverti jubeo. Ducite eum." See more instances in Thilo, *Codex Apoc. N. T.* p. 576: see also Note p. 268, *Ibid.* and Baronius, ad ann. 285, sec. 9.

Page 59, *l.* 1.—*The sentence.* ܐܦܘܦܣܣ, this is the Greek *αποφασις*. Compare Trajan's sentence on Ignatius in the Martyrdom of Ignatius, c. 2. *Patres Apost. Jacobson, edit.* IV. p. 580.

l. 14.—*A strap to be cast into the mouth.* Compare *χαλινον εμβαλειν*, in the Life of Euthymus in *Eccl. Græc. Monumenta*, Vol. II. p. 240, and Cotelerius' note thereon, *Ibid*, p. 623: "Immittebantur in ora reorum et servorum cami, funes, frena. Morem firmabo aliquot testimoniis, &c." See also the sentence against Habib, p. 82.

PAGE 60, *l.* 1.—*They gave him wine to drink.* Compare the Acts of Fructuosus: "Cumque multi ex fraterna caritate eis offerent, uti conditi permixti poculum sumerent, ait, &c." Ruinart, *Acta Martyr.* p. 220.

l. 29.—*A saw of iron.* See Suetonius, *Calig.* c. 27, "serra dissecuit," and notes thereon, *Edit. Varior. Lond.* 1826, p. 1555.

PAGE 61, *l.* 11. — *Young men.* ܥܠܝܡܐ, B. reads ܥܠܡܝܐ "laics."

l. 16. —*Notaries.* ܐܟܣܩܦܛܘܪܣ. This is the Latin word "Exceptores." They were also called Notarii: thus we read in the Acts of Genesius the Martyr: "Accidit autem ut eodem ante tribunal Judicis *Exceptoris* munus implente, impia atque sacrilega mandatæ persecutionis jussa legerentur: quæ cum devotus Deo repudiaret auditus, et imprimere ceris manus sancta respuerat &c." see Ruinart, *Acta Martyr.* p. 539: and in the Acts of Pionius, "Post hæc Polemon, cum ceræ Notarius, quæ respondebantur, imprimeret, ait ad Pionium: Quis vocaris? &c." *Ibid.* page 144.

l. 17.—*Where the charters of the Kings are placed.* After this the following passage is found in B.: "And that which was spoken by the Judge, those who stood in the Judge's presence wrote down; but all the rest, which took place outside the tribunal, the Sharirs of the city wrote down, and they went in and made it known to the judge, and he, according as he heard from them, gave orders in the legal manner, agreeably to the custom of the ordinances and laws of old. Thus these Acts were written, and deposited in the chamber of antient records. But there are fifty-two questions which the Judge asked Sharbil; and then they gave against him the bitter sentence of death, which is widely apart from the laws of the Romans, and from the sentence of their edicts. But this transaction of the Confession of Sharbil took place in the first consulate of Commodus and Cerealis."

l. 18.—*But this Barsamya.* The passage commencing thus to the end is evidently an addition by a later person not well acquainted with chronology; for it is stated at the beginning of these Acts, that what is here recorded took place in the 15th year of the reign of Trajan or A.D. 112; but Fabianus was not made Bishop of Rome before the reign of Maximinus Thrax, about the year 236; see Dodwell, *Diss. Sing. de Rom. Pontif.* page. 84.

l. 19.—*Binus.* ܒܝܢܘܣ: B. ܦܒܝܢܘܣ, "Fabianus," and so at p. 62 line 14. The introduction of this passage probably arose from the fact of Fabianus having instituted Notaries for the express purpose of searching for and collecting the Acts of Martyrs, as we learn from a letter of his own cited by Bishop Pearson: "Denique septem similiter Subdiaconos ordinavimus, qui septem Notariis imminerent, et gesta Martyrum veraciter in integro colligerent, nobisque rimanda manifestarent;" see *De Succ. prim. Romæ Episc.* p. 20.

PAGE 63, *l.* 3.—MARTYRDOM OF BARSAMYA. This also is taken from the same MS. as that in which the later copy of the Acts of Sharbil is found, Cod. Add. 14,645, fol. 233, vers. It is called ܣܗܕܘܬܐ: "Martyrdom" on the title, but in the work itself, p. 71, it is called ὑπομνήματα. See *Martyrolog. Rom.* Jan. 25. There is also an Armenian version or extract from this still in existence: see Dr. Alishan's letter cited p. 166 *above.*

l. 8.—*In the consulship of Commodus and Cyrillus.* Cyrillus is evidently a mistake for Cerealis; and this must be the consulate of Commodus Verus and Tutilius Cerealis, which was in the 9th year of Trajan, A.D. 106: see Clinton, *Fasti Romani*, 92. This agrees nearly enough with the year of the Greeks 416, or A.D. 105, but does not correspond with the 15th year of Trajan, which falls A.D. 112: see Tillemont, *Hist. des Emp.*, Vol. II. pp. 193. 202; Clinton, *Ibid.* p. 96.

l. 9.—*Lysinas.* In the Acts of Sharbil, p. 45, called Lysanias: see Note, page 181, *above.*

l. 23.—*Nebo.* At page 45 this name is given Labu.

PAGE 67, *l.* 5.—*The Christians to whom thou art gone, &c.* See Acts of Sharbil, p. 45.

PAGE 69, *l.* 26.—*Alusis* [Lusius]. This seems to be Lusius Quietus, Trajan's general in the East at this time: see Tillemont, *Hist. des Emp.*, Vol. II. page 199.

PAGE 70, *l.* 6.—We have here probably the most authentic copy of the Edict of Trajan, respecting the stopping of the persecution of the Christians. Tertullian, in speaking of this persecution, refers to the letter of Pliny to Trajan, and to the Emperor's reply to him, but not to the edict itself: see *Apologeticum*, c. ii. It is to the same, also, that Eusebius refers, *Ecc. Hist.* B. III. c. 33. But in these Acts we have, as it would appear, the words of the Edict itself, as they were taken down by the notaries at the time. Those who wish to refer more fully to this matter may read Lardner's *Credibility*, and Tillemont, *Mem. pour servir a l'Hist. Ecc.* Vol. II. page 174 seq.

l. 8.—*Sharirs.* This word, which occurs many times in the course of this volume, does not seem always to represent officers discharging the same functions. It is not apparent what was the Latin title of these officers. Pliny, from whom Trajan received the information to which this edict refers, and whose words even are cited, was ηγουμενος της επαρχιας, according to Eusebius. The etymology of the word *Sharir* is nearest to the Latin *Corrector*, which title the governors of some countries had. Thus we find Calvisianus Consularis, in the Greek *Corrector*, was the governor or judge before whom the martyr Euplius was tried; see Ruinart, *Acta Mart.* Note II. p. 406.

PAGE 71, *l.* 11.—*Notaries.* ܐܟܣܩܦܛܘܪܣ; the Latin "Exceptores:" see Note p. 185, above.

l. 12.—*Euterpes.* ܐܘܛܪܦܣ. This may perhaps be "Eutropius."

l. 15.—*But this Barsamya.* From this place to the end is a much later addition, evidently made by the same ignorant person as that at p. 61 above: see *Note* thereon.

l. 26.—*Dapius* [Pius]. This blunder evidently arose from supposing the prefix ܕ to be a part of the name.

PAGE 72, *l.* 3.—*The nineteenth year of the reign of Tiberius Cæsar in the consulate of Rufus and Rubelinus.* There seems to be a mistake here in reading ܬܫܥܣܪܝܬܐ, "nineteenth," for ܫܬܬܥܣܪܝܬܐ, "sixteenth," which agrees with what is stated by Julius Africanus, who assigns the death of our Lord to the sixteenth year of Tiberius: see Routh, *Reliq. Sacr.* Vol. II. p. 187. It also accords with the year of the Consulate of Rubellius Geminus, and Fufius Geminus, and with the year 341 of the Greeks, A.D. 29 or 30: see Clinton, *Fasti Romani*, p. 10. *Rufus and Rubelinus.* These names are given by Tacitus, *Ann.* V. 1. "Rubellio et Fufio Consulibus, quorum utrique Geminus cognomen erat." Tertullian, *Adversus Judæos*, cap. 8, writes, "Passio perfecta est sub Tiberio Cæsare, consulibus Rubellio Gemino et Rufio Gemino (Junius and Rigaltius from the *Fasti Cons.* read "Fufio Gemino"), mense Martio, temporibus Paschæ, die viii. Calendarum Aprilium." Augustine, *De Civitate Dei*, XVIII. 58. "Mortuus est ergo Christus duobus Geminis Consulibus, octavo Cal. April." See further, respecting these Consuls, Thilo, *Cod. Apoc. N. T.* p. 497.

l. 7.—*Register.* ܐܠܝܛܪܝܢ: the Greek Εληταριον: see Du Fresne, *Glossarium.*

l. 14.—MARTYRDOM OF HABIB THE DEACON. This is found in the same MS. as the preceding, Cod. Add. 14,645, fol. 238, vers. There is an account of the Acts of Habib, evidently taken from these, by Simeon Metaphrastes subjoined to the Acts of Shamuna and Guria, given in Latin by Surius at Nov. 15, p. 339, which I have reprinted in this volume, p. 113. Surius also gives another account, p. 345, "De Sanctis Christi Martyribus Samona, Guria, et Abibo, Arethæ Archiepiscopi Cæsariensis Oratio;" see also the Bollandists at Nov. 15.

l. 16.—*The consulate of Licinius and Constantine.* They were consuls together A.D. 312, 313, 315: see Clinton's *Fasti Romani*, pp. 360, 364, 368. Baronius puts the martyrdom of Habib in the year A.D. 316.

l. 18.—*In the rule of Julius and Barak.* ܒܐܣܛܪܛܓܘܬܐ, that is, while they were Στρατηγοι, *Magistrates;* or *Duumviri*, as Valesius renders it. "Στρατηγος is the word in the original, which the Latins called *Magistratus* or *Duumviri.* It is taken in this sense throughout the whole *Title Cod. Theodos de Decurionibus*, Et in *Optatus, Lib.* I. &c., in which places, and in many others, *Magistratus* and *Duumviri* are promiscuously used." See Valesius' Notes on Eusebius, *Hist. Eccl.* B. VIII. c. 11. *English Trans.*, p. 146. *Cona, Bishop of Edessa.* He is called Cognatus erroneously by Metaphrastes, see p. 113. This same Cona laid the foundation of the Church at Edessa, in the year of the Greeks, 624, or A.D. 313: see Chronicon Edess. in Assemani, *Bibl. Orient.* Vol. I. p. 394.

l. 9.—*Licinius made a persecution.* See, respecting this, Steph. Evod. Assemani, *Act. Mart.* Vol. II. p. 214.

l. 28. — *Telzeha.* This is called by Metaphrastes "Thelsæa." See page 122.

Page 74, *l.* 13.—*Theotecna*, or, in Latin, Theotecnus. There was a person of this name, Curator of Antioch, who urged on the persecution against the Christians: see Eusebius, *Hist. Eccl.* B. IX. c. 2, 3, 4, and Martyrdom of Theodotus in Ruinart, *Acta Mart.* p. 338. He was afterwards put to death by order of Licinius: see Eusebius, *Hist. Eccl.* B. IX. c. 11. The person here spoken of, although cotemporary, and of the same name, seems to have thought and acted very differently.

Page 77, *l.* 15.—*Ruler.* ܐܪܟܘܢ, Greek, αρχων.

l. 29.—*The band.* ܛܟܣܐ, Greek, ταξις, which is the same as the Latin word Officium: see Pancirolus, *Notitia Dignitatum.*

l. 30.—*And he began to interrogate him thus, and said to him, What is thy name.* This seems to have been generally the first question put by the judges to those accused of being Christians: see Martyrdom of Lucianus and Marcianus, A.D. 200. "Proconsul Sabinus dixit ad Lucianum: Quis diceris? Respondit: *Lucianus* . . . . Dixit ad Marcianum: Quis vocaris? Respondit:

Marcianus;" Ruinart, *Acta Mart.* p. 167. See also Acta Tarachi, Probi, et Andronici, circa A.D. 304: *Ibid*, p. 423, &c.

PAGE 83, *l.* 2. — *The cemetery which was built for Abshelama, Abgar's son.* Probably that in which Sharbil and Babai were buried; see p. 61 *above.* There was a church built at Edessa in honour of the martyrs Shamuna, Guria, and Habib in the 4th century: see Assemani, *Acta Mart.* Vol. I. p. 226.

PAGE 84, *l.* 3. — *The hill called Baith Allah Cucla.* In Simeon Metaphrastes this is written *Bethelabicla*, and is said to lie on the north side of the city: see p. 121. The copy which he followed would seem to have read ܒܟܠܐ for ܟܘܟܠܐ.

l. 19.—*The notaries.* ܐܟܣܩܦܛܘܪ̈ܘܗܝ: the Latin "Exceptores," called in Greek ταχυγραφοι: see Grabe, *Spicilegium*, Vol. I. p. 219; and *Note*, page 185.

l. 25.—*As I had also formerly written of Shamuna and Guria.* It seems probable that the account of these martyrs by this same Theophilus formed the basis of the history of their martrydom given by Simeon Metaphrastes, for the comparison of these Acts of Habib by Theophilus with the narrative of this martyr by Simeon Metaphrastes, shows that he made use of them: see p. 113.

PAGE 85, *l.* 6.—*Domitianus.* We might, perhaps, have suspected that the reading here should be *Diocletian.* We know, however, that Nero and Domitian were the first persecutors of the Christians, from Melito, in Routh's *Reliq. Sac.* Vol. I. pp. 111, 124, as well as from Tertullian, Lactantius, and Eusebius. See, respecting the persecution under Domitian, Tillemont, *Mem. Hist. Eccl.* Vol. II. p. 117.

PAGE 86, *l.* 1.—ORATION ON HABIB THE MARTYR, COMPOSED BY MAR JACOB. The MS. from which this is taken is Cod. Add. 17,158, fol. 30, vers. Mar Jacob, Bishop of Sarug, or Batnæ, was one of the most learned and celebrated among all the Syriac writers. He was born A.D. 452, made Bishop of Sarug A.D. 519, and died A.D. 521. He was the author of several Liturgical works, Epistles, and Sermons, and, amongst these, of numerous Metrical Homilies, of which the two printed here will serve as specimens. Assemani enumerates no less than 231 of such Homilies, and, amongst them, one on Habib, *Bibl. Orient.* Vol. I. p. 330, and that which follows on Shamuna and Guria, *Ibid.* p. 329. For a full account of Mar Jacob and his works the reader is referred to Assemani, *Ibid.* pp. 283—340. Ephraem Syrus also wrote a similar Homily on Habib, Shamuna, and Guria: see Assemani, *Ibid*, p. 50.

PAGE 90, *l.* 3.—Correct here a typographical error, and dele *at.*

l. 20.—*I am Habib.* Compare Martyrdom of Habib, p. 74.

PAGE 92, *l.* 4.—*A man I worship not.* Compare Martyrdom p. 80.

l. 7.—*The daughter of Abgar.* This seems to be a metonym for his city Edessa.

l. 12.—*My heart is captive with God who became man.* Compare Acts of Sharbil, p. 65.

PAGE 93, *l.* 27.—*Daughter of the Parthians.* Another metonym for Edessa.

PAGE 94, *l.* 2.—*A strap*: see p. 82, *l.* 24.

l. 21.—*She clad herself in white.* See p. 83.

PAGE 95, *l.* 5.—*Shamuni.* From the context this would appear to be the mother of the Maccabees.

l. 28.—*With Sharbil it began, with Habib ended in our Lord.* This passage is cited by Assemani, *Bibl. Orient.* Vol. I. p. 331, who, after quoting the passage from the Acts of Habib, by Simeon Metaphrastes, "Talem quidem vitæ finem" to the end, page 124, line 24, adds "Ubi manifeste alluditur ad relatam de Licinio victoriam anno Christo 324., de qua consule Pagium ad annum 317, sec. 5. Licinianam autem persecutionem ante annum Christi 319 inchoatam non fuisse, idem Pagius ostendit ad annum 316. sec. 6. Martyrio igitur defunctus est Abibus exeunte anno 323. quo persecutioni Licinianæ finis impositus fuit. Sarbelius vero, cujus a cæde initium duxisse persecutionem Sarugensis testatur, coronatus fuit sub Trajano Imperatore, de quo hæc in Martyrologio Romano die 29. Januarii. *Edessæ in Syria Sanctorum Martyrum Sarbelii et Barbææ sororis ejus, qui a Beato Barsimæo Episcopi baptizati, in persecutione Trajani sub Lysia Præside coronati sunt.* Et in Menologio Græcorum die 15 Septembris. *Sarbelius, idolorum Sacerdos, unacum Sorore Barbæa conversus est ad fidem Christi per Barsimæum Edessæ Episcopum, et ambo tenti; post gravissima tormenta Sarbelius inter duo ligna sectus est: soror autem capite truncata.*

PAGE 96, *l.* 12.—ORATION ON SHAMUNA AND GURIA, COMPOSED BY MAR JACOB. This is also taken from the same MS. as the preceding, Cod. Add. 17,158, fol. 23, vers. The Acts of Guria and Shamuna from Simeon Metaphrastes are given by Surius, from whom they have been copied in this volume at page 113. Their day is celebrated, as we learn from these and also from the Roman Martyrology, on the 15th of November: see Assemani, *Bibl. Orient.* Vol. I. p. 329. This accords with what we find in Cod. Add. 14,504, fol. 140. ܩܢܘܢܐ ܕܥܠ ܡܘܕܝܢܐ ܩܕܝܫܐ ܠܓܘܪܝܐ ܘܫܡܘܢܐ ܘܚܒܝܒ ܕܗܘܐ ܕܘܟܪܢܗܘܢ ܒܚܡܫܐ ܒܬܫܪܝ. "Canon on the Holy Confessors, Guria, and Shamuna, and Habib, whose commemoration day is on the fifteenth of Tishri."

Page 97, *l.* 5.—*On their own bodies—wrote.* Compare *Doctrine of Addæus*, p. 9, line 14.

Page 103, *l.* 9.—*For faith consisteth not in many words.* Compare *Doctrine of Addæus*, p. 11.

Page 105, *l.* 7.—*And from the necks of his bridegroom friends the spear demanded blood.* This is wrongly translated in consequence of my having been ignorant of the meaning of ܪܘܡܚܝܢܐ, which is written in the MS. so that it seems like ܪܘܡܚܐ, "spear." I have since ascertained the true sense of ܪܘܡܚܝܢܐ, which is the same word as we find under the root, ܪܘܡܐ in Castel's Lexicon. ' ܪܘܡܚܘܢܐ, strena nuptialis, *Off. Mar.* 474." Thus I have found in the Sermon of Mar Jacob Persa on ܩ̈ܛܠܗ ܡܫܝܚܐ Cod. Add. 14,619, fol. 36, vers. ܢܥܒܕ ܪܘܡܚܝܢܐ ܠܫܠܘܬܗ ܘܢܦܘܩ ܠܐܘܪܥܗ ܒܚܕܘܬܐ: "Let us prepare a nuptial gift for his marriage, and go out to meet him with joy;" and again, fol. 40, ܘܗܢܝܢ ܗܠܝܢ ܕܥܒܕ ܚܬܢܐ ܠܬ̈ܠܝܬ ܡܫܬܘܬܗ ܐܢܬ ܥܒܕ ܠܟ ܪܘܡܚܝܢܐ. ܘܥܒܕ ܢܦܫܟ ܠܐܘܪܥܗ: "And these same things which the bridegroom has prepared for the of his wedding feast, make thou for thyself a bridal gift, and prepare thyself to meet him." The word ܫܘܫܒܝܢܐ I find used in the marriage ceremony, given by Ebedjesu in Card. Mai, *Script. Vett. Coll. Nova*, Vol. X. p. 211, ܘܢܬܪܫܡܘܢ ܫܘܫ̈ܒܝܢܐ ܘܫܘܫܒܝܢܝܬܐ ܒܨܠܝܒܐ: "And let the groomsmen and the bridesmaids be signed with the sign of the cross." The line will therefore be corrected thus: "And he demanded of his wedding friends their neck's blood as a bridal gift."

Page 106, *l.* 13.—Canticle of Mar Jacob the Doctor upon Edessa. This is taken from Cod. Add. 17,158, fol. 56.

Page 107, *l.* 20.—*Abgar the Black.* See Note p. 144 above.

l. 22.—*Your envy.* Correct here a misprint, and read ܡܬܚܣܡܝܢ for ܢܬܚܣܡܝܢ.

Page 108, *l.* 5.—Extract I. This is found in Cod. Add. 14,535, fol. 1. An octavo volume, imperfect at the beginning and the end, consisting at present of 115 folia. The contents are miscellaneous: see *Corpus Ignatianum*, p. 359.

l. 13.—*Watchers.* That is, the Angels.

l. 24.—Extract II. This is from Cod. Add. 12,155, fol. 53 vers. It is a large volume in quarto, written in two columns, and has the following title prefixed, ܦܢܩܝܬܐ ܕܬܚܘܝܬܐ ܕܐܒܗ̈ܬܐ ܩܕ̈ܝܫܐ ܕܠܘܩܒܠ ܗܪ̈ܣܝܣ "Table of the Demonstrations of the Holy Fathers against Heresies." See *Corpus Ignat.* p. 359. This Extract II., from Addæus, is taken from a chapter with the following heading, ܥܠ ܪܓܫܬܐ ܕܢܦܫܐ ܒܬܪ ܦܘܪܫܢܗ̇ ܡܢ ܦܓܪܐ: "Touching the consciousness of the soul after its separation from the body." The part contained in this extract is wanting among some of the missing leaves of the manuscript from which the *Doctrine of Addæus* is printed. The same is also found in several other manuscripts in this Nitrian collection. It is written on the fly leaf of Cod. Add. 12,161, which is one of the books procured at Bagdad by the Abbot Moses, and presented to the Monastery of St. Mary at Nitria, being an antient copy of Chrysostom's Homilies on St. Matthew, containing Homilies 60—88. It is also quoted in Cod. Add. 14,532, fol. 139, which is a volume containing "Proofs from the Fathers against various heresies;" and in Cod. Add. 14,612, fol. 165, rect., a large quarto volume of miscellaneous contents, consisting of Homilies by Chrysostom and others. It is found, too, in Cod. Add. 17,193, fol. 37, vers., and in Cod. Add. 17,194, fol. 30, which is a small duodecimo volume bearing the title ܪ̈ܫܐ ܡܫܚܠ̈ܦܐ ܘܦܘܫ̈ܩܐ ܕܐܒܗ̈ܬܐ ܩܕ̈ܝܫܐ "Various chapters and explanations of the Holy Fathers."

Page 109, *l.* 7.—Extract III. is taken from Cod. Add. 17,193, fol. 36. It is a quarto volume, imperfect at the end, and at present consists of 99 folia. It bears the title ܦܢܩܝܬܐ ܕܬܚܘܝܬܐ ܘܕܟܢܘ̈ܫܝܐ ܘܕܡܐܡ̈ܪܐ: "A table of Proofs and of Collections and of Treatises." This Extract III. is found on fol. 36, vers., and is followed by Extract II. on the next page, with ܕܠܗ, "by the same," prefixed in red letters. According to this order it would appear that Extract III. preceded

Extract II. in the *Doctrine of Addæus*: this we find at page 19 above, line 7—16. The preceding Extract II. probably belongs to that part which has been lost from p. 20.

l. 26.—Extracts IV. and V. are taken from Cod. Add. 14,601, fol. 164. It is a large quarto volume in two columns, consisting at present of 182 folios, written apparently in the eighth century. Its contents are miscellaneous, containing Sermons by Basil, Gregory Theologus, John Chrysostom, Theodotus of Ancyra, Philoxenus, Severus of Antioch, &c. These extracts are found in a Chapter with the following heading, ܡܛܠ ܗܠܝܢ ܫܒܥܝܢ ܘܬܪܝܢ ܫܠܝܚܐ ܩܕܝܫܐ. ܘܡܛܠ ܫܠܝܚܐ ܕܓܠܐ ܕܗܘܘ ܒܙܒܢܗܘܢ. "Touching those Seventy-two Holy Apostles, and touching the false Apostles who were in their time." Extract IV. is also in the *Bee*, and is found in the page cited in *Note*, p. 163 above.

PAGE 110, *l.* 4.—Extract VI. is taken from Cod. Add. 14,484, fol. 19. It is a very antient quarto volume, in two columns, of the fifth or sixth century; imperfect, a few leaves have been added in a more recent hand. It is an apochryphal work relative to the Blessed Virgin, in six Books, of which the title is that given at the heading of the Extract. There is also bound up in the same volume another Codex of still older date, containing the Acts of Simeon Stylites.

PAGE 112, *l.* 4.—Extract VII. is taken from Cod. Add. 14,624. A quarto volume, imperfect at the beginning, the end, and in the middle. It at present consists of 56 leaves, apparently written in the ninth century, and contains various Homilies, &c., of Jacob of Sarug, and others.

l. 18.—Extract VIII. is taken from Cod. Add. 14,590. Homilies of the same Mar Jacob, of the eighth or ninth century.

PAGE 113.—MARTYRIUM SANCTORUM CONFESSORUM SAMONÆ, GURIÆ ET ABIBI, EX SIMEONE METAPHRASTE. The account of the martyrdom of these three persons, collected by Simeon Metaphrastes, I have reprinted exactly as I found it in the well-known work of Surius, "De Probatis Sanctorum vitis, quas tam ex MSS. Codicibus, quam ex editis Auctoribus, R. P. Fr. Laurentius Surius, Carthusiæ Coloniensis Professus Primum edidit, et in duodecim menses distribuit. NOVEMBER. Hac postrema editione multis Sanctorum vitis auctus et notis marginalibus illustratus. Coloniæ Agrippinæ, Sumptibus Ioannis Kreps et Hermanni Mylii. Anno clɔ.lɔc.xviii." I find no notice of the MS. whence this text was printed, nor of the author of the Latin translation. There are several obvious blunders in it, but having no other copy to correct them by, and inasmuch as they are such as in no way affect the facts related, I have reprinted this text verbatim, without proposing any conjectural emendations of my own. The learned reader will do this for himself. There is subjoined, p. 345, "De Sanctis Christi Martyribus Samona, Guria et Abibo Arethæ Archiepiscopi Cæsareensis Oratio: viro docto interprete. Habetur 3 Tomo Aloysii." This I have not thought it worth while to reprint here, because it supplies no additional facts, but merely corroborates those related in the preceding Tract.

PAGE 125.—MOÏSE DE KHORÈNE HISTOIRE D'ARMÉNIE. I have thought it more convenient to give all that is told by Moses Chorenensis relative to Abgar and the establishment of Christianity at Edessa, in a continued narrative, rather than to break it up and cite it in isolated passages in the Notes. The first translation that appeared in any European language of this work of the Father of Armenian History was in Latin, by the two brothers Whiston. "MOSIS CHORENENSIS HISTORIÆ ARMENICÆ LIBRI III. Accedit ejusdem Scriptoris EPITOME GEOGRAPHIÆ. Præmittitur Præfatio, quæ de LITERATURA, ac VERSIONE SACRA ARMENICA agit; et subjicitur APPENDIX, quæ continet EPISTOLAS DUAS ARMENICAS; Primam CORINTHIORUM ad PAULUM Apostolum, Alteram PAULI Apostoli ad CORINTHOS; nunc primum e codice MS integre divulgatas. Armeniace ediderunt, Latine verterunt, notisque illustrârunt GULIELMUS ET GEORGIUS GUL. WHISTONI filii, Aulæ Clarensis in Academia Cantabrigiensi aliquamdiu Alumni. LONDONI: 1736." I have, however, thought it more desirable to give the French Translation by M. Le Vaillant de Florival, which was made at a more recent period, after the Armenian had been longer studied, and with more available sources at hand. "MOÏSE DE KHORÈNE, auteur de Ve Siecle, HISTOIRE D'ARMÉNIE, texte Arménien et traduction Française, avec notes explicatives et précis historiques sur l'Arménie: ouvrage dédié a S. M. Impériale NIÇOLAS I., Empereur de toutes les Russies, par P. E. LE VAILLANT DE FLORIVAL. Paris, 8vo." There is also a more recent translation in Italian, but that language is perhaps not so generally read as the French.

PAGE 129, *l.* 11.—*Marinus.* Whiston has the following Note on this, p. 132, "Per hæc tempora Syriam administrabat Ælius Lamia, cui tamen provinciam suam adire non fuit permissum, ut scribit Tacitus, l. vi. c. 27., qui etiam Julii cujusdam Marini meminit, c. 10. an vero is idem fuerit atque hic Marinus, id omnino incertum."

The account of Abgar having heard of the miracles of Jesus through his envoy Ananias, who met with him when in Palestine, is also given by Simeon Metaphrastes, but with some variations from this by Moses Chorenensis. "Cum Dominus et Deus et Salvator noster Jesus Christus ad genus nostrum erigendum apud nos versaretur, erat, ut dicit Propheta, Multitudo pacis in terra, et fuerat dissipatus multorum principatus et administratio, cum tamquam ab una zona Romano Imperio cinctus esset universus orbis terræ, et subjectus esset uni gubernatori. Ideo erat omnium cum omnibus secura congressio, neque sibi videbantur homines terram habitare divisam, sed ut quæ ab uno Domino possideretur, et esset tota unius opificis: et collum primo illi servo inclinantes, pacem inter se agitabant. Quamobrem qui tunc quoque erat Edessæ Toparcha Abagarus, erat Ægypti Præsidi notus, et amicus, et alterius ad alterum veniebant utrinque ministri. Quocirca illo quoque tempore, quo Dominus noster et Deus, paternam implens voluntatem, salutarem doctrinam proponebat hominibus, et per insignia miracula ad fidem in eum habendam convertebat homines: accidit ut quidam ex ministris Abagari, nomine Ananias, in Ægyptum vadens per Palestinam, in Christum incideret: et eum procul contemplaretur verbis ab errore attrahentem multitudinem, et quæ omnem superabant opinionem facientem miracula. Postquam ergo iter suum confecisset in Ægyptum, et iis quæ mandata fuerunt tractatis rediret, cum recordaretur dominum suum diuturno articulari morbo tyrannice vexari, et nigra lepra consumi, et duplicem calamitatem, vel multiplicem potius morbum sentire, quod et articulorum affligeretur doloribus, et lepræ malis cruciaretur (aderat quidem pudor quoque deformitatis, propter quam ab hominibus non erat aspectabilis: et neque solummodo erat fere semper in lecto, sed amicos etiam qui veniebant ad eum aspiciendum, præ pudore celabat) propterea hæc laboravit scire diligentius, ut posset certo renunciare domino suo, quo ille quoque forte per eum sanitatem consequeretur. Invenit ergo rursus Dominum in eisdem locis mortuos excitantem: cæcis visum donantem: claudos ad ingrediendum integros efficientem; sanosque et firmos reddentem omnes qui aliqua laborabant infirmitate.

Postquam ergo persuasum habuit, et aperte cognovit hæc fieri a Domino, ea Abagaro reversus significavit, et pluribus ea quæ viderat et audierat, edocuit. Quamobrem ut qui rem in transitu comparasset majorem quam quæ ei commissa fuerat, et ut qui bona afferet nuncia, benignissime fuit exceptus, et habitus fuit unus ex maxime benevolis. Et quoniam qui alicujus rei desiderio tenetur, tamquam rapinam existimat, si quod promissum fuerit differatur, re quæ narratur, et spe ipsa hominum excitante, vehementique studio incitatur ad venandum id quod significatum fuerat. Idcirco Abagarus est excitatus, ut literis eum accesseret, qui talia dicebatur posse curare. Et protinus scripsit ad Dominum eam, quæ ubique circumfertur, epistolam. See "Constantini cognomento Porphyrogeniti, in Christo Romanorum Imperatoris, narratio collecta ex diversis histôriis de non manu facta Christi Dei nostri imagine, missa ad Abagarum, et ex Edessa translata in hanc beatissimam urbium Reginam Constantinopolim. *Per Simeonem Metaphrastem.*" In HISTORIA ALOYSII LIPOMANI EPISCOPI VERONENSIS DE VITIS SANCTORUM. Pars. I. p. 187.

ܡܢ ܬܫܥܝܬܐ ܕܒܝܬܐ

ܐܬܬܠܚܡܘܪ ܬܫܥܝܬܐ ܥܠ ܡܠܟܐ ܕܐܘܪܗܝ.

ܬܫܥܝܬܐ ܕܝܢ ܕܗܘܬ ܡܛܠ ܗܕܐ. ܕܐܝܟ ܗܠܝܢ ܗܘܐ ܠܦܘܣܐ. ܟܕ ܡܬܒܪܝܐ ܗܘܬ ܐܠܗܘܬܗ ܕܦܪܘܩܢ ܘܡܚܝܢ ܝܫܘܥ ܡܫܝܚܐ ܠܘܬ ܟܠܗܘܢ ܒܢܝ ܐܢܫܐ. ܡܛܠ ܚܝܠܐ ܬܡܝܗܐ ܕܥܒܕ ܗܘܐ. ܫܡܥܬܐ ܕܝܢ ܐܦ ܡܢ ܐܬܪ̈ܘܬܐ ܪ̈ܚܝܩܢ ܡܢ ܐܬܪܐ ܕܝܗܘܕ: ܕܐܚܝܕܝܢ ܗܘܘ ܒܟܘܪ̈ܗܢܐ ܘܒܟܐܒ̈ܐ ܕܠܐ ܚܠܡ. ܟܠ ܣܒܪܐ ܕܐܣܝܘܬܐ ܐܬܝܢ ܗܘܘ ܠܘܬܗ. ܐܦ ܐܒܓܪ ܡܠܟܐ: ܕܒܟܐܒ̈ܐ ܕܡܪܝܥܘ ܕܦܓܪܗ ܡܫܬܢܩ ܗܘܐ ܒܟܪܝܘܬܐ. ܐܬܚܒܠ ܗܘܐ ܦܓܪܗ ܒܟܐܒܐ ܩܫܝܐ. ܕܐܝܟ ܕܠܝܬ ܒܢܝ ܐܢܫܐ ܠܝܬ ܠܗ ܐܣܝܘܬܐ. ܘܟܕ ܫܡܥ ܘܝܠܦ ܫܡܗ ܕܝܫܘܥ ܘܥܠ ܚܝܠܐ ܕܥܒܕ ܗܘܐ: ܕܫܡܝܥܬ ܟܠܗ ܡܕܝܢܬ ܗܘܬ ܒܠܫܢܗ. ܫܕܪ ܐܓܪܬܐ ܕܒܥܘܬܐ ܒܝܕ ܓܒܪܐ ܕܠܗ ܘܡܗܝܡܢ ܗܘܐ ܠܗ ܕܢܐܬܐ ܢܐܣܐ ܐܢܘܢ ܡܢ ܟܘܪܗܢܗ. ܗܘ ܕܝܢ ܦܪܘܩܢ ܒܥܘ ܕܟܠܐ ܕܫܕܪܗ ܠܐ ܐܬܦܢܝ ܠܗ. ܠܐܓܪܬܐ ܕܝܢ ܐܫܘܗܝ. ܕܐܫܬܘܝ ܠܗ ܕܢܫܕܪ ܠܗ ܚܕ ܡܢ ܬܠܡܝ̈ܕܘܗܝ ܘܢܐܣܐ ܟܘܪܗܢܗ. ܘܚܠܦ ܠܗ ܚܝܐ ܘܠܟܠܗܘܢ ܩܪ̈ܝܒܘܗܝ. ܠܐ ܕܝܢ ܐܫܬܘܚܪ ܕܢܫܡܠܐ ܠܗ ܫܘܘܕܝܗ. ܡܢ ܒܬܪ ܕܝܢ ܕܩܡ ܡܢ ܒܝܬ ܡܝ̈ܬܐ ܘܐܬܥܠܝ ܠܫܡܝܐ. ܬܐܘܡܐ ܫܠܝܚܐ ܫܕܪ ܡܢ ܬܪ̈ܥܣܪ ܠܐܕܝ. ܗܘ ܕܡܬܡܢܐ ܗܘܐ ܐܦ ܗܘ ܡܢ ܫܒܥܝܢ ܬܠܡܝ̈ܕܘܗܝ ܕܡܫܝܚܐ. ܐܝܟ ܕܡܢ ܡܦܩܕܢܘܬܐ ܕܐܠܗܝܐ ܫܕܪܗ ܠܐܘܪܗܝ. ܕܢܗܘܐ ܟܪܘܙܐ ܘܡܒܣܪܢܐ ܕܣܒܪܬܐ ܕܡܫܝܚܐ. ܘܫܘܘܕܝܐ ܕܡܫܝܚܐ ܒܐܝܕܗ ܐܬܡܠܝ. ܐܬܐ ܠܗ ܒܚܝܠܬܐ ܗܝ ܕܡܪܘܬܐ ܕܝܠܗ ܕܐܫܬܠܛ ܡܢ

ܕܐܫܡܠܐ ܗܪܟܐ ܟܠ ܡܕܡ ܕܡܛܠܬܗ ܐܫܬܕܪܬ. ܘܡܢ ܒܬܪ ܕܡܫܡܠܐ ܐܢܐ ܗܝܕܝܢ ܐܣܬܠܩ ܠܘܬ ܗܘ ܕܫܕܪܢܝ. ܘܡܐ ܕܐܣܬܠܩܬ ܡܫܕܪ ܐܢܐ ܠܟ ܠܚܕ ܡܢ ܬܠܡܝܕܝ܆ ܕܟܐܒܟ ܢܐܣܐ. ܐܦ ܚܝܐ ܢܬܠ ܠܟ ܘܠܐܝܠܝܢ ܕܐܝܬ ܥܡܟ. ܠܗܘܢ ܕܝܢ ܠܗܠܝܢ ܐܚܪ̈ܝܬܐ ܐܦ ܗܠܝܢ ܢܣܒ ܠܗܘܢ ܒܠܥܕܝܟ ܐܪܡܝܐ. ܕܡܢ ܒܬܪ ܕܐܣܬܠܩ ܡܫܝܚܐ. ܫܕܪ ܠܗ ܝܗܘܕܐ ܬܐܘܡܐ ܠܐܕܝ܆ ܫܠܝܚܐ ܚܕ ܡܢ ܫܒܥܝܢ. ܘܟܕ ܐܬܐ ܫܪܐ ܗܘܐ ܠܘܬ ܛܘܒܝܐ ܒܪ ܛܘܒܝܐ. ܟܕ ܕܝܢ ܐܫܬܡܥܬ ܥܠܘܗܝ ܐܘܕܥܘܗܝ ܠܐܒܓܪ܆ ܕܐܬܐ ܫܠܝܚܐ ܕܫܕܪ ܠܗ ܝܫܘܥ ܐܝܟ ܕܟܬܒ ܠܟ. ܫܪܝ ܗܘܐ ܕܝܢ ܗܘ ܐܕܝ ܕܢܐܣܐ ܠܟܠ ܟܐܒ ܘܟܘܪܗܢ ܒܚܝܠܐ ܕܐܠܗܢ ܐܡܝܢܐ ܕܟܠ ܐܢܫ ܡܬܕܡܪ ܀ ܟܕ ܕܝܢ ܫܡܥ ܐܒܓܪ ܪ̈ܘܪܒܬܐ ܘܬܕܡܪ̈ܬܐ ܕܥܒܕ ܗܘܐ ܘܐܣܝܘ̈ܬܗ. ܐܬܪܥܝ ܕܗܘܝܘ ܗܘ ܕܥܠܘܗܝ ܟܬܒ ܘܐܡܪ ܠܗ. ܕܡܐ ܕܐܣܬܠܩܬ ܡܫܕܪ ܐܢܐ ܠܟ ܠܚܕ ܡܢ ܬܠܡܝܕܝ܆ ܕܗܘ ܢܐܣܐ ܟܐܒܟ. ܘܫܕܪ ܩܪܐ ܠܛܘܒܝܐ ܗܘ ܕܠܘܬܗ ܫܪܐ ܗܘܐ ܘܐܡܪ ܠܗ. ܫܡܥܬ ܕܓܒܪܐ ܚܝܠܬܢܐ ܐܬܐ ܘܫܪܐ ܒܒܝܬܟ. ܐܣܩܝܗܝ܆ ܗܟܝܠ ܠܘܬܝ. ܟܕ ܐܬܐ ܕܝܢ ܛܘܒܝܐ ܠܘܬ ܐܕܝ܆ ܐܡܪ ܠܗ. ܐܒܓܪ ܡܠܟܐ ܩܪܐ ܠܝ ܘܐܡܪ ܠܝ ܕܐܣܩܝܟ ܠܘܬܗ ܕܬܐܣܝܘܗܝ. ܘܐܡܪ ܐܕܝ܆ ܣܠܩ ܐܢܐ. ܡܛܠ ܕܒܚܝܠܗ ܠܘܬܗ ܗܘ ܐܫܬܕܪܬ. ܩܕܡ ܗܟܝܠ ܛܘܒܝܐ ܠܒܬܪܗ ܕܝܘܡܐ ܘܐܙܠ ܠܘܬ ܐܒܓܪ. ܟܕ ܕܝܢ ܣܠܩ ܐܕܝ ܐܬܟܢܫܘ ܗܘܘ ܩܕܡܘܗܝ ܪ̈ܘܪܒܢܘܗܝ. ܘܥܡ ܥܠܬܗ ܟܕ ܥܐܠ ܗܘܐ. ܚܙܘܐ ܪܒܐ ܐܬܚܙܝ ܠܐܒܓܪ ܒܐܦ̈ܘܗܝ ܕܐܕܝ܆ ܫܠܝܚܐ. ܘܟܕ ܚܙܐ܆ ܐܒܓܪ ܠܐܕܝ܆ ܣܓܕ ܠܗ. ܘܐܚܕ ܬܗܪܐ ܠܟܠܗܘܢ ܕܩܝܡܝܢ ܗܘܘ ܬܡܢ. ܡܛܠ ܕܠܐ ܚܙܐܘܗܝ ܠܗܘ ܚܙܘܐ. ܗܘ ܕܠܗ ܠܐܒܓܪ ܒܠܚܘܕܘܗܝ ܐܬܚܙܝ. ܘܫܐܠܗ ܡܫܐܠ ܗܘܐ ܠܗ ܠܐܕܝ. ܕܐܢ ܒܫܪܪܐ ܐܢܬ ܬܠܡܝܕܗ ܕܝܫܘܥ ܒܪܗ ܕܐܠܗܐ. ܗܘ ܕܐܡܪ ܠܝ ܕܡܫܕܪ ܐܢܐ ܠܟ ܠܚܕ ܡܢ ܬܠܡܝܕܝ. ܕܗܘ ܢܐܣܝܟ

ܗܦܪ ܒܡܗ̈ܕܝܢܐ ܕܐܝܬ ܗܘܐ ܒܐܘܪܗܝ. ܕܗܢܝܢ ܒܕܒܝܠ ܦܘܫܐ
ܗܘܬ ܡܠܟܘܬܗ. ܒܥܪ̈ܦܠܐ ܗܒܠ ܕܐܝܬ ܗܘܐ ܬܡܢ: ܕܐܝܬ
ܗܘܐ ܒܗܘܢ ܡܕܝܢ ܕܐܬܗܘܬܪ ܡܢ ܩܕ̈ܡܝܐ ܒܕܡܟܐ ܠܐܒܓܪ.
ܐܦ ܗܠܝܢ ܒܕܡܟܐ ܠܡܫܟܐ ܡܫܬܟܚܝܢ ܕܢܛܝܪ̈ܝܢ ܬܡܢ. ܠܝܬ ܕܝܢ
ܒܠܒܬܐ ܕܢܫܬܡܥ ܐܝܟ ܐܦ ܠܐܓܪ̈ܬܐ ܕܫܩܝܠ ܠܢ ܡܢ ܒܝܬ
ܐܪܟܐ. ܕܐܝܬ ܠܗܝܢ ܦܘܫܩܐ ܕܗܠܝܢ ܡ̈ܠܐ: ܕܡܦܫܩܢ ܡܢ
ܐܪܡܝܐ ܠܝܘܢܝܐ. ܀

ܦܘܚܡܐ ܕܐܓܪ̈ܬܐ ܕܟܬܝܒܐ ܡܢ ܐܒܓܪ ܡܠܟܐ ܠܝܫܘܥ.
ܘܐܫܬܕܪܬ ܠܗ ܒܝܕ ܚܢܢܝܐ ܛܒܠܪܐ ܠܐܘܪܫܠܡ ܀ ܐܒܓܪ
ܐܘܟܡܐ ܪܫ ܐܬܪܐ. ܠܝܫܘܥ ܐܣܝܐ ܛܒܐ ܕܐܬܚܙܝ
ܒܐܬܪܐ ܕܐܘܪܫܠܡ ܫܠܡ ܀ ܫܡܥܬ ܠܝ ܥܠܝܟ ܘܥܠ ܐܣܝܘܬܐ
ܕܗܘܝܐ ܒܐܝ̈ܕܝܟ ܕܠܐ ܣܡ̈ܡܢܐ ܘܥܩܪ̈ܐ. ܐܝܟ ܕܡܫܬܡܥ
ܓܝܪ. ܥܒܕ ܐܢܬ ܠܣܡ̈ܝܐ ܕܢܚܙܘܢ. ܘܠܚܓܝܣ̈ܐ ܕܢܗܠܟܘܢ.
ܘܠܓܪ̈ܒܐ ܡܕܟܐ ܐܢܬ. ܘܪ̈ܘܚܐ ܛܢ̈ܦܬܐ ܘܫ̈ܐܕܐ ܡܦܩ
ܐܢܬ. ܘܠܐܝܠܝܢ ܕܡܫܬܢܩܝܢ ܒܟܘܪ̈ܗܢܐ ܢܓܝܪ̈ܐ ܡܐܣܐ ܐܢܬ.
ܘܡܝ̈ܬܐ ܡܩܝܡ ܐܢܬ. ܘܟܕ ܫܡܥܬ ܥܠܝܟ ܗܠܝܢ ܟܠܗܝܢ.
ܣܡܬ ܒܪܥܝܢܝ ܚܕܐ ܡܢ ܬܪ̈ܬܝܢ. ܐܘ ܕܐܢܬ ܗܘ ܐܠܗܐ ܕܢܚܬܬ
ܡܢ ܫܡܝܐ ܘܥܒܕ ܐܢܬ ܗܠܝܢ. ܐܘ ܕܒܪܗ ܐܢܬ ܕܐܠܗܐ
ܗܠܝܢ ܥܒܕ ܐܢܬ. ܡܛܠܗܢܐ ܗܟܝܠ ܟܬܒܬ ܒܥܝܬ ܡܢܟ
ܕܬܫܬܡܚ ܘܬܐܬܐ ܠܘܬܝ. ܘܐܬܐܣܐ ܗܢܐ ܟܐܒܐ ܕܐܝܬ
ܠܝ. ܐܦ ܫܡܥܬ ܓܝܪ ܕܝܗܘܕ̈ܝܐ ܡܪ̈ܛܢܝܢ ܥܠܝܟ ܘܪܕܦܝܢ
ܕܢܒܐܫܘܢ ܠܟ. ܡܕܝܢܬܐ ܕܝܢ ܙܥܘܪܬܐ ܘܫܦܝܪܬܐ ܐܝܬ ܠܝ
ܕܣܦܩܐ ܠܬܪ̈ܝܢ. ܀ ܦܘܚܡܐ ܕܐܝܠܝܢ ܕܐܬܟܬܒ ܡܢ ܝܫܘܥ. ܒܝܕ
ܚܢܢܝܐ ܛܒܠܪܐ ܠܐܒܓܪ ܪܫ ܐܬܪܐ. ܀ ܛܘܒܘܗܝ ܠܐܢܫܐ
ܕܗܝܡܢ ܒܝ ܟܕ ܠܐ ܚܙܢܝ. ܟܬܝܒ ܓܝܪ ܥܠܝ. ܕܐܝܠܝܢ ܕܚܙܝܢ
ܠܝ ܠܐ ܢܗܝܡܢܘܢ ܒܝ. ܘܐܝܠܝܢ ܕܠܐ ܚܙܐܘܢܝ ܗܢܘܢ ܢܗܝܡܢܘܢ
ܘܢܚܘܢ. ܥܠ ܗܝ ܕܝܢ ܕܟܬܒܬ ܠܝ ܕܐܬܐ ܠܘܬܟ. ܘܠܐ ܗܘ

ܚܠܗ ܘܡܚ̈ܒܘܗܝ. ܘܥܠ ܐܪ̈ܙܐ ܕܡܠܠ ܒܠܒܗ. ܘܒܐܝܢܐ ܚܠܐ ܗܠܝܢ ܦܬܪ ܗܘܐ. ܘܥܠ ܒܪܘܪܘܬܗ ܫܪ̈ܬܐ ܘܥܠ ܕܒܘܪܬܗ ܘܡܗܡܢܘܬܗ. ܘܕܐܝܟܢܐ ܡܚܝܢ ܘܦܪܩ ܘܐܘܒܪ ܢܦܫܗ ܘܐܫܬܠܛ ܘܫܒܩܬ ܠܥܡܠ. ܘܦܬܚ ܗܝܟܠܐ ܕܡܢ ܒܠܡ ܠܐ ܐܬܦܬܚ ܘܐܫܟܚ ܡܬܝܬܐ. ܘܫܒܩܬ ܒܠܚܘܕܘܗܝ، ܘܗܠܡ ܒܒܢܝܐ ܗܝܟܠܐ ܠܗܬ ܐܒܘܗܝ ܀ ܀

ܗܕܐ ܗܝܠ ܐܡܪܢ ܕܐܠܝܦܪܐ ܬܬܦܢܩܘܢ ܒܠܗܘܢ ܟ̈ܠ ܡܕܝܢܬܗ. ܘܢܬܒܝܐܘܢ ܒܪܘܪܘܬܗ ܕܐܕܝ. ܘܟܬܒ ܗܢܝܢ ܗܟܢܐ ܕܢܬܬܥܗܕ ܠܗ ܕܗܘܟܢܐ ܘܗܐܡܟܢܐ. ܘܗܘ ܕܝܢ ܠܐ ܡܟܠ. ܘܐܡܪܢ. ܐܝܟܢܐ ܕܕܠܡ ܥܕܡ ܐܢܫܒܐ ܢܩܒ ܕܐܫܬ̈ܝܢܐ ܀ ܐܬܡܣܪ ܗܠܝܢ ܒܟܬܒܬ ܬܠܬܡܐܐ ܘܐܪܒܥܝܢ. ܕܠܘ ܕܝܢ ܗܪܡܝܐܝܬ ܢܩܡ ܗܠܝܢ ܒܟܠ ܦܬܟܡܐ ܡܢ ܐܪܒܥܐ. ܒܪܚܡܘܗܝ ܐܬܬܗܝܡ ܗܪܟܐ ܀ ܀ ܀

ܫܠܡ ܣܦܪܐ ܡܕܡܟܐ

ܡܠܦܢܘܬܐ ܕܐܕܝ ܫܠܝܚܐ

* * * * *

* * * * *

ܠܗ ܐܕܝ. ܡܛܠ ܕܗܒܢܐ ܗܘܡܢܘܬ ܗܘܐܡ ܐܝܢܐ ܐܢܐ ܐܕܝ ܒܠܝܟ. ܒܫܡܗ ܕܝܫܘܥ ܡܢ ܕܗܘܡܢܬ ܒܗ ܗܘܝܬܐ. ܘܒܗ ܒܚܝܠܐ ܕܗܘܝܬ ܗܘܐ ܐܝܕܗ ܒܠܗܘܢ. ܐܬܐܣܝ، ܡܢ ܢܣܝܢܐ ܕܟܐܒܐ ܕܐܝܬ ܗܘܐ ܠܗ ܢܩܪܐ. ܘܬܡܗ ܗܘܐ ܐܒܓܪ ܘܐܬܕܡܪ. ܕܐܝܟܢܐ ܕܫܡܥ ܗܘܐ ܠܗ. ܥܠ ܝܫܘܥ ܕܥܒܕ ܗܘܐ ܘܡܐܣܐ. ܗܟܢܐ ܘܐܦ ܗܘ ܐܕܝ. ܕܠܐ ܣܡܐ ܕܥܒܕ ܡܐܣܐ ܗܘܐ. ܒܫܡܗ ܕܝܫܘܥ. ܘܐܦ ܠܓܒܘ ܒܪ ܓܒܘ ܦܩܪܐ ܐܝܬ ܗܘܐ ܠܗ ܒܪ̈ܓܠܘܗܝ. ܘܐܦ ܗܘ ܣܡ ܗܘܐ ܠܗ ܐ̈ܝܕܗ ܥܠ ܪ̈ܓܠܘܗܝ. ܘܗܢ ܗܘܐ ܐܣܝܐ ܒܠܚܡ

ܘܫܐܠ ܠܝ ܚܝܐ. ܘܐܡܪ ܚܒܝܐ ܘܐܡܪ. ܡܛܠ ܕܐܘܪܚܐܝܬ
ܡܒܚܢܬ ܒܗ ܒܗܘ ܕܚܠܝܢ. ܡܛܠ ܗܢܐ ܐܫܬܠܚܬ ܠܘܬܝ.
ܘܬܘܒ ܐܢ ܬܗܘܝܢ ܒܗ ܢܗܘܐ ܠܝ ܫܐܠܬܗ ܕܠܒܝ. ܗܘܐ
ܐܒܘܗܝ ܐܡܪ ܠܗ. ܕܗܘܢܐ ܠܟ ܡܫܬܒܩ ܒܗ. ܐܝܟܢܐ ܕܐܦ
ܠܡܘܕܝܐ ܦܘܠܘܣ ܕܝܠܗܘܢ. ܟܬܒ ܕܐܡܪ ܚܠܝܐ ܘܐܫܬܘܒ
ܐܝܘܒ. ܐܠܐ ܠܐ ܕܐܬܬܠܝܬ ܡܛܠ ܡܠܘܬܐ ܕܗܘܡܢܐ.
ܘܐܡܪ ܐܡܪ. ܡܢܘ ܝܚܢܘ ܕܐܒܘܗܝ ܫܡܠܝ. ܘܟܕ ܫܡܠܝ
ܐܬܚܠܝ ܠܗܬ ܐܒܘܗܝ. ܐܡܪ ܠܗ ܐܡܪ. ܐܦ ܐܢܐ ܡܫܬܒܩ
ܒܗ ܘܟܐܒܘܗܝ. ܘܐܡܪ ܐܡܪ. ܡܛܠ ܗܢܐ ܗܟܢ ܐܢܐ ܚܠܝܢ
ܐܢܫ ܒܥܘܢ. ܘܟܕ ܚܙܐ ܗܕܐ. ܡܫܕܐ ܐܬܐܡܪ ܡܢ ܒܪܘܚܗ
ܘܗܘ ܒܐܒܐ ܕܐܝܬ ܗܘܐ ܠܗ. ܘܐܬܕܟܪ ܐܡܪ. ܕܐܝܟ
ܕܥܒܕ ܗܘܐ ܠܗ ܟܠ ܫܘܒ ܗܢܐ ܒܝܬ ܒܒܥܬܐ ܒܝܕ ܐܘܝ.
ܬܠܡܝܕܘ. ܕܕܠܐ ܫܘܬܦܘܬܐ ܘܒܥܘܬܐ ܐܫܬܡܥ. ܠܐ ܕܝܢ ܠܗ
ܒܠܚܘܕ. ܐܠܐ ܐܦ ܠܒܢܘܗܝ ܒܪ ܒܢܘܗܝ ܕܐܝܬ ܗܘܐ ܠܗ
ܦܘܩܕܢܐ. ܕܐܦ ܗܘ ܓܠ ܘܢܦܠ ܥܠ ܪ̈ܓܠܘܗܝ. ܘܟܕ ܝܠ
ܒܠܒܗ ܐܬܬܘܗܝ. ܘܐܬܦܬܚܘ ܦܬܓܡܐ ܥܠ ܡܬܚܫܒܬܗܘܢ
ܐܦܝ. ܘܟܕ ܗܢܐ ܕܘܪܫܐ ܘܡܚܝܪܝ. ܡܠܘܬܐ ܕܐܠܗܐ ܀ ܟܕ
ܗܠܝܢ ܐܡܪ ܠܗ ܐܡܪ. ܐܝܬ ܗܕܐ. ܒܚܝܠܐ ܕܐܠܗܐ ܗܠܝܢ
ܟܠ ܐܝܬ. ܐܦ ܚܝ ܐܬܕܡܪܬ ܒܗܠܝܢ. ܐܠܐ ܟܕ ܗܠܝܢ
ܠܗܘܢ ܒܢܝܐ ܡܢܝ. ܕܬܫܬܒܚ ܠܟ ܠܐ ܡܫܬܘܬܗ ܕܡܫܝܚܐ.
ܘܕܐܝܟܢܐ ܗܘܬ ܥܠ ܚܠܬܐ. ܘܕܟܐܡܢܐ ܚܠܝܐ ܗܠܝܢ ܕܫܡܥܬ
ܦܟܪ ܗܘܐ ܀܀

ܘܐܡܪ ܐܡܪ. ܗܢܐ ܥܒܕ ܐܢܐ. ܡܛܠ ܕܝܢ ܕܠܡܬܪܐܘ
ܡܠܬܐ ܕܐܠܗܐ ܐܫܬܠܚܬ. ܡܢܝ ܟܝܪ ܠܟ ܠܟܠ ܡܬܚܫܒܢ
ܒܠܒܘܟ. ܘܡܬܡܗܘܢ ܡܬܚܙܐ ܐܢܐ ܘܙܥ ܐܢܐ ܒܗܘܢ
ܡܠܬܐ ܕܚܝܐ. ܘܥܠ ܡܫܬܘܬܗ ܕܡܫܝܚ ܕܐܡܪܢܐ ܗܘܬ܆
ܘܥܠ ܫܠܡܘܬܗ ܕܡܛܠ ܐܢܫܐ ܐܫܬܠܚ ܡܢ ܐܒܘܗܝ. ܘܥܠ

ܕܟܘܠܗ ܒܪܘܬܐ ܐܚܪܢܬ ܗܘܬ ܘܚܫܒܬ ܒܪܘܚܐܘܬܗ ܕܗܘܬ ܫܠܝܢ. ܠܣܘܪܝܐ ܕܟܠܗܘܢ ܒܢܝ ܐܬܪܐ. ܘܐܫܬܟܚ ܗܘܐ ܡܢ ܐܓܝ ܡܠܟܐ ܘܥܡ ܪܘܪܒܢܘܗܝ ܘܐܚܝܢܘܗܝ. ܘܥܡ ܐܓܘܣܛܘܢ ܐܡܗ ܕܐܓܝ. ܘܥܡ ܫܠܝܛܬ ܒܪܬ ܡܙܝܕܬ ܐܢܬܬܗ ܕܐܓܝ. ܐܬ̈ܬܗ ܕܡܪܢ ܘܬܠܡܝܕ̈ܬܗ ܘܫܠܡܐ ܫܩܝܠܬܐ ܕܟܕܢ ܗܘܐ. ܘܢܦ̈ܫܬܗܘܢ ܐܠܗ̈ܝܐ. ܘܗܘܠܡܗ ܕܠܘܬ ܐܚܘܗܝ. ܕܐܚ̈ܝܢܐ ܡܟܠܘ ܗܘܘ ܣܠܩܐ ܘܡܠܦܢܐ. ܘܡܟܝܠܐ ܗܘ ܕܐܬܘܗܝ ܗܘܐ. ܕܟܡ ܗܘ ܟܕ ܣܠܩ ܐܝܟܢ ܗܘܐ ܠܐܓܝ. ܘܠܡܟܝܠܘ ܡܢ ܟܕܘ ܬܪܝܢܐ ܕܡܠܟܘܬܗ. ܘܐܡܝܢܐ ܐܘܟܝ ܐܝܟ ܕܣܬܦܠܐ ܠܚܪܬܐ ܕܩܝ̈ܡܐ. ܘܟܕ ܡܠܟܐ ܕܚܝܬܐ ܟܠܗܝܢ. ܘܐܘܟܝܐ ܘܡܫܬܡܥܐ ܕܒܬܪܐ ܕܐܬܗܘܐ ܠܟܠܗܘܢ ܒܢܝ ܐܬܪܐ. ܘܦܘܪܫܢܐ ܕܗܘܐ ܒܝܬ ܐܡܝ̈ܢܐ ܠܟܠܝ̈ܢܐ. ܘܒܝܬ ܡܫܡܫܢܐ ܠܡܦܘܪܫܐ. ܘܐܡܝܪ ܗܘܐ ܠܗܘܢ: ܕܡܛܠ ܕܬܪܥܐ ܕܫܠܐ ܦܬܝܚܐ ܗܘ. ܘܐܡܪܝܢܐ ܕܐܪܙܐ ܐܠܝܨܐ ܗܘ. ܡܛܠ ܗܢܐ ܕܠܝܠܝܐ ܐܝܟ ܡܫܡܫܢܐ ܕܡܫܝܚܐ. ܘܟܕ ܕܦܘܪܫ ܢܦܫܗ ܗܘ ܕܡܨܠܝܢܐ. ܡܛܠ ܗܢܐ ܡܨܠܝܢ ܐܝܟ ܕܥܠܝܐ ܕܡܨܠܝܢ ܠܫܡܝܐ. ܐܠܐ ܠܐ ܟܕ ܡܛܠ ܕܐܝܬ ܫܪܝܬ ܠܡܠܬܐ ܠܐܓܝ ܡܢ ܡܫܝܚܐ. ܠܐ ܫܒܩ ܗܘܐ ܡܪܢ ܡܢ ܥܠܡܐ. ܘܐܝܬ ܗܘܐ ܠܒܝܐ ܘܠܫܢܐ ܕܡܟܝܠܐ. ܘܐܝܬܐ ܗܘܐ. ܘܠܐ ܕܠܐ ܡܫܬܪܝ ܗܘܐ.

• • • •

• • • • •

• • • • •

ܕܡܫܡܫܢܘܬܐ ܕܡܫܕܪܢ ܕܐܠܗܐ ܐܦܣܩܘܦܐ • • • ܠܟܠܗܘܢ ܒܢܝ ܐܢܫܐ. ܘܐܦ ܐܢܫ ܐܠܗܐ ܕܠܐ ܢܥܒܕ ܕܢܬܦܠܛܘܢ ܠܟܠܗ ܥܠܡ. ܢܥܒܕܘܢ ܢܥܒܕ ܘܡܠܠܘܢ ܠܗ ܡܢܗ ܐܝܟܢܘܢ. ܕܐܬܩܢܘܬܗ ܕܡܦܪܫܢܐ ܐܬܪܚܡܘܢ • ܢܥܒܕ ܗܘܢܐ ܡܫܡܫܢܐ

ܘܐܘܕܝܗ ܗܘܐ. ܘܬܘܒ ܠܐ ܗܘܬ ܠܗ ܦܠܓܘܬܐ. ܘܐܦ ܒܡܕܝܢܬܐ ܟܠܗ̇ ܐܬܘ̈ܬܐ ܪ̈ܘܪܒܬܐ ܡܚܘܐ ܗܘܐ. ܘܫ̈ܠܐ ܬܕܡ̈ܪܬܐ ܡܚܘܐ ܗܘܐ ܒܗ̇. ܐܡܪ ܠܗ ܐܒܓܪ ܡܠܟܐ ܕܝܕܒ ܗܠ ܐܢܬ ܕܒܚܝܠܗ ܕܝܫܘܥ ܡܫܝܚܐ ܗܠܝܢ ܬܕܡ̈ܪܬܐ ܥܒܕ ܐܢܬ. ܘܗܐ ܬܡܝܗܝܢ ܐܢܚܢ ܒܥܒ̈ܕܝܟ. ܒܒܥܐ ܗܘܝܠ ܡܢܝ. ܕܬܫܬܥܐ ܠܝ ܥܠ ܡܐܬܝܬܗ ܕܡܫܝܚܐ. ܐܝܟܢܐ ܗܘܬ. ܘܥܠ ܚܝܠܗ ܡܫܝܚܐ. ܘܥܠ ܬܕܡ̈ܪܬܐ ܕܥܒܝܕ ܗܘܐ ܠܗ ܕܚܙܐ ܗܘܐ. ܐܝܠܝܢ ܕܐܢܬ ܚܙܝܬ ܐܢܬ: ܥܡ ܬܠܡܝ̈ܕܐ ܚܒܪ̈ܝܟ. ܐܡܪ ܠܗ ܐܕܝ. ܡܢ ܗܕܐ ܠܐ ܫܬܩ ܐܢܐ. ܕܐܡܪ. ܡܛܠ ܗܢܐ ܗܘ ܓܝܪ ܐܫܬܕܪܬ ܠܗܪܟܐ. ܕܐܡܪ ܘܐܠܦ ܠܟܠ ܗܘ ܕܨܒܐ ܕܢܫܡܥ ܐܝܟܘܬܟ. ܠܡܚܪ ܟܢܫ ܠܝ ܟܠܗ̇ ܡܕܝܢܬܐ. ܘܐܙܪܘܥ ܒܗ̇ ܡܠܬܐ ܕܚܝܐ. ܒܟܪܘܙܘܬܐ ܕܡܟܪܙ ܐܢܐ ܩܕܡܝܟܘܢ: ܥܠ ܡܐܬܝܬܗ ܕܡܫܝܚܐ. ܐܝܟܢܐ ܗܘܬ. ܘܥܠ ܫܠܝܚܘܬܗ ܕܠܡܢܐ ܘܐܝܟܢܐ ܫܠܝܚ ܗܘܐ. ܘܥܠ ܚܝܠܗ ܘܥܒ̈ܕܘܗܝ ܬܕܡ̈ܪܬܐ. ܘܥܠ ܐܪ̈ܙܐ ܥܫ̈ܝܢܐ ܕܡܐܬܝܬܗ. ܐܝܠܝܢ ܕܡܠܠ ܗܘܐ ܒܥܠܡܐ. ܘܥܠ ܫܬܩܘܬܐ ܕܟܪܘܙܘܬܗ. ܘܐܝܟܢܐ ܘܡܛܠ ܡܢܐ ܐܙܥܪ ܗܘܐ ܢܦܫܗ. ܘܐܡܟܝܟ ܗܘܐ ܐܠܗܘܬܗ ܡܪܝܡܬܐ. ܒܐܢܫܘܬܐ ܕܢܦܠ ܗܘܐ. ܘܐܙܕܩܦ ܗܘܐ ܘܢܚܬ ܗܘܐ ܠܫܝܘܠ ܡܝ̈ܬܐ. ܘܬܪܥ ܗܘܐ ܣܝܓܐ. ܗܘ ܕܡܢ ܥܠܡ ܠܐ ܐܬܬܪܥ ܗܘܐ. ܘܐܚܝ ܗܘܐ ܡܝ̈ܬܐ ܒܡܘܬܗ. ܘܢܚܬ ܗܘܐ ܒܠܚܘܕܘܗܝ. ܘܣܠܩ ܗܘܐ ܥܡ ܣܓܝܐܐ ܠܘܬ ܐܒܘܗܝ ܡܫܒܚܐ. ܗܘ ܕܥܡܗ ܐܝܬܘܗܝ ܗܘܐ ܡܢ ܥܠܡ ܒܚܕܐ ܐܠܗܘܬܐ ܡܪܝܡܬܐ. ܘܦܩܕ ܗܘܐ ܐܒܓܪ ܕܢܬܠܘܢ ܠܐܕܝ ܟܣܦܐ ܘܕܗܒܐ. ܐܡܪ ܠܗ ܐܕܝ. ܐܝܟܢܐ ܡܫܟܚܝܢ ܐܢܚܢ ܢܣܒ ܐܢܚܢ ܡܕܡ ܕܠܐ ܕܝܠܢ ܗܘ. ܕܗܐ ܡܕܡ ܕܝܠܢ ܗܘܐ ܫܒܩܢܝܗܝ. ܐܝܟ ܕܐܬܦܩܕܢ ܡܢ ܡܪܢ. ܕܕܠܐ ܟܝܣ̈ܐ ܘܕܠܐ ܬܪ̈ܡܠܐ. ܟܕ ܦܩܝܕܝܢ ܐܢܫܝܢ ܠܡܣܒ ܥܠ ܟܬܦ̈ܝܢ. ܐܬܦܩܕܢ ܕܢܒܕܪ ܣܒܪܬܗ ܒܟܠܗ̇ ܒܪܝܬܐ. ܗܘ

ܗܘ ܕܒܪܝܬܐ ܗܘܐ ܢܘܗܪܐ ܠܥܠܡܝܢ ܒܢܘܗܪܐ. ܘܒܗܘ ܒܪܢܫܐ
ܡܬܝܕܥܝܢ ܕܒܪ̈ܝܬܗܘܢ ܒܡܘܕܥܬܗܘܢ. ܘܗܘܝܢ ܦܪ̈ܝܫܝܢ ܡܓܠܐ
ܠܡܬ̈ܬܐ ܕܟܝܘܬܐ ܘܠܘܬ ܗܘܝܢ ܕܠܐ ܢܕܢ ܗܦܟܐ. ܡܛܠ
ܕܟܠܢ ܒܡܬ̈ܬܐ ܕܢܦܫܗ ܗܘܐ ܩܪܐ

* * *

* * * * *

* * * *

ܐܢܬܘܢ ܕܐܝܬ ܠܟܘܢ ܚܘܒܐ ܒܗܘ ܕܠܐ ܡܬܚܙܐ ܐܢܬܘܢ
ܗܘܝܬܘܢ ܠܟܘܢ ܐܦ ܐܢܬܘܢ ܐܚܝܬܗܘܢ ܕܠܐ ܚܙܝܢ ܘܠܐ
ܥܒܕܝܢ ܘܐܝܟܢܐ ܗܘ ܕܥܒܕܝܢ ܠܟܠܗܘܢ ܦܪ̈ܘܫܐ ܠܐܕܝܢܐ ܫܪܝܪܐ.
ܟܕ ܗܘܝܬܘܢ ܠܐ ܒܕܠܝܢ ܒܗܘ ܕܠܐ ܥܒܕܝܢ ܡܛܠ ܕܟܝܢܐ ܐܝܟܢ:
ܫܪܝܪܐ ܘܫܬܩܢܐ ܒܕܠܝܐ ܕܝܢ ܕܦܠܛܘܪܐ ܒܗ ܟܝܢܘܬܐ ܕܠܟܘܢ
ܗܘ ܕܠܐ ܝܕܥ ܐܢܬܘܢ ܕܬܬܒܝܢܘܢ. ܐܝܠܐ ܒܗܝܢܐ ܡܕܡ
ܕܚܝܢ ܐܢܬܘܢ. ܠܐ ܓܝܪ ܥܒܕܐ ܠܟܘܢ ܒܪܝܠܐ ܕܠܦܛܪܝܢ
ܕܦܪܘܫܐ ܥܠ ܦܪܨܘܦܟܘܢ ܕܬܒܝܢܘܢ ܢܗܘܪܐ ܫܡܫܐ ܕܐܝܬܘܗܝ,
ܒܗܝܢܐ ܕܝܕܥܬܐ. ܒܪܘܟܐ ܗܟܠ ܡܢ ܒܝ̈ܫܬܐ ܘܒܪ̈ܝܬܐ ܐܝܟ
ܕܐܬܩܪܝܬ ܠܟܘܢ ܕܒܗܝܢܐ ܗܘ ܒܠܝܘܕ ܡ̈ܬܦܪܝܢ ܐܠܗ̈ܐ ܒܕ ܠܗ
ܐ̈ܠܗܐ ܐܝܟ ܒܝܫܘܬܗܘܢ ܘܐܬܦܪܒܘ ܠܘܬ ܗܘܢܐ ܕܟܝܢܗ ܐܠܗܐ
ܐܝܬܘܗܝ ܗܘܐ. ܡܢ ܡܬܘܡ ܘܡܢ ܥܠܡ. ܘܠܐ ܗܘܐ ܒܒܪܐ ܗܘ
ܐܝܟ ܡܬܥܒ̈ܕܢܐ ܘܐܦ ܠܐ ܒܪܝܬܐ ܗܘ ܘܬܘܟܠܢܐ ܐܝܟ
ܨ̈ܠܡܐ ܗܠܝܢ ܕܡܫܬܡܫܝܢ ܐܢܬܘܢ ܒܗܘܢ. ܡܛܠ ܕܐܦ ܠܒܪ
ܦܓܪܐ ܗܘܐ ܐܠܗܐ ܐܝܬܘܗܝ, ܒܪ ܐܒܘܗܝ. ܒܪ̈ܝܬܐ ܓܝܪ ܕܐܬܒܪܝ
ܗܘ, ܒܡܠܬܗ ܘܐܬܪܟܒܘ ܗܘ, ܒܨܒܝܢܐ ܕܡܬܘܡ. ܗܘܝܘ ܗܟܢ
ܕܗܘܘ ܐܠܗܐ ܒܪܘܟܐ. ܠܐ ܗܘܐ ܓܝܪ ܚܠܦ ܒܪܢܫܐ ܕܡܢ
ܐܪܥܐ. ܐܠܐ ܚܠܦ ܗܘ ܕܐܡܪ ܗܘܐ ܐܪܥܐ ܥܠ ܡܬܝ̈ܐ ܘܠܐ
ܗܘܐ ܚܠܦ ܒܪܢܫܐ ܚܙܝ ܗܘܐ ܥܒܕܐ ܒܥܘܠܐ. ܐܠܐ ܚܠܦ
ܗܘ ܕܒܕܒ ܗܘܐ ܢܦܫܐ ܦܘܪ̈ܥܢܐ ܘܠܐ ܗܘܐ ܒܒܪ ܐܢܫܐ
ܐܬܚܫܒ ܗܘܘ ܒܐܬܪܐ ܘܐܕܘܫܐ. ܐܠܐ ܒܗܘ ܕܡܦܩ. ܗܘܐ

d

ܠܫܠܡܘܬܐ ܕܡܫܘܬܦܘܬܗܿ܆ ܐܦ ܟܕ ܠܐ ܡܪܚܡ ܗܘܝܬܘܢ ܒܒܝܬܐ ܕܝܫܘܥ ܕܡܫܝܚܐ ܐܠܐ ܒܫܡܗܐ ܕܫܡܥܝܢ ܗܘܐ ܘܫܡܥܬܘܢ܆ ܠܗ̇ ܐܬܒܫܪܘ ܥܠ ܓܪܘܫܐ ܪܒܐ ܕܗܘܐ ܒܗ̇ܘ ܒܒܝܬܐ ܕܐܘܣܛܬܗ ܕܗܘ ܕܦܪܫܬ ܗܘܬ ܡܦܪܬܗ ܒܟܠܗ ܐܪܥܐ ܒܐܬܪ̈ܘܬܐ ܕܒܒܝܢ ܠܡܫܒܚܘܬܗ܆ ܫܪܝܢ ܒܟܠܗ ܐܪܥܐ. ܘܐܠܠܝܢ ܕܒܒܪ̈ܝܬܐ ܗܘܘ ܘܠܥܝܢܐ ܗܘ ܕܒܒܪ̈ܝܬܐ ܕܠܝܬܝܢ ܗܘܘ ܒܗ ܕܟܡ ܗܘܘ ܒܠܫܘܢ ܗܘܐ ܡܩܒܠܐ ܡܡܠܠܝܢ ܒܟܠ ܠܫ̈ܢܝܢ ܕܥܡܡ̈ܐ ܕ̈ܫܡܝܐ ܘܢܫܡܥܘܢ܆ ܐܝܟ ܡܕ̈ܒܪܐ ܕܗܘܘ ܒܟܠ ܠܫ̈ܢܐ ܕܡܪ̈ܝܐ ܒܦܫܝܬܐ ܗܘܢܐ ܕܡܕܡܝܢ. ܘܗܘܘ ܡܠܦ ܒܐܡܝܢ܆ ܡܩܒܠܐ ܡܚܘܬܐ ܕܗܡܝܢܘܬܐ ܘܕܪ̈ܙܐ ܒܚܝ̈ܘܬܐ ܘܬܪ̈ܘܢܐ ܕܡܢ ܓܠܝܢܐ ܕܠܗܠܝܢܐ. ܐܦ ܐܝܠܐ ܟܕ ܕܫܡܥܬܘܢ܆ ܠܝ ܡܢ ܦܘܡܗ ܐܢܬ܆ ܡܢ ܐܬܪ ܕܢܦܩ ܡܕܢܚ ܢܗܪܐ ܘܐܬܓܠܝܬ ܒܗ ܫܪܪ܆ ܕܐܝܬܘܗܝ ܒܪܘܪܐ *

* * * *

* * * * *

* * * * *

ܐܝܠܐ ܟܕ ܐܝܟ ܕܦܩܕ ܠܝ ܡܪܝ܆ ܗܐ ܡܟܪܙ ܐܢܐ ܘܡܫܒܪ ܐܢܐ ܘܡܫܘܕܥ ܥܠ ܦܬܓܡܐ ܗܘ ܪܒܐ ܐܝܠܐ ܕܡܚܝܐ܆. ܘܙܪܥܐ ܕܡܠܟܘܬܗ ܙܕܩ ܐܝܠܐ ܒܐܪ̈ܚܬܐ ܕܟܠܗ ܘܐܡܠܝܢ ܕܝܗܒܝܢ ܕܢܫܒܩܘܢ܆ ܕܠܗܘܢ܆ ܗܘ ܦܘܪܩܢܐ ܠܟܠܐ ܕܐܬܪܚܡܬܐ. ܘܐܡܠܝܢ ܕܠܐ ܡܬܦܠܓܝܢ ܥܠܐ ܕܬܟܠ ܢܦܫ ܐܝܠܐ ܒܠܫܘܢ܆ ܐܝܟ ܕܐܬܦܩܕ ܠܝ. ܬܘܒ ܗܟܠ ܫܡܥܝܢ ܡܢ ܐܘܪܚܬܐ ܒܝܬܐ ܘܡܢ ܒܒܝܬܐ ܩܕܝܫܐ. ܘܐܬܦܢܘ ܠܘܬܗ ܒܪܚܡܐ ܠܟܠܐ ܘܫܦܝܪܐ. ܐܝܟ ܕܐܬܦܢܝ ܗܘ ܠܘܬܟܘܢ܆ ܒܫܡܐ ܕܝܫܘܥ ܡܫܝܚܐ. ܘܠܐ ܬܗܘܘܢ܆ ܐܝܟ ܕܪܐ ܡܕܡܝܐ ܕܒܝܫܐ. ܕܡܠܬ ܕܡܫܘ ܗܘܘ ܪܚܝܩܝܢ܆ ܡܢ ܕܠܐܬܗ ܕܐܠܗܐ ܡܠܘ ܗܘܘ ܡܢܘܡ ܒܪܫܐ ܠܗܝܢܬ. ܕܗܘܘ܆ ܢܬܪܘܢ܆ ܗܘܘ. ܘܐܡܠܝܢ ܕܐܬܝܢ ܒܬܪܗܘܢ܆ ܢܘܟܪܝܢ܆ ܘܡܫܠܡܝܢ܆. ܒܠܗ ܟܕ ܕܐܬܬ ܡܢܝ܆ ܠܟܠܡܐ. ܕܠܐ ܘܚܘܡ ܕܫܠܡܐ

ܐܢܫ ܡܕܡܟܟܘ ܐܝܟ ܕܡܫܠܡ ܡܢ ܡܗܝܡܢܘܬܗ ܕܡܪܝ ܐܘܓܝܢ
ܚܕ ܘܡܠܦ ܚܕ ܘܡܚܣܢ ܚܕ ܕܛܘܒܘܗܝ ܣܢܝܩܝܢ ܘܠܐ ܡܬܒܪܝܢ
ܙܘܬܪܐ ܒܝܘܡܝ ܕܚܝܘܬܐ. ܡܛܠ ܕܕܚܠ ܗܘ ܢܘܪܐ ܥܡܘܩܐ
ܟܪܝܘܬܐ. ܘܗܘܝܘ ܕܒܬܪܐ ܗܘܐ ܠܐܟܣܢܝܘܬܐ ܡܕ̈ܝܢܬܐ ܘܠܒܪ̈ܝܬܐ
ܘܠܩܕܫܐ. ܘܡܛܠ ܗܘܐ ܒܡܘܬܗ ܒܓܠܝܐ ܕܢܘܪܐ ܕܘܕܝܐ.
ܗܘܘ ܒܪ ܐܠܗܐ ܕܫܘܕܝܐ ܕܘܦܩܗ، ܘܢܦܩܐ ܙܟܝܐ ܠܗ ܗܘ
ܦܓܪܝܢ ܐܦ ܒܪ ܠܐ ܕܟܝܢ ܡܛܠ ܕܠܝܬ ܐܠܗܐ ܐܚܪܢܐ ܒܫܡܝܐ
ܘܒܐܪܥܐ ܗܘܐ ܘܠܝܬ ܠܗ ܡܬܕܪܫܢܘܬܐ ܡܢ ܐܪܥܐ ܒܢܝܢܘܗܝ
ܕܟܪܝܘܬܐ. ܗܢ ܡܛܠ ܥܒܕ ܐܝܢܝܟܘܢ ܡܕܡ ܕܠܐ ܥܒܕ
ܗܘܐ ܠܗܘܢ. ܘܗܐ ܬܘܒ ܚܙܝ ܒܢܝܟܘܢ ܡܕܡ ܕܠܐ ܡܬܚܙܐ
ܗܘܐ ܗܘܐ ܠܗܘܢ. ܠܐ ܡܛܠ ܬܗܘܘܢ ܡܠܝܟܐ ܠܡܕܡ
ܕܢܦܩܘܢ ܘܡܛܠܬܘܢ. ܐܟܙܢܐ ܡܢܝܢ ܐܢܫܐ ܡܪܘܕܐ
ܕܐܟܡܐ. ܘܫܪܪ ܢܦܫܗܘܢ ܡܢ ܥܠܡܐ ܕܢܦܠܬܐ ܕܡܬܠܚܡܐ
ܚܠܦܝܗܘܢ ܒܬܘܒܐ ܘܒܢܝܢܐ ܕܡܕܡ ܙܠܝܩܐ. ܘܬܬܠܠ ܠܗܘܢ
ܚܠ ܣܢܝܩܘܢ ܐܢܫܐ ܘܚܠ ܡܢܝܢ ܪܫܡܘܢ ܒܟܬܒܐ. ܘܗܘ
ܪܚܡܐ ܣܓܝܐܐ ܗܘ ܕܢܦܩ ܠܚܡܕܐ ܘܠܐ ܠܚܛܝܐܐ. ܗܘ ܕܝܢ
ܟܗ ܡܠܟܐ ܕܗܘܝܬܐ ܘܕܪܪܐ ܕܐܟܐ ܘܟܝܢܐ ܘܕܘܝܐ
ܕܗܘܕܝܐ ܒܪ ܬܗܘܡܝܢ ܘܬܫܡܫܘܢ ܒܪܘܚܐ ܬܠܬܝܬܐ
ܘܡܫܝܚܐ. ܗܕܐ ܗܝ ܒܪ ܡܫܠܡܢܘܬ ܘܫܪܪܘܬ. ܠܐ ܗܘܐ
ܒܪ ܒܡܚܒܝܢܘܬܐ ܡܬܗܘܡܝܢ ܫܪܪܗ ܕܡܫܝܚܐ. ܐܠܠܐ ܕܐܝܟ
ܕܬܬܚܫܒܘܢ ܠܡܫܝܚܐ. ܕܝܢ ܐܝܬܘܗܝ ܕܟܢܫܐ ܡܬܚܪܢܝܬܐ
ܬܠܬ ܟܠ ܡܕܡܝܢ ܕܐܬܠܦܘ ܘܬܬܚܫܒܘܢ ܒܟܠܡ ܕܡܫܝܚܐ
ܐܝܬܘܗܝ. ܘܐܢܫ ܚܕܐ ܒܗܕܐ ܐܝܟ ܐܪܥܐ ܕܚܕܐ ܒܫܡܝܐ
ܒܪܝܬܐ ܘܐܠܗܐ ܢܦܫܗ ܒܝܕ ܒܬܫܒܘܚܬܗܘܢ ܕܠܥܠܡ. ܒܪ ܐܝܬܘܗܝ
ܚܕ ܐܝܬܘܗܝ ܒܗܕܐ. ܐܦ ܐܢܫ ܕܡܠܦܝܢ ܚܕ ܠܗܘܢ ܗܕܐ.
ܠܐ ܡܬܦܠܓܝܢ ܐܪܥܐ ܒܪܝܬܐ ܕܗܕܐ. ܘܡܛܠ ܕܐܬܒܠ ܐܝܟܐ
ܕܗܘܘ ܐܪܥܐ ܒܪܝܬܐ ܐܝܟ ܕܢܚܘܢ ܕܟܪܝܐ ܡܫܝܚܐ.

ܫܘܠܛܢܐ ܕܡܠܟܘܬܐ ܡܢ ܝܘܢܝܘܬܐ. ܘܠܐ ܗܘܐ ܟܒܪ ܐܬܘܪܝܐ
ܐܝܟܢܐ، ܗܘܐ ܐܦ ܬܘܪܥܐ ܕܡܝܠܐ ܕܡܫܘܕܥܐ ܡܢ ܝܕ ܠܘܬ.
ܐܠܐ ܒܗܘ ܕܐܡܪ ܗܘܐ ܠܗܘܢ ܕܗܘܐ ܥܡܗ ܒܫܘܬܗܘܢ ܣܪ̈ܒܐ.
ܗܘܐ ܓܝܪ ܐܦܠܐ ܠܐ ܚܕ ܡܢܗܘܢ ܕܠܘܩܒܠܗ، ܕܒܪܗ ܗܘܐ ܕܐܠܗܐ
ܠܐ ܫܘܕܥܐ ܕܡܬܚܫܒܬܗܘܢ ܡܚܘܝܢ ܗܘܘ. ܐܦܠܐ ܗܘܐ ܐܟܠ
ܢܦܫܗܘܢ ܘܠܐ ܡܬܟܦܝܢ ܗܘܘ. ܐܦܠܐ ܓܝܪ ܐܦܠܐ ܙܟܘ ܗܘܘ
ܕܢܦܫܗܘܢ ܡܢ ܗܕܐ ܬܘܕܝܬܐ: ܥܒܕܘ ܗܘܘ ܠܗܘܢ ܓܘܢܚܐ
ܕܚܝܠܐ ܕܗܘܘ ܒܗܘ ܒܟܠܐ. ܗܘܐ ܓܝܪ ܐܦ ܡܢ ܒܢܝ̈ܗܘܢ
ܕܐܘܦܐ ܒܢܦܫܗܘܢ ܘܡܘܗܒܬܐ ܒܪ̈ܘܚܐ ܘܡܗܝܡ̈ܢܐ ܒܗܢ ܥ̈ܠܡܐ
ܣܓܝ̈، ܒܟܠܗ ܐܪܥܐ ܕܦܠܣܛܝܢܐ. ܘܒܬ ܡܕܝ̈ܢܬܐ ܘܒܟܠܗ
ܐܬܪܐ ܕܦܠܓܬܐ. ܘܩܢܝܢ ܬܘܕ̈ܝܐ ܕܫܘܒܚܐ. ܘܡܬܬܢܝܪ
ܘܫܘܒܚܐ ܕܡܫܝܚܐ. ܘܡܗܝܡܢ ܒܥܒ̈ܕܐ ܘܒܪ̈ܬܐ ܒܐܠܗܐ.
ܕܗܘܐ ܒܪ ܐܢܫܐ. ܐܦ ܒܬ ܒܪ ܐܢܫܘܬܗ، ܗܘܐ ܒܐܪܒܥܐ
ܫܘܒ ܡܢ̈ܝ ܡܫܝܚܘܬܗ ܗܘܝܘ ܒܗ ܕܒܪܗ ܗܘ ܕܐܠܗܐ
ܘܡܕܡ ܕܬܫܒܘܚܬܐ ܗܘܝܘ ܡܠܬܐ ܕܒܪܘܬܗ ܐܘܕܝܘ ܒܗ
ܕܐܠܗܐ ܗܘ. ܗܢܐ ܕܩܠܝ ܠܘܬ ܐܒܘܗܝ، ܘܫܝܢܘ ܐܬܬ̈ܐ
ܘܬܕܡܪ̈ܬܐ ܕܗܘܝ ܒܒܗܘܢ. ܘܡܠܬܐ ܕܒܪܬܗ ܫܒܚܘ
ܒܐܕܢ̈ܝܗܘܢ ܠܐ ܐܝܟ ܡܒܗܘܢ ܢܬܦܠܓ ܒܪܢܫܗ ܐܝܟ ܕܢܬܦܝܣ
ܠܬܗܘܢ ܫܘܕܥܐ ܕܟܘܪܗܢܗ ܕܥܠܝ ܠܗܘܢ. ܕܠܡܚܒܘ
ܕܡܫܝܚܘܬܗ ܒ ܒܪ ܠܐ ܚܝܬܘܗܝ. ܘܡܛܠ ܕܗܒܢܐ ܡܫܝܚܘܬܗ
ܒ ܒܪܬܐ ܕܒܪܝܢ ܐܝܬܘܗܝ ܒܗ ܢܘܗܪܐ ܒܪܝܟ ܘܒܠܒܒܐ
ܠܐ ܢܬܦܠܓ ܒܗ ܠܚܠܡ. ܠܐ ܗܘܐ ܬܘܦܝܐ ܡܢ ܡܫܝܚܘܬܗ
ܕܗܘܐ ܫܒܚܘܬܗ ܘܚܝܘܬܗ ܐܠܝܢ ܗܢܘܢ ܠܡܫܝܚܘܬܗ ܕܒܪܐ
ܗܘ ܦܪܘܩܐ ܘܐܠܗܐ ܗܘ ܡܫܝܚܐ. ܘܡܠܟܐ ܗܘ ܘܪܒܐ ܘܫܠܝܛܐ
ܗܘ ܬܘܩܦܐ. ܘܒܡܫܝܚܘܬܗ ܗܘ ܡܫܡܫ ܐܢܫ ܦܠܐ ܒܢ̈ܝܐ
ܕܒܢܝܢܐ ܫܪܝܪܐ ܘܡܬܬܣܝܡ ܕܟܠ ܦܢ ܕܡܟܪ ܠܒ̈ܪܢܬܐ ܘܠܟܢܐ
ܕܡܫܝܚܘܬܐ ܡܕܝܢ ܠܗ . . . . ܠܗܒܝܡ ܓܝܪ ܕܐܡܪܝܢ

ܐܫܘܪܝܐ ܕܗܘܝ ܒܥܕܢܗ ܗܠܝܢ ܐܬ̈ܘܬܐ ܘܬܕܡܪ̈ܬܐ. ܐܠܐ
ܒܫܠܡ ܕܡܫܝܚܐ ܕܡܗܝܡܢ ܐܝܬ ܠܗ ܒܗܘܢܬܐ ܘܒܫܪ̈ܪܐ.
ܘܡܛܠ ܠܗ ܗܘ ܩܛܠ܃ ܐܢܐ ܐܢܐ ܘܡܚܝܢܐ ܒܪ܆ ܘܐܝܟܢܘܬܐ
ܘܫܠܡܬ ܡܠܟܘܬܐ. ܘܡܛܠ ܗܠ ܐܢܫܐ ܕܒܥܠܬ ܒܢ ܕܘܟܬܐ
ܒܝܬ ܢܘܟܪܝܐ ܕܐܝܠܝܢ ܕܗܝܡܢܘ ܘܡܗܝܡܢܝܢ ܒܡܠܟܝܢ. ܘܐܝܟ
ܡܢܐ ܕܡܣܝܒ ܠܟ ܡܢ ܡܪܝܟ ܗܘܝܬ ܡܫܡܫ ܐܝܬ ܒܪ̈ܝܬܐ
ܒܬܠܬܐܝܬ. ܘܐܝܠܝܢ ܕܗܘܝܢ ܒܥܡܟ ܡܠܟ̈ܐ ܕܡܪ̈ܝܬܐ ܗܕܐ
ܕܡ̈ܠܐ ܙܘܕ̈ܩܐ ܡܬܠܝܢ ܐܢܐ ܕܐܬܠ ܠܗܘܢ ܕܗܕܝܡ ܒܡ
ܬܫܡܫܬܐ ܠܟ ܢܗܘܐ ܗ̇ܘ ܒܥܒܕܐ ܐܫܘܪܝܐ ܘܠܥܡܡܝܢ
ܕܡܬܬܒܥܐ ܠܟ ܠܬܩܘܬܗ ܕܒܫܬܐ ܐܢܐ ܢܗܒ ܐܢܐ ܠܟ ܕܠܐ
ܫܘܒܪ ܒܪ ܗܘܐ ܡܠܬܟ ܥܠܡܝܢܐ ܘܡܡܠܟܐ ܒܪܘܚܐ ܗܢܐ.
ܘܕܠܐ ܐܚܪ ܐܫܘܪܝܐ ܗܘܬ ܒܠܬ ܝܘܡܢ܆ ܡܬܠܝܬ ܠܐܬܘܪܝܐ
ܕܐܘܪܚ ܕܡܠܟܘܬ܆ ܘ . ܘ ܘܒܪ ܢܬܟ ܗܘܐ ܐܬܒܢܝ ܠܐܬܘܪܝܐ
ܕܡܠܟܘܬܗ. ܫܪܐ ܗܘܐ ܗܘ ܘܪܘܪܒܘܬܗ܆ ܒܥܡܗ. ܒܥܕܢܐ ܒܪ
ܒܥܕܢ ܦܟܪܐ. ܘܫܡܫܝܟܪܢ ܘܐܒܗܝ ܘܡܗܘܕܪܬ. ܒܡ ܫܪܒܐ
ܕܡܕܪ̈ܗܘܢ ܒܥܠܡܕܡ ܕܝܢ ܗ̇ܘ܆ ܒܝ̈ܬܗܘܢ ܘܫܒܚ ܗ̈ܘ܆ ܘܐܦ
ܐܪ̈ܥܗܘܢ ܘܒܢܘܬܐ ܕܠܗܘܢ ܡܫܒܚܝܢ ܗܘܘ ܐܦ ܗܢܘܢ
ܠܐܠܗܐ ܕܐܦܢ ܗܘܐ ܪ̈ܓܝܫܝܢ ܠܗܘܢ. ܒܪ ܒܫܪܝܢ ܗܘܘ
ܒܫܘܬܐ ܕܡܫܝܚܝܢ ܗܘܘ ܒܗ. ܘܡܗܕܝܢ ܗܘܘ ܒܥܒܪܬܐ
ܕܡܫܝܚܐ. ܘܒܪ ܒܢܝܐ ܗܘܐ ܐܝ̈ܕܐ܆ ܒܕܘܬܐ ܡܗܪܒܝܢ ܗܘܘ ܒܗ̇
ܢܕܪܐ ܘܩܘܪ̈ܒܢܐ ܗܢܘܢ ܘܫܘܬܐ ܕܡܕܢܚܐ. ܘܬܡܢ ܡܫܒܚܝܢ
ܗܘܘ ܥܠ ܩܘܡܬ ܫܒܚܗܘܢ. ܘܦܪܥ ܗܘܐ ܠܗܬܗ ܕܐܢܐ܆ ܒܗܢܕܐ
ܡܪ̈ܝܬܐ ܐܝܠܝܢ ܕܪ̈ܒܐ ܗܘܘ ܘܩܘܡܕܐ ܘܠܒܢ ܫܘܕܐ ܕܡܠ̈ܟܐ
ܘܡܫܬܐܠܝܢ ܗܘܘ ܠܗ ܥܠ ܥܪܒܗ ܕܡܫܝܚܐ ܕܐܬܡܪܬ ܠܗܘܢ
ܕܐܬܒܢܝܐ ܒܪ ܐܠܗܐ ܗܘܐ ܡܬܢܝܚܐ ܗܘܐ ܠܗܘܢ ܐܝܟ ܒܪ̈ܝܫܐ
ܬܫܒܘܚܬܐ ܠܟ ܡܫܒܚܝܢ ܗܘܘ܆ ܫܢܪܝܢ ܗܘܘ ܒܗ.
ܘܠܥܠܡ ܡܫܝܚ ܗܘܐ ܠܗܘܢ ܥܠ ܗܕܐ ܥܠ ܟܠ ܕܝܢ ܗܘ܆

ܡܛܠ ܗܢܐ ܝܠܗ ܝܠܗ ܕܪ̈ܓܠܝ ܕܐܬܐܡܪ ܠܝ ܕܢܦܩ ܒܠ ܒܪܒܐ ܕܠܐ ܡܡܟܠ ܩ̈ܠܝܢ. ܗܘܐ ܢܦܩܬ ܡܡܟܢܐ ܒܠ ܐܬ̈ܪܘܬܐ ܕܐ̈ܪܝܫܘܬܘܢ ܦܬ̈ܟܡܐ ܕܦܩ̈ܘܕܬ، ܕܟܡܘܢ ܝܘܡ ܡܟܐܬܘܬܗ ܕܡܫܝܚܐ ܕܗܘܬ ܐܦ ܕܒܬܘܪܐ ܕܬܗܘܐ. ܘܫܘܒܚܬܐ ܘܢܘܫܒܚܐ ܕܟܠܗܘܢ ܒ̈ܢܝܫܐ. ܘܦܘܪܫܢܐ ܕܗܘܐ ܒܝܬ ܡܗܘ̈ܡܢܐ ܠܦܘܪ̈ܐ. ܘܡܢܗܘܢ ܒܪܫܐ ܒܫܢܐ ܕܢܛܪ ܠܐܠܗܝܢ ܕܠܐ ܝܕܥܝܢ ܠܐܠܗܐ ܘܡܗܠܟܢܐ ܒܪ̈ܚܡܐ ܕܢܘܗܪܐ ܕܒܬܘܪ ܕܡܟܠܘܢ ܐܝܠܝܢ ܕܗܝܡܢܘ ܒܗ ܒܡܫܝܚܐ ܘܦܪ̈ܩܘ ܠܗ ܘܠܐܒܘܗܝ ܙܒܢܐ. ܘܐܘܕܘ ܒܗ ܘܒܪܘܚܐ ܕܐܠܗܘܬܗ. ܘܡܟܝܠ ܙܕܩ ܠܝ ܕܢܠܦ ܡܠܬܐ ܕܗܟܢܐ. ܘܐܝܠܝܢ ܕܡܟܠܘ ܡܠܬܗ ܕܡܫܝܚܐ. ܢܦܩܘ ܡ̈ܐܢܝܢ. ܘܐܦ ܐܝܠܝܢ ܕܪ̈ܒܝܢ ܕܢܬܘܬܦܘܢ ܒܗܢ ܒܝܠܘܬܐ ܘܒܝܢ ܢ̈ܐܘܠܘܢ ܠܒܬ̈ܗܘܢ ܘܫܝ ܗܘܝܐ ܒܗܕܐ. ܗܘ ܐܒܝ ܥܠܝܫܐ ܕܫܪܐ ܗܘܐ ܕܗܘ̈ܝܐܐ ܕܐܢܫܘܬܐ ܕܡܕܝܢܬܐ ܦܫܬ ܠܢ ܠܘܬܗ. ܘܕܠ̈ܝܠܐ ܗܘܐ ܗܘܘ ܐܝܠܝܢ ܕܠܐ ܗܘܘ ܗܘܘ ܒܗܘܢ ܒܪܢܐ ܒܕ ܐܦ ܗܘܢ ܕܠ̈ܝܠܐ ܒܬܪ ܗܢ̈ܬܐ ܡܠܠ ܡܢܠܘ ܗܘܐ ܠܩ̈ܠܘܗܝ. ܘܫܡܥܘ ܗܘܘ ܒܗܒܪ̈ܬܐ ܕܒܪܘܪ̈ܘܬܗ ܕܡܫܝܚܐ. ܘܟܕ ܐܡܪ ܗܘܐ ܗܠܝܢ ܐܒܝ ܥܠܝܫܐ ܗܘܝ ܒܠܗ ܒܪ̈ܒܐ ܕܐܘܪܗܝ. ܘܫܪܐ ܗܘܐ ܐܡ̈ܪܝܢ ܡܠܟܐ ܕܟܠܗ ܡܕܝܢܬܐ ܫܕܪܬ ܗܘܬ ܒܡܠܟܘܬܗ ܠܒ̈ܪܝܐ ܘܒ̈ܢܝܐ ܥܒܘܫܬ ܘܐܡܪܝܢ ܠܗ ܕܪܬܪ ܗܘ ܘܡܗܝܡܢ ܡܫܝܚܐ ܕܪ̈ܓܠܝ ܠܘܬܟ ܐܦ ܗܘ ܫܕ، ܗܘܐ ܠܒ ܒܗܘܕܐ ܒܕ ܡܫܒܚ ܗܘܐ ܠܐܠܗܐ. ܕܐܝܟ ܡܢܐ ܕܡܫܒܚ ܗܘܐ ܡܢ ܫܢ ܠܒܘܠܬܐ ܕܠܗ ܒܠ ܡܫܝܚܐ ܗܒܢܐ ܫܕܐ ܗܘܐ ܫܬ̈ܠܐ ܐܬ̈ܟܫܗܐ ܕܟܒܕ ܗܘܐ ܗܘ ܐܒܝ ܥܠܝܫܐ ܒܫܡܗ ܕܡܫܝܚܐ. ܘܐܡܪ ܠܗ ܐܦ ܗܘ ܐܡ̈ܪܝܢ ܡܠܟܐ ܕܐܝܟ ܡܢܐ ܕܥܠܝܫܬ ܠܗ ܠܡܫܝܚܐ ܒܐܪ̈ܙܘܬ ܕܠܐܬܗ. ܘܐܝܟ ܡܢܐ ܕܥܠܝܫ ܠܝ ܐܦ ܗܘ ܡܠܬܐ ܘܐܦ ܡܢܝ ܕܠܝ ܡܡܟܢܐ ܗܒܢܐ ܡܗܝܡܢ ܐܢܐ ܒܠ ܡܦ̈ܩܢ ܫܢܝ. ܘܟܕܘܡ ܒܗܠܝܢ ܡܗܘܐ ܐܢܐ ܒܕ ܡܕܬܒܗܪ ܐܢܐ ܡܛܠܠ ܕܐܦ ܝܕܒ ܐܢܐ ܕܠܬ ܝܠܗ

ܘܒܡܘܬܪ̈ܝܗܘܢ ܕܥ̈ܠܝܡܐ ܥܠܝܗܝ ܒܗܘܢ ܡܬܡܨܝܢ ܗܘܘ ܒܪ.
ܡܛܡܪ ܗܘܐ ܠܗܘܢ ܘܡܬܝܕܥܬ ܕܗܘܘ ܕܒܝܬ ܦܓܪ̈ܝܗܘܢ ܘܡܬܕܝܢ
ܠܡܫ̈ܒܚܘܬܗܘܢ. ܐܝܟ ܕܙܕܩ ܠܐܢܫܐ ܕܡܫܝܚ ܡܪܢ ܡܬܬܒܥܘܢ
ܕܐܠܗܐ. ܘܗܘܝܘܬܗܘܢ ܠܐ ܕܚܝܩ ܡܢ ܡܫ̈ܡܫܢܘܬܐ ܕܒܠܬܐ ܘܡܢ
ܡܠܠܐ ܕܪܘܚܢܐ. ܘܡܢ ܗܘܕܝܘܬܐ ܕܫܘܪܝܐ ܕܟܘܪܐ ܦܬܟܐ.
ܘܡܢ ܚܪ̈ܫܐ ܕܠܝܬ ܥܠܝܗܘܢ ܕܝܢܐ. ܘܡܢ ܚܫ̈ܟܐ ܘܡܢ̈ܥܬܐ
ܘܪܘܚ̈ܐ. ܘܡܢ ܚܠܦܐ ܘܡܢܬ ܠܒܐ ܕܡܫܬܒܗܪܝܢ ܒܗܘܢ ܩ̈ܠܝܐ
ܠܢܦܫܐ. ܘܡܢ ܒܣ̈ܒܪܐ ܘܡܠܦܢܐ ܕܬܚܠܝܢ ܥܠܝܗܘܢ ܬ̈ܒܥܐ.
ܘܐܪ̈ܚܘܬܐ ܡܒܢܝܗܘܢ ܡܢܗܘܢ ܒܐܦ̈ܝܐ ܕܒܘܠܝܐ. ܘܡܫܘܚܕܐ
ܘܬܘܪ̈ܒܝܐ ܕܡܬܚܣܒܝܢ ܒܗܘܢ ܕܦ̈ܐ. ܘܒܪ ܗܕܐ ܬܫܡܫܬܐ
ܕܐܬܪ̈ܝܬܘܢ ܠܗ ܠܐ ܬܘܒ ܢܗܘܐ ܠܗܘܢ ܦܠܚܘܬܐ ܐܪܝܟܐ
ܡܪܢܐ ܗܘ ܒܪ ܦܠܚܘܬܐ ܕܬܫܡܫܬܗܘܢ ܥܠ ܡ̈ܢܝܢ ܚܝ̈ܝܗܘܢ.
ܘܗܘܝܘܬܗܘܢ ܢܣܝܒܝܢ ܠܟܠܗ ܪܘܫܡܐ ܕܡܫܡܫܢܘܬܐ. ܘܠܐ
ܗܘܝܘܬܗܘܢ ܪܚܝܩܝܢ ܡܢ̈ܬܘܢ ܕܐܠܗܐ ܗܘܝܐ. ܘܗܘܝܘܬܗܘܢ
ܥܒܝܕ ܐܝܬܘܗܝ ܕܝܠܗ ܟܘܪܣܝܐ ܘܡܫܡܫܢܘܬܐ. ܘܠܐ ܬܗܘܘܢ
ܬܘܠܕܬܐ ܠܒܪ̈ܝܬܐ. ܕܐܠܗܐ ܢܬܚܙܐ ܒܗܘܢ ܥܒܕܗ ܕܗܘ
ܕܬܫܡ ܗܘܐ ܠܒܪ̈ܝܬܐ ܐܝܟ ܗܘܐ ܕܐܢܫ. ܥܠ ܕܗ̇ܘ ܗܒܠ ܕܐܢܫ
ܠܗܘܢ ܢܬܚܝܘܢ ܕܥܠܝܢ ܐܝܬܘܗܝ ܗܘ ܠܥܠܡܝܢ ܕܡܬܕܪܐ
ܐܝܬܘܗܝ ܘܡܠܝܢ ܐܝܬܘܗܝ. ܘܡܫܡܫܝܢ ܗܘܘ ܒܗܘܢ ܒܕܝܬܐ
ܕܒܢܐ ܗܘܐ ܗܘ ܐܝܕ. ܡܢ ܡܠܬܗ ܘܦܘܩܕܢܗ ܕܐܝܟܢ ܡܠܟܐ
ܒܪ ܡܬܦܪܢܣ ܗܘܘ ܡܢ ܕܡܠܟܐ ܘܡܢ ܕܐܝܪ̈ܘܗܝ. ܡܟܝܠ
ܠܒܬܐ ܕܐܠܗܐ ܘܡܢܗܘܢ ܠܦܘܪܫܢܐ ܕܩ̈ܘܕܫܐ. ܒܒܝܬ ܕܝܢ
ܡܚܙܝܢܐ ܥܠܝܗ ܒܗܘܢ ܒܢܝܢ ܐܬܬܝܢ ܠܝܠܘܬܐ ܕܬܫܡܫܬܐ.
ܘܠܬܫܡܫܬܐ ܒܬܘܕܝܬܐ ܘܫܘܒܚܐ ܕܕܝܠܗܘܢ ܘܒܢܝܬ ܩ̈ܝܬܐ
ܡܬܒܢܝܢ ܗܘܘ ܘܠܒܝ̈ܬܗܘܢ ܒܒܪ̈ܝܐ ܕܢܘܗܪܐ ܡܕܝܢ ܗܘܘ.
ܘܡܫ̈ܬܐ ܕܒܝܬܐ ܒܪܒܝܗܘܢ ܒܪܝܢ ܗܘܘ. ܘܥܠܝܗܘܢ ܒܗܘܪܐ
ܕܒܝܬܐ ܐܡܪܝܢ ܗܘܘ. ܘܗܘܒܪ̈ܝܐ ܕܙܕ̈ܩܬܐ ܗܒܪܝܢ ܗܘܘ

ܒܢ̈ܝܗܘܢ. ܘܥܠ ܟܠ ܡܐ ܕܥܒܕ ܗܘ̣ ܐܝ̈ܕܝܗܘܢ ܚܙܘ.
ܘܠܡܕܝܢܬܐ ܕܐܬܘܪ ܗܘܘ ܥܠܘܗܝ. ܢܫ̈ܐ ܐܦ ܐܢܝܢ ܗܘ̈ܝ ܡܕܡܝܢ̈ܢ
ܘܡܫܬܠܡ ܗܘܘ ܡ̈ܠܘܗܝ. ܒܗܝܡܢܘܬܐ ܘܡܗܝܡܢܘܬܐ ܘܠܘܬ ܗܘܐ
ܐܝܟ ܕܝܐܐ ܗܘܐ ܠܡܗܠܟܘ. ܠܐ ܓܝܪ ܥܒܕܝܢ ܗܘܘ ܢܟܝܠܐ
ܕܟܕܒ ܗܘܐ ܕܢܫܦܩ ܐܝܟ ܠܡܗܠܟܘ. ܥܡܐ ܕܝܢ ܘܟܗ̈ܢܘܗܝ
ܕ̈ܝܪܐ ܕܒܡܕܝܢܬܐ ܕܝܪܥܐ ܗܘܝܐ ܒܗ ܦܪܝܫܐ ܘܕܡܝܐ ܒܝ̈ܬܗܘܢ
ܟܕ ܚܙܘ ܗܘܘ ܐܬ̈ܘܬܐ ܕܥܒܕ ܗܘܐ ܪܗܛܝܢ ܗܘܘ ܘܡܫܬܪ
ܗܘܘ ܠܘܬ̈ܗ ܕܠܫܡܗܘܢ ܡܫܡܥܝܢ ܗܘܘ ܡܛܠ ܢܒܗ ܘܥܠ
ܐܠܗ̈ܘܬܗ ܠܒܪ ܡܢ ܟܠܗ ܐܪܥܐ ܕܡܬܚܙܝܐ ܟܪܟܐ ܘܡܢ ܗܘܘ
ܡܫܡܥܝܢ. ܕܬܪܥܝܬܗ ܕܗܘܢܐ ܕܠܡܕܝܢܬܐ ܕܗܘ ܐܪܥܐ ܡܫܡܥܐ
ܘܡܫܝܚܐ ܕܥܒܕܝܢ ܗܘܝܢ ܟܠ ܕܥܒܕ ܗܘܐ ܒܐܬܘ̈ܬܐ ܕܐܠܗܘܬܗ.
ܘܥܠ ܐܝܠܝܢ ܕܡܗܝܡܢܝܢ ܗܘܘ ܒܡܫܝܚܐ ܡܩܒܠ ܗܘܐ ܠܗܘܢ
ܐܕܝ. ܘܡܥܡܕ ܗܘܐ ܠܗܘܢ ܒܫܡ ܐܒܐ ܘܒܪܐ ܘܪܘܚܐ
ܕܩܘܕܫܐ. ܘܐܝܠܝܢ ܕܠܦܬܟܪܐ ܘܠܣܛܘܢܐ ܫܓܕܝܢ ܗܘܘ ܠܘܬ
ܨ̈ܠܡܘܗܝ ܦܠܚܝܢ ܗܘܘ. ܘܡܬܦܢܝܢ ܡܢ ܦܬܟܪܘܬܐ ܕܥܒܕܘܬܐ
ܕܣܢܝܬܐ. ܐܦ ܟܘ̈ܡܪܐ ܕܗܠܝܢ ܢܟܣܘ̈ܗܝ ܘܟܗ̈ܢܐ ܐܝܠܝܢ
ܕ̈ܦܛܚܐ ܡܕܒܚܝܢ ܗܘܘ ܐܦ ܗܢܘܢ ܐܬܦܢܝܘ ܗܘܘ
ܘܐܬܬܠܡܕܘ ܘܐܘܕܝܘ ܗܘܘ ܒܡܫܝܚܐ ܕܪܒܗ ܗܘ ܕܐܠܗܐ ܚܝܐ.
ܠܐ ܕܝܢ ܐܒܓܪ ܡܠܟܐ ܐܦ ܠܐ ܐܕܝ ܫܠܝܚܐ. ܚܝܠܐ ܗܘܐ
ܠܐܢܫ ܕܡܬܦܪܐܬ ܢܗܘܐ ܗܘܐ ܒܗ ܒܡܫܝܚܐ. ܡܛܠ ܕܐܠܐ
ܡܠܦܢܐ ܕܐܢܫ ܡܠܦܢܐ ܕܐܬܘ̈ܬܐ ܚܝܠܐ ܗܘܐ ܠܦܓܪ̈ܐ
ܕܢܫܡܥܘܢ ܗܘܘ ܒܗ. ܘܫܘܒܚܐ ܡܫܬܠܡ ܗܘܐ ܡܠܦܢܘܬܗ
ܠܗ ܐܬܪܐ ܗܢܐ ܕܒܗ ܢܗܪ ܘܦܫܛܬܐ ܒܠܒܗܘܢ ܕܐܢܫ̈ܘܗܝ, ܗܘܘ
ܐܦ ܕܝܢ ܒܒܝܬ ܫܐܕ̈ܐ ܘܦܬ̈ܟܪܐ ܕܡܠܟܐ ܘܡܠܦ ܘܒܪܝܠܡܐ
ܘܒܪܗܡܐ ܒܢ ܥܒܕܐ ܕܐܟܣܢܝܐ ܫܡ̈ܝܗܘܢ ܢܫܡܗ, ܗܘܘ
ܠܐܕܝ ܫܠܝܚܐ. ܘܡܛܠ ܐܢܘܢ ܘܐܫܬܘܝܘ ܐܢܘܢ ܒܗܘܢ ܒܫܘܫܛܬܐ
ܟܕ ܡܬܪܝܢ ܗܘܘ ܒܕܘܒܪܐ ܕܫܒܝܠܐ ܕܫܪܪܐ. ܘܕܝ̈ܢܐ

ܐܪܟܐ. ܘܐܟܠ ܗܘ̈ܘ، ܘܐܦ ܟܠܗܘܢ ܒܢ̈ܝܬܐ. ܘܐܝܟ ܕܗܘ
ܢܫ̈ܘܗܝ ܒܢܝܐ. ܘܡܢܝܢܐ ܐܘܟܝܬ ܗܘܬ ܠܗ̇ ܟܠܗ̇ ܒܢ̈ܬܐ
ܘܡܗܡܢܘܗ̇ ܕܒܢ̈ܬܐ. ܘܡܚܒܒ ܡܠܦܢܘܬܗ ܡܕܒܪܐ ܡܟܝܠܐ ܘܙܗ
ܕܬܫܡܫ ܥܠ ܒܥܒܐ ܕܡܫܘܕܥܐ ܕܘܠܝ ܟܒܕ. . .

ܘܥܒܕ ܗܘܐ ܦܠܚܘܗ ܡܢ ܘܕܝܪ ܗܘܐ ܠܐܦܝ̈ ܡܠܦܢܐ
ܘܗܒܢܐ ܟܒܕ ܠܗ.

ܕܐܢܬܬܐ ܕܢܪܘܬܝ ܕܠܗܬ، ܡܠܬ ܘܐܬܬܪܬ ܡܕܝܢ. ܟܠ
ܡܕܡ ܕܗܘܐ ܗܘܘ ܡܫܘܕܥܐ ܒܝܘܡܐ. ܐܦ ܥܠܠܗܘ ܡܢܗܘܢܐ
ܥܒܕ ܗܘܐ ܘܐܘܕܥܗ ܠܐܘܠܨܢܘܗ ܡܦܪܥܐ ܕܠܐ ܟܠܗܘܢ
ܕܠܗܘܢ ܕܘܠܝ ܕܥܒܕܬ ܠܝ. ܡܛܠ ܕܝܢ ܕܦܘܪܥܐ ܕܒܬܪ ܐܘܦܢܝܐ
ܕܡܕܪܘ̇ ܥܠ ܡܐܢ ܒܗܢܐ ܙܒܢܐ. ܡܛܠ ܗܢܐ ܠܐ ܐܫܟܚܬ
ܕܐܬܟܒܪ ܠܡܗܘܬܐ ܗܕܐ. ܡܠܦܢ ܐܢܐ ܕܝܢ ܕܟܕܐ ܕܗܘܐ
ܠܝ ܥܠܝܐ. ܐܫܡܫ ܟܠܗܘܢ ܢܡܘܣܐ ܥܠ ܡܫܘܕܥܐ ܕܠܐ
ܗܕܝܢ ܢܡܘܣܐܝܬ. ܘܡܛܠ ܗܢܐ ܐܦ ܥܠܠܗܘ ܕܟܕܡ ܗܘܐ
ܠܝ ܬܡܢ ܡܢܗܘܢܐ. ܫܪܝܬ ܠܫܡܗܘ، ܐܢܫܐ ܘܫܪܝܬܗ ܠܗ
ܒܢ̈ܝܐ ܥܠ ܕܢܦܩ ܡܢ ܢܡܘܣܗ. ܘܥܒܕ ܗܘܐ ܢ̈ܒܝܐ ܠܡܫܘܕܥܐ
ܘܢܦܩ ܗܘܐ ܠܡܥܒܕܢܐ ܠܢܫܘܗܝ ܕܡܫܘܕܥܐ. ܗ̇ܘ ܕܐܝܟ
ܕܥܒܕ ܐܢܐ ܟܠܗܘ، ܕܠܐ ܘܡܦܩܐ ܕܡܗܘܬܐ. ܕܬܘܒ ܗܘܐ
ܘܡܬܕܪ ܡܢܗܘܢ ܘܕܦ ܗܘܐ. ܬܘܪܐܝܬ ܕܝܢ ܕܡܢ̈ܝܢܘܗܝ ܚܝܢ
ܗܘܘ ܥܠ ܡܕܡ ܕܟܕܡ ܗܘܐ. ܐܝܬ ܕܝܢ ܐܝܟ ܫܪܘܬܝ ܕܠܗܬ،
ܘܡܢܟܐ ܫܪܪܐ ܕܠܝ ܘܕܐܢ̈ܫܝ. ܫܦܝܪ ܒܟܕܘ ܕܥܒܕܬ ܠܝ
ܗܒܢܐ.

ܘܡܠܠ ܗܘܐ ܐܦܝ̈ ܡܠܦܢܐ ܠܐܪܘܦܠܝܘܗ ܕܐܫܬܕܪ
ܗܘܐ ܡܢ ܦܠܚܘܗ ܡܢ ܢ̈ܐܕܘܗܝ. ܘܥܢܐ ܗܘܐ ܫܪܪܗ ܒܟܝ̈ܢܐ
ܕܐܡܪܐ ܕܙܘܡܢ ܠܗ̇ ܡܢ ܕܫܪܪܗ ܗܘܐ ܠܗܬܗ. ܘܡܢ ܐܘܪܚܗ،
ܐܝܠ ܗܘܐ ܠܬܫܡܫܬܐ ܐܡܬܐ ܕܐܬܠܗܘܢ، ܗܘܐ ܥܠܝܗ ܬܪܥܐ
ܕܡܠܟܐ. ܘܡܢ ܬܡܢ ܬܘܒ ܐܝܠ ܗܘܐ ܠܐܪܘܦܠܝܐ ܕܬܡܢ ܗܘܐ

ܢܚܬ ܒܪܘܚܐ ܘܫܠܝܛܐ ܐܝܟ ܡܠܟܘܬܗ ܕܐܪܝ ܓܐܕܝܘܗܝ.
ܘܟܢܘܫܝ̈ܗ ܕܡܫܝܚܝܐ ܚ̈ܕܬܐ ܡܬܒܢܝܢ ܗܘ̈ܝ. ܘܐܝܟܢܐ ܕܫܝܢܘܬܐ
ܡܫܬܠܡܝܢ ܗܘܘ ܡܢܗ ܩܘܪܒܢܐ. ܗܟܢܐ ܕܐܦ ܡܕ̈ܝܢܬܐ ܒܫܝܢܘܬܐ
ܕܬܚܘܬܐ ܠܡܠܟ ܪ̈ܗܘܡܝܐ ܚܟܝܡ ܗܘܘ ܕܢܣܒܘܢ ܗܘܘ ܐܬ̈ܘܬܐ
ܕܟܕ ܗܘܐ ܗܘ ܐܪܝ. ܘܐܝܠܝܢ ܕܡܬܬܠܡܕܝܢ ܗܘܘ ܡܫܬܠܡܝܢ
ܗܘܘ ܡܢܗ ܐܝܟܢܐ ܕܒܫܝܢܘܬܐ ܘܒܐܬܪܐ ܕܫܠܡܘ ܕܐܬܘܪ̈ܝܐ
ܠܒ̈ܢܝ ܒܝܬܗܘܢ ܡܬܬܠܡܕܝܢ ܗܘܘ ܘܟܬ̈ܒܐ ܕܝܘܠܦܢܐ ܗܘܝܢ ܒܝܘܡܐ
ܒܝܘܡ ܗܘܘ ܡܢ ܡܠܟܐ ܕܩܕܡ܆ ܠܒܪܐ ܘܥܡܗ܆ ܠܫܡܝܐ ܀
ܢܗܘ̇ ܕܝܢ ܡܠܟܐ ܕܐܬܘܪ̈ܝܐ. ܟܕ ܫܡܥ ܗܘܐ ܗܢܝܢ ܗܠܝܢ
ܕܚܙܐ ܗܘܐ ܐܪܝ ܥܠܝܡܐ. ܥܠܬ ܗܘܐ ܠܗ ܠܐܟܣܢܝܐ ܡܠܟܐ.
ܕܐܘ ܫܕܪ ܠܝ ܠܦܪܣܐ ܗܘ ܕܩܠܝܠ ܐܬ̈ܘܬܐ ܒܟܕ ܓܐܕܝܘܗܝ
ܕܐܣܝܘܬܗ ܘܐܫܬܡܥ ܡܠܬܗ ܐܘ ܥܠܘܗܝ ܠܝ ܟܠ ܕܣܢܝܩ ܕܒܟܪ
ܗܘܐ ܒܟܪܣܐ ܕܠܐܝ. ܘܟܬܒ ܗܘܐ ܐܓܪܬ ܠܦܪܘܗܝ، ܘܐܘܕܥܗ
ܗܘܐ ܥܠܘ ܬܫܒܘܚܬܐ ܕܦܪܣܗ ܕܐܪܝ، ܡܢ ܫܘܪܐ ܠܫܘܠܡܐ.
ܘܠܐ ܫܡܥ ܗܘܐ ܡܕܡ ܕܠܐ ܟܬܒ ܗܘܐ ܠܗ. ܟܕ ܕܝܢ ܫܡܥ
ܗܘܐ ܦܪܣܗ، ܐܝܠܝܢ ܕܐܬܟܬܒ ܥܠܘܗܝ ܠܗ. ܬܡܗ ܗܘܐ ܘܐܬܕܡܪ ܀
ܐܡܪ ܕܝܢ ܡܠܟܐ ܡܛܠ ܕܠܐ ܐܫܟܚ ܗܘܐ ܕܢܟܬܘܒ ܠܡܠܟ
ܪ̈ܗܘܡܝܐ ܘܢܐܙܠ ܗܘܐ ܠܦܝܠܝܦܘܣ ܘܢܦܠܛ ܗܘܐ ܠܫܘܕܥܐ
ܟܠ ܕܐܣܩܘܗܝ ܠܡܫܝܚܐ. ܟܬܒ ܐܓܪܬܐ ܘܫܕܪ ܗܘܐ ܠܡܠܟ
ܦܝܠܝܦܘܣ ܐܣܝ. ܟܕ ܟܬܒ ܒܗ ܗܟܢܐ.

ܐܡܪ ܡܠܟܐ ܠܡܪܝ ܦܝܠܝܦܘܣ ܐܣܝ. ܟܕ ܢܚܬ ܐܢܐ ܕܐܬܚܪܡ ܡܢ
ܡܠܟܘܬܟ ܠܐ ܡܬܟܬܫܐ. ܟܬܒ ܐܢܐ ܘܡܘܕܥ ܐܢܐ ܠܦܠܛܘܢ
ܕܫܠܐ ܘܪܒܐ ܕܗܘܕܝܐ ܕܬܫܒܘܚܬ ܐܝܟ ܕܐܡܪܝܢ ܒܐܬܪܐ
ܕܦܝܠܝܦܘܣ ܐܬܚܙܝ ܗܘܐ ܘܢܦܩ ܗܘܐ ܠܡܫܝܚܐ ܕܠܐ ܗܘܠܘܬܐ
ܕܡܠܟܐ. ܟܕ ܚܙܐ ܗܘܐ ܡܬܚܡܠܘ ܐܝܬܘܗܝ ܘܬܕܡܪܬܐ ܘܡܫܘܚܬܐ
ܗܘܐ ܠܗܘܢ ܚܙܝܐ ܡܩܒܠܐ. ܗܟܢܐ ܕܐܦ ܩܕܡܝܐ ܐܝܟ ܠܗܘܢ.
ܡܟܪܙܐ ܕܘܡܣܘܗܝ ܗܘܘ ܡܢܝ ܗܘܐ ܫܡܥܐ ܘܟܠ ܗܘܬ ܐܦ

ܥ̈ܠܝܡܐ ܢܨ̈ܝܚܐ. ܗܟܢܐ ܐܦ ܐܢܬܘܢ ܠܐ ܬܬܒܥܘܢ ܡܢܗܘܢ: ܘܠܐ ܬܬܚܪܘܢ ܥܡܗܘܢ ܒܕܝܢ. ܐܝܟܢܐ ܕܐܦ ܐܢܐ ܒܗܘܢ ܗܘ ܡܬܕܒܪ ܐܢܐ ܒܢܝܚܘܬܗܘܢ ܘܠܐ ܥܢܫܬ ܡܢܗܘܢ ܠܡܬܢܨܚܐ ܐܘ ܠܡܫܠܐ ܕܠܐ ܐܬܢܒܪܐ ܗܘܝܬ ܠܫ̈ܢܐ ܬ̈ܠܡܝܕܐ ܕܢܦܩܝܢ ܠܐܠܝܢ ܕܒܗܠܝܢ ܡܬܕܒܪܝܢ. ܐܙܕܗܪܘ ܗܟܝܠ ܒܬܫܡܫܬܐ ܗܕܐ ܕܐܫܬܠܡ ܐܢܬܘܢ ܘܒܕܝܠܝܬܐ ܘܒܪ̈ܬܬܐ ܗܘܝܬܘܢ ܡܢܟܘܢ ܐܢܬܘܢ ܒܗ ܘܡܫܡܫܝܢ ܒܠܚܘܕ. ܠܐ ܗܘܝܬܘܢ ܡܫܡܫܝܢ ܒܗ ܒܟܢܘܫܬܐ ܒܫ̈ܢܐ ܐܠܐ ܒܦܘܪ̈ܫܢܐ ܕܡܫܝܚܘܬܐ. ܘܬܫ̈ܡܫܘܢܗ ܕܡܫܝܚܐ ܡܢ ܦܘܩ̈ܕܢܘܗܝ ܠܐ ܬܒܛܠܘܢ. ܘܡܟܝܟܘܬܐ ܒܓܠܘܬܐ ܕܟ̈ܪܝܐ ܠܬܚܘܬܗܘܢ ܠܐ ܬܬܒܪܘܢ. ܐܙܕܗܪܘ ܒܥܪ̈ܐ ܕܐܫܬܕܪܘ ܐܢܬܘܢ ܘܒܫܘܠܛܢܐ ܕܡܫܚܬܐ ܕܩܒܠܬܘܢ. ܘܒܪܬܘܬܐ ܕܫ̈ܢܐ ܕܡܓܒܠ ܐܢܐ ܠܟܘܢ. ܡܛܠ ܕܡܕܡ ܒܝܫ ܕܡܫܝܚܐ ܡܬܬܒܥܝܢ ܐܢܬܘܢ ܠܗ. ܡܢܐ ܕܒܟܕ ܢܘܟܪܝܐ ܒܡ ܙܒܢܘܬܐ ܘܟ̈ܠܝܢܐ. ܘܡܢܐ ܕܢܬܒ ܒܗܦܗ ܡܢ ܬܓܪ̈ܐ ܒܪܝܫܬܐ ܕܡܬܚܙܝܢܐ ܒܪ ܡܠܟܐ ܗܘ ܒܪܝ ܘܐܙܠ ܕܢܬܒ ܡܠܟܘܬܐ ܘܢܗܦܘܟ ܘܢܐܬܐ ܘܢܒܒܕ ܢܘܫܟܐ ܠܟܠܗܘܢ ܬ̈ܡܢ ܐܢܫܐ. ܘܗܝܕܝܢ ܢܬܒ ܥܠ ܟܘܪܣܝܐ ܕܡܠܟܘܬܐ ܘܕܝܢ ܬ̈ܚܬܐ ܘܚ̈ܝܐ ܐܝܟ ܕܐܡܪ ܠܝ. ܚܢܢܐ ܗܫܬܐ ܕ̈ܚܢܝܟܘܢ ܡܢ ܙܘܥܐ ܠܐ ܬܬܬܟܝܢ ܕܠܐ ܢܦܠܘܢ ܬܘܩ̈ܠܬܟܘܢ ܒܟܐܪܘܙܐ ܕܠܝܬ ܒܗ ܬܘܩܠܬܐ. ܐܠܐ ܬܘܒܥܐ ܗܘܢܐ ܒܬ̈ܚܠܝܬܗ ܗܘܝܬܘܢ ܒܗܝܢ ܐܢܬܘܢ ܐܚ̈ܪܢܝܬܐ ܘܦܩܕܝܢ ܐܢܬܘܢ ܕܬܛܒܝܢ ܘܚܕܝܢ ܐܢܬܘܢ ܒܚܝ̈ܢܘܬܐ ܗܘܝܬܘܢ ܚܝܒܝܢ ܬܚܝܪܬܐ ܘܢܛܪܝܢ ܐܢܬܘܢ ܥܡ̈ܢܘܬܐ. ܡܛܠ ܕܟܐܪ̈ܝܒܘܢ ܡܬܬܒܝܢ ܢܦܘܬܗ ܕܡܫܝܚܐ. ܠܐ ܗܘܝܬܘܢ ܚܙܝܢ ܐܢܬܘܢ ܠܐܝܦܪܐ ܒܟܘܪܐ. ܙܒܢܐ ܒܪ ܕܢܫܪ ܕܢܬܦܪ ܡܢ ܡܪ̈ܚܘܬܗ. ܒܟܕ ܒܟܕ ܡܢܝܐ ܡܪ̈ܢܘܗܝ ܡܪܥܝܬܗ. ܬܗܘܐ ܗܦܟܬܐ ܒܠܒܘܬܟܘܢ ܥܠ ܐܡܪ̈ܐ ܥܒܪ̈ܐ ܕܡܠܐܩܝܗܘܢ ܚܙܝܢ ܦܪ̈ܝܘܦܗ ܕܐܒܐ. ܕܠܐ ܡܬܚܙܝܐ. ܘܠܐ ܬܗܘܘܢ ܩ̈ܐܦܐ ܕܬܘܩܠܬܐ ܘܡܕܡ ܒܡܪ̈ܐ. ܐܠܐ ܢܩܠ ܐܘܪܚܐ

ܠܛܝܒܪܝܘܣ ܩܣܪ. ܓܐܝܘܣ ܕܝܢ ܫܢ̈ܝܐ ܕܐܣܛܪܘܗܝ ܕܩܣܪ ܢܛܪ ܗܘܐ. ܘܐܫܬܡܥ ܗܘܐ ܐܦ ܗܘ ܐܪܣܛܝܕܣ ܡܢ ܛܝܒܪܝܘܣ ܥܠ ܚܝ̈ܠܐ ܕܥܒܕ ܗܘܐ ܐܕܝ، ܥܡ ܐܒܓܪ ܡܠܟܐ. ܘܡܟܐ ܕܗܘܐ ܗܘܐ ܠܗ ܥܠܬܐ ܡܢ ܦܪܟܐ. ܫܕܪ ܩܛܠ ܗܘܐ ܡܢ ܪ̈ܒܢܐ ܕܝܗ̈ܘܕܝܐ ܕܐܬܚܙܝ ܗܘܐ ܒܦܠܣܛܝܢܐ. ܘܟܕ ܫܡܥ ܗܘܐ ܐܒܓܪ ܡܠܟܐ ܚܕܝ ܗܘܐ ܒܗܕܐ ܛܒ. ܕܡܟܝܠ ܗܘܘ ܫܘܕܥܐ ܡܬܘܡ ܠܓܫܐ ܐܝܟ ܕܙܕܩ ○ ○ ○ ○

ܘܡܢ ܒܬܪ ܫܢ̈ܝܐ ܕܒܢܐ ܗܘܐ ܐܕܝ ܫܠܝܚܐ ܒܡܕܝܢܬܐ ܒܐܘܪܗܝ، ܘܐܬܬܩܢ ܗܘܐ ܒܟܠ ܡܕܡ ܕܙܕܩ ܗܘܐ ܠܗ ܘܬܠܡܕ. ܗܘܐ ܠܗܘܦܟܐ ܕܐܟܣܢܝܘܬܐ ܕܡܕܒܪܢܘܬܐ ܐܦ ܒܡܘܗܒܬܐ ܐܚܪ̈ܢܝܬܐ ܕܪ̈ܚܡܘܗܝ ܘܕܡ̈ܩܪܒܝܢ ܒܢܐ ܗܘܐ ܥܕ̈ܬܐ ܘܟܠܠ ܘܨܒܬ ܘܩܫ̈ܝܫܐ ܘܡܫ̈ܡܫܢܐ ܐܩܝܡ ܗܘܐ ܒܗܝܢ ܘܕܪܫ ܗܘܘ ܠܥܕ̈ܬܐ ܐܝܟ ܗܘܐ ܒܗܝܢ ܘܦܬ̈ܓܡܐ ܘܬܫܡܫܬܐ ܠܒܪ ܘܠܓܘ ܐܝܟ ܗܘܐ. ܒܬܪ ܗܠܝܢ ܟܠܗܝܢ ܐܬܒܪܗ ܗܘܐ ܒܗܝܡܢܘܬܐ. ܕܢܦܩ ܗܘܐ ܒܗ ܡܢ ܥܠܡܐ ܗܢܐ. ܘܩܪܐ ܗܘܐ ܠܐܓܝ ܩܕܡ ܟܠܗ ܟܢܫܐ ܕܥܕܬܐ ܘܩܪܒܗ ܗܘܐ ܘܥܒܕܗ ܗܘܐ ܡܕܒܪܢܐ ܘܦܩܘܕܐ ܒܕܘܟܬܗ. ܘܦܠܘܛ ܕܡܫܡܫܢܐ ܗܘܐ ܥܒܕܗ ܗܘܐ ܩܫܝܫܐ. ܘܠܥܒܕܫܡܝܐ ܕܩܫܝܫܐ ܗܘܐ ܥܒܕܗ ܗܘܐ ܡܫܡܫܢܐ. ܘܟܕ ܟܢܝܫܝܢ ܗܘܘ ܘܩܝܡܝܢ ܠܘܬܗ ܚܐܪ̈ܐ ܘܫܪ̈ܟܐ ܕܥܡܐ ܟܠܗ ܐܝܟ ܘܡܬܪܗܒ ܒܝ ܒܢܝ̈. ܘܦܘܫ ܒܝ ܚܘܒܐ ܘܫܪܪܐ ܒܝ ܦܠܘܛ ܥܡ ܫܪܟܐ ܕܡܪ̈ܥܝܬܗ: ܐܡܪ ܠܗܘܢ ܐܕܝ ܫܠܝܚܐ. ܕܗܒܝܢ ܐܚ̈ܝ ܘܗܘܕܡ ܟܠܗܘܢ ܕܫܡܥܬܘܢ ܠܝ ܕܟܠܡܕܡ ܕܡܟܪܙ ܗܘܝܬ ܠܟܘܢ ܘܡܠܠ ܗܘܝܬ ܠܟܘܢ ܘܫܡܥܬܘܢ ܗܘܝܬܘܢ ܡܢ ܗܘܢܐ ܐܬܕܟܪܘ ܒܠܒܟܘܢ: ܘܐܚܘܕܘܢ ܐܦ ܒܥܒܕ̈ܐ. ܡܛܠ ܕܗܟܢܐ ܦܩܕ ܠܝ ܡܪܢ. ܕܗܘ ܡܕܡ ܕܡܟܪܙ ܐܢܐ ܒܡܠܬܐ ܩܕܡ ܥܡܐ ܒܥܒܕܐ ܗܘܝܬ ܡܫܡܠܐ ܠܗ ܩܕܡ ܟܠܢܫ. ܘܐܝܟ ܦܘܩܕܢܗ ܘܢܡ̈ܘܣܐ ܕܡܫܝܚܐ ܠܬܠܡܝ̈ܕܐ ܒܐܘܪܫܠܡ ܘܬܠܡܕܝܢ ܗܘܘ ܒܗܘܢ ܐܦ

ܟܠܗܘܢ ܡܬܚܙܝܢ ܗܘܘ ܠܗܘܢ܆ ܐܠܐ ܐܦ ܡܫܘܕܥܐ ܘܡܢܗܪܐ
ܕܐܝܬ ܗܘܐ ܒܗ ܒܥܘܬܐ ܗܢܐ. ܐܡܪܝܢ ܕܝܢ ܡܠܟܐ ܠܒܪ ܡܢ
ܟܠܗ ܡܕܡ ܗܘܐ ܠܗܘܢ܆ ܗܘ ܕܪܘܪܒܢܐ ܕܡܠܟܘܬܗ. ܘܒܪܢܫܘܬܐ
ܕܪܚܡܘ ܥܠ ܗܘܐ ܘܒܥܘ ܠܐܣܘܪܗ ܕܡܠܟܘܬܗ ܒܗܘ ܙܒܢܐ.
ܘܒܙܒܢܐ ܫܢܝܩܘܬܐ ܚܙܐ ܗܘܐ ܠܗ ܒܪ ܟܠܝܢ. ܘܒܗܢܐ ܟܠܗ
ܕܒܝܫܘܬܐ ܕܗܢܐ ܗܘܐ ܠܗ ܡܬܕܟܪ ܗܘܐ ܒܗ ܕܒܗܢܐ ܥܠܡܐ
ܗܘܐ ܠܗܘܢ܆ ܘܒܐܣܘܪܐ ܪܒܐ ܘܒܫܬܐܪܐ ܐܝܬ ܗܘܐ. ܘܡܛܠܗ
ܐܝܟ ܚܕ ܡܢ ܪܘܪܒܢܐ ܡܢܐ ܕܡܠܐܟ ܗܘܐ. ܘܡܫܡܫ ܗܘܐ
ܒܡܕܝܢܬܐ ܪܒܐ ܕܡܠܟܐ ܕܝܩܝܪܬܐ. ܗܘ ܐܝܢܐ ܕܡܫܡܫ ܗܘܘ ܒܗ
ܕܒܝܬ ܐܒܘܗܝ ܕܐܒܗܘܗܝ ܕܐܡܪܝܢ ܡܠܟܐ. ܬܘܒ ܘܡܛܠܗ
ܗܘܐ ܡܫܬܐܠܬ ܒܪܝܫܘܬܐ ܘܒܫܘܠܛܢܐ ܪܒܬܐ. ܘܒܗܢܐ ܒܟܠܗ
ܕܒܝܬܐ. ܐܪܐ ܗܘܐ ܡܢ ܒܢܝܐ ܠܒܢܝܐ. ܘܡܛܠܐ ܗܘܐ ܬܘܒ
ܡܫܬܐܠܬ. ܘܢܘܟܪܝܐ ܕܒܝܬܗ ܒܪܝܟܝܢ ܗܘܘ ܡܢ ܥܒܕܐ ܠܥܒܕܐ.
ܐܝܟ ܦܘܩܕܢܐ ܘܫܘܠܛܢܐ ܕܡܫܡܠ ܗܘܐ ܠܗܘܢ ܢܝܫܗ ܐܒܪ
ܥܠܝܡܐ. ܘܐܝܟ ܡܠܬܗ ܕܐܒܘܗ ܕܗܘ ܗܘܐ ܡܕܒܪܢܐ ܘܦܩܘܕܐ
ܘܢܬܐ ܕܒܝܪܘܬܗ ܡܢ ܒܬܪܗ. ܒܐܝܕܐ ܕܫܘܠܛܢܘܬܐ ܕܡܫܡܠ ܗܘܐ
ܡܢܗ ܘܕܡ ܟܠܝܢ. ܐܦ ܗܘ ܒܗ ܒܐܝܕܐ ܕܡܫܡܠ ܗܘܐ ܡܢܗ ܒܪܕ.
ܗܘܐ ܒܫܘܢܐ ܘܡܕܒܪܢܐ ܒܟܠܗ ܐܬܪܐ ܗܢܐ ܕܒܝܬ ܢܗܪܝܢ.
ܐܦ ܗܘܝܘ ܒܬܪ ܐܒܘܗ ܕܐܒܪ ܥܠܝܡܐ. ܗܕܝܢ ܐܫܬܪܝ ܗܘܘ
ܡܠܬܗ ܘܡܫܬܡܥ ܗܘܘ ܘܡܫܡܠܝܢ ܐܝܟ ܢܝܫܐ ܦܬܓܡܐ ܘܡܗܝܡܢܐ
ܕܥܠܝܡܐ ܕܡܫܡܫܐ ܦܣܝܩܐ. ܒܗܢܐ ܕܝܢ ܘܕܡܘܬܐ ܡܢ ܐܝܟ ܠܐ
ܫܦܠ ܗܘܐ. ܘܡܫܬܥܝܬܐ ܕܪܘܪܒܢܐ ܠܐ ܡܬܝܢ ܗܘܐ ܦܐܪܘܗ
ܚܠܦ ܒܪ ܕܡܠܟܐ ܘܡܐܡܪܐ. ܒܥܒܕܬܐ ܕܡܫܡܫܢܐ ܡܫܬܪ
ܗܘܐ ܠܗ ܠܥܒܕܗ ܕܡܫܝܚܐ. ܡܛܠ ܕܝܢ ܟܠܗ ܕܒܪܢܐ ܘܕܝܢܐ.
ܢܦܩ ܗܘܘ ܘܩܡܝܢ ܘܡܫܬܥܝܢ ܗܘܘ ܘܕܒܩܝܢ. ܕܐܬܚܙܝܬ
ܘܡܦܣܝܬ ܒܚܙܝܢ ܗܘܘ ܕܠܐ ܦܘܠܫܐ. ܒܒܝܪܬܐ
ܕܡܬܟܬܫܬܐ ܘܡܬܝܬ ܒܫܠ ܦܘܠܚܢܐ ܕܠܘܬ ܡܫܒܚܢܐ

ܘܫܟ̈ܠܠܐ ܒܐܬܪܐ ܒܗܘܐ܂ ܒܝܕ ܫܘ̈ܪܝܐ ܘܗ̈ܦܟܐ ܘܫ̈ܘܦܝܐ ܠܒܢܝܐ܂ ܒܡ ܘܠܝܡ ܗܘ ܓܝܪ ܬܪ̈ܝܢ ܓܒܝܢ ܐܝܬ ܠܗܘܢ ܡܪ̈ܟܝܢ ܕܬܫܡܫܘܢ ܒܬ̈ܪܐ ܕܡܫܒܚܘܬܐ ܕܐܝܬܝܗܝܢ ܐܢܬܘܢ܂ ܘܟܕ ܫܠܝܡ ܐܢܬܘܢ ܚܬܝܬܝܢ ܡܗܝܡܢܘܬܐ ܘܡܫܪܪܬܐ ܗܘܝܬܘܢ ܡܦܪܫܐ ܠܡܫܚܘܢ܆ ܒܡ ܦܘܬ ܕܫܡܝ ܡܘܫܐ ܘܢܦܩܝܢ ܠܥܡܐ܂ ܠܐ ܬܗܘܘܢ ܡܬܦܫܝܢ ܠܡܫܡܥܘܬܐ ܐܦܢ ܒܬܪܐ܂ ܘܦܩ ܠܗܘܢ ܓܝܪ ܟܕ ܐܢܐ ܒܥܕܐ ܡܫܡܠܝܘܬܗܘܢ܆ ܠܐ ܬܬܒܥܘܢ ܒܡܘܫܒܚܐ ܘܬܢܐ ܕܡܬܢܟܠܐ ܕܠܐ ܬܗܘܘܢ ܒܬܪܥܐ ܡܢ ܡܫܝܚܘܬܐ ܕܠܒܫܝܢ ܐܢܬܘܢ܀

* * * *

* * * *

ܘܒܡ ܫܘܪܝܐ ܕܦܘܩܐ ܠܐ ܡܬܬܠܬܠܝܢ܂ ܘܢܬܬܪܬܐ ܗܪܐ ܕܡܫܠܡ ܡܢܝ ܠܐ ܡܬܪܦܝܢ܂ ܘܟܕ ܗܘ ܢܦܩܝܢ ܡܢ ܒܠܥܕܐ ܗܢܐ ܘܟܘܠܗܘܢ ܕܡܢ̈ܝ ܐܦܢ ܒܝܬ ܕܕܝܢܐ ܕܟܐܢܘܬܐ܂ ܬܘܒ ܢܦܫܐ ܠܝ ܢܬܬܪܬܐ ܗܪܐ ܐܝܟ ܕܐܡܪܬ ܠܝ܂ ܘܟܕ ܐܬܐܡܪ ܗܘ̈ܝ܆ ܗܢܝܢ ܗܠܝܢ܂ ܗܡ ܗܘܐ ܐܡܪ ܡܠܟܐ ܗܘ ܘܪܘܪܒܢܘܗܝ܆ ܘܫܪ̈ܘܗܝ܆ ܘܐܙܠ ܗܘܐ ܠܡܦܪܫܐ ܕܠܗ ܒܪ ܡܟܝܢ ܗܘܘ ܒܠܗܘܢ܆ ܒܠܗܘܢ ܕܒܐܬܐ ܗܘܐ܂ ܘܥܒܪ ܗܘܐ ܠܗ ܠܒܢܝܥܐ ܡܢܘܪܬܐ ܘܪ̈ܚܡܐ ܕܬܫܡܪ ܗܘܐ ܒܗܘܢ܀ ܘܟܕ ܒܝܬ ܐܢܘܢ ܐܒܐ܆ ܥܠܝ ܠܗ ܕܠܐ ܒܝܫ ܫܠܬ ܡܢܝ ܡܕܡ ܐܡܠܐ ܗܟܢܐ ܒܡܘܬ܆ ܫܠ ܐܢܐ ܡܢܝ ܡܕܡ ܘܠܐ ܡܓܒܠ ܐܢܐ ܒ ܡܠܬܗ ܕܡܫܝܚܐ ܕܐܡܪ ܠܝ ܕܠܐ ܬܫܒܘܢ܆ ܡܢ ܐܢܐ ܡܕܡ ܘܠܐ ܬܫܒܘܢ܆ ܡܕܡ ܒܠܥܕܝ ܗܢܐ ܀

ܘܡܢ ܒܬܪ ܬܠܬܐ ܝܘܡ̈ܝܢ ܐܚܪܢܐ ܕܐܬܐܡܪ ܗ̈ܘ܆ ܗܢܝܢ ܗܠܝܢ ܡܢ ܐܒܐ܆ ܥܠܝܡܐ ܘܫܡܥ ܗܘܐ ܘܩܒܠ ܣܗܕܘܬܐ ܕܡܠܦܢܘܬܐ ܕܦܪܘܫܘܬܗܘܢ܆ ܡܢ ܩܕܡ ܬܫܒܚܬܗ ܐܦܢ ܫܐܪܐ ܒܠܗܘܢ܆ ܢܗܡ ܗܘܐ ܡܢ ܒܠܥܕܐ ܗܢܐ܂ ܘܐܢܬܘܢ܆ ܗܘܘ ܢܘܡܐ ܗܘ ܫܡܥܐ ܡܢܐ ܒܐܪܒܥܘܢܐ ܒܐܢܫ ܐܢܫ܂ ܘܟܐܒܠܐ ܪܒܐ ܘܒܫܝܐ ܡܪܢܐ ܗܘܬ ܒܠܗܘܢ܆ ܒܠܗ ܡܢܝܚܘܬܐ܂ ܠܐ ܗܘܐ ܕܝܢ ܒܦܘܪܫܢܐ

ܗܘܐ ܠܟܠܗܘܢ ܘܠܟܢܫܐ ܕܡܕܝܢܬܐ ܗܘܝܐ ܕܡܛܠ ܒܢܝܢܗ ܗܘܐ
ܡܐܬ ܐܢܐ. ܟܕ ܫܡܥܘ ܘܒܟܘ ܘܐܬܟܪܝܘ. ܘܐܝܟ ܕܐܡܪ ܗܘܐ
ܗܟܢܐ ܘܗܟܢܐ ܗܘܐ. ܠܗ ܡܢ ܬܪܥܐ ܡܦܩܢܐ ܕܟܢܘܬܐ ܟܕ
ܒܪܬܐ ܠܒܪܐ. ܘܗܘܐ ܗܘܐ ܐܒܠܐ ܪܒܐ ܘܡܪܝܪܐ ܒܟܠܗ
ܒܝܬܐ ܘܟܠܗ ܡܕܝܢܬܐ. ܟܠ ܚܫܐ ܘܐܒܠܐ ܕܗܘܐ ܗܘܐ
ܒܓܘܗ. ܐܝܟ ܕܗܘܐ ܗܘܐ ܐܒܠܐ ܟܕ ܡܝܬ ܗܘ ܐܕܝ ܫܠܝܚܐ.
ܘܡܛܠ ܕܒܥܓܠ ܬܘܟܪܐ ܕܩܛܠܗ، ܡܝܬ ܗܘܐ ܠܗ ܪܗܒܐܝܬ
ܘܡܣܪܗܒܐܝܬ. ܠܐ ܐܝܬܝܗ ܗܘܐ ܕܢܣܝܡ ܐܝܕܐ ܥܠ ܦܠܘܛ.
ܐܙܠ ܗܘܐ ܗܘ ܦܠܘܛ ܠܐܢܛܝܘܟܝ ܘܩܒܠ ܗܘܐ ܐܝܕܐ
ܕܟܗܢܘܬܐ ܡܢ ܣܪܦܝܘܢ ܐܦܝܣܩܘܦܐ ܕܐܢܛܝܘܟܝ. ܗܘ ܕܐܦ
ܗܘ ܣܪܦܝܘܢ ܡܩܒܠܐ ܗܘܬ ܠܗ ܐܝܕܐ ܡܢ ܙܦܪܝܢܘܣ
ܐܦܝܣܩܘܦܐ. ܕܪܗܘܡܐ ܡܕܝܢܬܐ ܡܢ ܝܘܒܠܐ ܕܐܝܕܐ
ܕܟܗܢܘܬܐ ܕܫܡܥܘܢ ܟܐܦܐ. ܗܘ ܕܩܒܠ ܗܘܐ ܡܢ ܡܪܢ
ܘܗܘܐ ܗܘܐ ܐܦܝܣܩܘܦܐ ܬܡܢ ܒܪܗܘܡܐ ܥܣܪܝܢ ܘܚܡܫ
ܫܢܝܢ. ܒܝܘܡܝ ܣܘܝܪ ܗܘ ܕܐܡܠܟ ܗܘܐ ܬܡܢ ܬܠܬܥܣܪܐ
ܫܢܝܢ.. ܘܐܝܟܢܐ ܕܐܝܬ ܚܕܐ ܒܡܠܟܘܬܗ ܕܐܒܓܪ ܡܠܟܐ
ܘܟܠ ܫ̈ܠܡܘܗܝ ܕܠܡܕܝܢ ܕܦܫܛ ܡܠܟܐ ܘܟܠ ܡܕܡ ܕܡܬܐܡܪ
ܒܝܘܡܘܗܝ، ܡܬܟܬܒ ܘܡܬܬܣܝܡ ܒܝܬ ܡܘܕܥܢܐ ܗܟܢܐ ܐܦ
ܠܒܘܒܢܐ ܒܪ ܣܢܩ ܒܪ ܐܒܫܕܪ ܣܦܪܐ ܕܡܠܟܐ ܟܬܒ ܗܘܐ
ܗܘܝ ܗܠܝܢ ܕܐܕܝ ܫܠܝܚܐ ܡܢ ܫܘܪܝܐ ܠܫܘܠܡܐ. ܟܕ ܪܡܐ
ܗܘܐ ܐܝܕܐ ܕܣܗܕܘܬܐ. ܐܦ ܚܢܢ ܬܒܘܠܪܐ ܫܪܝܪܐ ܕܡܠܟܐ.
ܘܣܡ ܗܘܐ ܒܝܬ ܡܘܕܥܢܐ ܕܡܠܟܐ ܐܝܟܐ ܕܦܘܩܕܢܐ ܘܢܛܘܪܐ
ܣܝܡܝܢ ܘܕܟܝܪܝܢ ܘܡܬܩܪܝܢ ܬܡܢ ܢܛܝܪܝܢ ܒܡܘܕܥܢܘܬܐ ܕܠܐ
ܚܘܒܠܐ ܡܕܡ.

ܫܠܡܬ ܡܠܦܢܘܬܗ ܕܐܕܝ ܫܠܝܚܐ ܕܐܟܪܙ ܒܐܘܪܗܝ ܡܕܝܢܬܐ
ܡܗܝܡܢܬܐ ܕܐܒܓܪ ܡܠܟܐ ܡܗܝܡܢܐ.

ܒܡܘܟܟܝܗܘܢ ܕܠܘܬ ܟܪ̈ܝܗܐ. ܘܠܟܠܗܘܢ ܟܕ ܫܡܥܢܐ ܡܠܝܢ
ܗܘ̈ܝ ܡܢ ܫܪܪܐ. ܘܒܡܘܟܟܝܗܘܢ ܬܫܡܫܬܐ ܟܠܝܠܝܢ ܗܘܘ ܡܢ
ܢܟܪ̈ܝܐ. ܐܝܟܢܐ ܕܐܦ ܒܡܕܝܢܬܐ ܕܟܠܗ ܢܒܗ ܘܟܠ ܐܢܫ̈ܐ
ܠܗܘܢ ܦܠܚܝܢ ܗܘܘ. ܟܠܗܝܢ ܒܢܝܫܗܘܢ ܢܫܪܬܐ. ܒܡܟܠܬܗܘܢ
ܫܪܝܪܬܐ. ܒܦܪܗܣܝܐ ܕܐܝܬ ܗܘܐ ܒܡܬܪܘܬܗܘܢ. ܕܒܟܢܝܘܬܐ
ܠܐ ܟܪܝܗܐ ܗܘܬ. ܘܐܝܬܝܗ ܒܟܠܝܐ ܠܐ ܢܚܫܒܐ ܗܘܬ. ܠܐ
ܗܘܐ ܟܕ ܕܝܢܐ ܐܝܟ ܕܠܐ ܙܕܩ ܗܘܐ ܠܐܘܪܚܗܘܢ ܕܢܫܐܠ
ܗܘܐ ܥܠܝܗܘܢ ܢܦܫܬܐ. ܡܛܠ ܕܐܦ ܗܝ ܢܝܚܘܬܗܘܢ
ܥܠܡܐ ܦܪܫܐ ܗܘܬ ܟܠ ܝܘܡܐ. ܒܕܡܘܬ ܡܕܝܢܬܐ ܟܕ
ܦܪܫܘ ܗܘ̈ܝ ܬܠܝܗܘܢ ܕܥܡܐ ܟܠ ܡܕܝܢܬܐ. ܟܕ ܒܐܠܝܢ ܗܘܘ
ܠܒܗ ܡܢ ܦܠܓܐ ܕܡܫܬܐ ܘܕܝܪ̈ܐ. ܠܝܬ ܗܘܐ ܟܕ ܕܢܪܐ
ܗܘܐ ܠܗܘܢ ܘܟܘܠ ܡܢܗܘܢ ܒܕܠܐ ܘܟܪܝܢ ܗܘܘ ܡܕܡ
ܕܕܠܐ ܒܕܘܟܐ ܘܕܠܐ ܒܥܠܝܬܐ. ܘܟܕ ܗܠܝܢ ܟܠܝܢ ܗܘ̈ܝ
ܐܢ̈ܫܘܗܝ ܒܕܪܘܬܐ ܕܡܠܦܢܘܬܗܘܢ ܝܘܡ ܟܠܗ. ܗܘ ܟܕ
ܡܕܡ ܕܐܡܪܝܢ ܗܘܘ ܠܐܚܪ̈ܢܐ ܘܡܪܬܝܢ ܠܗܘܢ ܗܢܘܢ
ܒܟܒܕܐ ܡܫܘܚ ܗܘܘ ܠܗ ܒܡܘܡܣܗܘܢ ܘܥܕܡܐ ܕܢܝܚ
ܗܘܘ ܕܟܠ ܬܠܝܗܘܢ ܒܟܕܘܗܘܢ. ܕܠܐ ܦܫܘܐ ܦܘܩܕܢܐ
ܡܬܠܒܕܝܢ ܗܘܘ ܠܗܘܢ ܘܒܡܠܟܐ ܡܟܝܢܐ ܡܕܝܢ ܗܘܘ ܟܕ
ܡܥܟܒܝܢ ܗܘܘ ܠܐܠܗܐ ܕܐܦܩ ܐܢܘܢ ܠܢܘܗܪܗ ... ...

ܘܡܢ ܒܬܪ ܙܒܢܐ ܕܡܘܬܗ ܕܐܒܘܢ ܡܠܟܐ. ܡܢ ܗܘܐ ܚܕ ܡܢ
ܒܢܘܗܝ ܡܕܝܢܬܐ ܕܠܐ ܡܬܦܠܓܐ ܗܘܐ ܠܥܠܡܐ. ܘܫܠܚ ܠܗ
ܠܟܠ ܟܕ ܗܘܐ ܗܘܐ ܒܡܕܝܢܬܐ ܕܟܕ ܠܗ ܚܘܕܐ ܕܕܘܟܬܐ.
ܐܝܟ ܡܢܐ ܕܒܥܐ ܗܘܬ ܠܐܚ̈ܘܗܝ ܡܢ ܩܕܡ. ܫܠܚ ܠܗ ܐܝܟ.
ܕܠܐ ܡܢܦܩܐ ܐܢܐ ܬܫܡܫܬܗ ܕܡܫܝܚܐ ܕܐܬܟܠܬ ܠܝ ܡܢ
ܬܠܡܝܕܘܗܝ ܕܡܫܝܚܐ ܘܟܕ ܐܢܐ ܚܘܕܐ ܕܒܥܬܐ. ܘܟܕ ܚܙܐ
ܗܘܐ ܕܠܐ ܐܬܦܠܓܘ ܠܗ. ܫܕܪ ܗܘܐ ܠܘܬ ܗܘܐ ܫܒܩܗܝ
ܟܕ ܡܬܐ ܗܘܐ ܒܟܪܝܗܐ ܘܡܬܢܝܚ. ܘܟܕ ܡܟܐܬ ܗܘܐ. ܐܘܡܢ

ܗܢܘܢ ܬܠܡܝܕܐ ܒܥܘܡܩܐ ܗܘܐ ܙܥܝܪ ܗܘܘ ܕܐܡܝܢܐ ܢܛܪܘܢ
ܗܘܘ ܡܫܪܬܗ. ܠܟܢܫܐ ܢܡܘܣܐ ܕܠܐ ܡܕܒܪ ܗܘܘ ܠܗܘܢ. ܘܡܗܝܡܢܐ
ܐܡܪܝܢ ܗܘܘ ܚܕ ܠܚܕ ܕܐܢ ܫܠܝܐ ܘܬܕܡܪܬܐ ܬܚܠܝܢ ܚܝܢ ܕܒܒܐ
ܗܘ ܡܫܝܚܐ ܒܐܝܕܢ ܘܡܬܒܟܝܢܐ ܢܡܘܣܐ ܕܠܐ ܡܕܒܪܝܢ
ܠܥܡܗܘܢ ܐܦܠܐ ܗܢܘܢ ܡܩܒܠܝܢ ܒܠܥܕ. ܡܛܠ ܢܠܦ ܐܢܘܢ ܘܢܕܪܒ
ܐܢܘܢ. ܕܒܫܡܗ ܕܡܫܝܚܐ ܕܐܬܕܪܫ ܗܘܝܢ ܫܬܠܐ ܗܠܝܢ ܘܬܕܡܪܬܐ.
ܘܟܕ ܗܢܘܢ ܬܠܡܝܕܐ ܒܗܠܝܢ ܫܘܚܠܦܐ ܐܬܚܙܝܘ ܗܘܘ. ܡܢ
ܗܘܐ ܥܡܗܘܢ ܒܐܦܐ ܘܐܡܪ ܠܗܘܢ. ܐܫܘ. ܠܐ ܕܝܠܝ ܗܝ ܗܕܐ
ܕܐܡܝܢܐ ܢܛܪ ܡܫܪܬܗ ܐܠܐ ܕܡܪܢ ܗܝ ܕܗܘ ܡܕܒܪ ܐܡܝܢܐ
ܡܥܒܕܐ ܢܛܪ ܡܫܪܬܗ ܒܟܠܡܕܡ. ܬܚܠܝܢ ܕܝܢ ܟܠ ܒܬܠܡܝܕܘܬܗ
ܕܠܘܬܢ ܕܐܫܬܘܕܝ ܠܝ ܘܐܡܪ. ܕܡܐ ܕܫܠܡܬ ܠܘܬ ܐܒܐ ܡܥܕܪ
ܐܢܐ ܠܟܘܢ ܪܘܚܐ ܦܪܩܠܝܛܐ ܕܗܘ ܢܠܦܟܘܢ ܒܟܠܡܕܡ ܕܐܡܪ
ܠܟܘܢ. ܕܬܕܟܪܘܢ ܘܬܬܕܟܪܘܢ. ܘܟܕ ܗܘ ܥܡܗܘܢ ܒܐܦܐ ܗܠܝܢ
ܠܬܠܡܝܕܐ ܚܙܬܗܘܢ، ܐܡܪ ܗܘܐ ܘܡܚܘܐ ܗܘܐ ܠܗܘܢ. ܘܠܐ
ܕܗܘܐ ܐܫܬܡܥ ܗܘܐ ܠܗܘܢ. ܘܪܐܘܬܐ ܒܗܘܡܟܐ ܕܢܘܕܪ،
ܗܘܐ ܠܬܠܡܝܕܐ ܦܢ ܗܘܐ ܠܗܘܢ. ܘܠܫܢܐ ܕܢܘܪܐ ܒܝܬ ܦܠܐ
ܠܪܐܫܐ ܚܕܬܐ ܗܘܘ ܡܢ ܫܡܝܐ ܠܬܠܡܝܕܘܗܝ. ܘܪܒܘ ܗܘܘ ܟܠ
ܚܕ ܚܕ ܡܢܗܘܢ ܘܝܬܒܘ. ܘܐܝܟ ܠܫܢܐ ܕܢܦܠ ܗܘܐ ܟܠ ܚܕ
ܚܕ ܡܢܗܘܢ ܗܟܢܐ ܦܠܓ ܗܘܐ ܢܦܫܗ ܕܢܐܙܠ ܠܐܬܪܐ
ܕܡܬܡܠܠ ܘܡܫܬܡܥ ܒܗ ܠܫܢܐ ܗܘ. ܘܒܗ ܒܗܝܡܢܘܬܐ
ܕܪܘܚܐ ܕܐܬܝܗܒܬ ܗܘܬ ܠܗܘܢ ܒܗܕ ܝܘܡܐ. ܗܟܢܐ ܗܘܘ
ܦܫܛܘ ܘܢܦܩܘ ܐܝܠܝܢ ܕܫܠܝܚܝܢ ܗܘܘ ܠܟܪܙܘܬܐ ܕܣܒܪܬܗܘܢ:
ܘܠܬܘܠܡܕܐ ܥܒܕܐ ܘܡܗܝܡܢܐ ܕܫܠܝܚܘܬܗܘܢ ....

ܐ. ܗܟܢܐ ܗܘܝܠ ܫܠܝܚܐ ܕܠܡܫܝܚܐ ܗܘܘ ܡܟܪܙܝܢ. ܡܛܠ
ܕܐܝܟ ܒܪܢܫܐ ܕܒܪܬ ܡܢ ܡܕܝܢܬܐ ܘܡܬܚܙܝܐ ܒܗܝܟܠܐ ܠܡܕܢܚܐ
ܗܟܢܐ ܬܗܘܐ ܡܟܬܒܬܗ ܕܒܪܬ ܕܐܝܟܢܐ ܕܒܗܕܐ ܢܐܒ
ܘܬܗܡ ܕܕܡ ܡܕܝܢܬܐ ܡܬܚܙܝܐ ܡܢ ܫܠܝܚܐ ..

ܡܫܠܡܢܘܬܐ ܕܫ̈ܠܝܚܐ ܀

ܕܐܡܬܝ ܐܣܬܠܩ ܡܫܝܚܐ ܠܘܬ ܐܒܘܗܝ. ܘܐܡܝܢܐ ܡܛܠ ܫܠܝ̈ܚܐ ܡܗܝܡܢܘܬܐ ܕܪܘܚܐ ܘܦ̈ܬܓܡܐ ܘܢ̈ܡܘܣܐ ܕܒܥܕܬܐ ܘܕܠܐܝܟܐ ܐܙܠ ܗܘܐ ܚܕ ܚܕ ܡܢܗܘܢ ܕܫ̈ܠܝܚܐ. ܘܡܢ ܐܝܟܢܐ ܡܛܠ ܐܝܢܐ ܕܡܫܝܚܘܬܐ ܐܬܪ̈ܘܬܐ ܕܒܝܬ ܪ̈ܗܘܡܝܐ ◦◦◦

ܒܫܢܬ ܬܠܬܡܐܐ ܘܬܠܬ ܠܡܠܟܘܬܐ ܕܝܘ̈ܢܝܐ. ܒܝܪܚ ܢܝܣܢ ܒܗܘ ܐܪܒܥܣܪܐ ܒܗ. ܕܐܝܬܘܗܝ ܚܕ ܒܫܒܐ ܘܫܘܠܡܐ ܕܦܢܛܩܘܣܛܐ. ܗܘ ܒܣܘܡܐ ܗܘܐ ܐܬܘ ܬܠܡ̈ܝܕܐ ܡܢ ܢܨܪܬ ܕܓܠܝܠܐ ܡܢ ܐܬܪܐ ܕܐܬܒܣܪܬ ܒܗܘܢ ܕܡܪܢ ܠܛܘܪܐ ܕܡܬܩܪܐ ܕܒܝܬ ܙܝܬܐ. ܟܕ ܡܪܢ ܥܡܗܘܢ ܗܘܐ ܘܠܐ ܡܬܚܙܐ ܗܘܐ ܠܗܘܢ. ܘܒܥܕܢܐ ܕܨܦܪܐ ܪܒܐ ܐܪܝܡ ܗܘܐ ܡܪܢ ܐܝܕܘܗܝ ܘܣܡ ܗܘܐ ܐܝܕܘܗܝ ܥܠ ܪ̈ܫܝܗܘܢ ܕܚܕܥܣܪ ܬܠܡ̈ܝܕܐ. ܘܝܗܒ ܠܗܘܢ ܡܘܗܒܬܐ ܕܟܗܢܘܬܐ. ܘܡܢ ܫܠܝܐ ܥܢܢܐ ܢܗܝܪܬܐ ܡܛܠܬ ܗܘܬ. ܘܚܙܐܘܗܝ ܟܕ ܣܠܩ ܗܘܐ ܠܫܡܝܐ. ܘܝܬܒ ܗܘܐ ܡܢ ܝܡܝܢܐ ܕܐܒܘܗܝ. ܘܡܒܪܟܝܢ ܗܘܘ ܠܐܠܗܐ. ܕܚܙܘ ܗܘܠܝܢ ܐܝܟ ܕܐܡܪ ܠܗܘܢ ܘܚܕܝܢ ܗܘܘ ܕܡܛܠ ܗܘܘ ܡܣܒܪܝܢ ܕܡܘܗܒܬܐ ܕܒܫܢܬ ܡܘܒܠܐ ܐܡܪܘܗ̱ܝ. ܘܡܢ ܬܡܢ ܗܦܟܘ ܐܬܘ ܠܗܘܢ ܠܐܘܪܫܠܡ. ܐܝܟ ܕܦܩܕ ܗܘܐ ܡܪܢ ܠܗܘܢ ܗܟܢܐ. ܘܒܥܕܬܐ ܕܗܘܘ ܫ̈ܠܝܚܐ ܕܡܫܠܡ ܠܗ ܡܪܢ ܠܥܡܗܘܢ. ܬܡܢ ܗܘܘ ܫ̈ܠܝܚܐ ܐܦ ܕܐܡܪܢܐ ܢܦܩܘܢ ܗܘܘ ܟܪܘܙܘܬܗ ܒܥܠܡܐ. ܘܐܡܪܢܐ ܕܒܗ ܒܠܫܢܗ ܫܪܝ ܗܘܐ ܐܢܫ ܕܦܓܥܘܗ ܘܡܫܡܥ ܕܡܪܢ ܕܢܬܠܝ ܗܘܐ ܒܥܠܡܐ. ܗܟܢܐ ܐܦ ܡܢ ܬܡܢ ܥܕ ܗܘܐ ܡܠܦܢܐ ܕܒܪܝܘܬܗ ܕܥܠܝܠ ܗܘܐ ܒܥܠܡܐ. ܘܟܕ

ܗܘܘ ܐܪܡܝܐ ܗܢܐ ܐܪ̈ܟܘܢ ܡܘ̈ܬܢ ܢܦܩܘ ܗܘܘ ܐܦ
ܗܢܘܢ. ܘܦܩܕܝܢ ܐܢܘܢ.

ܗ. ܦܩܕܘ ܗܘܘ. ܬܘܒ ܫܠܝ̈ܚܐ. ܕܒܫܘܠܡܐ ܕܟܬ̈ܒܐ ܟܠܗܘܢ
ܬܬܩܪܐ ܐܘܢܓܠܝܘܢ ܐܝܟ ܡܫܠܡܢܘܬܐ ܕܟܬ̈ܒܐ ܟܠܗܘܢ. ܘܟܕ
ܩܝܡܝܢ ܟܠܗ ܥܡܐ ܥܠ ܪ̈ܓܠܝܗܘܢ ܢܫܡܥܘܢܝܗܝ. ܕܣܒܪܬܐ ܗܝ
ܕܦܘܪܩܢܐ ܕܟܠܗܘܢ ܒܢ̈ܝܢܫܐ ܀

ܘ. ܦܩܕܘ ܗܘܘ ܬܘܒ ܫܠܝ̈ܚܐ ܕܒܫܘܠܡܐ ܕܐܪܒܥܝܢ ܝܘ̈ܡܝܢ
ܕܡܢ ܒܬܪ ܩܝܡܬܗ ܗܘܘ ܥܒܕܝܢ ܕܘܟܪܢܐ ܕܣܘܠܩܗ ܕܠܘܬ
ܐܒܘܗܝ ܡܫܒܚܐ ܀

ܙ. ܦܩܕܘ ܗܘܘ ܫܠܝ̈ܚܐ ܕܐܠܐ ܐܢ ܕܬܗܘܐ ܠܬܫܡܫܬܐ
ܘܩܪܝܢܐ ܘܐܘܢܓܠܝܘܢ ܘܩܘܪܒܢܐ ܕܦܓܪܗ ܠܐ ܗܘܐ
ܡܬܩܪܒ ܥܠ ܥܡܐ ܟܢܫܬܐ ܀

ܚ. ܦܩܕܘ ܗܘܘ ܬܘܒ ܫܠܝ̈ܚܐ. ܕܐܢܫܐ ܕܠܐ ܢܕܘܢ
ܡܬܚܫܒܘܬܗ ܕܒܬܪܐ ܘܦܘܩܕܢܐ ܘܢܡܘܣܐ ܕܐܡܝܢ ܒܗ. ܠܐ
ܢܗܘܐ ܡܬܩܒܠܐ ܘܡܫܬܡܥܐ. ܘܐܢܫܐ ܕܚܕ ܠܗܘܢ ܘܥܒܕ
ܡܢܗܘܢ. ܠܐ ܬܗܘܐ ܢܣܒ. ܡܛܠ ܕܠܐ ܫܦܝܪ ܒܬܫܡܫܬܗ
ܕܐܠ ܀

ܛ. ܦܩܕܘ ܗܘܘ ܬܘܒ ܫܠܝ̈ܚܐ. ܕܐܢܫܐ ܕܥܒܕܐ ܐܘ ܡܬܓܠ.
ܐܘ ܡܬܛܘܠ ܦܘܠܚܢܐ ܕܟܘܡܪܐ. ܐܘ ܐܙܠ ܠܘܬ ܚܪ̈ܫܐ
ܘܡܓܘ̈ܫܐ ܘܟܠܕܝ̈ܐ ܘܡܗܝܡܢ ܠܒܠܗܐ ܘܠܘܬ ܬܠܝܐ. ܡܕܡ
ܕܐܣܘܪܝܢ ܐܝܟܢ ܕܠܐ ܝܕܥܝܢ ܠܐܠܗܐ. ܐܦ ܗܘ ܐܝܟ ܚܢܦܐ
ܕܠܐ ܝܕܥ ܠܐܠܗܐ ܢܬܕܪܐ ܡܢ ܬܫܡܫܬܐ ܘܠܐ ܢܫܡܫ ܀

ܝ. ܦܩܕܘ ܗܘܘ ܬܘܒ ܫܠܝ̈ܚܐ. ܕܐܢ ܐܝܬ ܐܢܫ ܕܡܠܝܟ ܥܠ
ܬܫܡܫܬܐ ܘܠܐ ܫܦܝܪܐ ܠܗ. ܗܢܐ ܬܗܘܐ ܠܐ ܢܫܡܫ. ܕܠܐ
ܫܦܝܪ ܠܗ ܡܢ ܕܬܫܡܫܬܐ. ܘܡܐܢܐ ܗܘ ܡܟܠܒܐ ܘܠܐ ܗܘܐ
ܟܐܠܗܐ ܗܘ ܕܠܐ ܬܗܘܐ ܢܟܬܒܐ ܒܫܡܗ ܀

ܝܐ. ܦܩܕܘ ܗܘܘ ܬܘܒ ܫܠܝ̈ܚܐ ܕܐܢܫܐ ܕܡܫܘܕܥ ܘܡܠ

ܒ. ܗܟܢܐ ܗܘܘ ܬܘܒ ܫ̈ܠܝܚܐ ܕܒܝܫ ܟܘܟܒܐ ܬܗܘܐ
ܬܫܡܫܬܐ ܘܦܪܢܣܐ ܕܬ̈ܒܝܠܐ ܡܕ̈ܢܚܐ ܘܡܥܪ̈ܒܐ. ܡܛܠ ܕܒܝܫ
ܟܘܟܒܐ ܡܢ ܗܘܐ ܡܢ ܟܠܗ ܡܕ̈ܝܢܬܐ ܡܢܗ. ܘܒܝܫ ܟܘܟܒܐ ܕܠܐ
ܗܘܐ ܒܠܡܚܐ. ܘܒܝܫ ܟܘܟܒܐ ܢܠܡ ܗܘ ܠܫܡܫܐ. ܘܒܝܫ
ܟܘܟܒܐ ܡܬܚܙܐ ܠܢܗܝܪܬܐ ܒܝܢ ܡܠܐܟ̈ܐ ܫܡܝܐ ⁘

ܓ. ܗܟܢܐ ܗܘܘ ܬܘܒ ܫ̈ܠܝܚܐ ܕܒܐܪܒܥܐ ܟܘܟܒܐ
ܬܗܘܐ ܬܫܡܫܬܐ ܡܛܠ ܕܒܗ ܗܘ ܟܠܐ ܗܘܐ ܠܗܘܢ ܡܢܗ
ܟܠ ܕܚܝܠܐ ܘܢܘܗܪܗ ܘܢܦܫܬܗ ܘܡܕܡܬܗ ܘܡܫܘܚܬܗ. ܘܗܘܘ
ܬܠܡܝ̈ܕܐ ܒܡܕܝܢܬܐ ܗܕܐ ⁘

ܕ. ܗܟܢܐ ܗܘܘ ܬܘܒ ܫ̈ܠܝܚܐ ܕܒܡܕܝܢܬܐ ܒܠܚܘܕ ܩ̈ܕܡ
ܬܗܘܐ ܬܫܡܫܬܐ. ܡܛܠ ܕܗܘ ܡܕܡ ܕܐܬܬܐܡܪ ܗܘܐ
ܒܐܪܒܥܐ ܟܘܟܒܐ ܟܠ ܚܕܐ ܕܦܪܘܩ ܒܡܕܝܢܬܐ ܐܬܬܚܪ
ܗܘܐ. ܟܕ ܐܝܟ ܗܘܘ ܩ̈ܠܝܠܐ ܘܡ̈ܕܝܢܬܐ ܘܚܝܠܗ ܗܘܘ ܢܗܝܪܐ
ܟܘܟܒܐ ⁘

ܗ. ܗܟܢܐ ܗܘܘ ܬܘܒ ܫ̈ܠܝܚܐ ܕܢܗܘܘܢ ܗܘܘ ܡܢ̈ܗܪܐ
ܘܡܫܬ̈ܒܚܢܐ ܐܝܟ ܠܗܢܐ. ܘܡܫܬܡܫܢܐ ܐܝܟ ܗܢܘܢ ܕܡܟܝܢ
ܗܘܘ ܩ̈ܕܡܝ ܕܪܬܐ ܕܒܝܬ ܡܘܕܝܗ ܕܡܠܟܐ. ܘܕܘܡܝܐ ܕܗܘܘ
ܡܬܒܪܢܐ ܕܟܠܗ ܒܒܒܐ. ܐܝܟ ܐܗܪܘܢ ܢܗܪܐ ܘܪܒܐ
ܕܟܠܗܘܢ ܒܢܝܢܐ ܘܠܗ̈ܘܢ ܕܟܠܗ ܡܕ̈ܝܢܬܐ ⁘

ܘ. ܗܟܢܐ ܗܘܘ ܬܘܒ ܫ̈ܠܝܚܐ ܕܗܘܘ ܒܒܝܬ ܡܘܡܐ ܕܕܝܢܗ
ܕܦܪܘܩ ܕܐܝܬܘܗܝ، ܢܗܪܐ ܕܟ̈ܐܢܘܬܗ ܕܒܝܬܐ. ܒܐܝܬܘܬܐ ܟܠܗܘܢ
ܐܝܟ ܒܡܝܢܐ ܡܬܚܝܢܐ ܕܒܢ̈ܝܐ ⁘

ܙ. ܗܟܢܐ ܗܘܘ ܬܘܒ ܫ̈ܠܝܚܐ ܕܐܬ̈ܟܝܢ ܩܕܡ ܡܕܡ ܡܘܡܐ
ܕܚܝܠܐ ܕܦܪܘܩ ܗܘܘ ܝܡܝܢ. ܘܗܢܘܢ ܒܟܢܫܐ ܠܗ ܠܥܘܡܟܐ
ܕܫܠܐ ܘܠܘܡܟܐ ܕܡܫܬܐ. ܡܛܠ ܕܐܝܟ ܗܘ ܡܢܗ ܡܢܗ
ܕܒܐܢܫܐ ܐܬ̈ܟܝܢ ܩܕܡ ܝܡ ܗܘܐ. ܘܡܫܟܚ ܘܐܠܘܢ ܕܠܒܫܢ

ܡܫܡܫܢܐ ܘܠܐ ܪܘܚܡ ܒܬܪ ܡܛܪܢܘ ܕܫܘܫܐ. ܗܢܘܢ ܗܘܘ ܡܬܟܬܫܝܢ ܘܡܬܬܪܝܢ ܠܡܫܡܫܘܬܗ ܕܡܕܒܚܐ ܀

ܟܐ. ܫܢܬ ܗܘܘ ܗܘܬ ܫܠܝܐ. ܕܒܗ ܐܬܐ ܡܠܟܐ ܕܐܬܘܪ ܒܐܓܪܬܗ ܕܠܐ ܒܙܒܢܐ ܢܦܠ ܡܫܡܫ ܒܝܬܐ ܒܙܒܢܐ. ܗܘ ܕܝܢ ܕܐܬܐܬܪ ܢܦܠܘ ܠܐܬܪܐ ܐܝܟ ܕܒܫܠܡܘܬܐ ܐܬܐܬܪ ܀

ܟܒ. ܫܢܬ ܗܘܘ ܗܘܬ ܫܠܝܐ. ܕܐܬܠܝ ܕܡܕܝܢ ܕܢܫܡܥܘܢ ܕܒܢܐ ܐܢ ܐܬܚܝܠܬ ܕܢܫܡܥ ܬܐܘܐ ܘܢܫܡܥ ܠܒܢܐ ܘܕܚܠ ܠܫܡܐ. ܠܐ ܗܘܬ ܢܫܡܥܘܢ ܕܡܠܐ ܐܚܪܢܐ. ܒܕ ܗܘܬ ܡܫܡܠܝܢ ܪܓܠܐ ܕܡܫܘܒ ܒܐܦܝܗܘܢ ܒܫܠܡܘܬܐ ܀

ܟܓ. ܫܢܬ ܗܘܘ ܗܘܬ ܫܠܝܐ ܕܐܬܠܝ ܕܪܡܝܢ ܒܪ̈ܚܡܘܗܝ ܘܡܫܡܠܝܢ ܒܫܬܪܘܬܐ ܕܫܒܘܪܘܬܐ ܠܐ ܢܬܪܦܘܢ ܠܡܫܡܫܘܬܐ. ܡܛܠ ܗܢ ܕܡܕܡ ܕܪܡ ܒܗ ܒܒܢܝܐ ܡܕܡ ܐܠܗܐ ܢܣܒ ܗܘ. ܘܫܠܡܘܢ ܐܡܪܐ ܐܦܣܝܩ ܗܘܪܢܐ ܒܠ ܐܠܝܢ ܕܡܬܟܢܫܝܢ ܀

ܟܕ. ܫܢܬ ܗܘܘ ܗܘܬ ܫܠܝܐ ܕܢܫܘܢ ܗܦܘܟܐ ܒܠ ܡܫܒܐ ܕܐܝܬ ܒܡܘܬܒܐ ܘܕܘܒܪܐ ܪܓܠܐ ܕܫܠܡܘܢ ܕܟܐܢܘܬܗ ܗܘܘ ܡܬܬܟܬܝܢ ܠܗܘܢ. ܐܦ ܫܡܘܐܝܠ ܓܒܪ ܗܘܢܐ ܦܬܪ ܗܦܟܐ ܡܢ ܕܘܟܐ ܠܕܘܟܐ ܘܦܣܩ ܗܦܟܐ . . .

ܟܗ. ܫܢܬ ܗܘܘ ܗܘܬ ܫܠܝܐ ܕܡܠܟܐ ܐܠܝܢ ܕܒܬܪܝܢ ܕܢܫܡܥܘܢ ܒܡܫܡܫܢܐ ܗܦܟܐ ܒܠܝܠܐ ܠܗܘܢ ܕܢܫܡܥܘܢ ܘܢܫܡܥܘܢ ܡܢ ܡܕܒܚܐ ܒܝܬ ܡܕܒܚܝܐ ܕܒܬܐ. ܡܛܠ ܕܐܦ ܕܘܢ ܦܐܠܝܢ ܕܐܦܫܘܬܗ ܗܘܘ ܗܠܝܢ ܗܘܘ ܘܡܫܡܥܝܢ ܗܘܘ ܡܢ ܡܕܒܚܐ ܀

ܟܘ. ܫܢܬ ܗܘܘ ܗܘܬ ܫܠܝܐ. ܕܠܐ ܐܢܫ ܢܣܒܪ ܘܢܫܡܥܘܢ ܡܢ ܒܫܘܠܛܢܐ ܕܡܫܡܫܢܘܬܐ ܕܠܐ ܒܙܒܢܐ ܘܕܠܐ ܒܫܠܡܘܬܐ. ܐܠܐ ܒܡܫܡܫܢܘܬܐ ܘܕܠܐ ܪܓܝܫܐ ܕܡܫܡܫܢ ܬܐܘܐ ܀

ܐܚܪܬܐ ܘܡܬܚܫܚ ܒܬܐܓܘܪܬܐ ܘܡܒܘܢܘܬܐ. ܗܢܐ ܠܐ ܢܗܘܐ ܢܩܪܒ ܘܠܐ ܢܗܘܐ ܒܡܫܡܫܢܘܬܐ ܀

ܡܗ. ܬܘܒ ܗܘܘ ܣܡܘ ܫܠܝܚܐ ܕܐܝܢܐ ܕܡܫܡܫ ܩܘܕܫܐ. ܐܝܟ ܬܕܪܘܦܬܐ ܕܢܝܫ ܐܢܘܢ ܐܘ ܠܚܢܦܐ ܕܟܢܫܝܢ ܠܒܝ̈ܬܐ ܫܠܡ ܒܪܘܚܐ. ܠܐ ܢܥܘܠ ܒܥܕܬܗܘܢ ܘܢܣܒ. ܐܦ ܕܝܢ ܐܢܬܬܗ، ܒܥܕܬܗܘܢ ܠܐ ܢܩܒܠܘܢܝܗ، ܐܠܐ ܕܢܬܦܪܫ ܡܢ ܥܕܬܗܘܢ ܘܠܐ ܬܗܘܐ ܢܣܒܐ ܒܥܕܗܘܢ ܀

ܡܘ. ܬܘܒ ܗܘܘ ܣܡܘ ܫܠܝܚܐ. ܕܐܦ ܐܢܫ ܡܢ ܩܘܕܫܐ ܐܘ ܡܢ ܩܢܘܢܐ ܐܬܬܐ ܘܡܬܦܠܛ ܒܥܕܬܗܘܢ ܘܐܦ ܡܢܐ ܕܐܬܦܠܛ ܒܥܕܬܗܘܢ ܦܢܐ ܘܐܙܠ ܠܗ ܢܗܘܐ ܠܒܪܐ ܕܐܝܟ ܗܘܐ ܒܗ. ܐܦ ܕܝܢ ܢܗܘܐ ܒܠܒ ܐܬܬܐ ܕܐܢ̈ܫܝܗܘܢ ܕܢܦܫܗ ܠܐ ܢܗܘܐ ܢܬܩܒܠ. ܐܠܐ ܐܝܟ ܓܒܪܐ ܕܐܬܬܘܗܝ، ܗܘܐ ܒܗ ܡܢ ܩܕܝܡ. ܡܚܝܐ ܗܘܘ ܣܓܝ ܒܗ ܐܠܗܐ ܕܩܒܠ ܠܗ ܀

ܡܙ. ܬܘܒ ܗܘܘ ܣܡܘ ܫܠܝܚܐ ܕܠܐ ܢܗܘܐ ܥܠܝܠ ܠܡܕܒܪܢܐ ܕܥܠܡܐ ܐܠܗܐ ܕܡܫܡܫܝܢ ܒܥܕܬܗ ܢܗܘܐ ܣܓܝ ܕܩܕܡܘܬܐ ܐܠܗܐ ܕܐܬܐܘܬܐ ܐܢܫ، ܐܠܐ ܒܡܠܟܐ ܕܥܠܡܘܢ ܢܗܘܐ ܦܘܪ ܦܘ ܘܡܣܬܒܪ ܗܘ ܡܫܡܫ ܕܥܠܡܘܢ ܡܚܝܢ ܒܗ ܘܠܐ ܡܚܝܢ ܀

ܡܚ. ܬܘܒ ܗܘܘ ܣܡܘ ܫܠܝܚܐ ܕܟܠ ܐܠܗܐ ܕܢܦܩ ܡܢ ܒܠܚܘܕ ܗܢܐ ܒܡܫܘܕܬܐ ܦܓܪܐ ܕܡܢܝܘܬܗ ܕܡܫܝܚܐ. ܘܒܐܘܠܝܢܐ ܕܟܠ ܫܢܐ ܗܘܘ ܒܕܝܢ ܠܗܘܢ ܕܡܕܝܢܐ ܒܗܘܦܟܐ ܕܦܠܚܘܢ ܀

ܡܛ. ܬܘܒ ܗܘܘ ܣܡܘ ܫܠܝܚܐ ܕܬܫܡܫܬܐ ܕܒܝܬܐ ܗܘܘ ܐܡܪܝܢ ܬܫܒܚܬܐ ܕܕܘܝܕ ܒܠܝܐ ܒܝܘܡ. ܡܛܠ ܗܢܐ ܕܐܡܪܝܢ ܠܡܪܢܐ ܒܠܠܝܐ. ܘܒܠܠܝܐ ܬܫܒܚܬܗ ܒܝܘܡܐ. ܘܐܫܬܡܥܐ ܠܗ ܘܡܠܠܐ ܐܪܢܐ ܘܐܡܪ ܘܐܫܬܡܥ ܥܠ ܡܕܡܝܢ ܀

ܢ. ܬܘܒ ܗܘܘ ܣܡܘ ܫܠܝܚܐ ܕܐܠܗܐ ܕܡܬܩܪܒ ܡܢ

ܕܒܬܪ ܐܝܟܢܐ ܬܗܘܘܢ ܢܚܙܘܢ ܡܕܡ ܐܠܗܝܐ ܘܬܬܒܗܘܢ ܒܗ
ܐܬܒܗܘܢ ܕܟܗ ܕܡܫܝܚܐ ܕܟܠܗ ܒܠܚܘܕܝܗܘܢ. ܠܐ ܓܝܪ
ܡܢܟܠܐ ܡܕܡ ܐܠܗܝܐ ܕܒܪ ܐܢܫܘܬܗܘܢ ܒܡ ܦܠܘܓܬܗ،
ܬܫܘܝ ܘܬܬܠܘܬܗܘܢ ܒܡ ܡܬܩܠܐ ܕܒܝܗ ܦܠܚܐ. ܐܝܟܢܐ
ܫܡܝܢ ܐܢܘܢ ܕܬܬܦܟܠ ܗܡܫܝܚܘܬܗܘܢ ܒܡ ܥܒܕܐ. ܟܕ ܒܡ
ܟܠܗ ܐܢܘܢ. ܐܠܐ ܙܕܩ ܗܘ ܠܗܘܢ ܕܐܝܟ ܐܢܫܐ
ܕܡܫܡܫܝܢ ܒܡܫܝܚܐ ܬܘܕܝ. ܓܠܝܐܝܬ ܒܫܡܫܘܬܐ
ܗܕܐ ܕܡܗܝܡܢ. ܘܟܕ ܥܒܕܘ ܗܘܘ ܗܢܝܢ ܟܠܗ ܡܢ ܬܠܡܝܕܐ
ܡܢܗ ܒܠܚܘܕ ܥܘܠܐܝܬ ܗܢܘܢ ܟܕ ܒܫܡܐ ܡܕܡ ܒܠܗ
ܒܗܢܐ ܕܟܠܝܢܐ ܕܡܫܝܚܐ ܕܐܙܕܩ ܡܗܝܡܢ ܘܡܫܡܫܝܢ ܗܘ
ܘܐܢܬܘܢ، ܡܢ ܡܬܘܡ ܒܪܐ ܕܐܠܗܐ ܡܗܝܡܢ. ܘܟܐܠܝܢ
ܕܐܡܬܝܢ ܘܢܩܫܘܢ، ܒܫܪܝܢ. ܐܦ ܓܝܪ ܒܫܡܗ، ܕܒܟܐ ܡܗܝܡܢ
ܐܢܘܢ ܒܫܡܐܬ ܒܡܫܝܚܐ. ܘܡܛܠ ܙܒܢܘܬܐ ܕܒܟܐ ܕܐܢܫܝܢ
ܠܗ. ܠܐ ܢܓܕܝܢ ܕܢܕܪܘܢ ܓܠܝܐܝܬ. ܘܦܩܕ ܠܗ، ܕܬܬܡܢܐ
ܕܢܡܠܟܬܐ ܗܘ ܡܪܝܐ ܘܠܐ ܬܗܝܢ ܡܕܡܗ، ܢܟܬܐ. ܟܕ
ܕܝܢ ܥܒܕܘ ܗܘܘ ܐܟܫܗܘܢ ܗܢܝܢ ܟܠܗ ܡܢ ܒܢܝܗܘܢ ܠܚܡܫܝܢ
ܗܘܘ ܠܗܘܢ ܓܒ. ܠܐ ܗܘܐ ܕܝܢ ܡܛܠ ܗܢ ܕܗܡܫܝܚܘ ܗܘܘ
ܒܡܫܝܚܐ. ܐܠܐ ܒܠ ܕܟܠܗ ܗܘܘ ܘܦܪܗܘ ܗܘܘ ܙܒܢܐ
ܕܐܒܫܡܗܘܢ ܡܕܡ ܒܬܪ ܒܡܫܗܘܢ. ܗܢܘܢ ܕܝܢ ܕܗܡܫܝܚܘ ܗܘܘ
ܢܦܩܘ ܗܘܘ ܠܗܘܢ ܠܬܠܡܝܕܐ ܘܡܢ ܓܐܕܗܘܢ ܠܐ ܡܫܝܢ
ܗܘܘ ܕܐܡܝܢ ܗܘܘ ܕܗܘܘ ܡܕܡ ܕܟܠܗܝܢ ܗܘܘ ܠܩܘܒܠܐ. ܗܢܘܢ
ܒܒܕܐ ܦܒܪܝܢ ܡܕܡ ܒܠ ܐܝܟ. ܘܐܡܬܝ، ܕܐܬܠܓܝܐ
ܘܪܕܘܦܝܐ ܡܐܡ ܩܘܐ ܒܠ ܬܠܡܝܕܐ ܚܕܝܢ ܗܘܘ ܕܬܬܐܠܓܝܢ ܗܘܘ
ܒܡܫܘܢ. ܘܒܫܘܕܘܬܐ ܢܟܪܝܐ ܦܫܘܫܝܐ ܡܡܟܠܝܢ ܗܘܘ
ܒܬܘܕܝܬܐ ܕܗܡܫܝܚܘܬܗܘܢ ܕܒܡܫܝܚܐ؛ ܘܥܠ ܡܩܡ ܚܝܘܗܘܢ
ܠܡܫܝܚܐ ܡܗܝܪܝܢ ܗܘܘ ܡܕܡ ܡܩܘܕܫܐ ܘܫܩܝܠܐ. ܘܡܢ ܒܬܪ
ܡܬܬܒܗܘܢ ܕܩܠܝܠܐ ܗܘܘ ܡܕܒܪܢܐ ܘܡܩܘܕܫܐ ܒܟܪܝܬܐ. ܘܗܘ

ܟܕ. ܗܟܢܐ ܗܘܐ ܬܘܒ ܥ̈ܠܝܡܐ ܕܠܫܡܥܐ ܕܡܘܪܒܐ ܒܗܘܢܐ ܕܡܬܬܐܦܐ ܢܗܘܐ ܟܠ ܡܕܡ ܕܟܣܝܐ. ܘܠܐ ܟܬܪ ܘܡܬܬܐ ܡܢܗ ܕܠܐ ܥܠܡ܀

ܗܠܝܢ ܕܝܢ ܟܠܗܝܢ ܠܐ ܗܘܐ ܠܢܦܫܗܘܢ ܗܘܘ ܗܟܢ ܥ̈ܠܝܡܐ. ܐܠܐ ܠܐܠܝܢ ܕܐܬܝܢ ܗܘܘ ܒܬܪܗܘܢ. ܦܫܝܛܝܢ ܗܘܘ ܓܝܪ ܕܒܬܪܝܢ ܐܝܟ ܕܐܒܗܐ ܕܠܒܢܝܗܘܢ ܠܒܢܝܐ ܕܐܡܪܬܐ ܠܗܘܢ ܓܝܪ ܗܘܦܟܐ ܗܘܬ ܙܘܥܐ ܦܘܠܚܢܐ ܕܟܠܗܘܢ. ܕܐܝܟ ܕܗܘܬ ܒܐܝܕܝܗܘܢ ܗܠܝܢ ܢܟܣܘܗܝ ܬܕܒܪ ܐܝܟ ܢܟܣܘܗܝ. ܗܘܘ ܓܝܪ ܕܟܠ ܗܘܘ ܡܢ ܡܢܟܘܢ ܚܝܠܐ ܘܫܘܠܛܢܐ. ܠܐ ܗܘܝܢ ܗܘܘ ܕܡܢ ܐܢ̈ܫܐ ܢܬܬܗܝܒܘܢ ܠܗܘܢ ܢܟܣܝܗܘܢ. ܐܦ ܦܠܚܘ ܓܝܪ ܘܦܠܚܬܐܗܘܢ ܟܕ ܡܬܬܒܪܝܢ ܗܘܘ ܒܐܬܪܘܬܐ ܕܗܘܪܐ ܘܕܠܝܠܝܐ ܠܗܘܢ ܠܗܠܝܢ ܦܩܘܕܐ ܘܢܛܘܪܐ ܕܥ̈ܠܝܡܐ ܘܕܥ̈ܒܕܐ ܠܬܚܘܢ ܕܐܬܬܣܝܡܘܢ ܗܘܘ ܬܘܒ ܐܝܟ ܐܚܪܢܐ ܕܥ̈ܠܝܡܐ ܡܟܝܠ ܗܘܘ ܠܓܒܪܐ ܕܐܬܪܘܬܐ ܕܡܕܒܪܝܢ ܗܘܘ ܒܗܘܢ ܘܡܫܬܪܝܢ. ܬܠܡܝܕܐ ܕܝܢ ܡܢ ܟܬܪ ܗܠܝܢ ܦܬܓܡܐ ܘܢܟܣܝܗܘܢ ܕܗܟܢ ܗܘܘ: ܠܐ ܥܠܝܢ ܗܘܘ ܡܢ ܒܪܘܪܬܐ ܕܗܒܪܬܐ ܘܡܢ ܚܝܠܐ ܬܘܟܝܢܐ ܕܒܪ ܗܘܐ ܡܢ ܐܒ̈ܗܝܗܘܢ. ܒܗܢܐ ܓܝܪ ܦܘܫܩܐ ܟܕ ܦܘܫ ܟܠܗܘܢ ܕܐܝܟܢ ܕܡܬܡܠܟܝܢ ܗܘܘ ܒܡܟܣܝܢܐ ܘܡܢ ܡܕܒܪܢܘܬܐ ܐܢ̈ܫܝܐ ܐܬܝܢ ܗܘܘ ܕܐܒܗܝܗܘܢ. ܘܫܒܩܝܢ ܗܘܘ ܡܠܘ̈ܗܝ ܘܡܡܠܠܝܢ. ܢܡܘܣܗܘܢ ܕܝܢ ܦܟܝܠܬܐܝܬ ܗܘܐ ܒܐܘܪܚܐ ܕܡܘܕܝܐ ܐܬܝܢ ܗܘܘ ܕܐܒܗܝܗܘܢ ܕܥ̈ܠܝܡܐ ܒܗܘܢܐ. ܟܕ ܥܠܝܢ ܗܘܘ ܠܡܠܦܢܘܬܗܘܢ. ܡܘܕܐ ܕܝܢ ܘܠܘ، ܘܦܪ، ܘܡܘܦ ܘܡܘܦܬܐ ܟܠ ܚܢܢܐ ܘܡܘܫܐ ܘܐܠܟܣܢܕܪܘܣ ܒܚܝܠܐ ܐܬܝܢ ܗܘܘ ܐܦ ܗܢܘܢ ܕܐܒܗܝܗܘܢ ܕܥ̈ܠܝܡܐ ܟܠܠܟܐ. ܟܕ ܡܟܝܠ ܗܘܘ ܒܡܫܝܚܐ ܕܒܪܐ ܗܘ ܕܐܠܗܐ ܘܡܢ ܟܠ ܒܟܠܗܘܢ ܕܥܠܝܢ ܗܘܘ ܕܢܟܠܘܢ ܙܕܝܩܘܬ ܕܠܗܘܬ ܬܠܡܝܕܐ. ܘܡܟܠ ܐܝܟ ܥ̈ܠܝܡܐ ܫܒܝܚܘܬ ܟܕ ܐܡܪܝܢ ܠܗܘܢ. ܠܐ ܡܫܠ ܢܦܫܬܐ ܘܕܠܝܬܐ

ܘܡܫܕܪܢܘܬܐ ܕܠܟܘܢ. ܡܢܘܬܐ ܕܟܠ ܚܕ ܡܩܒܠܝܢ ܗܘܘ. ܘܟܐܢܐ ܕܫܘܝܘܬܐ ܕܡܩܒܠ ܗܘܐ ܡܢ ܡܪܢ ܗܘܝܘ ܫܠܝܚܐ ܦܛܪܘܣ ܘܚܒܪܘܗܝ ܒܐܝܕܐ ܐܘܪܚܗ ܕܫܠܡܐ ܡܠܟܘܬܗ. ܘܟܕ ܗܟܢܐ ܗܘܘ ܠܩܕܝܫܐ ܡܫܡܫܝܢ ܗܘܘ ܠܩܕܝܫܐ ܀

ܡܛܠ ܐܝܕܐ ܕܫܘܥܝܬܐ ܐܘܪܫܠܡ. ܘܟܠܗ ܐܬܪܐ ܕܦܠܣܛܝܢܐ ܘܟܠܗ ܥܡܡܐ ܘܟܠܗ ܦܠܚܘܬܐ. ܘܐܬܪܐ ܕܒܪܝܐ ܘܕܝܘܢܐ ܘܟܠ ܡܕܝܢܐ ܡܢ ܝܘܡܢ. ܗܘ ܕܗܘܐ ܗܘܐ ܦܩܘܕܐ ܘܡܕܒܪܢܐ ܒܥܕܬܐ ܕܠܫܢܐ ܕܐܬܟܢܫ ܗܘܬ ܒܝܘܡܝ ܀

ܡܛܠ ܐܝܕܐ ܕܫܘܥܝܬܐ ܕܠܫܢܐ ܐܠܟܣܢܕܪܝܐ ܪܒܬܐ ܬܬܟܢܫ ܘܟܠܗ ܡܕܝܢ ܒܗܝܢܐ. ܘܟܠܗ ܐܬܪܐ ܕܡܨܪܝܢ. ܘܒܡܕܢܚܐ ܠܬܝܡܢܐ ܕܡܨܪܝܢ. ܡܢ ܡܪܩܘܣ ܡܫܒܪܢܐ ܗܘ ܕܗܘܐ ܗܘܐ ܬܡܢ ܦܩܘܕܐ ܘܡܕܒܪܢܐ ܒܥܕܬܐ ܕܒܢܐ ܗܘܐ ܬܡܢ ܘܫܡܫ ܗܘܐ ܀

ܡܛܠ ܐܝܕܐ ܕܫܘܥܝܬܐ ܕܟܠܝܫܐ. ܗܝܕܝܢ ܘܟܠܗܘܢ ܐܬܪܘܬܐ ܕܠܗ ܘܕܚܕܪܝܗ. ܒܝܕ ܐܝܟܢܐ ܐܡܝܪܐ. ܡܢ ܗܕܐ ܬܐܘܡܐ ܗܘ ܕܗܘܐ ܗܘܐ ܡܕܒܪܢܐ ܘܦܩܘܕܐ ܒܥܕܬܐ ܕܒܢܐ ܗܘܐ ܬܡܢ ܘܫܡܫ ܗܘܐ ܬܡܢ ܀

ܡܛܠ ܐܝܕܐ ܕܫܘܥܝܬܐ ܕܠܫܢܐ ܐܢܛܝܘܟ ܘܣܘܪܝܐ ܘܟܠܗ ܦܠܩܣ ܕܒܗ ܠܦܠܣܛ ܡܢ ܥܡܡܐ ܘܟܠܗ ܕܗܘܐ ܗܝ ܗܘܐ ܥܠ ܕܘܟܬܐ ܕܒܢܐ ܬܡܢ. ܘܫܡܫ ܗܘܐ ܘܫܡܫ ܗܘܐ ܬܡܢ ܒܥܕܬܐ ܠܟܠܗ ܕܟܠܗ ܗܘܐ ܡܢ ܬܡܢ ܠܪܘܡܝܐ. ܡܛܠ ܗܢܘܢ ܫܢܝܐ ܕܚܠܝܬܐ ܗܘܐ ܠܗܘܢ ܠܟܠ ܪܘܡܝܐ ܒܫܢܝܗܘܢ ܀

ܡܕܡ ܕܐܬܟܠܘ ܗܘܘ ܠܗܘܢ ܝ̈ܘܢܝܐ ܘܝܠܦܘ ܗܘܘ ܡܕܝܢܗܘܢ
ܟܠܗ ܙܒܢܐ ܕܚ̈ܝܝܗܘܢ ܡܠܟܝܢ ܗܘܘ ܠܡ̈ܠܟܐ. ܐܦ ܗܢܘܢ
ܬܘܒ ܒܡܠܟܘܬܗܘܢ ܐܬܟܠܘ ܗܘܘ ܘܐܫܠܡܘ ܗܘܘ ܠܬܠܡ̈ܝܕܝܗܘܢ
ܒܬܪܗܘܢ ܟܠ ܡܕܡ ܕܝܠܦܘ ܗܘܘ ܡܢ ܟ̈ܠܕܝܐ. ܐܦ ܡܕܡ ܕܝܠܦ
ܗܘܐ ܝܗܘܕ ܡܢ ܐܘܪܫܠܡ. ܘܝܠܦܘ ܡܢ ܪܗܘܡܝܐ ܡܕܝܢܬܐ.
ܘܗܢܝܢ ܡܢ ܐܦܣܘܣ. ܘܡܢܗܘܢ ܡܢ ܐܠܟܣܢܕܪܝܐ ܪܒܬܐ.
ܘܐܚܪ̈ܢܐ ܡܢ ܦܪܓܡܐ. ܘܠܘܩܐ ܡܢ ܡܩܕܘܢܝܐ. ܘܗܘܕܐ
ܬܘܡܐ ܡܢ ܗܢܕܘ. ܕܐܓܪ̈ܬܗ ܕܫܠܝܚܐ ܢܬܩܪܐ ܘܢܬܦܪܫ
ܒܟܬܒ̈ܬܐ ܕܟܠ ܐܬܪ ܐܝܟ ܕܡܬܦܪܫ ܢ̈ܦܫܐ ܕܡܗܝܡ̈ܢܝܗܘܢ
ܦܝܠܘܢ ܕܒܬܪ ܗܘܐ ܠܗܘܢ ܠܘܩܐ. ܕܡܫܕܐ ܢܬܕܒܪܘܢ ܝ̈ܘܢܝܐ
ܘܢܩ̈ܦܐ ܘܢܬܦܩܐ ܒܬܘܕܝܬܐ ܘܚܕܬܐ ܕܚܕ ܥܕܬܐ ܐܬܪܐ ܐܬܝܬܪ
ܒܠܒܗܘܢ ܕܚܕܐ ܪܘܚܐ ܡܠܠܬ ܒܠܒܗܘܢ ܡܢ ܚܕ ܐܠܗܐ
ܕܡܬܟܪܙ ܗܘܐ ܒܠܒܗܘܢ ܘܡܬܒܪܢܫ ܗܘܐ ܒܠܒܗܘܢ. ܘܡܟܠ
ܐܬܪ̈ܘܬܐ ܡܠܟܘܬܗܘܢ. ܒܠܒܕ ܦܝܠ ܕܐܬܦܠܠ ܡܢ
ܡܪܢ ܒܝܕ ܝ̈ܘܢܝܐ. ܘܝ̈ܘܢܝܐ ܐܫܠܡܘ ܗܘܘ ܠܬܠܡ̈ܝܕܝܗܘܢ
ܐܬܦܫܛܘ ܘܐܬܦܠܠ ܒܟܠ ܐܬܪ ܒܐܪܥܗ ܕܡܪܢ ܕܐܬܒܪ
ܠܗܘܢ. ܕܒܟܬܒܘܢ ܐܝܟ ܒܝܕܥܐ ܕܥܠܡ ܒܠܒܐ. ܒܗ ܕܝܢܫ
ܗܘܘ ܒܗ ܡܕܘܒܪܢܐ ܡܕܒܪ̈ܢܐ ܡܢ ܗܦܟܐ ܕܢܟܝܐ ܘܡܬܦܪܫ
ܗܘܘ ܐܦ ܒܗ ܚܦܝܐ ܠܟܝܢܐ ܒܚܠܝܐ ܕܫܠܝܐ ܕܒܕܝܢ ܗܘܘ
ܒܡܬܐ ܕܡܬܝܢܐ. ܒܡܫܟܢܐ ܒܪ ܒܠܒܗܘܢ ܐܦ ܗܢܘܢ ܕܒܡܬܪ
ܗܘܘ ܒܐܬܪ̈ܘܬܐ ܐܢܫ̈ܝܢܐ ܥܠܘ ܗܘܘ ܘܫܬܘ ܒܡܕܝܢܬܗ
ܕܡܬܢܝܐ. ܘܐܝܠܝܢ ܕܡܬܕܪܢ ܡܢܗܘܢ ܗܘܘ ܒܪܕܝܬܐ ܕܗܘܕܐ
ܪ̈ܕܝܦܘܬܐ ܕܡܬܕܒܪܢܐ ܬܘܕܝܐ ܗܢܐܓܪܐ ܫܠܝܛ ܕܗܘܝܢ
ܪ̈ܕܝܦܐ ܡܢ ܡܫܝܚ. ܐܝܬ ܗܘܐ ܒܪ ܡܫܡܗܘܢ ܕܡܬܦܬܐ ܕܗܘܕܐ
ܡܬܦܫܛ ܗܘܐ ܒܠܒܦ. ܘܐܝܬ ܗܘܐ ܡܫܡܗܘܢ ܕܡܕܡ ܕܝܕܥ
ܗܘܐ ܥܡܠ ܗܘܘ ܡܫܡܗܘܢ ܘܡܬܦܫ ܗܘܘ ܠܗܘܢ. ܘܥܡܗ
ܕܐܘܠܝܢܐ ܡܢܝܢ ܗܘܐ ܒܠܒܗܘܢ ܒܢܦܫܗܘܢ ܫܬܪܝܢ ܗܘܘ ܘܕܪܫܝܢ.

ܓܘܓ ܘܡܓܘܓ ܘܐܬܪ̈ܘܬܐ ܬܘܒ ܟܠܗܝܢ ܕܡܢ ܟܠ ܓܒ̈ܝܢ. ܡܢ ܐܓܝ ܥܒܕ ܫܝܪ̈ܝܐ ܬܠܡܝܕܗ ܕܐܕܝ ܫܠܝܚܐ ܀

ܫܪܟܐ ܕܝܢ ܕܚܒܪ̈ܝܗܘܢ ܐܚܪ̈ܢܐ ܕܫܠܝܚ̈ܐ ܐܙܠܘ ܗܘܘ ܠܐܬܪ̈ܘܬܐ ܡܪ̈ܚܩܬܐ ܕܒܪ̈ܒܪܝܐ. ܘܡܢ ܕܘܟܐ ܠܕܘܟܐ ܡܬܠܡܕܝܢ ܗܘܘ ܘܡܟܪܙܝܢ. ܘܬܡܢ ܫܡܫܘ ܗܘܘ ܒܟܪܘܙܘܬܗܘܢ. ܘܬܡܢ ܗܘܘ ܡܫܬܢܝܢ ܡܢ ܥܠܡܐ ܗܢܐ. ܟܕ ܬܪ̈ܝܢ ܘܬܠܡ̈ܝܕܝܗܘܢ ܒܬܪܗܘܢ ܥܕܡܐ ܠܝܘܡܢܐ. ܘܡܕܡ ܫܘܠܡܐ ܐܘ ܬܘܕܝܬܐ ܠܐ ܗܘܐ ܠܗܘܢ ܟܠ ܟܪܘܙܘܬܗܘܢ ܀

ܠܘܩܐ ܕܝܢ ܐܘܢܓܠܝܣܛܐ ܗܘܬ ܠܗ ܚܦܝܛܘܬܐ ܗܕܐ ܘܟܬܒ ܗܘܐ ܢܨ̈ܚܢܐ ܕܥܘܒܕ̈ܝܗܘܢ ܕܫܠܝܚ̈ܐ ܘܦܘܩܕ̈ܢܐ ܘܢܡܘ̈ܣܐ ܕܬܫܡܫܬܐ ܕܟܗܢܘܬܗܘܢ. ܘܠܐܝܟܐ ܐܙܠ ܗܘܐ ܚܕ ܚܕ ܡܢܗܘܢ. ܒܟܬܒܘܬܗ ܗܝ ܕܠܘܩܐ ܗܠܝܢ ܘܫܪ̈ܟܐ ܡܢ ܗܠܝܢ ܟܬܒ ܗܘܐ ܘܐܦ ܟܕ ܦܪܣܡܘ ܘܐܝܠܝܢ ܕܬܠܡܝܕܘܗܝ. ܘܠܡ ܗܘܘ ܠܗ ܒܥܕܬܐ ܠܝܘܡܢܐ ܕܟܢܘܫܬܗ ܐܝܟ ܕܠܐ ܗܘܐ ܠܫܘܠܡܗ ܦܘܩܕܢܘܗܝ ܘܐܪ̈ܟܠܗ ܕܡܢ ܠܘܬܦܛܪܐ. ܘܡܟܝܠܐ ܗܘ ܬܠܡܝܕܗ ܐܝܟܢܐ ܕܫܠܝܚܐ ܒܐܬܪܐ ܕܪܗܘܡܐ ܡܕܝܢܬܐ. ܕܢܦܩ ܗܘܐ ܠܘܬܗ ܦܝܠܠܘ ܪܘܡܦܪܐ. ܘܟܬܒܗ ܗܘܐ ܢܦܩ ܗܢܘ ܒܟܬܒܐ ܠܗ ܠܫܡܥܘܢ ܟܐܦܐ ܒܪܗܘܡܐ ܡܕܝܢܬܐ ܀

ܡܠܦܢܘܬܗ ܕܫܡܥܘܢ ܟܐܦܐ ܒܪܗܘܡܐ ܡܕܝܢܬܐ.

ܒܫܢܬ ܬܠܬ ܕܩܠܘܕܝܘܣ ܩܣܪ. ܢܦܩ ܗܘܐ ܫܡܥܘܢ ܟܐܦܐ ܡܢ ܐܢܛܝܘܟܝ ܕܢܐܙܠ ܠܗ ܠܪܗܘܡܐ. ܘܟܕ ܥܒܪ ܗܘܐ ܡܟܪܙ ܗܘܐ ܒܐܬܪ̈ܘܬܐ ܕܚܕܪ̈ܝܗ̇. ܘܟܕ ܡܛܐ ܗܘܐ ܕܢܥܘܠ ܗܘܐ ܠܗܠܝܢ: [ܫܡܥܘ ܗܘܘ ܐܚ̈ܐ ܕܒܪܗܘܡܐ ܘܢܦܩܘ ܠܐܘܪܥܗ. ܘܩܒܠܘܗܝ ܗܘܬ ܒܚܕܘܬܐ ܪܒܬܐ ܟܠܗ ܟܢܘܫܬܐ. ܘܡܢ ܪܘܪ̈ܒܢܐ ܕܡܕܝܢܬܐ

ܩܒܠܬ ܐܝܕܐ ܕܟܗܢܘܬܐ ܕܫܠܝܚܘܬܐ. ܪܗܘܡܐ ܡܕܝܢܬܐ
ܘܟܠܗ̇ ܐܝܛܠܝܐ ܘܐܣܦܢܝܐ ܘܒܪܛܢܝܐ. ܘܓܠܝܐ ܥܡ ܫܪܟܐ
ܕܐܬܪ̈ܘܬܐ ܐܚܪ̈ܢܐ ܕܚܕܪ̈ܝܗܘܢ܇ ܡܢ ܫܡܥܘܢ ܟܐܦܐ ܕܣܠܩ
ܗܘܐ ܡܢ ܐܢܛܝܘܟܝ. ܘܗ̣ܘܐ ܗ̣ܘܐ ܬܡܢ ܦܩܘܕܐ ܘܡܕܒܪܢܐ
ܒܥܕܬܐ ܕܒܢܐ ܗܘܐ ܬܡܢ ܘܒܣܘܪ̈ܝܗ̇ ܀

ܩܒܠܬ ܐܝܕܐ ܕܟܗܢܘܬܐ ܕܫ̈ܠܝܚܐ ܐܦܣܘܣ ܘܬܣܠܘܢܝܩܐ ܘܟܠܗ̇
ܐܣܝܐ ܘܐܬܪܐ ܟܠܗ̇ ܕܩܘܪ̈ܢܬܝܐ ܘܕܐܟܐܝܐ ܟܠܗ̇ ܘܕܚܕܪ̈ܝܗ̇. ܡܢ
ܝܘܚܢܢ ܐܘܢܓܠܣܛܐ ܗܘ ܕܐܣܬܡܟ ܗܘܐ ܥܠ ܚܕܝܗ ܕܡܪܢ. ܕܗܘ ܒܢܐ
ܗܘܐ ܥܕܬܐ ܬܡܢ ܘܫܡܫ ܗܘܐ ܬܡܢ ܒܡܕܒܪܢܘܬܗ ܕܬܡܢ ܀

ܩܒܠܬ ܐܝܕܐ ܕܟܗܢܘܬܐ ܕܫ̈ܠܝܚܐ ܢܝܩܝܐ ܘܐܢܛܝܘܟܝܐ ܘܟܠܗ̇
ܐܬܪܐ ܕܩܦܘܕܩܝܐ ܘܓܠܛܝܐ ܘܦܢܛܘܣ ܘܕܚܕܪ̈ܝܗ̇. ܡܢ
ܐܢܕܪܐܘܣ ܐܚܘܗܝ ܕܫܡܥܘܢ ܟܐܦܐ ܕܗܘ ܗܘܐ ܗܘܐ
ܡܕܒܪܢܐ ܘܦܩܘܕܐ ܒܥܕܬܐ ܕܒܢܐ ܗܘܐ ܬܡܢ ܘܒܗܝܢ ܗܘܐ
ܘܫܡܫ ܗܘܐ ܬܡܢ ܀

ܩܒܠܬ ܐܝܕܐ ܕܟܗܢܘܬܐ ܕܫܠܝܚܘܬܐ. ܒܐܘܪܫܠܡ ܘܟܠܗ̇ ܐܬܪܐ
ܕܬܝܡܢܐ ܘܕܚܕܪ̈ܝܗ̇. ܒܝܕ ܝܥܩܘܒ ܪܒܐ ܬܫܡܫܬܐ ܕܦܪܫ
ܟܠܗ ܒܪ̈ܢܫܐ ܡܢ ܠܘܩܒܠ ܫܠܝܚܐ ܕܗܘ ܒܢܐ ܗܘܐ ܒܥܕܬܐ
ܬܡܢ ܘܫܡܫ ܗܘܐ ܬܡܢ ܒܦܩܘܕܘܬܗ ܘܒܡܕܒܪܢܘܬܗ ܕܬܡܢ ܀

ܩܒܠܬ ܐܝܕܐ ܕܟܗܢܘܬܐ ܕܫ̈ܠܝܚܐ ܐܘܪܗܝ ܘܐܬܪ̈ܘܬܐ
ܟܠܗܘܢ ܕܚܕܪ̈ܝܗ̇. ܕܥܠ ܓܒ̈ܝܗ̇ ܘܨܘܒܐ ܘܥܪܒ ܘܟܠܗ̇
ܓܪܒܝܐ ܘܦܢ̈ܝܬܐ ܕܚܕܪ̈ܝܗ̇ ܘܬܚܘܡܝܐ ܘܒܝܬ ܢܗܪ̈ܝܢ ܟܠܗ̇
ܕܟܠܗ ܢܗܘܪ̈ܢ ܡܢ ܐܕܝ ܫܠܝܚܐ ܚܕ ܡܢ ܫܒܥܝܢ ܘܬܪ̈ܝܢ ܫܠܝܚܐ.
ܕܗܘ ܬܠܡܕ ܗܘܐ ܬܡܢ ܘܒܢܐ ܗܘܐ ܥܕܬܐ ܬܡܢ ܘܒܗܝܢ
ܗܘܐ ܘܫܡܫ ܗܘܐ ܬܡܢ ܒܡܕܒܪܢܘܬܗ ܕܬܡܢ ܀

ܩܒܠܬ ܐܝܕܐ ܕܟܗܢܘܬܐ ܕܫ̈ܠܝܚܐ ܦܪܣ ܟܠܗ̇ ܕܐܬܘܪ̈ܝܐ
ܘܕܐܪ̈ܡܝܐ ܘܕܡܕ̈ܝܐ ܘܕܐܬܪ̈ܘܬܐ ܕܚܕܪ̈ܝܗ̇ ܕܒܒܠ. ܘܗܘܙܝܐ
ܘܓܠܝܐ ܥܕܡܐ ܠܬܚܘܡ̈ܐ ܕܗܢܕܘܝܐ. ܘܥܕܡܐ ܠܒܝܬ

ܕܐܡܝܪܐ ܗܘ ܡܠܬܐ ܕܢܘܚܪ ܫܡܥܘܢ ܕܕܝ̈ܠܢ. ܟܐܦܐ
ܕܗܘܝܢ ܥ̈ܠ ܐܝܟܐ ܫܒܝܚܐ ܕܡ̈ܠܐ ܦ̈ܠܠܬܐ ܒܗ ܕܒܝܐ.
ܡܛܠ ܕܡܢ ܕܫܢ ܐܢܬܘܢ ܗܘܝܬܘܢ ܬ̈ܠܡܝܕܐ ܕܡܫܝܚܐ. ܘܠܐ ܗܘܐ ܫܦܝܪܐ
ܕܬܫܬܩܘܢ. ܡܛܠ ܗܢܐ ܗܘ ܐܡܪ ܠܝ. ܕܡܫܟܚ ܐܢܐ ܠܟܘܢ
ܙܘܥܐ ܫܪܝܪܬܐ. ܕܗܘ ܢܠܒܫܘܢ ܡܕܡ ܕܠܐ ܡܫܚܝܢ ܐܢܬܘܢ.
ܒܡܘܗܒܬܗ ܗܘ ܒܪܗ ܕܐܠܗܐ ܐܡܪܝܢ ܚܢܢ: ܐܝܠܝܢ ܕܡܫܡܫܝܢ
ܐܢܬܘܢ. ܘܡܢ ܬܘܒ ܡܬܦܪܢܣܝܢ ܒܡܕܝܢܬܐ ܠܒ̈ܢܝܗܝܢ ܘܫܘܠܛܢܐ
ܠܡܫܡܫܢܐ. ܘܡܢ ܢܨܚܢܐ ܕܡܠܟܘܬܗ ܘܡܢ ܒܡܕܝܢܬܐ ܕܫܠܝܚ.
ܬܫܡܫܘܢ ܒܡܫܝܚܐ ܕܐܢܬܘܢ، ܐܝܟܢܐ ܕܒܪܐ ܕܐܠܗܐ.
ܬܬܦܪܢܣܘܢ ܡܢ ܫܘܠܛܢܐ ܕܡܠܟܘܬܗ. ܘܬܬܠܒܫܘܢ ܠܗ
ܘܠܐܠܗܘܗܝ. ܘܬܫܒܚܘܢ ܠܙܘܥܐ ܕܐܠܗܘܬܗ. ܡܢ ܓܝܪ ܠܐܒܐ
ܡܫܒܚܝܢ ܚܢܢ. ܐܦ ܠܒܪܗ ܒܗܘ ܡܫܒܚܝܢ ܚܢܢ. ܘܡܢ ܠܒܪܐ ܣܓܕܝܢ
ܚܢܢ. ܐܦ ܠܐܒܐ ܒܗܘ ܣܓܕܝܢ ܚܢܢ. ܘܡܢ ܒܪܘܚܐ ܡܘܕܝܢ.
ܐܦ ܒܐܒܐ ܘܒܒܪܐ ܡܘܕܝܢ ܚܢܢ. ܡܛܠ ܕܚܕ ܐܒܐ ܘܒܪܐ
ܘܪܘܚܐ ܐܬܟܪܙܘ. ܕܢܚܘܐ ܠܐܝܠܝܢ ܕܡܗܝܡܢܝܢ ܕܢܚܘܢ ܠܥܠܡ ܀

ܒܪܘܗܝ ܗܟܝܠ ܡܢ ܡ̈ܠܐ ܕܫܡܥܘܬܐ ܕܗܢܐ ܥܠܡܐ ܕܠܗ
ܒܗܘܢ ܡܬܪܥܝܢ. ܘܢܬܦܪܫܘܢ ܠܘܬ ܐܝܠܝܢ ܕܡܪ̈ܢ ܘܡܫܡܫܝܢ:
ܘܡܩܒܠܝܢ ܡܢ ܐܠܗܐ. ܘܢܛܪ ܐܝܟܢܐ ܘܢܫܒܘܩ ܫܘܒܚܢ.
ܘܡܛܠ] ܕܢܚܘܐ ܠܗ ܢܘܗܪܐ ܒܢܘܗܪܬܐ. ܘܢܚܐ ܠܗ ܒܠܚܘܕ ܒܢܝܢܐ
ܕܢܚܫܐ ܕܢܚܘܐ ܟܠ ܐܢܫ ܘܢܬܒܢܐ: ܕܠܐ ܙܪܥ ܕܢܗܘܬܩܢ
ܒܪܬܐ ܢܠܦ ܒܪܘܚܐ ܐܚܪܬܐ ܡܢ ܒܪܘܚܐ. ܡܛܠ ܕܗܢܐ ܡܕܡ
ܕܒܪܬܐ ܗܘ ܫܦܝܪܐ ܗܘ ܕܒܗܘܢ. ܘܠܐ ܗܘܝ ܫܦܝܪܐ ܗܘ
ܐܝܟ ܒܪܘܚ. ܗܢܐ ܕܝܢ ܕܐܬܬܐ ܢܣܒܝܢ. ܐܠܗܐ ܗܘ ܓܝܪ ܐܠܗܐ
ܒܟܢܘ. ܐܦ ܐܠܗܘܬܗ ܢܛܪ ܗܘܝ ܒܢܦܫܬܗ ܕܢܦܫܬܗ ܢܩܘܬ
ܒܡܕܝܢܬܐ ܕܐܠܗܘܬܗ. ܘܡܛܠ ܗܢܐ ܙܪܥ ܗܘ ܠܝ ܕܢܫܬܘܕܥ ܠܗ.
ܡܛܠ ܕܫܦܝܪܐ ܗܘ ܒܢ ܐܟܡܐ. ܘܠܐ ܢܫܬܘܕܥ ܠܒܪܬܐ
ܕܐܬܬܝ، ܠܒܪܬܗ ܕܒܪܘܚܐ. ܗܘܘ ܓܝܪ ܐܠܗܐ ܕܡܫܬܐ

ܠܒܢ̈ܝ ܚܐܪ̈ܐ ܕܡܠ̈ܟܐ ܐܝܬܘ ܗܘܘ ܓܐܕܘܗܝ܂ ܕܢܚܙܘܢܗܝ ܘܢܫܡܥܘܢ ܗܘܘ ܡܠܘܗܝ܂ ܘܟܕ ܚܙܐ ܗܘܬ ܡܕܝܢܬܐ ܟܠܗ ܠܘܬܗ܂ ܡܢ ܗܘܐ ܕܢܬܟܠܠ ܒܫܡܗܘܢ܂ ܘܫܡܐ ܠܗܘܢ ܟܪܘܙܘܬܐ ܕܡܠܟܘܬܗ ܐܡܝܢܐ ܐܝܬܝܗ ܗܘܬ܂ ܘܟܕ ܗܘܐ ܕܢܐܡܪ ܠܗܘܢ ܗܟܢܐ܂ ܓܒܪ̈ܐ ܒܢ̈ܝ ܪܘܡܝܐ ܡܫܒ̈ܚܐ ܕܐܬܝܗܒܬ ܠܟܘܢ܂ ܫܡܥܘ ܡܕܡ ܕܐܡܪ ܐܢܐ ܠܟܘܢ܆ ܗܡܢܐ ܡܟܪܙ ܐܢܐ ܘܡܣܒܪ ܐܢܐ܂ ܠܫܘܒ ܒܪܗ ܕܐܠܗܐ܂ ܕܢܚܬ ܡܢ ܫܡܝܐ ܘܗܘܐ ܒܪ ܐܢܫܐ܂ ܗܘܐ ܒܟܠܡ ܐܚܘܬܢ ܘܟܕ ܫܠܝܐ ܦܬܓܡܘܗܝ܂ ܘܐܬܬܒܪ ܘܐܬܕܟܪܬܐ ܡܕܡܝܢ ܘܡܕܡ ܒܗܠܝܢ ܡܫܘܕܥܐ ܕܐܝܬ ܒܐܪܥܐ ܕܠܐ ܦܠܚܝܢ܂ ܟܕ ܐܦ ܐܢܘܢ ܫܡܥܝܢ ܗܘܘ ܩܘܡ ܗܠܝܢ ܕܟܬܒ ܗܘܐ܂ ܡܛܠ ܕܐܦ ܡܢ ܐܬܪ̈ܘܬܐ ܐܚܪ̈ܢܝܐ ܐܬܝܢ ܗܘܘ ܠܘܬܗ܂ ܟܠ ܠܚܙܝܐ ܕܐܬܘܬܗ܂ ܘܟܠ ܫܡܥܐ ܕܟܪܘܙܘܬܗ ܦܬ̈ܓܡܐ܂ ܘܟܠ ܡܢ ܕܫܡܥ ܗܘܐ ܠܗ ܡܬܗܝܡܢ ܗܘܐ ܒܡܠܬܗ܂ ܘܡܛܠ ܕܐܠܗܐ ܗܘܐ܂ ܥܡ ܐܘܝܘܬܗ ܐܦ ܦܘܠܐ ܫܒܩ ܗܘܐ܂ ܐܘܝܘܬܗ ܥܡ ܕܫܠܝܐ܂ ܗܝ ܗܕܐ ܟܠ ܫܘܒܚܗ ܟܠܗ܂ ܕܫܪܪ ܗܘ ܘܩܝܡܝܢ܂ ܠܗܢܐ ܟܕ ܫܡܥ ܡܟܪܙܝܢ ܗܘܘ ܢܦܫܐ ܟܪ̈ܝܗܘܢ܂ ܟܕ ܡܦܩܝܢ ܗܘܘ ܕܢܚܙܘܢܗܝ ܘܢܫܡܥܘܢ ܗܘܘ ܡܠܘܗܝ܂ ܕܗܘ ܕܐܝܬܘܗܝ ܗܘܐ ܥܡ ܐܒܘܗܝ ܡܫܬܘܬܦ ܘܡܢ ܟܠܡ܂ ܐܠܗܐ ܕܟܠܗ ܗܘܐ ܒܪܘܡܐ ܘܐܬܚܙܝ ܒܒܘܡܝܐ܂ ܒܪܐ ܫܒܝܚܐ ܕܡܢ ܡܠܦܢܗ܂ ܘܡܫܒܚ ܗܘܐ ܥܡ ܐܒܘܗܝ ܘܥܡ ܪܘܚܐ ܕܐܠܗܘܬܗ܂ ܘܫܠܝܛܐ ܕܢܝܠܐ ܕܡܪܘܬܗ܂ ܘܐܬܪܕܦ ܗܘܐ ܒܨܠܝܒܐ ܡܢ ܐܝܕ̈ܝ ܦ̈ܠܚܐ܂ ܘܐܬܥܠܝ ܗܘܐ ܠܘܬ ܐܒܘܗܝ܂ ܐܝܟ ܡܐ ܕܢܦܩܬ ܐܢܐ ܘܡܟܪܙ܂ ܘܟܬܒ ܗܘ ܕܬܘܒ ܢܐܬܐ ܒܫܘܒܚܐ ܕܝܠܗ ܘܥܡܗܘܢ ܡܠܐܟ̈ܘܗܝ ܩܕ̈ܝܫܐ܂ ܐܝܟ ܡܐ ܕܫܡܥܢ ܗܘܝܢ ܡܢܗ ܕܐܡܪ ܗܘܐ ܠܢ܂ ܠܐ ܓܝܪ ܡܫܟܚܝܢ ܕܢܐܡܪ ܡܕܡ ܕܠܐ ܫܡܥܢ ܗܘܐ ܠܢ ܡܢܗ܂ ܐܦ ܠܐ ܟܬܒܝܢ ܒܟܬܒܐ ܕܟܪܘܙܘܬܢ ܡܕܡ ܕܗܘ ܠܐ ܐܡܪ ܗܘܐ ܠܢ܂ ܡܛܠ

ܐܢܬܘܢ ܕܗܘܝܢ ܫܡܫܢ. ܠܐ ܬܬܟܫܠܘܢ ܘܫܡܥܘܢ ܚܙܝܐ
ܒܫܘܬܦܘܬܐ ܕܡܫܝܚܐ ܠܗܘܢ ܕܠܐ ܒܨܒܝܢܐ ܐܝܟ ܕܠܐܢܫܐ ܕܠܐ
ܗܘܢܐ. ܕܠܐ ܝܕܥܝܢ ܕܢܦܪܩܘܢ ܡܢܗ ܕܢܝܚ ܘܫܒܩܘܢ. ܫܪܝܪ
ܗܒܠ ܐܬܬܘܣܝ، ܐܝܟܐ ܕܒܢܝܐ ܥܠܘܗܝ ܡܬܢܣܒܝܢ. ܦܩܕܘ
ܠܗܘܢ ܫܬܐ ܡܕܡ ܕܒܠܒ ܡܢܗܘܢ. ܘܗܘ ܐܢܫܐ ܕܢܝܚ
ܐܢܬܘܢ ܕܒܥܐ ܠܗ ܠܗ، ܫܬܐ ܕܠܗܘܢ ܗܝ ܕܬܫܡܫܘܢ ܒܗ.
ܘܒܗ ܒܟܠܬܐ. ܫܪܝ ܐܬܬܘܣܝ ܗܘܐ ܠܫܡܥܘܢ ܣܒܐ. ܘܐܡܪ
ܗܘܐ ܠܗ ܐܢܫܐ ܩܕܝ ܦܘܡܗ. ܐܝܟ ܟܪܝܐ ܕܬܟܠܝܢ ܥܠܝܟ.
ܕܐܢܬ ܟܝܢ ܚܠܐ ܕܥܠܡܐ ܠܗܕܐ. ܒܟܠ ܫܬܐ ܡܕܡ ܡܢ
ܒܗܠܝ. ܘܢܝܐ ܗܘܐ ܫܡܥܘܢ ܟܠܠܐ ܕܡܦܪ ܠܡܫܝܚܐ. ܘܟܕ
ܡܢܗ ܐܡܪܝܢ ܗܘܐ ܠܗ ܐܬܬܘܣܝ ܒܟܪ ܗܘܐ ܡܠܬܐ ܚܕ
ܒܪܗ ܕܝܢ ܡܢ ܪ̈ܒܐ ܘܢܘ̈ܒܐ ܘܡ̈ܫܡܫܢܐ ܕܥܡܗܘܢ. ܘܐܡܪ
ܗܘܐ ܠܗ ܥܠܘܗܝ ܒܙ ܒܢܝܢ ܗܘܘ. ܕܐܝܢܐ ܡܢܗܘܢ ܕܡܢܗ
ܠܗ ܠܗܘܐ ܡܠܬܐ. ܗܘ ܗܘ ܫܦܝܪ ܘܡܫܦܝܪ ܘܡܫܡܠ.
ܘܒܬܪܗ ܐܢܠܝܢ ܥܠ ܒܠܚܘܕ ܕܐܡܪ ܠܝ. ܘܐܡܪ ܗܘܐ ܠܗ
ܠܫܡܥܘܢ ܣܒܐ ܡܠܠ ܕܐܢܬ ܗܘ ܡܕܡ ܐܢܬ ܠܫܡܥܘܢ
ܟܠܠܐ ܗܪܟܐ. ܘܠܝ ܗܘ ܡܕܝܢ ܡܫܡܫܢ. ܐܢܬ ܗܘܐ ܚܠܐ
ܕܠܗܐ ܠܝ ܡܫܡܫܢܬ. ܫܡܥܘܢ ܕܝܢ ܬܠܡܝܕܘܬ ܦܪܟ ܗܘܐ
ܠܐܒܗܘܗܝ ܕܡܠܬܐ ܘܫܡܥܘܗ̇ ܗܘܘ ܠܪ̈ܘܚܐ ܡܫܡܫܢܘܗܝ. ܘܚܙܪ
ܗܘܐ ܠܫܡܝܐ ܘܠܡܠܟܐ. ܘܫܡܫܐ ܡܬܒܣܡܐ ܗܘܐ. ܟܕ ܐܡܪ
ܗܘܐ ܡ̈ܠܐ ܦܬܓܡ̈ܐ. ܡܫܡܥ ܕܝܢ ܒܡܠܬܐ ܐܡܪ ܗܘܐ.
ܘܡܫܡܥ ܒܫܡܝܐ ܕܠܐ ܡܠܬܐ. ܘܐܦ ܗܘܐ ܦܬܓܡܐ ܦܬܓܡܐ
ܘܡܕܡ ܠܐ ܗܘܐ ܗܘܐ ܘܠܐ ܐܫܬܪܝ. ܘܡܠܬܐ ܗܝ ܒܠܒܗ
ܪܡܐ ܗܘܐ. ܘܒܗ ܒܫܒܬܐ ܕܝܢ ܗܘܐ ܫܡܥܘܢ ܒܐܦܐ
ܬܠܝܬܝܬ ܠܬܠܬܗ ܕܡܠܬܐ ܗܝ. ܘܡܠܐ ܗܘܐ ܡܕܡ ܥܠܘܗܝ ܒܢܝܐ
ܕܡܐܟ ܗܘܐ ܬܡܢ. ܒܫܡܗ ܕܣܘܒ ܡܫܝܚܐ ܗܘ ܕܐܦܣ ܗܝ.
ܣܗ̈ܕܐ ܒܐܘܪܫܠܡ ܘܐܝܢܐ ܡܫܒܚܢ ܚܕ ܠܗ. ܘܡܢ ܬܡܢ.

ܘܕܫܪܝܪ̈ܐ. ܗܘܘ ܕܝܢ ܡܕܡ ܠܡ̈ܠܟܐ ܘܒܪ̈ܬܐ. ܗܘܘ ܒܪܐ ܕܡܫܬܐ ܘܦܐܪ̈ܐ ܫܒܝܚܐ ܕܡܢ ܐܒܘܗܝ ܙܡܢܐ. ܐܠܐ ܚܢܢ ܐܢܬܘܢ ܚܒܝ̈ܒܐ ܬܫܡܫܬܐ ܕܠܘܬ̈ ܘܢܣܒܝܢ ܠܟܠܝܢ ܗ̇ܠܝܢ ܠܐ ܐܝܟ ܢܬܦܠܣܘܢ ܕܒܢܐ ܗ̇ܘ ܕܒܪܐ ܗܘܐ ܡܢ ܕܩܕܡ ܠܘܬ ܐܒܘܗܝ, ܘܫܪܘ ܐܢܚܢܐ ܦܪܘܩܢ ܡܫܪܝܬܗ ܒܟܠܗ̇ ܒܪܝܬܐ ܕܒܗܕܐ ܢܬܝܕܥ ܘܢܬܗܡܢ ܕܗܘܝܘ ܒܪܘܝܐ ܕܒܪ̈ܝܬܐ. ܘܒܪܝܗ ܩܕܡ ܒܪ̈ܝܬܐ. ܘܕܡܫܒܬܘܢ ܫܡܥܬܐ ܕܢܒܥܝܢ ܗܘܐ ܒܡܬܘܬܗ ܐܦ ܐܢܬܘܢ ܗܘܝܢ ܐܢܬܘܢ. ܐܝܟܢܐ ܕܝܢ ܕܐܬܬ ܗܘܬ ܒܡܠܬܗ. ܘܐܦ ܬܪܥܝܬܐ ܕܐܢ̈ܫܝܢ ܗܘܐ ܒܡܬܘܬܗ ܘܥܠ ܗ̈ܠܝܢ ܗܢܘܢ ܗܘܐ ܐܦ ܫܠܝܚܘ ܡܫܝܚܝܐ. ܕܗܘ ܫܒܩ ܗܘܐ ܘܐܘܕܝ ܗܘܐ ܠܡܪܢ ܘܐܬܡܠܟ, ܗܘ ܡܫܝܚܐ ܗܠܝܢ ܘܕܟܪ̈ܝܬܐ ܡܢ ܗܠܝܢ. ܘܡܕܡ ܦܘܪܫܢܗ̇ ܕܡܫܝܚܘܬܗ. ܘܡܛܠ ܗܢܐ ܢܦܩ ܗܘܐ ܗܘܢ ܥܠ ܫܠܝܚܘ. ܥܠ ܕܠܐ ܒܥܘܠܐ ܐܬܦܠܣ ܗܘܐ ܠܗܘܕ̈ܝܐ ܘܡܛܠ ܗܢܐ ܫܕܪ ܗܘܐ ܫܠܝܚ ܡܫܝܚ ܫܘܠܛܢܐ ܕܡܢ ܗܘܐ ܠܗ. ܘܗܝ ܗܕܐ ܐܬܦܠܣܬ ܘܐܬܬܕܟܪܬ ܒܟܠܗ ܐܬܘܬܐ ܕܡܫܝܚܘܬܐ. ܗ̇ܘ ܡܛܠ ܡܕܡ ܕܗܢܐ ܗܘܐ ܫܠܝܚܘ ܘܐܘܕܝ ܗܘܐ ܠܡܪܢ ܘܠܗܘܢܝܠܝܢ ܡܗܝܪܐ ܕܠܗܘܢ. ܠܗ ܗܘ ܡܫܝܚܐ ܐܢܐ ܘܥܠܡܝܢܐ ܢܒܝ̈ܐ. ܘܡܢ ܐܢܬܘܢ ܕܠܐ ܡܫܡܫ ܗܘܐ ܫܠܝܚܘ ܕܢܬܘܒ ܗܘܐ ܠܡܠܟܘܬܐ ܡܕܡ ܕܠܐ ܗܘܐ ܗܘܐ ܘܚܙܐ ܒܚܝܘܗܝ, ܐܠܐ ܗ̇ܘ ܡܕܡ ܕܗܘܐ ܗܘܐ. ܡܫܘܕܥ ܒܟܬܒܐ. ܗܘ ܗ̇ܘ ܒܬܪ ܗܘܐ ܘܐܘܕܝ. ܗܢܘܢ ܕܝܢ ܕܫܠܝܚܘ ܗ̇ܘ, ܬܘܒ ܘܢܛܘܪܐ ܕܡܪܢ. ܗܘܘ ܐܝܟ ܬܠܡ̈ܝܕܐ. ܘܟܕ ܐܫܬܐܠܘ ܗܘܘ ܡܕܡ ܫܠܝܚܘ ܗܢܘܢ ܢܛܘܪܐ ܐܘܕܝ ܗܘܘ ܡܕܡܘܗܝ, ܒܟܠܐ ܫܘܚܕܐ ܢܣܒܘ ܗܘܘ ܠܗܘܢ ܬ̈ܒܥ ܒܫ̈ܘܠܐ ܕܡܘ̈ܕܝܐ ܐܝܟ ܕܐܬܡܠܟܘ ܗܘܘ ܕܐܚܝܢ ܠܡܫܡܫܘܬܗ, ܒܟܠܗܝܢ ܫܠܝܚܐ ܕܡܫܝܚܐ. ܗܘܐ ܡܛܠ ܫܡܥܘܢ ܡܫܝܚܘܬܐ. ܗܢܘܢ ܕܝܢ ܠܐܠܝܢ ܕܫܡܥܘܢ ܠܐ ܝܕܥܝܢ ܐܢܬܘܢ ܕܐܬܦܠܣܘܢ. ܐܬܦܠܣܘ ܐܦ ܠܚܝܠܐ ܕܚܝܝܢ

ܕܫܠܡܘ. ܗܘܐ ܗܘܐ ܟܘܢܫܐ ܣܓܝܐܐ ܠܡܚܙܐ ܘܚܡܬܐ
ܡܕܝܢܬܐ ܟܠܗ ܕܒܝܬܐ. ܐܝܟ ܕܐܬܟܢܫܘ ܗܘܘ ܡܢ ܣܘܓܐܐ
ܕܥܠܡܐ. ܘܐܦ ܗܘܐ ܐܚܘܗ ܡܕܢܚܝܐ ܘܦܠܚ ܗܘܐ ܒܩܪܝܬܗ
ܟܠܠܝܐ. ܘܦܪܩ ܗܘܐ ܐܚܘܗ ܒܐܣܦܪܐ ܪܒܐ ܘܗܘܐ ܗܘܐ
ܬܡܢ ܥܡܗ ܢܘܚܐ ܠܡܫܝܚܐ. ܘܟܕ ܚܙܝܢܐ ܗܘ ܐܝܟ ܕܡܢ
ܕܢܚܐ ܕܢܘܬܐ ܥܡ ܗܘܐ ܢܦܩ ܡܠܟܘܬܗ ܘܚܝܐ. ܘܗܘܐ
ܥܠܝܐ ܘܠܠ ܡܢ ܪܘܚܐ ܕܐܘܚܕ ܗܘܐ ܠܒܗܘܢ ܢܦܩ ܡܗܪ.
ܘܡܢ ܒܬܪ ܥܕܢܐ ܡܟܫܦܬܐ ܕܡܠܠܗܘܢ ܪܒܐ ܕܫܠܝܚܐ
ܕܢܫܡܘ ܗܘܘ ܡܢ ܚܠܡܐ ܚܕ ܪܕܝܐ ܗܘܬ ܐܘܕܐ ܕܡܫܝܚܘܬܗܘܢ
ܒܟܠܗ ܪܗܘܡܐ ܘܒܟܠܗ ܐܬܠܝܐ. ܟܕ ܕܝܢ ܘܗܘܐ ܗܘܐ
ܒܫܢܐ ܪܒܐ ܒܪܗܘܡܐ ܡܕܝܢܬܐ.

ܫܠܡܬ ܡܠܘܬܗ ܕܫܡܥܘܢ ܒܐܫܐ.

ܗܘܦܘܡܢܡܛܐ ܕܫܪܒܝܠ. ܕܐܝܬܘܗܝ ܗܘܐ ܟܘܡܪܐ ܕܦܬܟܪܐ.
ܘܐܬܗܦܟ ܗܘܐ ܠܡܗܝܡܢܘܬܐ ܕܦܪܘܩܘܬܐ ܕܡܫܝܚܐ..

ܒܫܢܬ ܚܡܫܥܣܪܐ ܕܐܘܛܘܩܪܛܘܪ ܛܪܝܢܘܣ ܩܣܪ. ܘܒܫܢܬ
ܬܠܬ ܕܡܠܟܘܬܗ ܕܐܒܓܪ ܡܠܟܐ ܫܒܝܥܝܐ. ܕܐܝܬܘܗܝ ܫܢܬ
ܐܪܒܥܡܐܐ ܘܫܬܥܣܪܐ ܕܡܠܟܘܬܗ ܕܐܠܟܣܢܕܪܘܣ ܡܠܟܐ
ܕܝܘܢܝܐ. ܘܒܗܘܦܛܝܩܘܬܗ ܕܫܪܒܝܠ ܘܒܪܫܡܝܐ. ܦܩܕ ܗܘܐ
ܛܪܝܢܘܣ ܩܣܪ ܠܡܓܡܘܢܐ ܕܐܬܪܘܬܐ ܕܫܘܠܛܢܗ. ܕܢܬܓܘܢ
ܕܒܚܐ ܘܢܩܘܣܘܢ ܠܟܠܗܘܢ ܫܬܝܬܐ ܕܡܬܒܪܝܢܘܬܗܘܢ. ܘܐܝܠܝܢ ܕܠܐ
ܡܕܒܚܝܢ. ܢܬܠܟܕܘܢ ܘܢܫܬܠܡܘܢ ܠܢܓܕܐ ܘܠܣܪܩܐ ܘܠܐܣܩܠܝܛܐ
ܡܪܝܪܐ ܕܠܐ ܚܘܣ. ܘܢܬܕܝܢ ܢܫܠܡܘܢ ܣܝܦܐ ܕܩܛܠܐ.
ܘܟܕ ܐܬܐ ܗܘܐ ܦܘܩܕܢܐ ܠܐܘܪܗܝ ܕܐܝܟܢ ܕܐܬܐܡܪ. ܒܝܘܡܐ

ܘܒܡܫܡܗ ܕܡܠܦܢܘܬܗ ܕܝܫܘܥ ܚܝܐ ܗܘܐ ܡܫܬܐ ܗܘ ܥܡܡ ܗܘܐ
ܡܢ ܥܡܪܐ. ܘܚܙܐ ܟܠܗ ܥܡܐ ܘܐܬܕܡܪ. ܘܐܡܪܘ ܗܘܘ ܠܗ
ܠܝܫܘܥ. ܕܐܝܢ ܗܘ ܡܫܝܚܐ ܕܡܬܐ ܐܢܬ ܠܗ ܘܡܠܐ ܦܓܪܐ
ܘܐܡܪܘ. ܢܦܩܝܢ ܗܘܘ ܝܫܘܥ ܚܙܝܐ ܘܡܬܦܢܝܐ ܕܟܠ، ܘܝܫܘܥ
ܕܝܢ ܡܠܠܬܐ ܕܐܡܪ ܗܘܐ ܠܗ ܟܠܢ ܕܢܚܙܐ ܠܡܠܬܐ ܗܘ ܕܢܚܐ.
ܗܠܝܢ ܗܘܐ ܡܫܝܚܐ ܡܢ ܫܡܝܐ ܠܡܐܪܗ ܘܡܢ ܕܘܟܬܐ ܠܕܘܟܬܐ
ܘܠܐ ܢܦܠ ܗܘܐ ܒܐܬܪܘܬܗ ܒܗܘ ܥܘܡܩܐ. ܡܕܝܢܬܐ ܕܝܢ
ܟܠܗ ܐܬܬܙܝܥܬ ܗܘܬ ܠܝܫܘܥ ܒܐܘܪܚܐ ܘܟܠܗ، ܗܘܘ ܫܪܝܐܝܬ
ܘܡܣܒܪܢܝܬ. ܒܕ ܡܢ ܐܬܬܐ ܘܬܕܡܘܪܬܐ ܠܐ ܥܠܬܐ ܗܘܐ
ܕܠܒܒ ܒܫܡܗ ܕܡܫܝܚܐ. ܘܡܫܡܫܝܢ ܗܘܘ ܒܗ ܦܓܪܐ.
ܘܡܦܪܫܝܢ ܕܝܢ ܐܒܗܘܗܝ، ܕܗܘ ܕܢܚܐ ܗܘܐ ܐܘܟܠܗ ܗܘܐ
ܒܬܪ ܠܝܫܘܥ ܒܐܪܥܐ ܠܒܝܬܗ ܘܟܠܗ ܗܘܐ ܐܝܟ ܕܐܡܪ.
ܟܕ ܡܫܡܫܢ ܗܘܐ ܗܘ ܘܟܠ ܒܝܬܗ ܟܠܗܘܢ ܒܡܫܝܚܐ ܕܪܒܗ
ܗܘ ܕܐܠܗܐ ܚܝܐ. ܘܐܬܬܠܡܕܘ ܗܘܘ ܬܡܢ ܦܓܪܐ ܡܢ
ܡܢܕܥܐ ܘܢܦܫܐ. ܘܟܕ ܦܠܚܬ ܗܘܬ ܚܕܘܬܐ ܒܡܠܦܢܘܬܗ
ܒܟܠ ܗܘܐ ܬܡܢ ܒܕܘܬܐ ܒܪܘܡܐ ܘܡܬܒܪܢܝܘܬܐ ܕܚܕܪܘܗ
ܘܡܘܕܝܢ ܟܠܗܘܢ ܕܒܢܝ ܐܢܫܐ ܘܫܒܚܘ ܗܘܘ ܬܡܢ
ܕܐܠܗܐ ܕܡܬܒܪܢܝܬܐ ܕܡܕܝܢܬܐ ܒܫܪܪ ܘܫܒܚ ܥܡܗ. ܘܡܢ ܒܬܪ
ܗܠܝܢ ܥܢܝܐ ܠܒܡܗ ܗܘܐ ܢܦܩ ܡܢܗ. ܘܫܒܚܘ ܗܘܐ ܒܗܬ
ܐܡܪܐ. ܘܢܦܠ ܗܘܐ ܕܡܝܐ ܗܘܐ ܠܗ. ܘܡܪܐ ܗܘܐ ܠܐܢܫܘܗܝ
ܡܫܡܫܢܐ ܘܟܕܢܗ ܗܘܐ ܐܣܛܘܡܐ ܢܠܦܘܗ، ܒܪܘܚܐ.
ܘܗܢܝܢ ܗܠܝܢ ܐܡܪ ܗܘܐ ܗܘ ܝܫܘܥ ܘܫܒܚܐ ܬܘܒ ܐܦ
ܐܢܫܘܬܐ ܕܐܢܫܬ ܗܘ، ܠܗ ܦܓܪܗ ܗܘܐ ܠܐܢܫܘܗܝ ܕܗܘܐ ܡܠܦ
ܦܕܡ ܒܥܠܐ ܟܕ ܐܡܪ ܗܘܐ ܠܗ ܕܒܟܢ ܕܬܘܠܐ ܫܘܬܐ ܘܬܘܠܝܬܗ.
ܠܐ ܗܘܐ ܡܬܦܪܐ ܦܕܡ ܒܥܠܐ ܡܕܡ ܐܢܫܝܢܐ ܕܠܐ ܙܕܩ.
ܟܕ ܕܝܢ ܦܫܛ ܗܘܐ ܡܢܘܢ ܕܢܦܫܗ ܗܘܐ ܝܫܘܥ ܒܬܪ ܢܫܡ
ܐܝܟ ܕܗܘ ܒܥܠܐ ܗܘܐ ܡܢ ܡܢܘܢ ܘܢܦܫܬܐ ܗܘܐ ܢܫܡ

ܠܡܠܟܐ ܗܢܐ. ܕܗܘ ܐܠܗܐ ܐܡܪ ܠܝ ܕܐܡܪ ܠܟܘܢ ܕܡܛܠ
ܕܩܫܝܘ ܘܡܪܪܬܘܢ ܒܗ. ܐܢܐ ܥܒܕܐ ܒܐܬܪܟܘܢ ܗܢܐ.
ܘܥܠ ܐܡܪ ܒܗ ܐܢܐ ܗܕܟܐ ܪܘܚܐ ܒܐܪܥܟܘܢ. ܘܠܐ
ܦܪܫܝܢ ܗܘܘ ܕܢܣܒܘܢ ܡܢܗܘܢ ܕܡܠܟܘܬܐ ܡܠܟܐ ܐܝܬ ܒܗܘܢ.
ܡܛܠ ܕܥܡܒܐ ܐܝܬ ܠܗܘܢ ܘܠܐ ܡܬܠܠܝܢ. ܘܫܒܚܐ ܐܝܬ ܠܗܘܢ
ܘܠܐ ܣܝܡ ܒܗܘܢ. ܦܘܡܐ ܕܐܝܬ ܠܗܘܢ ܚܙܝܢ ܐܝܬܘܢ ܠܗܘܢ.
ܘܠܐ ܗܘܐ ܗܢܘܢ ܚܙܝܢ ܠܗܘܢ ܐܝܟ ܕܡܕܡ ܐܝܬܘܢ.
ܘܐܝܬܘܢ. ܠܗܘܢ ܡܥܒܕܝܢ ܐܝܬܘܢ ܫܐܕܐ. ܘܠܐ ܗܘܐ ܗܢܘܢ
ܡܬܕܪܝܢ ܠܗܘܢ. ܘܗܫܐ ܐܬܦܠܣ ܠܝ ܠܡܐܡܪ ܕܐܡܪ ܐܢܐ ܠܟ
ܘܡܠܟ ܐܢܐ ܠܟ. ܐܦ ܢܦܫܐ ܐܝܬ ܕܐܬܬܚܝܕ. ܫܡܥܘ ܫܐܕܐ
ܟܡܝܪܐ ܘܗܦܟܘ ܠܐܠܗܐ ܚܝܐ ܘܠܒܪܗ ܫܡܥܘ ܡܫܝܚܐ.
ܠܐ ܗܘܐ ܡܛܠ ܕܠܒܪ ܦܓܪܐ ܗܘܐ ܒܪ ܐܢܫܐ ܘܐܬܡܫܚ
ܥܠ ܪܘܚܐ ܕܩܘܕܫܐ ܫܡܥ ܡܢܗ ܘܠܐ ܐܬܗܦܟ ܠܗ. ܗܠܝܢ
ܟܕ ܫܠܡܘ ܕܡܟܪ ܡܦܠܓ ܚܝܠܘܬܐ ܗܘ ܕܟܠ ܐܢܫܐ
ܘܡܛܠ ܦܘܪܩܢܢ ܗܘ. ܗܢܐ ܟܕ ܕܠܒܪ ܦܓܪܐ ܐܠܗܐ
ܗܘ ܟܕ ܐܠܗܐ ܟܕ ܐܬܐܬܐ ܕܐܒܘܗܝ. ܘܟܕ ܚܢܢܐ ܕܠܘܬܗ.
ܘܡܫܚܐ ܗܘ ܟܕ ܡܫܝܚܐ ܕܐܠܗܘܬܗ. ܘܪܘܚܐ ܗܘ ܥܡܢܘܐ
ܕܟܘܠܗ. ܘܟܕ ܐܟܘܬܗ ܐܝܬܘܗܝ ܗܘܐ ܡܢ ܡܬܘܡ ܘܥܕ
ܥܠܡ. ܕܪܚܡ ܘܡܫܝܚ ܘܫܠܝܚ ܘܡܫܡܫܢ ܘܡܩܝܡܢ. ܘܪܘܚܐ
ܫܢܐ ܕܡܚܝܢ ܡܫܘܚܬܐ ܘܡܫܬܢܝܐ ܕܟܠܗܘܢ ܫܘܠܛܢܘܗܝ.
ܗܠܝܢ ܕܐܠܗ ܗܘܐ ܠܝ ܣܒܪܬ ܗܘ ܕܡܕܡ ܠܗ ܡܢܗܘܢ. ܘܟܕ
ܐܝܬ ܕܣܒܪܬ ܐܬܦܢܝܘ ܗܘܐ ܕܟܕ ܫܠܡܘ. ܘܐܬܟܪܙ ܡܠܟܐ
ܕܡܫܝܚ ܡܢ ܗܢܐ ܐܟܪܙ ܕܗܢܐ ܗܘ ܒܗܘܢ ܠܬܒܪܝܐ. ܘܗܟܢܐ
ܗܘܐ ܐܦ ܗܘ ܒܡܠܟܐ ܡܫܝܚܐ ܒܪܗ ܕܗܘܐ ܠܗ ܡܟܝܪ
ܕܫܠܡܘ ܐܠܗܐ. ܠܐ ܟܕ ܥܡܪ ܠܗܘܢ ܠܬܘܦܠܣܐ ܕܗܦܟܘ
ܠܡܐܡܪ ܕܒܫܘܒܚܐ ܗܘ. ܘܟܪܝܬܐ ܗܘ ܘܡܫܝܚܐ ܠܐ ܐܝܬܘܗܝ ܐܠܗܐ.
ܐܝܟ ܡܕܐ ܕܡܠܦܝܢ ܐܝܬܘܗܝ ܠܬܒܪܝܐ ܒܫܘܒܚܐ ܕܟܠ ܐܢܫܐ. ܦܘܢ

ܪ̇ܒܐ ܗ̇ܘܐ ܗ̇ܘܐ ܒܬܡܝܗܘܬܐ ܒܝܢܬܗܘܢ ܒܬܠܬܐ ܒܫܒܐ. ܒܢܫܬ ܗܠܝܢ ܡ̈ܕܝܢܬܐ ܓܝܪ ܠܬܠܬܐ ܪܒܬܐ ܕܐܝܬ ܗ̇ܘܐ ܒܡܨܥܬܗ ܕܪܒܐ ܠܡܦܠ ܒܗ ܬܪ̈ܥܐ. ܟܕ ܚܙܝܢ ܗܘܘ ܟܠܗܘܢ ܐ̈ܠܗܐ ܘܡܬܟܠܝܢ ܘܫܬܩܝܢ ܒܬܗܪܐ. ܘܢܟܐ ܘܟܠ ܚܡ ܣܓܝ̈ܐܘܗܝ ܘܟܘܡܪ̈ܐ ܟܠܗܘܢ ܡܬܚܪܝܢ ܗܘܘ ܒܣܓ̈ܕܬܐ ܘܢܩܘܫܐ ܘܪܘܫܐ ܕܗܘܬܐ ܗܐܝܕ ܗ̇ܘܐ. ܘܟܪ̈ܟܐ ܘܬܘܪ̈ܐ ܢܚܬܝܢ ܗܘܘ. ܘܥܠ ܘܥܙܐ ܘܦܠܓܐ ܒܟܠܗ ܟܪܟܐ ܡܬܬܡܟܟ ܗ̇ܘܐ. ܐܪܒܝܠ ܕܝܢ ܪܒܐ ܘܡܡܘܕܐ ܕܟܠܗܘܢ ܒܡ̈ܕܝܢܬܐ ܐܬܘܬܗ̇ ܗ̇ܘܐ. ܘܦܠܓ ܡܢ ܟܠܗܘܢ ܣܓܝ̈ܐܘܗܝ ܗܘ ܡܬܚܫܒ ܗ̇ܘܐ ܘܡܣ̈ܒܥܐ ܡܦܩ̈ܬܐ ܘܡܬ̈ܪܟܬܐ ܠܒܪ ܗܘܐ. ܘܫܘܕܐ ܕܚܘܡ ܗܘܐ ܒܪ̈ܘܬܐ ܕܕܗܒܐ ܒܪܫܗ ܣܝܡ ܗ̇ܘܐ. ܘܒܪ̈ܡܝܐ ܕܟܠܬܗ ܟܠ ܕܦܩܕ ܗ̇ܘܐ ܗܘܐ. ܘܐܟܚܕ ܡܠܟܐ ܒܪ ܐ̈ܠܗܐ ܒܪܫ ܟܥܐ ܦܐܝܡ ܗ̇ܘܐ. ܘܡܫܬܡܥܝܢ ܗܘܘ ܠܗ ܠܐܪܒܝܠ. ܡܛܠ ܕܐܬܪ ܡܢ ܟܠܗܘܢ ܣܓܝ̈ܐܘܗܝ ܗܘ ܩܪܝܒ ܗ̇ܘܐ ܓܝܪ ܐ̈ܠܗܐ ܟܠܗܘܢ. ܘܐܝܟ ܗ̇ܘ ܕܡܕܡ ܥܬܝܕ ܗ̇ܘܐ ܡܢ ܐ̈ܠܗܐ. ܗܬܡܢܐ ܠܟܠ ܐܢܫ ܡܩܝܡܐ ܗ̇ܘܐ. ܘܟܕ ܗܘܠܝܢ ܡܢ ܗܘܡܕܢܐ ܕܥ̈ܠܡܐ ܡܫܬܡܥܢ ܗ̈ܘܝ. . . . . ܒܪܘܡܒܐ ܐܣܘܡܣܐ ܕܒܪܘܦܛܝܐ ܗܦܠ ܗ̇ܘܐ ܓܐܕܘܗܝ ܕܐܪܒܝܠ ܗܘ ܘܬܕܪܬ ܡܫܟܐ ܘܥܠܡܐ ܡܫܡܫܢܐ. ܘܐܡܪ ܗ̇ܘܐ ܠܗ ܠܐܪܒܝܠ ܒܡܬܪܐ ܪܒܐ. ܢܬܒܒ ܡܠܟܐ ܡܫܝܚܐ ܒܐܬ̈ܪܘܗܝ ܗܘ ܕܫܝܫܘ ܥܡܡܐ ܘܐܬܪ̈ܐ؛ ܟܠܗܘܢ ܢܦܩܬܐ ܗܘܠܝܢ ܕܢܦܠܐ ܐܢܬ ܒܗܘܢ. ܘܡܦܠܐ ܐܢܬ ܠܗܘܢ ܘܡܗܘܝܢ ܐܢܬ ܠܗܘܢ ܡܢ ܓܝܪ ܐܠܗܐ ܕܗܘܝܬܐ ܘܕܪ̈ܪܐ. ܓܝܪ ܗܬܒܪܐ ܒܟ̈ܢܫܐ ܘܦܠܚ̈ܐ. ܗܢܘܢ ܕܠܐ ܗܘܗܐ ܒܐ̈ܪܥܬܗܘܢ ܡܕܡ ܠܡܟܢܫ. ܡܬܠܐ ܣܓܝ ܐܢܬ ܒܠ ܢܦܫ ܕܐܟܠܗ ܡܢ ܫ̈ܢܐ ܥܕܪ̈ܐ ܕܐܠܗܐ. ܘܡܫܡܪ ܐܢܬ ܠܗ ܠܒܢ̈ܫܐ ܗܘܝܐ ܕܬܐܪ̈ܐ ܚ̈ܪܝܐ ܘܡܟܠܠܝܢ ܒܟܝܢ. ܘܐܝܟ ܗܘ ܕܡܕܡ ܥܬܝܕ ܐܢܬ ܡܟܝܢܘܢ ܡܦܪܟ ܐܢܬ ܐܕܝܢ ܓܝܪ ܚܕ ܚܕ ܡܢܗܘܢ. ܘܐܡܪ ܐܢܬ

ܠܘܬܗ ܕܪܘܚܢܝܐ ܒܠܠܝܐ ܗܘ ܘܒܝܡ ܥܡܗ. ܘܐܬܡܛܠ ܗܘܐ
ܡܢ ܟܠܗ ܒܪܝܬܐ. ܘܐܡܪ ܗܘܐ ܠܗܘܢ ܕܢܪܒܘ ܚܠܦ ܝܠܘܬܐ
ܘܟܘܡܪܘܬܐ. ܕܫܡܥܬ ܠܝ ܡܥܢܝܢܐ ܥܠ ܕܝܬܩܢ ܠܗ ܒܗܝܢܐ
ܟܠܗ ܠܘܒܪܐ ܕܫܢܝܐ. ܘܡܛܠ ܕܡܫܝܚ ܗܘܘ ܡܢ ܙܪܘܥܐ.
ܡܥܡ ܗܘܘ ܘܝܗܒܘ ܠܗ ܦܘܪܥܢܐ ܕܫܢܝܐ ܒܪ ܡܗܘܪܐ
ܗܘܐ ܒܐܘܒܐ ܘܒܒܪܐ ܘܒܪܘܢܝܐ ܕܡܘܕܥܢܐ! ܘ. ܘ.
ܘܟܕ ܫܡܥܬ ܗܘܬ ܡܕܝܢܬܐ ܟܠܗ ܕܝܢܬ ܗܘܐ ܠܒܪܬܐ.
ܫܪܐ ܗܘܐ ܒܦܘܪܫܢܐ ܒܡܚܝܢ̈ܐ. ܘܡܥܡ ܗܘܘ ܘܝܢܬܘ
ܗܘܘ ܠܘܬܗ. ܘܝܘܢ ܗܘܘ ܠܗ ܕܠܒܫ ܗܘܐ ܕܡܘܬܐ
ܕܪܘܦܝܢܐ. ܘܐܡܪ ܠܗܘܢ. ܢܣܒܐ ܠܝ ܒܪܐ ܡܥܢܝܢܐ
ܥܠ ܫ̈ܦܠܗܐ ܕܢܦܩܬ ܒܗܘܢ. ܘܥܠ ܡܕܡ ܕܐܡܘܪܬܗܘܢ
ܕܐ̈ܠܗܐ ܡܥܠܠܝܢ ܒܗܘܢ ܒܪ ܠܐ ܡܥܠܠܝܢ. ܘܕܗܘܝܬ
ܠܗܘܢ ܒܠܝܐ ܘܫܢܝܬܐ. ܐܝܟܐ ܠܗܘܢ ܗܘܐ ܒܠܘܬܐ
ܥܡܪܬܐ. ܫܠܡ ܕܗܘܦܟܬܗܘܢ ܠܬܫܒ̈ܪܐ ܒܫ̈ܢܝܐ. ܬܘܦܝܩܘܢ
ܡܛܠ ܠܐܠܗܐ ܒܫܢܝܐ. ܘܟܕ ܥܡܪܘ ܗܘܘ ܗܠܝܢ. ܡܘܬ
ܠܗܬܗ ܒܢܥܐ ܘܦܘܠܐ ܕܒܪܐ ܘܪ̈ܥܝܐ. ܘܐܦ ܠܒܢ ܘܫܡܘ،
ܘܒܪܦܠܟܐ ܘܟܘܕܪܐ ܕ̈ܥܢܝܐ ܕܡܪܝܢܬܐ. ܐܡܪܘ ܗܘܘ ܠܗ
ܟܠܗܘܢ ܠܐܪܒܝܠ. ܕܡܛܠ ܘܐܦ ܚܢ ܒܥܝܢ ܐܢܫܝܢ ܒܡܕܝܢ
ܕܒܥܝܬ ܒܗ. ܘܡܫܬܐܠ ܚܢ ܒܟܠܗܝܢ ܡܥܢܝܢܐ ܕܐܘܪܚܬ ܒܗ. ܘ. ܘ.
ܠܘܩܢܝܐ ܕܝܢ ܕܢܟܐ ܕܐܬܬܪܐ ܒܪ ܥܡܕ ܗܘܐ ܕܗܪܐ ܒܓܪ
ܗܘܐ ܥܪܒܝܠ. ܥܒܪ ܗܘܐ ܒܠܠܝܐ ܘܫܦܝܗ ܗܘܐ ܡܢ
ܒܪܬܐ. ܘܦܠܚ ܗܘܘ ܒܗܘܢ ܒܪܘܦܝܢܐ ܦܓܪ̈ܝܐ ܘܬܒܥ ܗܘܐ
ܕܢܥܡܕܘܢ ܘܢܪܘܝܘܢ. ܡܪܝ ܒܠܗܐ ܕܡܬܓܒܬ ܒܪܝܐ ܐܡܬܐ
ܕܡܪܒܝܢ ܗܘܐ ܠܐ̈ܠܗܐ. ܘܐܡܪ ܠܗ. ܕܠܡܥܢܐ ܒܥܝܬ
ܕܐ̈ܠܗܐ ܕܦܓܪ ܗܘܬ ܠܗܘܢ ܘܡܪܒܝܢ. ܘܪܥܝܐ ܕܒܘܡܪܐ
ܒܥܝܢ ܗܘܬ ܠܗܝܢ ܘܗܝ ܡܪܕܘܬ ܘܡܥܢܐ ܡܥܡܪܢܝܐ ܕܥܒܪ
ܗܘܬ ܒܗ ܡܢ ܡܥܡ. ܝܘ ܓܝܪ ܕܪܘܦܝܢܐ ܦܘܩ ܕܐܝܠܬ

ܕܐܦ ܗ̇ܢܘܢ ܒܢ̈ܝܐ ܐܢܘܢ ܘܒܢ̈ܬܐ. ܐܬܦܠܓܘ ܗܟܝܠ ܠܗܠܝܢ ܕܐܡܪܬ ܠܟ: ܕܗܢܝܢ ܐܝܟ ܗܡܝܢܘܬܗ̇ ܕܒܪܬܐ. ܡܢ ܐܢܐ ܓܝܪ ܕܟܝ ܗܘ ܫܢܝܐ ܟܠܗ̇ ܗܕܐ ܐܢܫܘܬܐ. ܘܢܬܪܐ ܠܝ ܕܝܢ ܡܬܦܠܓܘ ܐܢܬ ܗܟܐ. ܘܓܒܪ̈ܐ ܡܬܦܠܓܝܢ ܒܟܝܢ ܀

ܐܡܪ ܠܗ ܝܘܣܦ. ܗܟܢ ܐܬܦܠܓ ܥܠ ܬܠܬܝܢ ܗܠܝܢ ܕܐܡܪܬ ܡܢܟ. ܘܐܬܦܠܓ ܥܠ ܙܘܥܐܝܬ. ܐܠܐ ܐܢܐ ܡܢ ܐܢܐ ܕܐܟܢܫ ܐܢܫ ܡܢ ܗܠܝܢ ܟܠܗܝܢ. ܘܬܘܒ ܠܝܬ ܠܝ ܐܚܘܬܐ. ܘܡܟܝܠ ܕܗܘܐ ܠܝ ܗܫܐ ܗܒܪܐ. ܡܢܐ ܠܐܝܬ ܒܡܬܐ ܗܫܐ ܕܠܝܬ ܗܒܪܐ ܕܢܫܡܥܐ ܠܡܬܘܬܗ. ܡܛܠ ܐܢܐ ܗܘ ܓܝܪ ܠܫܬܩܘܬܐ. ܘܗܘܝܬ ܠܝ ܡܬܬܗ ܕܟܝܢܐ ܒܒܥܝܐ ܘܟܢ̈ܘܫܝܐ ܕܠܝܚܘܬܐ ܓܡܝܪܬ ܟܠܗܘܢ ܡܢܗܘܢ ܫܢ̈ܝ ܀

ܘܟܕ ܫܡܥ ܗܘܐ ܗܠܝܢ ܒܪܘܡܝܐ ܐܦܘܣܩܐ. ܢܦܠ ܗܘܐ ܡܢ ܪ̈ܓܠܘܗܝ. ܘܐܡܪ ܠܗ. ܐܢܬ ܗܘ ܗܒܪܐ ܠܐܚ̈ܝܟ ܘܗܫܘܬܐ ܠܡܫ̈ܝܚܐ. ܐܢܐ ܚܙܐ ܐܢܐ ܠܟ ܥܠ ܪ̈ܫܢܐ ܫ̈ܦܝܪܐ ܕܗܒܪܐ ܡܫܝܚܐ. ܕܗܘ ܫܡܥ ܠܟ ܥܠ ܕܝܗܠܬ ܠܗ. ܕܡܫܒܚ ܘܡܢܬ ܠܒܪ̈ܝܬܗ ܣܠܩܗܘܢ. ܗ̇ܘ ܓܝܪ ܫܠܝܐ ܕܡܬܠ ܢܦܫܗ ܥܠ ܪܡܫܐ ܕܡܘܬܐ. ܠܐ ܟܠܐ ܚܝܠܗ ܡܢ ܕܩܢ̈ܬܐ. ܕܡܬܦܠܓܘܢ ܘܡܬܓܡܪܘܢ ܒܡܫܡܫܘܬܗ ܕܗܘܬ ܟܠܝܢ ܐܝܟ ܕܚܕ ܗܘܐ ܠܗܘܢ ܓܒܪܐ. ܡܫܡܫ ܗܘ ܕܒܟܠ ܐܢ̈ܫܝܢ ܘܐܦ ܓܝܪ ܐܝܠܝܢ ܕܐܡܬܝܢ ܐܝܟܢ. ܐܡܪ ܠܗ ܝܘܣܦ ܐܢܬ ܐܝܟ ܐܢܘܢ ܫܡܫܐ ܕܐܬܐ ܠܗ ܡܢ ܦܐܪܐ ܕܐܝܠܝܢ ܥܦܪ ܟܕ ܕܐܬܟܠܠ ܠܟ ܟܠ. ܗܟܢܐ ܕܝܢ ܡܬܠ ܕܟܕܐ ܗܘ ܡܢܝܢܐ ܕܡܟܐ ܗܢܐ ܕܟܠܢ. ܠܐ ܡܫܡܫ ܐܢܐ ܕܐܢܫܘܬ ܒܟܝܢ ܡܢܝܢܐ ܠܒܪܬܐ. ܐܠ ܫܘܬ ܐܢܬ ܒܐܦܪܐ ܘܠܒܫܪ ܟܠܠܐ ܫܘܬ ܐܢܐ ܓܝܪܝܢ. ܐܢܐ ܡܟܝܠ ܒܥܝܬ ܠܝ ܒܦ̈ܠܓܘܬܐ ܒܩܢ̈ܝܐ ܘܡܬܘܪ̈ܐ ܐܢܐ ܒܒܪܝܐ ܡܫܝܚܐ ܒܚܘܪܐ ܕܟܠܗܘܢ ܩ̈ܕ ܐܢܫܐ: ܘܒܬܪ ܡܢܝܢܐ ܡܢ ܗܘܐ ܝܘܣܦ ܘܢܫܩ ܗܘܐ

ܡܘܡܝܐ. ܕܠܐ ܡܨܐ ܐܢܐ ܟܝ ܥܠ ܐܝܠܝܢ ܕܗܝܡܢܘ ܐܫܬܘܕܝܬ܀
ܥܪܒܠ ܐܡܪ ܡܢ ܡܠܟܐ ܕܡ̈ܠܟܐ ܕܫܐܠ ܐܢܐ. ܘܡܢ ܡܠܟܐ
ܕܐܪܥܐ ܠܐ ܙܒܢ ܐܢܐ. ܘܐܦ ܠܐ ܡܢ ܠܘܩܒ̈ܠܝܗܘܢ ܕܠܘܬܝ.
ܕܗܘܐ ܡܬܠܒܫ ܐܢܬ ܐܠ ܦܓܪ̈ܘܗܝ ܕܡܫܝܚܐ ܕܐܘܪܚܬ ܒܗ
ܐܬܡܟܠ. ܘܗܘܐ ܡܬܕܝܢ ܐܢܐ ܡܬܠܬܗ ܘܡܬܟܢܫܐ. ܐܝܟ
ܕܐܬܕܝܢ ܗܘ ܡܛܠ ܬܘܠܕܬܐ ܕܕܝܢ ܠܝ܀ ܕܗܢܐ ܐܡܪ ܐܦ ܐܢܬ
ܠܐ ܚܙܐ ܐܢܬ ܥܠ ܢܦܫܝ ܐܠܐ ܐܢܐ ܚܙܐ ܐܢܐ ܗܘ
ܚܠܦܝ ܕܐܦܣܘܣ ܐܬܕܝܢ ܗܠܝܢ ܕܗܡܟܬ ܒܗܝܢ ܒܣܘܟܐ ܡܕܡ
ܫ̈ܠܡܐ. ܘܐܡܪ ܐܪ̈ܫܝܢ ܒܕܡܝܢ ܕܥܡܕ ܗܘ ܐܪ̈ܙܗܘܢ
ܘܥܠܝܢ ܕܐܬܒܪܝܬ ܘܦܫܛ ܠܝ ܦܬܓ̈ܡܘܗܝ ܡܚܫ̈ܘܗܝ ܗܘ ܗܘܐ
ܕܫܠ ܐܢܐ ܘܚܙܐ ܐܢܐ ܚܠܦܝ. ܐ̱ܠ ܕܝܢ ܗܘܝܐ ܡܗܝܡܢܘܬ
ܗܘܝܢ ܫ̈ܠܡܐ ܢܗܘܘܢ ܠܝ ܦܘܩܕܐ ܕܠܐ ܚܙܐ ܐܢܐ ܚܠܦܝ܀
ܥܪܒܠ ܐܡܪ ܐܝܟ ܒܪܢܐ ܕܕܫܠ ܐܢܬ ܡܢ ܡ̈ܠܟܐ ܘܐܝܟ
ܐܢܬ ܡܢ ܦܬܓܡܐ ܠܐ ܬܫܘܐ ܥܠ. ܐܢܐ ܒܪ ܠܐ ܡܒܪܐ ܐܢܐ
ܡܚܝܐ ܐܡܪ ܐܢܬ ܡܛܠ ܗܢܐ ܐܦ ܠܐ ܙܒܢ ܐܬܬܐܡܪ
ܘܐܬܪܗܒ ܒܐܝܠܝܢ ܕܐܡܪ ܐܢܬ. ܒܕ̈ܝܢܝ ܒܪ ܦܠܛܝܢ ܡܢ
ܕܒܟܐ ܕܒܬܪ ܥܠ ܐܝܠܝܢ ܕܠܐ ܦܓܕܝܢ ܠܟܕܡ. ܕܠܘ ܐܠܗܐ ܗܘ
ܒܚܝܠܗ܀ ܕܗܢܐ ܐܡܪ ܢܬܦܢܐ ܒܦܘܪܩܢܗ ܥܠ ܕܐܡܪܬ ܡܦܢܝܐ
ܠܡܦܢܝܘ ܠܝ ܦܬܓܡܐ ܘܐܡ ܠܘܩܒܠ ܦܘܩܕܢܐ ܕܡ̈ܠܟܐ ܘܠܐ
ܦܩܕ ܐܣܝܪܐ ܕܡܪܘܗܝ ܫ̈ܠܡܐ. ܕܗܘܐ ܒܗܪ ܒܗܘܢ. ܘܐܬܩܛܠ
ܡܢ ܒܗܪܐ ܕܠܒܫܝܢ ܗܘܘ ܠܗ ܐܝܟ ܦܘܩܕܢܐ ܕܕܝܢܐ܀
ܥܪܒܠ ܐܡܪ ܠܐ ܙܒܢ ܐܢܬ ܒܝܠܕܐ ܕܒܐܘܢܬܐ ܕܗ̇ܘ
ܚܠܡܐ ܕܒܬܪ. ܐܢܬ ܓܝܪ ܒܠܠܬ ܘܐܦ ܕܫ̈ܢܝܢ ܒܒܪܝܢ.
ܒܐܘܢܬܐ ܕܝܢ ܠܐ ܒܒܪܐ. ܘܬܒ̈ܥܬܗ ܠܐ ܒܒܪܢ܀ ܕܗܢܐ
ܐܡܪ ܗܟܢܐ ܙܒܢܬ ܒܗ ܒܒܪܘܦܘܣܘܬܐ ܒܕܡܟܐ ܕܠܐ ܬܬܒܪ
ܡܕܡ ܡܢ ܡܬܕܢܝܢ ܐܢܬ ܘܒܢ ܡܟܘܢ ܡܬܝܕܥ ܐܢܬ ܡܢ ܗܘܢ
ܕܒܣܘܪܝܢ ܗܘܘ ܠܝ ܡܢ ܡܕܡ ܘܦܓܕܝܢ ܗܘܘ ܠܒܣܘܪܝܘܬܝ

ܢܬܕܝܢܘܢ ܠܐ ܡܫܪܝܢ ܒܡܕܡ ܕܡܣܟܝܢ ܒܗ. ܐܝܟ ܡܢܐ ܕܣܒܪܬ ܐܢܬ. ܒܗܘ ܡܕܡ ܕܠܝܬ ܐܢܬ ܒܗ. ܐ̱ܠܐ ܣܒܪ̈ܝܢ ܠܟ ܫ̈ܠܡܐ. ܐܝܟܢܐ ܕܣܒܪܬ ܒܗܘܢ ܡܢܟܝܐ. ܐ̱ܠܐ ܕܝܢ ܠܐ ܣܒܪ̈ܝܢ ܠܟ ܐܝܟܢܐ ܕܫܒܩ ܐܢܬ ܒܠܝܫܘܢ ܐܝܟܢܐ ܡܕܒܫ ܗܘܝܬ ܠܗܘܢ ܘܫܦܝܪ ܗܘܝܬ ܠܗܘܢ. ܥܙܪܝܠ ܐܡܪ. ܟܕ ܗܘܝܢܐ ܗܘܝܬ ܒܪܚܡܐ ܫܦܝܪ ܗܘܝܬ ܠܡܕܡ ܕܠܐ ܝܕܥ ܗܘܝܬ. ܡܢܟܝܐ ܕܝܢ ܕܗܘܝܬ ܚ̈ܝܝܢܐ ܢܦܫܬܐ ܕܐܢܫܐ. ܠܝܬ ܠܗ ܡܦܪܢܐ ܡܚܝܠ ܕܐܬܬܘܠ ܒܡ̈ܟܐܒܐ ܚܠܘܦܬܐ ܐܘ ܕܐܢܫܐ ܗܘܒ ܒܠܗ ܬܘܠܬܐ ܠܐܢ̈ܫܝܐ. ܫܒܪܐ ܗܘ ܟܕ ܙܟܐ ܠܦܘܡ ܕܦܬܘܚ ܚ̈ܝܘܗܝ. ܘܐܙܠ ܢܦܠ ܒܚܘܫܟܐ ܡܟܒܕܢܐ .. ܕܢܝܐ ܐܡܪ. ܡܛܠ ܕܡܥܡܪܐ ܗܘܝܬ ܕܫ̈ܠܡܐ ܡܫܡ̈ܪܐ ܘܟܕ ܐܝܟܐ ܗܘܝܬ ܕܢܦܠܘܢ ܕܢܣܒܝܢ ܠܗܘܢ ܬ̈ܠܬܐ ܚܕܡܐ. ܡܛܠ ܐܢܫ ܪܘܚ ܒܟܝܢ ܕܬܬܦܢܫ ܠܝ ܘܠܐ ܬܬܒܥܐ ܡܢ ܬܫܡܫܬܐ ܕܫ̈ܠܡܐ. ܐ̱ܠܐ ܕܝܢ ܠܐ ܡܬܦܢܫ ܐܢܬ ܠܝ. ܒܗܘܢ ܒܫ̈ܠܡܐ ܕܣܒܪܬ ܒܗܘܢ ܡܟܐ ܐܢܐ. ܕܐܝܟ ܕܠܒܪܢܐ ܦܬܠܐ ܗܘܝܢܐ ܐܬܝܢ ܒܝ. ܘܐܬܒܥ ܡܢܝ ܠܡܦܢܝܢܐ ܕܫ̈ܠܡܐ ܕܡܣܒܪܬ ܠܒܝܫܘܢ ܘܣܒܪܬ ܒܗܘܢ. ܘܐܦ ܢܒܪܐ ܕܡܥܒܪ ܐܢܬ ܠܗܘܢ ܟܕ ܠܐ ܫܒܩ ܐܢܐ ܠܟ ܫܪܝܢ ܕܠܐ ܡܫܬܢܐ ܐܢܐ ܒܝ. ܘܐܝܟ ܕܗܘܐ ܗܘܦܐ ܐܢܫܝܢ ܡܢ ܦܘܡܝ. ܗܟܢܐ ܐܦܠܐ ܢܦܫܝ ܡܢܟܝܐ .. ܥܙܪܝܠ ܐܡܪ. ܘܐܦܠܐ ܐܢܐ ܡܚܝܠ ܐܢܐ ܕܬܬܚܘܪ ܒ ܐܝܟ ܕܡܢ ܦܘܡܝ ܕܗܘܐ ܗܘܝܬ ܠܫ̈ܠܡܐ ܚܠܝܢܐ. ܐ̱ܠܐ ܚܙܝ ܒ ܡܢܟܝܐ ܘܡܬܠܝܢ ܐܝܟ ܕܠܒܪܢܐ ܦܘܠܝܐ. ܒܬܪ ܒܗܬܬܐ ܘܡܒܪܐ ܒܬܠܬܐ ܡܫܒܚܐ .. ܕܢܝܐ ܐܡܪ ܐܝܟܢܐ ܠܐ ܕܝܢ ܐܢܬ ܡܢ ܬ̈ܠܬܐ ܘܠܐ ܒܗܘܬ ܐܢܬ ܡܢ ܐܠܗܝ ܕܒܟܢܫ ܕܐܝܟ ܕܬܐܡܪ ܕܒܪܦܠܢܐ ܐܢܐ. ܐ̱ܠܐ ܐܘܕܐ. ܕܡܟܒܪ ܐܢܬ ܠܫ̈ܠܡܐ ܒܟܢܫܐ ܡܦܪܣܝܢ. ܐܝܟ ܕܠܗܘܦܐ ܐܢܫܝܢ ܐܝܟ

ܬܠܡܝܕܘܗܝ ܘܣܥܘܪܘܗܝ ܟܢܫܘܗܝ. ܘܟܕ ܡܫܡܠܝܘܬܗ ܗܘܬ ܩܪܝܒܐ
ܗܘܐ ܘܐܡܪ. ܫܠܚ ܡܫܝܚܐ ܕܐܠܗܐ ܢܘܗܪܐ ܒܫܘܐܠܬ
ܒܫܘܒܚܬܗ ܕܪܒܢ. ܘܟܕ ܐܡܪ ܗܠܝܢ. ܫܟܒ ܬܘܒ ܕܝܠܗ
ܕܘܬܐ ܡܫܡܫܢܘܗܝ . . .

ܕܐܪܒܝܠ ܐܡܪ. ܗܘܐ ܕܬܫܬܝܢ ܡܢ ܐܝܬ ܥܠ ܕܠܐ ܡܕܒܪ
ܐܢܫܐ. ܘܠܐ ܕܐܬܕܝܢ ܬܘܒ ܥܠ ܕܡܕܒܪ ܗܘܬ ܠܟܠ ܐܬܪܐ
ܕܟܠ ܐܢܫܐ . . . ܕܝܢܐ ܐܡܪ ܬܬܒܥ ܘܡܕܢܗ ܠܟܘܬܪܗ.
ܘܬܘܦܪܐ ܒܪܘܟܐ ܒܐܬܪܘܗܝ ܘܡܕܒܪܢܘܗܝ. ܘܟܕ ܒܥܐ
ܠܟܘܬܪ ܢܬܒܥ ܥܠ ܒܪܘܗܝ. ܘܒܥܘܗܝ ܗܘܢܐ ܐܝܟ ܒܘܣܝܢ
ܕܝܢܐ. ܘܟܕ ܗܘܐ ܕܢܫܢ ܗܘܐ ܠܟܠ ܐܘܪܚܐ ܘܢܬܕܐ
ܗܘܐ ܒܟܘܒܐ ܢܣܘܒܐ. ܘܬܟܢܘܗܝ ܗܘܘ ܡܦܩܢܝܬܐ.
ܘܡܬܦܠܓܐ ܗܠܝܢ ܕܐܠܗܐ ܗܘܘ ܒܥܒܘ ܡܢ ܒܪܬܐ. ܡܛܠ
ܕܠܐ ܡܥܒܕ ܗܘܐ ܕܢܫܠܡ ܗܘܐ ܥܠ ܬܘܠܕܘܗܝ ܡܢ ܗܘ ܕܥܒܕ
ܗܘܐ ܠܟܘܬܪܗ. ܘܗܘܐ ܒܝܬ ܢܒܘܟܐ ܢܘܟܪܝܐ ܕܦܠܓܬܐ.
ܒܬܪܐ ܕܡ ܒܐܠܗܐ ܒܬܘܬܐ ܒܥܒܕܐ. ܡܢ ܗܘܐ ܕܝܢܐ ܘܢܫܬ
ܗܘܐ ܠܕܡܘܦܪܝܢ ܕܠܗ ܟܠܝܠܐ. ܘܟܠܗܘܢ ܒܢܝ ܐܘܣܝܢ ܐܝܬ
ܗܘܐ ܒܥܒܗ. ܘܟܕ ܗܘܐ ܠܒܦܪ ܒܝܬ ܐܬܘܪܐ ܘܐܬܟܢܘܗܝ ܗܘܘ
ܡܥܒܘܗܝ. ܘܐܡܪ ܠܗ ܕܝܢܐ. ܒܗܢܐ ܢܦܪܘܐ ܗܘܝܬ ܒܝܬ
ܐܬܘܪܐ. ܡܕܝܢܐ ܢܘܫܒܐ ܗܘܐ ܠܝ ܥܠ ܐܠܝܢ ܕܐܫܬܐܠܬ
ܗܘܝܬ ܡܥܡܪ. ܡܬܦܠܓܝܢ ܐܝܬ ܕܬܫܒܥ ܠܬܠܡܐ ܒܥܒܪܝ
ܡܥܡܪܐ ܐܝܟ ܒܘܣܝܢܐ ܕܬܠܡܐ . . . ܕܐܪܒܝܠ ܐܡܪ ܗܘܢܐ
ܢܘܫܒܐ ܗܘܐ ܠܝ ܒܝܬ ܐܬܘܪܐ ܕܗܘ ܡܥܡܪ ܕܐܪܒܬ ܗܘܬ
ܒܗ ܡܥܡܪܝ. ܒܗ ܐܫܠܡ ܒܥܒܕܐ ܠܡܪܬܐ. ܘܠܐ ܐܕܓܠ
ܒܡܠܬܗ. ܠܐ ܓܪ ܒܡܬܦܪܬܐ ܕܟܦܪܬ ܒܗܘܢ ܬܘܒ ܡܥܕܪܐ
ܐܢܫܐ. ܐܦ ܠܐ ܒܡܠܟܐ ܡܫܝܚܐ ܕܐܘܪܚܬ ܒܗ ܒܥܪ ܐܢܫܐ . . .
ܕܝܢܐ ܐܡܪ ܬܠܡܝܕܘܗܝ ܒܐܬܪܗ ܕܡܫܝܚܐ ܥܠ ܕܡܫܬܥܝ ܡܢ
ܚܘܣܢܐ ܕܠܐ ܬܘܒ ܢܦܫܗ ܒܗ ܒܡܥܒܕܐ ܒܥܡܕܐ ܠܘܬ

ܕܦ̈ܠܚܘܬܐ. ܟܠ ܡܢܐ ܗܘܝܬ ܐܡܪܐ ܘܫܡܥܬ ܝܬܝܪܐ ܗܘܐ. ܐܦ ܟܢ ܐܢܬ ܕܠܐ ܢܗܘܐ ܡܫܬܠܠ ܐܢܬ. ܐܠܐ ܐܝܢܐ ܠܐ ܡܬܚܫܚ ܐܝܢܐ ܕܐܫܬܐܠܐ ܡܢ ܢܦܫܗܘܢ ܕܦ̈ܠܚܐ .:. ܫܪܒܝܠ ܐܡܪ. ܐܝܟܢܐ ܕܐܢܬ ܚܙܪ ܐܢܬ. ܘܠܐ ܬܦܘܩ ܡܢ ܢܦ̈ܫܬܐ ܕܦ̈ܠܚܐ. ܘܐܢ ܕܝܢ ܢܦܩ ܐܢܬ. ܘܗܐ ܐܢܬ ܗܘ ܡܢܐ ܗܕܝܢ ܟܠܗܝܢ. ܗܟܢܐ ܐܦ ܐܢܐ ܚܙܐ ܐܢܐ ܕܠܐ ܐܬܘܠܐ ܡܢ ܢܦܫܗܘܢ ܕܗܘ ܕܐܡܪ ܕܠܐ ܬܬܟܦܪ ܠܟܠ ܝܠܕ ܘܠܟܠ ܕܡܗ. ܘܡܛܠ ܗܢܐ ܠܐ ܡܕܒܚ ܐܢܐ ܠܦܬܟܪ̈ܐ ܚܫܝܟ̈ܐ. ܗܦܟ ܟܢ ܕܝܢܐ ܡܠܟܐ ܕܕܒܚܬ ܠܗܘܢ ܒܗ. ܠܐ ܢܕܒܚ ܗܘܝܬ .:. ܕܝܢܐ ܐܡܪ. ܠܝ ܬܗܘܐ ܠܝ ܕܐܒܐ ܟܠ ܕܐܒܐ ܕܡܠܝܬ ܐܢܬ ܒܗ. ܗܘܝ ܠܝ ܕܐܡܪܬ ܕܠܐ ܡܕܒܚ ܐܢܐ. ܠܐ ܬܡܪܚ ܘܬܬܒܪ ܠܨ̈ܠܡܐ ܘܬܬܘܪܐ ܐܝܟ ܦܬܟܪ̈ܐ ܚ̈ܣܝܪܐ ܠܗܠܝܢ ܕܡܣܓܕܝܢ ܠܗܘܢ ܐܝܟ ܦ̈ܠܚܐ .:. ܫܪܒܝܠ ܐܡܪ. ܐܝܟ ܚܠܦ ܦ̈ܠܚܐ ܕܚܣܝܢ ܘܠܐ ܪܚܡܝܢ ܘܠܐ ܪܓܫܝܢ ܒܐܝܠܝܢ ܕܡܗܠܟܝܢ ܗܘܩ̈ܫܝܗܘܢ. ܐܡܪ ܐܢܬ ܠܝ ܕܐܬܪܚܡ. ܣܠܩ ܬܠܬܐ ܕܗܢܐ ܪܚܡܝܢ ܘܡܬܚܫܚܝܢ ܘܠܐ ܚܙܝܢ. ܐܝܟܢܐ ܐܡܪ ܐܢܬ ܠܝ ܕܐܬܪܚܡ. ܘܡܗܢܐ ܐܘܪܚܬ ܡܪܢ ܟܠܗ ܐܘܪܫܠܡ ܕܠܝ. ܕܡܛܠ ܕܦܘܡܐ ܐܝܬ ܠܗܘܢ ܘܠܐ ܡܡܠܠܝܢ. ܗܐ ܚܟܡ ܐܢܬ ܗܢܟܢܐ ܫܠܝܛܘܬܗܘܢ. ܗܢܘܢ ܕܐܝܟܘܬܗܘܢ ܢܗܘܘܢ ܥܒ̈ܕܝܗܘܢ ܘܟܠ ܡܢ ܕܬܟܠ ܥܠܝܗܘܢ ܐܝܟܘܬܗܘܢ .:. ܕܝܢܐ ܐܡܪ. ܠܐ ܗܘܐ ܠܡܕܐ ܐܬܦܪܣܬ ܡܢܟ ܕܬܣܒ ܐܦܝܐ ܕܐܢܡ ܬܓܪ ܠܦ̈ܠܚܐ. ܘܠܨ̈ܠܡܐ ܡܪܘܒ ܘܪܚܡ ܘܫܘܐ ܟܠ ܢܦܫ ܡܓܪ ܢܦܫܗ .:. .:. .:.

ܫܪܒܝܠ ܐܡܪ ܡܢܐ ܡܬܒܥܐ ܗܘ ܒܢ̈ܝܬܐ ܕܐܬܐܠܨܬ. ܒܬܪ ܗܝ ܕܐܡܪܬ ܠܝ ܕܠܐ ܡܕܒܚ ܐܢܐ ܘܪܡܝܬܢ ܡܓܪ ܢܦܫܗ. ܐܬܦܘܩ ܕܝܢ ܡܢ ܦܠܚܘܬ. ܗܘܐ ܗܘܐ ܠܝ ܗܢܐ ܙܒܢܐ. ܡܓܪܬ ܗܟܢܐ ܢܦܫ ܕܐܟܢܫܐ ܗܘܝܬ .:. ܕܝܢܐ ܐܡܪ.

ܘܐܬܬܪܝܡ ܥܠ ܡܪ̈ܘܡܗܘܢ، ܡܫ̈ܒܚܐ ܘܡܠܘܫܐ ܘܫܠܡܐ ܡܫܬܒܚܝܢ
ܒܡܪ̈ܘܡܐ ܕܫ̈ܡܝܐ. ܘܐܡܪ ܠܗ ܠܐ ܬܕܚܠ ܒܫܠܡܐ ܕܡܪܝܐ
ܗܘܝܬ ܒܗܘܢ . . . ܥܙܪܝܠ ܐܡܪ. ܗܘ ܠܝ ܬܘܒ ܕܐܡܪܬ ܕܐܝܬ
ܫܠܡܐ ܘܫ̈ܝܢܐ ܘܫܠܡܐ ܘܦܝܫ ܬܠܬܐ. ܐܠܐ ܡܪܝܐ ܐܝܟ
ܒܗ̇ ܫܠܡܐ ܕܟܠܗ ܥܠܡܐ ܘܐܝܟܢܐ ܘܫ̈ܡܝܐ ܘܟܠ ܕܐܝܬ
ܒܗܘܢ. ܘܒܟܝܢ ܕܒܪܝܗ ܡܠܟܐ ܡܫܝܚܐ . . ܕܢܟܐ ܐܡܪ ܠܐ
ܗܘܐ ܟܠ ܗܕܐ ܐܫܬܐܠܬ ܡܢܟ ܕܡܠܟܐ ܗܝ ܡܫܝܚܘܬܐ
ܕܪ̈ܘܚܢܝܐ ܕܐܘܕܥܬ ܒܗ̇. ܐܠܐ ܢܚܙܐ ܗܘ ܐܡܪܬ ܠܝ. ܕܠܐ
ܬܕܚܠ ܒܫܠܡܐ ܗܠܝܢ ܕܒܟܝܢ ܗܘܝܬ ܠܗܘܢ ܒܡܪܝܐ . .

ܥܙܪܝܠ ܐܡܪ: ܐܝܟܢܐ ܗܘ ܫܡܥܬܟ ܘܡ̈ܠܟܐ ܕܫܠܡ ܐܝܬ
ܒܗܘܢ ܕܠܟܠ ܐܢ̈ܫܐ ܕܐܘܡܢܐ ܡܢܗܘܢ ܐܝܬܝܗܘܢ ܘܡܢܗܘܢ
ܐܝܬܝܗܘܢ. ܘܠܗܘܢ ܠܐܘܡܢܐ ܕܟܠܗ ܐܢܘܢ ܠܬܫܡܫܬܐ ܡܢܗܘܢ
ܐܝܬܝܗܘܢ ܒܫ̈ܠܡܐ ܘܒܫܬܐܣܬܐ ܕܐܬܒܢܝ ܐܝܬܝܗܘܢ ܒܠܗܘܢ.
ܐܘܡܢܐ ܡܐܢ ܡܢ ܡܕܡ ܠܐܘܡܢܢ ܕܝܠܢ. ܘܐܝܟ ܡܐܢ
ܐܝܬ ܡܕܡ ܒܟܠܗ ܕܐܘܡܢܐ ܘܡܢܗ ܐܝܬ ܠܗ ܘܗܘܢ ܐܝܬ
ܠܗ . . . . ܕܢܟܐ ܐܡܪ. ܠܐ ܗܘܐ ܬܫܒܘܚܬܐ ܐܝܬ ܕܫܠܡ:
ܡܬܬܒܥܘ ܕܝܢ ܡܬܬܒܥ ܐܝܬ. ܕܟܠ ܡܢܝܢܐ ܒܫܪܪ ܒܫܠܡܐ
ܘܠܐ ܢܦܫܐ ܐܝܬ ܕܬܗܘܐ ܠܗܘܢ ܒܫ̈ܡܝܐ ܐܝܟ ܒܡܪܝܐ
ܫܡ̈ܝܢ . . . ܥܙܪܝܠ ܐܡܪ. ܡܘܬܐ ܕܡܛܠ ܗܕܐ ܫܡܝܐ ܐܝܟܘܢ
ܥܒ̈ܕܐ. ܠܐܝܠܝܢ ܕܡܘܕܝܢ ܒܡܠܟܐ ܡܫܝܚܐ ܘܐܦ ܗܘ ܡܘܕܐ
ܒܗܘܢ ܡܕܡ ܐܒܘܗܝ، ܫܡܝܐ . . . ܕܢܟܐ ܐܡܪ. ܟܠܢ ܡ̈ܠܟܐ
ܕܢܘܪܐ ܘܡܬܒܪܝܢ ܠܫ̈ܡܝܗܘܢ، ܘܠܡܠ̈ܟܐ ܕܪ̈ܘܡܗܘܢ. ܘܡܕܡ
ܗܢܐ ܦܘܪܐ ܡܠܐܟܐ . . . ܥܙܪܝܠ ܐܡܪ ܥܒܪ ܡܘܡܪ ܐܝܬ
ܠܝ ܒܢܘܪܐ ܗܕܐ ܕܐܬܦܪܫܬ ܡܢ ܗܝ ܢܘܪܐ ܕܠܐ ܕܒܚܐ ܘܬܘܠܕܐ
ܕܠܐ ܡܫܬܬܐ. ܗܝ ܕܠܫܡܝܐ ܠܐܝܠܝܢ [ܕܡܬܡܢܝܢ ܠܡܠܟܘܬܐ
ܫܠܡ ܡܠܟܘܬܐ. ܠܐ ܓܝܪ ܒܥܝܪ ܠܗܘܢ ܠܪ̈ܘܚܢܝܐ: ܕܢܦܪܩܘܢ
ܘܢܦܪܩܘܢ. ܠܡܢܝܢ ܕܠܒܪ ܡܢ ܚܝܘ ܗܘ ܕܐܠܗܐ ܡܪܢܝܐ.

ܕܡܬܦܫܩܐ ܐܚܝܗ ܗ̇ܘ ܕܫܡܥ ܗܘܐ ܡ̇ܢ ܠܐ̈ܠܗܐ. ܒܠ ܕܗ̇ܘ ܒܫܘܕܐ ܡܠܬܗ. ܘܟܕ ܬܠܐ ܗܘܐ ܒܐܝܕܗ ܕܐܠܗܗ̇ ܘܐܡܪܝܢ ܠܗ̇. ܡܬܬܦܝܣ ܐܝܟ ܕܬܒܥ ܠܐ̈ܠܗܐ. ܗܘ̇ ܕܝܢ ܠܐ ܡܫܟܚ ܗܘܐ ܕܢܦܠܐ ܠܗܘܢ ܡܬܒܥܝܐ ܡܢ ܦܘܫܩܐ ܕܕܝܢܗ. ܘܟܕ ܗܘܐ ܕܢܫܐ ܘܒܢܘܗܝ ܗܘܘ ܘܐܚܘܬܗ. ܘܠܐ ܡܫܟܚ ܗܘܐ ܕܢܦܩ ܗܘܐ ܕܕܝܢܗ ܠܒܝܬܗ ܒܥܘܬܐ ܕܒܢܝܢܗ ܗܘܘ ܡܫܬܦܠܢܝܢ ܘܐܦܣܗܘܢ ܠܒܝܬܗ. . . .

ܕܢܠܐ ܐܡܪ. ܗܢܘ ܒܗܘܢ̈ܐ ܘܠ ܠܐܠܗܐ ܕܡܪܐ ܐܝܬ. ܘܠܐ ܐܝܟ ܚܦܝܐ ܠܟ ܕܬܗܘܐ ܬܗܘܐ ܒܗܡܝܪܐ. ܐܘ ܠܐ ܚܦܝܐ ܐܝܬ ܕܐܡܪܝܢ ܡܢ ܗܠܝܢ ܡܫܚܘܐ ܐܢܐ ܠܟ. . . . ܫܦܝܪ ܐܡܪ ܐ̈ܠܗܐ ܕܫܡܝܐ ܘܐܪܥܐ ܠܐ ܥܒܕ ܢܐܒܕܘܢ ܡܢ ܬܚܝܬ ܫܡܝܐ ܗܠܝܢ. ܐܝܬ ܕܝܢ ܠܐ ܗܘܬ ܚܕܐ ܒܡ̈ܠܐ ܕܠܡܫܝܚܐ ܐܠܗܐ ܚܠܦ ܡ̈ܠܐ ܫܘܐ ܐܝܕܗ ܒܟܬܒܐ ܕܠܡܫܝܚܐ. ܕܠܐ ܬܗܘܐ ܐܫܟܚ ܡܢܟ ܕܡܫܟܚ ܐܝܬ ܥܡܟܐ ܕܐ̈ܠܗܐ ܫܪܟܐ . . . ܕܢܠܐ ܐܡܪ ܕܬܗܘܐ ܒܩܘܩܐ ܕܢܘܪܐ ܡܝܬܪܐ ܒܝܬ ܒܢܘܗܝ ܘܒܢܝ̈ܗܘܢ. ܘܒܬܪܗ ܡܫܬܦܠܢܐ ܗܘܢܐ ܒܢܘܡܐ ܕܚܠܦ ܪܝܫ ܒܡܘܬܐ ܒܠܗ ܒܬ ܕܢܒܝܐ. ܘܠܐ ܦܟܐ ܕܬܒܥܗ. ܫܦܝܪ ܐܡܪ ܥܡܟܬ ܠܟ ܡܢ ܕܐܡܪܬ ܠܟ ܕܠܐ ܪܚܡ ܐܝܬ ܒܟܦܪܐ ܕܠܦܘܚܝܐ ܕܢܘܪܐ ܕܡܠܒܟܐ ܠܐܢܠܝܢ ܕܡܒܪܝܢ ܒܡܬܦܪܐ ܒܚܒܪܐ ܐܚܪܬܟ. ܘܡܦܪܢ ܒܐܠܗܐ ܚܝܐ ܒܕܡܘܬܟ. . . . ܕܢܠܐ ܐܡܪ. ܡܢܘ ܐܠܦܟ ܗܠܝܢ ܒܗܠܝܢ ܕܬܐܡܪ ܡܕܡ ܗܟܢܐ ܒܒܪܐ ܕܐܡܬܝܟ ܗܘܬ ܪܘܚܐ ܕܐ̈ܠܗܐ ܘܒܠܒܒܗ ܕܡܫܝܚܐ. ܕܗܐ ܒܟܕ ܐܝܬ ܦܢܝܬܗ . . . ܫܦܝܪ ܐܡܪ. ܡܫܝܚܐ ܕܐܘܕܝܬ ܒܗ. ܗܘܐ ܐܠܦܢ ܕܐܡܪ ܗܟܢܐ. ܠܐ ܓܒܪ ܗܘܝܘ ܕܐܡܪܘܗ ܠܗ ܦܢܝܬܐ. ܪ̈ܘܚܗ, ܓܒܪ ܐܬܢܘܗܝ ܦܘܪܫܢܐ ܡ̈ܠܠܐ ܣܠܩ ܣܬܟܐ ܕܕܡܝܢ ܠܗ. ܗܘܢܘܢ ܡܟܝܠ ܕܢܗܘܘܢ ܣܠܩ ܒܟܝܢܐ ܒܡܘܬܐ ܕܗܘܝܢ ܒܗ ܦܘܩܕܢܐ ܠܟܠܗ. . . . ܕܢܠܐ ܐܡܪ ܢܬܬܠܐ

ܐܝܬ ܒܡ̈ܠܟܐ ܕܐܝܬ ܕܝܢܐ. ܘܐܢܐ ܦܩܘܕܐ ܐܝܬ ܠܝ ܒܟܬܒܐ.
ܕܫܠܛ ܗܘ ܕܝܢܐ ܕܒܥܠܕܒܒ. ܡܢ ܗܢܐ ܕܡܕܡ ܒܥ̈ܝܢܝ ܕܗܘܐ
ܡܫܝܡ ܐܝܬ ܒܗ. ܗܘܝܬ ܕܐܬܐ ܘܫܐܠ. ܘܠܐ ܐܬܦܢܝܬ ܐܬܡܠܠ
ܡܕܡ ܀ ܫܪܒܝܠ ܐܡܪ ܡܢ ܕܢܝܚܐ ܕܢܦܫܟ ܐܠܗܐ ܡܕܡ ܒܥܝܢܘܗܝ.
ܒܡܐܢܝܢ. ܗܘ ܐܠܗܐ ܗܘܐ ܡܢ ܡܢܝܢܘ. ܘܐܢܐ ܠܐ ܕܢܠ ܐܢܐ
ܡܢ ܠܘܬܟܬܒܐ ܕܩܕܡܐ ܕܢܡܘܣ ܐܝܬ ܘܡܕܢܚ ܐܝܬ ܠܝ ܒܗܘܢ ܀
ܕܝܢܐ ܐܡܪ. ܢܦܪܘܢ ܡܟܝܠܐ ܕܐܘܕܝܬ ܒܗ. ܡܢ ܟܠ ܡܕܡ
ܕܐܫܬܘܕܝܬ ܒܗ. ܘܕܒܥܬܘ ܐܢܐ ܗܘܝܬ ܕܐܫܬܘܕܝ ܒܗ܆ ܘܢܦܩܐ
ܦܘܪܫܢܗ ܠܘܬܟ ܒܠܒܝܫܘܬ܆ ܘܢܗܘܢ ܡܢ ܐܝܕܝ ܀
ܫܪܒܝܠ ܐܡܪ. ܗܢܐ ܗܘ ܦܘܪܫܢܗ ܫܪܝܪܐ ܕܡܫܝܚܐ ܕܐܬܦܪܫ.
ܢܦܠܐ ܒܗܘܢܐ ܗܢܐ ܕܢܦܩ ܠܝ. ܕܐܬܦܢܝܬ ܠܡܕܡ ܕܡܫܬܐܠܬ
ܡܢ. ܘܥܠ ܡܕܡ ܕܗܝܡܢܐ ܒܥܒܕܝ ܕܐܬܦܢܝܬ ܒܗ. ܘܥܠ
ܦܠܓ ܒܝܫܬ ܗܘܝܬ. ܠܐ ܢܦܫܬ ܕܐܬܦܪ ܡܠܬܝ ܀ ܕܝܢܐ ܐܡܪ.
ܐܒܥܘܬܗ ܡܢ ܡܕܡܝ. ܘܬܬܠܐ ܒܥܡܘܕܐ ܒܬܪ ܪܝܫܗ
ܗܟܢܐܝܬ. ܘܢܦܠܘ ܒܥܬܝܕܘܬܐ ܒܪ ܬܪܬܐ. ܘܡܢܕܘ ܠܗ
ܗܦܠܘܢܐ ܗܘܝܢܐ ܒܬܪܬܝܐ ܕܒܝܬ ܕܝܢܐ ܀ ܀ ܀
ܘܦܩܕ ܗܓܡܘܢܐ ܘܐܟܠܘܗܝ ܡܢ ܩܕܡܘܗܝ ܘܐܡܪ ܗܘܐ
ܠܗ. ܕܢܦܩ ܠܐܠܗܐ ܘܢܗܘܐ ܢܛܝܪܐ ܕܩܛܠܐ. ܒܫܪܟܐ: ܕܢܦܩܐ
ܐܣܝܪܐ ܘܢܛܪ ܢܛܘܪܐ ܣܓܝܐܐ ܀
ܫܪܒܝܠ ܐܡܪ. ܡܢܐ ܗܘܐ ܠܝܬ ܡܠܬܟ ܘܐܡܪܬ ܐܝܬ
ܕܐܬܕܟܪ: ܒܬܪ ܗܦܟܢܘܬܐ ܕܢܦܩܬ ܡܢܝ ܕܠܐ ܗܘܬ ܦܪܥܘ
ܐܢܐ. ܠܐ ܗܘܐ ܒܪ ܡܠܬܐ ܕܦܘܪܫܢܐ ܥܠܝ ܡܢ ܕܩܕܡ
ܐܠܐ ܫܪܪܘܗܝ ܗܘ ܦܘܡܝ ܡܢ ܐܘܟܡܬܐ ܕܣܘܦܬܐ ܀ ܕܝܢܐ
ܐܡܪ. ܢܦܠ ܒܟܘܒܐ ܕܦܪܙܠܐ ܐܝܟ ܦܩܘܕܐ. ܘܐܬܬܪ ܡܠܘܦܝܢ
ܐܝܟ ܚܕ ܩܒܪܬܐ. ܘܡܢܕܘ ܡܦܠܘܢܐ ܗܘܢܐ. ܒܬܫܐ
ܕܠܐ ܗܘܬ ܒܗ ܕܘܟܬܐ ܕܫܪܪܐ ܀ ܫܪܒܝܠ ܐܡܪ. ܗܠܝܢ ܩܕܝܫܐ
ܕܥܒܕܬ ܐܝܬ ܒܠܒܘܢ ܕܟܐܢܘܬܐ. ܡܢ ܟܕ ܡܫܪܘܬܗܘܢ

ܡܕܡ ܕܝܢ ܕܟܣܐ ܗܘ ܘܓܠܝܐ ܗܘ. ܡܬܕܪܟܐ ܗܘ ܕܟܣܝܐ ܗܘ.
ܘܠܐ ܗܘܐ ܡܬܕܪܟܐ ܗܘ ܡܢ ܒܪܢܫܐ ܐܝܟ ܕܦܓܪܢ ܐܢܬ ܀ ܀

ܡܬܕܡܪܢܐ ܐܡܪ. ܠܐ ܗܘܐ ܗܘܐ ܕܦܩܕܘ ܠܝ ܡ̈ܠܐܟܐ
ܕܐܬܒܥ ܡܐܒ̈ܗܝܟ: ܕܐܝܟܘ ܕܐܝܬ ܕܡܝܐ ܘܐܬܒܥܬܐ ܒܬܪ
ܦܬܓܡܗܘܢ ܕܩܢܘܡܐ. ܐܦ ܠܐ ܟܠ ܗܘܐ ܓܠܝܠ ܠܝ: ܕܐܝܟ
ܗܘ ܕܡܬܚܡܪ ܒܟܘܕܐ ܘܐܝܟ ܠܐ ܡܬܚܡܪ. ܠܝ ܗܘܐ ܗܘ ܦܩܕܘ
ܠܝ ܡ̈ܠܐܟܐ. ܕܟܠ ܡܢ ܕܠܐ ܡܬܚܡܐ ܠܬܠܡܝ̈ܕܐ ܘܦܬܓܡ ܠܗܘܢ
ܒܦܘܡܐ ܒܓܠܝܐ ܘܡܣܬܪܐ ܘܦܫܝܛܐ ܫܪܝܪܐ ܐܬܝܗܒ
ܒܟܘܢ ܀ ܀ ܀

ܓܒܪܝܠ ܐܡܪ. ܡܠܟܐ ܕܗܘܐ ܠܡܠܟܐ. ܟܕ ܗܘܐ ܗܘ ܠܡܠܟܐ
ܠܒ̈ܢܝ ܐܢܫܐ. ܡܠܟܐ ܕܝܢ ܕܡ̈ܠܐܟܐ ܠܗܘܢ: ܗܘ ܓܠܝܐ
ܘܟܢܘ. ܠܝ ܕܐܝܬ ܠܡܠܟܐ ܐܢܫܐ ܘܕܡܐ ܕܝܠܝ. ܕܟܢ ܗܘܐ
ܦܘܪܫܐ ܒܝܬ ܐܢܫܝܢ ܕܠܒܫܘ ܠܐܠܗܐ: ܠܐܢܫܝܢ ܕܠܐ ܠܒܫܘܗܝ،
ܘܠܐ ܐܘܕܥܘ ܟܗ. ܡܛܠ ܗܢܐ ܡܟܐ ܐܢܝ. ܕܠܐ ܬܘܒ ܡܬܚܙܝܢ
ܐܢܐ ܠܬܠܡܝ̈ܕܝ. ܘܠܐ ܡܬܚܘܐ ܐܢܐ ܠܥܠܡܐ. ܘܠܐ ܡܬܚܡܪ
ܐܢܐ ܠܡ̈ܠܐܟܐ ܀ ܕܢܝܐܝܠ ܐܡܪ. ܬܪܝܢ ܦܬܓܡܐ ܕܩܕܡܝܐ ܒܝܬ
ܒ̈ܢܝܗܘܢ ܕܡܠܟܐ: ܘܐܬܝܕܥ ܠܗܘܢ ܡܠܟܐ ܕܡܬܚܡܐ ܠܗ ܐܝܟ
ܒܪܐ ܠܡܠܟܘܬܐ. ܘܡܬܪܘ ܠܗ ܡܣܬܒܪܢܘܬܐ ܗܕܝܐ. ܟܕ
ܡܣܬܒܪ ܗܘܐ ܥܠ ܢܒ̈ܝܐ ܕܢܒܝܐ ܕܡܬܐܡܪܝܢ ܗ̇ܘ، ܟܢ
ܫܘܒܚܐ ܀ ܓܒܪܝܠ ܐܡܪ. ܦܠܓܐ ܢܦܩܬ ܒܝܬ ܒ̈ܢܝ ܐܢܫ ܡܢܐ
ܕܐܬܩܢܝ ܗܘ، ܦܠܓܐ ܒܐܝ̈ܕܘܗܝ، ܕܗܘ ܐܪܕܟܠܐ ܡܬܟܢܫܐ
ܕܒܬܘܠܬܐ. ܡܛܠ ܗܢܐ ܐܚܐ ܗܘܐ ܘܪܚܡ ܒܢܝܐ ܒܠܗܘܢ
ܕܒܬܘܠܬܐ ܒܗܘ ܒܪܢ. ܗܠܝܢ ܕܝܢ ܕܗܘܐ ܡܬܚܙܝܢ ܐܢܬ ܒ.
ܗܢܝܢ ܗܘ ܕܝܠܐ ܕܒܬܘܠ ܠܗ ܡܕܡ ܐܚܪܝܢ. ܐܝܠܝܢ ܕܝܢ ܕܬ̈ܢܝܢ
ܐܪܒܥܬܗܘܢ ܒܠܚܘܕ: ܡܛܠ ܕܠܝܬ ܕܝܠܗ ܕܐܠܗܐ ܡܕܡ
ܒ̈ܢܝܗܘܢ. ܡܛܠ ܗܢܐ ܐܝܠܝܢ ܕܐܝܬܝܗܘܢ، ܐܠܗܝܢ ܡܬܚܘܝܢ.
ܡܐܡܠܐ ܗܘ ܡܬܘܕܐ ܒܗܘܢ ܀ ܀ ܕܢܝܐܝܠ ܐܡܪ. ܐܝܬ ܐܡܪ

ܘܦܘ̈ܩܕܢܐ ܕܡ̈ܠܟܐ ܕܐܡܪܬ ܐܢܬ. ܐܠܐ ܕܡܫܬܒܚܝܢ ܒܠܚܘܕ
ܐܠܗ̈ܝܐ ܦܬܟܪ̈ܐ ∘∘∘ ܫܪܒܝܠ ܐܡܪ. ܐܢ ܫܪ̈ܝܪܢ ܠܝ
ܫܒܐ ܡܢ ܬܫܒܘܚܬܗ ܕܚܕ ܡܢ ܐܠܗ̈ܝܢ. ܒܡܫܬܐ ܗ̄ܝ ܕܐܡܪܬ
ܕܐܡܝܢܐ ܐܢܬܘܢ. ܚܙܝ ܓܝܪ ܗܘܐ ܚܒܝܫܐ ܒܗ ܫ̈ܒܝܠܐ. ܡܕܡ
ܕܠܐ ܙܕܩ. ܘܐܡܝܢܐ ܚܕ ܡܢ ܒܬܘܠܬܐ ܕܐܬܓܠܝܬ ܒܐܬܠܝܐ.
ܐܝܟ ܕܐܡܪܬ ܬܫܒܘܚܬܗܘܢ ܕܒܣܬܪ̈ܐ ∘.∘ ܕܝܢܐ ܐܡܪ. ܗܘܝܐ
ܕܡܫܡܥܐ ܗܘܐ ܕܐܠܗ̈ܐ ܡܢ ܦܘܡܟ ܘܡܦܩܝܢ ܝܬܝܪ ܐܢܘܢ
ܦܫܟܐ. ܘܠܐ ܕܝܠ. ܘܒܬܪ ܐܦ ܫܘܡܕܢܐ ܕܡ̈ܠܟܐ ܘܠܐ ܝܕ.
ܐܫܬܡܥܘ. ܒܠ ܓܪ̈ܓܠܬܐ ܒܙ ܛܝܒܘܬܐ ܒܫܘܪܐ. ܘܒܒܙܘ
ܡܓܠܦܪ̈ܐ ܡܒܠܝܐ. ܒܙܒܢܐ ܕܦܣ ܗܘܐ ܬܫܘܬܐ ܕܓ̈ܠܘܗܝ ∘.∘
ܫܪܒܝܠ ܐܡܪ. ܐܦ̄ ܒܓܪ̈ܒܝܗܘܢ ܗܠܝܢ ܘܗܪ̈ܝܢܐ ܕܐܠܗ̈ܝܢ
ܘܠܐ ܪܓܫܝܢ ܒܗܘܢ ܒܪ̈ܝܢܗܘܢ ܒܙܒܢܐ ܗܕܪ ܕܝܢ ܠܝ ܕܐܬܒܗܬ.
ܗܐ ܓܝܪ ܐܦ̄ ܐܢܐ ܗܟܢ ܡܕܡ ܕܗܒܪ ܚܕ ܡܢ ܐܠܗ̈ܝܢ
ܘܡܒܠܝܢ ܠܗ ܡܕܡܝܢ. ܡܕܡܬܐ ܗܘ̇ ܐܢܬ ܒܠܗܘܢ ∘.∘ ܕܝܢܐ
ܐܡܪ. ܡܡܒܠܐ ܬܒܒ ܐܢܐ ܡܒܝܢ ܒܓܢܒܝܢ ܕܒܠ ܐܠܗ̈ܐ
ܘܡܪ̈ܘܬܐܝܢ ܕܓܪ̈ܒܬ ܐܦ ܠܡ̈ܠܟܐ. ܘܠܐ ܡܫܬܐ ܐܢܐ ܡܒܝܢ
ܒܓܢܒܐ ܕܐܘܡܝܬ ܐܢܬ [ܠܗܘܢ ܒܩܘܡܐ ܒܢܒܢܝܢ ܩ̈ܘܡܐ ∴ ∴
ܫܪܒܝܠ ܐܡܪ. ܡܢܐ ܒܗܘܢ ܒܓܪ̈ܓܝܢ ܗܒܠ ܘܠܐ ܦܘܫܬ
ܬܕܓܠ. ܘܫܘܐ ܓܝܪ̈، ܒܒܙܢܐ ܫܘܠܛܢܐ ܕܡ̈ܠܟܐ ܕܡܗܘ
ܠܝ. ܘܠܐ ܬܓܪܫܐ ܐܢܬ ܠܦ̈ܠܚܐ ܒܓܠܘܬܝܢ: ܘܐܬܬܒܩ ܘܐܦ
ܐܢܬ] ܒܒܢܝ ܐܘܦܫܡ ܕܠܝܢ ∘.∘ ܕܝܢܐ ܐܡܪ. ܝܬܝܪ ܕܒܠ
ܐܠܗܐ ܘܡܪܘܬܝܢ ܕܠܘܬ ܡ̈ܠܟܐ. ܐܬܪܘ ܒܠܝܢ ܫܪ̈ܒܐ ܗܘܠܝܢ
ܕܡܒܝܡ ܐܢܬ ܒܗܘܢ. ܗܐ ܬܘܒ ܡܫܘܦ ܐܢܬ ܒܠ
ܡܪ̈ܘܬܝܢ. ܬܘܒ ܡܬܬܘܦܝܡ ܒܠܝܢ ܐܠ̈ܗܝܢܐ. ܕܗܢ ܗܠܝܢ
ܡܪܝܪ̈ܝܢ ∘.∘ ܫܪܒܝܠ ܐܡܪ ܫܒܝܩ ܐܢܬ ܐܝܟ ܕܝܢܐ. ܒܟܕ ܡܕܡ
ܦܝܫܐ ܐܢܬ ܘܠܐ ܬܫܘܒ ∘.∘ ܕܝܢܐ ܐܡܪ. ܗܢ ܕܒܠ ܦܓܪܟ
ܠܐ ܚܘ ܕܢܫܡܪ ܒܗ ܗܠܝܢ ܫܪ̈ܒܐ. ܐܡܝܢܐ ܡܫܡܫ ܕܝܠ

ܢܚܬܝܢ ܠܝ ܢܓܕܐ ܕܦܘܪܥܢܐ ܘܪܘܓܙܐ: ܒܣܘܓܐ ܕܩܫܝܫܘܬܐ
ܕܠܥܠܡ ܀ ܗܟܢܐ ܐܡܪ. ܢܬܬܘܣܦܘܢ ܫܢܝܐ ܕܩܕܡܝܐ
ܘܟܠܝܠܐ ܒܗ ܢܚܬܐ ܕܐܒܗ̈ܘܗܝ: ܘܬܬܚܝܢܘܢ ܚܠܝܡܘܢ
ܡܢܝܐܝܬ. ܘܒܬܪ ܠܗ ܗܒܠܐ. ܒܪܡܫܐ ܕܢܦܩ ܗܘܐ ܕܢܚܐ
ܡܢ ܬܚܝܬ ܠܓܢܐ] ܕܢܬܚܙܘܢ ○○○ ܫܪܒܝܠ ܐܡܪ. ܐܦ ܠܐ
ܗܒܠܬ ܚܝܝ ܡܢ ܥܒܘܕܗ̇ ܕܡܠܟܬܐ ܬܘܒ ܐܘܣܦ ܠܗ ܥܠ
ܥܒܘܕܗ̇ ܡܛܘܠ ܕܢܦܠܐ ܐܝܬ ○○○ ܕܢܫܐ ܐܡܪ ܢܬܐܡܪ ܢܬܚܙܐ
ܕܐܒܗ̈ܘܗܝ ܘܐܬܬܒܥܘܗܝ ܥܠ ܐܪܒܐ ܘܩܘܒܪܐ ܐܒܗ̈ܘܗܝ ܥܠ
ܒܩܒܪܗܘܢ. ܘܐܒܠܘ ܡܫܝܚܐ ܬܚܝܬ ܒܩܒܪܗܘܢ. ܘܐܒܕ ܥܠ
ܦܓܪܐ ܕܐܒܗ̈ܘܗܝ. ܘܬܠܐܘܗܝ ܒܐܟܠܘܗܝ ܒܗ ܒܥܡܡ ܒܬܪ ܙܒܢ.
ܘܬܠܓܐ ܒܠܒܢܐ. ܘܒܬܪܗ ܠܗ ܗܒܠܐ ○○○ ܫܪܒܝܠ ܐܡܪ.
ܠܐ ܡܫܒܚܝܢ ܐܝܟ ܐܠܗܝܢ ܕܒܗ ܐܠܗܐ ܡܫܪܝܢ ܘܠܐ ܡܢܝܢ
[ܫܡܝܢ] ܐܠܗܝܢ ܕܐܠܗܐ ܗܘ ܬܘܕܝܬܗܘܢ ܘܡܛܠ ܗܢܐ ܐܡܪ
ܐܢܐ. ܕܠܐ ܢܘܪܐ ܘܠܐ ܡܝܐ ܘܠܐ ܡܘܬܐ ܘܠܐ ܚܝܐ. ܘܠܐ
ܪܘܚܐ ܘܠܐ ܒܣܡܐ. ܡܫܒܚܝܢ ܦܓܪܝܢ ܠܗ ܠܐܒܘܗܝ ܡܢ
ܫܡܫܐ ܕܐܠܗܐ ܕܒܪܢܫܐ ܕܥܒܕ ܡܫܝܚܐ ○○○ ܕܢܫܐ ܐܡܪ
ܐܝܟܢܐ ܐܘܪܚܐ ܕܐܒܪܗܡ ܘܕܝܢܐ ܘܫܡܫܐ ܬܚܝܬ ܥܒܕܘܗܝ.
ܘܒܬܪܗ ܗܒܠܐ ܒܪܡܫܐ ܕܐܬܚܝܕ ܗܘ ܪܒ ܬܠܡܝܕܘܗܝ ○○
ܫܪܒܝܠ ܐܡܪ ܕܒܢܝܢ ܐܝܟ ܡܫܝܚܝܢ ܕܐܝܟܢ ܡܢ ܫܡܝܢ
ܕܠܗܬ. ܐܠܐ ܫܡܝܢ ܗܘܬ ܕܒܪܝܐ ܘܡܫܝܚܝܢ ܗܘܐ ܪܘܚܢܝܝܢ ○○
ܕܢܫܐ ܐܡܪ. ܠܐ ܫܠܡ ܐܢܬ ܠܝ ܒܥܠܡ ܕܐܡܪ ܐܢܬ. ܐܢܬ ܗܘ
ܒܪ ܐܢܬܬܐ ܒܪܝܫ. [ܕܢܒܓܪ ܪܘܚܝ. ܘܐܝܟܐ ܒܠ ܡܕܡ ܕܟܝܢ
ܘܦܝܫܐ ܡܟܪܙ. ܐܝܟܢܐ ܒܥܘܠܡܐ ܕܦܓܪܝ. ܒܠ ܕܠܐ
ܡܬܠܒܫ ܐܢܬ ܕܬܬܒܢܐ ܠܬܠܡܝܕܐ ܕܢܣܒ ܗܘܝܬ ܠܗܘܢ ܀ ܀ ܀
ܫܪܒܝܠ ܐܡܪ. ܐܠܗܝܢ ܕܐܡܪܬ ܘܬܚܝܬ ܡܫܝܚܝܢ: ܠܐ ܝܕܥ ܐܢܬ
ܕܒܡܫܪܝܢ] ܕܬܫܒܘܚ ܐܝܢ. ܐܡܪܢܐ ܐܠܗܝܢ ܕܐܝܬ ܒܪܝܫ
ܗܒ ܐܢܬ ܕܢܒܥ ܐܢܬ ○○ ܕܢܫܐ ܐܡܪ ܠܐ ܡܫܒܚܝܢ ܠܟ

ܕܬܬܝܠܕ ܕܒܒܪ ܐܢܬ ܗܘ ܝܠܕܐ ܕܫܠܝܐ . . ܕܝܢܐ ܐܡܪ
ܢܬܪܡ ܒܥ̈ܡܡܗ܇ ܘܒܟ̈ܬܒܐ ܕܢܒ̈ܝܘܬܗ܆ ܘܒܢܘ ܡܦܠܓ̈ܢܐ
ܗܒܢܐ܆ ܒܝܘܡܐ ܕܝܕܐ ܘܢܣܒ ܕܡܗ ܒܠ ܐܪܒܥܐ . . . ܓܒܪܐܝܠ
ܐܡܪ. ܫܦܪ ܒܒܪ ܐܢܬ ܠܝ ܗܒܝܐ. ܡܛܠ ܕܫܡܥܬ ܠܝ ܕܝܢ
ܡܢ ܫ̈ܠܝܚܘܗܝ ܕܒܝܬܐ ܐܡܪ ܗܘܐ ܕܫܘ̈ܒܚܬܐ ܠܟ ܕܦܓܪ܇
ܕܐܬܬܐ ܠܡܫܝܚܐ ܕܡܢ ܒܝܬ ܫ̈ܒܛܝ. ܘܐܢܐ ܕܡܫܝܚܐ ܗܘܝܬ
ܒܡܟܐ܇ ܗܐ ܐܘܠܝܨܝ ܡܢܝܫܟܢ ܠܝ . . . ܕܝܢܐ ܐܡܪ.
ܢܬܪܡ ܒܥ̈ܡܡܗ܇ ܕܠܐ ܒܡܬ ܡܢ ܗܦܟܐ ܕܢܝܫ ܒܝܬ ܒ̈ܢܝܗ܇
ܘܦ̈ܪܘܩܗ܇ ܒܟ̈ܬܒܗ܇ ܘܢܣܒ ܗܦܟܐ ܕܢܝܫ ܒܡܗ . . ܓܒܪܐܝܠ
ܐܡܪ. ܠܐ ܡܬܬܡܟܢ ܐܢܐ ܠܫ̈ܠܝܚܐ ܕܡܢܗ ܕܢܦܩܘܢ. ܘܬܘܒ
ܡܕܡ ܕܠܘ ܡܢ ܒܢܝ ܗܘ ܕܐܠܗܐ. ܘܠܘ ܐܠܗܐ ܗܘ ܒܒܢܝ
ܐܠܐ ܒܒܪܐ ܗܘ ܕܒܪܘܚܗ . . . ܕܝܢܐ ܐܡܪ. ܐܝܟ ܕܢܒܝܐ
ܫ̈ܠܝܚܐ ܘܟܠܗ ܐܦ ܐܢܬ. ܐܝܟ ܕܡܫܡܪ ܕܝ̈ܢܐ ܦܪ ܐܦ
ܐܢܬ . .

ܓܒܪܐܝܠ ܐܡܪ. ܘܐܢ ܐܢܐ ܡܘܟܪ ܐܢܐ ܠܡܕܡ ܕܒܒܪܐ
ܗܘ ܕܒܢܝ ܐܢܫܐ. ܕܠܐ ܙܒܢ ܘܠܐ ܫܢܐ ܒܡܕܡ. ܐܢܬ ܠܐ
ܬܟܪܙ ܠܐܠܗܐ ܒܒܪܐ ܕܟܠ. ܘܬܬܦܓܪ ܒܒܢܗ ܠܡܕܡ ܕܠܘ
ܡܢܗ ܗܘ. ܘܡܢܒܪ ܠܢܦܫܗ . . . ܕܝܢܐ ܐܡܪ. ܗܒܢܐ ܡܠܟ
ܠܗܘܢ ܘܠܫ̈ܡܝܢ ܗܢܐ. ܕܗܘܬܘܢ ܡܟܪܙܝܢ ܐܦ ܠܢܒܝܐ
ܕܡܢܝܘܡܝܢ ܠܟܠ ܦܬܓܡܐ ܕܐܪܒܥܐ . . . ܓܒܪܐܝܠ ܐܡܪ. ܐܦ ܠܐ
ܒܬܡܟ ܠܝ ܕܢܟܪ ܐܢܫܝ ܐܠܐ ܒܬܡܟ ܗܘ ܠܝ ܕܠܐ ܢܬܟܪ
ܠܗܘܢ ܘܠܐ ܢܦܪ ܐܢܫܝ. ܒܪ ܕܒܒ̈ܢܝܐ ܐܢܫܝ. ܒܬܠܐ ܗܘ
ܒܪ ܗܘܐ ܡܠܘܐ ܕܢܬܟܪ ܒܒܢܝܐ ܒܡ ܒܒܪܗ. ܘܟܪܐ
ܗܘ ܠܒܒܢܝܐ ܕܢܬܦܪܫ ܒܒܢܗ ܒܬܪ̈ܬܗ . . . ܕܝܢܐ ܐܡܪ.
ܒܡܫܝܚܐ ܐܬܬܠܝ ܡܫܝܚܐ ܕܐܘܪܬ ܒܗ. ܘܒܡܫܝܚܐ ܬܬܠܐ ܐܢܐ
ܠܝ ܐܝܟ ܕܠܢܝ. ܘܬܬܠܐ ܒܗ ܒܠ ܡܫܝܚܐ ܦܠܓܐ ܗܘܒܥܐ . . .
ܓܒܪܐܝܠ ܐܡܪ. ܡܫܝܚܐ ܕܗܘܐ ܡܒܝܢ ܐܢܬ ܒܗ. ܫܪܝ ܕܠܐ

ܐܘ ܒܗܬܬ ܕܢܬܡܚ ܠܗܓܡܘܢܘܢ ܕܡ̈ܠܟܐ... ܫܪܒܝܠ ܐܡܪ. ܫܦܝܪ ܐܡܪܬ ܕܠܐ ܒܗܬܬ ܐܢܐ. ܡܛܠ ܕܡܪܝ ܗܘ ܡܥܕܪܢܝ. ܘܫܠܝܛܐ ܗܘ ܥܠܘ ܬܪܥܝܬܝ ܠܗܘܢ. ܕܐܝܬܝܗܘܢ ܠܒܪ ܡܢ ܒܕ̈ܝܢܐ ܕܦܬ̈ܓܡܐ. ܡܬܒܥܐ ܐܢܐ ܠܗ ܠܡܬܒܥܐ ܒܐܘܠܨܢܐ ܕܦܘܣܩܝ. ܥܒܕܐ ܗܘ ܓܝܪ ܙܒܝܢܐ ܝܫܘܥ. ܐܠܗܐ ܕܗܘܐ ܒܪ ܐܢܫܐ... ܕܢܚܐ ܐܡܪ. ܠܥܒܕܐ ܗܘ ܗܟܝܠ ܡܫܬܐܠ ܐܢܐ ܘܠܥܒܝܕܐ ܕܠܐ ܠܡܡܬܐ. ܘܟܡ ܡܘܬܐ ܕܡܘܬ ܗܘܐ ܡܬܚܠܠ ܐܢܐ... ܫܪܒܝܠ ܐܡܪ. ܐܦ ܫܪܒܐ ܗܝ ܕܥܒܕܐ ܐܢܐ. ܠܐ ܡܬܕܢ ܡܬܒܥܠܐ. ܐܢܬ ܓܝܪ ܥܒܕܐ ܕܡܫܬܐܠ. ܡܬܪܐܡܬ ܓܝܪ ܡܘܬܐ ܐܢܐ ܕܡܘܬ ܐܝܟ ܕܐܡܪܬ... ܕܝܠܐ ܐܡܪ ܐܡܪܢܐ ܐܘܣܩܦ ܡܘܬܐ ܕܗܘ ܡܢܗ ܕܠܐ ܡܬܒܥ ܐܢܐ...

ܫܪܒܝܠ ܐܡܪ. ܐܦ ܐܢܐ ܠܐ ܡܕܡ ܐܢܐ ܐܡܪܢܐ ܐܦܠܐ ܠܝ ܦܬܓܡܐ ܕܡܪܝ ܡܘܬܐ. ܘܗܦܟܝ ܐܢܬ ܡܫܟܚ ܐܢܬ ܠ ܐܝܟ ܫܢܐ... ܕܝܠܐ ܐܡܪ. ܫܦܝܪ ܡܪܝܢ ܡܘܬܐ ܕܡܫܝܚܐ ܕܒ̈ܠܚܝܢ ܘܠܐ ܟܠܗ ܠܝ ܘܡܣܬܩܠ ܐܩܦܝ ܘܗܢܘܢ ܐܢܬ. ܘܡܣܡܡ ܩܠܐ ܟܠ ܟܡ̈ܬܝܢ ܘܠܐ ܫܡܥ ܠܝ. ܘܡܬܚܫܚ ܐܠܗܝ ܡܢ ܟܠ ܗܕܐ ܘܡܦܪܢ ܐܢܬ ܠܬ̈ܟܠܐ. ܘܡܬܠܝܢ ܥܠܘ ܦܓܪܝ ܘܡܣܘܪܩ ܒܦ̈ܓܪܐ ܘܡܦܪܩ ܐܢܬ ܠܟ ܐܠܗܐ. ܘܡܛܠ ܕܗܘܬ ܦܓܪܝ ܗܐ ܐܡܪ ܐܢܬ ܥܠܡܪܝܡ ܕܥܒܪ ܠܝ... ܫܪܒܝܠ ܐܡܪ. ܗܐ ܐܢܐ ܕܗܡܪܬ ܗܠܝܢ ܦܘܬܝ ܡܪܝܫܐ. ܐܢܬ ܕܗܡܪܬ ܐܢܝܢ ܝܬܝܪ ܐܝܟ ܕܐܦܢܝܬ ܡܬܡܪܐ ܒܟܠܝܢ ܘܡܬܦܠܐ ܒܟܠܝܢ... ܕܠܐ ܐܡܪ ܗܐ ܝܬܝܪ ܠܬ̈ܟܠܐ ܘܐܦ ܠܐܠܗܐ. ܘܗܐ ܐܦ ܠ ܡܦܪܢ ܐܢܬ. ܐܝܟ ܕܐܬܡܘܣ ܟܠܝܢ ܡܘܬܐ ܡܠܠܬܐ. ܫܠܐ ܗܕܐ ܕܝܢ ܕܥܒܪ ܐܢܬ ܡܬܠܥܒ ܐܢܐ ܗܘ ܕܗܘܒ ܥܕܪ ܡܪܝܐ ܘܦܬܝܐ ܐܝܬܝܢ ܒܝ... ܫܪܒܝܠ ܐܡܪ. ܡܕܡ ܐܢܬ ܗܘ ܕܐܡܪܬ ܠܝ ܕܦܠܚܬ ܗܝܟܠܬܐ ܕܫܠܡ ܓܒܪܐ ܕܠܘܬܗ ܗܘ ܟܠܢܫ ܕܠܘܬܗ ܗܘܬ ܡܫܘܐ ܓܝܪ..

ܡܫ̈ܝܢ ܒܗܘ ܕܐܬܚܙܝ. ܘܐܠܐ ܢܦܩܬ ܗܘܬ ܠܗ ܒܬܪ̈ܥܐ
ܘܢܦܠܬ ܗܘܐ ܠܗ ܘܐܦ ܡܢ ܥܬ̈ܪܐ ܐܚܪ̈ܢܐ. ܚܦܪ ܗܘ̣ܐ
ܘܐܫܬܘܬܗ، ܘܟܕ ܚܙܐ ܗܘܐ ܕܢܝܐ ܕܐܬܥܬܬܗ ܗܘ̣ܐ ܠܗ ܘܠܐ
ܡܥܒܕ ܗܘ̣ܐ ܕܬܘܒ ܢܦܠܐ ܠܗ ܦܬܓܡܐ. ܐܬܗܡܝ ܗܘ̣ܐ
ܡܢܗ ܡܠܟ ܚܕ̇ ܒܟܐܠܐ ܒܗ ܢܦܫܗ. ... ܫܒܘܪ ܐܡܪ. ܟܠ
ܡܟܢܐ ܢܦܩܬ ܟܠ ܐܦ ܗܢܐ ܒܙܢܐ ܕܒܣܪܐ. ܘܟܠܠܬܝ ܡܢ
ܘܬܪܥܐ ܕܡܕܝܢܬܐ ... ܡܒܗܘܢܐ ܐܡܪ. ܠܐ ܡܫܡܫ
ܫܡܥܬ ܟܠܢ ܘܐܫܡܥܬ ܡܠܟ. ܫܡܥܢ ܗܘ ܒܪ ܥܠܝܢ ܡܠܟ.
ܘܐܠܐ ܡܢܐ ܗܘܬ ܠܒܪ ܡܢ ܢܦܫܐ ܕܡ̈ܠܟܐ ܡܢܗ ܗܘܬ
ܕܐܫܬܘܩܬ ܡܢ. ܐܝܟ ܕܐܬܬ ܐܬܦܢܝ ܡܢܝ ܒܙܢܐ ܕܠܘܬ
ܐ̈ܠܗܐ. ܕܫܠܬܝ ܒܪ ܠܐ̈ܠܗܐ ܫܠܬ. ܘܐܦ ܐܢܐ ܡܦܪܥܢܟ
ܘܐܫܬܘܝܬ ܡܢ ܗܡܢܐ. ܐܝܟ ܒܪܢܐ ܕܐܦܐ ܗܡܢܐ. ܘܦܩܕ
ܗܘܐ ܕܢܬܐ ܘܢܦܠܬ ܗܘܬ ܘܠܐ ܡܢ ܫܠܛܐ ܒܟ̈ܦܘܗܝ، ܒܙܢܐ
ܕܒܣܪܐ. ܘܐܬܩܡ ܗܘܐ. ܘܬܡ ܗܘ̣ܐ ܐܦܝܣܩܘ ܕܢܬܠ ܗܘ̣ܐ
ܟܠܗ̇، ܟܠܝܠܬ. ܘܗܘܟ ܡܢ ܫܠܝܐ ܐܬܦܫܬܬ ܗܘܬ ܘܠܐ.
ܘܡܟܐ ܗܘ̣ܐ ܕܢܐ ܘܐܡܪ. ܫܒܘܪ ܗܢܐ ܕܐܬܗܘܝ، ܗܘ̣ܐ
ܡܢ ܩܕܡ ܒܡܕܝܢܬܐ ܕܐ̈ܠܗܐ ܘܡܦܝܢ ܒܬܪ ܡܡܠܠܐ ܒܐ̈ܠܗܐ
ܘܦܓܥܐ ܕܒܪܘܦܫܢܐ ܐܢܐ. ܘܠܐ ܚܕ ܡܢ ܐ̈ܠܗܐ ܘܢܚ.
ܘܐܦ ܡܢ ܦ̈ܠܓܐ ܠܐ ܕܚܠ ܡܢ ܦܘܕܩܢܘܗܝ. ܘܐܡܪܬ ܠܗ
ܕܢܟܢ ܠܐ̈ܠܗܐ ܒܢܝܗ ܡܕܒܚܐ ܘܠܐ ܕܒܚ. ܘܟܬܒ ܐܢܘܢ
ܐܦ ܡܟܬܒ. ܣܦܪ ܘܣܡܗ ܕܢܬܠܐ ܕܗܠܟ ܒܬܪ ܘܐܦܠܐ
ܐܢ ܡܥܒܕ ܙܕܩ ܕܢܗܘܘܢ ܟܠܗܘܢ ܢܗܪ̈ܐ. ܘܠܐ ܙܕܩ ܕܢܗܘܐ
ܥܒܕܐ ܕܩܘܪ̈ܗܘܢ. ܟܠ ܕܐܡܘܠ ܢܬܦܘܫܘܢ. ܦܩܕܬ ܕܐܝܟ
ܕܡܢ ܢܦܫܐ ܕܡ̈ܠܟܐ. ܬܘܒ ܒܪܬܐ ܒܦܘܡܗ ܕܡܢܒܪܝܐ
ܐܝܟ ܕܦܩܕ ܡܠܟܐ. ܘܢܦܩ ܠܒܪ ܡܢ ܡܕܝܢܬܐ ܕܡ̈ܠܟܐ
ܡܦܪܣܟܢܬ ܐܝܟ ܕܐܡܪ ܠܡܪܝܢ ܕܡܕܝܢܬܐ ܘܠܐ̈ܠܗܐ
ܕܫܠܛܢ ܟܠܢ. ܦܩܕܬ ܕܢܬܦܪܫ ܒܡܒܘܥܐ ܕܡܝܐ. ܘܡܟܐ

ܡܢܗܘܢ ܘܡܢܗܘܢ، ܐܠܗܝܟ ܘܦܬܟܪܐ: ܕܗܐ ܫܒܩܬ ܘܡܣܬܠܩܬ.
ܘܟܠܗܝܢ ܒܢܝܐ ܘܡܘܬܐ ܡܢ ܐܝܠܝܢ ܕܦܠܚܝܢ ܗܘܘ ܠܗܘܢ
ܡܢ ܡܕܡ ... ܕܢܬܐ ܐܡܪ. ܐܡܝܢܐ ܒܐܠܗܐ ܚܕ ܐܝܬ
ܘܒܡܫܝܚܐ ܡܗܕܐ ܐܝܬ ܗܘ ܕܐܬܬܠܝ، ܥܠ ܨܠܝܒܐ... ܫܪܒܝܠ
ܐܡܪ. ܒܩܘܒܪܗܘܢ ܗ̈ܢܐ ܕܦܪܘܛܠܝܢܐ ܗܘܐ ܩܘܪܒܐ ܕܡܫܝܚܐ.
ܕܟܗ ܗܘ ܗܘܐ ܦܘܪܢܐ. ܕܢܫܐ ܠܟܠܗܘܢ ܦܬܓܡܘܗܝ. ܘܟܗ
ܗܘ ܗܘ ܚܕܢܐ ܢܗܝܪܬܐ. ܕܠܐ ܗܘܘ ܦܬܓܡ ܠܒܪܢܫܐ ܟܡ
ܒܪܢܐ... ...

ܗܓܡܘܢܐ ܐܡܪ. ܫܡܥܘܗܝ ܕܒܪܢܫܐ ܢܬܦܪ ܒܣܘ
ܐܢܫܝܢ ܘܡܩܕܡܐ ܡܢ ܐܝܕܝܟ ܠܐ̈ܠܗܐ ܢܬܦܪܥܘܢ... ܫܪܒܝܠ
ܐܡܪ ܠܐ ܡܚܣܢܝܢ ܐܝܠܝܢ ܕܦܪܝܩ ܒܪܘܡܐ ܕܬܘܒ ܢܫܬܘܢ
ܘܢܠܒܫܘܢ ܠܬܘܒܪܐ ܚܕܬܐ ܕܦܘܠܚܢܐ. ܒܬܪܐ ܗܟܝܠ ܠܒܪܢܫܐ
ܠܐ ܡܚܣܢܐ ܦܬܓܡܐ. ܡܛܠ ܕܐܦ ܗܘ ܦܬܓܡܐ ܗܘ ܕܟܡ
ܕܟܒܪܗ ܘܢܫܬܟܚ ܟܡ ܒܟܒܪܗ ܝܗܒܐ ܗܘ ܠܟܒܪܗ. ܐܝܟ
ܕܐܡܪܬ ܘܐܡܪܬ ○ ܗܓܡܘܢܐ ܐܡܪ ܫܡܥ ܒܬܪܟܝܢ ܕܐܠܗܝܟ
ܗܢܘܢ. ܘܟܕ ܦܘܩܕܢܐ ܕܡܠܟܐ ܕܠܐ ܬܫܡܥ ܡܢ ܢܦܫܟ
ܕܡܠܟܐ... ܘܫܪܒܝܠ ܐܡܪ ܘܗܕܐ ܗܝ، ܒܐܝܢܬܐ ܕܡܠܟܐ
ܕܫܬܪ ܐܝܬ ܒܗܘܢ ܕܢܟܒܘܢ ܢܦܫܗ ܕܐܠܗܐ ܘܢܬܒܪ
ܢܦܫܗܘܢ... ܗܓܡܘܢܐ ܐܡܪ ܬܢܝܢܐ ܕܟܬܒܐ ܕܗܝܡܢܬ
ܒܗܘܢ ܗܢܘܢ ܕܬܢܝܬ ܡܛܠܗܘܢ. ܗܘܢ ܐܡܛܝܗܘܢ ܒܐܘܪܝܢܐ
ܗܠܝܢ. ܐܠܐ ܟܪ ܦܩܕ ܒܟܬܒܐ ܠܐ̈ܠܗܐ ܦܬܓܡܐ ܗܟܢܐ ܐܡܪܝܢ
ܐܝܟ ܡܕܡܢܐ ܐܝܟ ܒܡܕܝܢܬܐ ܕܐܠܗܐ... ܫܪܒܝܠ ܐܡܪ
ܠܐܢܫܝܢ ܒܦܘܪܐ ܡܣܬܟܪܝܢ ܗܠܝܢ. ܐܝܟ ܗܘ ܕܐܘܠܝܢܐ
ܐܡܝܢ. ܠܐܢܫܐ ܟܪ ܫܪܝܪܐ ܐܘܠܝܢܐ ܡܗܝܡܢܘܬܐ ܡܫܝܚܝܐ.
ܘܟܠܗ ܐܦ ܒܗܘܢ ܘܡܢܗ ܕܒܗܘܢ ܦܪܝܐ ܕܡܗܝܡܢܘܬܐ...
ܗܓܡܘܢܐ ܐܡܪ ܬܠܐܘܗܝ: ܘܣܪܩܘܗܝ، ܥܠ ܦܬܓܡܘܗܝ، ܘܡܫܚܐ.
ܘܫܡܥܬܗ ܕܕܢܚܐ ܕܠܘܬ ܦܬܓܡܐ. ܘܐܬܚܒܠ ܗܘܘ ܕܐܦ

ܘܬܫܥܝܬܐ ܕܙ̈ܟܘܬܗ ܕܡܫܡܫܢ ܗܘܐ ܘܡܫܡܫ ܘܕܡܐ ܕܣܗ̈ܕܐ
ܕܐ̈ܒܗܘܗܝ ܘܕܒ̈ܢܘܗܝ ܘܕܫܠ̈ܝܚܘܗܝ ܘܕܬ̈ܠܡܝܕܘܗܝ ܕܕܪܐ ܗܘܐ ܘܢܣܒܬ.
ܐܝܬܝܗ ܗܘܬ ܡܫܝ̈ܚܐ ܕܝܠܕܐ ܘܐܪܚܡܝܢܘܗܝ، ܠܗ ܒܡܫܟܢܐ
ܕܡܫܡܫܐ. ܘܣܝܡ ܟܠܗܝ ܒܪܡܫܐ ܕܟܠܠܐ ܗܘܐ ܒܝ̈ܡܫܐ ܕܒܬ̈ܚܘܡܘܗܝ
ܡܢ ܐܠܦܝ̈ܢܐ. ܘܐܬܡܢܝܘ ܗܘܘ ܟܠܗܘܢ ܡܫܝܪܐ ܕܩܪ̈ܝܬܐ.
ܘܫܪܝܘ ܗܘܘ ܢܫܕܪܘܢ ܠܗ. ܘܟܕ ܩܪܒ ܗܘܐ ܕܢܣܒܬ ܕܡܠܟܐ
ܗܘܐ ܠܗ ܡܫܘܪܐ ܚܕ ܦܘܡܗ. ܡܫܐܠܘܗܝ ܗܘܘ ܒܫܘܦܐ
ܘܒܟܠܗܘܢ، ܦܪܨܐ ܕܝ ܐܬܚܝ ܗܘܐ ܒܗ ܒܬܒܝܠ ܒܡܫܟܠܝܐ. ܘܡܪܬܗ
ܗܘܬ ܕܝܢ ܚܕܐ ܘܦܪܘܬ ܗܘܬ ܒܫܡܗ ܘܡܠܟܬ ܗܘܬ ܠܕܡܗ.
ܘܐܡܪܬ ܠܗ ܕܬܫܠܚ ܪܘܚ ܒܟ ܪܘܚܐ. ܦܢ ܡܫܝܚܐ ܕܒܚܝܠܗ
ܘܡܬܟܢܫ ܒܗ. ܘܪܗܛܘ ܗܘܘ ܫܪ̈ܝܪܐ ܕܡܫܝܚܝܘܬܐ. ܘܟܠܗ ܗܘܐ
ܘܐܘܕܝܘܗܝ. ܠܒܢܝܐ ܐܝܟ ܕܐܡܪ ܗܘܐ ܫܪܒܝܠ ܒܟܠܗܬܗ.
ܘܕܐܡܒܝܢܐ ܡܟܠܬ ܫܡܗ ܠܕܡܗ. ܘܟܕ ܗܘܐ ܠܗܘܢ ܕܢܗܐ
ܕܢܬܦܫܩ ܗܘܘ ܘܢܐܡܪܘܢ ܠܦܝܠܘܣܘܦܐ ܕܒܕܘܟܬܐ ܕܡܟܠܬ
ܠܕܡܗ ܕܐܝܣܘܥ ܬܡܟܠ ܐܦ ܗܝ ܡܛܘܠ ܒܝܫܐ ܕܪܒܘܬܐ.
ܘܠܟܡܘܬܗ ܗܘܘ ܦܝܠܘܣܘܦܐ ܘܟܠ ܚܕ ܚܕ ܡܢܗܘܢ ܠܡܟܠܗ
ܡܫܬܚܠܦ ܗܘܐ ܒܗ. ܘܟܕ ܚܙܝܢܐ ܗܘܬ ܠܕܡܗ ܕܐܝܣܘܥ.
ܢܦܫܗ ܡܢܗ ܦܪܫܬ ܗܘܬ. ܘܫܠܛܘܗܝ ܕܡܢܗ ܒܡ ܕܠܗ ܘܟܕ
ܟܠ ܗܘܘ ܦܝܠܘܣܘܦܐ ܠܡܫܝܚܘܬܐ. ܪܗܛܘ ܐܢܫܐ ܘܐܢܫܐ
ܒܠܒܗܘܢ. ܘܚܒܪܘ ܗܘܘ ܫܪܒܐ ܕܬܡܝܗ̈ܘܬܗ ܘܗܘܦܟܐ ܗܘܘ ܐܝܟ
ܒܬܪ ܡܫܘܪܐ ܕܐܒܗܘܗܝ ܕܒܫܠܡܐ ܐܦܝܣܩܘܦܐ ܒܡܫܝܚܘܬܐ
ܕܐܬܠܠ ܒܗܘܢ ܕܬܘܒܬܐ. ܒܬܪܗ ܗܘܦܘ̈ܡܢܛܐ ܗܠܝܢ
ܒܐܪܥܐ ܐܝܟ ܡܫܝܚܐ ܘܐܬܠܠܘ ܐܦܝܣܩܘܦܐ. ܘܡܢ
ܐܝܟ ܒܬܪ ܐܪܒܥܐ ܕܡܫܝܚܘܬܐ ܐܡܪ ܕܒܪܢܫܐ ܕܐܬ̈ܠܝܐ
ܡܢܗܘܢ.. ܗܘܐ ܕܝܢ ܒܪܡܫܐ ܐܦܝܣܩܘܦܐ ܬܠܡܝܕܗ ܗܘܐ
ܠܫܪܒܝܠ ܒܡܕܝܢܐ. ܐܬܬܝܗܝ ܗܘܐ ܕܝܢ ܒܝܘܡܬܐ ܒܝܘܡܐ
ܐܦܝܣܩܘܦܐ ܕܪܗܘܡܐ ܗܘ ܕܒܢܝܗܘܢ، ܒܫܢܬ ܗܘܬ ܒܗܠܝܢ

ܕܪܡܝ ܕܢܚܘܬ ܗܕܝܢ ܢܬܬܠ ܪܫܗ. ܒܣܘܦܐ ܕܦܠܚܘܬܐ. ܘܟܕ ܒܥܒܕܐ ܢܦܠܬ ܒܪܘܬܐ ܒܣܘܟܠܗ ܡܢ ܥܠܝܐ. ܘܫܠܡܗ، ܡܦܠܘܬܐ. ܘܒܬܟܠܗ، ܕܢܒܥ ܡܣܪܗܒܐܝܬ ܡܬܪܗܒܝܢ ܗܘܘ ܠܗ. ܘܠܒܪ ܡܢ ܡܕܝܢܬܐ ܡܥܡܪ ܗܘܐ ܠܗ ܒܪ ܪܗܛܐ ܗܘܬ ܐܢܫܬܐ ܠܒܪܝܗ. ܘܡܫܟܢܐ ܗܘܬ ܘܝܪܬܐ ܗܘܬ ܕܢܚܫ ܒܟܠ ܝܘܡ ܘܬܡܢܝܢ ܗܘܘ ܕܠܐ ܚܙ ܗܘܐ ܒܐܘܠܨܢܗ. ܒ̈ܝܬܗ، ܒܪ ܕܩܝܡ ܗܘ، ܗܢܘܢ ܗܘ، ܒܠ ܚܕܘܬܐ ܕܐܒܘܗ. ܘܒܪ ܡܠܟܘ ܗܘܘ ܡܦܠܘ̈ܬܐ ܠܕܘܟܬܐ ܗܝ ܕܡܥܒܠ ܗܘܐ ܒܗ ܡܥܡܪ ܒܪܢܫܐ ܕܡܕܘܬܐ. ܐܡܬܝ ܗܘܘ ܒܥܡܗܘܢ ܩܕܝܫ ܡܕܝܢܬܐ ܕܢܨܝܒܝܢ ܟܠ ܐܝܟ ܕܩܕܡ ܗܘܐ ܕܢܐܐ ܒܒܝܬ ܗܘܘ. ܘܕܢܫܒܚܘܢ ܡܢܐ ܐܡܪ ܗܘܐ ܥܒܕܠ ܒܒܢܝܐ ܗܘ ܐܝܟ ܕܢܘܕܘܢ ܗܘܘ ܠܕܢܐ ܕܐܬܪܐ. ܘܡܚܒ ܗܘܘ ܠܗ ܣܓܝܐܐ ܕܢܫܬܐ ܐܝܟ ܒܪܢܐ ܕܢܬܩܝܡ ܡܠܟܘܬܐ. ܘܐܡܪ ܠܗܘܢ ܕܠܐ ܥܒܕܬ ܐܢܫ. ܡܛܠ ܕܝܕܥܐ ܐܢܐ ܗܘ ܕܐܪܥܐ ܒܢܘܪܐ ܕܢܗܝܡ ܐܢܘܢ ܠܝ. ܘܣܘܦܐ ܕܡܒܒܪܝܢ ܐܢܘܢ ܒܠ ܡܕܝ. ܐܠܐ ܫܠܡ ܗܢܐ ܣܓܝܐ ܕܠܐ ܡܒܕܪ ܠܝ. ܗܒܘ ܠܝ ܡܠܟ ܒܢܝܐ ܕܐܝܟܢܐ ܒܪ ܣܒܝܢ ܐܢܘܢ. ܘܡܢ ܗܘܐ ܘܚܪ ܗܘܐ ܠܡܒܝܢܐ ܘܐܡܪ ܗܘܐ ܠܗ ܘܐܡܪ. ܥܒܘܕ ܠܝ ܡܥܝܢܐ ܒܠ ܕܢܦܠܬ ܠܝ ܘܒܠ ܕܐܬܒܥܬܟ ܒܪܥܝܢܐ ܦܬܝܟܐ ܕܬܒܥܬܐ ܚ̈ܝܠܬܐ. ܘܫܡܘ ܒܠ ܫܢܝ. ܘܩܪܒ ܡܢ ܕܢܐ ܕܒܬܪ ܘܫܘܢ ܐܝܟ ܕܢܗܘܐ ܠܣܡܘܟܐ. ܘܡܠܝܢ ܐܝܟ ܬܘܒܥܐ ܕܩܝܡ ܘܐܬܦܢܝܘ ܒܐܕܡܟ ܘܕܐܬܦܢܝܬ ܒܐܕܡܘܢ. ܘܕܒܠܬ ܒܢܒܥܘܬܐ ܥܬܝܡ ܠܒܪܡܟ. ܫܠܡ ܕܢܐ ܦܠܓ ܡܢ ܒܐܢܘܬܐ. ܡܛܠ ܕܒܠܟ ܬܠܢܐ ܗܘ ܢܫܡ ܡܦܠܘܬ، ܒܣܘܡܟܐ ܕܡܟܐܬܘܟ. ܘܒܪ ܗܠܝܢ ܥܒܕܗܘ ܗܘܘ ܥܕܢܪܐ ܕܡܕܝܢܬܐ. ܐܬܢܨܚܘ ܗܘܘ ܒܠ ܡܦܠܘܬܐ ܒܠ ܕܥܒܕܗܘܢ، ܗܘܘ ܕܢܦܠܐ. ܘܒܪ ܢܦܩ ܗܘ، ܗܟܢܐ ܕܒܝܬ ܗܘ، ܒܬܪ ܚܒܝܒܗ، ܘܡܬܢܝܚ ܗܘ، ܬܠܡܝܕ ܡܢ ܒܬ ܗܘܡܐ. ܘܡܢ ܡܕܝܢܬܐ ܕܟܐܡܗ،

ܫܒܝܚܐ. ܘܡܫܡܫܝܢ ܐܢܫܝܢ ܒܫܘܒܚ ܡܠܟܐ ܒܪܗ ܕܐܠܗܐ
ܗܘ ܕܐܬܐ ܘܒܬܪ ܕܗܘܒ ܢܬܬܐ ܘܐܠܘ ܐܢܬ ܗܘܝܐ ܡܠܟܘܬܐ
ܐܚܪܢܐ ܒܪܘܡܐ ܘܒܠܗܘܢ ܐܬܠܝܐ. ܐܦ. ܗܠܝܢ ܒܟܬܪ ܗܘܘ
ܒܡܠܟܘܬܗܘܢ ܐܝܟ ܕܟܬܒ ܗܘܘ ܣܦܪܐ ܘܡܫܒܚܬܐ ܕܥܠܡܐ
ܕܡܬܒܪܢܐ ܗܘܬ ܒܟܢܘܫܬܐ ܡܕܒܪ ܗܘܘ ܀

ܫܠܡܬ ܗܘܦܡܢܝܛܐ ܕܥܪܒܠ ܡܟܕܢܐ ܀

.o:o. .o:o. .o:o. .o:o. .o:o. .o:o.

ܬܘܒ ܫܘܕܥܬܐ ܕܒܪ ܫܡܥܐ ܐܦܝܣܩܘܦܐ ܕܐܘܪܡܝ ܡܕܢܚܐ ܡܒܪܟܬܐ.

ܒܫܢܬ ܐܪܒܥܡܐܐ ܘܐܬܚܡܫܝܢ ܕܡܠܟܘܬܐ ܕܝܘܢܝܐ:
ܘܐܬܬܗ ܥܢܬ ܫܡܥܘܢܝܐ ܕܡܠܟܘܬܗ ܕܐܘܦܪܛܪ ܡܪ
ܦܪܝܣܘ ܩܝܪ. ܒܗܘܦܢܐ ܕܒܘܟܪܘܗ ܘܕܘܪܠܝܘܣ ܒܐܪܝܢ
ܐܬܠܬ: ܒܗܘܢ ܫܡܥܬܐ ܒܗ: ܒܬܪ ܗܘܡܐ ܕܐܬܒܥ ܗܘܐ
ܠܗܘܫܥ ܕܢܝܐ ܕܐܬܪܐ ܠܥܪܒܠ ܒܡܕܝܢܐ: ܒܕ ܢܦܩ ܗܘܐ ܗܘ
ܕܢܝܐ ܒܕܘܦܛܪܝܢ ܕܝܠܗ: ܒܠܘ ܗܘܘ ܡܕܡܘܗܝ. ܫܪܝܪܐ
ܕܡܕܝܢܬܐ ܘܐܬܟܪܝܢ ܠܗ. ܕܡܬܕܒܪܝܢ ܡܕܡ ܪܒܘܬܟ: ܒܠ ܒܪ
ܫܡܥܐ ܡܕܒܪܢܐ ܕܒܪܘܦܛܐ ܕܗܘ ܩܠܘ ܗܘܐ ܟܕ ܥܪܒܠ
ܒܡܕܝܢܐ: ܒܕ ܡܩܝܡ ܗܘܐ ܘܡܫܡܫ ܗܘܐ ܡܕܡ ܐܠܗܐ ܡܫܝܚܐ.
ܘܫܕܪ ܗܘܐ ܘܦܢܝܗ ܗܘܐ ܠܘܬܗ ܒܫܐܠܬ: ܘܡܠܠ ܗܘܐ
ܒܫܡܗ ܡܢ ܒܬܒܥܐ: ܕܦܩܕܐ ܒܫܡܗ ܒܟܬܒܐ ܕܒܥܠ ܒܥܠܕܒܒܘܗܝ.
ܘܬܒܥܐ ܗܘܐ ܠܗ ܡܫܡܠܝܘܬܗܘܢ ܕܒܪܘܦܛܐ: ܘܐܡܪ ܗܘܐ
ܠܗ. ܕܠܐ ܙܕܩ ܠܝ ܕܐܬܦܓܪ ܠܬܠܡܝܕܐ ܡܣܟܢܐ. ܐܠܐ ܐܢ

ܐܢܫܘܬܐ ܕܪܗܘܡܝܐ. ܘܟܕ ܗܘܘ ܠܗܦܪܟܐ ܕܡܕܝܢܬܗܘܢ
ܘܐܡܪܝܢ ܠܗ. ܕܐܟ̈ܣܢܝܐ ܘܬܪ̈ܐ ܐܝܬ ܒܗ̇ ܒܡܕܝܢܬܢ ܘܗܢܘܢ
ܒܒܬܝܢ ܒܚܢܘܬܐ ܘܒܫܘܩܐ ܕܠܡܒܬܘ. ܐܠܐ ܒܪ ܒܒܬܝ ܚܕ ܡܢܗܘܢ
ܕܬܦܩܘܕ ܢܦܘܩ ܡܢ ܡܕܝܢܬܐ. ܘܟܕ ܦܩܕ ܗܘܐ ܕܢܦܩܘܢ ܡܢ
ܡܕܝܢܬܐ. ܐܬܒܥܝܘ ܗܘܘ ܗܢܘܢ ܐܟ̈ܣܢܝܐ ܘܐܡܪܝܢ ܠܗ
ܠܗܦܪܟܐ ܒܪ ܒܒܬܝ ܚܕ ܡܢܗܘܢ ܡܪܝ. ܦܩܘܕ ܕܐܦ ܠܟܪ̈ܝܗܐ
ܕܬܫܬܡ ܒܗܢ ܢܦܫܗ. ܘܦܩܕ ܗܘܐ ܠܗܘܢ ܕܢܗܘܘܢ ܗܘܘ
ܟܪ̈ܝܗܘܢ ܕܬܫܬܐ ܘܢܦܩܘܢ ܘܐܬܒܥܝܘ ܗܘܘ ܒܠܗܘܢ
ܐܟ̈ܣܢܝܐ ܠܡܫܩܠ ܟܪ̈ܝܗܘܗܝ ܕܒܡܕܝܢܬܐ ܟܐܦܐ ܘܕܦܠܛܘܗ
ܥ̈ܠܝܡܐ ܘܐܡܪܝܢ ܠܗܘܢ ܟܕ ܪܗܘܡܝܐ ܠܐ ܡܫܟܚܝܢ ܐܢܫܝܢ
ܠܗܘܢ ܟܪ̈ܝܗܘܗܝ ܕܥ̈ܠܝܡܐ. ܘܐܡܪܝܢ ܠܗܘܢ ܗܢܘܢ
ܐܟ̈ܣܢܝܐ. ܕܢܠܒܘ ܘܢܗܘܘ ܕܟܪ̈ܝܗܘܢ ܕܡܬܦܪܫܐ ܒܟܐܦܐ ܡܢ
ܒܝܬ ܡܕܝܢܬܐ ܗܘ ܕܓܠܝܠܐ. ܘܦܠܛܘܗ ܥ̈ܠܝܡܐ ܡܢ ܬܪ̈ܥܘܗܝ ܗܘ
ܡܕܝܢܬܐ ܕܫܠܝܚܐ. ܘܟܕ ܫܡܥ ܟܠ ܪܗܘܡܝܐ ܕܡܟܝܢܐ ܗܘ
ܡܫܬܘܬܐ ܗܕܐ. ܐܝܟ ܗܘ ܕܒܟܘܠ ܐܝܟܢ ܘܟܕ ܩܒܠܘ ܐܝܟܢ
ܘܫܡܥ ܗܘܐ ܡܢ ܕܬ̈ܫܡܫܬܗܘܢ ܒܗ ܒܫܒܬܐ ܗܕܐ ܗܕܐ ܘܟܬܒܐ
ܪܟܐ. ܘܡܠܟ ܗܘܐ ܡܕܝܢܬܐ ܕܡܕܝܢܬܐ ܠܡܟܠ. ܘܦܪܫܐ ܗܘܬ
ܠܡܬܦܩܕܘ. ܘܟܕ ܚܙܐ ܗܘܐ ܟܠ ܪܗܘܡܝܐ. ܗܦܟܘ ܟܠܗ ܡܢ
ܐܟ̈ܣܢܝܐ ܕܢܦܩܘܢ ܗܘܐ ܒܡܕܝܢܬܗܘܢ ܘܕܬܫܡܫܘܢ ܗܘܘ
ܟܪ̈ܝܗܐ ܒܬܫ̈ܡܫܬܗܘܢ. ܘܟܕ ܚܙܝܬ ܗܘܐ ܟܪ̈ܝܗܐ ܕܥ̈ܠܝܡܐ
ܠܬܫ̈ܡܫܬܗܘܢ ܗܕܐ ܥܠܬܐ. ܘܫܡܥ ܗܘܐ ܪ̈ܚܡܐ ܘܡܠܟ ܗܘ
ܪ̈ܘܚܐ ܘܢܛܪܬ ܗܘܬ ܐܝܟ ܘܐܬܦܢܝܬ ܗܘܬ ܠܘܬܗ ܡܕܝܢܬܐ
ܗܝ. ܘܟܕ ܚܙܐ ܡܫܘܕܥܐ ܘܢܦܩܐ. ܪ̈ܚܡܘ ܘܩܒܠܘ ܗܘܘ ܗܢܘܢ
ܟܠ ܪ̈ܚܡܘܗܝ ܕܒܝܬܗܘܢ ܐܦܝܣܩܘܦܐ ܕܡܕܝܢܬܗܘܢ ܒܪ ܡܟܝܢ
ܗܘܐ ܡܫܘܕܥܐ ܕܡܟܝܢ ܐܢܫܝܢ ܒܡܫܝܚܐ ܕܢܡܫܚ ܒܪܬ ܗܘ
ܕܐܠܗܐ ܚܝܐ. ܗܘ ܕܡܠܠܗܘܢ ܢܦܫܐ ܒܐܪ̈ܙܘܗܝ ܘܡܟܐ ܐܦ
ܚܠܦܐ ܘܐܡܪܝܢ ܠܗ ܕܒܥܝܢ ܒܪ̈ܚܡܐ ܘܩ̈ܛܝܢܐ ܕܠܝܬ ܒܗܘܢ

ܬܫܡܫܬܐ ܕܐܢ̈ܫܐ ܕܡܟܝܢ ܗܘܘ: ܕܒܢ ܒܝܘܡܬܐ ܡܢܬܗܝܢ. ܘܟܕ
ܢܦܩܘ ܗܘܘ ܕܢܬܒܥܘܢ ܐܢܘܢ ܠܐܢ̈ܫܐ ܗܠܝܢ: ܘܒܥܘ ܗܘܘ
ܠܗܘܢ ܐܝܠܝܢ ܕܡܟܝܢ ܗܘܘ ܡܢܗܘܢ: ܘܠܐ ܡܫܟܚܝܢ ܗܘܘ
ܠܡܫܟܚ ܐܢܘܢ ܠܬܫܡܫܬܗܘܢ. ܕܒܥܘ ܗܘܘ ܠܗܘܢ.
ܕܡܛܠ ܕܡܢ ܟܠ ܟܬܒܝܢ ܐܬܝܐ ܗܘܬ ܠܗܘܢ: ܕܡܛܠܬܗ ܗܘܘ
ܡܛܠ ܡܫܟܚܐ ܠܗ ܒܪܘܡܝܐ. ܘܟܕ ܒܥܐ ܗܘܐ ܠܗ ܢܘܟܪܝܐ
ܕܐܢܫܘܬܐ. ܦܩܕ ܗܘܘ ܥܒ̈ܕܐ ܕܡܕܝܢܬܐ. ܘܟܠܗ ܗܘܘ ܠܗܘܢ
ܠܗܘܬ ܕܢܐܠܐ ܘܐܫܬܟܚ ܠܗ. ܠܐ ܡܫܟܚܝܢ ܕܢܬܘܒ ܐܢܘܢ
ܠܬܫܡܫܬܐ ܕܐܢ̈ܫܐ ܕܡܟܝܢ ܠܟܢ. ܡܛܠ ܕܗܘ ܟܬܒܝܢ ܐܢܘܢ ܕܠܐ
ܡܫܟܚܐ ܀ ܘܦܩܕ ܗܘܐ ܕܢܐܠܐ ܕܢܗܘܐ ܗܘܐ ܒܪܘܡܝܐ. ܠܒܝܬ
ܐܣܝ̈ܐ. ܐܝܟ ܕܬܬܒܪܐ ܗܘܬ ܐܣܝܘܬܐ ܕܟܢܫܝܢܐ ܗܘܬ
ܓܘܫܡܗܘܢ. ܕܕܠܡܐ ܒܪܘܡܝܐ ܕܦܓܪܐ ܬܗܘܐ ܗܘܬ ܒܝܬܐ
ܡܕܝܢ ܒܡܕܝܢܬܐ. ܘܟܕ ܫܠܡ ܗܘܐ ܠܒܝܬ ܫܡܫܝ̈. ܦܩܕ
ܗܘܐ ܠܗܬܝܡܐ ܐܝܠܝܢ ܕܒܡ ܥܪ̈ܒܠ ܐܬܬܠܟܕܘ ܗܘܘ. ܘܡܢ ܒܬܪ
ܕܗܘܐ ܗܘܐ ܡܫܡܫܬܐ ܦܓܪܢܝܬܐ: ܡܢ ܗܘܐ ܕܢܐܠܐ ܒܪܘܡܝܐ
ܘܢܣܒ ܠܐܝܣܛܪܛܝܓ ܕܠܗ. ܐܝܟ ܕܢܫܡܫܗ ܗܘܐ ܠܒܪܘܡܝܐ.
ܘܦܩܕ ܗܘܐ ܕܢܐܠܐ ܘܢܬܪܡܐ ܡܢ ܒܝܬ ܐܣܝ̈ܐ: ܘܟܠ ܗܘܐ
ܘܡܢ ܕܢܦܩܘܢ. ܠܚܡܐ ܐܬܝܢ. ܗܘܐ ܡܬܐ ܡܢ ܪܒܘܬܝ.
ܕܢܐܠܐ ܐܡܪܝ. ܐܝܬ ܗܘ ܒܪܘܡܝܐ ܕܟܠܢ ܐܝܬ ܦܩܘܕܐ
ܘܡܕܒܪܢܐ ܠܟܠܗ ܕܒܪܝܬܐ: ܘܐܬܠܒܫܬܗ ܠܥܪ̈ܒܠ
ܒܡܪܝܐ ܪܒܐ ܕܐܠܗ̈ܐ ܕܗܟܢ ܗܘܐ ܠܗܘܢ: ܀ ܒܪܘܡܝܐ
ܐܡܪ. ܐܢܐ ܐܢܐ ܕܟܬܒܬ ܗܕܐ ܘܠܐ. ܦܩܕ ܐܢܐ ܘܡܬܠܒܫ
ܐܢܐ ܕܐܫܟܚܬ ܟܠ ܐܦ ܥܒ̈ܕܘܗܝ ܕܗܘܝܐ ܀ ܕܢܐܠܐ ܐܡܪ. ܐܡܪܢܐ
ܠܐ ܕܝܠܗ ܡܢ ܦܓܪܗ ܕܠܗܠܐ: ܕܟܕ ܬ̈ܠܡܝܕܐ ܦܩܕܝܢ ܕܢܒܥܘܢ ܚܠܦܝ:
ܐܝܬ ܠܥܪ̈ܒܠ ܒܡܕܝܢܬܐ ܕܒ ܡܫܝܢ ܗܘܐ ܘܡܕܒܪ ܗܘܐ ܠܬ̈ܠܡܝܕܘܗܝ:
ܘܦܩܕ ܗܘܐ ܠܗܘܢ ܬܫܡܫܬܐ: ܒܒܪܘܬܗ ܕܢܦܫܗ ܒܗܘ ܡܕܡ
ܕܬܫܒܘܚܬܐ ܗܘܐ ܒܗ: ܘܝܗܒܬܐ ܒܬܫܡܫܬܐ ܕܟܪܝܗܐ ܗܘܐ ܒܗ ܀

ܠܘܬ ܐܠܗܐ؛ ܘܠܒܪܗ ܝܫܘܥ ܡܫܝܚܐ: ܒܝܕܐ ܕܬܠܡܝܕܘܗܝ
ܗܘܐ: ܘܒܝܕܗ ܗܘܐ ܕܢܦܩܘܢ ܒܫܠܡܐ ܕܩܠܝܕ ܗܘܐ ܠܗܘܢ
ܡܢ ܐܕܝ. ܘܒܬܝܒܘܬܗ ܕܝܠܗ ܕܫܪܒܝܠ ܐܦ ܩ̈ܠܝܪܐ ܐܬܬܠܡܕܘ
ܗܘܘ ܘܢܦܩܘ ܠܒܪܝܬܐ. ܘܗܘܐ ܫܡܥܐ ܗܕܐ ܒܡܫܝܚܝܐ. ܘܐܦ
ܒܡܕܝܢܬܐ ܘܒܗ ܘܒܪ ܟܠܗ̇ ܘܫܦܘܗ̇؛ ܡ̈ܗܝܡܢܐ ܘܪ̈ܫܢܐ
ܕܡܕܝܢܬܐ: ܫܠܡܘ ܗܘܘ ܠܗ ܠܫܪܒܝܠ ܒܥܕܬܐ. ܘܣܡ ܐܝܟ
ܐܢܫ̈ܐ ܪ̈ܫܢܐ ܕܡܕܝܢܬܐ. ܡܫܒܚܝܢ ܩܕܡ ܢܡܘܣܟ. ܕܠܐ
ܢܦܠ ܡܢܗܘܢ ܟܢܫܐ ܐܝܟ ܬܫܒܘܚܬܐ؛ ܕܠܐ ܚܠܦܝܢ ܩܕܡ
ܢܡܘܣܟ؛ ܐܝܠܝܢ ܕܐܬܬܟܠܠ ܒܟܗܢܐ ܡܢ ܫܪܒܝܠ؛ ܡܢ
ܒܪܫܡܝܐ ܡܕܒܪܢܐ ܕܥܕܬܐ ܀ ܡܚܒܠ ܢܡܘܣܟ ܡܪܢܐ:
ܐܡܝܢܐ ܕܐܦ ܕܬܦܘܠ ܡܠܟܘܬܗ ܕܥܕܐ. ܘܟܕ ܫܡܥܗ ܕܐܚܕ
ܗܘܐ ܕܝܢܐ ܗܠܝܢ؛ ܫܕܪ ܗܘܐ ܐܝܬܝ ܠܪ̈ܫܢܐ ܕܡܕܝܢܬܐ:
ܘܡܢ ܩܕܡ ܐܘܦܝܢ ܒܥܡܗܘܢ؛ ܕܢܦܩܘܢ ܗܘܘ ܠܒܪܝܬܐ.
ܘܢܫܡܥܘܢ ܠܒܪܫܡܝܐ ܡܢ ܒܝܬܐ. ܘܒܪܘܪܗ ܗܘܘ ܘܫܠܡܘ
ܠܗܓܡܘܢܐ ܕܝܠܗ ܕܕܝܢܐ. ܘܫܠܡܘ ܗܘܘ ܒܝܕܗ ܠܗܓܡܘܢܐ
ܩ̈ܠܝܪܐ. ܟܕ ܐܚܝܕܝܢ ܗܘܘ. ܕܐܦ ܗܘ ܡܚܬܢ ܒܗܘܢ
ܕܪ̈ܗܘܡܝܐ. ܡܛܠ ܕܐܦ ܗܘ ܫܠܡܝܢ ܗܘܐ ܒܗܘܢ: ܒܬܘܠܡܕܐ
ܕܬܠܡܝܕܗ ܗܘܐ ܠܫܪܒܝܠ. ܘܟܠ ܡܕܡ ܕܡܛܠ ܗܘܐ ܒܗܘܢ.
ܘܒܟܠ ܡܕܡ ܕܦܓܥ ܗܘܐ ܡܢܗ. ܘܐܬܦܠܣܘ ܗܘܐ ܠܗ:
ܘܡܚܒ ܗܘܐ ܝܠܦ ܡܕܡ ܕܫܡܥ ܗܘܐ ܡܢܗ. ܘܟܠܗ ܗܘܘ
ܫ̈ܪܪܐ ܕܡܕܝܢܬܐ. ܘܐܡܪܘ ܗܘܘ ܠܗ ܠܕܝܢܐ. ܕܪ̈ܗܘܡܝܐ
ܕܦܩܕܬ ܢܡܘܣܟ؛ ܗܐ ܡܩܝܡ ܥܠ ܬܪܥܐ ܕܒܝܬ ܕܝܢܐ
ܕܫܠܝܛܝܢ. ܘܪ̈ܫܢܐ ܡܗܝܡܢܐ ܕܡܕܝܢܬܐ ܕܐܬܬܠܡܕܘ ܗܘܘ
ܡܢ ܫܪܒܝܠ: ܗܐ ܡܫܡܫܝܢ ܠܐܠܗܗ ܕܪ̈ܗܘܡܝܐ ܘܩܝܡܝܢ ܕܠܐ
ܡܢܬܗܝܢ ܒܥܡܗ ܕܪ̈ܗܘܡܝܐ. ܕܐܢܬܘܢ ܡܠܟܝܢ ܘܡܕܒܪܝܢ ܀ ܀
ܘܟܕ ܫܡܥ ܗܘܐ ܕܝܢܐ؛ ܗܠܝܢ ܕܐܡܪܘ ܗܘܘ ܠܗ ܫܪ̈ܪܐ
ܕܡܕܝܢܬܐ. ܦܩܕ ܗܘܐ ܠܗܘܢ ܕܢܩܘܡܘܢ ܗܘܘ. ܘܢܦܩܘܢ

ܕܐܝܠܝܢ ܕܟܦܪܝܢ ܒܗ. ܟܦܪ ܡܫܝܚܐ ܟܦܪܝܢ ܠܗܘܢ: ܐܘ ܐܝܟܢܐ
ܚܝܠܐ ܕܡܫܝܚܐ ܢܥܘܩ ܠܗܘܢ. ܐܘ ܠܡܫܡܫܢܝ ܕܠܝ ܡܠܟܐ
ܟܕܒܝܢ ܠܗܘܢ. ܠܗܢܘܢ ܕܥܒܕ ܕܬܗܘܐ ܒܠܒܗܘܢ ܕܢܬܟܬܘܢ:
ܐܝܟ ܗܘ ܕܟܬܒܬܗܘܢ ܡܢ ܟܢܫܘܬܗܘܢ. ܘܠܗ ܗܘ ܡܦܩܝܢ
ܚܠܦܝܗܘܢ ܀ ܕܝܢܐ ܐܡܪ. ܠܐ ܬܬܠܐ ܒܣܒܪܗ ܕܡܫܝܚܐ ܗܢܐ
ܕܐܣܬܩܦ ܕܝܠܟ. ܐܠܐ ܫܠܘ ܗܕܐ. ܐܫܬܡܥ ܠܦܘܩܕܢܐ
ܕܡܠܟܐ: ܕܦܩܕܘ ܠܡܕܒܚܘ ܠܐܠܗܐ ܀ ܒܪܫܡܝܐ ܐܡܪ. ܐܦ
ܗܘ ܠܐ ܢܛܪܬ ܣܒܪܗ ܕܡܫܝܚܐ ܡܕܝܚܐ: ܣܒܪܗ ܕܡܫܝܚܐ ܓܝܪ
ܗܘ ܘܡܚܝܐ ܠܟܠܗܘܢ ܕܡܫܝܚܐ. ܘܬܒܪ ܡܢ ܟܠ ܕܡܣܒܪ
ܐܝܬ ܠܦܘܩܕܢܝܗܘܢ ܕܡܠܟܐ. ܫܡܥܝܢ ܒܪܘܡܢܐ ܠܡܫܝܚܐ
ܡܠܟܐ ܕܡܠܟܐ ܀ ܕܝܢܐ ܐܡܪ. ܗܐ ܐܫܬܡܥܬ ܠܗ
ܠܡܫܝܚܟ. ܘܗܒܬ ܠܗ ܒܪܡܫܐ ܠܦܘܩܕܢܐ. ܡܛܠ ܐܫܬܡܥ
ܠܗܘܢ ܠܡܠܟܐ. ܘܗܒܘ ܠܐܠܗܐ ܕܦܩܕܝܢ ܠܗܘܢ ܡܠܟܐ ܀
ܒܪܫܡܝܐ ܐܡܪ. ܐܡܟܢܐ ܐܫܬܡܥܬ ܠܝ ܕܐܫܒܘܩ ܒܕܡܝܢ ܕܠܝܬ
ܐܢܐ ܒܗ: ܕܗܐ ܠܫܪܒܝܠ ܫܡܥܬ ܒܐܝܕܗ ܘܐܫܬܡܥܬ ܠܗ:
ܕܟܠ ܡܠܟܐ ܒܫܪܬ ܒܫܘܒܚܐ ܕܐܠܗ ܐܢܬ ܒܗ: ܘܐܫܬܕܪܬ
ܒܪܘܚܢܝܘܬܐ ܕܐܠܗ، ܗܘܝܬ ܠܗ. ܗܐ ܓܝܪ ܐܦ ܡܢ ܩܕܡ
ܕܐܬܟܠ ܡܕܡ ܒܝ. ܐܝܬ ܦܩܕܬ ܘܫܘܕܬ ܘܐܫܬܡܥܬ ܠܗ ܠܫܪܒܝܠ.
ܕܒܪܘܚܢܐ ܕܐܠܗܐ ܢܬܒܪܟܘܢ. ܠܐ ܒܥܝܢ ܒܗܘ ܡܕܡ
ܕܠܝܬ ܒܗ ܘܡܫܚܢ ܒܗ. ܦܘܐ ܗܘܝܠ ܓܝܪ ܡܠܬܐ ܕܐܫܬܡܥܬ
ܗܘܝܬ ܀ ܕܝܢܐ ܐܡܪ. ܢܬܬܟܢܫ ܒܪܫܡܝܐ. ܒܠ ܕܫܪܪ ܒܠ
ܦܘܩܕܢܐ ܕܡܠܟܐ: ܘܐܫܬܪܪ ܒܝܕܗ ܐܘܦ ܠܐܠܗܐ ܕܦܩܕܝܢ
ܗܘܘ ܠܗܘܢ ܠܡܠܟܐ. ܘܒܪ ܐܬܟܢܫ ܗܘܐ ܡܢ ܫܡܥܝܢ ܐܡܪ
ܠܗ. ܠܐ ܬܦܠܐ ܦܘܩܕܢܐ ܕܡܠܟܐ: ܘܬܬܟܪ ܠܐܠܗܝܗܘܢ
ܕܡܠܟܐ ܀ ܒܪܫܡܝܐ ܐܡܪ. ܗܟܢ ܒܥܘܪ ܡܕܡ ܕܝܢܐ:
ܘܐܦ ܕܡܠܟܐ ܕܫܡܥ ܠܝ ܒܩܠܝܢܐ. ܘܠܐ ܡܬܬܩܝܡ
ܠܗܘܢ ܐܝܠܝܢ ܕܒܠܝܢ. ܘܠܐ ܡܬܬܚܝܢ ܐܝܬܝܗܘܢ. ܕܗܠܝܢ

ܒܪܗܡܢܐ ܐܡܪ. ܟܠܗ ܕܟܬܒ ܐܢܐ ܪܚܡܐ ܕܒܢܝ̈ܫܟ.
ܠܐ ܗܘܐ ܡܛܠ ܐܝܠܝܢ ܕܡܫܚܝܢ ܟܠܫܘܕ: ܐܠܐ ܐܦ ܡܛܠ
ܐܝܠܝܢ ܕܪܚܝܩܝܢ ܡܢ ܬܪܥܐ ܕܗܝܡܢܘܬܟ. ܕܒܥܘܕܝܢ ܡܬܟܠܬܐ
ܠܐܢܫܐ ܕܝܩܘܬܟ. ܘܐܠܐ ܠܐ ܕܬܠܡܝܕܘܬ ܗܘܝܬ ܠܥܪܒܝܠ
ܒܐܝܕܝ̈ ܗܘ ܕܝܠܗ ܡܬܬܥܒܕ ܗܘܐ ܕܝܢ. ܘܐܠܐ ܠܐ ܡܫܬܒܩ
ܗܘܐ. ܡܫܝܚܐ ܗܘܝܬ ܡܢ ܕܝܢ ܀ ܕܢܚܐ ܐܡܪ. ܘܥܕܡܐ ܕܡܢ
ܕܐܘܕܝܬ ܕܐܝܬ ܗܘ ܬܠܡܝܕܘܬܗ ܠܥܪܒܝܠ: ܒܐܝܕܝ̈ܟ ܗܘ ܕܝܠܟ
ܬܥܒܕ ܐܢܐ ܠܗ ܠܡܫܬܘܬܗ. ܘܡܛܠ ܗܢܐ ܕܪܫ ܗܘ ܕܝܬܝܪ ܡܢܗ
ܬܬܕܝܢ ܘܕܡܢ: ܕܡܢ ܐܝܕܝ̈ܟ ܡܢܝܬ ܗܘܐ ܩܘܬܝ ܩܕܡܝܐ ܕܩܕ̈ܝܫܐ
ܩܕܝܫܐ. ܕܥܒܕ ܗܘܐ ܦܘܪܫܢܐ ܕܩܛܠܐ: ܘܐܫܬܡܥ ܗܘܐ
ܠܩܛܠܝ̈ܟ ܕܠܝ ܀ ܒܪܗܡܢܐ ܐܡܪ. ܠܘ ܠܩܛܠ ܐܬܬܠܡܕ ܗܘܐ
ܥܪܒܝܠ. ܐܠܐ ܠܡܩܠܬܗ ܕܐܠܗܐ ܕܐܡܪ. ܕܠܐ ܬܗܦܟܘܢ
ܠܦܠܚܐ ܘܕܟܝܘܬܐ ܕܩܕܝܫܐ. ܘܠܐ ܗܘܐ ܐܢܐ ܟܠܫܘܕ
ܡܫܚ ܐܢܐ ܕܐܡܡܢܬ ܡܢܬܗ ܕܥܪܒܝܠ ܕܡܬܕܝܢܬܗ ܕܒܡܫܝܚܟ.
ܐܠܐ ܐܦ ܟܠܗܘܢ ܒܪܘܚܢܐ ܩܕܝ ܒܥܬܐ ܢܪܥܡ ܬܘܒ ܒܗܕܐ
ܕܡܢܚܡ ܕܫܡܫܘܗܝ ܡܫܚܝܢ ܘܒܡ ܐܠܗܐ ܒܗܕܐ ܀ ܀ ܀ ܕܢܚܐ
ܐܡܪ. ܠܐ ܬܦܢܐ ܠܝ ܦܬܓܡܐ ܗܢܢܐ ܐܝܟ ܥܪܒܝܠ
ܬܠܡܝܕܟ: ܕܠܐ ܗܘܘ ܩܕܝܫܝܢ ܥܩܘܒܝ̈ܟ ܕܠܝ ܡܢܝܬ ܡܢ ܕܝܠܗ.
ܐܠܐ ܐܫܬܘܕܝܬ ܕܐܡܪܬ ܐܢܬ ܘܒܡ ܐܠܗܐ ܫܠܡܘܗܝ ܀ ܀
ܒܪܗܡܢܐ ܐܡܪ. ܥܪܒܝܠ ܕܠܐ ܢܕܥ ܗܘܐ ܠܐܠܗܐ: ܐܠܦܬܗ
ܕܢܕܥ: ܐܢܐ ܕܠܐܠܗܐ ܢܕܥ ܡܢ ܛܠܝܘܬ: ܐܘܕܥܬ ܠܝ
ܕܐܬܩܪܒ ܒܐܠܗܐ. ܗܘ ܠܝ ܡܢ ܐܠܗܐ ܕܐܬܝܗܒ ܗܘܐ ܀ ܀
ܕܢܚܐ ܐܡܪ. ܐܝܬܘܗܝ ܬܠܡܝܕܘܬܟ ܠܟܠ ܒܪܬܐ ܠܢܘܠܡܘ
ܕܡܫܝܚܐ: ܘܗܐ ܦܪܫ ܒܐܠܗ̈ܐ ܩܛܠܐ. ܕܩܛܠܝܢ ܗܘܘ
ܠܗܘܢ ܩܛܠܐ. ܒܬܪ ܡܢ ܗܢܐ ܪܚܡܢܐ. ܕܠܐ ܐܢܫ ܒܢ
ܩܛܠܐ ܕܢܫܝܢ ܠܝ ܝܘܡܢܐ: ܘܪܚܡܐ ܕܩܕܝܫܝܢ ܥܠܘܗ̈ܝ
ܕܕܝܢܟ ܀ ܒܪܗܡܢܐ ܐܡܪ. ܟܠ ܐܠܗܐ ܒܥܒܕܝܢܐ ܗܘ

ܕܡܫܡܫܐ: ܠܗܘܡܢܐ ܕܠܐ ܡܥܡܫ ܫܪܐ ܠܗ. ܘܕܠܐ ܚܒܠܐ
ܕܡܚܪܒ. ܠܐ ܡܥܡܫܐ ܕܢܬܪܘܢ ܠܫܡܥܘܗܝ. ܕܚܙܝܐ ܗ̇ܕܐ
ܕܚܙܝܐ ܗܘ ܕܐܠܗܐ: ܕܠܐ ܡܥܡܫ ܕܢܫܐ ܢܗܘܐ ܠܟܘܠܗܝܢ ܀
ܕܢܝܐ ܐܡܪ. ܡܢܐ ܕܐܬܚܙܝܬ ܒܗ ܐܚܡܢܐ ܕܬܘܢܝ. ܡ ܗܘ
ܚܬܒ ܐܝܟ ܚܠܝܢ ܠܥܠܡܐ ܐܝܟܐ ܢܚܙܐ ܚܙܝܬ ܠܐܠܗܐ.
ܕܐܬܚܙܝܬ ܠܥܝܢܐ ܒܗܡܢܐ ܡܗܝܪܢܘܬܐ ܕܐܠܗܐ: ܘܕܥܬܠܝܢ
ܐܝܬܘܗܝ ܢܗܘܡܢܘܢ ܕܥܠܡܐ. ܘܕܠܐ ܢܥܡܝܢ ܐܝܬܘܗܝ ܠܙܒܢܐ
ܕܐܬܪܬܐ: ܘܐܝܟ ܒܙܒܢܐ ܒܥܙܝܢ ܐܝܬ ܒܗܘܠܝܢܐ
ܕܪܘܡܢܐ ܀ ܀ ܒܪܘܡܢܐ ܐܡܪ. ܠܐ ܡܥܡܠ ܐܝܬ ܠ
ܒܗܠܝܢ ܕܐܡܪ ܐܝܬ. ܐܦ ܠܥܠܡܐ ܠܐ ܡܢܗ ܐܝܬ ܗܘܡܢܐ.
ܐܠܐ ܡܢ ܥܘܠܝܢܐ ܕܗܘܐ ܠܝ ܥܠܡܐ. ܗܐ ܦܐܡ ܐܝܬ
ܗܒܐ ܘܡܬܬܕܡ ܐܝܬ. ܚܠ ܕܐܡܪܬ ܕܠܐ ܚܙܐ ܐܝܬ
ܒܐܠܗܐ ܕܗܢܘܢ ܥܠܡܐ ܘܐܪܒܐ: ܘܚܙܪܘ ܢܗܒ ܡܗܝܢܐ
ܥܠܡܐ ܕܠܥܠ ܐܪܒܐ ܀ ܕܢܝܐ ܐܡܪ. ܐܢ ܗܘ ܕܫܪܪܐ ܠܝ
ܗܕܐ: ܕܗܕܡ ܥܘܠܝܢܐ ܕܥܠܡܐ ܦܐܡ ܐܝܬ ܘܡܬܬܕܡ: ܐܬܥܒܕ
ܠܥܠܡܝܢܘܢ ܘܠܐ ܬܡܛܪ ܚܠ ܢܗܘܡܢܘܢ. ܕܠܐ ܐܝܟ
ܡܬܘܕܐ ܡܚܒܠ ܐܝܬ ܡܗܘܡ ܒܪܥܐ ܕܡܗܘܬܐ ܀ ܒܪܘܡܢܐ
ܐܡܪ. ܘܐܢ ܐܝܠܝܢ ܕܡܬܕܡܝܢ ܚܠ ܥܠܡܐ: ܗܕ ܒܐܝܢܐ ܡܬܕܡܝܢ:
ܡܗܘܬܐ ܢܚܡܝܢ ܐܝܟ ܕܐܡܪ ܐܝܬ: ܐܝܠܝܢ ܕܥܠ ܐܠܗܐ ܥܠܡܐ
ܕܥܠܡܐ ܡܬܕܡܝܢ: ܘܗܪ ܗܘ ܠܗܘܢ. ܘܐܦ ܡܗܘܡ ܒܪܥܐ
ܕܡܗܘܬܐ ܕܗܘܒܐ ܀ ܕܢܝܐ ܐܡܪ. ܠܐ ܗܘܐ ܕܬܬܪܓܡ
ܒܗܘܡܢܝܢ ܕܠܐ ܚܠܬ ܡܢܗ. ܡܛܠ ܕܕܢܚܐ ܕܦܐܡ ܐܝܬ ܒܗ.
ܪܫܡ ܗܘ ܡܢ ܬܘܪܓܡܐ: ܘܡܪܒ ܠܡܗܘܡ ܒܪܥܐ ܕܡܗܘܬܐ:
ܠܐܝܠܝܢ ܕܡܬܕܡܝܢ ܠܥܠܡܐ ܘܠܐ ܡܬܦܫܡܝܢ ܠܡܗܘܡܢܘܢ ܀ ܀
ܒܪܘܡܢܐ ܐܡܪ. ܡܛܠ ܕܠܝܬ ܐܠܗܐ ܡܢ ܚܒܡܘܗܝ. ܘܐܦ
ܠܐ ܡܛܬ ܐܠܗܐ ܢܚܡ ܐܝܬܘܗܝ ܠܡܒܥܒܘ. ܘܥܠܡܐ ܕܠܝܬ
ܗܘܘ ܢܚܫܘ: ܕܗܘܡܢܐ ܐܝܬ ܠܗܘܢ ܘܠܐ ܡܬܠܠܝܢ: ܐܝܟ

ܒܪܬܐ ܗܝ ܘܟܪܬܗ ܠܗ ܠܡܫܝܚܐ: ܘܠܝ ܐܡܪܬ ܠܝ. ܕܠܐ
ܬܘܟܠ ܠܗ. ܐܝܟ ܗܘ ܕܐܢܫ ܗܘ ܒܠܚܘܕ ܫܒܩ ܐܢܫ ܠܗ.
ܠܗܘ ܕܒܥܐ ܟܠܗ ܫܒܩܝܢ ܠܗ ܒܪܗܡܢܐ ܀ ܕܢܝܐ ܐܡܪ.
ܘܐܢ ܠܟܘܠܗܘܢ ܐܠܗܝܢ ܐܝܟ ܕܗܘܘ ܫܒܩܝܢ ܠܗ ܠܡܫܝܚܐ.
ܠܟܠܗ ܥܠܡܐ ܐܝܟ ܐܝܠܝܢ. ܕܗܘܘ ܫܒܩܝܢ ܠܗ ܠܡܫܝܚܐ ܀
ܒܪܗܡܢܐ ܐܡܪ. ܗܢܘܢ ܐܢܘܢ ܟܠܗܘܢ: ܦܩܘܕ ܘܐܠܗܐ
ܐܢܘܢ ܠܬܫܡܫܬܐ: ܥܠ ܕܢܦܫܐ ܫܒܩܬܗ ܕܟܠܗܐ ܡܫܝܚܐ:
ܕܫܒܩܝܢ ܠܗ ܘܠܐܒܘܗܝ. ܥܡ ܪܘܚܐ ܕܐܠܗܘܬܗ ܀ ܕܢܝܐ
ܐܡܪ. ܫܡܥܘ ܗܠܝܢ ܕܐܬܝܢ ܠܟܘܢ: ܘܡܠܦܝܢ ܐܢܬܘܢ ܐܦ
ܠܐܚܪ̈ܢܐ. ܘܐܬܦܢܝܘ ܠܐܝܠܝܢ ܕܝܗܒܘ ܡܠܟܝ. ܘܠܐ
ܬܦܠܘܢ ܢܦܩܘܢ. ܕܠܐ ܬܬܦܠܓܘܢ ܒܪ ܗܘܐ ܡܢ ܢܘܗܪܗ
ܕܫܡܫܐ ܗܢܐ ܡܛܠܐ ܀ ܒܪܗܡܢܐ ܐܡܪ. ܢܘܗܪܐ ܕܫܡܫ
ܘܠܐ ܫܡܫܢ. ܠܐ ܗܘܐ ܢܘܗܪܐ ܗܘ ܫܪܝܪܐ. ܐܠܐ ܕܡܫܡܫ
ܗܘ ܕܗܘ ܢܘܗܪܐ ܫܪܝܪܐ. ܕܠܐ ܦܪܝܫ ܡܢܗ ܠܘܬ ܐܠܗܘܬܗ:
ܕܝܠܗ ܘܒܗ ܠܒܪܘܝܐ ܫܪܝܪܐ ܕܡܫܝܚܐ. ܀ ܕܢܝܐ ܐܡܪ.
ܠܐ ܬܐܡܪ ܘܕܝܢ ܡܕܡ ܥܠܝ ܡܕܡ ܕܐܬܒܥܐ. ܕܠܐ ܡܢ
ܫܡܫܐ ܠܒܘܬܐ ܡܫܝܚܐ ܐܢܫ ܠܝ: ܥܠ ܕܡܫܪܬ ܒܢܘܗܪܐ ܗܢܐ
ܕܡܬܒܥܐ ܘܫܘܕܥܐ ܐܢܬ ܒܐܢܫܐ ܕܠܐ ܡܬܒܥܐ ܀ ܒܪܗܡܢܐ
ܐܡܪ. ܠܐ ܡܫܟܚ ܐܢܫ ܕܢܦܫܐ ܗܘ ܡܕܡ ܕܡܫܟܚ ܐܢܬ
ܠܝ. ܘܐܡܪ ܥܠ ܡܕܡ ܕܠܐ ܡܫܟܚ ܐܢܬ ܠܝ. ܐܢܬ ܗܘ
ܐܡܪܬ ܠܝ ܡܛܠ ܢܘܗܪܗ ܕܫܡܫܐ. ܘܐܡܪܬ ܡܕܡ. ܕܐܢܬ
ܗܘ ܢܘܗܪܐ ܒܪܗܡܢܐ ܕܡܢܗܪ ܒܢܘܗܪܗ ܡܢ ܗܢܐ ܕܫܡܫܐ
ܕܫܡܫ ܐܢܬ ܘܡܢܗܪ ܐܢܬ ܠܗ. ܡܬܬܒܥܬ ܒܪ ܥܠܡ ܗܕܐ:
ܕܡܬܒܥܐ ܠܚܝܘܬܟ ܥܠܡ ܐܠܗܐ ܒܪܘܚܝ ܀ ܕܢܝܐ ܐܡܪ. ܠܐ
ܬܬܒܪ ܘܐܦ ܠܫܡܫܐ ܢܘܗܪܐ ܕܒܝܬܐ: ܘܬܬܠܠ ܒܫܘܪܝܐ
ܕܟܠܗܐ: ܘܬܫܘܡ ܒܚܝܘܬܐ ܠܥܠܡ ܡܢܗܘܢ ܕܐܬܬܐ: ܕܗܝܢ
ܥܠܡܝܢ ܒܗ ܀ ܒܪܗܡܢܐ ܐܡܪ. ܡܢܐ ܡܕܡ ܢܘܗܪܗ

ܕܫܠܡܘܬܗܿ. ܘܐܦ ܐܢܐ ܫܠܝܐ ܠܗܘܢ ܡܢ ܒܬܪ ܗܢܐ ܦܘܩܕܢܝ: ܗܿܘ
ܫܘܫܐ ܕܦܘܠܝ ܗܘܐ ܠܝ ܕܢܟܬܘܒ ܥܠ ܐܝܠܝܢ ܕܫܠܝܚ ܦܘܩܕܢܝ.
ܗܿܘ ܗܘ ܦܘܩܕܢ ܕܢܟܬܘܒ ܥܠ ܐܝܠܝܢ ܕܡܫܬܠܡܝܢ ܠܗܢܐ ܦܘܩܕܢܐ
ܕܡܪܘܡܝܘܬܗܿ ܀ ܘܟܕ ܐܬܦܪܣ ܗܘܐ ܗܢܐ ܦܘܩܕܢܐ
ܕܡܪܘܡܝܘܬܐ ܕܫܠܡܐ: ܢܦܩ ܥܠܘܗܝ ܡܪܗܛܘܬܐ. ܕܦܘܐ ܗܘܐ
ܥܠܝܐ ܘܢܘܫܐ ܥܠ ܥܠܝܐ. ܘܡܛܐ ܗܘܐ ܕܢܬܐ ܘܢܐܪܘܗܝ ܗܘܘ
ܠܪܘܡܝܐ ܕܢܦܩܬ ܗܘܐ ܠܒܝܬܗ. ܘܫܠܡܘ ܗܘܘ ܒܪܘܚܢܝܐ
ܩܕܡܝܐ ܠܒܝܬ ܕܢܝܚ. ܘܗܘܟܢܐ ܗܘܐ ܕܐܢܫܘܬܐ ܕܡܪܗܛܘܬܐ.
ܘܡܫܠܡܘܗܝ ܗܘܘ ܠܪܘܡܝܐ: ܟܐܢܫܐ ܗܘܐ ܘܡܪܗܛܐ. ܟܕ
ܐܦܪܝܢ ܗܘܘ ܡܕܡܘܗܝ ܡܟܝܢܐ ܐܝܟ ܫܪܒܘܢ. ܘܚܙܐ ܕܪܒܝܐ.
ܕܫܡܫܐ. ܘܫܒܩܝܢ ܗܘܘ ܘܢܩܦܝܢ ܗܘܘ ܠܗ ܓܠܝܐ. ܘܦܪܫ
ܗܘܘ ܠܗ ܡܢܝܢܐ ܪܒܐ. ܣܓܝܐ ܕܢܦܫܐ ܗܘܐ. ܘܐܟܢ
ܗܘܐ ܠܗܘܢ. ܪܒܐ ܐܝܟ ܐܣܟܡܐ. ܡܢ ܩܕܡܝܐ ܕܝܢ
ܗܘܐ ܕܢܦܫ ܘܒܓܘܗ ܪܘܚܐ ܐܢܫܐ. ܘܐܦܪܝܢ ܗܘܘ ܠܗ.
ܕܡܫܡܫ ܗܘ ܠܝ ܡܢܝ: ܕܐܟܢ ܡܠܟܐ ܕܒܝܬܝ. ܐܝܟ ܒܢܝܐ
ܐܝܟ ܡܢܐ ܕܐܬܬܘܗܝ ܗܘܠܐ ܗܘ ܡܬܦܬܠ ܀ ܘܟܕ ܥܠ ܗܘܐ
ܠܒܝܬܐ: ܗܿܘ ܘܟܠܗ ܒܡܢܐ ܕܐܝܬ ܗܘܐ ܒܗܘܢ. ܡܢ ܗܘܐ
ܘܠܐ. ܘܦܪܫ ܗܘܐ ܘܢܦܩ ܐܝܟ ܕܢܐܙܠ ܠܦܘܬܗܘܢ. ܟܕ
ܢܦܫ ܘܡܫܡܫ ܠܐܠܗܐ: ܒܦܘܪܫܢܐ ܕܒܝܬ ܗܘܐ ܠܗܘܢ
ܘܠܒܝܬܐ. ܘܡܢ ܒܬܪ ܝܘܡܐ ܕܐܙܠ ܗܘܐ ܐܒܝܐ: ܠܗܘܢܐ
ܕܝܠܐ ܕܐܬܪܐ ܒܗܘ ܦܘܪܫܢܐ ܗܘܝ: ܐܫܬܪܝ ܗܘܐ ܠܗ ܡܢ
ܥܡܠܗ. ܐܝܟܐ ܕܝܢ ܕܫܡܥܘ ܘܦܪܫܘ ܐܣܩܘܦܐ ܕܘܪ
ܕܬܚܝܢ ܗܘ ܦܘܪܫܢܐ ܗܘܝ: ܟܕ ܗܕܝܢ ܒܟܢ ܒܐܝܕ
ܐܒܝܐ. ܕܢܦܪܘܫ ܡܢܝܢܐ ܣܓܝܐܐ ܕܡܪܗܛܘܬܐ. ܐܝܟ ܕܦܩܕܝ
ܢܦܩܘܗܝ ܩܕܡܝܐ ܕܫܠܡܐ ܩܕܡܝܐ ܀ ܗܢܐ ܕܝܢ ܪܘܡܝܐ
ܐܦܝܣܩܘܦܐ ܕܐܘܪܗܝ: ܗܿܘ ܕܬܠܡܝܕܗ ܗܘܐ ܠܪܒܘܠܐ ܒܡܟܝܢܐ
ܥܠܗܿ ܕܡܪܗܛܘܬܐ: ܕܐܬܘܗܝ ܗܘܐ ܒܡܕܝܢܬܐ ܕܐܘܪܗܝ ܐܦܝܣܩܘܦܐ

ܗ̇ܘ ܕܡܫܬܠܠܝܢ ܚܫܚܝܢ ܠܗܘܢ. ܡܛܠ ܕܒܗܢ ܗܘ ܡܕܒܚܝܢ ܒܫܘܒܚܐ ܕܣܓܘܕܬܐ ܕܡܫܝܚ ܐܠܗܢ ܒܗ̇ ܀ ܕܢܝܐ ܐܡܪ. ܫܡܥܘ ܐܝܟ ܕܐܡܪܬ ܕܠܐ ܡܬܒܪܝܢ ܠܢ ܡܢܟ. ܘܫܠܡܘ ܠܫܠܡܐ: ܟܕ ܠܐ ܐܝܬܝܟ ܚܠܦܝܢ ܣܘܪܚܐ ܡܬܬܪܝܐ ܘܡܬܬܒܥܐ ܦܝܫܐ ܀ ܒܪܘܡܝܐ ܐܡܪ. ܫܡܥܘ ܐܝܬ ܫܘܐܠܐ ܦܓܥܐ ܕܗܘܐ ܡܫܐܠ ܐܢܐ ܠܟ. ܘܫܡܥ ܥܠ ܬܚܘܐ ܘܗܘܝܐ ܕܢܚܡ ܐܢܐ ܒܗܘܢ ܥܠ. ܠܐ ܓܝܪ ܡܕܒܪܝܢ ܠܢ ܩܠܝܠ ܐܝܟ ܡܢܐ ܕܡܕܒܪܝܢ ܠܟ ܐܩܠܝܠܝܢ ܀ ܕܢܝܐ ܐܡܪ. ܫܬܐܠܬܐ ܒܪܘܡܝܐ ܘܫܐܠܬܗ. ܘܒܗ ܒܕܘܟܐ ܗܘ ܐܬܬ ܗܘ، ܠܗ ܐܓܪܬܐ ܡܢ ܓܡܪ ܐܠܗܘܗܝ ܗܘܦܪܟܐ ܪܒܐ ܐܒܐ ܕܩܠܝܠܐ ܀ ܘܫܡܥ ܗܘܐ ܡܐܬܝܬܘܗܝ ܗܘܘ ܠܒܪܘܡܝܐ. ܘܠܐ ܐܬܬܪܡ ܗܘܐ. ܘܐܪܫܝܡܘܗܝ ܗܘܘ ܠܒܪ ܡܢ ܒܝܬ ܕܝܢܐ. ܘܫܡܥ ܗܘܐ ܗܘ ܕܝܢܐ. ܕܢܓܠܘܢ ܗܘܘ ܡܕܡܘܗܝ ܫܪܪܐ ܘܪܘܪܒܐ ܘܡܟܬܪܐ ܕܡܕܝܢܬܐ: ܕܢܓܒܗ ܗܘܐ ܡܢܐ ܦܣܝܩܐ ܐܬܦܩܕ ܗܘܐ ܡܢ ܩܠܝܠܐ: ܟܕ ܦܘܩܕܢܐ ܡܕܝܢܝܐ ܕܐܬܬܪܝܬܐ ܕܫܘܠܛܢܐ ܕܪܗܘܡܝܐ ܀ ܘܐܬܒܛܠܘ ܕܢܫܒܘ ܗܘܘ ܩܠܝܠܐ ܒܕ ܦܘܩܕܢܐ ܠܕܝܢܐ ܕܐܬܬܪܝܬܐ: ܕܡܢ ܕܫܡܥܬ ܩܠܝܠܐ ܕܢܦܩܐ ܦܘܪܣܐ ܥܠ ܚܡܫܐ ܕܪܗܘܡܝܐ: ܫܡܥܝܢ ܘܠܒܝܢ ܡܢ ܥܡܝܪܐ ܕܐܝܬ ܠܝ ܒܐܬܬܪܝܬܐ ܕܐܘܪܗܝ ܕܩܠܝܠܐ: ܕܚܡܫܐ ܕܪܗܘܡܝܐ. ܐܬܥܠܝܐ ܐܠܗܢ ܕܪܘܡܝܢ ܡܢ ܡܠܟܐ. ܘܡܢ ܚܝܠܐ. ܘܡܢ ܟܘܪܐ. ܘܡܢ ܟܢܫܬܐ. ܘܡܢ ܥܡܘܕܐ ܘܢܓܠܐ. ܘܐܝܠܝܢ ܕܐܦ ܢܩܘܫܘܢ ܕܩܠܝܠܬܐ ܬܬܒܝܢ ܡܫܡܫ ܟܪܝܗܐ ܡܢ ܐܝܠܝܢ ܕܡܬܢܝܢ ܠܗܘܢ. ܫܢܝ ܕܝܢ ܒܟܐܢܘܬܗ ܕܐܪܝܘܛܐ ܡܩܪܝܢ. ܕܡܛܠ ܗܠܝܢ ܢܓܠܐ ܡܚܝܢܘܗܝ ܙܪܘܥܐ ܕܗܘܝܐ. ܘܢܦܩܘ ܢܘܫܐ ܘܥܠܝܐ ܒܟܠܗ ܐܘܪܚܝܢ. ܟܕ ܗܘܝܢ ܡܫܡܫܝܢ ܒܟܗܢܘܬܗܘܢ ܘܠܐ ܐܝܟ ܢܓܠܐ ܐܠܗܢ. ܠܐ ܗܘܐ ܕܝܢ ܒܠܚܘܕܝܗܘܢ ܟܗܢܝܢ ܬܒܝܥܝܢ. ܐܠܐ ܥܠ ܢܩܘܫܘܗܝ ܐܝܠܝܢ ܕܥܠܝܢ ܠܢܩܘܫܐ

ܗܕܪܘܬܐ ܕܡܫܝܚܐ ܡܫܡܫܢܐ.

ܒܐܝܕܐ ܐܒ: ܕܫܢܝܬ ܫܘܬܦܘܬܐ ܘܡܫܘܕܥ ܕܡܠܟܘܬܗ
ܕܐܠܗܘܬܗ ܡܫܘܕܥ: ܒܗܘܦܟܐ ܕܠܒܫܗ ܘܕܡܘܗܒܬܗ:
ܕܐܬܓܠܝ ܫܘܬܐ ܕܐܬܬܠܝ ܗܘܐ ܒܗ: ܒܐܘܪܫܠܡܬܐ ܕܗܘܠܝܐ
ܘܕܟܪܗ: ܒܫܘܡ ܡܘܫܐ ܐܦܣܘܩܐ ܕܐܘܪܗܝ. ܓܒܪ ܗܘܐ
ܗܘ ܠܒܫܗ ܙܕܘܩܐ ܠܒܪܬܐ: ܘܠܗܘܢܐ ܟܠܗ ܕܒܪܘܦܝܐ:
ܟܕ ܙܕܘܩܐ ܗܘ ܡܕܡܐ: ܕܓܒܪ ܗܘܐ ܕܘܠܦܢܗ ܡܠܟܐ.
ܘܓܒܪ ܗܘ ܠܒܫܗ ܡܠܟܐ. ܕܢܗܘܘܢ ܗܘܘ ܕܟܝܐ ܘܢܩܝܐ:
ܘܡܠܘܬܐ ܒܟܠ ܕܘܟܐ ܢܬܩܢ ܗܘ. ܒܩܘܡܐ ܘܠܗܘܢܬܐ ܘܕܡ
ܙܘܗ ܢܬܠܙܘܢ ܗܘܘ. ܘܟܕ ܡܬܙܕܩܝܢ ܗܘܘ ܦܓܪ̈ܐ. ܗܢܝܢ
ܡܟܝܢ ܗܘܘ ܒܫܐܪܬܗܘܢ ܕܒܪܘܦܝܐ ܐܚܝܢ: ܘܠܐ ܕܢܠܝܢ
ܗܘܘ ܡܢ ܙܕܘܩܐ. ܡܛܠ ܕܦܓܪ̈ܐ ܗܘܘ ܗܢܘܢ ܕܡܬܙܕܩܝܢ
ܗܘܘ ܡܢ ܗܢܘܢ ܕܙܕܩܝܢ ܗܘܘ. ܫܡܥܢ ܕܝܢ ܐܝܟܐ ܕܐܝܬܘܗܝ ܗܘܐ
ܡܢ ܬܠܝܬܐ ܡܐܬܐ: ܘܡܫܡܫ ܗܘܐ ܡܫܡܫܢܐ: ܘܡܕܒܪ ܗܘܐ
ܠܚܘܬܐ ܕܒܡܘܪܝܐ ܒܗܝܟܠܐ. ܘܡܫܡܫ ܗܘܐ: ܘܩܪܐ ܗܘܐ
ܒܬܒܐ: ܘܡܠܒܒ ܗܘܐ ܘܡܚܝܠ ܗܘܐ ܒܡܠܬܗ ܠܦܓܪ̈ܐ.
ܘܡܕܗܪ ܗܘܐ ܠܗܘܢ. ܕܢܬܦܫܩܘܢ ܗܘܘ ܒܐܪܙܐ ܕܡܫܝܚܘܬܗܘܢ.
ܘܠܐ ܢܥܢܘܢ ܗܘܘ ܡܢ ܙܕܘܩܐ. ܘܡܦܩܕ ܗܘܐ ܠܗܘܢ.
ܘܟܕ ܦܓܪ̈ܐ ܡܬܬܢܝܚܝܢ ܗܘܘ ܒܡܠܘܗܝ. ܘܡܬܦܨܠܝܢ ܗܘܘ
ܡܢ ܚܫܗܘܢ ܣܓܝܐܐ: ܟܕ ܘܫܬܪܝܢ ܗܘܘ: ܕܠܐ ܢܬܟܪܘܢ
ܗܘܘ ܒܡܢܝܢܐ ܕܝܘܡܝܢ ܗܘܘ ܒܗ. ܘܟܕ ܫܡܥܘ ܗܘܘ ܫܪܪܐ
ܕܡܫܝܚܘܬܐ: ܐܝܟܢ ܕܗܘܝܘ ܫܒܩܝܢ ܗܘܘ ܡܬܠܠܬܗ ܕܢܟܘܬܐ
ܗܕܐ. ܟܠܗ ܗܘܘ ܐܘܕܝܘܗܝ ܠܠܒܘܫܗ ܡܫܝܚܝܐ ܕܐܝܬ
ܗܘܐ ܒܥܕܬܐ ܕܐܘܪܗܝ. ܘܐܡܪܝܢ ܠܗ. ܕܫܡܥܢ ܐܝܟܐ
ܕܐܝܬܘܗܝ ܡܫܡܫܢܐ ܒܬܠܝܬܐ ܡܐܬܐ. ܡܬܒܪܟ ܘܡܫܒܚ

ܕܪ̈ܗܘܡܝܐ ܡܕܝܢܬܐ: ܘܡܫܬܠܡܐ ܗܘܬ ܐܝܕܐ ܕܟܗܢܘܬܐ ܠܗ ܠܒܪܫܡܝܐ ܡܢ ܒܫܠܡܐ ܕܗܘܐ ܐܦܣܩܘܦܐ ܒܐܘܪܗܝ. ܘܒܫܠܡܐ ܡܫܬܠܡܐ ܗܘܬ ܠܗ ܐܝܕܐ ܡܢ ܦܠܘܛ ܡܕܝܢܐ. ܘܦܠܘܛ ܡܫܬܠܡܐ ܗܘܬ ܠܗ ܐܝܕܐ ܡܢ ܣܪܦܝܘܢ ܐܦܣܩܘܦܐ ܕܐܢܛܝܘܟܝ. ܘܣܪܦܝܘܢ ܡܫܬܠܡܐ ܗܘܬ ܠܗ ܐܝܕܐ ܡܢ ܙܦܘܪܝܢܘܣ ܐܦܣܩܘܦܐ ܕܪ̈ܗܘܡܝܐ. ܘܙܦܘܪܝܢܘܣ ܕܪ̈ܗܘܡܝܐ ܩܒܠ ܗܘܐ ܐܝܕܐ ܡܢ ܒܝܩܛܘܪ ܕܬܡܢ ܕܪ̈ܗܘܡܝܐ. ܘܒܝܩܛܘܪ ܩܒܠ ܗܘܐ ܐܝܕܐ ܡܢ ܐܠܘܛܪܘܣ. ܘܐܠܘܛܪܘܣ ܩܒܠ ܗܘܐ ܡܢ ܣܘܛܪ. ܘܣܘܛܪ ܩܒܠ ܗܘܐ ܡܢ ܐܢܝܛܘܣ. ܘܐܢܝܛܘܣ ܩܒܠ ܗܘܐ ܡܢ ܦܝܘܣ. ܘܦܝܘܣ ܩܒܠ ܗܘܐ ܡܢ ܐܓܝܢܘܣ. ܘܐܓܝܢܘܣ ܩܒܠ ܗܘܐ ܡܢ ܛܠܣܦܘܪܘܣ. ܘܛܠܣܦܘܪܘܣ ܩܒܠ ܗܘܐ ܡܢ ܐܠܟܣܢܕܪܘܣ. ܘܐܠܟܣܢܕܪܘܣ ܩܒܠ ܗܘܐ ܡܢ ܐܘܪܣܛܘܣ. ܘܐܘܪܣܛܘܣ ܩܒܠ ܗܘܐ ܡܢ ܩܠܝܡܝܣ. ܘܩܠܝܡܝܣ ܩܒܠ ܗܘܐ ܡܢ ܐܢܘܣ. ܘܐܢܘܣ ܩܒܠ ܗܘܐ ܡܢ ܫܡܥܘܢ ܟܐܦܐ. ܘܫܡܥܘܢ ܟܐܦܐ ܩܒܠ ܗܘܐ ܡܢ ܡܪܢ. ܥܡ ܫܠܝܚܐ ܚܒܪ̈ܘܗܝ. ܒܝܘܡܐ ܕܦܢܛܩܘܣܛܐ ܕܣܘܠܩܗ ܕܡܪܢ ܕܠܘܬ ܐܒܘܗܝ ܡܫܒܚܐ. ܕܐܝܬܘܗܝ ܗܘ ܐܪ̈ܒܥܐ ܒܚܙܝܪܢ: ܕܐܝܬܘܗܝ ܫܢܬ ܬܫܥܣܪܐ ܕܡܠܟܘܬܗ ܕܛܝܒܪܝܘܣ ܩܣܪ ܒܗܘܦܛܝܐ ܕܪܘܦܘܣ ܘܪܘܒܠܝܘܣ. ܕܐܝܬܝܗ̇ ܫܢܬܐ ܗ̇ܝ ܫܢܬ ܬܠܬܡܐܐ ܘܐܪ̈ܒܥܝܢ ܘܫܬܐ. ܒܚܘܫܒܢܐ ܕܝܘ̈ܢܝܐ ܚܕ ܘܬܠܬ. ܗܘܐ ܕܝܢ ܗܘ ܕܦܘܠܘܣ ܒܡܠܟܐ ܐܝܟ ܗܘܕܝܬܐ ܕܐܚܝܕܝ ܚܢ ܒܐܠܦܝܢ ܥܢܝܢܐ ܕܒܝܬ ܐܪ̈ܒܥ. ܕܠܐ ܦܠܓܐ ܡܕܡ ܕܠ ܡܕܡ ܡܘܕܥ.

ܫܠܡܬ ܣܗܕܘܬܐ ܕܒܪܫܡܝܐ.

ܐܦܣܩܘܦܐ ܕܐܘܪܗܝ ܀

ܗܐ ܓܝܪ ܢܦܘܩ ܡܢ ܗܪܟܐ. ܡܘܬܐ ܕܟܝܢܐ ܦܪܩ ܗܘ ܠܗ ܠܟܠ ܐܢܫܐ ܕܐܙܠ: ܘܕܢܦܠܛ ܡܢܗ ܠܐ ܡܫܟܚ. ܡܛܠ ܕܓܙܪܬܐ ܗܝ ܗܕܐ ܕܥܠ ܟܠܗܘܢ ܝ̈ܠܘܕܝ ܕܐܢܫ ܀ ܘܟܕ ܗܘܐ ܚܒܝܒ ܘܐܬܐ ܠܐܘܪܗܝ، ܒܟܣܝܘܬܐ. ܗܘ ܡܚܙܝܢ ܗܘܐ ܢܦܫܗ ܠܬܪ̈ܥܐ ܡܢܗܘܢ، ܠܗܝܡܢ̈ܐ. ܘܡܫܡܫ ܗܘܐ ܠܟܢܫܐ ܕܢܘܪܐ. ܘܐܙܠ ܗܘܐ ܠܗ ܒܝܬܐ. ܠܘܬ ܐܦܛܪܘܦܐ ܗܦܟܐ: ܐܢܫܐ ܕܫܡܥܐ ܗܘܐ ܕܠܘܩܘܣ ܗܓܡܘܢܐ: ܘܐܡܪ ܗܘܐ. ܕܐܢܐ ܐܢܐ ܚܒܝܒ ܕܡܢ ܬܠܡܝܕܐ ܕܒܥܝܢ ܐܢܬܘܢ ܠܝ. ܘܐܡܪ ܗܘܐ ܠܗ ܗܘ ܐܦܛܪܘܦܐ. ܐܝܟ ܗܘ ܕܠܐ ܝܕܥ ܐܢܐ ܕܐܝܬܝܟ ܚܒܝܒ: ܐܫܬܡܥ ܠܝ ܕܐܡܪ ܐܢܐ ܠܟ. ܘܩܘܡ ܙܠ ܠܐܘܪܚܐ ܕܐܝܬܝܟ ܗܘܝܬ. ܘܗܘܝ ܬܡܢ ܒܥܝܢܐ ܗܢܐ ܘܗܕܐ ܕܐܝܬܝܟ ܚܒܝܒ، ܘܡܛܠܬ ܒܥܝ. ܘܡܠܬܟ ܗܢܝܐ: ܐܢܐ ܠܐ ܢܟܪ ܘܠܐ ܢܓܪ. ܘܕܐܫܬܡܥܬܟ ܘܕܟܪ ܡܪܝܬܟ ܠܐ ܬܬܪܦܐ ܡܕܡ. ܠܐ ܓܝܪ ܐܢܐ ܡܚܦܪ ܠܗܘܢ ܡܕܡ. ܘܡܛܠ ܗܘ ܕܣܥܪܬܐ ܩܘܡ ܒܒܝܬ ܚܒܘܫܝܐ. ܘܡܚܦܪ ܠܗܘܢ ܗܓܡܘܢܐ. ܡܛܠ ܕܟܠܗܘܢ ܠܐ ܦܩܕܘ ܡ̈ܠܟܐ ܡܕܡ ܕܟܕ ܩܦܘܣܐ. ܘܐܢܬ ܠܐ ܡܬܦܠܣ ܐܢܬ ܠܝ ܒܡܠܝܟ ܕܐܡܪܬ ܠܝ: ܡܛܠ ܐܢܐ ܡܢ ܕܡܟܝ. ܡܛܠ ܕܐܝܟ ܗܘ ܕܐܬܬܚܝܒܐ ܠܕܝܢܐ ܕܐܬܝܢ. ܡܢ ܡܘܬܐ ܕܢܘܪܐ ܠܐ ܦܠܛ ܐܢܬ. ܐܝܟ ܩܘܡܝܢܐ ܕܡ̈ܠܟܐ ܕܦܩܕܘ ܥܠܝܟ ܀

ܐܡܪ ܠܗ ܚܒܝܒ ܠܐܦܛܪܘܦܐ. ܐܢܐ ܠܐ ܗܘܐ ܡܛܠ ܐܢܫܘܬ، ܘܕܟܪ ܡܪܝܬ، ܐܬܓܠܠ ܠܝ: ܐܠܐ ܥܠ ܚܕ ܕܠܐ ܢܐܟܦܘܢ. ܐܦ ܥܠ ܗܕܐ ܐܬܬܟܣܝܬ ܗܟܝ: ܕܠܐ ܐܬܬܦܟܠ ܗܘܝܬ ܒܪܘܚܝ، ܒܡܘܡܬܐ ܕܟܠܢ ܗܘܐ ܗܓܡܘܢܐ. ܘܡܛܠܬܝ ܗܐ ܩܪܒ ܩ̈ܒܠܢܐ ܒܦܬܓܡܐ. ܘܐܬܬܟܪܝܬ ܠܗ ܐܝܟ ܒܪܢܫܐ. ܡܛܠ ܗܢܐ ܓܝܪ ܗܘ ܕܠܐ ܡܬܦܠܣ ܐܢܬ ܠܝ ܕܐܬܟܠܝܬ ܡܢ ܗܓܡܘܢܐ: ܐܢܐ ܒܠܫܢܝ، ܐܙܠ ܐܢܐ ܘܡܬܚܙܐ ܐܢܐ ܠܗ ܀ ܘܟܕ ܫܡܥ ܗܘܐ ܐܦܛܪܘܦܐ ܕܗܟܢܐ ܐܡܪ ܗܘܐ ܠܗ. ܠܟܢܫ ܗܘܐ ܚܝܠܐ.

ܒܓܠܐܝܬ ܒܟܠ ܕܘܟ. ܘܡܣܪܗܒ ܠܡܒܛܠ ܦܘܩܕܢܐ ܕܡܠܟܐ ܘܠܐ ܕܚܠ. ܘܟܕ ܚܙܐ ܗܘܐ ܗܓܡܘܢܐ ܗܠܝܢ. ܐܬܚܡܬ ܚܡܬܐ ܥܠܘܗܝ ܕܚܒܝܒ. ܘܟܬܒ ܗܘܐ ܐܓܪܬܐ. ܘܫܕܪ ܗܘܐ ܘܐܘܕܥ ܗܘܐ ܠܠܝܣܢܝܘܣ ܡܠܟܐ ܥܠ ܐܝܠܝܢ ܕܥܒܕ ܗܘܐ ܚܒܝܒ. ܘܕܢܐܠܦ ܗܘܐ ܘܢܦܩܐ ܡܢܗ ܦܘܩܕܢܐ ܡܬܦܩܕ ܗܘܐ ܥܠܘܗܝ. ܘܥܠ ܐܝܠܝܢ ܕܠܐ ܨܒܝܢ ܕܢܕܒܚܘܢ. ܐܦ ܦܘܩܕܢܐ ܦܩܝܕ ܗܘܐ ܕܢܬܩܛܠ ܗܘܐ ܒܚܪܒ: ܐܠܐ ܠܐ ܦܩܕ ܗܘܐ. ܕܒܢܘܪܐ ܢܬܘܩܕ ܗܘܐ: ܠܐܝܠܝܢ ܕܠܐ ܡܬܪܟܢܝܢ ܗܘܘ. ܡܛܠ ܕܫܡܥܘ ܗܘܘ: ܕܗܘܦܛܝܩܘܣ ܐܢܛܘܠܝܐ: ܒܡܠܝܐ ܘܒܐܘܦܣܝܐ ܒܐܦܪܟܝܐ ܐܝܬܝܗܘܢ ܘܠܐ ܡܬܟܢܫ. ܘܦܩܕ ܗܘܐ ܠܝܣܢܝܘܣ ܡܠܟܐ ܠܠܘܣܢܝܘܣ ܗܓܡܘܢܐ. ܕܐܝܢܐ ܕܡܫܬܟܚ ܐܫܬܟܚ ܗܘܐ ܘܡܚܪ ܗܘܐ ܥܠ ܦܘܩܕܝܢ. ܦܩܕܗ ܡܠܟܘܬܗ ܕܢܘܩܪܐ ܢܗܘܐ. ܘܫܪܝܐ ܕܐܣܝܪܝܢ ܐܝܠܝܢ ܕܠܐ ܡܬܦܝܣܝܢ ܕܢܕܒܚܘܢ ܒܡܕܝܢܬܐ ܕܐܘܪܗܝ ܢܬܩܛܠܘܢ ⁘ ⁘

ܟܕ ܕܝܢ ܐܬܐ ܗܘܐ ܗܢܐ ܦܘܩܕܢܐ ܠܐܪܥܐ ܕܐܘܪܗܝ. ܚܒܝܒ ܐܝܢܐ ܕܡܬܠܬܗ ܗܘܬ ܗܘܬ ܐܘܦܪܐ. ܒܥܪ ܗܘܐ ܠܐܬܪܐ ܕܩܣܛܠܝܢܐ ܕܢܦܩ ܗܘܐ ܐܦ ܗܘ ܒܡܫܡܫܢܘܬܗ. ܘܟܕ ܫܡܥ ܗܘܐ ܗܓܡܘܢܐ ܫܡܗ ܒܩܪܝܬܗ: ܘܟܠܗ ܐܬܪܐ ܕܫܪܝܪܘܗܝ ܘܠܐ ܐܫܬܟܚ. ܦܩܕ ܗܘܐ ܕܢܬܬܠܕܢ ܗܘܬ ܐܢܫܘܬܗ ܘܟܠ ܩܪܝܒܘܗ. ܘܠܐܡܗ ܗܘܘ ܘܐܚܘܗܝ ܐܦ ܗܢܘܢ ܒܫܪܝܬܐ ܠܐܣܝܪܗ ܘܠܩܪܝܒܐ ܕܐܝܬܘܗܝ. ܘܐܦ ܡܢ ܟܠ ܩܪܝܒܘܗܝ. ܘܐܬܬܣܝܡܘ ܐܢܘܢ ܠܒܝܬ ܐܣܝܪܐ. ܘܣܡܐ ܐܢܘܢ ܒܒܝܬ ܐܣܝܪܐ. ܘܟܕ ܚܙܐ ܗܘܐ ܚܒܝܒ ܗܕܐ ܕܗܘܬ ܗܘܬ. ܐܬܢܝܚ ܗܘܐ ܒܪܘܚܗ ܘܐܙܠ ܗܘܐ ܒܐܬܪܘܬܗ. ܕܦܩܕ ܗܘ ܠܗ ܕܢܐܙܠ ܘܐܬܐ ܠܡܕܝܢܬܐ ܕܐܘܪܗܝ. ܘܥܠ ܡܢ ܗܘܐ ܕܐܦܩܘܗܝ ܒܚܘܫܒܐ: ܘܐܬܠܘ ܐܚܝܢܐ ܘܡܬܟܠܠܘ ܒܟܠܗ: ܘܐܬܬܚܒܫ ܠܗ ܒܒܝܬܐ ܪܒܐ. ܡܢܝܐ ܟܕ ܡܢܗ ܠܗ ܫܡܥܐ ܕܦܪܝܫܘܬܐ ܠܐܢܫܐ ܕܚܙܐ ܡܢ ܩܕܡܘܗܝ ܕܦܪܝܫܘܬܐ.

ܕܢܓܠܐ ܗܘܐ ܒܠܒܗ܁ ܐܫܬܡܥܬ ܗܘܬ ܠܗܘܢ ܠܒܪ̈ܢܫܐ ܕܡܫܝܚܘܬܐ܆ ܘܐܘܕܥܗ܁ ܠܒܢܝܐ ܥܠ ܡܕܡ ܕܫܡܥܘ ܗܘܘ܁ ܘܐܬܬܥܝܩܬ ܗܘܬ ܕܒܢܝܐ ܥܠ ܐܝܠܝܢ ܕܐܬܚܪܡܘ ܗܘܘ ܠܗ ܠܝܫܘܥ܁ ܕܥܠ ܡܢܐ ܐܬܚܫܬ ܘܐܬܬܚܝܒܬ ܠܒܢܝܐ܆ ܕܠܐ ܒܡܦܠܚܢܐ ܕܐܠܗ ܕܕܝܢܐ܁ ܘܠܗܓܡܘܢܐ ܐܡܪ ܗܘܐ ܠܗ. ܕܠܐ ܙܕܩ ܗܘܐ ܠܟܗܢ̈ܐ ܕܚܒܫ ܙܟܝܐ ܠܡܩܛܠܗ܆ ܕܗܟܢܐ ܥܬܝܕ ܗܘܐ ܥܠ ܐܪܥܗ ܕܠܗ܆ ܘܢܦܠ ܗܘܐ ܦܘܩܕܢܐ ܕܡ̈ܠܟܐ܆ ܕܢܦܩܘ ܥܠ ܝܫܘܥ ܡܬܘܪܐ ܕܒܗܘܪܐ ܢܦܩܘ܀ ܘܐܦ ܗܓܡܘܢܐ ܐܡܪ ܠܗ ܗܘܐ ܥܠ ܝܫܘܥ܁ ܐܬܬܚܠܬ. ܘܐܦ ܠܐ ܕܐܬܦܠܛ ܦܘܩܕܢܐ ܕܐܬܚܪܡ ܡ̈ܠܟܐ ܥܠܬ. ܐܠܐ ܟܕ ܡܢܐ ܐܢܬ܁ ܡܢ ܢܒܝܘܬܟ܆ ܕܗܘܐ ܡܬܚܙܐ ܗܘܬ ܕܐܬܒܥܝ. ܡܫܬܐܠ ܕܝܢ ܫܐܠܬܗ. ܐܚܪܢܐ ܕܐܦ ܢܒܝܘܬܟ ܡܬܚܙܝܐ ܗܘܬ ܒܐܦ̈ܝܗ܆ ܕܐܬܝܠܕ ܗܘܬ ܘܐܢܫܐ ܕܐܝܟ ܗܘ ܕܒܐܝܪܘܬܗ ܐܝܬܝܗ ܠܗܪܕܘܣ. ܐܦ ܕܠܐ ܠܡܐ ܡܠܦܢܐ ܕܒܢܒܝܘܬܟ ܐܬܚܙܝܗ ܗܘܐ ܒܗ ܐܝܣܪܐܝܠ. ܘܒܪ ܫܡܥܬ ܗܘܬ ܡܢܗ. ܕܗܘ ܒܝܫܘܥ ܐܝܟ ܗܘܐ. ܫܐܠܬܗ ܐܢܬܬܗ ܠܬܪܥܐ ܡܫܡܫܢܐ ܕܒܡܦܘܩܝܢ ܕܐܪܙܘܬܟ܀

ܘܦܩܕ ܗܘܐ ܗܓܡܘܢܐ ܡܢ ܥܠܝܐ. ܘܐܬܟܠܝܗ܁ ܗܘܘ ܠܝܫܘܥ ܘܫܡܗܘܢ܁ ܀ ܗܓܡܘܢܐ ܐܡܪ ܗܘ ܡܢܘ ܕܝܢ ܢܒܝܘܬܟ. ܘܬܒܪ܁ ܗܘܐ ܕܒܫܬܐܠܗ ܗܓܡܘܢܐ. ܘܐܡܪ ܠܗ. ܕܐܡܪܢܐ ܫܡܥܟ ܘܡܢ ܐܢܫܐ ܐܢܬܟ. ܘܡܢ ܐܢܬܟ. ܐܡܪ ܠܗ ܝܫܘܥ ܫܡܥ. ܘܐܢܬ܁ ܡܢ ܬܠܝܐ ܛܠܝܬܐ. ܘܒܒܪ ܐܢܫܐ ܡܫܡܫܢܐ ܀ ܀ ܀

ܗܓܡܘܢܐ ܐܡܪ. ܡܛܠ ܡܢܐ ܒܒܪܬ ܥܠ ܦܘܩܕܢܐ ܕܡ̈ܠܟܐ. ܘܡܫܡܫ ܐܢܬ ܒܫܒܬܟ. ܡܕܡ ܕܠܐ ܦܩܕ ܠܟ ܡܢ ܡ̈ܠܟܐ. ܘܠܐ ܝܕܥ ܐܢܬ ܠܡܪ̈ܕܘܬܐ ܠܗܘ ܕܦܩܕܢ ܠܗ ܡ̈ܠܟܐ ܀ ܝܫܘܥ ܐܡܪ. ܝܢ ܒܡܘܠܦܢܐ. ܠܐ ܗܘܐ ܠܡ̈ܪܕܐ ܕܟܢܫܐ ܦܩܕܢ ܫܒܩ. ܩܘܡܘ ܕܠܐ ܗܘܘ ܡܕܡ. ܘܐܦ ܠܐ ܠܡܪ̈ܕܘܬܐ ܡܕܡ. ܐܠܐ ܦܩܕܢ ܠܐܠܗܐ ܕܒܥܐ ܐܢܘܢ

ܘܐܫܠܡܗ ܗܘܐ ܠܒ̈ܢܝ ܒܝܬܗ. ܘܐܘܟܠܘܗܝ ܗܘܘ ܒܒܝܬܗ
ܠܢܡܘܣܝܢ ܕܡܫܡܫܢܘܬܐ. ܘܟܠ ܗܘܐ ܗܘ ܬܐܓܡܘܢܐ. ܘܐܘܕܒܗ
ܗܘܐ ܠܡܫܡܫܢܘܬܐ ܘܐܡܪ ܗܘܐ ܠܗ: ܕܐܬܐ ܚܝܒ ܕܡܢ
ܬܠܝܬܐ: ܐܢܫܐ ܕܒܥܝܐ ܗܘܬ ܠܗ ܪܒܘܬܟ. ܘܐܡܪ ܗܘܐ
ܡܫܡܫܢܐ: ܕܢܒܥ ܗܢܐ ܕܐܢܬܬܗ ܘܐܡܗܐ ܐܢܫܝܗ̇ ܗܘܘ.
ܘܡܫܢܐ ܓܒܪ ܐܢܫܐ ܕܐܢܬܬܗ, ܗܘܐ ✣ ܐܡܪ ܠܗ ܬܐܓܡܘܢܐ.
ܦܘܩ ܒܫܪܪܬܗ ܐܬܐ ܠܬܪܥܐ ܕܠܐ ܡܬܝܪܐ ܕܐܙܠ. ܟܕ
ܠܐ ܐܢܫ ܐܬܟܠ ܒܗ. ܘܟܕ ܫܡܥ ܗܘܐ ܡܫܡܫܢܐ:
ܐܬܡܪܡܪ ܗܘܐ ܥܠܘܗܝ ܛܒ. ܘܗܟܢܐ ܐܡܪ ܗܘܐ. ܕܗܢܐ
ܕܗܟܢܐ ܓܒܪ: ܡܫܡܫܢܘ ܒܥܐ ܥܠ ܡܫܠܡ. ܘܫܡܥܬ ܐܝܟ ܠܐ
ܕܢܫܐ. ܘܡܛܠ ܕܗܟܢܐ ܓܒܪ: ܠܐ ܙܕܩ ܕܢܗܘܘܢ ܥܠܘܗܝ
ܪ̈ܚܡܐ. ܘܐܦ ܠܐ ܕܐܬܦܬܚܘܢ ܘܢܩܘܡ ܥܠܘܗܝ ܡܚܘܬܐ
ܐܚܪܢܐ ܕܢܩܘܡ ܥܠܘܗܝ ܡܢ ܡ̈ܠܟܐ. ܐܠܐ ܙܕܩ ܗܘ ܠܝ ܕܐܬܟܪ
ܪܘܚܐ ܒܒܗ: ܐܝܟ ܕܡܬܪܐܬ ܢܦܫܗ ܥܒܘܕܘܗܝ ܘܕܝܢܘܗܝ
ܡܫܡ̈ܫܢܐ. ܘܐܡܪ ܒܗ ܦܓܥܬܐ: ܕܬܗܘܐ ܠܐ ܢܬܢܬܘܢ
ܠܡܢܐ ✣ ܘܟܕ ܦܓܥܬܐ ܒܫܥܬ ܗܘܐ ܘܦܣܩܬ ܥܠܘܗܝ ܟܠ
ܬܪܥܐ ܕܒܝܬ ܕܝܢܐ: ܡܫܡ̈ܫܢܘ ܕܝܢ ܡܢ ܩܕܡ ܐܘܦܝܣܝ. ܘܡܫܡ̈ܫܢܘ
ܡܢ ܩܕܡ ܡܬܥܕܝܐ. ܐܝܬ ܗܘܐ ܕܝܢ ܡܫܡ̈ܫܢܘ ܕܐܬܚܪܝܢ ܗܘܘ
ܠܗ. ܕܒܥܠܐܬ ܓܒܪܐ ܕܐܢܬܬܗ ܘܐܬܩܒܠܬ ܠܐܫܠܡ ܕܢܦܠ ܗܘܘ
ܠܟ ܕܠܐ ܡܬܝܪܐ ܕܕܝܢܐ. ܘܐܝܬ ܗܘܐ ܬܘܒ ܕܐܬܚܪܝܢ ܗܘܘ
ܠܗ. ܕܥܒܕ ܒܓܒܪܐ ܕܒܫܪܪܬܗ ܐܝܟ ܬܘܬ ܐܬܩܒܠܬ. ܡܛܠ ܡܢ
ܗܘ ܕܬܐܓܪܐ ܕܕܝܢܐ ܢܬܠܘܢ ܗܘܐ. ܗܟܢܐ ܗܘ ܟܕ ܡܬܬܕܒܪܐ
ܡܫܡܫܢܘܬܗ ܕܡܫܡܫܢܐ: ܕܐܬܟܢܝ ܗܘ, ܘܠܐ ܗܘܐ ܕܬܐܓܪܐ
ܕܚ̈ܫܐ ✣ ✣

ܩܕܡ ܕܝܢ ܕܫܡܫܐ ܗܘܘ ܥܕ̈ܡܐ ܕܡܬܝܗܒܐ ܡܢ ܐܢܫ ܕܐܬܚܪܝܢ
ܠܗ: ܟܕ ܦܣܩܬ ܗܘܐ ܥܠ ܬܪܥܐ ܕܒܝܬ ܕܝܢܐ. ܘܐܦ ܗܘ
ܗܢܐ ܕܐܝܬܝܐ ܗܘܐ ܒܫܪܪܬܗ ܝܬܝܪ ܬܐܓܡܘܢܐ: ܘܠܐ ܝܬܒܐ

ܕܝܢ ܒܐܝܠܘܠ: ܣܓܝ ܗܘܐ ܡܗܝܡܢܐ. ܘܐܬܬܘܗܝ ܗܘܘ ܡܢ
ܒܗ ܐܘܪܚܐ. ܘܐܡܪ ܗܘܐ ܠܗ. ܦܩܕ ܐܢܬ ܒܗܘ ܡܕܡ ܕܐܡܪ
ܐܢܬ ܒܗ: ܘܡܫܬܡܥ ܐܢܬ ܠܗܝܡܢܘܬܐ ܕܐܚ̈ܝܢ ܩ̈ܠܝܠܐ.
ܘܐܦ ܕܝܢ ܠܐ ܡܫܬܡܥ ܐܢܬ. ܒܗܘܢܐ ܡܪ̈ܝܪܐ ܚܒܪ ܐܢܐ
ܠܝ ܕܬܫܬܡܥ ܠܗܘܢ ܀

ܡܫܝܚ ܐܡܪ. ܠܐ ܐܫܬܡܥܬ ܠܗܘܢ. ܘܐܦ ܠܐ ܕܐܫܬܡܥ
ܠܗܘܢ ܦܩܕܐ ܒܪܚܡܘܬܐ. ܘܐܦ ܠܐ ܐܢ ܗܘ ܕܪ̈ܓܝ ܐܢܬ
ܠ ܒܪܢܫܐ ܕܪܒܝܥ. ܐܦ ܡܢ ܐܝܠܝܢ ܕܦܩܕܘ ܩ̈ܠܝܠܐ ܀ ܡܗܝܡܢܐ
ܐܡܪ. ܒܩ̈ܠܝܠܐ ܢܦܫܐ ܐܢܫ. ܕܐܢ ܠܐ ܬܬܪܥܝ ܠܐ
ܐܬܒܥ ܡܕܡ ܕܦܩܕܐ ܘܡܟܝܪ ܕܠܐ ܐܫܬܡܥ ܒܝ. ܘܢܒܝܐ
ܐܢ ܦܬܡ ܠܝ ܡܫܝܚܐ ܗܘ ܕܦܩܕ ܐܢܬ ܠܗ ܀

ܡܫܝܚ ܐܡܪ. ܒܠܗܘܢ ܐܝܠܝܢ ܕܦܩܕܬ ܠܡܫܝܚܐ ܦܪ̈ܘܫܐ
ܐܝܟ ܕܡܫܝܚܐ. ܕܠܐ ܗܘܘ ܦܩܕܝܢ ܠܒܪܢܫܐ ܒܡ ܕܪܘܚܐ
ܕܪ̈ܘܚܬܐ ܀ ܡܗܝܡܢܐ ܐܡܪ. ܫܡܥܬ ܘܢܛܪܬ ܒܩܛܠܬܐ.
ܒܪܡܐ ܕܠܐ ܦܓܥܬ ܗܘܬ ܕܢܦܠܬ ܒܚܙܘܗ ܕܠܐ ܩܠܝܠ ܗܘܐ
ܒܗ ܀ ܡܫܝܚ ܐܡܪ. ܗܠܝܢ ܐܘ̈ܠܝܢܐ ܕܐܘܪ̈ܚܬ ܒܠܗܘܢ
ܕܡܪ̈ܢܝܢ ܒܬ̈ܪܝܗܘܢ. ܡܢܗܘܢ ܡܬܬܒܠܝܢ ܩ̈ܠܝܠܐ ܕܪܘܚܬܐ.
ܠܐܝܠܝܢ ܕܡܫܬܡܥܝܢ ܠܗܘܢ ܀ ܡܗܝܡܢܐ ܐܡܪ. ܐܝܟܢܐ
ܠܐܘ̈ܠܝܢܐ ܦܬܝܪ ܐܢܬܘܢ ܠܗܘܢ ܪܘܚܬܐ. ܘܠܦ̈ܘܩܕܢܐ
ܕܦܬܓܡܘܢ ܫܡܥܝܢ ܐܢܬܘܢ ܠܗܘܢ ܒܠܠܐ ܕܪܘܚܬܐ ܀

ܡܫܝܚ ܐܡܪ. ܠܐ ܕܝܠܝ ܗܝ ܗܕܐ ܕܐܫܬܐܠܬ ܒܠ ܗܠܝܢ.
ܡܛܠ ܕܠܐ ܥܘܩܐ ܒܥܘܪܬܟ ܕܐܫܬܡܥ ܦܘܩܕܢ ܕܝܠܝ. ܕܠܐ
ܡܫܡܥ ܐܢܐ. ܐܡܪܬ ܘܐܡܪ ܐܢܐ ܀ ܡܗܝܡܢܐ ܐܡܪ. ܐܢܬ
ܡܛܠ ܕܥܒܕܬ ܠܗܘܢ ܦܩܕܬ ܒܗܠܝܢ ܕܪܒܝܥ. ܐܢܐ ܫܡܥܬ ܐܢܐ
ܚܢܢ: ܗܠܝܢ ܕܐܡܪ̈ܢ ܒܗܘܢ ܗܘܐ. ܘܠܐ ܕܐܝܟ ܡܕܡ.
ܘܡܫܡܥ ܐܢܐ ܐܢܫܝܢ: ܕܫܡܥܝܢ ܢܦܫܗܘܢ ܕܩ̈ܠܝܠܐ ܘܠܐ
ܐܡܪ ܀ ܡܫܝܚ ܐܡܪ. ܐܢܬ ܗܘ ܒܠܒܐ ܐܚܪܢܐ ܠܐܠܗܐ.

ܠܥܢܝܢܐ. ܀ ܦܝܠܣܘܦܐ ܐܡܪ. ܠܐ ܬܫܡܥ ܒܡܠܐ ܕܢܫܐ:
ܗܘ ܐܢܫܐ ܕܐܬܦܬܟ ܒܗ ܢܐܙܠ. ܘܬܬܒܪ ܠܗܘ ܚܘܒܫܗܘܢ
ܦܪܐ ܕܡܠܟܐ ܀ ܀ ܣܢܕܒܢ ܐܡܪ. ܐܠܐ ܐܬܬܘܗ. ܘܗܘ ܗܢܐ
ܫܬܦܪܐ ܒܕܒܪܐ ܕܢܫܝܐ. ܥܒܕ ܐܡܪ ܐܢܬ ܕܬܣܒܪ ܐܢܐ
ܠܗ. ܐܝܟ ܕܐܢ ܟܠܗܘܢ ܕܢܫܐ ܘܦܓܥܘ ܕܒܢܝܢܐ: ܦܓܥ
ܚܠܗܝ ܕܒܢܝܢ ܗܘ: ܐܡܬܝ ܐܡܪ ܐܢܬ ܠܝ ܕܡܣܒܪ ܐܢܐ
ܠܗ: ܕܗܘܐ ܢܦܪܘܩ ܡܢܗ ܘܟܠܗܝ. ܀ ܦܝܠܣܘܦܐ ܐܡܪ. ܒܗ
ܒܗܕܐ ܕܠܐ ܢܦܠܐ ܐܢܬ ܕܬܬܚܒܪ ܠܗ ܡܣܒܪ ܐܢܬ ܠܗ ܀
ܣܢܕܒܢ ܐܡܪ. ܘܡܢ ܡܛܠ ܕܠܐ ܦܠܚ ܐܢܐ ܠܗ ܡܣܒܪ
ܐܢܐ ܠܝ. ܒܗܢܐ ܕܝܢ ܢܦܪܘܩ ܒܪܒܪ ܗܘܐ ܠܗ ܢܦܠܐ: ܕܟܠܗܘܢ
ܗܘܐ ܒܒܥܬܐ ܕܦܪܘܠܐ: ܘܡܫܝܐ ܕܡܫܝܚܝ ܗܘܐ ܘܡܒܥܒܥ
ܗܘܐ ܒܢܝܢܐ ܀ ܘܒܪ ܥܒܕ ܗܘܐ ܦܝܠܣܘܦܐ ܕܗܢܐ ܐܡܪ
ܗܘܐ. ܦܬܪ ܗܘܐ ܕܬܬܒܪ ܕܠܐ ܢܫܩܘܢ. ܘܒܪ ܐܬܬܒܪ ܗܘܐ
ܡܢ ܫܡܥܐ ܐܡܪ ܠܗ. ܡܬܦܩܕ ܐܢܬ ܗܟܢܐ ܠܡܠܟܐ: ܗܘ
ܕܝܢ ܠܐ ܡܬܦܩܕ ܐܢܬ. ܡܦܪܫ ܦܪܫ ܐܢܐ ܠܟ. ܘܟܠ ܫܢܝܢ
ܡܬܠܬ ܐܢܐ ܠܟ: ܘܡܢ ܗܘ ܠܐܣܝܘܬܐ ܦܬܪ ܐܢܐ ܚܠܝܢ
ܕܟܘܪܐ ܬܐܡܪ. ܀ ܀

ܣܢܕܒܢ ܐܡܪ. ܗܠܝܢ ܠܡܫܡܥܐ ܕܗܘܐ ܡܢܐܠ ܐܢܬ ܠܝ
ܟܠܗܘܢ: ܐܦ ܚܕܐ ܘܚܒܝܝܢ: ܡܢ ܐܝܠܝܢ ܕܦܪܫܬ ܗܘܝܬ
ܦܪܫܬ ܒܪܒܢܢ ܕܐܬܬܟܪܝ. ܘܗܝ ܕܝܢ ܗܘ ܐܬܬܠ ܘܐܬܚܝܠܬ ܠܝ ܀ ܀
ܦܝܠܣܘܦܐ ܐܡܪ. ܐܬܐܡܝܗ ܒܡܠܐ ܕܦܪܘܠܐ ܕܩܛܠܬܐ.
ܘܬܬܒܪ ܐܝܟ ܕܫܩܠ. ܘܒܪ ܡܬܬܒܪ ܗܘܐ ܐܡܪܝܢ ܠܗ. ܕܝܢ
ܠܬܠܡܐ. ܘܦܬܚ ܗܘܐ ܘܐܡܪ. ܕܫܡܥܐ ܐܢܘܢ ܦܬܪܘܗܝ.
ܘܦܫܘܢ ܕܢܦܩܘܢ ܠܗܘܢ ܒܒܝܬܗܘܢ ܐܬܬܦܩܘܢ. ܘܥܒܕ ܗܘܐ
ܦܝܠܣܘܦܐ: ܘܬܫܡܫܬܗܘܢ ܗܘܐ ܠܒܝܬ ܐܒܗܬܐ. ܘܠܐ ܝܕܥܘ
ܗܘܘ ܠܗ ܕܢܦܠܠ ܥܡ ܐܢܫܘܬܗ ܘܒܢܝ ܒܝܬܗ. ܐܝܟ ܦܘܩܕܢܗ
ܕܡܠܟܐ. ܘܡܠܟܐ ܕܝܢ ܐܬܬܘܗ ܗܘܐ ܐܢܬܐ ܕܡܠܟܐ ܀ ܫܬܦܪܐ

ܕܥܠܘܗܝ ܕܠܡܦܠܚ ܐܢܬ. ܘܩܘܡ ܩܕܡܝܗܘܢ ܨܠܡܝ ܐܠ̈ܗܬܐ
ܕܡ̈ܠܟܝܢ: ܘܐܦ ܡܢ ܐܝܠܝܢ ܕܣܓܕܘ ܡ̈ܠܟܐ ܀ ܚܒܝܒ ܐܡܪ.
ܐܦܠܐ ܠܐ ܕܐܬܪܚܡܬ ܒܗܘܢ ܕܡܚܕ̈ܪܢ ܠܝ: ܘܐܦ ܠܐ ܡܣܐܡܪ
ܐܡܪ ܗܘܝܬ ܒܗܘܢ ܘܒܡܠܟܝܗܘܢ ܀ ܗܓܡܘܢܐ ܐܡܪ. ܐܝܟܢܐ ܡܬܚܬܡ
ܐܢܐ ܠܗܘܢ ܠܩܠܝܢ. ܒܥܕ ܚܕܢܐ. ܘܡܬܪܓܐ ܐܢܐ ܠܟ
ܠ̈ܐܠܗܐ ܕܠܐ ܬܣܓܘܕ ܠܗܘܢ. ܘܡܚܣܢ ܐܢܐ ܠܟ ܡ̈ܠܟܐ.
ܥܠ ܕܫܝܛܬ ܥܠ ܦܘܩܕܢܝܗܘܢ ܀ ܚܒܝܒ ܐܡܪ. ܠܐ ܕܝܠ ܐܢܐ
ܡܢ ܡܠܬܐ ܕܡܫܐܠ ܐܢܬ ܠܝ ܒܗ. ܐܦܠܐ ܒܪ ܕܝܠ ܗܘܝܬ
ܡܢܗܘܢ. ܠܐ ܗܘܐ ܒܥܬ ܩ̈ܛܠܐ ܡܬܒܥܝܢ ܗܘܝܬ ܘܡܬܡܟܟ ܗܘܝܬ:
ܗܘ ܕܡܛܠ ܗܢܐ ܡܬܟܪܟ ܗܘܝܬ ܀ ܗܓܡܘܢܐ ܐܡܪ. ܐܡܪܢܐ
ܠܒܪܢܫܐ ܗܝܟ ܐܢܬ ܘܡܝܬܪ ܐܢܬ. ܘܠܗܘ ܗܢܐ ܠܐ ܢܟܦܐ
ܐܢܬ ܕܬܬܗܦܟ ܠܗ ܘܬܣܓܘܕ ܀ ܚܒܝܒ ܐܡܪ. ܠܒܪܢܫܐ ܠܐ
ܦܠܚ ܐܢܐ. ܡܛܠ ܕܒܬܪܗ ܗܘ ܠܝ. ܕܠܝܬ ܗܘ ܥܠ ܟܠ
ܕܡܬܬܚܠ ܥܠ ܒܪܢܫܐ. ܠܐܠܗܐ ܕܝܢ ܕܥܒܕ ܫܡܝܐ ܘܐܪܥܐ
ܒܪܢܫܐ ܦܠܚ ܐܢܐ ܘܡܫܒܚ ܐܢܐ ܀ ܀ ܗܓܡܘܢܐ ܐܡܪ.
ܐܢܬ ܡܕܡ ܕܨܒܘ ܡ̈ܠܟܐ ܥܒܕ. ܘܗܝ ܕܐܢܬ ܒܪܚܡܝܢ ܕܠܝ
ܗܝ. ܐܢ ܢܟܦܐ ܐܢܬ ܕܬܬܦܫܐ. ܘܐܢ ܠܐ ܢܟܦܐ ܐܢܬ ܠܐ
ܬܥܒܕܗ ܀ ܚܒܝܒ ܐܡܪ. ܠܐ ܡܥ̈ܒܕܝܢ ܕܢܗܘܘܢ ܬܬܝܗܘܢ ܡܛܠ
ܕܡܘܕܝܢ ܗܘ ܒܟܘܪܐ ܠܡܘܬܐ. ܘܕܐܬܐ ܠܗ ܡܢ ܬܪܥܝܬܐ
ܗܝ ܕܡܚܒܐ ܒܪܚܡܝܢ ܠܐ ܡܚܒܝܢܐ ܀ ܗܓܡܘܢܐ ܐܡܪ.
ܒܐܠ̈ܗܘܬܐ ܡܪ̈ܬܐ ܘܩܢܝܐ ܥܒܕ ܐܢܐ ܠܟ ܕܬܬܚܪܪ ܡܢ
ܬܪܥܘܬܟ: ܗܝ ܕܐܬܪܓܫܬ ܕܡܚܒܐ ܒܪܚܡܝܢ. ܚܒܝܒ ܐܡܪ.
ܗܠܝܢ ܐܠܗܘܬܐ ܕܥܒܪ ܐܢܬ ܥܠܝܗܘܢ ܕܢܗܘܘܢ ܡܬܬܪܥܐ
ܡܢ ܬܪܥܘܬܝ. ܢܗܘܘܢ ܗܘ ܡܬܢܨܚܝܢ ܒܗ ܬܪܥܘܬ. ܐܝܟ
ܐܠܗܐ ܕܠܚܡ ܒܐܪܥܐ. ܀ ܗܓܡܘܢܐ ܐܡܪ. ܡܛܠ ܡܕܡ ܕܡܕܢܚ
ܬܟܠܐ ܘܫܘܪܐ ܠܗܘ ܐܠܗܝ. ܘܐܢܐ ܕܡ ܚܕܢܐ ܕܗܦܟ
ܐܢܐ ܥܠܘܗܝ ܢܘܪܐ ܠܡܝܢܘ ܕܠܐ ܢܫܘܢ ܀ ܚܒܝܒ ܐܡܪ.

ܗܘ ܕܟܦܪ ܐܢܬ ܒܗ ܗܪܟܐ. ܘܬܬܒܥ ܡܬܒܥܬ ܒܗ ܒܥܠܡܐ. ܒܪ
ܬܘܒ ܗܦܟܬ ܟܦܪ ܐܢܬ ܒܗ ܀ ܗܓܡܘܢܐ ܐܡܪ. ܫܡܥܘ ܗܘ
ܠܡܠܟܐ ܕܐܦܩܕܬ ܠܟܘܢ. ܘܣܘܦ ܫܡܫܐ ܕܗܘܢܐ ܕܒܥܐ ܕܗܘܐ
ܡܩܝܡ ܐܢܬ ܒܗ ܕܠܝܬ ܡܢ ܕܡܫܝܙܒ ܦܪܘܩ ܠܟ ܡܢܗ. ܐܠܐ
ܐܢܘܢ ܕܦܪܩܘܟ ܐܠܗܐ ܐܢܘܢ ܡܫܒܚ ܐܢܬ ܠܗܘܢ. ܀ ܫܡܘܢܐ
ܐܡܪ ܐܝܠܝܢ ܕܫܒܩܝܢ ܡܛܠ ܫܡܗ ܕܡܫܝܚܐ: ܘܠܐ ܦܠܚܝܢ
ܠܒܪܝܬܐ ܘܠܒܪܘܝܗ̇. ܫܒܩܘܢ ܡܫܝܚܢ ܡܢ ܐܠܗܐ. ܘܐܝܠܝܢ
ܕܪܚܡܝܢ ܚܝܐ ܕܒܥܠܡܐ ܗܢܐ ܡܢ ܗܪܟܐ. ܫܒܩܘܗܝ ܕܠܥܠܡ ܗܘ.
ܘܟܕ ܗܘܐ ܗܓܡܘܢܐ ܘܬܠܡܝܕܘܗܝ ܗܘܘ ܘܫܪܘܗܝ. ܘܟܕ
ܫܪܝܢ ܗܘܘ ܠܗ ܡܫܬܐܠܝܢ ܗܘܘ ܠܗ. ܘܗܘܐ ܬܠܬܐ ܗܘܐ
ܛܘܪܐ ܗܘܢܝܐ: ܒܝܘܡܐ ܕܫܒܬܐ ܗܘܘ ܬܒܥܐ ܕܕܪܟܗܘܢ.
ܐܡܪ ܠܗ ܗܓܡܘܢܐ. ܡܬܛܦܫ ܐܢܬ ܐܦ ܗܫܐ: ܕܬܗܘܐ
ܒܩܫܝܐ ܡܢ ܗܢܐ ܗܘܝܐ. ܫܡܘܢܐ ܐܡܪ. ܡܢ ܫܒܩܐ ܗܘܝܢ
ܠܐ ܐܬܛܦܫܬ ܠܟ: ܗܫܐ ܕܗܘܐ ܫܒܩܬ ܐܢܘܢ: ܐܡܠܟܐ ܦܩܕ
ܐܢܬ ܕܡܬܛܦܫ ܐܢܐ ܠܟ: ܕܐܦܠܚ ܒܗܘܢ ܗܘ ܡܕܡ
ܕܐܫܬܡܫܬ ܒܗܘܢ ܀ ܗܓܡܘܢܐ ܐܡܪ. ܒܪܢܫܐ ܕܫܒܩܝܢ
ܘܡܬܪܓܡ ܡܢ ܗܠܝܢ ܡܠܟܐ. ܐܢܐ ܕܐܫܬܡܥܟ: ܐܝܟ ܦܘܩܕܢܐ
ܕܡܠܟܐ. ܒܥܡܟܐ ܕܢܦܫܘܗܝ ܬܒܒ ܀ ܫܡܘܢܐ ܐܡܪ. ܐܢܬ
ܒܢܝ ܐܢܬ ܠܝ ܒܠ ܕܠܐ ܐܫܬܡܥܬ ܠܦܘܩܕܢܐ ܕܡܠܟܐ. ܕܗܐ
ܐܦ ܐܢܬ ܕܐܘܪܒܢܟ ܡܠܟܐ ܘܡܒܪܘܢܟ ܕܢܝܐ. ܒܥܒܕܬ ܒܠ
ܦܘܩܕܢܘܗܝ. ܒܗ ܕܠܐ ܒܥܒܕܬ ܠ ܡܕܡ ܕܦܩܕ ܠܟ ܡܠܟܐ ܀
ܗܓܡܘܢܐ ܐܡܪ. ܒܠ ܕܐܬܒܪܬ ܪܘܚ ܒܡܟ ܐܥܒܕܬ ܗܓܢܐ.
ܐܝܟ ܒܢܝܐ ܡܡܠܟܢܐ ܀ ܫܡܘܢܐ ܐܡܪ. ܐܠܘ ܠܐ ܕܢܚܬܬ
ܘܫܒܩܬ ܘܪܡܬ ܘܐܪܒܥܬ ܬܠܝܠ ܒܗܪܐ. ܐܢܬ ܗܘܐ
ܠܡܫܝܢܘ ܕܐܥܒܕܬ ܪܘܚܟ ܒܟܢ. ܐܠ ܕܝܢ ܗܠܝܢ ܐܝܬ
ܒܡܫܝܚܘܬܐ. ܐܡܟܐ ܗܝ ܡܥܒܕܬ ܪܘܚܐ ܕܠܒܬܝ ܕܐܥܒܕܬ.
ܗܓܡܘܢܐ ܐܡܪ. ܠܐ ܡܟܝܒܢ ܠܟ ܗܠܝܢ ܕܐܥܒܕܬ: ܡܛܠ

ܘܠܘܬ ܕܢܬܦܐ ܒܐܝ̈ܕܘܗܝ ܘܐܡܪ ܠܗ ܡܢܐ ܥܒܕ
ܐܢܬ ܀ ܀

ܡܫܡܫܢܐ ܐܡܪ. ܠܗܕܐ ܡܪܘܚܬܟ ܕܒܪ ܗܘ ܡܘܬܐ
ܕܣܝܦܐ. ܡܠܝܟ ܐܢܐ ܗܘ ܕܝܢ ܕܡܘܬܐ ܕܡܢܝܪ ܡܢ ܣܝܦܐ
ܢܦܫܝ ܥܠܝܟ ܀ ܚܒܝܒ ܐܡܪ. ܐܢܐ ܕܝܢ ܠܗܘ ܡܘܬܐ ܕܝܬܝܪ
ܡܬܚܫܒ ܡܢ ܕܣܝܦܐ ܚܫܝܒ ܐܢܐ: ܕܢܦܫܝ ܥܠ ܒܥܘܢܐ ܕܢܦܠܐ
ܐܢܬ ܀ ܘܡܢ ܒܬܪ ܗܠܝܢ. ܦܩܕ ܗܘܐ ܗܓܡܘܢܐ ܕܢܬܠ ܗܘܐ
ܥܠܘܗܝ ܐܦܘܦܣܝܣ ܕܡܘܬܐ. ܘܡܦܩܐ ܗܘܐ ܩܕܡ ܐܘܦܣܝܣ
ܕܠܗ ܘܐܡܪ. ܟܕ ܫܡܥܝܢ ܗܘܘ ܠܗ. ܘܐܦ ܚܐܪܐ ܕܡܕܝܢܬܐ.
ܚܒܝܒ ܗܢܐ ܕܟܦܪ ܒܐܠܗ̈ܐ; ܐܝܟ ܕܐܦ ܫܡܥܬܘܢ ܡܢܗ.
ܘܨܥܪ ܬܘܒ ܠܡܠܟ̈ܐ. ܘܐܦ ܗܘ ܕܐܬܦܩܕܘ ܚܝ̈ܘܗܝ ܡܢ ܬܚܘܬ
ܥܒܕܐ ܗܘܐ ܡܛܫܝ. ܘܠܐ ܢܒܥܐ ܢܬܚܙܐ ܗܘܐ ܚܙܝܐ
ܕܐܠܗ̈ܐ. ܘܐܠܘ ܠܐ ܕܦܩܕ ܗܘܐ ܠܡܠܟܐ ܩ̈ܕܡܝܐ: ܕܐܬܦܩܕܘ
ܥܠܝܗܘܢ ܕܩܛܠܝܢ. ܘܐܦܠܐ ܕܐܬܦܩܕ ܗܘܬ ܥܠܘܗܝ ܕܢܗܘܐ
ܙܕܩ ܗܘܐ. ܡܛܠ ܕܢܘܟܪܝܐ ܐܡܪܝܢ ܗܘܐ. ܦܩܕܬ ܕܬܬܠ
ܚܪܬܐ ܒܣܘܦܗ ܐܝܟ ܕܒܢܡܘܣ ܡܠܟ̈ܐ. ܘܐܡܪ ܟܪܘܙܐ
ܪܚܡܬܟ. ܗܘ ܕܐܬܚܪ ܡܬܚܝܒ. ܕܢܬܩܛܠ ܒܣܝܦܐ ܕܢܦܩܬܗ. ܘܢܦܩ
ܗܘܐ ܡܢ ܩܕܡ ܗܓܡܘܢܐ ܟܕ ܙܩܝܦܐ ܚܪܬܐ ܒܣܘܦܗ.
ܘܗܡܠܐ ܕܐܢܫ̈ܐ ܕܡܕܝܢܬܐ ܪܗܛܐ ܗܘܬ ܠܪܓܠܗ.
ܒܬܘܠܬܐ ܕܝܢ ܚܕܝܢ ܗܘܘ ܕܠܐ ܥܒܕ ܗܘܐ ܘܠܐ ܓܒܪ ܡܢ
ܡܒܚܬܗ. ܘܫܘܒܚܐ ܠܫܒܚܝܢ ܗܘܘ ܠܗ. ܟܠ ܕܠܐ ܢܟܪܐ ܗܘܐ
ܕܢܒܥ. ܘܒܪܘܗܝ ܡܢ ܬܪܥܐ ܡܕܝܢܬܐ ܕܩܘܫܬܐ. ܠܗܘܟܠ
ܡܘܡܠܢܝܢ. ܗܘ ܕܚܒܝܒܐ ܗܘܬ ܠܡܒܠܥܗ ܒܪ ܐܠܗܐ. ܐܡܗ ܕܝܢ
ܠܒܝܫܐ ܗܘܬ ܚܘܪ̈ܐ ܘܢܦܩܬ ܗܘܬ ܥܡܗ. ܘܟܕ ܢܦܩ ܗܘܐ
ܕܝܢ ܠܡܫܬܘܬܐ ܗܘ ܕܟܠܗ ܡܦܩܕܝܢ ܗܘܘ ܠܗ. ܡܢ ܗܘܐ ܘܢܦܠ
ܗܘܐ. ܘܟܠ ܐܢܫ ܕܒܥܐ ܗܘܘ ܒܥܒܕܗ. ܘܐܡܪ ܗܘܐ. ܟܠܗܘܢ
ܡܫܝܚܐ: ܕܕܝܠܟ ܗܘ ܟܠܗ ܗܢܐ: ܘܕܝܠܟ ܗܘ ܟܠܗܘܢ

ܠܐ ܗܘܐ ܒܐܝܠܝܢ ܕܣܥܪ ܐܝܬ ܐܢܐ. ܡܛܠ ܕܒܐܝܠܝܢ ܗܘ ܕܩܝܡ ܡܬܬܒܥܐ ܐܢܐ. ܘܡܛܠ ܗܢܐ ܥܒܕ ܐܢܐ ܝܨܝܦܐ ܒܐܠܗܐ ܚܒܪܝ. ܘܠܐ ܕܐܬܦܪܐ ܒܥܕܬܐ. ܗܘ ܕܐܦܠܐ ܒܡܕܡ ܚܕܐ ܀ ܡܟܣܝܡܘܣ ܐܡܪ. ܡܛܠ ܕܗܟܢܐ ܥܒܪ ܒܐܠܗܐ ܕܢܛܪܝܢ ܠܗܘܢ ܩܠܝܠܝ. ܬܬܦܘܣܘܢ ܗܪܟܐ ܥܠ ܗܘܦܟܗܘܢ ܩܕܡܝܐ. ܒܫܘܐܠܐ ܕܝܢ ܩܕܡܝܐ ܕܐܬܪܬ ܙܘܥ ܒܡܢܐ ܘܫܬܠܗ. ܠܡܢܐ ܐܝܟ ܠܗܘܦܟܗܘܢ ܩܕܡܝܐ. ܘܡܢ ܦܘܪܫܢܐ ܗܘ ܠܗ ܡܢܐ ܗܘܐ ܘܐܡܪ. ܕܠܐ ܥܒܕ ܢܦܫܗ ܕܥܒܕܐ ܗܢܐ: ܠܬܫܡܫܬܐ ܐܝܕܐ ܕܒܬܪܟܢ ܕܐܬܬܚܒܠ ܒܐܝܠܝܢ ܕܐܢܫܘܗܝ ܠܡܫܝܚܐ. ܘܡܢ ܝܕܥ ܗܘܐ ܡܟܣܝܡܘܣ ܕܐܦܠܐ ܒܗܠܝܢ ܐܬܠܝܢܐ ܙܟܝܐ ܗܘܐ ܕܢܨܚ. ܐܡܪ ܠܗ ܗܟܢܐ ܐܝܟ ܠܗܘܢ ܡܠܝܟܘܢ ܕܗܘܝܬܘܢ ܦܠܚ ܐܝܬܝܟܘܢ ܡܫܬܡܗܝܢ. ܀ ܫܡܥܘ ܐܡܪ ܠܐ ܗܘܐ ܦܫܝܩ ܗܟܢ. ܡܛܠܗ ܗܘ ܕܐܡܪ ܗܘ ܠܝ: ܕܡܢ ܕܐܠܗܐ ܢܦܫ ܢܦܫܗ. ܐܠܐ ܐܦ ܐܫܬܘܬܐ ܒܬܒܥܐ ܠܝ. ܕܠܐ ܢܛܠ ܡܘܕܥܐ ܠܥܠܡܝܢ. ܘܠܐ ܢܦܩܐ ܡܬܚܣܢܬܐ ܡܢܟ ܫܪܝܪܐ ܀܀܀ ܡܟܣܝܡܘܣ ܐܡܪ. ܢܗܘܐ ܐܢܐ ܕܠܗ ܕܐܡܪ ܐܝܬ ܗܟܢܐ. ܐܝܟ ܕܢܦܫ ܙܥܘܪ. ܘܫܬܐ ܕܥܒܕ. ܘܐܫܟܚ ܟܠܗ ܦܘܩܕܢܐ ܘܠܠܐܒܘܬ. ܠܐ ܝܕܥ ܦܘܬܪܗܘܢ ܐܢܐ ܥܠ ܗܕܐ ܕܥܒܕܬ. ܐܠܐ ܦܪܘܩ ܐܢܐ ܙܘܥ: ܠܐ ܗܘܐ ܠܢܦܫܝ. ܐܠܐ ܐܝܟ ܕܠܡܫܝܚܐ ܐܘܠܝܢܐ ܕܥܒܕܝ. ܘܬܒܥܐ ܒܡܪܝ ܡܢ ܢܛܪ ܡܫܡܫܝ: ܒܡܪܝܐ ܕܚܒܝܫ ܥܠ ܚܛܗܝ ܀܀ ܫܡܥܘ ܐܡܪ. ܐܦ ܐܢܐ ܠܗܕܐ ܗܘ ܣܥܪ ܐܢܐ. ܕܬܦܘܩ ܬܫܒܘܚܬܐ ܒܐܝܕܝ ܕܐܬܦܪܫܬ ܀܀

ܡܟܣܝܡܘܣ ܐܡܪ. ܐܬܩܢܝܘ ܠܬܟܠܝܬܐ ܕܐܝܬ ܠܗܘܢ ܥܘܠܝܟܝ. ܕܠܡܥܒܕ ܕܪܝܫ ܚܒܝܫ ܀܀ ܫܡܥܘ ܐܡܪ. ܠܗܝ ܡܢ ܒܝܫܬܐ: ܕܠܡܥܒܕ ܕܪܝܫ ܚܒܝܫ. ܐܠܐ ܐܦ ܐܠܗܐ ܗܘ ܕܥܘܠܝܟܝ ܒܡܫܡܫܐ: ܘܒܠܗܘܢ ܒܡܫܪܝܢ ܕܐܪܥܐ.

ܒܢ̈ܝܢ ܕܪ̈ܝܢ ܗ̈ܘܘ. ܟܕ ܥܡܘܕܐ ܚܠܝܫ ܡܢܗ ܗܘܐ ܠܐܠܗܐ: ܕܢܦܠ ܥܡܗ ܡܢܗ ܗܘܐ ܦܓܪܗ ܠܡܕܢܚܐ ܕܢܘܪܐ.܀

ܐܝܬܘܗܝ ܗܘܐ ܕܝܢ ܡܥܪܬܐ ܕܚܕܐ ܗܘܐ ܒܗ ܒܛܘܪܬܐ ܟܬܝܒܐ ܒܐܝܪܚ ܐܠܘܠ. ܒܡܥܪܬܐ ܗܝ ܕܐܫܬܟܚ ܗܘܐ ܒܗ. ܕܩܘܦܠܦܠܘܣ ܐܒܐ: ܕܝܢ ܗܘܐ ܕܢܦܩ ܡܢ ܠܗ ܐܘܟܝܢܐ: ܕܢܦܩܬ ܗܘܐ ܠܗܘܡܢܐ ܡܕܝܢܬܐ ܕܐܦܠܝܛܐ. ܐܝܟ ܕܢܦܩ ܗܘܐ ܒܗ ܠܝܘܡܢ: ܗܢܐ ܕܡܬܩܪܝܐ ܡܕܝܢܬܐ ܒܐܩܐ ܡܕܢܚܝܬܐ ܒܗ ܕܚܘܡܨܐ. ܘܗܘܐ ܡܕܝܢܬܐ ܐܝܬܝܪܬܐ ܕܥܠ ܟܠܗܝܢ. ܕܠܐ ܐܝܟ ܢܒܝܐ ܐܢܫܐ ܡܢܗܘܢ ܕܒܗ. ܘܡܫܡܫܐ ܒܫܘܠܛܢܐ ܕܡܠܟܘܬܗ. ܘܟܗܢܐ ܠܟܠ ܗܢܘܢ ܕܠܝܬ ܕܘܟܝܐ ܡܢ ܥܠܡܐ. ܐܦܝܣܩܘܦܐ ܕܝܢ ܕܬܡܢ ܗܘܘ ܥܠ ܡܕܡ ܕܫܡܥܝܢ ܗܘܘ ܡܢ ܕܢܒܝܐ. ܘܟܗ̈ܢܐ ܕܡܕܝܢܬܐ ܕܬܡܢ ܗܘܘ. ܫܪܟܐ ܕܐܢ̈ܫܝܢܬܐ ܕܡܬܐܡܪ̈ܝܢ ܗ̈ܘܘ، ܠܒܪ ܡܢ ܬܪܥܐ ܕܒܝܬ ܕܢܒܝܐ. ܘܐܝܟ ܟܒܝܪܐ ܕܐܝܬ ܗܘܐ. ܟܠ ܕܫܡܥܝܢ ܗܘܘ ܘܟܠ ܕܚܙܝܢ ܗܘܘ. ܡܫܒܚܝܢ ܗܘܘ ܠܢܒܝܐ. ܘܡܬܬܟܝܢ ܗ̈ܘܘ ܒܗܘܡܢܘܬܐ ܕܠܗܘܢ ܠܟܠ ܕܒܗܘܢ ܀ ܐܢܫܐ ܬܐܘܦܝܠܐ ܐܢܫܐ ܕܦܓܪܗ ܗܘܬ ܒܬܪܬܝܬܐ ܒܫܢܬܐ ܕܐܬܝܗܒ. ܘܐܬܕܢܚܬ ܒܡܥܝܢܐ. ܐܬܓܠܝ ܠܝ ܘܦܬܚܬ ܫܡܥܐ ܕܗܘܦܩܢܘܬܐ ܗܠܝܢ ܕܝܘܚܢܢ ܐܝܟ ܡܐ ܕܦܬܚܬ ܗܘܬ ܡܢ ܩܕܡ: ܕܟܠܗܝܢ ܘܕܫܘܠܛܢܐ ܕܗܘܕܝܐ ܚܕܝܘܗܝ. ܘܕܗܘܒܐ ܗܘܐ ܠܗܘܢ ܠܟܠܢܐ ܒܟܬܒܐ ܕܦܫܝܩܘܬ. ܐܬܕܪܟ ܗܘܐ ܠܗܘܢ ܐܦ ܗܘ ܒܣܘܪܐ ܕܡܕܝܢܬܐ ܕܟܠܠܗ. ܘܦܬܚܬ ܬܪܥܐ ܘܪܗܛܐ: ܘܡܫܝܚܐ ܕܒܠܠܗܘܢ ܕܗܘܕܝܐ ܗܠܝܢ: ܠܐ ܡܛܠ ܐܝܠܝܢ ܕܐܬܒܛܠ ܚܕ ܟܢܫܝܢ. ܐܠܐ ܡܛܠ ܕܢܐܠܦܘܢ ܐܝܠܝܢ ܕܐܬܝܢ ܒܬܪܢ. ܐܢܫܐ ܗܘܐ ܕܒܗܘܢ ܕܗܘܕܝܐ ܗܠܝܢ: ܗܢܝܢ ܐܢܘܢ ܘܐܦ ܒܗܘܦܩܢܘܬܐ ܕܗܘܕܝܐ ܩܕܡܝܐ ܕܒܢܝܢ ܕܡܠܝܘܗܝ ܡܠܟܐ. ܘܕܪܟܐ ܕܡܠܟܐ ܐܚܪܢܐ. ܐܝܠܝܢ ܕܐܦ ܦܘܢ ܟܕܘ ܗܘܘ ܬܪܥܝܐ ܠܒܪܬܐ. ܘܡܛܠ ܗܘܐ ܘܐܦ ܠܦܠܚܐ: ܒܬܪܬܐ ܘܒܗܘܪܐ ܘܒܐܘܠܨܢܐ ܡܬܕܪܝܐ:

ܕܡܠܟܘܬܗ. ܢܣܒ ܘܣܪ. ܕܟܕ ܡܫܡܫܐ ܗܘܬ ܕܐܚܘܗܝ ܗܘܬ ܡܢ
ܦܝܠܝܦܐ ܩܠܝܠ: ܠܐ ܫܪܝܪ ܕܬܣܒܝܗ̇ ܠܐܢܬܬ ܐܚܘܟ. ܠܐ ܫܠܝܛ
ܗܘܬ. ܡܛܠ ܕܠܐ ܢܘܪܐ ܗܘܐ ܕܝܢ ܐܢܐ ܗܘ. ܠܦܘܪܫܢܐ
ܡܫܡܥܢܝ: ܐܝܟ ܕܐܬܬܦܝܣ ܡܢ ܢܘܪܐ ܗܘ ܕܠܐ ܕܥܟܐ. ܘܡܛܠ
ܕܘܟ ܡܫܡܥܢܝ: ܫܪܘܝ ܐܠܗܘܬܟ ܒܪܐ ܕܡܫܝܚܐ ܕܐܠܗܐ
ܘܚܝܐ. ܘܟܕ ܢܚܬ ܗܘܐ. ܐܬܚܒܠ ܗܘܐ ܘܒܪܟܬ ܐܢܘܢ. ܘܡܘܡܐ
ܗܘܐ ܠܗ ܫܠܡܐ. ܟܕ ܦܪܩ: ܒܪܢܫܐ ܘܒܥܝܪܐ، ܘܐܬܩܪܝ ܠܗ.
ܦܪܩ ܟܠܗ ܡܕܡ ܡܫܬܝܟ: ܕܢܒܥܐ ܚܝܠܐ ܒܡܥܡܕ. ܘܢܣܒܬܐ
ܠܦܪܘܫܘ ܕܚܝܐ̈. ܘܟܕ ܡܩܝܡ ܗܘܐ ܚܝܠܐ: ܢܚܬܘ ܗܘܘ
ܕܡܠܟܘܬܐ ܚܕܐ. ܘܐܬܚܙܝ ܗܘܘ ܘܐܣܬܟܠܘ، ܗܘܘ ܒܟܠܗ.
ܘܡܠܟܐ ܗܘܘ ܒܫܡܗ ܡܫܝܚܐ ܚܝܐ. ܘܐܬܬ ܕܢܣܒܘܢܝܗ، ܒܗ ܒܗܘ
ܡܫܝܚܐ. ܘܐܡܪ ܠܗܘܢ: ܠܐ ܡܫܬܠܐ ܐܢܐ ܡܢ ܕܡܠܟܘܬܐ ܗܕܐ
ܕܫܡܝܐ ܐܬܬܘܢ ܠܝ ܒܗ. ܘܐܬܬܚܝܒ ܗܘܘ ܩܕܡܝ. ܘܦܩܕ ܗܘܘ
ܘܫܡܥܘ ܐܢܘܢ ܡܢ ܟܠ ܒܢܝܗܘܢ. ܘܟܕ ܐܬܟܢܫܘ ܗܘܬ ܢܘܪܐ.
ܘܫܠܡ ܗܘܐ ܕܠܗ ܫܘܒܚܐ. ܘܒܗ ܠܗ ܦܬܚ ܦܘܡܝ. ܘܟܕ
ܒܡܠܬܐ ܕܦܬܚ ܦܘܡܗ ܫܠܡܬ ܗܘܬ ܢܦܫܗ، ܘܡܠܟܘ ܗܘܘ
ܒܪܢܫܐ ܘܥܝܪܐ ܒܡܠܝܐ ܕܡܠܟܐ. ܘܚܙܘ ܗܘܘ ܘܐܬܕܡܪܘ، ܡܢ
ܢܘܪܐ. ܟܕ ܐܬܚܙܝ ܗܘܘ ܒܠܗܘܢ، ܩܠܐ ܦܬܝܐ. ܘܡܫܝܚܐ ܒܬܪܗ
ܘܒܫܡܝܐ. ܘܡܫܬܠܛܝܢ ܗܘܘ ܡܢ ܩܕܡܐ ܕܡܥܡܕܢܐ. ܘܫܠܡܘ، ܗܘܘ
ܐܝܟ ܐܦܪܝܐ ܠܒܝܬܐ، ܘܡܫܡܫ ܗܘܘ ܘܡܒܪܟܝܢ، ܠܗܘܢ
ܒܢܘܪܐ ܘܫܡܫܐ ܩܕܝܫܐ: ܒܡܥܡܕܐ ܗܘ ܕܐܬܩܪܝ ܗܘܐ ܒܗ.
ܒܪܝܟܐ ܕܡܠܟܘܬܐ ܕܫܡܝܐ ܠܗ ܘܠܐ. ܟܕ ܐܬܩܪܝ ܗܘܘ ܒܠܗܘܢ،
ܡܢ ܡܥܡܕܐ ܘܡܫܪ ܥܠ. ܘܐܬܚܙܝ ܗܘܐ ܦܓܪܐ ܕܡܥܡܕܢܐ ܫܡܫܐ ܕܝܘܡܐ
ܘܡܫܝܚܝܬܐ. ܘܐܦ ܡܢ ܢܘܪܐ ܘܫܡܫܐ. ܐܫܬܘܕܥ ܗܘܘ ܠܡܥܡܕ
ܘܠܡܫܡܫ ܦܓܪܗ ܥܡ ܐܢܫܐ ܒܪܘܚܢܐ. ܒܗܘ ܕܝܢ ܒܝܘܡܐ ܕܡܥܡܕܢܐ:
ܘܐܦ ܒܚܝܐ ܕܡܠܟܝܢ ܗܘܘ ܠܗ. ܚܕܐ ܚܕܬܐ ܕܡܠܟܘܬܐ
ܦܪܫܬܐ ܗܘܬ ܥܠ ܟܠܗܘܢ ܘܥܠ ܟܠܢܫ. ܕܡܫܝܚܐ ܕܝܢ ܡܢ ܥܠ

ܥܘܩܪܘܗܝ ܕ̈ܐܠܗܐ. ܡܢ ܒܬܪ ܡܬܚܪܝܢ ܢܦܠ ܫܝܢܐ ܒܫܠܡܘܬܐ.
ܕܠܦܢ ܕܡܟܐ ܘܐܡܝܢ ܡܬܬܚܪܝܢ ܥܡ ܚܝ̈ܘܬܐ. ܐܝܟܘ ܝܠܬ ܗ̇ܢ ܚܪ̈ܝ
ܕܬ̈ܠܡܐ ܒܬܪ ܐܬܘܬܐ. ܥܡ ܚܫܘܟܐ ܐܣܦܩ ܚܒܝܒ ܠܐ ܝܕܥ
ܐܢܐ. ܗܘܐ ܠܐ ܐܡܪܘ ܗܠܝܢ ܬܘܒ ܘܐܡܝܢ ܕܟܬܐ. ܗܢܐ ܠܗܠܝܢ
ܕܗܘܐ ܗܢܐ ܘܬ̈ܠܡܐ ܠܐ. ܡܢ ܟܕ ܥܦܪ ܚܒܝܒ ܡܘܕܐ ܐܘ
ܒܪܬܐ. ܒܗܘܢ ܠܝ ܝܠܕܐ ܒܠ ܕܐܢܫܪ ܒܗ ܠܐ ܝܕܥ ܐܢܐ.
ܗܐ ܡܬܐܡܠ ܠܐ ܐܡܪ. ܗܘܐ ܡܢ ܒܪܬܬܐ. ܘܚܒܝܒ
ܐܡܪ ܘܐܡܠܐ ܥܦܪ ܠܕܝܪ ܒܗ. ܡܢܘ ܡܬܚܪܝܢ ܢܐܡܪ
ܕܗܢܐ ܗܢܐ ܐܘ ܗ̇ܘ. ܐܘ ܠܐ ܥܦܪ ܗܢܐ ܐܝܟ ܗ̇ܘ ܠܕܝܪܐ
ܠܗ. ܬܠܬܐ ܒܢܘܪܐ ܘܠܐ ܡܪܟܐ ܠܗܘܢ ܥܠܡܢܝܬܐ. ܚܕ ܕܝܢ
ܐܡܪ ܘܐܡܝܢ ܐܗܦܟ ܠܡܟܠܠܘ. ܕܪܟܒܟܐ ܗ̇ܝ ܗ̇ܘ ܕܝܠܗ
ܗܘܐ ܠܟܘ ܐܬܘܬܐ. ܕܝܠܕ ܝܠܕܐ ܠܚܒܝܒ ܬܘܒ ܥܡ ܕܬܠܬܐ.
ܡܢܟ ܗܘ ܠܗ ܕܡܟܬܐ ܒܢܘܪܐ ܠܗ̇ܘ ܕܐܡܪ ܗܘܐ. ܕܪܟܒܟܐ
ܚܠܦܘܗܝ ܒܗܘܐ ܝܕܥ ܕܟܬܐ. ܘܗܝ ܕܬܠܬܐ ܚܝܝܢ ܥܘܩܪܐ ܕܗ
ܠܐ ܐܡܪܘ. ܗܢܐ ܕܐܡܪ ܐܡܝܢ ܠܐ ܣܠܩܬ ܥܡ ܚܝ̈ܘܬܐ.
ܐܠܐ ܥܠܝܟ ܐܢܬ ܐܘ ܢܐܡܪ ܐܘ ܠܐ ܢܐܡܪ. ܗܢܐ ܕܐܡܪ ܪܡ
ܗܘܐ ܥܘܩܪܗ ܡܢ ܕܬܠܬܐ. ܐܠܐ ܡܛܠ ܕܐܝܬܘܗܝ ܕܡܬܪܐ
ܡܬܒܪܢܘܬܐ. ܗ̇ܘ ܡܫܬܒܚ ܐܡܟܐ ܕܟܝ̈ܢ ܘܐܡܟܐ ܕܐܫܠܡ.
ܝܒܝܫܐ ܕܝܢ ܐܦ ܕܬܠܬܐ ܕܠܐ ܐܡܪܘ ܗܘܘ. ܘܕܗܘ ܕܐܡܪ ܚܕ
ܗܘ ܘܣܒܪ ܗܘ ܗܪܟܐ ܘܠܗܠ. ܘܐܠܐ ܦܩܕ ܠܗ̇ ܡܪܗ̇ ܠܒܪܬܐ
ܕܬܘܩܕ ܐܢܘܢ. ܠܬܠܬܝܗܘܢ ܡܢ ܝܐܕܝܗܘܢ ܡܩܕܡ ܗܘܘ.
ܘܐܠܐ ܪܡܐ ܠܗ̇ ܕܐܦ ܠܗ ܠܗ̇ܘ ܚܕ ܠܐ ܬܘܩܕ ܗܘܬ. ܠܐ
ܡܕܝܢ ܗܘܐ ܘܠܐ ܕܠܗ ܗܘܬ ܢܬܦܝܐ ܗܘܐ. ܕܒܟܠܗܘܢ ܠܒܪܬܐ
ܕܝܟܣܘܢ ܗܘܬ ܒܗ ܒܐܠܝܢ ܠܗ̇. ܕܠܐ ܕܝܢ ܐܡܪܘ ܡܪܗ̇
ܕܒܪܬܐ ܝܒܫܐ ܘܦܩܕ ܠܗ̇. ܡܕܝܢ ܚܕ ܗܘ ܥܘܩܪܐ ܕܐܝܟܐ
ܕܐܡܪ. ܘܕܠܐ ܐܡܪ ܡܛܠ ܕܥܒܐ ܗܘ ܐܦ ܝܒܫܐ ܗܘܕܐ
ܪܫܡܬܐ. ܪܡ ܗܘ ܕܪܟܝܟ. ܘܦܫܐ ܟܠܠܟ

ܘܣ̈ܪܩܐ ܚ̈ܪܝܦܐ: ܘܒܥܘܪܐ ܕܢܘܪܐ: ܘܫܢ̈ܢܐ ܕܚܝܠܐ ܘܡܬܚܠܠܢ ܕܠܐ ܪ̈ܚܡܐ. ܘܗܠܝܢ ܟܠܗܝܢ ܘܐܝܠܝܢ ܕܕ̈ܡܝܢ ܠܗܝܢ. ܥܠ ܣܒܪܐ ܕܦܘܪܥܢܐ ܕܥܬܝܕ. ✣ ܐܬܠܚܨܘ ܕܝܢ ܕܣ̈ܗܕܐ ܗܠܝܢ. ܘܐܝܠܝܢ ܕܡܫܒܚܬ ܗܘܬ ܒܠܗܘܢ: ܦܓܪܗ ܚ̈ܒܫ ܕܥܠ ܬܐܘܦܝܠܐ ܘܢܗܪܘ ܪܒܢܐ. ܘܐܘܕܝܬ ܒܡܫܝܚܐ. ܕܒܪܗ ܗܘ ܕܐܠܗܐ ܘܐܠܗܐ ܐܬܘܗܝ. ܘܢܠܐ ܕܪ̈ܚܡܘܗܝ ܕܣ̈ܗܕܐ ܗܠܝܢ: ܕܦܠܚܬ ܗܘܬ ܒܗ ܪܘܚܬ ܠܪ̈ܚܡܘܗܝ: ܒܟܢܫܐ ܕܢܦܫܢ ܗܘܘ ܡܬܬܠܠܝܢ: ܢܥܒܕ ܠܗ ܕܦܪܥܬ ܗܘܬ ܒܗ. ܘܢܘܕܐ ܒ ܕܒܡ ܦ̈ܓܪܘܗܝ ܕܐܘܕܝܬ ܒܗ ܡܫܝܚ ✣

ܒܫܘܠܡܐ ܕܝܢ ܕܒܫܢܝܢ ܘܡܥܒܕܐ: ܕܐܬܥܠܝ ܗܘܐ ܕܢܝܚܐ ܠܚܒܝܒ. ܗܟܢ ܗܘܐ ܟܠܗ ܐܦܣܩܘܣ ܕܦܬܚܬܐ ܕܡܕܢܚܐ ܕܢܘܪܐ.

ܫܠܡܬ ܣܗܕܘܬܐ ܕܚܒܝܒ:

✣ ܡܫܡܫܢܐ ✣

ܬܘܒ ܡܐܡܪܐ ܕܥܠ ܚܒܝܒ ܣܗܕܐ. ܕܣܡ ܠܡܪܝ ܝܥܩܘܒ.

ܚܒܝܒ ܣܗܕܐ ܠܒܫ ܟܠܝܠܬܐ ܚܕܐ ܡܢ ܢܘܪܐ. ܕܐܦ ܠܗ ܐܝܟ ܝܠܕܐ ܕܫܘܦܪܐ ܒܡ ܢܘܗܪܐ. ܥܒܪ ܕܒܝܬܐ ܗܘܐ ܪܚܡ ܠܗ ܡܢܕܥܐ. ܕܐܟܡܐ ܕܠܫܘܒܚܐ ܕܒܪܗ ܐܚܪܢ ܡܬܚܠܠ. ܒܫܡ ܒܡܐܡܪܐ ܦܬܚ ܒܚܪܐ ܘܗܘܐ ܦܘܐ ܠܗ. ܐܝܟ ܝܠܕܐ ܘܠܐ ܡܫܟܚܐ ܠܗ ܠܫܒܘܚܬܐ. ܫܡܥ ܡܪܢ ܐܦ ܫܡܫܐ ܡܫܬܘܕܐ ܘܢܘܗܪ ܦܩܕܐ ܘܡܢ ܦܩܕ ܠܗ ܕܢܬܠܐ ܫܡܫܐ. ܐܠܐ ܒܫܘܒܚܐ ܗܘ ܕܠܗܘܕܐ ܒܢܘܪܐ ܣܡܗ. ܠܐ ܐܝܟ ܡܣܟܢ ܢܬܠܐ

ܐܘܦ ܕܐܟܠܐ ܘܦܪܙ. ܡܢܗ ܫܘܚܬ ܥܠܡܐ. ܘܗܦܟ ܬܘܪܒܬܐ
ܘܣܓܠ ܐܡܪܬܐ ܟܠܝܠܘܗܝ. ܢܦܩ ܒܥܐܝܬ ܠܒܒܐ ܬܘܚܝܢ
ܠܚܘܫܒܬܐ. ܫܠ ܬܘܚܝ ܘܐܪܬ، ܬܘܚܝ ܘܗܦܟܬ ܐܬܝ. ܘܣܓܠ ܕܢܚܐ
ܕܡܬܚܘܒܬܐ ܥܠܒܪ ܐܬܝ. ܕܠܐ ܢܬܪܗܘܢ ܡܢ ܫܦܘܬܐ
ܕܦܠܚܐ ܗܘܬ. ܒܪܬܐ ܕܒܝܬ ܕܒܪ ܐܠܗܐ ܡܬܝܪܒܝ ܗܘܘ.
ܡܢ ܬܪܘܦܐ ܘܠܒܒ ܠܐܡܪܬܐ ܘܠܩܘܬܐ. ܘܗܘܐ ܦܢܝܪܬܐ
ܠܒܝ ܒܝܬܐ ܕܡܬܚܘܒܬܐ. ܘܐܠܦ ܐܢܘܢ ܕܠܐ ܢܬܪܗܒܘܢ ܡܢ
ܬܪܘܦܐ. ܐܠܦ ܐܢܘܢ ܕܗܘܘ ܪܗܛܝܢ ܠܗܘܒܠ ܡܘܬܐ. ܒܪ
ܠܐ ܕܢܠܝܢ ܠܗ ܡܢ ܫܦܐ ܘܠܐ ܡܢ ܢܘܪܐ. ܒܡܠܦܘܬܗ ܕܒܪ
ܐܠܗܐ ܡܬܬܒܪ ܗܘܐ ܕܗܘܬ ܪܗܛܐ ܡܬܚܘܬܗ ܕܠܐ ܗܘܪܕܐ.
ܘܫܡܥܬ ܛܠܝܐ ܦܢܝܬ ܘܥܢܬ ܘܡܛܠܬܗ. ܘܫܦܬ ܒܬܪܗ
ܐܬܐܣܪ ܒܐܪܒܥܐ ܕܡܟܐ ܪܟܝܐ. ܐܒܠ ܡܪܝܐ ܕܦܝܐ ܠܟܘܠܗ
ܕܒܝ ܐܢܫܐ. ܢܠܐ ܠܗ ܦܫܐ ܕܢܓܠܘܢ ܠܐܬܪܐ ܡܢ ܚܢܘܢ.
ܦܝܐ ܥܬܝܪܐ ܢܦܩ ܗܘܐ ܒܬܪܗ ܠܡܬܚܬܬܗܝܢ ܕܢܥܠܐ ܘܠܗ ܡܢ
ܘܠܦܠܐ ܕܒܝܬ ܐܠܗܐ. ܘܪܒܬ ܛܠܝܐ ܕܢܡܘܬ ܫܒܝܒ ܒܠ
ܕܗܝܟܢ ܘܪܗܛܬ ܒܐܒܠܐ ܘܡܒܝܐ ܗܘܬ ܠܗ ܕܢܦܫܗ ܬܫܬܒܩ.
ܘܐܬܬܪܝܒ ܥܪܒܗ ܘܡܢ ܕܢܦܠܐ ܫܦܝܐ ܕܐܬܪܐ. ܘܣܓܠܐ
ܠܦܠܠܐ ܛܠܝܐ ܪܣܝܡܐ ܒܘܦܪܐ ܪܒܐ. ܘܕܒܫܦܘܬܐ ܘܛܠܝ
ܗܘܐ ܬܦܠܐ ܦܒܪ ܗܘܐ ܡܡܘܬܐ ܡܛܠ ܫܒܝܒ ܒܠ ܕܡܠܐ
ܗܘܐ ܡܬܚܘܒܬܐ. ܘܒܪ ܦܘܡܪܐ ܡܛܠܐ ܠܪܢܝܐ ܐܪܪܝܢ ܗܘܐ.
ܒܡܬܐ ܘܦܠܓܐ ܘܒܬܪܒܝܬܐ ܕܢܘܗܐ ܠܡܪܒܐ ܘܐܝܟ ܢܝܪܐ
ܕܠܐܚܠܐ ܒܠܡܒܐ ܢܒܪܐ ܪܚܡ. ܒܬܪ ܫܒܝܒ ܢܦܩܝܢ ܗܘܘ
ܠܡܢܝܢܘ. ܗܘ ܕܡܢ ܟܢܪܐ ܒܪܘܪܐ ܗܘܐ ܕܡܬܚܘܒܬܐ. ܕܒܐܘܪܫܗ
ܪܒܬܐ ܕܪܘܦܬܐ ܡܬܒܪ ܗܘܐ. ܘܢܘܬܪ ܗܘܐ ܒܡܠܦܘܬܗ
ܠܒܝ ܒܝܬܗ. ܠܒܢܝ ܗܘܐ ܒܢܝܗ ܒܐܬܪܘܬܐ ܕܫܪܝܪ ܠܗ.
ܘܒܪ ܢܦܩܬ ܗܘܬ ܒܬܪܗ ܛܠܝܐ ܠܐ ܐܫܒܚܬܗ. ܠܗ ܕܒܝܬܗ
ܗܘܐ ܐܠܐ ܕܢܦܩ ܠܡܦܩܪܘ. ܘܡܛܠ ܫܒܬܐ ܕܫܦܐ ܕܪܒܐ

ܘܫܠܛ ܥܕܟܢ ܒܪ̈ܘܚܐ. ܕܗܟܢܐ ܐܝܟ ܕܒܥܐ ܘܒܪܐ
ܒܡܬܝܢ ܘܐܘܪܚ ܫܘܦܪܗ. ܗܘܐ ܒܠܠܝܗ ܕܡܠܟܐ ܚܙܐ ܐܝܟ
ܡܢ ܐ̈ܢܫܐ. ܦܠܚܐ ܠܦܠܚܐ ܕܒܫܠܝܘܗ ܕܟܪ ܐܠܗܐ. ܗܘܠ
ܐܝܟ ܠܦܘܠܐ ܡܠܠ ܥܘܦܪܐ ܕܡܫܝܚܘܬܗ. ܫܒܝܒ ܗܘܕܝܐ
ܡܠܦܢܐ ܗܘܐ ܕܝܗ̈ܘܕܝܘܬܐ. ܐܦ ܒܙܘܪܐ ܕܡܠܟܐ ܦܘܩܕܗ
ܗܝܡܢܘܬܐ. ܟܕ ܗܘܐ ܘܚܙܐ ܘܡܠܦܢ ܗܘܐ ܒܡܠܦܢܘܬܗ.
ܠܒ̈ܢܝ ܥܡܬܐ ܕܒܝܬ ܐܠܗܐ ܒܗܝܡܢܘܬܗ. ܢܗܘܪܐ ܡܠܟܐ ܗܘܐ
ܘܡܬܬܥܒܕ ܗܘܐ ܡܢ ܫܘܒܚܐ. ܕܢܦܩܘܗ ܠܐܬܪܐ ܡܢ ܫܘܒܘܬܐ
ܕܐܫܬܥܝܬܗ ܗܘܬ. ܘܗܕܪܬܗ ܕܒܪܐ ܡܠܟܐ ܗܘܐ ܦܘܩܕܗ
ܒܟܬܝܒܬܐ. ܘܐܝܟ ܗܕܐ ܟܕ ܗܘܐ ܠܗܘܪ̈ܐ ܒܪܝܟܐ
ܕܡܠܟܘܗ. ܠܦܢܐ ܗܘܐ ܕܢܩܒܠ ܗܘܐ ܠܗ ܥܠ ܡܠܦܢܐ. ܐܠܗܐ
ܕܥܡܡ ܠܒܪܐ ܕܡܫܝܚܘܬܐ. ܒܪܝܬܐ ܕܢܟܐ ܙ̈ܘܓܐ ܕܫܘܦܐ ܗܘܐ
ܠܡܫܬܪܪܐ. ܘܡܬܬܦܠܓ ܗܘܐ ܟܕ ܢܩܫ ܒܗ ܘܠܐ ܕܟܝܢ ܗܘܐ.
ܥܒܕ ܗܘܐ ܘܡܠܟܐ ܢܣܒܬ ܡܪܗ ܘܩܒܠ ܗܘܐ ܠܗ. ܡܠܠܘܬܗ
ܕܡܠܠܗ ܗܘܐ ܠܐ ܕܗܘܝܐ. ܒܟ̈ܠܐ ܕܠܒܫ ܐܝܟ ܒܐܬܪܐ
ܡܢ ܫܘܒܬܐ. ܘܒܟܠܐ ܕܡܫܡܫ ܟܕ ܗܘܐ ܠܗܘܢ ܒܡܠܠܘܬܗ.
ܡܠܦ ܡܢܗܪܐ ܘܡܫܪܪ ܗܘܐ ܒܡܫܝܚܘܬܐ. ܠܡܫ̈ܝܚܐ
ܕܡܬܐܠܨܝܢ ܗܘܘ ܡܢ ܙ̈ܕܘܩܐ. ܠܗܘܠ ܗܘܩܐ ܘܠܗܘܠ ܢܘܪܐ
ܡܬܬܥܝܪ ܗܘܐ. ܒܣܘܦܐ ܕܣܡܟ ܐܝܟ ܕܒܐܠܗܐ ܘܠܐ
ܕܢܠ ܗܘܐ. ܐܝܟ ܗܘܦܪܐ ܕܐܬܪܝ ܦܘܩܕܢܗ ܢܘܩܐ ܗܘܬ.
ܗܡܫܝܚܘܬܗ ܘܠܗܘܠ ܠܦܢܝ ܡܬܬܥܒܕ ܗܘܐ. ܫܡܪܐ ܒܒܝܫ
ܗܘܐ ܒܗܘܢܐ ܐܬܪܐ ܕܦܠܛ ܗܘܐ ܠܗ. ܒܢܫܡܬ ܬܠܡ̈ܝܕܐ
ܕܪܘܡܘܬܐ ܕܐܒܠܬ ܠܦܢܝ. ܗܘܐ ܐܝܟ ܡܠܝܐ ܒܡܠܦܢܘܬܗ
ܠܦܢܝܢܘܬܐ. ܠܗܕܐ ܦܢܝܬܐ ܕܒܫܘܡܬ ܗܘܬ ܠܗ ܒܒܫܘܪܬܐ.
ܡܫܡܫܢܐ ܗܘܐ ܘܡܠܠ ܕܗܘܬ ܒܗܘܢܐ ܪܒܐ. ܒܟܪܘܙܘܬܐ
ܘܒܡܠܦܢܐ ܕܝܗ̈ܘܕܝܘܬܐ. ܗܘܐ ܠܗ ܠܒܢܐ ܪܒܐ ܠܦܠܚܐ ܒܗ
ܚܠܝܐ ܗܘ. ܘܢܦܫ ܗܘ ܗܘܐ ܫܠܝܡ ܕܒܢܐ ܒܗ ܢܦܠ ܠܗ.

ܕܒܝܬܘܢܝ ܗܘܐ ܡܬܘܡ ܐܢܐ. ܘܐܬܬܪܒܝ ܚܝܠܐ ܘܐܚܝܕܗ
ܬܘܪܐ ܘܐܬܬܪܝܒ ܒܗ. ܡܫܪܪܐ ܕܠܐ ܕܝܠ ܠܐ ܡܢ ܗܦܟܐ
ܘܠܐ ܡܢ ܢܘܪܐ. ܟܕ ܦܩܕ ܗܘܐ ܕܡܫܪܪ ܒܪܝܫ ܟܠ ܒܢܝ ܒܗ.
ܘܐܦ ܕܢܐ ܕܥܝܢܘܗܝ ܕܠܒܝܒ ܠܗܘܒܠ ܡܘܬܐ. ܬܠܡܝܕܘܗܝ ܗܘ
ܕܟܪ ܐܠܗܐ ܗܘ ܕܐܡܪ ܗܘܐ. ܕܡܘܡܐ ܬܘ ܢܐܙܠ ܕܗܘܘ
ܕܡܟܠܡ ܠܝ ܗܘܐ ܦܓܪ ܠܗ. ܘܠܢܩܘܫܐ ܬܘܒ ܐܡܪ ܗܘܐ ܠܗܢ
ܒܢܝ ܐܢܬܘܢ ܐܡܪܝܢ ܠܝܫܘܥ ܘܐܡܪ ܗܘܐ ܠܗܘܢ ܕܐܢܐ
ܐܢܐ. ܟܕ ܐܠܗܐ ܗܘ ܒܝܬܝܗ ܐܬܐ ܠܢܦܫܐ. ܘܟܗ ܚܕ
ܦܬܪܐ ܘܐܢܬ، ܗܘ ܠܗ ܦܬܡ ܕܢܐܐ. ܘܒܝܘܡܝ ܚܝܠܐ
ܘܐܬܟܠܝ ܗܘܐ ܘܐܬܡܛܪܪ ܗܘܐ. ܘܦܠܛ ܪܒܝܢܗ ܘܟܢܝ
ܒܝܬܘܗ ܡܪܝܒ ܒܥܕܠܐ. ܘܐܝܟ ܕܡܫܪܪܐ ܕܐܟܝܢ ܒܐܪܥܐ
ܕܡܟܐ ܕܩܛܠܐ. ܡܫܐܠ ܗܘܐ ܠܗ ܡܫܪܪܐ ܚܫܐ ܘܠܐ
ܒܗܬ ܗܘܐ. ܟܕ ܫܡܥ ܠܗ ܘܡܟܕܢܠ ܠܗ ܘܡܩܦܪ ܠܗ. ܘܬܢܝܢܐ
ܫܒܐ ܕܡܠܒܟܝܢ ܠܗ ܡܛܠܬܗ. ܗܘ ܕܝܢ ܚܝܒܝܢ ܟܕ ܡܫܬܐܠ
ܠܐ ܕܢܠ ܗܘܐ. ܠܐ ܒܗܬ ܗܘܐ ܘܠܐ ܡܬܗܦܪ ܡܢ ܠܘܩܒܠ
ܟܕ ܪܡ ܘܠܗ ܐܘܕܝ، ܒܫܘܒܚ ܒܪ ܐܠܗܐ ܕܐܝܬܘܗܝ، ܒܟܝܢܗ
ܘܐܝܬܘܗܝ، ܒܟܝܢܗ ܘܡܫܡܫܢܘܬܗ. ܒܫܡܬܐ ܕܫܒܩܐ ܟܕ ܢܗܡܐ
ܒܗ ܐܝܟ ܐܪܘܬܐ. ܠܐ ܐܦ ܢܦܠܐ ܡܢ ܬܘܕܝܬܗ ܕܒܪ ܐܠܗܐ.
ܡܬܒܠܒ. ܗܘܐ ܘܡܬܪܕܐ ܦܓܪ ܚܝܒܝܢ ܠܗ. ܕܐܠܦ ܘܠܠ ܡܢ
ܡܫܘܬܗ ܕܒܪ ܐܠܗܐ. ܟܠ ܠܡܗܡܝܢܐ ܘܚܪ ܗܘܐ ܒܟܪܝܗ
ܕܐܦ ܠܗ ܚܝܒܝܢܘܗܝ. ܘܚܙܝ ܠܗܘܢ ܕܒܐܘܪܚܐ ܕܫܡܝܗ ܫܪܝ ܪܕܐ.
ܘܦܠܛ ܗܘܐ ܠܡܝܬܐ ܘܦܪܩܢ ܗܘܘ ܠܗ ܘܢܗܪܬ ܢܦܫܗ. ܕܐܝܟܐ
ܕܢܦܠܘܗܝ، ܪܕܦܐ ܕܫܒܐ ܕܪܡܘܬܐ. ܒܐܘܪܚܐ ܕܡܘܬܐ ܗܘ
ܗܘܐ ܫܡܘܗܝ، ܠܡܫܠܡܘ. ܘܡܢ ܒܬܪܐ ܗܘܐ ܕܢܒܝܗ ܗܘܐ
ܒܗ ܐܠܐ ܫܒܐ. ܢܘܪܐ ܕܕܩܝܩܐ ܡܚܝܪܐ ܗܘܬ ܠܗ ܘܠܗ
ܚܒܪ ܗܘܐ. ܗܘ، ܫܪܝܬ ܠܗ ܦܘܪܩܐ ܘܢܨܚܢܐ ܘܟܠܝܠܐ ܢܨܝܚܐ.
ܟܕ ܐܬܬܐ ܗܘܬ ܫܪܝܬ ܚܝܠܐ ܕܟܠܬܗܘܢ. ܢܗܘܐ ܡܠܒܟ

ܗܝ ܡܢ ܥܠܝܬܐ. ܠܒܢܝ̈ ܚܝܠܗ ܘܠܐܡܗ ܠܒܬܗ ܗܘܘ ܡܫܬܠܛܗ.
ܠܡܥܒܕ ܐܝܬܝܬܐ ܐܟܡܐ ܕܫܪܪܐ ܡܢ ܗܝ ܕܐܬܐܡܪ. ܕܥܠ
ܡܢܗ ܠܚܡܘܕ ܣܒܘܬܐ ܒܥܠܬܐ. ܡܛܠ ܕܬܡܢ ܠܐ ܡܠܟ
ܥܒܝܕܐ ܡܢܐ ܬܡܢܘܬܐ. ܗܐ ܬܡܢ ܠܐ ܬܘܕܝ ܫܪܪܐ ܕܢܗܘܐ
ܕܒܢܝܐ. ܐܝܟ ܐܝܟ ܦܐܪܐ ܣܠܩܐ ܠܒܝܬ ܡܘܬܒܐ. ܕܒܢܝܢ
ܙܢܝܢ ܕܢܗܘܐ ܒܛܝܪܐ ܠܐܠܗܘܬܐ. ܫܬܐ ܦܐܝܬܐ ܘܚܒܠܐ
ܐܝܟ ܡܢ ܒܪ ܕܐܝܬܘܗܝ ܕܠܗܘܢܐ ܢܗܘܐ ܣܒܪܗ ܕܥܠܐ
ܠܡܥܒܕ ܥܒܕܐ ܗܘܐ ܐܟܪܐ ܕܒܢܝܢ ܗܘܘ ܠܗ ܢܗܘܐ ܕܒܢܝܐ
ܘܠܘܝܢ ܘܐܬܐ ܛܢܐ ܠܒܢܝܐ ܒܪ ܚܕܐ ܗܘܐ. ܥܒܕ ܕܐܬܚܪܐ
ܗܘ ܡܬܐܠܝܢ ܗܘܘ ܡܫܬܠܛܗ. ܘܐܬܐ ܢܛܪ ܫܥܐ ܕܠܗ ܣܠܩ
ܫܒܝܐܐ. ܦܪܬܐ ܡܫܬܠܛܗ ܕܗܘ ܒܠܗܘܕܘܗܝ ܢܗܘܐ ܕܒܢܝܐ.
ܘܢܘܪܐ ܕܕܒܢܝܐ ܠܗ ܣܢܐ ܗܘܬ ܒܪ ܐܬܬܐ ܗܘܐ. ܡܢ ܫܒܝ̈ܐܐ
ܕܣܒܥܝܢ ܗܘܘ ܡܫܬܠܛܗ. ܐܦ ܠܐ ܚܪ ܐܝܟ ܐܬܬܝܚ. ܕܢܚܘܬ
ܐܠܐ ܐܢ ܗܘ. ܗܘ ܓܒܪܐ ܗܘܐ ܐܦ ܫܘܕܥܬܐ ܠܗ ܢܛܪܐ
ܗܘܬ. ܘܐܝܟ ܢܣܠܘܩ ܗܘܐ ܕܢܚܬ ܫܪܪܐ ܠܐ ܡܟܝܟ ܗܘܐ.
ܘܡܛܠ ܗܢܐ ܗܘ ܒܪܝܫܗ ܐܝܟ ܢܦܫܗ. ܝܘ ܕܢܝܐ ܕܐܬܬܝܚ.
ܘܢܚܘܬ ܡܛܠ ܥܘܡܕ. ܒܥܒܕ ܕܒܐܒܘܗܝ ܘܐܬܐ ܕܐܬܬܝܚ. ܐܝܟ
ܕܒܐܒܘܗܝ. ܘܐܒܠ ܗܘ ܠܗ ܡܘܬ ܕܢܝܐ ܘܛܠܝܢ ܐܦܘܗܝ. ܠܐ
ܐܬܬܠܒ ܘܠܐ ܝܕܥ ܕܒܪܘܡ ܡܢ ܕܢܝܐ. ܕܢܗܘܐ ܗܘܐ ܘܡܢ
ܫܘܒܚܐ ܠܐ ܚܙܘ ܗܘܐ. ܠܐ ܒܢܝܐ ܘܠܐ ܡܠܬܐ ܘܠܐ
ܒܢܝܐ. ܘܠܐ ܒܪ ܠܠܝܐ ܕܥܠܗ ܙܪܩܗ ܒܐܡܘܡܐ ܗܘܐ.
ܠܡܘ ܢܚܘܡ ܗܘܐ ܡܢ ܡܪܒܝܬܐ ܙܒܢܐ ܠܒܢܐ. ܘܢܪܦܐ
ܒܢܐ ܒܪ ܡܬܐܠܝܢ ܡܢ ܒܢܝܐ. ܠܡܘ ܒܪܘ ܗܘܐ ܐܘܪܐ
ܕܢܩܘ ܡܬܐܘܐ ܒܐܒܢܐ. ܘܠܦܬܓܡܬܐ ܒܪܝܫ ܒܕܡܘܬܗ ܕܒܠ
ܐܠܗܐ. ܒܠܗܘܢ ܐܦ̈ܝܐ ܗܘܐ ܒܪܝܐ ܘܠܒܢܐ ܪܒܐ.
ܘܠܗܘܒܠ ܡܘܬܐ ܙܘܦܠ ܒܪ ܚܕܐ ܡܛܠ ܥܘܡܕ. ܒܠ ܗܘܐ
ܡܢ ܠܗ ܡܘܬ ܕܢܝܐ ܒܪ ܐܡܪ ܠܗ. ܐܝܟܐ ܐܝܟܐ ܚܢܢܝ

ܕܓܫܬ ܦܓܪܐ ܘܗܘܐ ܐܢܫܐ. ܠܗ ܚܙܬ ܐܢܫܐ ܐܚܪܝ ܗܘܝܐ
ܒܡܠܐ ܙܒܢܐ. ܡܢ ܡܩܕܫܢܐ ܦܪܝܫܐ ܡܫܡܗܐ ܥܩܠܐ ܩܠܝܠܐ.
ܘܡܠܟܐ ܒܟܝܢܐ ܠܘܬ ܐܒܘܗܝ ܡܫܝܚܘܬܐ. ܘܩܒܠܐ ܠܡܪܢ
ܕܐܦ ܐܠܗܐ ܗܘ ܒܪ ܐܠܗܐ. ܘܠܘܬ ܘܐܘܕܝܬ ܕܓܫܬ ܦܓܪܐ
ܕܗܘܐ ܐܢܫܐ. ܠܘ ܡܢ ܦܓܪܐ ܚܫܝܒܐ ܠܘܬ ܡܫܝܚܘܬܐ. ܡܠܟܗ̇
ܐܠܗ̇ ܦܘܪܩܢܗ̇ ܐܠܗܘܬܗ ܘܐܘܕܝܬ ܐܝܟ. ܘܐܦ ܡܬܓܠܝܐ
ܕܠܒܪ ܐܢܫܐ ܦܓܪܐ ܡܬܚܙܐ. ܠܦܘܪܩܢܗ̇ ܡܚܝܐ ܕܡܬܚܙܐ
ܣܠܩܬ, ܥܠ ܕܐܠܗܐ ܗܘ. ܠܒܪ ܐܢܫܐ ܠܡ ܠܐ ܚܙܬ ܐܢܫܐ
ܐܡܪ ܫܡܥܘܢ. ܡܛܠ ܕܚܙܐ ܕܠܘܬ ܗܘ ܕܡܬܬܚܝܠ ܒܟܠ ܒܪ
ܐܢܫܐ. ܥܠ ܕܐܠܗܐ ܗܘ ܚܙܬ ܐܢܫܐ ܠܗ ܐܦ ܗܝ ܐܢܫܐ.
ܡܛܠܬܗ ܘܠܐ ܚܙܪ ܐܢܫܐ ܒܡܫܝܚܘܬܗ. ܗܢܐ ܥܒܪܐ ܠܒܢܝܐ
ܐܚܪܢ, ܡܢ ܛܠܝܘܬܗ. ܘܒܡܫܝܚܘܬܗ ܠܐ ܡܫܠܡܐ ܠܗ ܒܪܬ
ܡܩܕܫܐ. ܡܠܟܗ̇ ܒܟܢܝܐ ܗܘܐ ܠܗ̇ ܦܓܪܐ ܘܡܛܠ ܠܘܬ.
ܡܛܠ ܡܪܢ ܕܒܪ ܐܠܗܐ ܗܘ ܐܦ ܐܠܗܐ. ܐܚܪ ܕܐܢܫܬ,
ܒܛܘܬܗ ܕܚܛܝܬܐ ܘܫܡܥ ܠܗ̇ ܒܐܝܕܗ̇. ܗܟܢ ܡܒܪܟܗ̇ ܠܒܪ
ܐܠܗܐ ܕܡܚܝܢܐ ܗܘ. ܥܪܒܠ ܒܡܟܪܐ ܕܝܠܗ, ܘܟܠܗ ܠܒܘܠ
ܬܠܡܝܕ. ܣܠܩ ܐܠܗܐ ܕܗܘܐ ܐܢܫܐ ܡܚܛ ܐܝܟ ܕܐܡܪ.
ܥܡܘܕܐ ܘܦܓܪܐ ܡܛܠܬܗ ܕܡܚܝܢܐ. ܒܫܡܗ ܒܪ̈ܝܫܘܗܘ
ܘܣܠܩܘܗܝ ܡܢ ܥܠ ܕܐܠܗܐ ܗܘ. ܘܫܡܥ ܗܢܐ ܡܠܟܐ
ܗܘܐ ܕܒܪܢܫܐ. ܘܕܓܫܬ ܦܓܪܐ ܘܗܘܐ ܐܢܫܐ ܡܒܪ
ܗܘܐ ܠܗ. ܣܠܩ ܒܪ ܐܢܫܐ ܗܢܐ ܒܩܘܪܐ ܠܐ ܡܫܪ ܗܘܐ.
ܐܚܪܐ ܐܡܪ ܣܠܩ ܐܠܗܐ ܕܗܘܐ ܐܢܫܐ. ܘܗܢܐ ܐܚܪܢ
ܕܡܢ ܐܚܪܢ ܒܪ ܡܫܪ ܗܘܐ. ܘܡܢ ܛܘܒܬܗ ܕܗܢܐ ܕܐܡܪ
ܡܚܐ ܒܪܘܟ. ܠܟܠ ܕܚܣܝܢ ܡܬܚܙܐ ܘܡܚܐ ܡܫܝܚܘܬܐ.
ܕܢܗܘܐ ܡܠܟܐ ܘܠܐ ܡܬܚܙܝܐ ܒܪ ܛܠܝܐ. ܒܦܓܪܐ ܠܒܢܝܐ
ܕܛܠܝ ܠܒܪܐ ܕܠܘ ܐܠܗܐ ܗܘ. ܘܠܟܢܝܐ ܕܐܡܪ ܕܠܐ ܕܓܫܬ
ܦܓܪܐ ܕܗܘܐ ܐܢܫܐ. ܒܡܫܝܚܘܬܐ ܕܡܠܟܐ ܥܒܪܐ ܡܢ ܒܠ

ܕܗܟܢܐ ܕܦܓܥܬ ܒܗ ܠܐ ܬܪܝܨܗ ܗܘܬ. ܓܪܦܗ̇ ܣܓܝܐ ܕܗܟܢܐ
ܕܟܘܪܐ ܠܗ ܥܠܘܒܝܬܐ. ܠܐ ܢܗܘܐ ܐܝܬ ܡܕܡ ܪܓܬܐ
ܕܦܓܥܢ ܒܐܝܕܐ. ܘܗܒܪ ܐܝܟ ܠܚܠܦܝܗܘܢ ܛܥܝܢܐ ܒܗܘܢ
ܒܪܘܡܐ ܐܝܟ ܢܗܘܐ ܘܡܣܬܒܪܐ ܗܘܐ. ܕܐܬܕܪܟ ܗܘܐ ܒܗ.
ܘܡܚܫܒ ܗܘܐ ܒܪ ܚܙܐ ܗܘܐ ܠܫܡܝܐ ܕܢܦܠ. ܡܛܐ ܗܘܐ
ܓܝܪ ܕܒܫܘܠܛܢܗܘܢ ܡܬܘܬܐ ܡܥܡܝ. ܘܠܐ ܕܢܠ ܗܘܐ ܘܠܐ
ܡܢ ܡܬܘܬܐ ܘܠܐ ܡܢ ܚܝܠܐ. ܕܒܗ ܣܓܝܪܗ ܕܐܘܣܦܬܐ ܪܘܐ
ܗܘܐ ܠܗܘܢ. ܥܠܗ ܠܦܓܪܐ ܒܪ ܡܬܚܙܐ ܡܢ ܕ̈ܘܟܐ. ܘܠܡܫܕܡܘܗ̇
ܒܪ ܡܬܦܫܩ ܡܢܐܬܐ. ܫ̈ܕܐ ܒܫܝܢ ܗܘܦܐ ܒܪ̈ܢܫܐ
ܗܕܐ ܒܪ̈ܓܠܘܗܝ. ܘܢܘܪܐ ܠܣܦܪܠܗ ܘܠܒܢܝ ܘܡܠܐ ܗܝܡܢܘܬܐ.
ܡܫܘܕܥ ܗܘܐ ܕܠܒܪ ܐܢܫܐ ܗܘ ܦܓܪ ܐܝܬ. ܘܐܡܪ ܗܘܐ
ܗܘ ܕܠܒܪ ܐܢܫܐ ܠܐ ܦܓܪ ܐܢܐ. ܠܐܠܗܐ ܓܝܪ ܕܢܣܒ ܦܓܪܐ
ܘܦܓܪܐ ܐܢܫܐ. ܠܗ ܦܓܪ ܐܢܐ ܒܠ ܕܐܠܗܐ ܗܘ ܒܗ ܢܠܕܗ.
ܗܝܡܢܘܬܗ ܕܚܢܢ ܗܘܕܝܐ ܢܛܪܐ ܡܠܟܐ. ܘܟܕ ܢܗܘܪܐ
ܐܘܪܝܗ, ܡܠܦܬ ܗܝܡܢܘܬܐ, ܒܪܬܗ ܕܐܒܪܗܡ ܕܐܡܪ ܐܢ.
ܠܗܝܡܢܘܬܐ. ܒܗ ܗܘ ܢܡܘܣܗ ܒܗ ܗܘ ܓܙܪܗ ܘܗܝܡܢܘܬܗ.
ܡܠܟܘܬܗ ܡܢܗ ܗܘܪܢܗ ܡܢܗ ܓܙܪܗ ܡܢܗ. ܐܦ ܡܠܟܘܬܐ
ܕܗܝܡܢܘܬܐ ܡܢܗ ܐܝܬܝܗ. ܐܒܪܗܡ ܗܘܝܢ ܕܐܠܗܐ ܐܝܬ ܒܪ
ܐܠܗܐ. ܘܥܒܕ ܠܒܢܐ ܡܛܠ ܫܘܦܪܐ ܕܗܝܡܢܘܬܗ ܓܙܪܬܗ
ܗܘܕܝܐ ܒܪ ܐܒܪܗܡ ܬܘܒ ܐܡܪ ܗܘܐ. ܕܚܙܐ ܗܘ ܝܘܡܝ
ܓܝܪ ܐܠܗܐ ܕܗܘܐ ܐܢܫܐ. ܘܫܒܚܝ ܗܘܕܝܐ ܕܐܦ ܗܘ
ܒܐܘܪܗ, ܐܬܓܠܠ ܗܘܐ ܡܠܟ ܐܘܕ, ܕܢܣܒ ܦܓܪܐ ܘܗܘܐ
ܐܢܫܐ. ܕܒܪ ܐܠܗܐ ܗܘ ܐܦ ܐܠܗܐ ܗܘ ܘܗܘܐ ܐܢܫܐ.
ܡܛܠ ܐܘܪܗ ܡܢ ܡܠܟܘܬܐ ܕܕܪ̈ܬܐ. ܡܠܦܘ ܐܠܗܘ ܗܘܕܝܐ
ܐܠܦܘ ܗܝܡܢܘܬܐ. ܘܠܡܠܟܘܬܐ ܐܚ̈ܪܢܝܐ ܕܐܘܣܦܐ ܠܗ
ܡܬܬܡܟܐ. ܚܢܢ ܗܘܕܝܐ ܒܐܘܕܝܗ ܕܐܘܪܗ, ܗܘ ܦܟܐ.
ܡܢ ܒܗ ܢܘܪܐ ܕܠܒܪ ܐܢܫܐ ܠܐ ܦܓܪ ܐܢܐ. ܠܐܠܗܐ ܓܝܪ

ܘܗܘ̇ ܕܐܠܗܐ. ܚܙܐ ܒܚܙܘܐ ܕܢܦܩ ܢܬܬܘܣܡ ܥܠ ܫܘܠܛܢܐ. ܘܥܠ ܕܐܝܬ ܗ̱ܘܐ ܒܗ̇ ܪܘܚܐ ܡܪܢܝܐ ܠܐ ܚܙܐ ܗܘܬ. ܪ̈ܘܚܐ ܕܪ̈ܘܚܗ ܕܐܡܟܐ ܐܟܢ ܡܛܠ ܦܐܪܗ̇. ܘܡܫܬܘܕܐ ܠܗܘܢ ܦܩܘܕܘܬܐ ܕܠܐ ܢܬܟܢܫܘܢ. ܚܝܠܐ ܡܛܠܠ ܥܠ ܗܕܡܐ ܕܦܪܫ ܡܢܗ. ܘܫܡܥܗ ܕܡܪܝܐ ܡܪܝܐ ܠܢܫܐ ܕܠܐ ܬܪܥ ܒܗ. ܚܕ ܗܘܐ ܚܝܠܐ ܘܐܫܬܟܚ ܡܪܝܐ ܒܕܪܐ ܢܝܫܬ. ܒܢܦܫܗ ܕܐܡܟܐ ܕܠܐ ܬܬܡܪܡܪ ܥܠ ܢܦܫܗ. ܘܠܘ ܚܙܐ ܡܠܐ ܪ̈ܚܡܘܗܝ ܥܠ ܬ̈ܪܘܬܐ. ܘܠܘ ܐܟܠܐ ܒܫ̈ܝܢܬܐ ܫܟܝ̈ܢܐ ܢܦܫܐ ܗܘܬ. ܘܡܠܟܐ ܠܗ ܕܐܢܐܠ ܢܐܘܣ ܘܫܬܪܐ ܗܘܬ. ܡܛܠ ܕܒܗ ܐܫܬܟܚ ܡܪܝܐ ܠܗܘܢ ܕܚܝܠܐ. ܘܒܫܘܪܐ ܐܝܟ ܕܠܫܬܝܐ ܫܠܠܬܐ ܒܒܕܬ. ܐܡܟܘ ܕܗܘܕܐ ܘܦܩܝܚܐ ܗܘܬ ܡܬܠܬܠܬܗ. ܥܡܗܘܢ ܕܬܬ̈ܐܡ ܢܦܪܘܗ ܠܗܘܕܐ ܦܐܟܝܫܘܬܐ. ܕܐܠܘ ܐܡܘܕܘ ܥ̈ܒܕܐ ܫܠܘ ܚܕ ܗܘ ܗܘܐ ܠܗ̇. ܚܕ ܐܝܬ ܗܘܐ ܠܗ̇ ܘܗܟܘܬܗ ܕܗܘܐ ܠܢܘܪܐ ܠܫܡܟܐ. ܘܐܝܟ ܕܠܗܘ ܚܕ ܐܠܘ ܐܝܬ ܗܘܐ ܥ̈ܒܕܐ ܡܗܡܢ. ܢܦܠ ܥܠ ܢܘܪܐ ܘܚܪܬܗ ܗܘܬ ܫܠܗܒܝܬܐ. ܘܚܙܐ ܐܡܟܐ ܘܠܐ ܒܐܟܝ ܠܗ̇ ܥܠ ܡܗܕܡ. ܚܝܠܐ ܐܚܪܬܐ ܗ̇ܝ ܕܡܕܡܟܐ ܥܠ ܒܩܝܬܐ. ܐܝܬ ܗܘܐ ܠܢܦܫܗ ܘܥܠ ܗ̇ܝ ܪܘܚܬ ܒܕ ܡܦ̈ ܗܘܐ. ܦܬܓ̈ܡܐ ܕܗܘܪܐ ܕܐܝܬ ܒܡ̈ܠܠܐ ܕܗܘܦܪܐ ܚܪܬ. ܘܒܬܫܒܘܚܬܐ ܕܢܛܪܐ ܠܗܘܢ ܡܢ ܫ̈ܒܝܗܘܢ. ܘܦܬ̈ܓܡܐ ܡ̈ܠܝܟܐ ܕܢܬܬܡ ܬܟܢ ܒܐܘ̈ܠܝܨܘܢ. ܘܒܪ ܐܠܗܐ ܕܡܠܟ ܢܗܘܪܐ ܠܡܪ̈ܚܡܘܗܝ. ܘܒܗܦܪܐ ܡܩ̈ܒܠܐ ܕܗ̇ ܡܠܟܘܬܐ ܕܠܐ ܡܬܬܦܪܐ. ܘܬܪܒܐ ܪܒܐ ܕܦܬܚ ܢܟܠܘܢ ܥܡ ܐܠܗܐ. ܒܗܠܝܢ ܚܙܬ ܐܡܟܗ ܕܗܘܕܐ ܒܕ ܡܦ̈ ܗܘܐ. ܘܚܕܬ ܪܘܪܬ ܘܒܗܘܪܐ ܒܒܟܗ ܢܦܫܬ. ܚܙܐ ܗܘܬ ܒܗ ܒܕ ܗ̇ܘ ܦܘܦܐ ܦܬܟܡܗ ܢܘܪܐ. ܘܥܠ ܕܠܠܠܗ ܪܒ ܗܘܐ ܦܓܪ ܠܐ ܡܟܘܝܐ ܗܘܬ. ܢܦܠ ܒܡܪܐ ܫܠܝܐ ܒܢܘܪܐ ܠܟܠ ܡܢ ܦܬܟܡܪܐ. ܘܗܘܐ ܦܠܓܐ ܘܒܪ ܠܐܐܪ ܡܢ ܦܬܟܡܘܬܐ. ܡܢ ܬܘܒܐ ܕܕ̈ܒܫܐ ܐܐܪ

ܢܘܪܐ. ܘܗܘܐ ܒܦܓܪܐ ܘܐܦ ܒܪܘܚܗ ܠܒܪ ܐܠܗܐ. ܒܟܠ ܬܘܠܕܝܗ ܘܒܟܠ ܚܝܘܗܝ ܘܒܟܠ ܫܘܒܚܗ. ܗܢ ܐܡܪ. ܘܗܢ ܐܠܦܗ̇ ܠܡܟܪܙܘܬܐ. ܘܗܢܐ ܫܪܪܐ ܠܟܠܗ ܐܘܪܚܗ, ܡܛܠ ܡܪܢ. ܐܦ ܕܐܠܗܐ ܗܘ ܘܒܪܗ ܕܐܢܫܐ ܗܘܐ ܡܢ ܡܪܝܡ. ܘܗܢܐ ܒܠܬܐ ܠܐܢܫܐ ܕܟܦܪ ܒܐܠܗܘܬܗ. ܘܒܣܪܐ ܘܡܬܚܙܝܐ ܠܐܢܫܐ ܕܛܠܡ ܦܪܘܩܘܬܗ. ܢܣܓܕܘܢ ܠܗ ܚܕ ܒܐܠܗܘܬܗ ܘܒܐܢܫܘܬܗ. ܐܝܟܢܐ ܕܦܩܕܗ ܡܪܗ ܠܗ ܡܬܦܪܫ. ܘܗܘܐ ܠܘܬ ܒܪܬ ܩܠܝܡܐ ܠܡܫܡܫܘ. ܘܗܘܐ ܐܟܪܙ ܘܗܘܐ ܡܠܦܐ ܠܬܠܡܝܕܘ ܠܗ. ܦܛܪ ܗܘܐ ܗܟܢ ܗܘ ܕܢܫܐ ܡܠܐ ܚܣܝܘܬܐ. ܕܗܘܐ ܢܐܡܪ. ܗܘܕܐ ܒܩܘܪܐ ܕܦܛܪܐ ܠܗ. ܘܡܫܕܪܐ ܒܪܘܬܐ ܒܣܗܕܘܬܗ ܢܦܠܬ ܐܝܟ ܡܦܠܬܐ. ܒܕ ܬܘܕܝܬܗ ܒܠܒܗ ܢܦܫܪܐ ܝܕܥ ܐܠܗܐ. ܘܢܦܫܗ, ܘܢܦܩ ܡܢ ܒܝܬ ܕܐܢܫܐ ܒܕ ܫܪܐ ܗܘܐ. ܕܡܛܠ ܥܒܕܬܐ ܕܐܢܬܬܐ ܒܠܒܬܐ ܠܡܫܡܫܘܬܗ. ܘܢܦܩ ܒܗܝܢ ܒܢܝܐ ܕܐܢܫܐ ܕܠܘܩܒܠܗ. ܒܕ ܚܙܝܬ ܒܗ ܠܘ ܐܝܟ ܡܬܬܐ ܕܡܬܠܬܐ ܗܘܐ. ܐܠܐ ܓܒܪܐ ܕܐܙܠ ܢܗܘܐ ܒܢܘܪܐ ܚܕܬܐ. ܘܐܢܬܬܐ ܒܠܒܬܐ ܕܢܦܪ ܗܘܐ ܠܗ ܡܢ ܒܐܢܬܬܐ. ܚܙܝܬ ܗܘܘ ܒܗ ܐܝܟ ܕܓܒܪܐ ܕܥܠ ܠܡܪܟܒܐ. ܘܚܙܝܘܗ, ܒܐܪܐ ܘܐܘܡܢܐ ܘܫܡܫܐ ܘܢܓܪܐ ܐܝܟ. ܫܐܠܘܗ, ܕܡܠܠ ܐܝܟ ܐܬܠܚܡܬܐ ܡܢ ܐܓܘܢܐ ܘܒܓܘܬܐ ܐܬܘ ܠܗ ܟܠܠܐ ܡܢ ܫܡܝܐ. ܚܙܝܢ ܗܘܘ ܒܗ ܕܢܓܪܐ ܠܐܪܥܐ ܘܠܫܘܠܛܢܐ. ܕܒܓܘ ܕܝܢ ܒܒܝܬ ܒܠܗܘܢ ܘܐܒܕܗ̇ ܐܢܘܢ. ܙܒܢ ܗܘܐ ܒܗ ܒܠܗ ܒܢܝܐ ܕܡܫܝܚܐ. ܕܐܝܟ ܓܒܪܐ ܕܡܫܝܚܘܬܐ ܒܡܠܐ ܕܗܒܠ. ܢܦܩ ܒܗܝܢ ܒܕܘܬܐ ܒܠܘܬܐ ܡܠܟܬ ܢܘܗܪܐ. ܘܟܠܗܝܢ ܐܦܝܗ ܒܗܘܕܐ ܙܘܒܢܐ ܕܐܬܬܘܗܝ ܠܗ. ܗܕܡ ܐܡܗ ܡܛܠ ܕܗܘܐ ܫܠܡܐ ܠܒܪܗ. ܢܦܩܬ ܢܦܫܗ ܒܫܢܬܐ ܕܚܡܫ ܡܢ ܕܝܢܐ. ܕܠܐ ܫܟܝܚ ܗܘܐ ܟܐܢܐ ܢܨܚܐ ܠܟܠܗ ܡܫܬܘܬܐ. ܒܠ ܢܘܪܐ ܟܐܢܐ ܠܒܝܬ ܓܢܣܝܘܬܐ. ܗܪܟܐ ܠܕܪܐ ܢܦܩ ܙܒܢܬܐ ܠܡܬܬܠܡ. ܒܫܡܫ ܕܐܡܝܐ ܗ̇ܘ, ܕܒܢܝܐ

ܠܡܪܟܐ ܐܝܟ ܒܢܝܢܐ. ܘܡܬܬܪܥܢ ܐܬܚܝܠܘ ܒܗ ܒܡܐܪܘܬܐ
ܕܕܡܟܐ. ܗܠܝܢ ܕܗܘܘ ܡܠܝܫܐ ܠܐܬܪܐ ܘܐܬܟܢܫܘ ܒܗ. ܘܐܬܘ
ܠܒܝܬܗ ܕܟܒܫ ܗܘܐ ܠܗ ܒܟܦܘܪܬܐ. ܝܬܝܪ ܕܗܟܢܐ ܕܡܠܝܢ
ܡܚܫܒܗ ܕܐܘܦܩܬܐ. ܕܢܣܪܬ ܡܢܗܘܢ ܒܢܝܬ ܥܠܗ ܕܢܬܒܟܐ
ܗܘܬ. ܬܪܝܢ ܠܡܦܩܕܘ ܕܒܝ ܢܒܝ ܗܘ، ܠܘܬܗܘܢ ܕܘܝܐ. ܕܥܠܗ
ܠܒܝܬ ܠܐ ܐܙܝܠ ܗܘ، ܢܗܪܝܗܘܢ. ܦܓܠܐ ܬܠܡܝܕܐ ܕܡܢ
ܫܪܝܗ ܕܗܘܡܐ ܦܠܛܘ ܒܗ. ܒܚܕܡܐ ܒܪܡܫܐ ܕܒܝܬ ܐܠܗܐ
ܕܕܡܝܟܬ. ܫܪܝܘܗܝ ܕܐܬܪܐ ܕܒܝܬܗ ܠܗ ܐܝܟ ܗܘܬܪܐ. ܡܢ
ܟܠ ܒܢܝܗܘܢ ܕܟܠ ܕܪܐ ܕܪܚܡܝܢ ܠܗ. ܠܡܐܟܠܐ ܕܢܦܫܐ ܐܦ
ܒܝܬ ܓܘܡܐ ܕܟܠ ܕܢܦܫܢ. ܘܡܫܡܫܝܢ ܙܒܢܐ ܕܟܠ ܡܢ ܕܗܘܐ
ܟܠ ܒܗܕܪܐ. ܡܬܒܝܢܬܐ ܡܫܪܬܐ ܐܬܪܐܝܬ ܕܗܘ،. ܓܒܘܬܐ
ܠܟܠܬܐ ܕܪܒ ܐܟܒܪ ܒܪ ܐܪܒܥܐ. ܡܠܦܢܐ ܗܘܘ ܕܠܗܠܦܢܘܗܝ
ܒܕܡܟܐ ܕܪܫܐ. ܘܡܬܒܢܝܢܘܗܝ ܡܢ ܫܪܫܘܗܝ ܡܬܥܒܕܐ ܗܘܬ.
ܟܠ ܦܓܪܗܘܢ ܒܬܒܗܘܢ ܥܒܕܗ ܕܒܪ ܐܠܗܐ. ܒܫܘܪܗܘܢ
ܘܒܦܓܪܗܘܢ ܕܗܒܝܢ ܗܘܘ. ܗܘܘ ܫܘܒܗܘܢ ܠܐ ܗܘܐ
ܒܡܠܐ ܕܦܘܡܐ ܒܠܫܘܢ. ܐܠܐ ܒܥܒܕܐ ܘܒܦܘܫܩܐ
ܕܗܕܡܝܗܘܢ. ܫܠܚ ܐܣܟܡܬܗ ܕܒܪ ܐܠܗܐ ܡܢܗ ܦܓܪܗܘܢ.
ܕܒܐܪܐ ܠܐܣܟܡܐ ܕܫܠܚ ܐܣܟܡܗ ܢܫܠܡ ܢܦܫܗ. ܢܛܪܐ ܘܣܦܩܐ
ܒܢܝܗ، ܗܘܐ ܠܫܘܒܚܗܘܢ ܕܒܡܟܐ ܫܪܪ. ܘܠܒܫ ܡܢ ܗܕܡܐ
ܕܒܝܫ ܒܐܪܒܥܐ ܫܦܪ ܝܘܪܩܘܢ. ܫܪܘ ܒܐܠܗܐ ܘܡܠܦܠ
ܕܫܪܘ ܫܘܦܪܗ، ܕܡܟܐ. ܟܠ ܗܘ ܐܡܟܝܪ ܟܠ ܫܒܝܗܘܢ
ܡܠܠܬܗ. ܕܒܝܕ ܗܘܐ ܫܡܫܐ ܕܕܘܟܬܐ ܒܪܝܫܝܗܘܢ.
ܘܢܗܪ ܒܢܘܗ ܘܠܫܘܒܚܐ ܒܢܘܗܪܐ ܕܪܘܚܗ، ܠܫܡܗ ܟܠ
ܬܠܡܝܕܐ ܕܗܝܡܢܘܬܐ ܕܐܬܟܠܬ ܠܒܝܬܝ. ܒܡܫܝܚܘܬܐ ܕܒܪ
ܐܠܗܐ ܕܡܠܟܐ ܢܗܘܪܐ. ܙܠܝܩܬ ܡܢܪܐ ܗܘܬ ܐܝܟ ܢܘܪܐ
ܒܪܫܝܢܘܗܝ. ܘܠܐ ܐܦ ܠܗ ܕܝܢ ܥܠܘ ܡܢܪܐ ܕܒܬܪܘܬܐ.
ܐܘܪ ܗܘܐ ܫܘܒܚܗ ܕܝܢ ܐܠܗܐ ܕܠܐ ܡܬܚܙܐ. ܘܟܠ

ܐܬܦܠܓܐ ܗܘܐ. ܘܡܢ ܡܕܡ ܕܗܘܐ ܗܘܕܐ ܐܬܝܕܥ ܗܘܐ.
ܗܪܐ ܗܘܐ ܙܒܢܐ ܡܢ ܕܒܥܘܬܐ ܕܟ̈ܠܘܬܐ. ܘܦܠܛ ܙܕܩܗ
ܫܠܡܐ ܕܗܘܕܐ ܘܐܬܒܣܡ ܒܗ. ܘܟܠܠ ܕܒܢܝܐ ܗܘܐ ܫܒܝܐ
ܒܒܝ̈ܫܬܐ. ܘܗܘܬ ܚܙܒܐ ܕܠܐ ܬܗܘܐ ܬܚܘܒ ܠܡܫܝ̈ܚܐ.
ܒܥܕܢ ܥܪܝܬ ܒܡܕܝܢܬ ܫܠܝܛܬ ܒܐܬܪܐ ܕܝܠܗ. ܘܡܢܗ ܘܠܒܐ
ܠܐܢܫ ܠܐ ܡܫܠܛ ܡܢ ܕܐܡܪ ܗܘܐ. ܐܡܠܟ ܗܘܐ ܠܗ
ܘܡܫܠܛܢܘܬܗ ܙܒ ܙܒܢܐ. ܘܒܒܝܬ ܕܝܢ ܠܬܠܬܐ ܕܡܠܟܐ ܘܡܢ
ܟܠ ܦܪܣ. ܐܬܬܒܪܬ ܗܘܬ ܡܪܝܗ ܘܡܠܬܐ ܕܒܬܪܘܬܐ. ܘܡܢ
ܡܕܡ ܕܗܘܕܐ ܘܠܒܐ ܠܐܢܫ ܠܐ ܕܦܪܬ. ܦܠܛ ܬܚܝܬ ܘܗܘܐ
ܒܠܢܐ ܠܐܠܗܘܬܐ. ܘܐܫܬܒܩ ܒܗ ܐܝܟ ܕܕܠܝܠ ܡܢ ܣܘܦܘܬܐ.
ܘܒܡܕܝܢܬܐ ܐܬܝܕܥ ܗܘܐ ܐܬܪܐ ܟܠܗ. ܒܪܝܟ ܗܘ ܡܢ ܠܗ
ܟܠܠܐ ܘܫܘܒܚܐ ܘܝܩܪܐ ܠܥܠܡ.

ܫܠܡ ܡܐܡܪܐ ܕܥܠ ܚܝܒܝ ܗܘܕܐ

. . ܕܫܡܥ ܠܡܪܝ ܡܘܫܐ . .

ܡܐܡܪܐ ܕܥܠ ܟܘܪܗܢܐ ܘܫܘܒܩܢܐ

ܕܫܡܥ ܠܡܪܝ ܡܘܫܐ

ܫܘܒܩܢܐ ܘܟܘܪܗܢܐ ܗܘܕܐ ܕܢܝܫܘ ܒܐܘܠܝܢܘܣ.
ܒܗܘܟܐ ܬܫܡܫ ܠܡܫܠܠܘ ܢܫ̈ܩܘܢ. ܕܢ ܐܬܠܬܠܐ
ܕܡܫܡܫܢܘܬܐ ܡܪܝ ܝܘܠܝܢܐ. ܐܫܟܚ ܐܢܫܐ ܐܪ̈ܟܘܢܘ
ܘܩ̈ܠܝܠܘ. ܟ̈ܕ ܡܫܝܢܐ ܕܒܢܝܢܐ ܕܪܐ ܒܗ ܗܘܠܐ. ܡܪܐܘܢ
ܡܢ ܕܐܬܐ ܬܘܪܐ ܕܬ̈ܐܘܡܣܝܢܘ. ܗܘ̈ܟܐ ܒ̈ܢܪܐ ܕܟܠܗ

ܦܬܘܫܐ ܬܪܝܢܐ ܠܡܘܬܐ ܢܦܠ. ܐܦ ܗܘ ܕܝܢ ܠܫ̈ܢܐ ܘܕܝܫܝܢ
ܥܠ ܒܪ ܐܢܫܐ؛ ܐܦ ܓܢܣܐ ܚܝܘܬܐ ܡܠܝܠܬܐ ܕܗܝ ܡܠܝܠܘܬܐ.
ܫܩܠ ܡܠܝܠܘܬܐ ܘܪܟܒܬ ܓܢܣܬܐ ܕܡܠܝܠܐ ܦ̈ܠܓܐ. ܐܦ ܕ̈ܢܝܐ
ܕܚܘܠܐ ܠܡ̈ܫܕܐ ܒ̈ܢܝ ܡܫܝܚܐ. ܡܛܠ ܦܘܡܐ ܬܒܥܘ ܗܘܘ
ܒܠܚܘܕ ܠܡܓܕܦܘ. ܘܐܝܟ ܫ̈ܪܪܐ ܕܠܒܝܫܝܢ ܗܘܘ ܡܫܝܚܘܬܐ.
ܠܐ ܢܣܒܘ ܡܠܬܐ ܕܐܬܬܫܝܡ ܒܗ̇ ܒܦܘܪܬܐ. ܫܡܘܥܐ
ܫܦܝܪܐ ܕܡܫܝܚܘܬܟ ܡܢ ܡܘܡܐ ܠܟ. ܕܐܡܪ ܗܘ ܠܟ
ܦܘܡܟ ܘܒܪܝܪ ܗܘ ܠܟ ܕܐܬܬܡܠܠ ܒܗ. ܫܪܝܪܝܢ ܫܦܝܪܝܢ ܥܠܝܟ
ܢܫܝܢ ܒܥܬܪܝܢ ܠܓܒܪܝܢ. ܘܒܩ̈ܫܝܫܘܬܟ ܢܝܚܝܢ ܫܦܝܪܐ
ܕܐܬܬܠܠܝܢ. ܫܘܪ ܒܟ ܐܬܪ ܐܝܟ ܕܒܓܪܐ ܕܡܠܐ
ܕܗܒܐ. ܕܒܘܬܪܐ ܐܝܬ ܠܡ ܘܡܣܡܟܬܐ ܣܡܟܬܐ ܕܠܐ
ܡܬܒܥܝܐ. ܒܘܪܟܐ ܗܘܕܐ ܒܒܪ ܚܝܠܐ ܕܡܫܝܚܘܬܟ. ܡܢ
ܗܦܟ ܠܟ ܢܘܚܐ ܫܦܝܪܝܢ ܥ̈ܠܡܐ. ܗܐ ܬܫ̈ܢܝܐ ܒܟܒܪܝܢ
ܘܡܟܝܢ ܐܝܟ ܒܪ̈ܘܠܐ. ܘܡܦܩܐ ܒܝܘܪܢ ܐܝܟ ܗܡܝܢܘܬܐ
ܕܕܗܒܐ ܒܓܒܐ. ܕܡܟ ܥܠ ܒܓܘܫܡܟ ܐܗܦܠܠ ܫܘܒܚܐ
ܕܡܠܟܐ ܫܘܦܪܐ. ܘܒܓܕܐ ܕܣܝܡ ܠܟ ܠܚܘܒܐ ܕܫܘܒܚܐ ܠܐ ܦܢܝܡ
ܠܗ. ܗܕܪ ܐܢܬ ܘܦܐܐ ܒܗܠܝܢ ܫ̈ܢܝܐ ܕܡܒܟܝܢ ܠܟ. ܘܢܝܚܝܢ
ܫܘܦܪܝܢ ܡܛܠ ܒ̈ܢܝܐ ܕܒܥܝܢ ܒܟ. ܫܡܘܥܐ ܒܬܪ̱
ܒܬܪ ܐܢܬ ܗܘ ܡܢ ܒܬܪܐ. ܕܗܐ ܒܬܪܐ ܒܬܪܝܢ ܦܘܡܝܢ
ܬܡܡܬܟ ܐܢܘ̱. ܘܒܘܪܟܐ ܦܪܬܟ ܘܡܡܫܡܝܢ ܐܬܪܟ ܘܡܓܘ
ܡܫܒ ܠܟ. ܕܡܒܪ ܦܘܪܫܐ ܘܡܫ̈ܝܚܬܐ ܠܟ ܒܬܫܦܪܐ. ܗܐ
ܕܢ̈ܫܐ ܠܒ̈ܢܝ ܥܡܗܘܢ ܘܒ̈ܢܝ ܫܘܬܦܘܬܗܘܢ. ܒܦܪܐ ܫܡܠܝܢ ܡܢ
ܐܫܟܚܬܟ ܐܝܟ ܗܘ ܫ̈ܢܝܐ. ܘܢܦܩܐ ܒܬܪ ܘܠܡܓܕ̈ܘܬܗܘܢ
ܐܫܟܚ ܒܬܪܐ. ܘܡܫܒܚܘܬܗ ܠܟܠܗ ܒܬܪܗ ܕܟܠܡܐ ܒܥܘܪܬ.
ܫܡܘܥܐ ܘܓܒܪܐ ܒ̈ܢܝ ܡܫܡܫܢܐ ܗܐ ܒܬܪ̈ܝܢܘܗܝ. ܕܓܢ ܒܬܪܐ
ܕܢܫܒܘܗܝ ܡܫܒܚܘܗܝ ܘܗܢܘܢܩܫܘܗܝ̈ ܒܪ ܐܠܗܐ ܒܡܫܒܚܘܬܐ
ܘܒܡܫܝܚܘܬܐ. ܫܘܝ ܠܟܠܡܐ ܕܒܟܠܗ ܒܬܪܗ ܠܗ ܡܢܟ ܗܘ.

ܗ̇ܝ ܐܦܠܘ ܥܠ ܡܫܘܚܬܐ ܕܪܘܚܐ ܠܡܬܚܐ. ܒܡܬܡܫܚܢܘܬܐ
ܘܒܪܡܫܚܘܬܐ ܡܫܚ ܒܗ̇ ܕܢܒܐ. ܐܝܟ ܕܐܬܦܫܪܘ ܡܢ ܡܟܝܠܐ
ܕܝܪܬܘܬܐ. ܗܢ ܥܦܠܘ ܐܬܪܝܘ ܟܕܘܢܐ ܘܦܠܡܫܘܡܐ ܬܫܡܫ̈ܬܐ
ܗܘܘ. ܘܕܠܐ ܚܫܒ ܗܘܐ ܠܗܘܢ ܡܫܝܚܐ ܘܠܐ ܡܬܪܢܐ. ܒܗ̇
ܕܢܒܐ ܠܥܠ ܒܒܪܡܫܝܚܘܬܐ ܕܫܘܘܬܐ. ܘܗܝܕܝܢ ܗܘܘ ܒܗ̇
ܒܡܫܝܚܘܬܐ ܕܒܗ̇ ܐܠܗܐ. ܐܝܟܢܐ ܕܡܬܬܚܝܕ ܚܝܠܐ ܘܟܠܗ
ܪܫܡ ܢܦܫ. ܘܡܫܠܡ ܥܒܕ ܠܗ ܦܓܪܗ ܡܢ ܐܫܘܕܗ. ܘܡܫܚܐ
ܕܢܦܫ ܪܫܡܗ ܢܦܫܗ ܒܗ ܡܫܝܚܐ. ܐܦ ܕܝܢ ܪܫܡܐ ܢܦܠܘܢ
ܥܒܕܬ ܢܦܫܐ ܠܐܟܒܪ. ܪܫܡܐ ܕܢܦܫܐ ܡܫܝܚܘܬܐ ܕܒܢܝ ܐܢܫܐ.
ܘܐܦ ܗܝ ܢܦܫܐ ܒܗ̇ ܡܬܢܦܫܝܢ ܐܦ ܫܡܫܐ. ܘܐܦ
ܡܬܒܣܡܐ ܒܟܠܗ ܦܓܪܐ ܡܢ ܡܫܝܚܘܬܐ. ܒܡܐ ܕܢܦܫܐ
ܡܫܝܚܘܬܐ ܢܦܫܐ ܚܝܐ ܗܝ. ܐܦ ܕܝܢ ܒܠܒܗ ܡܫܝܚܘܬܐ
ܒܒܣܝܡܘܬܐ. ܐܟܙܢܐ ܢܦܫܐ ܦܓܪܘ ܚܝܐ ܡܢ ܒܪܢܫܐ.
ܢܦܫܐ ܘܦܓܪܐ ܒܡܫܝܚܘܬܐ ܐܝܟ ܕܒܪ ܐܢܫܐ. ܘܗܝܕܝܢ
ܗܘܘ ܒܗ̇ ܕܠܐ ܬܟܠܝܬ ܗܘܬ ܡܢ ܕܪ̈ܘܫܐ. ܡܕܡ ܗܘܘ ܚܙܝ
ܕܐܦ ܡܬܚܙܝܐ ܡܫܝܚܘܬܐ. ܢܦܫܐ ܘܦܓܪܐ ܢܛܪܝܢ ܐܦܘ
ܡܢ ܐܟܕܢܐ. ܘܡܛܠ ܗܢܐ ܕܡܫܝܚܘܬܗܘܢ ܡܫܝܚ ܗܘܘ.
ܕܗܒ ܠܐ ܬܟܠܝܬ ܕܒܗ̇ ܗܘ ܒܗܝ ܗܘܘ ܐܦ ܫܡܫܘܢ. ܡܕܡ
ܦܓܪܗܘܢ ܘܠܢܦܫܬܐ ܘܠܡܫܝܚܐ. ܘܠܗܠ ܢܦܫܝܢ ܕܠܐ ܬܟܠܝܬ
ܗܘܬ ܡܫܝܚܘܬܐ. ܘܐܝܟ ܕܐܦ ܚܘܐ ܡܛܠܒܐ ܪܫܡܗ ܡܢ
ܡܫܝܚܘܬܐ. ܡܢ ܛܒܥܗ ܠܡܫܝܚܘܬܐ ܢܦܩ ܠܒܢܝܗܘܢ. ܘܟܠ
ܦܓܪܐ ܘܢܦܫܐ ܢܫܒܐ ܘܛܠܡ ܫܒܐ. ܘܠܐ ܐܬܡܫܝܚܬ
ܡܫܝܚܘܬܐ ܕܒܠܚܘܕܝܗܘܢ. ܦܓܪܐ ܡܫܠܡ ܢܦܫܐ ܠܡܫܝܚܘܬܐ
ܡܢܐ ܕܡܫܠܠ. ܘܟܠܢܫܐ ܐܝܟ ܕܒܦܓܪܐ ܡܛܠܐ ܒܒܪ. ܘܡܫܡܗ
ܢܦܫܝܢ ܫܒܐ ܘܡܫܚܬܐ ܠܟܠ ܐܢܫܐ. ܦܓܪ ܡܫܝܚܐ ܡܫܚܐ ܕܫܒܐ
ܘܫܠܡ ܗܘ ܠܗ. ܒܦܓܪܐ ܡܫܝܚܐ ܗܘ ܘܡܬܕܡܪܐ ܕܢܦܫܐ ܫܒܐ.
ܘܫܠܡ ܦܓܪܐ ܥܠ ܬܪܬܝܗܘܢ ܐܝܟ ܕܢܫܐ. ܘܟܠܗ ܦܓܪܐ

ܐܬܠܝܚ ܕܢܦܫ ܐܢܘܢ. ܪܘܪܒ ܚܠܡܘܗܝ ܕܣܘܪܪܐ ܘܥܘܫܠܐ.
ܐܦ ܒܡܪܥܝܬܐ ܢܬܝܢ ܐܢܘܢ ܠܡܕܒܪܐ. ܐܬܬܠܝܬܐ ܕܝܢ
ܥܠܗ ܠܡܪܥܝܬܐ ܘܠܒܘܫܠܐ. ܘܠܚܕܐ ܕܝܠܗ ܘܠܟܠ ܩܘܕܫܝܢ ܦܪܝܫܐ.
ܘܡܬܚܒܢ ܗܘܘ ܠܡܥܪܬܐ ܘܬܥܕܐ ܘܠܡܫܡܫܘܬܐ. ܘܠܡܬܪܥܝܐ
ܘܠܢܛܘܦܐ ܘܠܡܣܟܢܐ. ܐܦ ܠܡܥܕܢܐ ܐܦ ܠܐܣܘܪܐ
ܘܠܟܘܠ ܚܒܝܫ. ܘܠܟܠ ܥܩܘܪ ܘܠܟܠ ܫܟܝܚ ܒܗ ܣܓܝ ܗܘܘ.
ܠܐ ܐܣܬܪܩܘ ܘܠܐ ܐܬܒܛܠܘ ܘܠܐ ܐܬܥܟܒܘ. ܘܠܐ ܟܕ
ܐܢܘܢ ܒܥܒܕܐ ܕܥܘܕܪܐ ܠܡܕܒܪܐ. ܠܡܪܥܝܬܐ ܥܠܡܘܗܝ ܘܐܝܟ
ܕܠܟܠܐ ܕܐܪܥܐ ܫܒܩܘܗܝ. ܡܕܝܢ ܗܘܘ ܒܪ ܕܒܥܝܐ ܕܟܠܒ
ܥܘܩܪܗ ܘܚܒܐ. ܘܡܢܚܐ ܕܐܘܒܠ ܚܠܦ ܕܢܥܐ ܢܦܪܕ ܐܢܘܢ.
ܐܘܚܕܘ ܒܦܪܘܗܝ ܒܕ ܠܐ ܕܢܠܝܢ ܡܢ ܠܘܩܒܠܗܘܢ. ܬܢܐ ܗܘܐ
ܠܗܘܢ ܕܒܥܒܕܐ ܥܢܝܕܐ ܠܚܒ ܠܗܘܢ. ܘܐܬܥܝܢ ܗܘܘ ܠܗ
ܟܠ ܒܥܘܬܐ ܕܢܛܪܐ ܠܗ. ܒܥܠܝܡ ܕܐܬܝܢ ܡܢܥܒܕ ܗܘܐ ܠܗܘܢ
ܠܡܕܒܪܐ. ܘܗܢܘܢ ܐܡܪܝܢ ܡܛܠ ܕܝܠܗ ܕܢܦܠܐ ܕܠܘܬ.
ܥܙܪܐ ܢܦܫ ܠܒܢ ܡܢ ܬܟܠܐ ܣܘܓܦܬܐ. ܘܩܠܝ ܗܢܝܐ ܒܗܒܐ
ܕܬܬܠܒܬ ܕܠܠܘܬܐ. ܥܒܕܘܢܐ ܘܒܘܪܟܐ ܥܙܪܐ ܐܘܗܒܘ
ܠܡܬܠܠܘ. ܒܕ ܕܢܝܐ ܒܬܠܘܬܐ ܡܬܢܫܝܢ ܗܘܐ. ܘܡܛܠ ܗܢܐ
ܠܐ ܕܢܠܝܢ ܗܘܘ ܡܢ ܠܘܩܒܠܗ. ܕܗܘܠܐ ܚܒܝܒ ܗܘܐ ܥܠܗ
ܒܡܥܒܕ ܨܒܐ ܥܙܝܙܐ. ܠܡܣܒܪܘ ܕܟܠܡܐ ܥܠܡܘܗܝ ܒܥܘܪܘܗܝ
ܘܐܬܘܠܐ ܒܥܡܗܘܢ. ܘܕܢܦܩܘܢ ܠܗ ܠܐ ܒܥܝܢ ܗܘܘ ܐܘ ܢܕܠܘܢ
ܠܗ. ܡܢ ܒܬ ܕܝܠܐ ܗܡܗ ܬܘܩܠܘܢ ܠܡܥܢܝܘ. ܠܘ ܒܬ
ܘܥܕܐ ܕܒܠܗܘܢ ܫܢܐ ܕܟܠܡܐ ܣܓܝܬܐ. ܠܐ ܪܢܝ ܗܘܘ ܠܐ
ܒܩܝܢܐ ܘܠܐ ܒܒܢܝܢܐ. ܘܠܐ ܒܣܘܬܪܢܐ ܕܗܢܐ ܟܠܡܐ
ܡܠܐ ܒܝܬܐ. ܟܠܠ ܢܘܗܪܐ ܐܘܪܐ ܗܘܐ ܠܗܘܢ ܒܝܕ
ܐܠܗܐ. ܘܠܘ ܠܗܘ ܐܬܪܐ ܗܘ ܬܘܩܠܘܢ ܠܡܥܢܝܘ. ܘܢܦܩ
ܗܘܘ ܠܗ ܠܥܘܦܐ ܕܢܐܬܐ ܘܡܗܘܐ ܒܪܐ. ܘܟܕ ܐܢܘܢ
ܒܝܕ ܐܠܗܐ ܕܡܫܡܫ ܠܗ. ܠܗܢܐ ܟܠܡܐ ܐܝܟ ܠܡܬܠܬܐ

ܥܠ ܢ̈ܨܚܢܐ ܥܠ ܡܦܩܢܐ ܥܠ ܬܘܒܢܐ. ܥܠ ܕܡܢܨܚܝܢ ܗܘܘ
ܢ̈ܨܚܢܐ ܠܡܫܝܚܘܬܗ. ܠܡܐ ܢܨܚܢܐ ܕܐܦ ܗ̇ܝ ܩܪܝܬܗ ܒܢܬ
ܢ̈ܨܚܢܐ ܗ̇ܘ. ܒܒܢܘܗ̇ ܪܥܐ ܠܬܪܥܝܬܗ ܐܦ ܪܒ ܒܢܬܐ. ܠܡܐ
ܠܛܠܝܬܐ ܕܥܕܡ ܕܒܢܐ ܪܕܘܦܐ ܗܘܐ. ܫܦܝܪ ܘܒܒܢܘܗ̇ ܡܒܝܢܐ
ܒܒܢܐ ܠܡܫܝܚܘܬܐ. ܢܨܚܢܐ ܘܦܘܪܫܐ ܐܬܘ ܡܢ ܡ̈ܪܝܐ
ܕܠܐ ܒܫܘܠ. ܗܘܐ ܒܡܕܝܢܬܐ ܪܒܬܐ ܒܒܢܝܢ ܡܪ̈ܘܬܐ.
ܘܡܢܗܝܢ ܪ̈ܫܝܗ ܐܦ ܕܢܫܗ ܥܠ ܬܪ̈ܥܝܗܘܢ: ܘܒܒܝܢ ܡܢܗܘܢ
ܪ̈ܫܝܢܐ ܢܦܠܘܢ ܦܘܠܚܢܗܘܢ. ܡܢ ܬܘܕܝܬܐ ܕܡܫܝܚܘܬܗ
ܕܒܪ ܐܠܗܐ. ܡܢܘ ܦܘܪ̈ܫܐ ܗܠܝܢ ܒܗܘܪܐ ܕܠܐ ܡܬܕܪܟܝܢ.
ܐܬܡܠܟܝܢ ܗܘ ܘܠܡܦܩܢܐ ܒܒܪ ܒܬܘܠܬܐ: ܗܘܐ ܒܬܘܠܬܐ ܒܗܠܝܢ
ܒܪܬܐ ܒܡܫܝܚܘܬܗ. ܫܡܥܐ ܦܫܝܛܐ ܕܪܐ ܒܒܢܘ ܗܘܘ ܠܗܘܠ
ܦܘܒܝܢ. ܘܡܬܘܕܝܬܗ ܕܒܪ ܐܠܗܐ ܘܡܢ ܐܝܟ ܦܪܘܫܐ. ܒܠܘ
ܐܘܕܝܘ ܒܗ ܡܢܘ ܕܒܢܐ ܒܠܥܘܬ ܫ̈ܒܚܐ. ܕܝܕܥ ܒܗܘܢ ܗܘ ܐܝܟ
ܕܐܘܕܝܘ ܒܗ ܡܢܘ ܢܠܕܗ. ܡܢ ܠܗܘܒܠܗܘܢ ܡܐܪܥܐ ܕܫ̈ܢܝܐ
ܐܝܟ ܡܫܒܠܢܐ. ܘܗܦܟܐ ܕܘܒܪܐ ܡܚܪܝܢܘܬܐ ܘܕܒܪ ܐܢܘܢ.
ܡܬܬܒܒܝܢ ܗܘܘ ܠܡܒܒܢܘ ܠܫ̈ܠܝܚܐ ܩ̈ܕܝܫܐ. ܘܠܐ ܢܦܩܝܢ
ܗܘܘ ܡܢ ܬܘܕܝܬܗ ܕܒܪ ܐܠܗܐ. ܢܚܬ ܪܘܚܐ ܕܡܬܪܥܝܬܐ
ܥܠ ܐܩ̈ܝܗܘܢ. ܘܗܘܘ ܡܢܗܘܢ ܫ̈ܘܒܚܐ ܦ̈ܫܝܛܐ ܡܕܡ
ܥܠܥܠܐ. ܐܝܟ ܕܪܘܚܬܐ ܦܘܒܝܢ ܫܦܝܛ ܐܢܘܢ.
ܘܥܠ ܕܐܬܬܪܬܘ ܒܝܘܡܬܐ ܠܐ ܢܦܩ ܐܢܘܢ. ܐܒܝ ܒܝܫܐ
ܥܠܝܗܘܢ ܥܠ̈ܝܗܝ ܢܨܚܘܢ ܐܢܘܢ. ܘܥܠ ܕܐܝܬ ܗܘܐ ܠܗܘܢ
ܫܦܝܪܐ ܘܠܒܐ ܠܥܠܡܘܢ ܐܒܪܘܟ ܘܡܢܗ ܫܒܝ ܠܡܥܠܠܘ
ܐܦ̈ܘܝܗܘܢ. ܐܘ ܢܫ̈ܝܗܘܢ ܐܘ ܦܓܪܗܘܢ ܕܫ̈ܒܝܚܝܗܘܢ. ܐܘ
ܡܢ ܡܟܝܢ ܢܝܪ ܥܠܡܐ ܠܥܠܝܗܘܢ. ܕܐܡܟܢܐ ܫܠܡ ܡܢ
ܐܦܘܢܐ ܒܪ ܢܝܫܢ. ܠܕܒܢܐ ܒܠܘ ܗܘܘ ܘܠܕܢܝܢܐ ܠܐ ܢܟܒܫܘܢ
ܗܘܘ. ܘܠܐ ܢܦܩܝ ܗܘܘ ܕܡܒܢܐ ܢܐܡܪܘܢ ܒܪ ܐܢܫܬܐܠܘ.
ܓܡܝܪ ܕܢܒܝܐ ܘܐܫܟܚ ܡܠܠ ܒܪ ܡܬܠܝܢ. ܘܦܠܓܐ ܫ̈ܢܝܐ ܘܥܠ

ܒܥܠܕܒܒܘܬܐ. ܘܡܟܝܢܐ ܢܒܒܪ ܥܘܕܪܐ ܕܠܐ ܡܟܐ ܕܢܡܠܠ ܗܘܐ.
ܡܟܐ ܕܡܫܬܐܠ ܕܠܐ ܢܪܟܐ ܗܘܐ ܠܡܕܒܫܗ. ܡܫܠܐ ܫܠܡ
ܗܘܐ ܗܦܟܐ ܡܠܝ̈ܢ ܡܣܟܢܘܬܐ. ܘܡܢ ܐܘܠܨܢܐ ܠܐ ܗܦܩ
ܗܘܐ ܠܡܡܠܠܘ. ܘܡܫܬܐܠܝܢ ܗܘܘ ܘܐܡܪܝܢ ܬܗܘܐ ܕܐܢ ܫܠܐ
ܐܢܫ. ܡܟܐ ܕܡܫܬܐܠ ܐܦ ܫܠܡ ܗܘ ܠܕܡܬܐܡܪܝܢ. ܘܕܠܐ
ܢܗܘܘܢ ܗܦܟܐ ܗܢܘܢ ܕܫܠܡܝܢ ܐܢܘܢ. ܡܕܝܢ ܐܡܪܘܗ̇
ܠܡܠܬܐ ܕܐܠܝܨܐ ܕܬܬܡܠܠ ܗܘܬ. ܪܫܡܘܢ ܐܢܫܘ ܘܫܠܦ ܡܠܬܐ
ܒܐܡܪܐ ܫܘܡܘ. ܗܘ ܓܒܝܐ ܕܗܘ ܒܪ ܐܢܫܐ ܫܪܝܬܐ ܕܠܒܗ. ܬܠܘ
ܪ̈ܫܡܘܢ ܒܪ ܐܡܪܝܢ ܗܘܘ ܒܐܘܠܨܢܗܘܢ. ܕܠܐ ܡܕܒܫܝܢ
ܗܘܘ ܘܠܦ ܟܠ ܐܢܫ ܪ̈ܚܫܘܢ. ܒܪ ܐܢܬ ܗܘܐ ܒܗܘܢ
ܐܬܪܐ ܠܡܠܬܐ ܒܡܠܬܐ ܕܐܘܪܝܐ. ܘܒܪ ܐܫܬܐܠܬ ܡܢ ܐܘܠܨܢܐ
ܒܡܕܪܐ ܡܠܘ. ܠܡܫܡܥܘܬܐ ܡܠܘܗ̇ ܒܡܠܐ ܘܕܠܐ ܡܠܐ.
ܕܡܟܐ ܕܡܡܠܠܝܢ ܐܦ ܡܟܐ ܕܫܠܡ ܥܒܪܐ ܗܘܘ. ܡܢ ܠܐ ܢܬܗܪ
ܒܐܘܪܚܐ ܕܚܝܐ ܒܡܟܐ ܡܢܝܢܐ. ܘܡܟܐ ܐܠܝܨܐ ܠܐܢܫܐ
ܕܢܪܟܐ ܕܢܫܠܛ ܒܗ̇. ܦܢ ܠܐ ܢܬܡܟܘܢ ܕܠܝܩܝܢܐ ܕܒܪ
ܘܡܠܒܒ. ܦܬܚ ܪܘܫܐ ܘܡܠܟܐ ܢܗܘܪܐ ܠܕܪܕܐ ܒܗ̇. ܫܪܝܪܘܗ̇
ܕܐܘܪܚܐ ܦܫܝܬܐ ܡܠܟܐ ܐܦ ܗܘܬܐ. ܘܡܠܠ ܡܢܗ̇ ܐܢ
ܡܗܘܠܐ ܐܢܫ ܡܠܘ ܦܫܬܐ. ܪܡܕܐ ܗܘ ܒܠܫܘܕ ܒܢܬ ܡܢܝܢܐ
ܘܠܡܡܠܐ. ܘܒܐܡܝܢ ܘܡܠܐ ܡܢܝܢܐ ܫܠܝܛܬܐ ܘܪܕܝܘܬܐ.
ܒܪܡܕ ܒܠܫܘܕ ܪܡܕܘ ܠܦܬܢܐ ܕܠܐ ܡܕܒܫܝܢ ܗܘܘ. ܘܡܢ ܫܪ
ܪܡܕܐ ܢܠܬ ܐܢܘ ܐܘܪܚܐ ܠܒܪܝܢ. ܘܗܘ ܗܘ ܪܡܕܐ ܐܠܘ
ܐܪܒܡ ܘܢܦܠܐ ܡܠܝܠ. ܠܚ̈ܦ ܒܗܡܡܐ ܐܘܪܚܐ ܕܦ̈ܫܐ
ܠܚܡܢܐ ܗܘܬ. ܠܒܠ ܪܡܕܝܢ ܗܘܘ ܕܠܒܠ ܢܦܫܗܘܢ ܐܬܦܠܒܗ
ܗܘܘ. ܘܡܢܗܘܢ ܕܪܡܕܐ ܗܠܡܐ ܘܐܫܠܛܘ ܒܡ̈ܡܢܐ. ܒܢܬ ܪܡܕܐ
ܠܪܡܕܐ ܒܢܬܐ ܐܦ ܒܡܢܐ. ܪܡܕ ܕܠܐ ܡܕܒܫܝܢ ܘܗܘܘ
ܡ̈ܬܐ ܒܢܬ ܡܠܒܡܘܬܐ. ܘܒܪ ܫܬܡܥ ܗܘܐ ܠܗ ܗܢܐ ܒ̈ܢܐ ܠܒܪ
ܐܠܗܐ. ܕܠܘ ܡܢ ܗܘܒܐ ܕܒ̈ܠܐ ܡܢܝܢܐ ܡܣܟܢܘܬܐ. ܗܘ

ܕܟܘܪܬܐ ܢܣܒܘܗܝ. ܘܠܗܘ ܕܠܡܠ ܐܝܟ ܠܡܦܣܢܘܬܐ ܕܡܠܟܐ
ܫܦܝܪܐ. ܘܐܬܗܡܟܝܢ ܗܘܘ ܠܡܣܟܢܘ ܒܣܘܓܐ ܡܕܡ. ܠܐܬܪܐ
ܕܗܘܝܐ ܕܡܠܟܐ ܦܬܟܐ ܠܐܟܪܝܢ ܠܗ. ܦܩܕ ܕܢܬܠ ܕܐܬܠܐ ܐܢܘܢ
ܒܪܚܡܘܗܝ. ܘܕܠܐ ܙܒܢܐ ܡܬܠܣ ܗܘܘ ܐܢܘܢ ܡܢܐܪܬܐ.
ܫܢܬܐ ܕܗܘܐ ܢܩܫܬ ܙܒܢܐ ܒܛܘܒ ܕܢܐ. ܘܡܬܪܡܪܬܐ ܗܘܬ
ܥܠ ܫܢܝܐ ܕܢܦܫܘ ܐܢܘܢ. ܘܒܬܪ ܙܒܢܐ ܠܒܗܬܬܐ ܡܬܦܩ
ܗܘܐ ܕܢܬܠܘܢ ܐܢܘܢ. ܘܗܘܘ ܬܗܘܪܐ ܠܬܪܝܢ ܚܛܝܢ ܕܡܣܟܢܐ
ܗܒܪܘ. ܒܣܘܓܐ ܕܒܝܬܐ ܥܡܟܐ ܘܐܪܓܐ ܬܗܘܪܐ ܗܘܬ.
ܡܟܐ ܠܡ ܫܢܐ ܘܠܐ ܡܛܠ ܗܘܐ ܡܢ ܐܘܠܨܢܐ. ܘܬܠܝ
ܘܢܬܗܡ ܦܬܪܐ ܡܫܠܛܐ ܒܪܚܡܘܗܝ. ܘܐܒܕܐ ܥܠܝܐ ܘܠܝܬ
ܕܡܛܠ ܐܦ ܕܡܛܠ. ܬܗܘܢ ܗܘܘ ܥܠ ܫܘܩܐ ܒܐܟܣܢܝܘܗܝ.
ܕܒܫܘܩܐ ܡܬܚܙܝܐ ܒܟܐ ܗܒܪܘ ܗܘܘ ܥܠ ܐܘܠܨܢܝܢ. ܬܗܪ
ܗܘܐ ܒܗܘܢ ܐܦ ܗܠܝܢ ܒܟܦܢܐ ܢܦܫܐ. ܕܒܟܐ ܢܗܘܪܐ ܠܒܢܘ
ܒܐܘܠܨܢܐ ܕܠܐ ܪܘܚܡܐ. ܦܝܣܝܢ ܗܘܘ ܕܝܢ ܐܦ ܡܠܟܘܬܐ
ܒܗܘ ܫܘܡܠܝܐ. ܕܒܟܐ ܐܟܪ ܗܘ ܐܟܣܢܝܐ ܕܫܠܚܐ ܕܗܘܐ.
ܐܬܠܝܛܐ ܕܝܢ ܕܡܬܗܡܝܢ ܗܘܘ ܠܡܬܠܝܘܗܝ. ܠܐ ܚܠܦ ܗܘܬ
ܡܣܟܢܘܬܐ ܠܬܚܝܬܘܗܝ. ܠܕܢܚ ܟܢ ܡܣܟܢܬ ܗܘܬ ܠܗ
ܐܦ ܐܬܕܡܪ. ܘܠܬܡܝܗܐ ܠܐ ܡܣܟܢܬ ܗܘܬ ܒܐܘܠܨܢܝܗܘܢ.
ܢܫܠ ܐܢܘܢ ܕܐܦ ܝܬܒܝܢ ܗܘܘ ܠܡܣܟܢܘ. ܘܠܐ ܡܫܟܚ ܗܘܐ
ܦܘܡܐ ܢܫܠܠ ܡܢ ܐܘܠܨܢܐ. ܗܝܟ ܐܟܘܬܗ ܘܐܘܠܝܘ ܐܢܘܢ
ܕܪܦܫܘܢ. ܒܕܡܟܐ ܕܠܐ ܢܗܘܐ ܐܬܪܐ ܠܡܠܬܐ ܕܬܬܡܠܠ
ܗܘܬ. ܥܠܝܐ ܗܘܐ ܦܘܡܐ ܡܢ ܐܘܠܨܢܐ ܕܗܘܪܡܘܗܝ ܝܬܒܝܢ ܕܝܢ
ܐܝܟ ܚܛܝܐ ܒܟܠܗ ܢܦܫܗܘܢ. ܐܘ ܠܪܕܘܦܐ ܒܟܐ ܚܠܝܡ
ܗܘܘ ܡܢ ܒܐܘܬܐ. ܘܟܠ ܢܗܘܪܐ ܒܟܐ ܠܡܣܟܢܝܢ ܗܘܘ
ܡܣܟܢܘܬܐ. ܬܒܟܝܢ ܡܠܬܐ ܒܕ ܠܝܬ ܐܬܪܐ ܠܡܬܠܠܘ. ܕܫܠܛܐ
ܗܘܬ ܡܠܠ ܦܘܡܐ ܡܢ ܐܘܠܨܢܐ. ܕܪܡܐ ܗܘܐ ܦܬܪܐ ܘܫܬܦ
ܦܘܡܐ ܘܠܐ ܡܫܟܚ ܗܘܐ. ܕܢܛܠ ܡܠܬܐ ܒܕ ܡܫܬܐܠ

ܐܘܪܫܠܡ ܠܪܘܡܝܐ ܠܘܬ ܡܠܟܘ̈ܬܐ. ܒܡܢܐ ܕܐܘܠܨܢܐ ܦܓܥܐ
ܗܘܐ ܠܗ ܠܫܘܕܐ ܚܒܝܫܐ. ܥܠ ܬܘܕܝܬܐ ܡܢ ܗܦ̈ܩܬܗ
ܡܫܬܡܥܢܐ ܗܘܬ. ܗܘܝܘ ܠܗ ܗ̈ܘܕܐ ܠܗܘܟܐ ܠܛܝܒܐ
ܣܒܝܪܐܝܬ. ܘܒܚܝܠ ܗܘܐ ܠܗ ܐܝܟ ܕܠܫܡܥܬܐ ܕܡ̈ܠܟܐ
ܒܥܘܬܪܐ. ܒܡ̈ܕܐ ܣܓܝܐܐ ܒܓܒ ܒܗ ܒܩܛܠܗ ܒܪ ܐܠܗܐ.
ܕܡܘܬܐ ܕܫܠܝܐ ܢܗܘܐ ܪܘܚܐ ܡܢ ܦ̈ܓܥܐ. ܐܢܫܐ
ܕܪܗܛܝܢ ܠܗܘܒܠ ܗܦܟܐ ܠܗ ܐܫܬܡܥܬ. ܐܠܐ ܗܠܝܢ
ܕܐܬܠܝ ܫܘܒ ܒܙܩܝܦܘܬܗ. ܕܡܚܪ ܡܘܬܐ ܒܠ ܐܢܫ ܢܕܒ
ܗܐ ܡܢ ܒܠܡ. ܠܫܘܕܐ ܒܠܝܘܙ ܠܐ ܡܨܐ ܗܘܐ ܒܙ ܡܬܡܠܠܝܢ.
ܚܫܝܢ ܗܘܘ ܠܗ ܠܗܘܟܐ ܠܛܝܒܐ ܡܢܐ ܕܢܐܘܗܝ. ܘܦܪܝܫܝܢ
ܒܗ ܕܗܘ ܗܘܐ ܒܠܬܐ ܠܦܠܝܠܘܬܗ. ܐܝܟ ܕܠܗܘܢܐ ܫܒܝܩ
ܗܘܘ ܠܗ ܠܦܫܡܬܐ ܢܒܠܒ. ܘܟܕ ܪܫܝܡ ܠܗ ܠܐ ܗܫܒܘܗܝ
ܗܘܘ ܡܢ ܐܘܠܨܢܐ. ܠܗܘܟܐ ܗܟܝܠ ܘܢܦܩ ܗܦܟܐ ܘܥܠܠ
ܐܝܟ. ܕܠܗ ܣܓܝܡ ܗܘܘ ܘܐܬܦܬܚ ܠܗܘܢ ܐܝܟ ܕܒܟܐܘܗܝ.
ܒܪ ܐܠܗܐ ܩܛܠܗ ܠܡܘܬܐ ܒܙܩܝܦܘܬܗ. ܘܥܠ ܕܩܛܠ ܗܘ
ܡܘܬܐ ܠܫܘܕܐ ܠܐ ܡܨܐ ܗܘܐ. ܒܫܘܠܐ ܕܦܢܝܢ ܡܫܬܡܥܢܐ
ܗܘ ܐܢܫ ܒܙ ܠܐ ܕܢܠ. ܠܐܪܥܐ ܕܩܛܠ ܚܒܪܗ ܗܘ ܠܗ ܐܦ
ܫܠܝܐ. ܠܫܘܠܐ ܙܟܐ ܡܪܢ ܗܟܢ ܒܙܩܝܦܘܬܗ. ܠܐܪܥܐ ܕܫܠܝܐ
ܒܪ ܐܠܗܐ ܒܫܝܢ ܩܛܠܗ. ܠܡܘܬܐ ܗܟܝܠ ܘܪܫܡܗ ܘܒܙܗ
ܒܬܪܟܐ ܕܫܘܠ. ܘܥܠ ܗܢ ܕܟܒܐ ܦܬܟ ܐܝܟ ܒܗ ܒܠ ܕܩܛܠ
ܗܘ. ܫܡܘܫܐ ܩܕܘܪܐ ܐܢܫܐ ܗ̈ܘܟܐ ܒܡܘܬܐ ܐܝܟ.
ܒܐܡܬ ܒܐܪܥܐ ܗܘ ܕܩܛܠ ܗܘܐ ܠܒܪ ܐܠܗܐ. ܠܙܪܥܐ ܙܟܐ
ܕܩܛܠܗ ܠܐܕܡ ܒܝܬ ܫ̈ܠܝܐ. ܡܢ ܠܥܠ ܗܘܐ ܒܙ ܠܐ ܫܘܬܐ
ܗܘܐ ܕܡܛܠ ܕܢܦܩܐ. ܒܪ ܐܠܗܐ ܙܟܐ ܬܫܢܐ ܒܙܩܝܦܘܬܗ.
ܗܘܐ ܡܫܠܡ ܒܗ ܩܠܝܐ ܘܗܘ̈ܟܐ ܒܫܘܠܐ ܕܦܢܝܢ. ܕܓܢ
ܗܘ ܐܪܥܐ ܒܪܘܡܝܐ ܕܕܫܘܗ ܕܒܪ ܐܠܗܐ. ܘܥܠ ܡܢ ܕܟܒܐ
ܕܫܘ ܘܩܛܠܗ ܐܦ ܐܝܟ ܒܗ. ܒܪ ܐܠܗܐ ܗܘܝܘ ܒܠܬܐ ܕܒܠ

ܫܘܡܠܝܗܘܢ ܬܘܕܝܬܐ ܗܘܬ ܕܡܠܝܐ ܡܠܬܐ. ܘܐܝܟ ܕܒܦܘܡܐ ܦܬܝܚܐ ܐܡܪܘܗ̇ ܠܡܫܝܚܘܬܐ. ܘܥܒܕ ܟܠ ܐܢܫ ܡܟܝܟܐ ܡܡܠܠܝܢ ܒܗ ܫܬܐܣܝܢ. ܘܒܬܪܗ̇ ܡܪܒܬ ܡܫܝܚܘܬܐ ܕܟܠܗ ܐܠܗܐ. ܘܒܗܬܬ ܠܗܘܢ ܕܟܬܝܒܝܢ ܗܘܝܢ ܕܒܗ ܠܐ ܡܠܠܘ. ܕܟܐܘܗ̇ ܘܫܬܐܣܘ ܘܡܫܬ ܕܠܗܘܢ ܡܫܝܚܘܬܐ. ܘܟܕ ܡܫܬܡܥܝܢ ܩܠܐ ܫܦܝܪ̈ܐ ܡܢ ܕܢܚܐ. ܘܟܕ ܦܘܪܩܢܐ ܕܡܠܟܐ ܕܫܠܝܡ ܐܦ ܒܝܘܡܝܢ. ܘܟܕ ܫܦܘܬܐ ܟܠܝܢ ܬܪ̈ܝܢ ܘܦܬܝܚ ܦܘܡܗ̇. ܘܐܡܪܐ ܡܠܬܗ̇ ܘܫܠܡ ܩܠܐ ܡܢ ܐܘܠܝܢܐ. ܒܛܠ ܦܘܪܩܢܐ ܘܐܫܬܡܗ، ܗܘܐ ܡܢ ܕܢܚܐ. ܘܕܠܐ ܡܠܬܐ ܪܘܚܐ ܕܗܘܪܐ ܫܒܠ ܢܝܚܐ. ܡܡܠܠܐ ܘܪܘܚܐ ܘܡܠܐ ܕܢܓܕܐ ܡܢ ܗܘܟܐ. ܘܫܠܝܐ ܪܘܚܐ ܘܫܟܐ ܕܟܐܡ ܡܢ ܡܚܢܐ. ܘܟܕ ܪܘܚܐ ܕܠܐ ܡܬܠܐ ܩ̈ܠܐ ܠܟܠ ܕ̈ܒܫܘܢ. ܐܬܬܪܝܡ ܕܒܪܗ̇ ܕܡܫܝܚܘܬܐ ܘܟܗܬܬ ܠܗܘܢ. ܫܟܐ ܕܡܡܠܠܝܢ ܘܠܫܬܘܩܐ ܗܘܐ ܢܝܚܐ. ܕܕܠܐ ܡܠܐ ܘܡܪܬܗ، ܡܐܡܪܐ ܕܡܫܝܚܘܬܐ. ܘܐܝܟܘ ܐܢܘܢ ܡܛܠ ܕܒܗ ܒܗ ܫܬܐܣܝܢ. ܘܫܡܥܘ ܐܢܘܢ ܒܗ ܠܒܘܫܝܢ ܗܘܘ ܢܒܘܢ ܐܢܘܢ. ܫܡܘܢܐ ܠܓܘܪܝܐ ܘܓܘܒܐ ܕܟܠܝܢ ܡܢ ܢܘܪܐ. ܠܐ ܫܒܩܘ ܗܘܐ ܠܗܘܢ ܐܠܐ ܢܘܪܐ ܕܠܐ ܡܫܬܡܥܝܢ. ܘܕܠܐ ܠܫܡܥܐ ܘܕܠܐ ܩ̈ܠܐ ܘܕܠܐ ܢܘܪܐ. ܗܢ ܗܘܐ ܠܗܘܢ ܡܛܠ ܫܡܥܗ ܕܒܪ ܐܠܗܐ. ܦܘܩ ܕܢܚܐ ܕܒܬ̈ܚܠܝܗܘܢ ܢܬܠܘܢ ܐܢܘܢ. ܒܬܪ ܕܫܡܥܘ ܒܥܒܕܐ ܕܪܫܡ ܡܢ ܒܐܢܘܬܐ. ܬܠܝܐ ܗܘܐ ܫܡܘܢܐ ܒܬܪ ܪܥܘܗ̇ ܘܡܬܠܐ ܗܘܐ. ܢܨܚܘܬܐ ܕܫܡܥܐ ܘܡܬܠܠܐ ܡܢ ܐܘܠܝܢܐ. ܦܐܪܐ ܫܦܝܪܐ ܬܠܐ ܗܘܐ ܒܫܘܫܐ ܒܗܘ ܒܬ ܕܝܢܐ. ܘܠܓܘܪܝܐ ܪܕܝܗ ܐܬܒܪܗ̇ ܐܢܘܢ ܠܓܘܪ̈ܝܐ. ܐܠܝܨ ܗܘܐ ܦܓܪܗ ܘܫܠܝܚܐ ܗܘܬ ܡܫܝܚܘܬܗ. ܥܒܪ ܗܘܐ ܠܓܘܫܡܗ ܘܥܒܪܐ ܨܠܘܬܗ ܒܠ ܘܥܕܡܐ. ܨܠܘܬܐ ܓܒܪ ܠܐ ܡܟܪܙ ܠܗ ܐܦ ܠܐ ܡܕܡ. ܘܠܐ ܡܟܘܪ ܠܗ ܐܦ ܠܐ ܫܡܥܐ ܐܦ ܠܐ ܢܘܪܐ. ܓܘܫܡܐ ܗܦܟܝܢ ܗܘܐ ܗܘܝܢ ܨܠܘܬܐ ܕܡܫܝܚܐ ܗܘܬ. ܘܐܬܪܚܝܩ ܗܘܬ

ܣܠܩ ܒܫܝܢܘܬܐ. ܠܐ ܕܝܢ ܗܘܘ ܠܡܪ̈ܝ ܒܥܠܬܐ ܬܪܝܢ ܕ̈ܝܠܗ. ܐܦ ܠܐ ܐܘܪܚܗ ܕܡܫܝܚܐ ܠܝܘܚܢܢ ܕܐܦ ܗܘ ܙܒܢܬ. ܗܘ ܐܒܘܬܗ ܗܪܟܢ ܗܟܢܐ ܐܦ ܡܪܘܬܢ. ܘܐܫܬܡܥ ܒܐܬܪܐ ܕܡܟܐ ܘܡܢܐ ܒܥܠܬܗ. ܒܫܠܡ ܗܘܐ ܕܗܘܬܐ ܘܡܫܬܐ ܗܘܐ ܡܬܡܠܠ. ܒܪܝܟ ܗܘ ܕܝܗܒ ܠܝ ܫܘܡܠܝܐ ܕܟܠܝܠܘܗܝ.

ܫܠܡ ܡܐܡܪܐ ܕܥܠ ܫܘܪܝܐ ܘܫܘܠܡܐ.

ܗܘܟܝܬ ܕܡܪܝ ܡܪܩܘܣ ܡܠܦܢܐ : ܥܠ ܐܘܪܚܗ

ܟܕ ܥܢܕ ܠܡܪܝ ܕܐܬܐ ܠܗ.

ܐܘܪܚܗ ܥܢܝܕ ܠܡܫܝܚܐ ܒܐܓܪܬܐ ܕܐܬܬ ܠܗ ܘܚܙܘܪܗ. ܣܠܩ ܠܩܘܡ ܒܬܫܡܫܬܐ ܩܘܫܬܐ ܒܥܕܬ ܠܗ ܕܢܦܩܐ ܠܝܘܚܢܢ ܕܗܘܬ ܘܐܬܬܐ ܠܗ ܠܘܬ ܒܬܫܡܫܬܐ ܕܐܘܚܕܗ ܀ ܫܕܪܬ ܠܐܒܘܗ ܘܡܢܬܗ ܕܢܬܟܠܠ ܒܡܥܒܕ ܒܪܗܡܬܐ. ܒܕ ܡܠܟܐ ܒܐܝܢܐ ܩܘܫܬܐ ܒܥܕܬ ܠܗ. ܕܢܦܩܐ ܠܗ ܡܢ ܒܥܕܐ ܘܝܕ ܒܬܫܡܫܬܐ ܢܬܪܝܢ ܗܘܐ ܡܬܥܠܘ ܀ ܡܢ ܟܠ ܡܠܟܝܢ ܫܕ ܡܠܟܐ ܫܡܫܐ ܒܪܬ ܒܬܫܡܫܬܐ ܐܫܬܡܥܬ. ܐܫܟܚܐ ܒܥܕܬܗ ܠܡܪܝܗ ܥܢܝܕ ܒܗ. ܬܐ ܠܟ ܢܐܕ، ܐܠܦܐ ܒܟ ܠܬܪܬܝܢ ܘܠܡܠܟܘܬܐ ܠܥܠܡ ܀ ܫܒܩܬ ܠܟܘܢ ܡܢ ܪܘܡܐ ܘܚܬܐ ܕܒܫܡܝܐ ܡܢܗ. ܠܚܝܘܬܐ ܒܪܘܚܢܝܐ ܫܒܝܪܬܐ ܡܠܟܐ. ܪܘܚܗ ܐܪܗܘ ܒܕ ܪܘܚ ܘܫܠܛܗ ܕܠܟܘܢܘܢ ܢܠܗ ܀ ܢܫܟܢ ܫܬܝܐ ܐܪܝܟܐ ܐܝܢܐ ܒܢܫܡܬܐ ܕܦܡܗ ܡܕܪܫܐ. ܫܡܥܬܗ ܡܢ ܪܘܡܐ ܐܝܟܘܗܝ، ܡܢ ܡܘܪܒܐ. ܘܐܗܘܡ ܦܩܘܕ، ܒܠ ܕܠܗ ܘܐܬܒܗܡ ܒܝܬܗ ܒܡܠܟ ܀ ܬܕܥܝܢ ܠܟܝܢ ܠܐ ܡܢ ܚܡܪܐ ܕܪܚܡ ܒܗܘܡܝܢ ܫܢܐ ܗܘ ܠܟܠܡܐ. ܒܫܠܡܝܢ ܐܬܪܟܐ ܒܪܚܡܝܢ ܐܬܟܢܫܡ. ܡܢ ܬܝܒܐ ܕܬܪܬܝܢ ܕܒܪܚܡܗ ܘܗܘܒܐ ܐܘܪܚܗ ܀ ܒܚܡܢ ܒܬܪܝܢ ܠܚܪܬܝܢ ܕܥܡܐ

ܦܬܓܡܐ. ܘܠܐ ܢܣܒܢ ܠܗܘܢ ܦܘ̈ܡܐ ܠܡܫܬܥܝܘ. ܗܘ ܡܕܝܢ ܚܠܦܐ ܕܒܡܕܒܪܐ ܕܕܝܪܐ ܡܢ ܡܫܝܚܘܬܗ. ܘܠܫ̈ܟܝܢܘܗܝ ܐܝܟ ܙܘܡܢܝܐ ܕܡܠܟܐ ܕܦܘܪܫܢܘܗܝ. ܡܢܐ ܫܘܠܠܐ ܗܠܝܢ ܒܪܫܟܐ ܒܐܟܣܢܝܘܬܐ. ܘܥܠ ܡܢ ܕܐܬܐ ܕܢܘܗܪܐ ܫܒܝܚܐ ܕܒܗ ܐܡܪ ܠܗ. ܫܡܥܘܢܐ ܦܘܪܫܐ ܡܢܗ ܦܓܪ̈ܝܗܘܢ ܡܬܠܬܗ. ܠܚ̈ܫܐ ܘܫ̈ܢܩܐ ܘܠܬ̈ܘܕܝܬܐ ܕܥܠ ܐܘ̈ܠܨܢ. ܟܕ ܚܙܝܢ ܗܘܘ ܒܗ ܡܬܟܪܝܢ ܡܢ ܟܐ̈ܒܐ. ܘܥܠ ܗܿܝ ܗܕܪܐ ܗܠܝܢ ܒܝܫܐ ܕܠܐ ܪܘܚܡܐ. ܒܬܪܬ ܐܘܪܗܝ ܡܢ ܦ̈ܠܓܘܬܗܘܢ ܐܘ ܦܘ̈ܪܫܢܐ. ܕܐܬܬܘܬܗ ܒܦܠܓܘ̈ܬܗܘܢ ܘܟܢܫܝܗܘܢ. ܫܘܦܪܗ ܐܬܘܢ ܫܘܦܪܗ ܐܬܘܢ ܡܠܟܗ ܐܬܘܢ. ܒܬܪܗ ܗܘ ܡܬܠܬܗ ܐܦ ܫܘܒܚܗ ܘܫܘܠܛܢܗ ܒܗ. ܐܬܘܢ ܐܝܟ ܕܝܢ ܟܠܗܐ ܕܡܫܝܚܘܬܐ. ܕܟ̈ܢܫܝܗܘܢ ܐܠܗܘܬܗ ܠܟܠܗܐ ܫܘܦܪܐ. ܒܪܬ ܦܘܬܚܐ ܕܐܬܡܟܪܬ ܗܘܬ ܠܡܫܝܚܐ. ܟܕ ܗܘ ܫܪܪܐ ܕܫܘܠܛܢܗ ܗܘܐ ܢܗܝܪܐ. ܗܐ ܓܒܪܝܗ ܐܬܘܢ ܫܘܦܪܐ ܕܪܥܐ ܒܗ ܫܡܥܘܢ. ܠܟܠܗ ܦܓܪܗ ܒܗ ܙܡ ܡܠܗ ܒܫܘܪܝܬܐ. ܗܠܝܢ ܗܘ̈ܝܐ ܕܒܪܬ ܒܒܪܝܬܐ ܟܕ ܒܥܠܬܐ ܗܘܘ. ܗܘ̈ܝܐ ܕܫܘܦܪܐ ܕܡܠܠܐ ܠܢܦܫܗ ܒܗ ܡܫܬܐܠ. ܕܬܪܬ ܐܘܪܗܝ، ܒܬܪܝܢ ܗܘ̈ܝܗ ܟܠܗ ܫܘܦܪܐ. ܕܗܘܘ ܗܘ̈ܝܐ ܠܒܪ ܐܠܗܐ ܘܡܫܝܚܐ ܐܝܟ ܢܦܫܗ. ܬܪ̈ܝܢ ܗܘܘ ܬܡܢ ܘܬܪ̈ܝܢ ܗܘܪܐ ܐܢܫܐ ܗܘ̈ܝܐ. ܘܗܠܝܢ ܗܘ̈ܝܐ ܘܗܠܝܢ ܗܘ̈ܝܐ ܡܬܐܡܪܝܢ ܗܘܘ. ܢܫܐ ܗܘܫܐ ܐܝܠܝܢ ܗܘ̈ܝܐ ܟܕܝܢ ܠܐܠܗܐ. ܘܐܢܫܐ ܡܫܝܚܐ ܙܘܓܐ ܒܗܘ̈ܝܗ ܘܒܢܦ̈ܫܬܗ. ܗܐ ܟܕ ܒܗܠܝܢ ܕܡܠܠ ܠܢܦܫܗ ܗܘ̈ܝܐ ܐܝܟ. ܘܗܪܟܐ ܫܡܥܘܢܐ ܦܘܪܫܐ ܗܘ̈ܝܐ ܬܘܒ ܐܬܘܢܗܘܢ. ܢܫܐ ܗܘܫܐ ܐܝܠܝܢ ܗܘ̈ܝܐ ܘܐܝܠܝܢ ܗܘ̈ܝܐ. ܘܐܢܫܐ ܡܫܝܚܐ ܟܠܝܢ ܬܫܘܢ ܡܫܢ ܐܠܗܐ. ܟܕ ܒܥܠܬܐ ܗܘܘ ܗܠܝܢ ܗܘ̈ܝܐ ܕܗܢ ܙܢܘܬܐ. ܘܗܐ ܒܗܘܬܗܘܢ ܦܪܝܫܐ ܠܗ ܒܟܫܡܫܘܢ. ܗܟܢܫ ܗܘ̈ܝܫ ܕܐܘܪܗܝ، ܒܬܪ̈ܝܢ ܐܦ ܕܕܝܢ. ܠܢܦܫܗ ܕܟܝܢ ܕܡܠܠ ܐܦ ܗܘ

ܦܓܪܐ ܠܒܫ ܗܘܐ ܟܕ ܕܗܘܐ ܒܕܡܘܬܗ ܕܦܓܪܐ. ܗܘ ܟܕ ܓܒܝܠܐ ܕܐܝܕܘܗܝ ܠܒܫܗ ܕܡܢ ܒܬܘܠܬܐ. ܗܘ ܗܘܐ ܬܫܒܘܚܬܗ ܠܫܡܝܐ ܕܢܚܬܬܗ ܀ ܘܡܢ ܒܬܪ ܟܠܠ. ܀ ܐܦ ܟܕ ܚܙܝܬܘܢ ܕܫ̈ܠܝܚܐ ܗܘܬ. ܐܠܐ ܚܙܘ ܘܐܬܒܩܝܘ ܘܫܘܠܛܢܗ ܕܐܠܗܘܬܐ ܗܘܐ.

ܒ. ܡܢ ܡܠܦܢܘܬܐ ܕܐܕܝ ܫܠܝܚܐ. ܕܐܬܐܡܪܬ ܒܐܘܪܗܝ ܡܕܝܢܬܐ ܀

ܡܕܝܢ ܐܚܝ̈ܢ ܕܐܬܚܙܝܬ ܠܟܘܢ. ܕܠܘܬܗܘܢ ܢܦ̈ܫܬܐ ܕܢܦܩ ܡܢ ܦ̈ܓܪܐ ܕܒܢܝ̈ܢܫܐ. ܬܗܘܐ ܡܢܬܟܘܢ ܠܐ ܬܗ̈ܘܝܢ. ܐܠܐ ܚܝܝܢ ܘܩܝܡܝܢ. ܘܐܝܬ ܠܗܘܢ ܐܘ̈ܣܝܐ ܘܡܢܬ ܡܟܝܪܐ ܕܢܦܫܐ. ܠܐ ܟܕ ܦܠܠܐ ܡܫܡܫܬܐ ܕܢܦܫܗ ܘܠܐ ܡܕܡܐ. ܡܛܠ ܕܝܠܗܐ ܐܝܬܝܗ ܕܐܠܗܐ ܠܐ ܡܝܘܬܐ. ܠܐܝܟ ܟܕ ܕܠܐ ܥ̈ܒܕܐ ܒܡܡܘܬܐ ܕܦܓܪܐ: ܗܘ ܕܠܝܬ ܠܗ ܡܫܪܝܘܬܐ ܕܢܦܠܘܢ ܗܘ ܕܐܬܩܠܝ ܒܗܘܢ. ܘܦܪܫܐ ܕܝܢ ܘܐܦܪܫܐ ܠܐ ܡܦܠܠܐ ܒܠܒܐ ܡܢ ܦܓܪܐ: ܡܛܠ ܕܢܦܫܐ ܠܘ ܕܠܝܗ ܗܘ ܒܠܘܚܘܗܝ. ܐܠܐ ܘܦܓܪܐ ܗܘ ܕܡܬܪܬ ܒܗ ܒܢܦܫ. ܠܐ ܡܬܦܫܛܐ ܕܝܢ ܕܠܐܠܗܐ ܠܐ ܡܕܥܐ: ܕܠܐ ܡܘܬܪ ܗܘܕܝܢ ܡܬܬܘܝܢ ܀

ܓ. ܡܢ ܐܓܪܬܐ ܕܐܕܝ ܫܠܝܚܐ ܕܥܠܠ ܒܐܘܪܗܝ ܡܕܝܢܬܐ.

ܐܘܕܝܘ ܒܡܫܡܫܬܐ ܗܕܐ ܕܐܫܠܡܢ ܐܚܝ̈ܢ. ܘܒܝܕܥܬܐ ܘܒܐܪܬܬܐ ܗܘܝܬܘܢ ܦܫܝܢ ܒܗ. ܘܡܫܡܫܝܢ ܒܠܘܩܝ. ܠܐ ܗܘܝܬܘܢ ܡܫܡܫܝܢ ܐܚܝ̈ܢ ܒܗ ܦܬܓܡܐ ܩܠܝܠܐ. ܐܠܐ ܒܦܘܪܫܢܐ ܕܗܝܡܢܘܬܐ. ܘܬܫܡܫܘܢ ܕܡܫܝܚܐ ܡܢ ܦܘܩܕ̈ܢܘܗܝ ܠܐ ܬܦܠܠ. ܘܒܐܝܡܢܘܬܐ ܒܚܕܝܐ ܕܪܘܚܬܐ ܠܬܫܡܫܘܢ ܠܐ ܬܬܘܪܒ. ܐܘܕܝܘ ܡܢܗܪܐ ܗܘ ܕܐܫܠܡܢ ܐܚܝ̈ܢ: ܘܒܫܘܠܡܐ

ܐܝܟ ܠܒܘܫܬܐ ܒܥܠܡܐ. ܒܬܪ ܕܦܠܓܬ ܐܢܐ ܐܝܟ ܘܡܘܬܟ
ܒܒܢܐ ܐܢܐ. ܕܡܬܠܠ ܒܗ ܡܫܝܚܐ ܗܘ ܕܡܛܐ ܠܐܒܘܗܝ
ܕܐܬܬܒܝܗ ܀ ܫܒܩܐ ܘܫܪܝ ܒܪܬܐܠ ܒܡ ܒܢܝܐ ܕܟܠܗܝܢ
ܠܗܘܢ. ܒܢ ܪܢܐ ܠܒܐ ܕܠܒܪܬܐ ܒܒܝܬܐ. ܒܠ ܓܠܝܬܟ
ܠܫܒܘܗܝ ܕܡܫܝܚܐ ܗܘ ܕܡܛܐ ܠܐܒܘܗܝ ܀ ܠܒܗ ܗܘ ܫܡܥܟ ܡܢ
ܫܒܪܐ ܘܡܢ ܬܐܦܐ ܕܐܬܪܝܐ ܪܫܡܬܟ. ܒܫܒܪܐ ܠܐܕܪܟ
ܕܒܥܠܐ ܕܕܡܟ. ܫܒܝܐ ܫܬܐܐ ܐܢܫܘܬ ܘܐܬܪܝܐ ܥܒܫܘ
ܠܪܫܡܬܟ ܀ ܒܕܬܐ ܐܢܐ ܕܡܢ ܒܢܝܢܐ ܘܪܫܡܬܗ ܠܐܢܫܘܬܐ
ܕܐܬܒܠܝ. ܕܡܫܘܪܬܗ ܦܠܛܗ ܐܢܐ ܫܒܚܬܗ. ܘܒܐܢܫܝ ܐܒܓܪ
ܐܘܡܢܐ ܡܫܘܚܐ ܐܢܐ ܕܢܝܚܬܐ ܠܝ ܘܫܒܪܢ ܀ ܐܘܡܢܐ
ܐܝܟ ܘܡܢܐ ܐܢܐ ܒܥܬ ܢܦܫܝ ܕܒܢܝܐ ܗܘ ܢܛܘܡܢܝ.
ܕܡܒܪܢ ܒܪ ܒܐܢܐ ܕܒܠܝܢ ܠܒܢܘܗܝ. ܘܒܕ ܦܢܝܐ ܐܢܐ ܪܫܡ
ܠܝ ܕܡܥܒܕ ܗܘ ܕܡܢ ܬܒܐ ܢܥܒܪܢ ܀ ܐܘܡܢܘܬܐ ܐܢܐ ܒܫܠܡܘܬܐ
ܘܡܢܐ ܐܢܐ ܕܐܬܒܢܬ ܘܐܬܦܢܝܬ. ܥܠܝܬܗ ܒܒܢܝܐ ܠܗܘ ܠܒܢܝܐ
ܦܢܝܐ. ܕܡܪܝܡ ܒܪܘܚܗ ܘܒܢܐ ܦܪܘܩܐ ܕܒܪܝܬܐ ܥܠܡܝܢ ܀
ܫܠܡ ܦܘܫܩܐ ܡܢ ܦܘܠܚܢܐ ܕܥܠ ܐܘܪܗܝ.

ܦܘܫܩܐ ܕܡܢ ܟܬܒܐ ܡܫܝܚܝܐ
ܕܥܠ ܐܒܓܪ ܡܠܟܐ ܘܐܕܝ ܫܠܝܚܐ.

ܐ. ܕܬܫܥܝܬܐ ܐܕܝ ܫܠܝܚܐ. ܡܢ ܡܠܦܢܘܬܐ ܕܥܒܕ ܒܐܘܪܗܝ
ܥܡ ܐܒܓܪ ܡܠܟܐ ܘܒܢܝܐ ܕܡܕܝܢܬܐ.

ܘܟܕ ܥܠ ܠܡܕܝܢܬܐ. ܐܬܚܙܝ ܗܘܐ ܘܫܡܗ ܡܢ ܡܕܝܢܬܐ ܟܡ
ܩܕܡܝܐ ܘܐܡܠܟ ܕܢܣܩܘܢ ܗܘܘ ܠܡܕܝܢܬܐ. ܠܐ ܫܘܐ ܐܡܝܢܐ ܢܦܩ
ܗܘܐ ܡܢ ܡܕܝܢܬܐ. ܘܫܠܝܐ ܕܐܘܪܚܐ. ܫܩܠ ܗܘܐ ܒܐܘܪܚܐ
ܘܡܣܬܒܪܢܐ. ܕܡܫܬܡܥ ܕܐܝܠܝܢ ܠܐ ܝܕܥ ܠܐ ܡܫܬܟܚ ܗܘܐ. ܡܛܠ
ܕܡܪܗ ܗܘ ܕܫܘܬܐ ܡܫܡܫܐ. ܘܐܝܠܝܢ ܠܐ ܕܥܒܪ ܠܗ: ܐܦ ܠܐ

ܘܒ̈ܬܠܗܘܢ. ܘܫܠܡ ܢܫܬܐ ܕܓܘܫܐ ܕܠܚܒ ܗܘܐ: ܘܦܪܫܘ
ܐܢܘܢ ܡܛܠ ܕܕܚܠܘ ܗܘܘ. ܕܕܠܡܐ ܠܡ ܐܢܫ ܡܢ ܡ̈ܠܟܐ ܐܘ
ܡܢ ܪ̈ܒܢܐ ܢܐܬܘܢ ܘܢܫܩܠܘܢ ܡܛܠ ܦܓܪܗ ܕܡܫܝܚܐ. ܘܟܠܗ
ܝܠܘܕܝܗ ܘܐܡܪܘ ܠܚܫܘܟܐ. ܕܐܬܘܬܐ ܡܕܝܢ ܒܐܘܪܗܝ ܘܒܢܝ̈ܦܐ
ܘܡܕܝ̈ܢܬܐ ܐܚܪ̈ܢ. ܘܗܘܬ ܫܡܥܐ ܒܐܬܪ̈ܘܬܐ ܡܛܠ ܡܕܡ،
ܡܕܝܢ. ܘܐܬܘܗ ܚܫܘܟܐ ܝܘܡ ܕܢܚܐ ܘܐܬܩܪܝ ܠܗ. ܡܢܘ ܚܕ
ܦܘܪܫܢ ܠܡܕܝܢ ܕܠܐ ܬܬܐܠ ܬܪܝܠܐ ܝܘܡ ܡܕܝܢܐ ܘܡܓܙܠܘܬܐ.
ܘܟܕ ܦܘܠܚܢ ܡܬܦܫܟܝܢ. ܗܐ ܐܓܪܬܐ ܐܬܬ، ܡܢ ܐܒܓܪ
ܡ̈ܠܟܐ ܕܐܘܪܗܝ، ܡܛܘܒܬܐ ܠܥܡܡܐ ܐܣܦܢܝܐ ܕܡܪܕܘ ܗܘܘ
ܠܛܝܒܪܝܘܣ ܡ̈ܠܟܐ ܘܒܪܘܡܐ ܠܩܪܬ ܢܪܣܐ. ܐܝܬ ܗܘܐ ܠܗ ܥܡ ܠܛܝܢܐ
ܠܥܡܡܐ ܐܣܦܢܝܐ. ܘܡܛܠ ܕܢܦܩ ܗܘܐ ܐܕܝ ܫܠܝܚܐ. ܚܕ
ܡܢ ܫܒܥܝܢ ܘܬܪ̈ܝܢ ܫ̈ܠܝܚܝܢ ܘܚܕܐ ܒܒܝܬܐ ܒܐܘܪܗܝ. ܘܐܦ
ܒܐܝܕܐ ܕܐܬܐ ܗܘܐ ܠܗ ܠܐܒܓܪ ܡܠܟܐ. ܘܟܬܒ ܗܘܐ ܠܗ
ܒܪ ܐܒܓܪ ܡܠܟܐ ܠܝܫܘܥ ܡܫܝܚܐ. ܘܡܫܬܐܠ ܗܘܐ ܒܟܠ
ܝܘܡ ܡܫܠܡܢܘܬܗ. ܘܟܕ ܡܝܬ ܡܫܝܚܐ ܘܩܒܠ ܐܒܓܪ ܡܠܟܐ
ܕܒܘܫܟܐ ܡܛܠܘܗܝ، ܘܡܫܡܫܢܘܬܗ. ܒܪܬܗ ܠܗ ܦܠܓ. ܘܩܡ ܐܒܓܪ
ܘܫܡܥ ܘܐܬܐ ܒܝܘܡܐ ܠܩܪܬ ܢܪܣܐ. ܕܟܬܒܐ ܗܘܐ ܕܢܦܩ
ܥܠ ܐܪܥܐ ܘܒܝܬܐܘܗ. ܘܟܕ ܐܬܐ ܐܒܓܪ ܘܫܠܡܐ ܢܪܣܐ
ܦܪܩ ܐܬܘܬܝܢ ܗܘܐ ܒܐܝܕܘܗ ܕܗܝ ܒܬܪ ܐܬܝܐ ܗܘܐ ܠܗ
ܒܠܒܒܘܬܐ ܒܬ ܠ ܠܛܝܒܪܝܘܣ ܡܠܟܐ. ܘܟܬܒ ܐܒܓܪ ܐܓܪܬܐ
ܘܫܕܪ ܠܗ ܠܥܡܡܐ ܐܣܦܢܝܐ ܘܗܘܢܝܐ ܒܬܪ ܐܝܟ ܠܛܝܒܪܝܘܣ
ܡܠܟܐ. ܗܘܝܐ ܒܬܪ ܟܬܒ ܗܘܐ ܠܗ ܐܒܓܪ ܠܛܝܒܪܝܘܣ
ܡܠܟܐ. ܡܢ ܐܒܓܪ ܡܠܟܐ ܕܐܘܪܗܝ، ܡܒܝܬܐ. ܫܠܡܐ ܡܪܢܐ
ܠܡܠܟܘܬܟ ܡܪܢ ܛܝܒܪܝܘܣ. ܡܛܠ ܕܠܐ ܬܬܦܫܩ ܡܠܟܘܬܟ
ܝܕܥܐ ܠܟ ܚܙܝܬ ܢܪܣܐ ܦܪܬ. ܕܚܟܐ ܗܘܝܬ ܕܐܬܝܗ ܥܠ
ܐܘܪܫܠܡ ܘܐܬܢܨܚܬ ܥܠ ܕܡܛܠܬ ܠܡܫܝܚܐ ܐܝܟܐ ܢܫܡܥܐ.
ܐܠܐ ܐܢܬ ܐܝܟ ܡܠܟܐ ܪܒܐ ܕܫܠܝܛ ܐܢܬ ܥܠ ܟܠܗ ܐܪܥܐ

ܕܡܫܬܐ ܕܦܘܩܕܢܘܗܝ. ܘܡܠܟܘܬܐ ܕܫܡܝܐ ܕܡܦܩܕ ܐܢܐ ܠܟܘܢ.
ܡܛܠ ܕܗܘܝܬ ܒܐܘܪܚܐ ܕܡܫܝܚܐ ܡܬܬܠܡܕܝܢ ܐܢܬܘܢ ܠܗ. ܡܢܐ
ܕܒܥܐ ܕܢܫܬܘܙܒ ܡܢ ܕܝܢܬܐ ܘܫܠܡܐ. ܘܡܢܐ ܕܢܦܩ ܒܗܘܢ
ܡܢ ܬܟܬܝܐ ܒܝܫܬܐ ܕܫܠܝܚܐ. ܒܪ ܡܠܟܐ ܗܘ ܓܝܪ ܘܐܙܠ
ܕܢܣܒ ܡܠܟܘܬܐ ܘܢܗܦܘܟ ܘܢܐܬܐ. ܘܥܒܕ ܢܘܗܪܐ ܠܟܠܗܘܢ
ܒ̈ܢܝܢܫܐ.

ܕ. ܐܢܐ ܐܡܪ ܒܐܘܪܗܝ، ܘܒܗ ܢܗܘܪܬܐ. ܐܝܬܘܗܝ، ܗܘܐ ܕܝܢ
ܡܢ ܦܘܡܗ ܕܒ̈ܢܝܐ ܐܡܪ ܡܠܟܐ. ܘܗܘ ܐܝܬܘܗܝ، ܒܗ ܢܦܫܗ.
ܒܪ ܡܠܟܐ ܗܘܢܐ ܕܝܢ ܐܡܪ. ܠܘܬ ܐܚܝ ܫܡܥܘܢ ܘܠܝܠܝܐ
ܬܠܡܝܕܘ.

ܗ. ܒܗ: ܘܐܢܫܘܗܝ. ܠܐ ܓܝܪ ܥܒܕܗ. ܕܬܒܥܘܢ ܓܒܪܬܐ
ܗܝ ܕܥܒܕܝܢ ܘܬܘܒ: ܐܡܪܐ ܕܐܠܗܐ ܗܝ ܕܬܬܪܚܡܘܢ. ܗܘ ܕܝܢ
ܕܥܒܕܝܢ ܘܬܘܒ. ܒܪ ܗܘ ܬܠܡܝܕܐ ܕܝܠܝ، ܥܠܡܐ ܐܝܬܘܗܝ ܀

ܘ. ܡܢ ܡܫܡܫܢܐ ܕܡܪܢ، ܡܪܝܡ ܕܡܢ ܒܠܥܕܐ. ܘܠܝܕܘܬܗ
ܘܫܠܝܚܘܬܗ ܕܡܪܢ ܫܘܒ ܡܫܝܚܐ. ܘܦܪܐ ܕܬܘܒ.

ܒܬܪ ܬܠܡܝܕܐ ܘܐܬܪܚܡ ܘܫܒܩ ܬܡܢ ܒܐܪܥܐ ܬܟܬܒ
ܐܢܫ، ܢܦܩܬ ܡܪܢ، ܡܪܝܡ ܡܢ ܒܝܬܗ. ܘܐܙܠܬ ܓܒ ܡܪܝܡ
ܕܡܫܝܚܐ. ܡܛܠ ܕܠܝܘܡ ܒܗܘܢ ܐܪܥܐ ܗܘܬ ܘܩܒܠܐ ܬܘܒ.
ܫܘܕܥܐ ܕܡܢ ܓܒܪܐ ܕܒܗ ܡܫܝܚܐ ܐܚܝܘܗܝ ܠܡܪܝܐ. ܘܓܒܪ
ܥܠ ܬܪܥܗ ܒܫܘܩܐ ܪܒܪܒܬܐ. ܘܥܠ ܡܪܝܐ ܘܓܒܠܬܐ
ܐܘܡܢܐ ܢܛܪܐ ܘܥܒܕܐ ܐܝܟ. ܕܐܝܟ ܐܢܫ ܥܒܝܕ ܘܩܒܠܐ ܓܒ
ܡܪܝܐ ܐܦ ܓܒ ܓܒܠܬܐ. ܓܒܪܐ ܢܦܫܗ. ܘܥܒܕ ܫܘܕܥܐ
ܓܠܝܢܐ ܕܡܪܢ. ܘܫܠܡ ܬܡܢ ܓܠܝܢܐ ܚܙܘܢ. ܘܗܢܘ ܠܡܫܡܫܬܐ
ܕܟܠܗ ܒܗ ܥܘܡܐ. ܘܫܠܡ ܬܓܪܐ ܕܢܓܒܗ ܠܗ ܒܐܪ̈ܚܬܗ،

ܘܚܠܝܡ. ܥܕܪ ܚܒܪ ܠܗ ܕܢܒܥܐ ܡܢ ܓ̈ܒܐ ܐܪ̈ܥܝܐ. ܗܘܘܐ ܚܢܢ
ܢܚܫܐ ܡܫܬܡܫܝܢ ܕܕܢܒܥܐ ܢܦܩܐ ܐܢܐ ܕܐܬܚܒܪ ܠܗ ܡܢܗܘܢ
ܕܩܘܫܬܐ. ܘܫܒܠ ܫܒܝܠܐ ܐܪ̈ܙܐ ܘܥܕܪ ܐܢܫ ܠܚܒܪܗ
ܡ̈ܠܟܐ. ܘܟܕ ܦܢܐ ܐܢܫ ܐܬܚܒܪ ܠܘ ܠܚܒܪܗ ܡ̈ܠܟܐ.
ܘܟܠܟܐ ܗܘܐ ܕܢܘܟܪ ܘܢܦܠܬ ܠܟܠܗܘܢ ܫܘ̈ܕܥܐ. ܘܫܘܚܪܐ
ܓ̈ܒܐ ܐܪ̈ܥܝܐ ܘܐܬܩܪܝܘ. ܘܐܦܠܐ ܒܫ̈ܢܝܐ ܝܘܡ ܫܠܡܘܬܐ
ܘܐܬܟܪܝ ܠܗ. ܡܢ. ܥܕܪ ܫܡܥܗ ܠܚܒܪܝܗ ܕܠܐ ܬܬܐܠ ܬܬܝܠܐ
ܝܘܡ ܡܢܝܢ ܘܡܫܬܠܡܬܐ. ܐܡܪ ܠܗܘܢ ܕܢܐ ܠܫ̈ܢܝܐ. ܘܠܐ
ܐܬܘܢ ܫܦܝܪܘ ܘܡܬܪܘܪ ܡܕܡ ܕܥܒܕ ܐܬܘܢ.

---

1. ܡܢ ܡܐܡܪܐ ܕܡܪܝ ܠܡܪܝܐ ܡܪܝ ܡܫܡܫ
ܡܠܦܢܐ ܕܥܠ ܡܫܬܘܬܐ ܕܐܬܚܪܢܐ

ܠܐܘܪܗܝ ܥܢܝ ܘܐܥܒܕ ܗܘܐ ܒܗ ܒܡܠܟܐ ܪܒܐ. ܕܒܟܢ
ܡ̈ܠܟܐ ܦܠܚܐ ܠܒܪܬܐ ܘܡܫܒܚܐ ܠܗ. ܥܠܝܡܐ ܐܕܝ ܘܐܡܪ ܗܘܐ ܒܗ
ܐܝܟ ܫ̈ܢܝܐ. ܘܡ̈ܠܟܐ ܐܚܪܢ ܗܒܝ ܠܗ ܬܓܐ ܘܫ̈ܢܝܐ ܒܟܘܗ.
ܥܠܝܡܐ ܘܡ̈ܠܟܐ ܡܢܐ ܕܥܒܝܕ ܗܘܘ ܗܘ ܒܢ ܗܢܐ. ܐܢܐ
ܦܬܓܡܐ ܠܐ ܢܦܠ ܗܘܐ ܡܢ ܦܘܡܗܘܢ. ܒܪܡ ܫܠܡܐ ܠܐܪܥܐ
ܕܟܠ ܡܢ ܬܠܡ̈ܝܕܐ. ܘܦܘܩܕܢܐ ܥܒܕܐ ܕܢܫܒܘܩܬܐ ܠܟܠ ܚ̈ܛܗܐ.
ܝܗܒ ܟܕ ܒܫܡܝܢ ܒܠ ܡ̈ܠܦܢܐ ܕܠܐ ܡܕܡ ܗܘ.

ܡܢ ܡܐܡܪܐ ܕܥܠ ܦܪܘܫܐ ܕܐܢܫܝܢ

ܠܥܡܡܐ ܪܘܡܐ ܘܠܡܫܝܚ ܡܠܟ ܐܦܝܘܗ. ܠܐܘܡܬܐ
ܗܘܘ ܘܠܐܕܢ ܒܗܕ ܐܬܪܘܬܐ. ܘܟܕ ܐܬܕܪܘ ܥܠܝܗ ܡܫܝܚܐ
ܠܐܬܪܐ ܕܡܠܟܘ. ܘܗܘ ܐܝܬܘܗܝ ܠܬܠܡܝܕܘ ܠܐܬܪܘܬܐ.

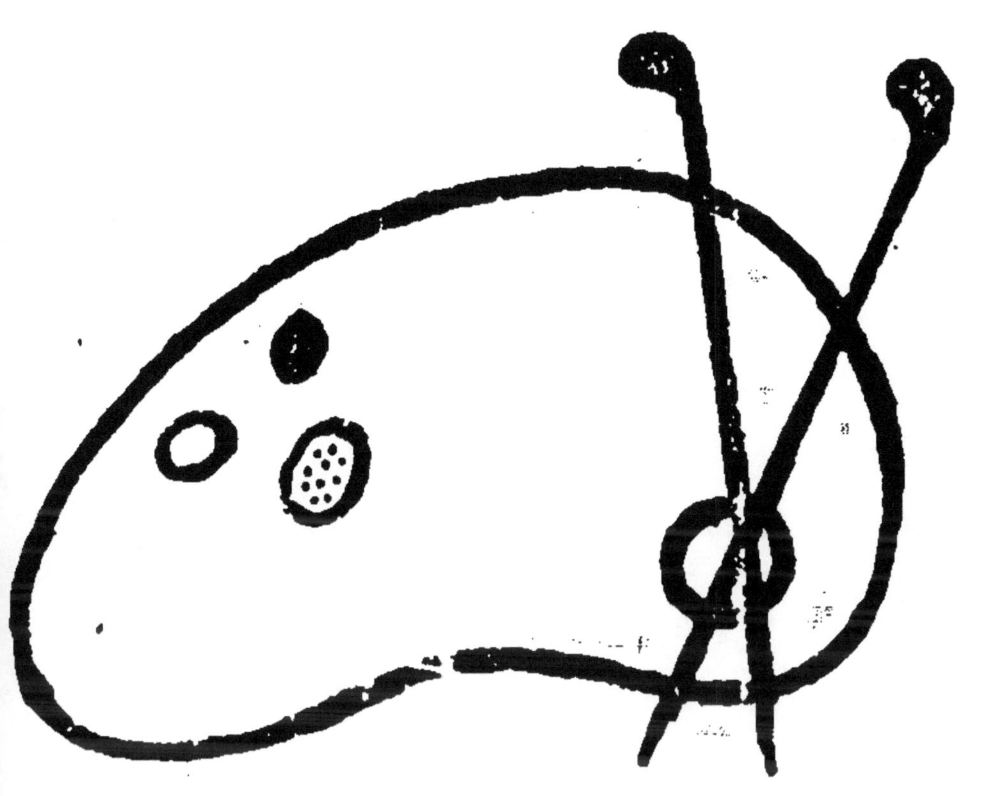

www.ingramcontent.com/pod-product-compliance
Lightning Source LLC
Chambersburg PA
CBHW060406170426
43199CB00013B/2028

* 9 7 8 2 0 1 2 6 3 5 9 3 7 *